LONDON

THE BLUE GUIDES

LONDON

Edited by
STUART ROSSITER
M.A.

*Atlas of 32 pages and
18 other maps and plans.*

LONDON
ERNEST BENN LIMITED

RAND McNALLY & COMPANY
CHICAGO, NEW YORK, SAN FRANCISCO

[First Edition (*London*) 1918]
First Edition (*Short Guide to London*) 1924
Second Edition 1928
Third Edition 1933
Fourth Edition 1938
Fifth Edition 1947
Sixth Edition 1951
Seventh Edition 1953
Eighth Edition 1956
Ninth (enlarged) Edition (*London*) 1965
Tenth Edition 1973
Eleventh Edition 1978

Published by Ernest Benn Limited
25 New Street Square, London EC4A 3JA
& Sovereign Way, Tonbridge, Kent TN9 1RW

Rand McNally & Company
Chicago · New York · San Francisco

ISBN 0 510 01600–6
      0 510 01610–3 (*paperback*)
      528 84637–X (*USA*)
      528 84638–8 (*paperback USA*)

PREFACE

This, the eleventh, edition of the BLUE GUIDE TO LONDON celebrates the book's diamond jubilee. For sixty years, in successive revisions and rewritings, the Blue Guide has assisted Londoners and visitors alike to a better appreciation of England's capital city.

Each decade has a new way of looking at the past. The period undergoing maximum revaluation is about three generations away. Putting it crudely, each young generation finds its grandparents' nostalgic views incomprehensible and boring reminiscence; but what happened before any living memory is susceptible to imaginative interpretations, and so can be viewed more dispassionately from today's standpoint. It becomes antique rather than antiquated, innovatory rather than old-fashioned, worthy of being considered for preservation rather than for destruction. People also come into perspective, seeming in retrospect more, or perhaps less, important. Whether or not a current viewpoint comes nearer some philosophical or historical truth is debatable, but provided it is not obviously evanescent or commercially 'trendy', there is no alternative but to acknowledge and reflect its existence.

As the era before the First World War slips from living memory (and one needs to be over 70 to *remember* even 1914), the theatres we patronize, the tubes in which we travel, have increasingly respectable historical origins and are taken less for granted. In addition, most of our amenities took hold (give or take ten years) around the turn of the century – the telephone, the motor-car, buses, trams, gas, electricity, the aeroplane.

Accordingly, collecting has taken new turns; museums reflect new tastes and new interests; we look at street-scapes with an eye for the new quaint or the newly historical. Ironically many things that are culturally disregarded while still in use come into prominence as soon as obsolete: London's Docks are a good example, Covent Garden another. The passing world begins to look at structures it has previously passed by insensitive or with eyes deliberately averted.

It is hoped many new interests are reflected in this edition, as other new interests have been in previous editions; but without upsetting the balance by elevating them (just because topical) to a status comparatively above their intrinsic merit.

So much for the 'new old'; what about the new? The Victoria Line has shortened many underground journeys; the Heathrow Central extension is open; the Fleet Line first stage may be by the time this books appears (dubbed 'Jubilee' to disarm criticism since its reaching Fleet St. seems still a matter of faith). The cost of parking has become prohibitive and the Blue Guide's arrangement for sightseeing on foot is more than ever valid. Traffic flow has thereby been eased. Ironically, however, most improvements in mobility have been largely negated in the summer by the huge increase of tourists, so that paradoxically those most likely to read these words are least likely to believe them.

5

Inconveniences brought about by sporadic acts of terrorism, a madness on the increase everywhere, are the continuing lack of luggage lockers and the searches that have become an accepted part of admission to public buildings.

If external changes have been slower of late, internal changes in the great collections have been numerous. The Museum of London, just included in the last reprint, receives the extended treatment it so richly deserves. The National Gallery extension has been opened.

This edition has posed particular difficulties in that many museums and galleries today adopt a policy of attracting the public by change at ever shorter intervals, with the result that any account of internal arrangement is obsolete as soon as written. In the larger collections this might be expected not to apply, but in several of these building extensions are evoking major rearrangements. The re-hanging of the National Gallery is sufficiently far advanced to be satisfactorily recorded; unpredictable delays to the Tate Gallery extension have brought a period of uncertainty reflected in unsatisfactory temporary displays which it is pointless to chronicle; the British Museum faces not only the opening in 1978 of a new building, but upheaval (at some unspecifiable date) when the British Library moves elsewhere.

Many long-term plans, of which mention was confidently made a decade ago, seem no nearer fruition. Some, such as London's third airport, the course of the Fleet Line, the British Library's move, and the future of Covent Garden have been killed, resurrected, and radically altered so often that to speculate on their future requires clairvoyance. Getting advance information accurate enough to print is almost impossible.

The preparation of this edition has depended more than usually on its editor alone, and omissions are inevitable since London offers a range of activities that could never be encompassed in a single volume.

The maps and plans drawn by **John Flower** have been brought up-to-date by his hand.

Corrections and suggestions for the improvement of future editions will be welcomed.

CONTENTS

III. THE SOUTH BANK

IV. THE THAMES AND SOUTHERN ENVIRONS

V. THE NORTHERN ENVIRONS

MAPS AND PLANS

EXPLANATIONS

TYPE. The main routes are described in large type. Smaller type is used for branch-routes and excursions, for historical and preliminary paragraphs, and (generally speaking) for descriptions of greater detail or minor importance.

ASTERISKS indicate points of special interest or excellence.

DISTANCES in the environs of London are given in miles cumulatively from Hyde Park Corner (for Western routes) and London Stone, Cannon St. (for Southern routes). POPULATIONS are given according to the preliminary figures of the 1971 census.

PLANS. References in the text (Pl. 1;1) are to the 20-page Atlas at the back of the book, the first figure referring to the page, the second to the square. There is a generous overlap between one page and another: the reference most convenient for the direction being described has been given. Ground Plan references are given as a bracketed single figure.

ABBREVIATIONS. In addition to generally accepted and self-explanatory abbreviations, the following occur in the Guide:

A.A. = Automobile Association
Abp. = Archbishop
Adm. = Admission, Admiral
Bp. = Bishop
BH. = Bank Holiday
B.R. = British Rail
c. = circa (about)
C = century
E.E. = Early English
E.R. = Eastern Region (British Rail)
exc. = except
fl. = floruit (flourished)
G.L.C. = Greater London Council
H.A.C. = Honourable Artillery Company
H.M.S.O. = Her Majesty's Stationery Office
incl. = including
I.T.A. = Independent Television Authority
L.M.R. = London Midland Region (British Rail)
L.P.O. = London Philharmonic Orchestra
L.S.O. = London Symphony Orchestra
L.T. = London Transport
m. = mile(s)
M.C.C. = Marylebone Cricket Club

min. = minutes
M.W.B. = Metropolitan Water Board
N.T. = National Trust
O.E. = old English
Pl. = Atlas Plan
P.L.A. = Port of London Authority
pron. = pronounced
R.A. = Royal Academician
R.A.C. = Royal Automobile Club
R = rooms
R.A.F. = Royal Air Force
R.C. = Roman Catholic
Rest. = restaurant
Rfmts = refreshments
R.H.S. = Royal Horticultural Society
Rte = Route
seq. = sequentia, etc. (following)
S.R. = Southern Region (British Rail)
SS = Saints
St = Saint
St. = Street
Stn. = station
tel. = telephone
W.R. = Western Region (British Rail)
Y.H. = Youth Hostel
Y.M.C.A. = Young Men's Christian Association
Y.W.C.A. = Young Women's Christian Association.

LONDON

London, the capital of England and in the wider sense also of Great Britain and its remaining colonial territories, is situated on the *Thames,* about 40 m. as the crow flies from the mouth of the river, or 60 m. by the windings of the stream. The name London has in the past had no single fixed and definite meaning, though since the formation in 1965 of the Greater London Council, the administrative area has more nearly coincided with the actual extent of the huge conurbation previously defined only by the extent of the Metropolitan and City Police District jurisdiction. This great urban county has 7,379,000 inhab., and now rates fifth in population of the world's great cities. Of its 625 sq. m., nearly one-third is still free of buildings, and the urban density is considerably lower (and the extent correspondingly greater) than that of the first four (Shanghai, Tokyo, New York, and Peking). A tiny 'square mile' (actually 1.03 sq. m.) in the centre represents the *City of London* with a population of 4230.

The whole area is roughly divided into a N. half and a S. half by the river, which flows through it from W. to E., though with many windings. Of the two, the more important for the tourist is still the N. half, though increasingly the South Bank is claiming its fair share of interest; in the sphere of entertainment, it is beginning to aspire once more to the position it held in the first Elizabethan age.

The conventional division of London to the N. of the Thames into 'the City' and the 'West End', though still current (especially on signposts), is no longer adequate and is therefore puzzling to the stranger. London is too complex to be contained in so simple a formula, which ignored the growth of the metropolis to the S. and W. The City has extended its commercial influence far beyond its historic limits. The Strand and Holborn have as much in common with the City as with the West End to which they formally belong, and the East End is larger than the City itself. Bloomsbury and Soho, though topographically in the West End, belong in character neither to it nor to the City: they are districts by themselves.

As manufacturing industry moves farther out to 'trading estates' in the country, offices invade 'fashionable' areas, and the character of boroughs changes with migrations (internal and from the Commonwealth), the once marked differentiation between E. (commercial) and W. (residential) becomes more blurred; but it is still generally true to say that it is thought socially desirable in the inner districts to live W. of a line drawn from Waterloo Bridge N.W. up Hampstead Road, rather than E. of it; and fashion in shops tends farther to the W.

Besides the officially recognized administrative areas and the smaller older established parishes (Putney, etc.), there are various districts with vague limits but with well-known names (Pimlico, St John's Wood, Mayfair, etc.), a knowledge of which is as necessary as an awareness of the locations of various taverns, past and present (Angel, Elephant), that mark important road junctions.

On all sides, except perhaps the E., London is fringed by agreeable suburbs, some of them recognizably the successors of historic villages. Those best favoured by their geographical situation, on the river such as Greenwich, to the E., and Hampton Court, to the w., attracted the sovereign, whose palaces remain. Others, equally well favoured, attracted the rich and powerful and conserve round a rural nucleus a patrician air and corresponding amenities to this day: among them Hampstead to the N., Richmond to the s.w., Dulwich to the s., and Blackheath to the s.E. Farther out London now incorporates places, formerly towns in their own right in Middlesex or Surrey, which still preserve in their compact centres a character markedly urban rather than suburban: among these are Bromley, Croydon, and Kingston to the s., and, to the N., Enfield and Barnet. These are nevertheless essentially parts of the great community, having little visible break in the continuous series of streets and houses that connects them with central London. This necessary break is provided at irregular intervals by the tracts of country and formal parks that intersperse the area and, to an extent, are protected as a 'green belt' from the encroachment of building. These open spaces culminate in the outer areas in such wide expanses as Richmond Park, Enfield Chase, and Epping Forest, and survive even quite near the centre in Hampstead Heath, Wanstead Flats, Clapham Common, and Wormwood Scrubs.

As the true Londoner is well aware, every district of London has a character, interest, and attraction of its own, derived partly from physical survivals of its past, partly from the interplay of continuity and change in its population. "When a man is tired of London, he is tired of life; for there is in London all that life can afford".

London, in addition, by virtue of its frequent suburban and inter-city train services, makes a convenient base for exploring farther afield. Among places of special interest within easy reach for a day excursion are Marlow and the Thames Valley, the Chiltern Hills, St. Albans, Hatfield House, and Colchester; Chessington Zoo, Box Hill, Guildford, Hindhead, the South Downs, and Brighton. These and an ever widening range of attractions are all described in the 'Blue Guide to England'.

PRACTICAL INFORMATION

I APPROACHES TO LONDON

Airports. The main airport of London is c. 15 m. w. of the centre at Heathrow. Some scheduled services and charter flights use Gatwick (27 m. s. of London) and Luton (33 m. N.W.). The auxiliary airport at Stansted (33 m. N.) is, however, named as the third official airport.

Heathrow. Frequent regular connecting COACHES to *West London Air Terminal*, Cromwell Road (for European flights); and to *Victoria Airways Terminal*, Buckingham Palace Road, for flights from U.S.A., etc. Because of restrictions on night flights there are no regular night coaches; passengers on delayed flights arriving at night may not find immediate transport. Transport facilities at Terminals, see below.

UNDERGROUND (Piccadilly line).

TAXIS may be hired at the authorized rank outside each Terminal Building at Heathrow. On journeys of over 6 miles but within the Metropolitan Police District (the area roughly covered in this Guide, including the environs) the driver may refuse to take the hire, but if he accepts it, he can charge only the fare shown on the meter. The fare to the centre of London (Piccadilly) in 1978 was approximately £6·50. If the destination is outside the Metropolitan Police District (e.g. Windsor), the driver is entitled, before he accepts the hire, to bargain with the customer to determine the fare (this should be agreed *before* beginning the journey). The British Airports Authority warns against private car drivers who are not licensed to ply for hire; licensed taxis display a special 'Hackney Carriage' number plate on the rear of the vehicle, and the driver wears a numbered badge.

CAR HIRE. The only companies allowed to operate within Heathrow are Avis, Hertz and Godfrey Davis (booking offices in each Terminal).

CAR PARKING. Multi-storey parking near the terminal buildings for any period up to 24 hrs (approx. 20p per hour); car parks (uncovered) on perimeter road for over 24 hrs (£1 per day), with ferry service to terminal buildings.

HOTELS, see p. 19; RESTAURANT in No. 3 Terminal (Departures).

TOURIST INFORMATION is available from the British Airports Authority in all three terminals at Heathrow (7 a.m.–10 p.m.).

Gatwick. Airport station with direct trains (every 20 min; hourly during the night) to *Victoria Station*. Tourist Information (24 hr service) is available at the airport. HOTELS, see p. 19.

Charter services using Stansted and Luton almost always operate connecting bus services to the North London Air Terminal, Finchley Rd, or to Victoria Station.

Stansted. Bus to Bishop's Stortford Station; frequent trains to *Liverpool Street Station.*

Luton. Bus to railway station, whence trains to *St Pancras Station.*

Air Terminals. The B.A. Victoria Terminal and the West London Air Terminal are both in central London and have refreshment facilities. Avis and Hertz car hire agencies have offices only at the Victoria Terminal. Taxis are nearly always available at both Termini.

The *West London Air Terminal* (Pl. 11; 5) is 2 min. N. of Gloucester Road Underground Station (comp. Atlas 22), and on the 74 (and 97 at night) bus routes.

The *Victoria Terminal* (Pl. 17; 2) is 2 min. w. of Victoria Station (Underground) and on the 11 and 39 bus routes.

The *North London Air Terminal*, 202 Finchley Road, N.W.3, is 5 min N. of Finchley Road Underground Station (comp. Atlas 22), and on the 2, 2B, 13, 113 and 26 bus routes. Taxis are sometimes available in Finchley Rd.; a mini-cab office operates inside the Terminal. Refreshments are available.

Seaports. Passenger liners no longer navigate the Thames beyond Tilbury. Travellers by liner arrive at Tilbury, Southampton, or Liverpool; from the Continent by steamer at various ports.

TILBURY, see p. 279. Boat trains to *Fenchurch Street Station*.
SOUTHAMPTON. Boat trains from Docks to *Waterloo Station*.
LIVERPOOL. Local buses from Pierhead to Lime St. Stn., whence express train service to *Euston Station*.

Passengers arriving from the Continent viâ DOVER, FOLKESTONE, and NEWHAVEN will find connecting trains to *Victoria Station*; viâ WEYMOUTH to *Waterloo Stn.*; viâ HARWICH and FELIXSTOWE to *Liverpool Street Stn.*; and from the NORTHERN PORTS to *King's Cross*.

Hovercraft Terminal. RAMSGATE (from Calais). Special connecting bus service to *Victoria Coach Station*.

Arrival by Car. The only airport of entry is SOUTHEND (22 m. E. of London); cars are also carried on the Ramsgate hovercraft. DOVER, FOLKESTONE, NEWHAVEN, SOUTHAMPTON, WEYMOUTH, PLYMOUTH, HARWICH, FELIXSTOWE, and the NORTHERN PORTS have facilities for landing cars. For the road routes from ports to London, see the 'Blue Guide to England'.

Railway Termini. It is important for the traveller to London to ascertain beforehand at which station his train arrives. The following is an alphabetical list of the chief London termini:

CHARING CROSS (Pl. 15; 3), West End terminus of the Southern Region.
EUSTON (Pl. 6; 2), terminus of the London Midland Region, serving Liverpool and Manchester.
KING'S CROSS (Pl. 7; 1), terminus of the Eastern Region, and services from Newcastle and Hull.
LIVERPOOL STREET (Pl. 9; 4), terminus of the Eastern Region (E. lines).
PADDINGTON (Pl. 4; 7) is the terminus of the Western Region.
VICTORIA (Pl. 17; 2), the chief West End terminus of the Southern Region, is the station for the continental routes viâ Folkestone, Dover, etc.
WATERLOO (Pl. 15; 6) is another terminus of the Southern Region, where the boat-trains from Southampton arrive.

All the termini are directly connected by passages or subways with the system of Underground Railways. 'Red Arrow' single-decker buses also connect the main railway stations during the day; nightly buses run on a circular route at frequent intervals between Paddington, Euston, St Pancras, King's Cross, Liverpool Street, Waterloo and Victoria.

International Travellers Aid provides advice at Victoria Station (Platform 10; 3–5, 6–9).

Health. Vaccination certificates are not normally required by visitors arriving direct from Europe, Canada, U.S.A., Australia, or New Zealand.

Foreign Exchange. Most airports and seaports of entry are equipped with Bureaux de Change, which are open during the period of arrival of international services. Exchange may be effected at most banks during normal banking hours (see p. 43). An increasing number of bureaux are open in central London: among these are Trafalgar Square Post Office (Mon–Sat, 9 a.m.–9.30 p.m.); Chequepoint Services, 89 Gloucester Rd, S.W.7 (daily 8.30 a.m.–midnight) and elsewhere in S.W. London; Credit Change Ltd, 4–5 Charing Cross, S.W.1 (9 a.m.–9 p.m., Sun from 10 a.m.); Victoria Station (daily 8.15 a.m.–9 or 10.30 p.m.); Liverpool St Stn (Mon–Sat 8 a.m.–8 p.m.). International credit cards are widely accepted in shops, restaurants, and hotels; and the larger hotels and stores (Harrod's, Barker's, Lewis's, Selfridge's) normally change certain currencies and travellers' cheques for their clients.

The **London Tourist Board** (the regional office of the English Tourist Board) with an information centre for tourists (open Mon–Fri 9.15 a.m.–5.30 p.m.) at 26 Grosvenor Gardens, S.W.1, issues a free 'Travellers' Guide to Britain' and willingly supplies convenient and useful information. It maintains information offices at Victoria Station (near Platform 15; open daily 9 a.m.–9 p.m.; 8 a.m.–10.30 p.m. in summer), and at the Victoria Airways Terminal (May–Sept only 9 a.m.–2 p.m.). A Student Centre (open daily 9 a.m.–5.30 p.m.; 8 a.m.–11 p.m. in summer) at 8–10 Buckingham Palace Road helps young people on arriving in London.

The **British Tourist Authority,** 64 St James's St., S.W.1, and 680 Fifth Avenue, New York, was founded with the object of increasing the number and promoting the comfort of visitors from overseas. The Association has offices also in Chicago, Los Angeles, Sydney, Melbourne, Toronto, Vancouver, Capetown, and most West European capitals. They will provide detailed information for those planning a trip outside the London area.

Travellers who wish to save the bother of making their own arrangements will be advised to do so through a **Travel Agent,** choosing a reputable member of the Association of British Travel Agents. These organizations, for a small fee, obtain travel tickets, make hotel reservations, and, if desired, arrange tours for individuals or parties. Among agents in London are: *Thomas Cook & Son*, 45 Berkeley St., W.1, and many branches; *American Express*, 6 Haymarket, S.W.1, 89 Mount St., W.1, etc.

II HOTELS AND RESTAURANTS

Although a number of large new **Hotels** have been built in London in recent years, advance booking is always advisable (especially in summer). The majority of hotels of the highest class are to be found in Mayfair and Piccadilly and in Knightsbridge and Kensington. Other first-class hotels are in the Strand, and in Bloomsbury, where there are also many less expensive ones. Accommodation is still virtually non-existent on the South Bank, but a few new hotels are now being sited in the City, and in North London. There is an increasing number of small private hotels in suburban areas. Many of the new hotels and motels on the outskirts of London (often 20 miles from the centre) have been built for the convenience of the businessman travelling from other centres in Britain.

Our list below includes most of the well-known hotels, and some of the less expensive ones. It is by no means exhaustive; omission does not imply any adverse judgment. The visitor is strongly advised to obtain from the English Tourist Board their latest lists of hotels and restaurants (for which there may be a small charge).

Both the principal motoring organizations publish excellent detailed guides to their recommended hotels and restaurants in Britain (the *Royal Automobile Club* and the *Automobile Association*). In addition there may be mentioned 'Egon Ronay's Guide' and the 'Good Food Guide' of the Consumers' Association, unofficial and often stringently critical surveys of the state of gastronomy in Britain.

The *Accommodation Service* of the London Tourist Board at 26 Grosvenor Gdns, S.W.1 (Tel. 730 3450) provides information on hotels in London. Advance bookings should be made at least six weeks before the date of reservation. An emergency service caters for visitors unable to find accommodation on first arrival in London.

The Board also runs a *Private Accommodation Bureau* for visitors wishing to live with a family. Such accommodation is only to be found in the suburbs; the minimum period is one week, and the maximum 3 months.

Hotels in Britain have neither official categories nor nationally standardized prices, and it is advisable when booking to have a precise understanding of the charges. Breakfast is now not always included in the cost of the room, but no extra charge is made for baths taken in a public bathroom. A service charge of 10, $12\frac{1}{2}$, or 15 per cent is now often added to or included in the bill; in such circumstances additional tipping is necessary only for exceptional personal service or where porterage is specifically not included. Where no percentage is added, equivalent remuneration should be divided among individual staff who have given service. Normally visitors are required to vacate their rooms before 12 noon.

Many hotels have restaurants. The better-known with a non-resident clientèle operate to a late hour, but in some hotels, especially the smaller ones, it may be difficult to dine after 8.30 in the evening.

There remains a notable lack of good second-class hotels and of small hotels in the central London area. New hotels tend to be very large, often with a high proportion of double rooms, and some become swamped by tourist groups at the expense of the individual traveller.

Hotels with more than 200 rooms (200 R) have been indicated in the list below; those with around 50 rooms or less are termed 'small'. Those not providing a full meals service have been marked '†'. The plan references are to the atlas section where many hotels are marked 'H'.

1. Hotels de luxe and large First-class Hotels

The following are hotels de luxe, sumptuously appointed, with private bathrooms attached to all the rooms, suites of rooms, restaurants, and grill-rooms, and corresponding charges. Some hotels in this group advertise no fixed tariff; others (in 1978) charge £28–£60 per night for a single room, and £35–£65 per night for a double room. Breakfast is *not* now usually included in the prices quoted by luxury and first-class hotels. Some de luxe hotels demand a deposit when a room is taken.

*Berkeley (Pl. 13; 5)Wilton Place, Knightsbridge; ***Claridge's** (Pl. 13; 2), Brook St., Mayfair, old-established with distinguished clientele, 250 R; ***Connaught** (Pl. 13; 2), Carlos Place, Grosvenor Square; **Dorchester**, 285 R, **Grosvenor House**, 467 R, **Inn on the Park**, 250 R, all in Park Lane (Pl. 13; 3, 4); ***Hyde Park** (Pl. 13; 5), 66 Knightsbridge, 201 R; **Ritz** (Pl. 14; 5), Piccadilly, overlooking Green Park; ***Savoy** (Pl. 15; 3), Strand, overlooking the Thames, 500 R; ***Westbury** (Pl. 14; 3), New Bond St. and Conduit St., 243 R; **Hilton** (Pl. 13; 4), Park Lane, 500 R; **Churchill** (Pl. 5; 7), 30 Portman Sq., 489 R; **Portman-International** (Pl. 5; 7), 22 Portman Sq., 282 R; **Holiday Inn**, 134 George St., Marble Arch, 243 R.

2. Other Hotels arranged topographically

The following groups include both first-class hotels and those of a simpler character. They are listed so that the less expensive ones are mentioned towards the end of each group.

Hotels near Piccadilly, and in Mayfair, Belgravia, and Knightsbridge (groups a, b, and c) usually charge higher prices than those elsewhere in London. In 1978 a single room with bath and breakfast in these areas cost £12–£25 (first-class hotels up to £40), and a double room with bath cost £16–£30.

Hotels in the rest of London (groups d–k) tend to be less expensive: here a single room with bath in 1978 cost from £8, and a double room with bath from £12·50 (often with breakfast included), though some now rival those more central.

(a) *Near Piccadilly*

*Stafford, Duke's (Pl. 14; 5), 16 and 35 St James's Place, both small; ***Meurice and Quaglino's** (Pl. 14; 5), 15 Bury St., a small hotel; ***Brown's** (Pl. 14; 3), 21 Dover St.; **Bristol** (Pl. 14; 5), 1–3 Berkeley St.; **Athenaeum** (Pl. 13; 4), 116 Piccadilly; **Cavendish**, Jermyn St., 255 R; **Park Lane** (Pl. 13; 4), 112 Piccadilly, 400 R; **Piccadilly** (Pl. 14; 3), 21 Piccadilly, 219 R; **Washington** (Pl. 13; 4) 6 Curzon St.; **Royal Angus** (Pl. 14; 4) 39 Coventry St.; **Fleming's** (Pl. 13; 4), Half Moon St.; **Green Park** (Pl. 13; 4), Half Moon St.

(b) *In Mayfair*

Londonderry (Pl. 13; 4), Park Lane; **May Fair** (Pl. 13; 4), Berkeley St., 392 R; **Curzon** (Pl. 13; 4), 2 Stanhope Row; **Chesterfield**, 35 Charles St; **Britannia**, 436 R, **Europa**, 273 R, both in Grosvenor Sq. (Pl. 13; 2).

(c) *In Knightsbridge and Belgravia*

Carlton Tower (Pl. 13; 7), Cadogan Place, Sloane St., 260 R; **Sheraton Park Tower**, 101 Knightsbridge, 293 R; **Belgravia Royal** (Pl. 13; 7), Chesham Place; ***Capital** (Pl. 13; 5), 22–24 Basil St., small; **Lowndes** (Pl. 13; 5), Lowndes St.; **Cadogan** (Pl. 13; 7), 75 Sloane St.; **Basil Street** (Pl. 13; 5), Knightsbridge; **Royal Court** (Pl. 17; 1), 8 Sloane Sq.; **Wilbraham** (Pl. 17; 1), Wilbraham Place, small; **Ninety Nine** (Pl. 13; 8), 99 Eaton Place, small.

(d) *Near Victoria*

Royal Westminster (Pl. 18; 3), 49 Buckingham Palace Rd.; ***Goring** (Pl. 13; 8), 15 Ebury St.; **St Ermin's** (Pl. 14; 8), Caxton St., 252 R; **Eccleston** (Pl. 17; 2), Eccleston Sq. and Gillingham St.; **Rubens** (Pl. 18; 3), Buckingham Palace Rd.; ***Ebury Court** (Pl. 17; 2), 24 Ebury St., small; **St James's** (Pl. 18; 1), Buckingham Gate, 505 R.

(e) *In Kensington*

*Kensington Palace (Pl. 11; 3), 2 De Vere Gardens, 310 R; **Kensington Close** (Pl. 10; 6), Wright's Lane, 539 R; **Kensington Hilton**, Holland Park Avenue, 610 R; **Royal Garden** (Pl. 11; 3), Kensington High St., 500 R; **Royal Kensington** (Pl. 10; 5), 380 Kensington High St.; **London International** (Pl. 11; 7), Cromwell Rd., 337 R; **London Tara,** Wright's Lane, 840 R; **De Vere** (Pl. 11; 3), 60 Hyde Park Gate; **Blakes** (Pl. 11; 8), 33 Roland Gardens, small; **Prince of Wales** (Pl. 11; 3), 16 De Vere Gardens, 301 R; **London Penta,** Cromwell Rd., 914 R; **Regency,** 100 Queen's Gate; **Buckingham** (Pl. 11; 6), 100 Cromwell Rd.; **The Edwardian** (Pl. 11; 7), 40–44 Harrington Gdns.; **Eden Plaza** (Pl. 12; 7), 68–69 Queensgate; **Elizabetta** (Pl. 11; 7), Cromwell Rd.; **Bailey's** (Pl. 11; 7), 140 Gloucester Rd.; **Embassy House** (Pl. 12; 7), 31 Queensgate; **Norfolk** (Pl. 12; 7), 2 Harrington Rd.; **Rembrandt** (Pl. 12; 8), Thurloe Place; **Suncourt** (Pl. 10; 6), 57 Lexham Gdns.; **Milestone** (Pl. 11; 3), Kensington Court; **Queensbury Court** (Pl. 16; 1), 7–11 Queensberry Place, small†; **Gloucester** (Pl. 11; 7), Harrington Gdns. – In EARL'S COURT: **Barkston** (Pl. 11; 7), Barkston Gdns.; **Kensington Court** (Pl. 10; 8), 33–35 Nevern Place, small; **Lily, West Centre** (beyond Pl. 10; 8), both Lillie Rd. – IN NORTH

KENSINGTON: **Portobello** (Pl. 10; 2), 22 Stanley Gdns., small.—Also **Cunard International,** Shortlands, Hammersmith.

Among the numerous RESIDENTIAL HOTELS may be mentioned: *Crofton, Onslow Court, Gore,* all in Queensgate (Nos. 14, 108, and 189; Pl. 12; 7 and 11; 8); *Tudor Court, Milton Court, Vanderbilt,* all in Cromwell Rd. (Nos. 58, 68, and 76; Pl. 11; 6) *Stanhope Court* (Pl. 11; 8), Stanhope Gdns.; *Harrington Hall* (Pl. 11; 7), 11 Harrington Gdns.

(f) *Near Charing Cross and the Strand*

Howard, Temple Place; **Waldorf** (Pl. 7; 7), Aldwych, on the verge of the City, 310 R; **Charing Cross** (Pl. 15; 3), Charing Cross Station, 217 R; **Royal Trafalgar,** Whitcomb St.; **Royal Horseguards** (Pl. 15; 5), Whitehall Court, 286 R; **Strand Palace** (Pl. 7; 7), 372 Strand, 777 R; **Drury Lane,** High Holborn, **Fielding** (Pl. 7; 7), 4 Broad Court (N. of Covent Garden), small †; **Pastoria** (Pl. 14; 4), St Martin's St., small; **Royal Adelphi** (Pl. 14; 4), 21 Villiers St., small †.

(g) *In Marylebone*

Selfridge, Oxford St., 298 R; **London Metropole,** Edgware Rd., 555 R; **Rathbone,** 30 Rathbone St.; **Sherlock Holmes** (Pl. 5; 5), 108 Baker St.; **Cumberland** (Pl. 13; 1), Marble Arch, 898 R; **Georgian House** (Pl. 5; 7), 87 Gloucester Place, small; **Londoner** (Pl. 5; 8), Welbeck St.; **Mount Royal** (Pl. 5; 7), Bryanston St., near Marble Arch, 694 R; **Clifton-Ford** (Pl. 5; 6), 47 Welbeck St.; **St George's** (Pl. 6; 5), Langham Place; **Great Western Royal** (Pl. 4; 7), Paddington Station; **Montcalm** (Pl. 5; 7), Great Cumberland Place; **Regent Centre** (Pl. 6; 3), Carburton St., 350 R; **Clarendon Court** (Pl.4; 3), Edgware Rd.; **Colonnade** (beyond Pl. 4; 3), Warrington Crescent, small; **Durrant's** (Pl. 5; 5), 26 George St.; **Mandeville** (Pl. 5; 8), 8 Mandeville Place; **Mostyn** (Pl. 5; 7), 19 Portman Street; **Bryanston Court** (Pl. 5; 7), 56 Great Cumberland Place, small.—Opening shortly: **London Metropole,** Edgware Rd.; **Harewood,** Harewood Row; and **Rathbone Piccadilly,** Charlotte St.

(h) *In Bayswater* (with many residential hotels)

Royal Lancaster, Lancaster Terrace, 436 R; **Henry VIII,** 19 Leinster Gdns., **Hertford** (Pl. 11; 1), 104 Bayswater Rd.; **White's** (Pl. 11; 2), 90 Lancaster Gate; **Hotel International** (Pl. 11; 1), Lancaster Gate; **Charles Dickens** (Pl. 12; 1), Lancaster Gate; **Park Court** (Pl. 12; 1), 75 Lancaster Gate, 250 R; **Kingshill** (Pl. 4; 7), 55 Westbourne Terrace; **Parkway** (Pl. 11; 1), Inverness Terrace; **Central Park** (Pl. 11; 1), 49 Queensborough Terrace, 360 R; **Lancaster Gate,** 106 Lancaster Gate; **Leinster Towers,** 25 Leinster Gdns.; **London Elizabeth,** Lancaster Terrace, small; **Norfolk Towers,** Norfolk Place, small; **Royal Eagle,** 26 Craven Rd.; **Coburg** (Pl. 11; 1), 129 Bayswater Road; **Inverness Court** (Pl. 11; 1), 1 Inverness Terrace, small †.

(i) *In Bloomsbury and neighbourhood*

Russell (Pl. 7; 3), Russell Sq., a large old hotel, 328 R; **Imperial** (Pl. 7; 3), 61 Russell Sq., another large house; with Turkish baths, 462 R; **Bedford** (Pl. 7; 3), 83 Southampton Row; **Tavistock** (Pl. 6; 4), Tavistock Sq., 300 R; **Bloomsbury Centre** (Pl. 7; 3), Coram St., 250 R; **Kingsley** (Pl. 15; 1), 36 Bloomsbury Way; **Bonnington** (Pl. 7; 5), 90 Southampton Row, 268 R; **New Ambassadors** (Pl. 6; 2), Upper Woburn Place; **Berners** (Pl. 14; 1), Bergers St., 245 R; **White Hall** (Pl. 7; 5), 9–11 Bloomsbury Sq. and 2–5 Montague St.; **Montague** (Pl. 7; 5), 12–17 Montague St.; **Bedford Corner** (Pl. 6; 6), Bayley St.; **County and Cora,** both Upper Woburn Place (Pl. 6; 2); **St Margaret's** (Pl. 7; 3), 26 Bedford Place †; **Ivanhoe** (Pl. 6; 6), Bloomsbury St., 263 R; **Kenilworth** (Pl. 7; 5), 92 Great Russell St., 210 R; **Waverley** (Pl. 7; 5), 132 Southampton Row.

(j) *The City and South Bank*

Central City (Pl. 8; 2), Central St., E.C.1, 580 R; **Tower** (Pl. 21; 2), St Katharine's Way, Tower Hill; **Great Eastern** (Pl. 9; 6), Liverpool Street Station; **Devereux** (Pl. 7; 8), Devereux Court (Temple), small.—**London Park** (Pl. 20; 6), Elephant and Castle, S.E.11, 375 R; **Queen's,** Church Road, Crystal Palace, S.E.19; **Aerodrome,** Purley Way, Croydon.

(k) *North London*

Kennedy (Pl. 6; 2), 43 Cardington St., N.W.1, 321 R; **Great Northern** (Pl. 7; 1), King's Cross; **Royal Scot** (Pl. 7; 2), Percy Circus, 356 R; **London Ryan** (Pl. 7; 2), Gwynne Place, 213 R; **White House** (Pl. 6; 3), Albany St., 746 R; **Westmoreland at Lords,** Lodge Rd., N.W.8, 350 R.—IN HAMPSTEAD: **Post House** (Atlas 24), Haverstock Hill, N.W.3; **Charles Bernard** (Atlas 24), 5 Frognal, N.W.3, small; **Clive** (Atlas 24), Primrose Hill Rd.; **West Lodge Park,** Cockfosters Rd., Hadley Wood; **Royal Chase,** The Ridgeway, Enfield.—IN HARROW, **Cumberland.**

(l) *South-Western Environs*

RICHMOND: **Roebuck, Richmond Hill, Richmond Gate,** on Richmond Hill; **Star & Garter,** Petersham Rd.; **White Cross,** Cholmondeley Walk. — WINDSOR: **The Old House,** Thames St., small; **Ye Harte & Garter, Castle,** High St.

Hotels at or near Airports

Heathrow. On the Bath Road which skirts the N. side of the Airport: *Sheraton-Skyline*, 360 R; *Heathrow*, 680 R; *Skyway*, 443 R; *Excelsior*, 662 R; *Arlington*, Shepiston Lane, Hayes; *Berkeley Arms*, Bath Rd., Canford, small; *Holiday Inn*, 280 R, *Post House* (Motel), 594 R, both West Drayton.

Gatwick. *Copthorne, Gatwick Shillbey, Gatwick Ambassador; Gatwick Piccadilly* and *Excelsior.*

Luton. *Esso Motor Hotel, Crest Motel*; *Strathmore*, Arndale Centre.

The *Royal Overseas League*, Vernon House, Park Place, St James's St., S.W.1 and the *English-Speaking Union*, 37 Charles St., W.1, provide limited accommodation for their members.

The *Y.M.C.A.* and *Y.W.C.A.* maintain the **Y-Hotel** (open to all), Gt. Russell St., W.C.1, and hostels in London at 30 Leinster Sq., W.2 (for overseas students); 233 Earls Court Rd., S.W.5; 14 Endsleigh Gdns., W.C.1; 39 Ennismore Gdns., S.W.7, etc. All enquiries to headquarters at 16 Great Russell St., W.C.1 (580 0478).

The *Youth Hostels Association* (national office, Trevelyan House, 8 St Stephen's Hill, St Albans, Herts) runs four hostels in London at 36 Carter Lane, E.C.4; the King George VI Memorial Hostel, Holland House, Holland Walk, Kensington, W.8; 38 Bolton Gardens, Earls Court, S.W.5; and 84 Highgate West Hill, N.6. Membership of the association costs 85p per annum for those from 5 to 15, £1·50 for those over 16 and under 21, and £2·50 for those 21 or over. All information is detailed in the Y.H.A. Handbook (free to members). Members of foreign Youth Hostels Associations need not join the English Y.H.A. The *Y.H.A. Travel Bureau* at 29 John Adam St., W.C.2, will give advice.

CAMPING AND CARAVANNING. Information can be obtained from the *Camping Club of Great Britain and Ireland*, 11 Lower Grosvenor Place, S.W.1. or the *Caravan Club*, 55 St James's St., S.W.1; the R.A.C. and A.A. also publish useful handbooks. A camping site (booking necessary in July and August) is situated at North Parade, Crystal Palace, S.E.19.

Restaurants of all classes abound in London, and nearly all hotels admit non-residents to luncheon or dinner. Service is now often included in the bill; at least 15 per cent is now the normal addition to the cost of the meal. A small extra tip may be left for specially good service.

Restaurants are normally open from 12 to 2.30 (sometimes till 3.30), and from 6.30 to 11.30. It is always advisable to book, especially in the fashionable West End restaurants (busiest times 8.30–10.30).

The fashionable eating areas are still in St James's, Mayfair, and the West End, though better value gastronomically is often to be found in the less pretentious restaurants of Soho, Chelsea, or the Charlotte Street area. Many of the suburbs such as Hampstead, Wimbledon, and Richmond are now also provided with restaurants.

The standard of light meals and refreshments served at coffee-houses and snack-bars is generally low. The food provided at pubs is often more imaginative, with good cold buffet counters supplemented by one or two modest dishes of the day.

The following list, without attempting to be comprehensive, aims at providing the traveller with a reasonable choice of restaurants within the routes covered by the Guide. The omission of a name from the list does not imply any derogatory judgment. In each section the restaurants are roughly arranged in the order of their charges, the cheaper restaurants being named last. Those termed 'less expensive' in the list are comparatively so only within each group. A reasonable but not exotic three-course lunch or dinner with wine will cost £4–£15 per head.

Most of the luxury and first-class hotels have excellent restaurants which have not usually been included in our list. Department stores in the West End often have well-run restaurants and coffee-shops (convenient for the hurried traveller).

Routes 1–4. *Westminster and Whitehall*
There is a notable lack of restaurants in the area. **Locket's**, Marsham St. (closed at week-ends). – Less expensive: **Vitello d'Oro**, Gt. Smith St., and restaurant in Central Hall.

Rte 5. *Charing Cross and Trafalgar Square*
See Rtes 17 and 14.

Rte 6. *St James's Park. The Mall and Buckingham Palace*
See Rte 7.

Rte. 7. *Pall Mall and St James's*
Lafayette, King Street; **Wiltons**, 27 Bury St.; **Quaglino's**, Bury St.; **Overton's**, St. James's St. (seafood); **L'Ecu de France**, 111 Jermyn St. – Less expensive: **Hunting Lodge**, 18 Lower Regent St.; **Frank's**, 63 Jermyn St.; **Stone's Chop House**, Panton St.; **Casa Mario**, 4 Duke of York St.

Rte 8. *Piccadilly*
*Martinez, 25 Swallow St. (Spanish); **Bentley's**, 11–15 Swallow St. (seafood); **Manetta's**, Half Moon St.; **Vine**, 3 Piccadilly Place; **Sands**, 30 New Bond St.; **Fortnum and Mason**, Piccadilly.—Less expensive: **Ceylon Tea Centre**, 22 Regent St.; **Pizza e Pasta**, Regent St.; **Royal Academy**, Burlington House; **Swan and Edgar** and **Simpson's**, both department stores in Piccadilly. Butteries and coffee-shops in Albemarle St.

Rte 9. *Park Lane and Mayfair*
The luxury hotels in the area have good restaurants and coffee-shops (some open all night). **Cunningham's**, 17 Curzon St. (for fish); ***Mirabelle**, 56 Curzon St.; **Tiberio**, 22 Queen St.; **Scott's**, 20 Mount St. (seafood); ***La Napoule**, North Audley St.; ***The Empress**, 15 Berkeley St. (not cheap); **Number Ten**, 10 Lancashire Court (New Bond St.).—Less expensive: **Vendôme**, 20 Dover St. and **Sovereign**, 17 Hertford St., both for seafood; **Guinea Grillroom**, 30 Bruton Place; **La Recolte**, 67 Duke St.; **La Terrasse Tio Pepe**, 13 Shepherds Place, Upper Brooke St.; **Golden Carp**, 8a Mount St. (seafood); **The Marquis**, 121a Mount St.; **Le Coq d'Or**, Stratton St.; **Richoux**, 41a South Audley St.; **Tiddy Dols Eating House**, 2 Hertford St.; **The Snooty Fox**, 52 Hertford St.; **Serafino**, 8 Mount St.; **Marlborough Head**, 24 North Audley St.; **Tandoori**, 37 Curzon St. (Indian).

Rte 10. *Hyde Park, Knightsbridge, and Belgravia*
*Le Grand Vefour, Pont St.; ***Le Gavroche**, Lower Sloane St.; **Mr Chow**, Knightsbridge; ***Parke's**, 4 Beauchamp Place; **Michael's**, 3 Park Close (Hawaiian); ***San Lorenzo**, 22 Beauchamp Place; **La Popôte**, Walton St.; **Land's**, Walton St.; **Marcel**, 14 Sloane St.; **Kir**, 11 Sloane St.; **Poissonerie de l'Avenue**, Sloane Ave.; **Pergola**, in Hyde Park; **Massey's Chop House**, 38 Beauchamp Place; **Minotaur**, Sloane Avenue; **Carafe**, 15 Lowndes St.; **The Other Bistro**, 27 Motcomb St.; **Coq au Vin**, 8 Harriet St.; **Trois Canards**, Knightsbridge Green; **13½ (Cantina Marchigiana)**, Beauchamp Place; **Chezan**, 16 Cheval Place (Pakistani). – Less expensive: **Fiddlers Three**, 22 Beauchamp Place; **German Food Centre**, Knightsbridge; **Spaghetti House**, Knightsbridge; **Upstairs**, Basil St.; Tea is served at **Bendick's** in Sloane St.

Rte 11. *Kensington and Bayswater*
Leith's, 92 Kensington Park Rd. (not cheap); **Le Bressan**, 14 Wright's Lane; **Chez Moi**, 3 Addison Ave.; ***Brompton Grill**, 243 Brompton Rd.; **L'Artiste Affamé**, 243 Old Brompton Rd.; **Ponte Vecchio**, Old Brompton Rd.; **Au Bon Accueil**, 27 Elyston St.; **Wheeler's Alcove**, 17a Kensington High St.; **Mr Chow's Montpelier**, 13 Montpelier St.;

Le Coq Hardi, 353 Kensington High St.; Kuchini, Kensington Court; The Ark, Kensington Court; Chez Luba, 116 Draycott Ave. (Russian); La Speranza, 179 Brompton Rd.; Le Chalet, 5 Campden Hill Rd.; Shangri La, 233 Brompton Rd. (Chinese); Chez Cleo, 11 Harrington Gdns.; Medusa, 38 Kensington Church St.; Trattoo, 2 Abingdon Rd.; Beoty, 14 Wright's Lane (off Kensington High St.); L'Artiste Assoiffé, 122 Kensington Park Rd.; Capability Brown, 53 Old Brompton Rd.; *Piccola Venezia, 39 Thurloe Place; Chez Kristof, 12 St Alban's Grove; Chanterelle, 119 Brompton Rd.; Star of India, 154 Old Brompton Rd. (Indian); La Toque Blanche, Abingdon Rd.; Marynka, 232 Brompton Rd. (Austrian); La Paesana, 30 Uxbridge Rd.; Gondoliere, 3 Gloucester Rd.; Tether's, 6 Portland Rd.; Norway Food Centre, 166 Brompton Rd.; Chez Franco, 3 Hereford Rd. — Less expensive: *Kalamaros, Inverness Mews (Greek; unlicensed); Bun Penny, Brompton Rd.; Elegant Bistro, 272 Brompton Rd.; Le Bistingo, 7 Kensington High St.; The Loose Box, Cheval Place; Jamshid, 6 Glendower Place (Indian); Al Ristoro, 205 Kensington Church St.; Contented Sole, 19 Exhibition Rd.; Luba's Bistro, 6 Yeoman's Row.

Rte 12. *Victoria and Pimlico*

La Poule au Pot, 231 Ebury St.; Massimo, 42 Buckingham Palace Rd.; *Como Lario, Holbein Place; Midas, 71 Ebury St.; Mimmo d'Ischia, 61 Elizabeth St.; Avocado, 22 Charlwood St. (off Belgrave Rd.); Chez Gaston, 36 Buckingham Palace Rd.; Overton, opposite Victoria Stn. (sea-food); Polonia, 27 Grosvenor Gdns. (Polish); Bushbys, 79 Royal Hospital Rd.; Grumbles, Churton St.— Less expensive: Bumbles, 16 Buckingham Palace Rd.; Alpino, Buckingham Palace Road; Edelweiss, 15 Eccleston St. (Swiss).

Rte 13. *Chelsea*

Don Luigi, King's Rd.; *Le Francais, 259 Fulham Rd.; Daisy, 40 King's Rd.; Au Fin Bec, 100 Draycott Ave.; Daphne's, 112 Draycott Ave.; Au Père de Nico, 10 Lincoln St.; Charco's, 1 Bray Place; Ox on the Roof, 353 King's Rd.; Minotaur, Chelsea Cloisters (Sloane Ave.); Casserole, 338 King's Rd.; Marco Polo, 95 King's Rd. (Chinese); Nick's Diner, 88 Ifield Rd.; Choy's, 172 King's Rd. (Chinese); Le Carrosse, 19–21 Elystan St.; Alvaro, 124 King's Rd.; Melita, 153 King's Rd.; '235', King's Rd.; Alexander's, 138a King's Rd.; Provan, Fulham Rd.; La Rêve, 330 King's Rd.; Casse Croute, 1 Cale St.; Sans Souci, 68 Royal Hospital Rd.; San Frediano, 66 Fulham Rd.; Patricia's, 9 Park Walk (off Fulham Rd.; with dancing); Da Angela, Sydney St.; Spot Three, 14 Fulham Rd.; '430', King's Rd.; Tandoori, 153 Fulham Rd. (Indian). — Less expensive: Nineteen, 19 Mossop St.; Dominic's Bistro, King's Rd.; Red Onion, Fulham Rd.; American Haven, King's Rd.; Peter Jones (department store), Sloane Sq.

Rte 14. *Soho and Shaftesbury Avenue*

Braganza, 56 Frith St. (seafood); Kettner's, 29 Romilly St. (not cheap); *Trattoria Terrazza, 19 Romilly St.; Gennaro's, 44 Dean St.—Less expensive: Casa Pepe, 52 Dean St. (Spanish); Chez Victor, 45 Wardour St.; Beoty's, 79 St Martin's Lane; Chez Solange, 35 Cranbourn St.; Mon Plaisir, 21 Monmouth St.; Estoril da Luigi e Fiorello, 3 Denman St.; Sheekey's, 29 St Martin's Court (seafood); Romano Santi, 50 Greek St.; Jardin des Gourmets, 5 Greek St.; L'Epicure, 28 Frith St.; Isola Bella, 15 Frith St.; La Capannina, 24 Romilly St.; Cranks, Marshall St.; Manzi's, Lisle St.; Swiss Centre, Leicester Square; Choy, 45 Frith St. (Chinese); Hungarian Csarda, 77 Dean St.; Ley On, 91 Wardour St.; Moulin d'Or, 27 Romilly St.; Boulogne, 27 Gerrard St.; Shafi, 18 Gerrard St. (Indian); Ashoka, 22 Cranbourn St. (Indian); Ganges, 40 Gerrard St. (Indian); Gay Hussar, 2 Greek St. (Hungarian); L'Escargot, 48 Greek St.; Trattoria Toscana, 14 Frith St.; Canton, 11 Newport St. (Chinese); Lee Hoo Fook, 15 Gerrard St. (Chinese); China Garden, 66 Brewer St. (Chinese); Hostaria Romana, 70 Dean St.; Young's Chinese, 13 West St.; Benoit's, Old Compton St.

Rte 15. *Regent Street, Marylebone*

*White Tower, 1 Percy St. (Greek); Odin's, 27 Devonshire St.; Lacy's, 26 Whitfield St. — Less expensive: L'Etoile, 30 Charlotte St.; Elysée, 13 Percy St.; Christophe, 9 St Christopher's Place, W.1; Shirreff's, 15 Great Castle St.; Nibub Lokanta (Turkish), 112 Edgware Rd.; Trat West, 143 Edgware Rd.; La Récolte, 67 Duke St.; Genevieve, 13 Thayer St.; Le Petit Montmartre, 15 Marylebone Lane; Oslo Court, Prince Albert Rd.; Barcelona, 17 Beak St. (Spanish); Verrey, 233 Regent St.; Diamond's (Greek; evening only), 134 Marylebone Rd.; Trattoria dei Pescatori, 57 Charlotte St.; Rose Garden, Regent's Park; Zoological Gardens Restaurant; Le Rendez Vous, 12 Great Castle St.; Boulevard, 56 Wigmore St.; Hellenic, 30 Thayer St. (Greek); Cock and Lion, 62 Wigmore St.; A la Gargouille de Notre Dame, 130 Regent's Park Rd.; Cooper Grill, 60

Wigmore St.—Less expensive: **Agra,** 135 Whitfield St. (Indian); ***Bertorelli,** 19 Charlotte St.; **New Kebab House, Anemos,** and **Kebab and Houmos** (all Greek), in Charlotte St.

Rte 16. *Bloomsbury*
See Rte 15.

Rte 17. *The Strand and Covent Garden*
Rule's, 35 Maiden Lane; ***Neal Street,** 26 Neal St.; **Boulestin,** 25 Southampton St.; ***Ivy,** 1 West St.; ***Inigo Jones,** 14 Garrick St.; **Simpson's,** 100 Strand, in the 'Old English' style; **La Scala,** Southampton St.; **Nag Head,** Floral St.; **L'Opéra,** Great Queen St.

Rte 18. *The Inns of Court*
Terrazza-Est, 125 Chancery Lane; ***Le Gaulois,** 119 Chancery Lane; **Devereux,** 20 Devereux Court.

Rte 19. *Fleet Street to St Paul's*
*Brasserie Benoits, Old Bailey; **City Friends,** 34 Old Bailey (Cantonese); **Le Bistingo,** 65 Fleet Street; **Cheshire Cheese** and **Cock Tavern,** both in Fleet Street.

Rte 20. *St Paul's*
See Rte 19. Modest restaurants and sandwich bars and good pubs with food (e.g. the **Master Gunner** and **Christopher Wren)** in the new piazza North of the cathedral.

Rte 21. *High Holborn to the Bank*
Royal Connaght, 267 High Holborn; ***Le Poulbot,** 45 Cheapside; **Williamson's,** Groveland Court, Bow Lane; **Taverna Etrusca,** Bow Lane; **Akiko,** 5 Cathedral Place (Japanese).

Rte 22. *Smithfield and Clerkenwell*
See Rte 21.

Rte 23. *Guildhall London Wall, and Barbican*
Old Dr Butler's Head, Mason's Ave., Coleman St.; **The Baron of Beef,** Gutter Lane (not cheap); **City Yacht,** London Wall.—Less expensive: **Elisabeth,** Wood St.; **City Diner,** Foster Lane.

Rte 24. *Bank of England, Mansion House, Stock Exchange*
Stock Exchange Grill, Birch's, 3 Angel Court, both in Throgmorton St; **Aykoku-kaku** (Japanese), Walbrook. See also Rte 29.

Rte 25. *Bank to the Angel*
See Rte 23 for the first part of the route; also, **Ravello,** 46 Old St.—IN ISLINGTON: **Robert Carrier, *Frederick's,** and **Portofino,** in Camden Passage, all first-class restaurants.—The **Camden Head,** in Camden Passage, and the **Island Queen** in Noel Rd. are pubs serving good food.

Rte 26. *The Thames Embankment*
'Hispaniola' and **'Old Caledonia'** river-boat restaurants.

Rte 27. *From Blackfriars to the Tower*
Rte A: **Armoury,** 44 Cannon Street; ***Sweeting's,** 39 Queen Victoria St.; ***Wheeler's,** 19 Great Tower St., both for seafood; **Cotillion Room,** Bucklersbury House, Walbrook; **Omar Khayyam,** 50 Cannon St. (Persian); **Ye Olde Wine Shades,** 6 Martin Lane (off Cannon St.).

Rte B: ***Samuel Pepys,** Brooke Wharf, 48 Upper Thames St.; **Mermaid Theatre,** Puddle Dock; **Bridge House,** London Bridge; **Southwark Bridge** restaurant.

Rte 28. *Tower of London*
On the piazza to the w. of the Tower: **Tower Room,** and **Castle.** Restaurant-Cafeteria in the Tower. See also Rte 27.

Rte 29. *From the Bank to Aldgate*
Essex, Duster House, Mincing Lane; **Falstaff,** 12 Philpot Lane; **Viceroy,** Colonial House, Mark Lane; **Wheelton Room,** 62 Crutched Friars; **George,** 86 Fenchurch St.; **Lucullus,** Plantation House, Mincing Lane; **Bull's Head,** Leadenhall St.

Simpson's, Ball Court (38½ Cornhill), an English-style eating-house for city businessmen; **George and Vulture,** 3 Castle Court, Birchin Lane.

Rte 30. *Bishopsgate and Shoreditch*

Executive, Winchester House; ***Palmerston**, 49 Bishopsgate; **Poor Millionaire**, 158 Bishopsgate; **Bill Bentley's Oyster Bar**, Swedeland Court (opposite Liverpool St. Stn.), and **Dirty Dick's**. Modest restaurants in Old Broad St.

Rtes 31–32. *The East End*

Bloom's, Whitechapel High St. (Jewish); **Friends** (Chinese); **Beefeater, Captain's Cabin, Dickens Tavern**, all St Katherine's Dock; **Mr Toad**, Grand Union Canal, 228 Old Ford Road.

RESTAURANTS IN THE ENVIRONS OF LONDON
A. *The North and North-West*

ST JOHN'S WOOD: **Froops**, 17 Princess Road; **Au Bois St Jean**, 122 St John's Wood High St.; **Rossetti**, Barrack St.; **Abbots**, 3 Blenheim Terrace.—HAMPSTEAD: **Le Celier du Midi**, Church Row; **Keats**, 3 Downshire Hill; **Huntsman**, 13 Flask Walk; **La Baita**, 200 Haverstock Hill; **Hampstead 8444**; **Ah! Bistro**, 66 Heath St. (dinner only). Pubs in Spaniards Rd., Downshire Hill, Holly Mount, and Well Walk.—FINCHLEY: **L'Aubergade**, 816 Finchley Rd.; **Da Fernando**, 34 Ballards Lane, N.3.—SOUTHGATE: **Ye Olde Cherry Tree**, The Green, N.14.—ENFIELD: **Robin Hood**, Botany Bay; **West Lodge; Jolly Farmers**.—HARLESDEN: **Kuo Yuan**, 217 High Road, N.W.10; **Kwan Yin**, The Broadway, Mill Hill.—STANMORE: **The Alpine, Romano**, Stanmore Hill.—HARROW: **Starlight Grill, The Etonian**.

B. *The South and South-West*

SOUTHWARK: **Anchor**, Bankside; **George Inn**, Borough High St.—LAMBETH: **Crispin's**, 219 Kennington Rd. (unlicensed).—BATTERSEA: **Five-Five-Five**, 555 Battersea Park Road; **Pooh Corner**, 246 Battersea Park Road.—CLAPHAM: **Wine and Dine**, 50 Battersea Rise, S.W.11.—WIMBLEDON: **Le Café Royal**, 72 High St.; **Fisherman's Wharf**.—BARNES: **Le Petit Bedon**, 89 Rocks Lane, S.W.13.—RICHMOND: **Le Chien au Feu; Oscars**, 149 Kew Rd.; **Valchera, Rendezvous** (Chinese), Hawkes' Wine Bar, Le Veranda, West Lodge, Jaspers Bun in the Oven, 11 Kew Green.—HAMPTON COURT: ***Bastians**, Hampton Court Rd.—EWELL: **The Spring**.—EGHAM: **Great Fosters**, Stroude Road.

C. *The West*

EALING: **The Hay Loft**.—UXBRIDGE: **Denham Lodge**.—WINDSOR: numerous restaurants in High St., **La Taverna**, River St.—OLD WINDSOR: **Bells of Ouseley**.—ETON: **House on the Bridge**, and restaurants in High St.

D. *The South-East*

NEW CROSS: **Marmara**, 29 Clifton Rise; **Casa Cominetti**, 129 Rushy Green, Catford.—GREENWICH: **Trafalgar Tavern**, Park Row.—Also in BLACKHEATH, several near the Station.

Public Houses vary considerably with the area of London in which they are situated. The most 'fashionable' (but often the most pretentious) pubs are found in Belgravia, Knightsbridge, and some parts of Chelsea; others with more character may be found in the City or along the river. Many serve good light meals, though often not on Sundays. Most pubs are 'tied' to a particular brewery, which controls the brew (and sometimes the brands of liquor) it sells; a 'Free House' is not so tied. In general the Public Bar is less well appointed and is patronized by the regular locals (male) and may be the scene of darts-playing, etc.; the Saloon, Private Bar, Lounge, are progressively more select (and usually less animated). Children under 14 years old are not admitted and those under 18 allowed only non-alcoholic drinks (except that those over 16 may have certain types of alcoholic drink with a meal). Unaccompanied ladies are not served in some city houses. 'Off-licences' sell liquor for consumption off the premises.

Licensing Hours. The 'permitted hours' during which alcoholic liquor may be supplied at restaurants or public houses vary in different districts, but the total number of such hours on weekdays is 8, unless specially extended to $8\frac{1}{2}$. Generally speaking, it is not possible to purchase liquor before 11 a.m., or between 3 and 5.30, or after 10.30 p.m. Restaurants may supply liquor for consumption with a meal for one hour after the ordinary hours. On Sundays the sale of liquor is permitted from midday to 2 p.m. and 7 to 10.30. These restrictions do not apply within their own hotels to visitors staying overnight.

III TRANSPORT

For the visitor to London the most informative means of transport (after walking) is by bus. Much of London may be seen from the top deck of a bus en route to a particular destination, although patience is needed to queue at bus stops for irregular services. A more efficient and faster means of communication between set points is provided by the London Underground. Care should be taken to avoid where possible the use of public transport from 8–10 a.m., 12–2, and 4.30–6.30 p.m., when the London 'rush-hour' is at its height.

The visitor is strongly advised to obtain the free London Transport bus and underground maps (revised frequently) issued at 55 Broadway, S.W.1.

Taxicabs cruise in central London and are generally adequate in number except during wet weather. Visitors with a car will find parking in central London an ever-increasing expense and experience periods of unaccountable congestion in the main traffic arteries.

Although Rtes 1–33 in the Guide are intended to be followed on foot, an indication of the public transport serving each area, and parking places, is given at the beginning of each route.

Up-to-the minute bulletins about transport (strikes, delays, cancellations, accidents, diversions, etc.) are broadcast by B.B.C. Radio London at intervals throughout the day.

Buses. The London red double-decker bus services are arranged in a system of numbered routes (buses; 1–299). A free list and map is issued by London Transport. Care should be taken to note the destination displayed on the front of the bus which may be short of the usual terminus of the service. If the halt is a 'request' stop the bus will only stop if hailed by a passenger (or if the bell is rung once by a passenger wishing to alight).

A disciplined procedure of 'queueing' is voluntarily observed at bus stops. On the type of bus used in the central area in which a conductor collects fares only 5 passengers are allowed to stand. Outside the centre newer buses with automatic fare machines are in use. Smoking is allowed on the top deck only.

FARES vary according to distance, and are usually cheaper than the equivalent Underground fare. Children under 15 may travel any distance for 5p after 9.30 a.m. Tickets should be retained until the end of the journey as they are often checked by inspectors.

Monthly Season tickets for unlimited and unrestricted travel on red buses may be purchased. A red bus '*Rover*' ticket gives a day's unlimited travel on all bus routes after 9.30 a.m. Mon–Fri or any time on Sat, Sun, and BH. Such tickets can be purchased from bus garages, Underground stations, or any London Transport Travel Enquiry Office. – '*Go-as-you-please*' Tourist tickets may be purchased for travel on all London Transport buses, and the Underground, for 4 days, 7 days, or a month. These are sold at the Tourist Ticket Office, St James's Park Stn., or L.T. Travel Enquiry offices. All fares are to be increased in June 1978. Photographs for an identity card are necessary for '*Go-as-you-please*' tickets.

On most routes the buses operate from 6 or 6.30 a.m. (earlier in outer areas) to 11.30 or 12 p.m. A few all-night buses (double fare between 12.30 and 4.30) run irregular services, except on Sat night/Sun morning.

RED ARROW single-decker buses connect the main railway stations with limited stops en route. They operate on a flat fare (10p) paid on entering. There are separate entrance and exit doors operated by the driver. No smoking is allowed.

Green Line Coaches. The environs of London within a radius of c. 30 miles are served by the comfortable Green Line Coaches of the National Bus Company, most of the routes of which intersect the whole length or breadth of London, while a few have termini at Aldgate or Victoria. In central London these coaches pick up passengers only at certain fixed points, i.e. Hyde Park Corner, Marble Arch, Notting Hill Gate, Baker St. Stn., Oxford Circus, Eccleston Bridge (Victoria), Albert Hall, High St. Kensington, etc.

Information on coach travel (including Green Line services and country buses) may be obtained from *National Travel Ltd.* (Mon–Fri 8 a.m–9 p.m., Sat 10–9, Sun & BH. 11–9; Tel. 730 0202) at Victoria Coach Station, Buckingham Palace Road, S.W.1. Information may also be obtained from *London Country Bus Services*, (daily 8.30–5.50), Eccleston Bridge, S.W.1.

A 'Master Ticket' for visitors may be purchased for 7 consecutive days' travel on London Country Bus services, coaches, etc.

Underground Railways (the 'tube') provide the most efficient and rapid means of public transport. The stations (about 250 in London and its suburbs) are indicated by 'Underground' signs. At their points of inter-section the underground railways are connected with each other by subways, and they communicate directly in the same way with most of the railway termini. A plan of the Underground system in London is provided in the Atlas section of the Guide.

Tickets for the final destination (even if a change of line is involved) must be purchased before the journey from a machine or ticket office in the station. At many stations automatic barriers have been introduced which operate with yellow tickets. At the beginning of a journey the platform is reached through a barrier opened by the insertion of a ticket into a machine; it must be remembered to retrieve the ticket as you pass through. The ticket is surrendered at the end of the journey.

Trains run frequently between 5.30 a.m. and 12.15 p.m. (Sundays until 11.30 p.m.) from the central area. There are no all night services. Certain stations are closed at weekends (comp. the Plan).

Season tickets may be purchased, and cheap Day Return tickets may be bought for journeys after 10 a.m. where the single fare is 35p or more. For tourist tickets, see p. 24. Children under 14 travel at half-fare or 20p, whichever is less.

London Transport Inquiry Offices (open daily, incl. Sun, 8.30 a.m.– 9.30 p.m.) are situated in the following Underground Stations: Heathrow Central, Victoria, Oxford Circus, Piccadilly Circus, St James's Park, King's Cross, and Euston. Public Relations Officer, 55 Broadway, S.W.1. A 24 hr telephone information service is maintained (222 1234).

Suburban Railways. The overground services still reflect the pattern of their independent pre-grouping era. The lines most convenient for the environs are listed at the beginning of each route (Nos. 34–48). For the main railway termini in London, see p. 14.

The termini for trains operated by the **Southern Region** include Waterloo, Victoria, Charing Cross and Cannon Street (Pl. 9; 7), London Bridge (Pl. 21; 3), and Holborn Viaduct (Pl. 8; 5). Cross-exchange between any of them and most suburban destinations can be effected by changing at one of the main suburban junctions at Beckenham, Mitcham, East Croydon, and Clapham.—The termini for the **Eastern Region** include Liverpool Street, Fenchurch Street (Pl. 9; 8), King's Cross, and Broad Street (Pl. 9; 3).—The **London Midland Region** operates from St Pancras (Pl. 7; 1), Euston, Broad Street, and Marylebone (Pl. 4; 6).—The **Western Region** operates local lines from Paddington.

The *British Rail Travel Centre* in Lower Regent Street, S.W.1 issues tickets and information about British Rail services throughout Britain.

Taxicabs. Cruising taxis may be hailed in central London, or local taxi ranks (listed under 'Taxicab' in the telephone directory) may be telephoned. Numerous radio cab services operate; among the most efficient are: 289 1133, 286 4848, and 272 3030 (the charge of the journey to pick up the passenger is added to the fare).

Charges are prominently displayed and taxi-drivers and their cabs have registered numbers.

Motoring. To import a car for tourist use into the United Kingdom for a period not exceeding 12 months, no formalities are necessary except the possession of (*a*) a valid National Driving Licence or International Driving Permit; (*b*) an International Motor Insurance Card (Green Card) valid for the U.K. (otherwise British Insurance must be effected immediately). No one under 17 years of age may drive a motor-car in Great Britain, and no one under 16 may ride a motor-cycle.

The rule of the road throughout the United Kingdom is 'keep to the left and overtake on the right', which is the reverse of the procedure in most parts of Europe and in America. There is a general speed limit of 30 miles per hour on roads in built-up areas (i.e. those areas with street lighting), except where otherwise indicated; and a maximum speed limit on all roads and motorways of 70 m.p.h. Penalties for driving under the influence of alcohol or drugs have recently been increased. For all information on road conduct motorists should consult 'The Highway Code' (H.M.S.O.).

Motorists are strongly advised to join one or other of the national motoring organizations: the *Automobile Association of Great Britain* (A.A.), Fanum House, Leicester Square, W.C.2; or the *Royal Automobile Club* (R.A.C.), Head Office: 89 Pall Mall, S.W.1. A slight reduction in membership fee is granted to members of affiliated overseas organizations such as the American Automobile Association, and free reciprocal membership is offered in some cases to Commonwealth visitors.

Signposting is in miles and British-made cars have mileometers and speedometers reading m.p.h. A change to kilometres is not likely during the currency of this volume. Continental readers hardly need to be reminded that 5 miles are almost exactly equal to 8 kilometres.

PARKING. On weekdays (8 a.m.–6.30 p.m.; Sat to 1.30 p.m.), parking in central London is controlled by meters. Charges vary according to district but tend everywhere to increase, while the maximum time allowed is now more usually two hours than four. A free meter is often hard to find, especially near the main shopping areas. Car parks (marked 'P' on the sectional plans) are mentioned at the beginning of each route in central London. Information on *National Car Parks* (including late-night garages) is obtained by telephoning 723 3400. Parking is forbidden on a yellow line; on a double yellow line stopping at all, even to set down or pick up a passenger, is forbidden. A 'ticket' (meaning an eventual fine) is likely for the former; towing away or a more severe penalty for the latter. The local police station (see Telephone Directory) will inform a driver to which 'pound' his car has been towed.

CAR HIRE. When hiring a car, visitors must present a valid driving licence free from endorsement (and, usually, have had driving experience for at least a year). Hire companies usually stipulate that the hirer of a self-driven car must be between 21 and 65 years old. Most of the International Car Hire firms have agents in London (for car hire at London Airport, see p. 13). Information may be obtained at the motoring organizations. Cars may also be hired through the *American Express*, *B.E.A.*, and the *Car Hire International*, Swallow St., Piccadilly. Chauffeur-driven cars may also be hired through many car hire firms and garages.

Thames Passenger Services. Daily motor launch services operate in April–September from *Westminster Pier* to Putney, Kew Gardens, Richmond, and Hampton Court Palace; and for most of the year from *Westminster* or *Charing Cross Pier* to the Tower of London and Greenwich. For details, see Rtes 38, 28, 34B. The *Thames Passenger Services Federation* operates from Charing Cross Pier and *Westminster Passenger Service Association* from Westminster Pier. A hydrofoil service operates throughout the year between the Tower and Greenwich.

Tours. The 'Round London' sightseeing tour operated by *London Transport* covers c. 20 miles of the West End and City and lasts about 2 hrs. It may be joined at Piccadilly Circus or at Victoria (Buckingham Palace Rd.). In summer some of the buses have an open top deck. It runs daily 10 a.m.–9 p.m. (in winter, after 4 p.m. from Piccadilly only). Fare £1·30 (children 80p). The 'Vintage Bus' tour (No. 100; an ST type vehicle of the 1930s) follows a circular route in the West End, starting at Horse Guards Avenue. It operates daily every hour on the hour from 10 a.m. to 7 p.m. (fare according to distance).

London Transport in summer also run three conducted coach tours (3 hrs) of London from Victoria Coach Station: Westminster and the West End (£3·50; children £2·50) daily exc. Sun, 18 Mar–13 Oct, 10 a.m.; the City and Tower (£5; children £3) daily incl. Sun, 18 Mar–13 Oct, 2 p.m.; also Mon, Wed and Fri, 15 May–22 Sept at 10 a.m.; Cockney East End & London Dungeon (£4·50; children £3) Weds, 22 Mar–11 Oct; Mon and Fri, 15 May–22 Sept; starting at 2 p.m. – A 7-hr combined tour of Westminster and City (£8·70; children £6, inc. lunch) runs daily exc. Sun, 18 Mar–13 Oct, starting at 10 a.m. – A 6-hr tour of Windsor and Hampton Court (£7·20; children £6, inc. lunch) runs daily, incl. Sun, 18 Mar–13 Oct, starting at 10.15 a.m.; also daily incl. Sun, 6 May–29 Sept, starting at 1 p.m. All prices listed are current for 1978.

London Transport run a number of other guided and unguided day tours during the summer from Victoria Coach Station to places of interest outside London. Details from any London Transport Travel Enquiry Office.

Other coach tour operators include: *American Express*, 6 Haymarket; *Thos. Cook & Son*, 45 Berkeley St., Piccadilly; *Evan Evans*, 41 Tottenham Court Road, W.1; and *Frames' and Rickards'*, 46 Albermarle St., W.1.

Helicopter. Sightseeing trips (£21 per person) are made daily by Helicopter Tours (London) Ltd, 94 Jermyn St., S.W.1. The fare includes transport to and from Battersea Heliport (bookings 24 hours in advance: Tel. 930 0261).

River Excursions. Evening cruises of the Pool of London operate in summer from Westminster Pier (7.30–9.30). River trips from Kingston upon Thames to Windsor and Oxford; from Waterloo and Paddington stations (May–Sept) combined rail and steamer trips to Windsor, Hampton Court, Kingston upon Thames, etc. Thames Valley Mini-cruises from Windsor to Oxford (with overnight stay at Caversham).— Cruises by hydrofoil twice daily May–Sept from Greenwich to Lambeth and back (2 hrs) and to Hampton Court on Sun.

Boat Trips on the Regent's Canal operate from Little Venice (see p. 169) and Camden Town (p. 322). A water-bus runs between Little Venice and the Zoo in Regent's Park (p. 170).

Guides, registered with the British Travel Association, can be contacted through travel agents, or the *Guild of Guide Lecturers Booking Bureau*, Royal Commonwealth Society, 18 Northumberland Avenue, W.C.2 (open in summer, Mon–Fri, 9.30 a.m.–5.30 p.m.).

Car Tours provide a car driven by a chauffeur/guide. Operators include: *Guides of Britain Ltd.*, 71 Burlington Arcade, W.1, and *University Guides*, 151 Kensington High St., W.8 (visitors conducted by a member of a British university).

SPECIALIST GUIDES. *Off-Beat Tours of London*, 66 St Michael's St., W.2, organize walks (often advertised in the Sunday press) mostly on Sundays. Other guided tours include: Pub Tours and City Strolls; Antique Tours; Horse-drawn carriage tours of residential London; children's tours (including Junior Jaunts, 13A Harriet Walk, S.W.1). For further information apply to the London Tourist Board.

IV AMUSEMENTS

For regular annual events, see p. 39. By dialling 246 8041 the visitor will be told the main events of the day in London. The well-known theatres and concert halls are described in more detail in the text (comp. the index).

Theatres and Concert Halls. Performances are given on Mon–Sat and usually begin at 7.30–8.30 p.m. and end at about 10.15 p.m. The centre of London becomes congested at these hours, and taxis and parking places are hard to find. It is wise to allow extra time for such conditions; latecomers to the theatre are often obliged to watch the first act on close-circuit television in the foyer; similarly, concertgoers are not admitted once the performance has begun until the end of the first movement. Matinée performances (often on Wed) start at 2.30–2.45 p.m. Some theatres give two performances on Saturday (c. 5.30 and 8.30 p.m.). Smoking is not usually permitted during a performance. Most theatres and concert halls have a bar serving light refreshments; orders for the interval may often be placed before the performance to avoid the necessity of queuing.

TICKETS may be obtained in advance from the theatre box-office (no extra charge; open from 10 a.m.–8 p.m.) or by telephone (in which case they must be collected at least $\frac{1}{2}$ hr before the performance). Otherwise tickets may be purchased (with a commission charge) at one of the numerous ticket-agents' offices (at the principal hotels, in the large stores, at music shops, etc.). These include Keith Prowse & Co. Ltd., 93 Knightsbridge, S.W.1, Mayfair Hotel, Berkeley St., W.1, etc; and Alfred Hays Ltd., 4 Charing Cross Road, S.W.1. Tickets may also now be booked through Computaticket, 242 Tottenham Court Rd., W.1.

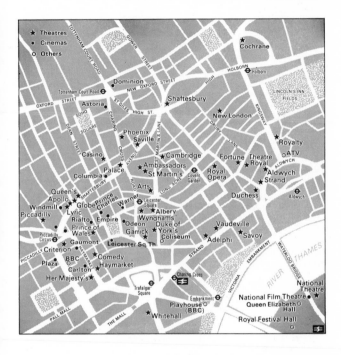

Special advance booking services. The *National Theatre* will send a programme of performances on request which allows booking before the general box office opens. The *Aldwych* (Royal Shakespeare Company) operates an advance booking service for members of its club (fee). At the *Festival Hall* tickets may usually be booked one month in advance; a subscription scheme with vouchers for 10 concerts also operates. Booking at *Covent Garden* is generally open c. 6 weeks in advance; for certain performances a day for postal bookings is advertised. At the *Royal Albert Hall* priority bookings may be made by those subscribing to the mailing list.

A weekly London Theatre Guide is available free at most theatre box offices, hotels, etc., and a copy is displayed at railway stations. Daily newspapers print an 'Amusement Guide'; a fuller and more detailed programme is given in the week-end press, and in the London evening papers. The British Tourist Authority publishes 'London Week', and the G.L.C., 'Looking for Leisure'. Newsagents also sell 'Time Out', and 'What's On', etc. (weekly publications).

A Plan of theatres and large cinemas in central London is given above;

those outside this area are indicated on the atlas (to which the plan references below refer).

London Theatres:
ADELPHI, 411 Strand, between Bedford St. and Southampton St.
ALBERY (formerly the New), St Martin's Lane (w. side)
ALDWYCH, Aldwych, at the corner of Drury Lane
AMBASSADORS, West St., Shaftesbury Avenue
APOLLO, at the corner of Shaftesbury Ave. and Rupert St.
CAMBRIDGE, Seven Dials
COMEDY, Panton St., Haymarket
CRITERION, Piccadilly Circus (s. side)
DRURY LANE (Theatre Royal, Drury Lane), Catherine St., at the corner of Russell St., Covent Garden
DUCHESS, Catherine St., Aldwych
DUKE OF YORK'S, St Martin's Lane (w. side)
FORTUNE, Russell St., opposite Drury Lane Theatre
GARRICK, at the s. end of Charing Cross Road
GLOBE, at the corner of Shaftesbury Ave. and Rupert St.
HAYMARKET (Theatre Royal, Haymarket), on the E. side of Haymarket
HER MAJESTY'S, on the w. side of Haymarket
JEANNETTA COCHRANE (Pl. 7; 5), Southampton Row, at corner of Theobald's Rd.
LYRIC, 29 Shaftesbury Avenue (N. side)
MAYFAIR (Pl. 13; 4), Stratton St.
MERMAID (Pl. 8; 7), Upper Thames St., near Blackfriars Bridge
NATIONAL THEATRE, South Bank
NEW LONDON, Parker St., off Drury Lane
OLD VIC (Pl. 19; 2), Waterloo Rd. (s. bank)
OPEN-AIR THEATRE (Pl. 5; 3), Queen Mary's Gardens, Regent's Park, Performances of Shakespeare in summer
PALACE, Cambridge Circus, Shaftesbury Avenue
PHOENIX, near the N. end of Charing Cross Road
PICCADILLY, 8 Sherwood St., Piccadilly Circus
PRINCE OF WALES, Coventry St., between Leicester Square and Piccadilly Circus
QUEEN'S, Shaftesbury Avenue
REGENT, Regent St., near B.B.C.
ROYAL COURT (Pl. 17; 1), Sloane Square
ROYALTY (Pl. 15; 1), Portugal St., off Kingsway
ST MARTIN'S, West St., Shaftesbury Avenue
SAVILLE, Shaftesbury Avenue, at the corner of Stacey St.
SAVOY, Savoy Court, Strand
SHAFTESBURY, Shaftesbury Avenue, at the corner of High Holborn
SHAW (Pl. 6; 2), 100 Euston Road
STRAND, Aldwych, at the corner of Catherine St.
THEATRE UPSTAIRS (Pl. 17; 1), Royal Court, Sloane Street
VAUDEVILLE, 404 Strand (N. side)
WESTMINSTER (Pl. 18; 1), Palace St., Buckingham Gate
WHITEHALL (Pl. 14; 6), Whitehall, near Charing Cross
WYNDHAM'S, Charing Cross Road and Cranbourn Street
YOUNG VIC, The Cut, Waterloo Road (s. bank)
The *Globe Playhouse*, Bankside holds performances of Elizabethan plays in June–Aug.

Theatres away from the centre of London often used by touring companies, or specializing in experimental plays, include: *The Roundhouse*, Chalk Farm, N.W.1; *Theatre Royal*, Angel Lane, Stratford; *Streatham Hill Theatre*; *Greenwich Theatre*, Crooms Hill, S.E.10; *Richmond Theatre*, Richmond Green; *Ashcroft Theatre*, Park Lane, Croydon; *Theatre Workshop*, Stratford, E.15; *Wimbledon Theatre*, The Broadway, S.W.19; *The Cockpit*, Gateforth St., N.W.8 – Open-air performances in summer at *Marble Hill* and *Richmond Terrace Gardens.*

In addition, a number of theatre clubs (with varying conditions of membership; new members can often join at the door, or 48 hrs in advance) exist for the purpose of staging modern or unusual plays, etc. They are licensed to play on Sun. Among the best known are: *The Arts*, 6 Great Newport St. (with performances for children on Sat & Sun); *Hampstead Theatre Club*, Swiss Cottage Centre, N.W.3; *Tower*,

Canonbury Tower, Islington; *King's Head*, Upper St., Islington; *Almost Free Theatre*, 9 Rupert St., W.1; *Open Space*, 32 Tottenham Court Rd.; *Players*, Villiers St. (old-time variety); *Irving*, Irving St.; and *Questor's*, Mattock Lane, Ealing.

The *Little Angel*, 14 Dagmar Passage, Cross St., Islington is a Marionette theatre.

VARIETY, now almost wholly transferred to the television screen, may still be seen at the *Palladium*, 7 Argyll St., Oxford Circus; *Victoria Palace*, Victoria St., near Victoria Station; and at the *Talk of the Town*, Cranbourn St., Charing Cross Road.

Concerts, Ballet, and Opera. ROYAL FESTIVAL HALL (Pl. 15; 6): concerts almost nightly by the London Symphony Orchestra, the London Philharmonic Orchestra, etc., with recitals also in the afternoons. Short Ballet seasons (usually at Christmas; sometimes in summer) include performances by the London Festival Ballet. Chamber music and recitals in the associated QUEEN ELIZABETH HALL and PURCELL ROOM.— COVENT GARDEN (Pl. 7; 7): nightly performances by the Royal Opera and Ballet Company from mid-Sept to early Aug, with matinées on Sat and occasional visits from other companies.—COLISEUM (Pl. 14; 4): the English National Opera Company give performances (sung in English) from Aug to March. In April–June the theatre is used by visiting national and international theatre companies (usually ballet). Lunchtime talks on the arts are given (often on Mon).—ROYAL ALBERT HALL (Pl. 12; 5): symphony concerts at intervals throughout the year (esp. on Sun evenings); Promenade concerts in July–Sept, nightly exc. Sun. The Hall is also used for recitals, etc.

A new hall for the London Symphony Orchestra is to be built on the Barbican site in the city.

Other concert halls (often used for chamber music and song recitals) include: *Fairfield Halls*, Park Lane, Croydon; *Wigmore Hall*, 36 Wigmore St.; *Conway Hall*, Red Lion Square; *St John's Church*, Smith Square, S.W.1 – The London Festival Ballet sometimes use the *New Victoria Theatre*, Vauxhall Bridge Rd.; and the London Contemporary Dance Theatre give performances at *The Place*, 17 Dukes Rd., W.C.1 – Occasional concerts (usually in winter) are held in *Central Hall, Westminster* and at *Alexandra Palace*, Wood Green. Informal recitals (harpsichord, clavichord, etc.) are given at *Fenton House*, Hampstead (see p. 323). Concerts are usually held at *Kenwood* in June and July on Sat evenings (open-air symphony concerts, and recitals in Orangery); at *Crystal Palace* in July (on Sun); and at *Holland Park* in Aug (on Sun).

Lunch-time Concerts at St John's, Smith Square, S.W.1 (Mon, exc. in Aug); Bishopsgate Institute, 230 Bishopsgate, E.C.3. (Tues); St Martin in the Fields, Trafalgar Square (Mon & Tues); Holy Sepulchre, Holborn Viaduct (Wed, exc. in Aug); St Stephen, Walbrook (Fri); and other City churches.

Church Music. Most days at *Westminster Abbey*, *St Paul's*, and *Westminster Cathedral* (R.C.). Also (on Sun and holy days) at *St Bartholomew the Great*, Smithfield; *St Michael*, Cornhill; the *Temple* Church; *St James's*, Piccadilly; *St Paul*, Knightsbridge; and *Brompton Oratory* (R.C.).

Cinemas are found in all parts of London. The minimum prices charged in central London are now comparable to those in the theatre. Often only the more expensive seats are bookable; the first showing of a new film is usually difficult to get into without a long queue. Performances are continuous from c. 10.30 a.m. until 11 p.m. (on Sun from c. 2 to 3 p.m.). Late-night films at week-ends begin at 11 or 12 p.m. Smoking is permitted.

The following is a list of the principal cinemas in London, some of which are named on the Plan, p. 29. *A. B. C. 1*, *A. B. C. 2*, Shaftesbury Ave.; *Bloomsbury*, Brunswick Gdns. (opposite Russell Sq. Underground station); *Carlton*, Haymarket; *Cinecenta* (4 small theatres), Panton St., off Leicester Sq.; *Columbia*, 93 Shaftesbury Ave.; *Curzon*, Curzon St.; *Dominion*, Tottenham Court Rd. (s. end); *Empire* and *Empire Two*, 6 Leicester Sq. (N. side); *Gala-Royal*, Marble Arch; *Leicester Square Theatre* (on s. side of the square); *London Pavilion*, Piccadilly Circus; *Metropole*, 160 Victoria St.; *Odeon*, Haymarket; *Odeon*, Leicester Sq. (E side); *Odeon*, Marble Arch (10 Edgware Rd.); *Odeon*, St Martin's Lane; *Plaza and Paramount*, Lower Regent St.; *Prince Charles*, Leicester Place (off Leicester Sq.); *Rialto*, 3 Coventry St.; *Studio One, Studio Two*, 225 Oxford St. (near Oxford Circus); *Universal*, Piccadilly Circus; *Warner Rendezvous* and *Warner West End*, Leicester Sq. (N. side).

Academy One, Two, and *Three*, 165 Oxford St., the *Continentale* and the *Berkeley*, 36 and 30 Tottenham Court Rd., make a speciality of foreign films. The *Everyman*, Hampstead, *Paris-Pullman*, 65 Drayton Gdns., S.W.10, the *Classic* cinemas, Baker St., Chelsea, Notting Hill Gate, Hampstead, etc., often show foreign films and old films. Other cinemas outside central London include: *The Screen*, 83 Upper St., Islington, and the *Gaumont*, 103 Notting Hill Gate.

The *National Film Theatre* (Pl. 15; 6) is open to members and their guests only (Restaurant). Overseas visitors may become members for 1 month. Foreign films, silent films, etc. are shown here in two theatres twice nightly (and often all night on Sat).

Art Exhibitions. The *Hayward Gallery* (p. 267) on the South Bank is leased to the Arts Council of Great Britain for its exhibitions (shows are changed every few months). Outstanding loan exhibitions are held at the *Tate Gallery*, *Victoria and Albert Museum*, *British Museum*, the *Queen's Gallery*, and the *National Portrait Gallery*. Also at the *Guildhall Art Gallery* and the *Imperial War Museum*. In outer London, exhibitions are held in the *Whitechapel Art Gallery*, the *South London Art Gallery*, *Kenwood*, *Osterley*, *Marble Hill*, *Orleans House*, *Bethnal Green Museum*, *National Maritime Museum*, *Camden Arts Centre*, etc.

The Royal Academy of Arts (p. 101) holds an annual summer exhibition of contemporary works of art; in winter important loan exhibitions are held. The Mall Galleries of the *Federation of British Artists* hold exhibitions by members of the *Royal Institute of Oil Painters*, *Royal Institute of Painters in Watercolours*, *Royal Society of British Artists*, *Royal Society of Portrait Painters*, etc. At 26 Conduit St., W.1 are held the exhibitions of the *Royal Society of Painters in Watercolours* (April and Sept) and the *Royal Society of Painter-Etchers* (in early spring).

Art exhibitions (mostly small 'one-man shows', etc.) are held at various galleries and picture-dealers' shops in and near Bond Street and St James's (adm. usually free). It should not be forgotten that superb collections of art pass through the hands of the auctioneers, *Sotheby's* and *Christie's* (for viewing days, see pp. 103, 100). Particulars of sales and exhibitions are advertised in the newspapers.

The *Institute of Contemporary Arts* in the Mall organizes a more or less continuous sequence of exhibitions of varying character.—The *Serpentine Gallery* in Hyde Park is used by the Arts Council for exhibitions of contemporary work by young artists.—The *Design Centre* of the Council of Industrial Design at 28 Haymarket (Mon–Sat, 9.30–5.30, until 9 p.m. on Wed & Thurs), and the *British Crafts Centre* at 12 Waterloo Place, S.W.1 and 43 Earlham St., W.C.2 (Mon–Fri, 10–5, Thurs till 6; Sat 10–1) hold changing exhibitions.—Occasional open-air exhibitions are held in Holland Park, Battersea Park, Victoria Embankment Gdns., and The Terrace, Richmond Hill.—The *Heinz Gallery* of the Royal Institute of British Architects (21 Portman Sq.) holds changing exhibitions of architects' drawings.—The *Photographers' Gallery*, 8 Great Newport St., Leicester Sq. has exhibitions in 2 galleries (changed every month); it is open Tues–Sat, 11–7, Sun 12–6. Periodic exhibitions are also held at the *Kodak Centre*, 246 High Holborn.—The *National Book League* holds exhibitions at 7 Albermarle St.

Spectator Sports. The visitor to London at the appropriate season has many opportunities of seeing interesting and even world-famous sporting events and competitions, a few particulars of which are here given. The two main sports centres in London are at Crystal Palace, and the Empire Stadium, Wembley. Athletics, badminton, football, gymnastics, hockey, judo, swimming, etc. take place at the *National Sports Centre, Crystal Palace* (Norwood, S.E.19); football, hockey, badminton, show-jumping, wrestling, boxing, ice-skating, etc. at the *Empire Stadium and Pool, Wembley* (Middlesex).

ATHLETICS are governed by the *Amateur Athletic Association*, 70 Brompton Rd., S.W.3. The championships, open to amateurs of all nations, are generally held about the second Sat in July at *Crystal Palace.* The Oxford and Cambridge contests are held here usually on a Sat in May.

BADMINTON. The All-England Championships (last week in March) are held at the *Empire Pool, Wembley.*

BOXING. Amateur championships held in April or May at the *Empire Stadium, Wembley.* The only other important bouts (amateur and professional) are now held in the *Albert Hall.* The dilettante would do well to attend the bouts of the various local amateur boxing clubs (Battersea, Croydon, etc.), and can obtain information as to dates and places from the *Amateur Boxing Association*, 10 Storeys Gate, S.W.1. Professional boxing is controlled by the *British Boxing Board of Control* (1 Hills Place, W.1).

CRICKET. The cricket season begins in May. The *Marylebone Cricket Club* (M.C.C.), the governing body, has its headquarters at *Lord's*, St John's Wood Road, where one of the Test matches with Commonwealth touring teams is always played. It is also the home ground of the county of Middlesex. The Eton and Harrow and the Oxford and Cambridge matches here in July are notable events in the social season. The Surrey County matches are played at *Kennington Oval.* 'Kent' and 'Essex' are nomadic teams. A first-class cricket match lasts for three days, usually beginning about 11.30 a.m. each day; although one-day matches (e.g. the Gillette Cup) are also played (often on Sun).

FOOTBALL is played from Aug to May. The chief professional league clubs in London under the Association code ('Soccer') play on Sat afternoons and sometimes on Wed evenings. They are: *Chelsea* (Stamford Bridge, S.W.6), *Tottenham Hotspur* (White Hart Lane, N.17), *Arsenal* (Highbury, N.5), *Orient* (Brisbane Rd., Leyton, E.10), *Fulham* (Craven Cottage, S.W.6), *Millwall* (New Cross, S.E.), *Charlton Athletic* (The Valley, Floyd Rd., S.E.7), *Queen's Park Rangers* (Loftus Rd., Shepherd's Bush, W.12), *Brentford* (Griffin Park), *West Ham United* (Upton Park, E.), and *Crystal Palace* (Selhurst Park, Croydon). The final F.A. cup-tie usually takes place in early May at Wembley Stadium. RUGBY UNION FOOTBALL ('Rugger') is played exclusively by amateurs, the chief clubs being the *Harlequins* (Twickenham, where international matches and the Oxford and Cambridge match are played), *Blackheath* (Rectory Field, S.E.), *Richmond* and *London Scottish* (Richmond Athletic Ground), *London Welsh* (Old Deer Park, Richmond), *London Irish* (The Avenue, Sunbury-on-Thames), and *Rosslyn Park* (Roehampton). The final of the Rugby League Championship (North-Country professional) is held at Wembley Stadium in early May.

GREYHOUND RACING. Tracks at *Catford, Hackney, Harringay, New Clapton, Walthamstow, Wembley, White City, Wimbledon,* etc.

HORSE RACING. The flat-racing season lasts from March to Nov; in winter hurdle-racing and steeplechasing prevail. The chief event of the year is the *Derby,* run at *Epsom* (14 m. s.s.w. of London) in early June. The enormous and animated crowds that assemble on Epsom Downs on this occasion afford a unique spectacle. Two weeks later the fashionable *Ascot Week* begins at *Ascot Heath* (5 m. s.s.w. of Windsor). The chief day is Thursday (Gold Cup Day), when Royalty usually drives up the course in state, attended by the master and huntsmen of the Royal Buckhounds.—Other race-meetings that may be conveniently visited from London are at *Sandown Park* (adjoining Esher station). *Kempton Park* (2½ m. w. of Hampton Court) is being rebuilt. Tattersall's Ring, for which an extra charge is made, is the best place for seeing at all meetings.

LAWN TENNIS. The controlling body is the *Lawn Tennis Association* (Barons Court, W.14). The premier club is the *All-England Lawn Tennis Club* (Church Rd., S.W.19), at Wimbledon; and the amateur championship of the world on grass is held there towards the end of June. Tickets for Wimbledon fortnight are issued by the All-England Lawn Tennis Club. Other championships take place at *Queen's Club* (Pallisser Rd., W.14), and the *Albert Hall*.

MOTOR-RACING. Circuits at *Crystal Palace*, and *Brands Hatch* (off the A20 Fawkham, Kent).—Stock-car Racing at *White City, Walthamstow*, and *Wimbledon*.

RACKETS, SQUASH RACKETS and ROYAL TENNIS are played at *Queen's Club* and *Lord's*. The chief rackets championships are played at Queen's; the Amateur Squash Rackets Championship are contested at the *Lansdowne* and *R.A.C.* Clubs.

ROWING. The *Oxford and Cambridge Boat Race*, usually rowed shortly before Easter, between Putney and Mortlake (4¼ m.), is the chief event of the rowing year and attracts enormous crowds. The ordinary spectators line the banks of the river or pay for a position on an anchored barge, a pier, or in the Duke's Meadows, Chiswick. The *Head of the River Race*, one week earlier, is rowed over the same course in the reverse direction.—*Henley Regatta*, the premier Thames regatta and a gay and fashionable gathering, is held early in July (see the 'Blue Guide to England').—*Doggett's Coat and Badge*, presented in 1715 by Thomas Doggett, the actor, is rowed for annually by Thames watermen on the last Mon in July. The course is from London Bridge (Millwall) to Chelsea (5 m.).— The *Amateur Rowing Association* headquarters is at 160 Great Portland St., W.1; the *Wingfield Sculls* (Amateur Championship) is rowed between Putney and Mortlake (in July).

Participant Sports. Most of the public parks in outer London have sports facilities (cricket, football, tennis, etc.) for the public. The *G. L. C. Parks Department* (Room 89, County Hall, S.E.1) give information. The public may also join the *National Sports Centre at Crystal Palace* (£2·50 per annum) which is equipped with facilities for lawn tennis, swimming, badminton and judo, and provided with squash courts, athletics stadium, and an artificial ski-slope.

CYCLING. The environs of London still include some charming country, with excellent roads. The main roads, however, especially on Sat and Sun, are apt to be crowded. The *Cyclists' Touring Club* (13 Spring St., W.2) have an information bureau. The chief racing body is the *British Cycling Federation*, 70 Brompton Rd., S.W.3; the chief racing track is at Herne Hill (Burbage Rd., S.E.24).

FISHING on the Thames downstream from Staines is free; upstream from Teddington the river is controlled by the *Thames Conservancy Board*, Nugent House, Vastern Rd., Reading, Berks. Information from the *London Anglers Association*, 183 Hoe St., E.17. A day permit is required for fishing in the parks administered by the G.L.C. The Serpentine, Hampton Court ponds, and Richmond Park ponds are controlled by the *Department of the Environment*, Royal Parks Division, Gaywood House, Great Peter St., S.W.1. Fishing is also available in some reservoirs, such as Aldenham (Elstree), and South Norwood Lake. The close season for coarse fishing is from 15 March to 15 June.

GOLF is played all the year round on numerous courses near London. At most of these introduction by a member is essential. Clubs are listed in the 'Golfers' Handbook' and the 'Golf Course Guide'. There are public golf-courses at *Whitewebbs* (Enfield); *Ruislip* (Ickenham Rd.); *Haste Hill* (The Drive, Northwood); *Harefield Place* (The Drive, Uxbridge); *Brent Valley* (Church Rd., Greenford Av., Hanwell, W.7); *Beckenham Place* (Beckenham Hill Rd., S.E.); *Hainault Forest* and *Chingford*. Putting-courses are to be found in many public parks.

ICE SKATING. Rinks at *Queen's*, Queensway, W.2; *Richmond*, Clevedon Road East, Twickenham; and *Silver Blades*, Streatham High Rd., S.W.16.

RIDING. Horses for Hyde Park from the *Knightsbridge Riding School*, 11 Elvaston Mews, S.W.7; for Hampstead Heath from *Strawberry Vale Riding School*, North Circular Road, Finchley, N.2.

SKI-ING. Dry ski slopes at *Alexandra Palace* (Wood Green, N.22); *Crystal Palace National Sports Centre* (Norwood, S.E.19); and *Simpson's* of Piccadilly.

SQUASH. *Squash Rackets Association*, 70 Brompton Rd., S.W.3. There are squash courts attached to many clubs, as well as to many modern blocks of flats. Public courts at *Bramley Sports Ground* (Chase Side, N.14); *Civic Centre, Swiss Cottage* (N.W.3); *Dolphin Square* (Grosvenor Rd., S.W.1); *Ealing Squash Club* (Haven Green, W.5.); *Holland Park Squash Court* (W.8); and *St Marylebone Public Baths* (Seymour Place, W.1).

SWIMMING. Most districts of London boast at least one covered municipal swimming bath open all the year, and many old baths have been replaced by new (Putney, Richmond, Ladywell, Morden Park, Southgate, etc.). Centrally placed are those in Westminster (Marshall St.), St Marylebone (Seymour Place), and Finsbury (Ironmonger Row); but among the most modern and best equipped are also those at Swiss Cottage and Crystal Palace, where competitions and championships are now held. The controlling body, the *Amateur Swimming Association*, has its headquarters at Loughborough in Leicestershire. In summer, open-air pools are to be found in most parts of London, many of them sited in parks (e.g. Victoria Park, Southwark Park, Parliament Hill Fields). Most readily accessible from the centre are the Serpentine, the 'Oasis' (Endell St., Holborn; with covered pool also) and Brockwell Park (Herne Hill Station). A more exclusive swim may be had in the privately-owned pools (covered) at Dolphin Sq., the White House and the Kensington Close Hotel.

TENNIS. Public tennis-courts in Lincoln's Inn Fields, Battersea Park, Archbishops Park, Lambeth, and most public parks.

V THE SIGHTS OF LONDON

A Table of the hours of admission to the principal sights of London is given below. When alternative hours of closing are indicated, the earlier hours refer to winter (usually Oct–April), the latter to summer. No galleries are open on Sun morning. Most public collections are closed on Good Fri and on Christmas Eve, Christmas Day, and Boxing Day. The Table is intended to group together the main sights for easy reference; more details of opening times, services, lectures, etc. will be found in the pages referred to in the list.

Admission Fees. Most of the privately-owned houses and galleries charge an admission fee. Precise sums have not been indicated in the text unless they are exceptionally large, but the existence of a charge has generally been indicated by the word 'fee'. Season tickets are available for properties of the Department of the Environment; membership of the National Trust gives free entrance to its properties.

An 'Open to View' season ticket is now available for overseas visitors (obtainable from Thos. Cook & Son Ltd. in the U.S.A., Canada, and Australia), entitling the holder to free admission to all properties owned by the Dept. of the Environment, the N.T., and also some 100 privately-owned houses in Britain.

The annual A.B.C. Publications: 'Historic Houses, Castles, and Gardens' and 'Museums and Galleries' (available from booksellers) are useful in providing up-to-date information about opening hours. The B.T.A. booklet 'National Museums' is also helpful.

Guide Lecturers. At fixed hours at some of the galleries visitors are conducted round one or more of the departments by competent official guide-lecturers (no fees). Anyone may join such a party.

	Weekdays	Sundays	Notes
Apsley House (p. 104)	10–6	2.30–6	Closed Mon & Fri
Banqueting House (p. 71)	10–5	2–5	Closed Mon
Bethnal Green Museum of Childhood (p. 261)	10–6	2.30–6	Closed Fri
British Museum (p. 176)	10–5	2.30–6	Closed Christmas Eve & Boxing Day
Carlyle's House (p. 151)	11–1, 2–6	2–6 or dusk	Closed on Mon & Tues & in Dec. Closes 3.30 Jan, Feb & Nov
Chelsea (Hospital p. 149)	10–4.30	—	Closed 12–2. Open Sat, 2–4
Chiswick House (p. 308)	9.30–4, 5.30	9.30–4, 5.30	Closed Mon & Tues, Oct–Mar
Courtauld Institute (p. 172)	10–5	2–5	
Dickens House (p. 175)	10–5	—	
Dulwich Gallery (p. 286)	10–4, 5, 6	2–5, 6	Closed Mon & Sun in winter
Geffrye Museum (p. 259)	10–5	2–5	Closed Mon
Ham House (p. 296)	2–6	2–6	Closed Mon. Oct–Mar, 12–4
Hampton Court (p. 302)	9.30–4, 5, 6	11, 2–4, 5, 6	
Hayward Gallery (p. 267)	10–6, 8	12–6	Mon; 1–8. Closed between exhibits
Johnson's House (p. 207)	11–5, 5.30	—	
Keat's House (p. 324)	10–6	2–5	
Kensington Palace (p. 114)	10–4, 5, 6	2–4, 5, 6	
Kenwood (p. 325)	10–4, 5, 7	10–4, 5, 7	
Kew Gardens (p. 298)	10–dusk	10–dusk	
Museum of London (p. 225)	10–6	2–6	Closed Mon
National Army Museum (p. 150)	10–5.30	2–5.30	
National Gallery (p. 75)	10–6	2–6	
National Maritime Museum (p. 282)	10–5 or 6	2.30–6	
National Portrait Gallery (p. 83)	10–5 or 6	2–6	Sat, 10–6
Natural History Museum (p. 132)	10–6	2.30–6	
Osterley House (p. 310)	2–6	2–6	Closed Mon. Oct–Mar, 12–4
Parliament, Houses of (p. 64)	10–4	—	Sat only. Also BH & Mon, Tues & Thurs in Aug & Sept
Queen's Gallery (p. 94)	11–5	2–5	Closed Mon except BH
Record Office Museum (p. 203)	1–4	—	Closed Sat & Sun
Royal Academy (p. 101)	10–6, 8	10–6	
Royal Mews (p. 94)	2–4	—	Wed & Thurs only. Closed Ascot Week
St Paul's Cathedral (p. 209)	8–5, 6, 7	Services	
Science Museum (p. 134)	10–6	2.30–6	Closed Fri
Soane Museum (p. 201)	10–5	—	Closed Sun & Mon
Syon House (p. 309)	2–4.15	1–5	See p. 309. Closed Fri & Sat
Tate Gallery (p. 141)	10–6	2–6	
Tower of London (p. 244)	9.30–4, 5	(2–5)	Sun in summer only
Victoria & Albert Museum (p. 117)	10–6	2.30–6	Closed Fri
Wallace Collection (p. 163)	10–5	2–5	
War Museum (p. 270)	10–6	2–6	
Wesley's House (p. 234)	10–4	—	Closed 1–2
Westminster Abbey (p. 50)	8–5, 6	Services	On Wed till 8. Closed Sat, 2.45–3.45
Westminster Hall (p. 69)	see p. 69	—	
Zoological Gardens (p. 158)	9, 10–dusk or 7	9, 10–dusk or 7	Closed Christmas Day

The **National Trust** FOR PLACES OF HISTORIC INTEREST OR NATURAL BEAUTY ('N.T.' in the text; 42 Queen Anne's Gate, S.W.1), founded in 1895, acts as trustee of properties acquired by the nation to be preserved intact for future generation. It preserves from destruction and damage an ever-increasing number of national treasures. The minimum subscription is £5 (family £10, under 23, £2) allowing free access to N.T. properties where a charge is normally made.

Many other historic monuments have been scheduled for preservation by Act of Parliament, and numerous ancient buildings are under the efficient care of the former *Ministry of Public Building and Works* (Ancient Monuments Dept.) now incorporated in the **Department of the Environment.** Information centre: 36 Parliament St., S.W.1 (open Mon–Fri, 10–6; in summer also Sat & Sun, 11–6).

The **British Waterways Board** own and manage c. 2000 miles of canals and rivers in Great Britain. Information about the Board's waterways is obtainable from the General Manager, Melbury House, Melbury Terrace, N.W.1. The Board also publishes maps and cruising guides to its waterways. The *Inland Waterways Association,* 114 Regent's Park Road, N.W.1, an unofficial body of enthusiasts, champions the use of waterways for pleasure purposes. Information on the hire of boats may be obtained from (and bookings made through) *Boat Enquiries Ltd.,* 12 Western Road, Oxford.

The **National Art-Collections Fund** (24 Bloomsbury Way, W.C.1), supported by subscriptions, donations, and bequests, assists public art-collections in the United Kingdom and Commonwealth to acquire works of art and objects of historical importance (annual subscription).

The CIVIC TRUST, an independent and unofficial body, was founded in 1957 to encourage high quality in architecture and planning; to preserve buildings of artistic distinction or historic interest; to protect the beauties of the countryside; to eliminate and prevent ugliness, whether from bad design or neglect; and to stimulate public interest in the good appearance of town and country and to inspire generally a sense of civic pride. Its headquarters are at 17 Carlton House Terrace, S.W.1.

Members of the *Victorian Society* (Priory Gdns., W.4) and the *Georgian Group* (2 Chester St., S.W.1) are concerned with the study and protection of Victorian, Edwardian, and Georgian architecture and other arts.

The *Residence Recitals Society* (34 Hillgate Place, W.8) organizes programmes of recitals in houses (mostly private) in which famous writers and composers lived.

Parks and Gardens. The parks of central London are a special feature of the city affording a welcome respite from noise. Most of them have now been enclosed and are locked at night; St James's Park, however, is always open. The flower beds in St James's Park, Kensington Gardens, and Regent's Park are beautifully maintained.

Among the less well-known parks, incorporating the fine gardens of old mansions are: *Holland Park*; *Brockwell Park,* nr. Tulse Hill and the *Rookery,* adjoining Streatham Common in S. London; *Waterlow Park* and *Clissold Park,* in N. London; also *Golders Hill, Victoria Park, Hackney Marsh, Avery Hill,* and *Dulwich Park.*

Spectacular flower gardens may be seen at the *Royal Botanic Gardens at Kew*; *Hampton Court Palace*; *Ham House*; and *Syon House* (with a Gardening Centre). The private gardens of about 50 London houses are thrown open to the public on certain days in summer (usually 11–7, Sun 2–7; adm. fee). The resultant funds are administered by the Queen's institute of District Nursing, for the Retired District Nurses' Benefit Fund and the National Trust and Royal Horticultural Society Gardens scheme. Particulars from the NATIONAL GARDENS SCHEME, 57 Lower Belgrave St., S.W.1, which publishes an annual illustrated guide.—The Royal Horticultural Society's garden at Wisley, Ripley, Surrey (20 m. from London) is open daily, 10–dusk.

Flower Shows. The Chelsea Flower Show (Royal Horticultural Society) is held in May in the grounds of the Royal Chelsea Hospital; smaller fortnightly shows are held in the Royal Horticultural Society Hall, Vincent Square. The Royal National Rose Society holds a June show at Alexandra Palace.

The beautiful squares and gardens in central London are usually kept locked. Residents in the area may apply for a key.

Specialized Museums and Collections. The following list groups museums by their content under a few major specialist subject headings:

Aircraft	R.A.F. Museum, Hendon; Science Museum, Exhibition Rd.; Imperial War Museum
Bibles	British and Foreign Bible Society, 146 Queen Victoria St.; British Museum
British furniture, porcelain, etc.	Victoria and Albert Museum; Geffrye Museum; Soane Museum; Fenton House
Chinese ceramics	David Percival Foundation of Chinese Art, 53 Gordon Sq.; British Museum
Clocks	Guildhall Museum; British Museum; Victoria and Albert Museum
Costume	Victoria and Albert Museum; Bethnal Green Museum; Museum of London; Madame Tussaud's; Law Courts (legal)
Cricket	M.C.C. Museum at Lord's
Fire-fighting equipment	Chartered Insurance Institute, Aldermanbury
Industrial equipment	Industrial Health and Safety Centre, 97 Horseferry Rd.
Jewish History	Woburn House, Tavistock Square
London History	Museum of London; Guildhall Museum
Manuscripts, records, charters, etc.	British Museum; Record Office Museum; Somerset House; British Science Library (Patent Office); British Records Association; Society of Genealogists; College of Arms
Maritime History	National Maritime Museum, Greenwich; Science Museum; Cutty Sark, Greenwich
Medicine	Wellcome Historical Medical Museum, Euston Rd.; Hunterian Museum, Royal College of Surgeons; Gordon Medical Museum, St Thomas St., S.E.1; Museum of Pharmacy, 17 Bloomsbury Square
Musical Instruments	Victoria and Albert Museum; Donaldson Collection, Royal College of Music; Horniman Museum; Piano and Musical Museum, Brentford; Fenton House
Police History	Metropolitan Police Historical Museum, Bow Street
Stamps and Postal History	National Postal Museum, King Edward St.; British Museum; Bruce Castle, Tottenham; National Maritime Museum
Telephones	Telephone Museum, Shoe Lane, E.C.4
Television	I.T.A. Gallery, 70 Brompton Road
Theatre	British Theatre Museum, Holland Park Road; Victoria and Albert Museum; Bear Gardens Museum
Toys	Pollock's Toy Museum, Scala St.; Bethnal Green Museum; Museum of London
War relics and trophies	National Army Museum; Imperial War Museum; Tower of London; Guards' Museum, Wellington Barracks; Rotunda Museum, Woolwich; HMS 'Belfast'; Royal Air Force Museum, Hendon.

VI CALENDAR OF EVENTS

The following is a list of some annual events of interest taking place in and near London on fixed or approximately fixed dates. For other annual sporting fixtures, see p. 33.

January	New Year's Day.
1	International Boat Show, Earls Court (for 10 days in early Jan)
6	Royal Epiphany offering in the Chapel Royal.—Baddeley Cake cut at Drury Lane Theatre
26	Australia Day. Service at St Clement Danes
30	Decoration of Charles I's statue, Trafalgar Square; commemoration service at St Mary le Strand
February	
6	New Zealand Day. Service at St Lawrence Jewry
9 (about)	Cruft's Dog Show, Olympia (2 days)
March	
1	St David's Day. Leeks given to Welsh Guard at Windsor, attended by the Duke of Edinburgh
(early)	Stampex, R.H.S. Hall, Vincent Square (4 days)
6 (about)	Ideal Home Exhibition, Olympia (for c. 3 weeks)
17	St Patrick's Day. Shamrock distributed to the Irish Guard
(end)	Oranges and Lemons service at St Clement Danes
SHROVE TUESDAY	'Tossing the pancake' at Westminster School
ASH WEDNESDAY	Stationers' Company attend service at St Paul's
TUES IN HOLY WEEK	Bach's 'Passion Music' at St Paul's
MAUNDY THURSDAY	Royal Maundy distributed (usually) in Westminster Abbey
GOOD FRIDAY	Holiday. Widow's dole at St Bartholomew's
before EASTER	Oxford and Cambridge Boat Race (often on 2nd Sat before Easter)
EASTER SUNDAY	Parade in Battersea Park
EASTER MONDAY	Bank Holiday. Easter procession at Westminster Abbey.—Harness Horse Parade in Regent's Park
after EASTER	'Spital sermon' at St Mary Woolnoth (Wed after Easter week)
April	
	Festivals of London (until July), initiated by the G.L.C., with 33 London boroughs, and the City of London taking part
(1st week)	Shakespeare Birthday Festival, Southwark
(mid; sometimes in March)	Spring Antiques Fair, Chelsea Old Town Hall (c. 10 days)
6	Stow Memorial service at St Andrew Undershaft
19	Primrose Day; decoration of Disraeli's statue in Parliament Square on Sat nearest
23	St George's Day; Shakespeare's birthday, service at Southwark Cathedral, and St George's, Windsor
25	Anzac Day. Service at Westminster Abbey
May	
1	Labour Day: processions to Hyde Park. Cricket season begins
(1st Sat)	Royal Academy opens (to public on Mon)
5 (about)	Football Association Cup Final, Wembley
12 (about)	Rugby League Challenge Cup Final, Wembley
(3rd or 4th Sat)	London to Brighton Walk (starts Westminster Bridge)
21	Commemoration of the death of Henry VI at the Tower (flowers laid on spot where he died), and at Eton
23 (about)	Chelsea Flower Show, Royal Hospital, Chelsea (3 days)
(last Mon)	Bank Holiday. American Memorial Day; wreaths at the Cenotaph and grave of the Unknown Warrior (nearest Sat); service in American church of St Mark's, N. Audley St. (nearest Sun)

29	Oak-Apple Day at Royal Hospital, Chelsea
30 (about)	Pepys Memorial service at St Olave, Hart Street
Ascension Day	Bound beating at Tower (next in 1978, 1981)

June

2 (about)	Queen's official Birthday; 'trooping the colour' on Horse Guards Parade
4	Speech Day at Eton
6 (about)	The 'Derby', Epsom, Surrey
9 (about)	The 'Oaks', Epsom, Surrey
14 (about)	Globe Playhouse Trust Festival, Bankside (until c. 1 Sept)
19 (about)	Ascot week
(2nd Wed)	Antique Dealers' Fair at Grosvenor House (2 weeks) National Rose Society Annual Show, Alexandra Palace
(end)	Lawn Tennis Championships at Wimbledon (2 weeks)
(end)	Garter Ceremony attended by the Queen at St George's Chapel, Windsor
(end)	Midsummer Day; presentation of the Knolly Rose (All Hallows by the Tower)
24	Election of Sheriffs of the City of London at Guildhall

July

(early)	Henley Regatta (4 days)
(2nd week)	Royal Tournament, Earls Court (c. 2 weeks)
(mid)	City of London Festival (c. 2 weeks; biennially, next in 1974)
(end)	Henry Wood Promenade Concerts, Royal Albert Hall (until mid-Sept)
	Royal International Horse Show, Wembley (6 days)
(2nd Thurs)	Road sweeping by Vintners Company, at St James Garlickhythe
(3rd week)	Swan Upping (census of swans taken between London Bridge and Henley)
(last week)	Doggett's Coat and Badge Boat Race between London Bridge and Chelsea (often on last Mon)

August

(early)	R.H.S. Summer Flower Show, Vincent Square
(last Mon)	Bank Holiday; fair on Hampstead Heath
BH, Sat & Sun	Greater London Horse Show, Clapham Common Cart Marking, Guildhall Yard

September

(mid)	Autumn Antiques Fair, Chelsea Old Town Hall (c. 10 days)
15	Battle of Britain Day. Fly-past of aircraft over London about midday. Thanksgiving service at Westminster Abbey at 3 p.m. following Sun
21 (about)	Boys of Christ's Hospital attend service at St Sepulchre, Holborn, and visit Mansion House
(late)	Election of Lord Mayor of London, Guildhall; Lord Mayor and Corporation attend service at St Lawrence Jewry
(late)	R.H.S. Great Autumn Show, Vincent Square

October

1 (about)	Law Courts open; services at St Margaret's, Westminster and Westminster Cathedral
(early)	Harvest Festival for the 'Pearly Kings and Queens of London', St Martin in the Fields
8 (about)	Horse of the Year Show, Wembley
16	'Lion Sermon' at St Katherine Cree
(mid)	International Motor Show, Earls Court (10 days)
21	Trafalgar Day: decoration of the Nelson monument
(late; or early Nov)	State opening of Parliament; the Queen is driven in a coach from Buckingham Palace to the House of Lords
(late)	British Philatelic Exhibition, Seymour Hall

November	
(1st Sun)	London to Brighton Veteran Car Run (depart Hyde Park Corner)
2 (about)	Horse of the Year Show, Wembley (6 days)
5	Guy Fawkes Day; fireworks at night (at Crystal Palace on 4th)
9 (or Sat nearest)	Lord Mayor's Show
11	Armistice Day. Service at Cenotaph at 11 a.m. on nearest Sun. Poppies sold in streets for benefit of ex-servicemen
(mid)	Kensington Antiques Fair (5 days)
22	St Cecilia's Day; musical service at St Sepulchre, Holborn
30	St Andrew's Day
December	
4 (about)	Royal Smithfield Show, Earls Court (5 days)
1st Tues in Advent	Handel's 'Messiah' at St Paul's Cathedral
12 (nearest Tues)	Oxford and Cambridge 'Rugger' match
25	Christmas Day (Holiday)
26	Boxing Day; Bank Holiday (if not Sun; otherwise on 27th)
26, 27, 28	Carol service and procession at Westminster Abbey
31	'Hogmanay' gathering of Scots outside St Paul's at midnight. Festivities at Trafalgar Square

VII USEFUL ADDRESSES

The information services and publications provided by the following organizations should not be overlooked by any visitor to London:

The *London Tourist Board*, 26 Grosvenor Gardens, S.W.1 (Tel: 730 0791). The Board is the regional office of the *British Tourist Authority*, 64 St James's St., S.W.1 (Tel: 629 9191).

The *Greater London Council*, County Hall, S.E.1 (Tel: 633 3000).

The *City of London Information Office*, St Paul's Churchyard, E.C.4 (Tel: 606 3030).

London Transport, 55 Broadway, S.W.1 (Tel: 222 1234).

Public Libraries. London is renowned for the excellence of its library system. Any visitor from another part of Great Britain will usually be issued with books on production of his tickets. Visitors from abroad may also be issued with books, provided that they can present a guarantor. Most of the libraries are equipped with reference libraries. Well-known reference libraries are at the Guildhall and Westminster (St Martin's St.).

Many required London addresses may be turned up in 'Kelly's Post Office London Directory' or in the 'London Telephone Directory'. A classified telephone directory ('London Yellow Pages') is now published annually by the Post Office. Particulars about people of eminence or social position are given in 'Who's Who'.—The *Daily Telegraph Information Bureau* (Tel: 353 4242) provides general information.

Street names are usually, but not always, shown on corner houses. The numbering of the houses is unsystematic. In some streets the numbers run up one side and down the other; in others the odd and even numbers are on opposite sides.

Clubs. The following is a list of the most important and historical clubs; most are described in more detail in Rtes 7 and 8 (comp. the index). Membership is in general by proposal and election only.

Army and Navy, 36 Pall Mall, S.W.1.—*Arts*, 40 Dover St., W.1.—*Athenaeum*, 107 Pall Mall, the leading literary and learned club.—*Boodle's*, 28 St James's St., S.W.1.—*Brooks's*, 60 St James's St.—*Carlton*,

69 St James's St., the premier Conservative club. — *Cavalry and Guards'*, 127 Piccadilly, W.1. — *Constitutional*, 86 St. James's St., Conservative. — *Garrick*, 15 Garrick St., W.C.2, dramatic, literary, and legal. — *National Liberal*, Whitehall Place, S.W.1. — *Naval and Military*, 94 Piccadilly. — *Pratt's*, 14 Park Place, S.W.1. — *Reform*, 104 Pall Mall, the premier Liberal club. — *Royal Air Force*, 128 Piccadilly. — *Savage Club*, 9 Fitzmaurice Place. — *Travellers'*, 106 Pall Mall. — *Turf*, 5 Carlton House Terrace, S.W.1. — *United Oxford and Cambridge*, 71 Pall Mall. — *White's*, 37 St James's St.

The *Royal Commonwealth Society*, 18 Northumberland Avenue, W.C.2, serves many of the purposes of a club. — The *Royal Overseas League*, Vernon House, Park Place, S.W.1, the *English-Speaking Union*, 37 Charles St., W.1, and the *Victoria League*, 38 Chesham Place, S.W.1, offer many advantages to strangers without private friends in London.

Embassies, Consulates, and High Commissioners.

Australia, Australia House, Strand, W.C.2.
Belgium, 103 Eaton Square, S.W.1.
Canada, Canada House, Trafalgar Square, S.W.1.
France, 58 Knightsbridge, S.W.1.
Irish Republic, 17 Grosvenor Place, S.W.1.
Italy, 38 Eaton Place, S.W.1.
Netherlands, 38 Hyde Park Gate, S.W.7.
New Zealand, New Zealand House, Haymarket, S.W.1.
South Africa, South Africa House, Trafalgar Square, S.W.1.
Switzerland, Montagu Place, W.1.
United States, 24 Grosvenor Square, W.1.
West Germany, 23 Belgrave Square, S.W.1.

Police Headquarters. New Scotland Yard, near St James's Park Station (in emergency, dial 999).

Lost Property should be inquired for at the *Lost Property Office*, 15 Penton St., N.1 (including articles left in taxis); articles left in buses or in the Underground should be applied for at 200 Baker St., N.W.1 (10–6; Sat 10–1).

Medical Attention. *St George's Hospital*, Hyde Park Corner, S.W.1 and the *Middlesex Hospital*, Mortimer St., W.1 have a 24-hr casualty service. — Boots chemist at Piccadilly Circus is open 24 hrs. Bayswater Pharmacy, 108 Westbourne Grove, W.2 is open Mon–Sat 9 a.m.– 11 p.m., and Sun 10–9; H. D. Bliss, 54 Willesden Lane, N.W.6, for 24 hrs; John Bell and Croyden, 50 Wigmore St., W.1, daily from 8.30 a.m. to 10 p.m.

VIII GENERAL HINTS

Season. The London Season proper extends from the beginning of May to the end of July. Parliament is then sitting, the Royal Academy and other annual exhibitions are open, the opera and the theatres are at their best, and social gaiety is at its height. August and September are perhaps the busiest tourist months. The chief characteristic of the climate is changeability; although long periods of fine weather occur each year, their incidence cannot usually be forecast with accuracy, and a little rain may be experienced at any season.

The LONDON WEATHER CENTRE, 284–286 High Holborn, from which the forecasts are televised, maintains display panels with up-to-the-minute data about weather, actual and forecast, for England and elsewhere.

Summer Time. A brief flirtation with Central European Time having proved unacceptable, Britain has reverted to the general use of Greenwich Mean Time. From about mid-April to mid-September the clocks are advanced one hour to give 'Summer Time'.

Business hours in London offices are usually 9.30–5.30 (sometimes 9–5) on Mon to Fri, with a one-hour break for lunch at 12 or 1. Business is suspended all over England on Good Friday and Christmas Day, and also on *Bank Holidays*, viz. New Year's Day, Easter Mon, first Mon in May, last Mon in Aug, 26 Dec, if not Sun (when 25 or 26 Dec is Sun, the holiday falls on 27 Dec). On bank holidays, however, museums, public galleries, and places of amusement remain open, though private collections are sometimes closed. On Sunday museums, collections, etc. are almost invariably closed in the morning.

Money. In 1971 a decimal system was adopted in Britain which left the exchange value of £1 sterling unaltered, while redividing it into 100 new pence. The denominations of 'silver' coins are 50p, 10p, and 5p; and of copper coins 2p, 1p, and ½p. The old sixpence (worth 2½p) is still in circulation. Four values of notes exist: £20 (rarely seen), £10, £5, and £1.

BANKS are open Mon–Fri, 9.30–3.30; also 4.30–6 on one night a week.

Tipping. In a restaurant, according to the quality of the service, the waiter should be rewarded with 10–12½ per cent of the bill; somewhat less where a considerable proportion of the bill is for a single bottle. If a service charge is included in the bill a small amount extra may be left for specially good service. Hotels now usually include a service charge of 10–12½ per cent (15 per cent in some of the larger hotels) in the bill. Cloak-room attendants expect to be tipped unless a charge is made. Taxi-drivers expect about 20 per cent of their fare (minimum 10p); barbers and hairdressers 20–30 per cent of their charge. Barmen in pubs (unlike those in hotel cocktail bars), usherettes at cinemas and theatres, and attendants in public lavatories are not tipped.

Postal Information. All letter-post to the continent of Europe (including Turkey and Cyprus) goes by airmail without surcharge. The Post Office issues a free multi-lingual leaflet explaining its range of services (obtainable at post offices, and the London Tourist Board).

POST OFFICES are normally open Mon–Fri, 9–5.30; some are open also on Sat morning. The Post Office at Trafalgar Square is open 24 hours, and the *London Chief Office*, King Edward St., W.C.1 on Mon–Fri, 8 a.m.–8 p.m., Sat, 9–4. Here letters addressed 'Poste Restante' without mention of any special post office should be called for.

Telephones. Call-boxes take 2p and 10p coins. The subscriber trunk dialling (S.T.D.) system, whereby 2p buys time according to distance, now covers the greater part of Britain; it is also available to most countries throughout the world (though generally not beyond Europe from coin boxes). Charges can be transferred (reversed) to most countries in Europe, Canada, and the U.S.A. Calls are cheaper 6 p.m.–8 a.m. and all day Sat and Sun. The operator is usually obtained by dialling 100. For emergencies (Fire, Police, Ambulance) dial 999. The dialling code for London is 01, but should be omitted when calls are made within the London area.

Shopping. The main high quality shopping streets are Bond St., Regent St., and Piccadilly. Other good shops are to be found near Knightsbridge and Sloane St. More popular shops are in Oxford St. and Kensington High St. Normal shopping hours are now Mon–Sat, 9–5.30; some shops still close on Sat afternoons. Late evening shopping (until 7 p.m.) on Wed in Knightsbridge and Chelsea, and on Thurs in the rest of the West End, and Kensington High St. A detailed guide 'Shopping in London' is available from the British Tourist Authority.

Among the best-known stores, where every ordinary want of the traveller may be met on the premises are: *Harrods*, 87–135 Brompton Rd., S.W.1; *Selfridges*, 398–429 Oxford St.; *Liberty's*, 210 Regent St.; *Peter Jones* and *John Lewis*, Sloane Square and Oxford St.; *Fortnum and Mason*, 181 Piccadilly; *Marshall and Snelgrove*, Oxford St.; *Dickens and Jones*, Regent St.; *Harvey Nichols*, Knightsbridge; and *Army and Navy*, 105 Victoria St.

The numerous branches of *Marks and Spencer* (main store, 458 Oxford St.) are famous for inexpensive and good quality clothes, etc.

Among the main bookshops are: *Hatchards*, 187 Piccadilly; *Foyles*, 119 Charing Cross Rd. (also for foreign books); *Dillon's*, 1 Malet St., W.C.1; and *Truslove and Hanson*, 205 Sloane St. *H.M. Stationery Office* has a shop at 49 High Holborn (for official government publications). Maps and plans are best sought at *Stanford's* in Long Acre.

I THE WEST END AND NORTH-WEST

The WEST END, in the colloquial sense, comprehends the regions extending w. from Charing Cross (Pl. 14; 6) to Campden Hill, with Westminster, Belgravia, and Brompton on the s., Hyde Park and Mayfair in the centre, and Bayswater and (less distinctly) Marylebone on the N. Within these limits lies the traditional London of fashion and leisure.—To the N. of Charing Cross lies *Soho*, with *Bloomsbury* (including the British Museum) farther to the N.E.—*Chelsea* lies on the river, to the s.w.

1 WESTMINSTER

STATIONS: *Westminster*, *St James's Park*, on the Circle line.—BUSES: 3, 11, 12, 24, 29, 39, 59, 76, 77, 88, and 159.—CAR PARKING: Abingdon St. Underground Car Park (entered from Great College St.); parking meters in Smith Sq. area.

The official area of the City of Westminster since 1965 includes practically all that is understood by the term 'West End' from Temple Bar to Chelsea and from Paddington and Marylebone to the Thames. But in the everyday usage of the Londoner the name **Westminster** refers to a much smaller area, in the immediate neighbourhood of Westminster Abbey and the Houses of Parliament.

Whitehall and its continuation Parliament Street terminates at the open PARLIAMENT SQUARE (Pl. 18; 2), created in 1926 as the first 'roundabout' in London. On the s.e. are the dignified buildings of the Houses of Parliament (Rte 3) with Westminster Hall in front of them; while due s. the towers of Westminster Abbey (Rte 2) rise beyond St Margaret's Church. The Middlesex Crown Court and the Royal Institution of Chartered Surveyors, both dating from the beginning of this century, are on the w. side, and on the N. is the flank of the huge Home Office building. Across the river to the e. may be glimpsed the County Hall, the home of London's Civic Parliament.

Round the lawn in the centre of the square are statues of eminent statesmen: *Field-Marshal Smuts* (1870–1950), by Epstein, *Lord Palmerston* (1784–1865), by Thos. Woolner, *Lord Derby* (1799–1869), by Matthew Noble, *Disraeli* (1804–81), by Mario Raggi, and *Sir Robert Peel* (1788–1850), by Noble. In front of the Middlesex Court stands *Abraham Lincoln* (1809–65), a replica of the statue by Saint-Gaudens at Chicago, and *George Canning* (1770–1827), by Sir Richard Westmacott. Disraeli's statue is annually decorated with primroses, his alleged favourite flower, on 19 April ('Primrose Day'; the anniversary of his death). The N.E. corner is occupied by Ivor Roberts–Jones' bronze of *Churchill.*

St Margaret's Church, dating from 1485–1523, has been repeatedly altered and restored. Founded before 1189 as the parish church of Westminster, it is also (since 1621) the 'national church for the use of the House of Commons'. It is a fashionable church for weddings; Samuel Pepys was married here in 1655, Milton (for the second time) in 1656, and Winston Churchill in 1908. Sir Walter Raleigh, who was executed in 1618 in front of the Palace of Westminster, is buried in the chancel; and in the church or churchyard rest also William Caxton (p. 49) and Wenceslaus Hollar (1607–77), the Bohemian etcher who depicted London before the Great Fire. The peaceful interior is adorned with

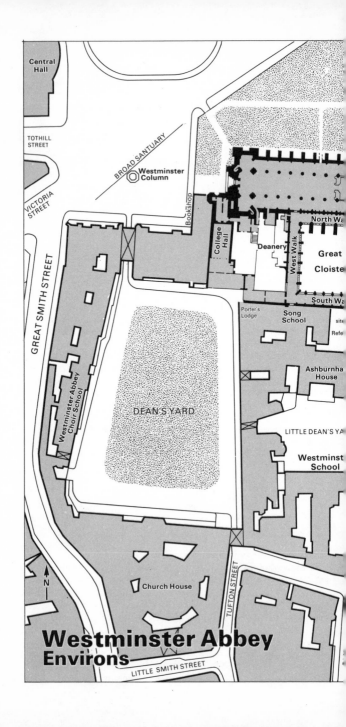

Central
Hall

TOTHILL
STREET

VICTORIA
STREET

BROAD SANTUARY

Westminster
Column

Bookshop

College
Hall

Deanery

North Wa

West Walk

Great

Cloiste

South Wa

Porter's
Lodge

Song
School

site

Refe

GREAT SMITH STREET

Westminster Abbey Choir School

DEAN'S YARD

Ashburnha
House

LITTLE DEAN'S YA

Westminst
School

N

Church House

TUFTON STREET

Westminster Abbey
Environs

LITTLE SMITH STREET

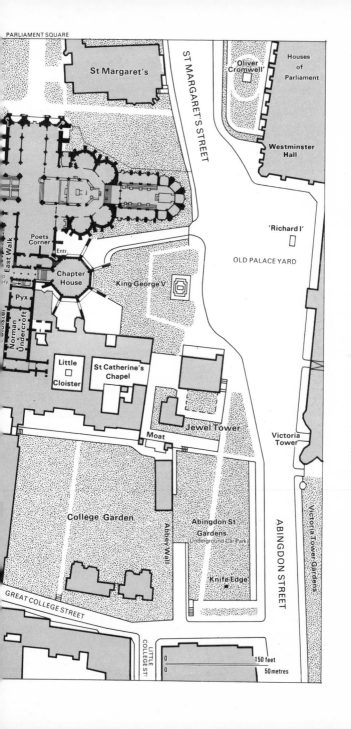

PARLIAMENT SQUARE

St Margaret's

ST MARGARET'S STREET

'Oliver Cromwell'

Houses of Parliament

Westminster Hall

Poets Corner

Entr.

East Walk

Chapter House

'Richard I'

OLD PALACE YARD

King George V

Pyx

Norman Undercroft

Cloister

Little Cloister

St Catherine's Chapel

Jewel Tower

Victoria Tower

Moat

College Garden

Abbey Wall

Abingdon St Gardens.
Underground Car Park

ABINGDON STREET

Victoria Tower Gardens.

Knife Edge

GREAT COLLEGE STREET

LITTLE COLLEGE ST.

0   150 feet

0   50 metres

unobtrusive Elizabethan and Jacobean wall monuments. The font, in the
s. aisle, is by Nicholas Stone (1641). At the E. end of the s. aisle is the
notable tomb of Lady Dudley (d. 1600), and on the E. wall, memorials
to Caxton and Raleigh. Over the w. door is a large window dedicated
by Americans to the memory of Raleigh (inscription by J. R. Lowell);
while that at the w. end of the N. aisle, with an inscription by Whittier,
commemorates Milton. The richly coloured *East Window, made in
Holland before 1509, celebrates the betrothal (1501) of Catherine of
Aragon to Prince Arthur, Henry VII's eldest son. It was bought for St
Margaret's in 1758. On the external E. wall is a leaden bust of Charles I
(c. 1800).

Opposite the E. end of St Margaret's is Westminster Hall (p. 69), by
the side of which is a *Statue of *Oliver Cromwell*, by Sir Hamo Thornycroft (1889). To the s. opens OLD PALACE YARD where an admirable
bronze equestrian *Statue of *Richard I*, by Marochetti (1860), stands in
front of the House of Lords.

Facing the Lords, beyond a pathway anciently connecting the Abbey
with the Palace of Westminster, stands a memorial to *George V*, by Sir
W. Reid Dick and Sir Giles Scott (1947), backed by fine plane-trees and
the chapter house. Immediately behind the attractive early-19C mansion flanking it is the low, moated **Jewel Tower** (1366), a survival of the
medieval Palace of Westminster (adm. weekdays, 10.30–4). Built by
Edward III as a royal treasure-house, it served in 1621–1864 as the
Record Office of the Lords, and thereafter until 1938 as an assay office
of weights and measures. It retains fine original bosses in the vaulting.
The three stories house capitals (c. 1090) from Westminster Hall, finds
from the moat (Saxon sword), and medieval carvings from Whitehall
Palace.

We may follow the ragstone wall (1374; 20 ft high) of the Abbey
precincts, crossing Abingdon St. Gardens (underground car park) past
'Knife Edge', a sculpture by Henry Moore (1967), and turn right into
Great College Street.

To the s. are quiet Georgian streets. *Barton Street* (where at No 14 lived T. E.
Lawrence) and its continuation Cowley St. lead to Great Peter St., whence Lord
North St. conducts to *Smith Square* (1726; plaque on No. 5). Here are the headquarters of the Conservative Party (Central Office) and the Labour Party (Transport House). The eccentric shape of the Baroque church of *St John the Evangelist*,
completed in 1728 by Thomas Archer, was likened by Dickens to "a petrified
monster on its back with its legs in the air". The four angle towers are said to have
been designed to ensure that the swampy foundations settled uniformly. Restored
after bomb damage, it is used for concerts and lectures.

Millbank follows the Thames s. to the Tate Gallery (Rte 12). Fine views of the
river may be had from the flanking *Victoria Tower Gardens*. Here are a bronze
replica (1915) of a *Group by Rodin (erected at Calais in 1895), representing the
devoted *Burghers of Calais*, who surrendered themselves to Edward III in 1340 to
save their city from destruction, and memorials to *Mrs Emmeline Pankhurst* (1858–
1928) and her daughter *Dame Christabel Pankhurst* (1881–1958), leaders of the
militant women's suffrage movement.

At the end of Great College St. an archway (r.) leads into DEAN'S
YARD, once a portion of the Abbey gardens. On the E. side are entrances
to the cloisters of the Abbey and to **Westminster School,** or *St Peter's
College*, the ancient monastic school, referred to as early as 1339, refounded by Queen Elizabeth in 1560, and now one of the great public
schools. The school is built round *Little Deans' Yard*, on the site of the
monks' quarters, relics of which remain. Visitors are admitted on writ-

ten application to the bursar. The College Hall with a fine hammerbeam roof dates from the time of Edward III and was formerly the abbey refectory. The Great School Room was the monks' dormitory. *Ashburnham House* dates from the 14C, but was refaced c. 1660 when the magnificent interior decoration (notable staircase and panelling) was carried out by John Webb.

Westminster School now educates over 400 boys and 40 foundationers or Queen's Scholars. The boys enjoy certain privileges in connection with the Abbey, and shout the 'Vivats' at coronations. They attend a daily service there. In summer every other year the Queen's Scholars, together with the majority of the classical seventh, remove and sixth (senior boys), perform a comedy of Terence or Plautus, with a topical Latin prologue and epilogue. On Shrove Tuesday 'tossing the pancake' takes place in the Great School Room, the boy securing the largest fragment being rewarded with a guinea. In the long list of famous pupils are the names of Giles Fletcher, Hakluyt, Ben Jonson, George Herbert, Cowley, Dryden, Locke, Wren, Cowper, Charles Wesley, Lord Mansfield, Warren Hastings, Gibbon, Southey, Lord Raglan, G. A. Henty, A. A. Milne, and Sir Henry Tizard.

On the s. side of Dean's Yard is *Church House*, by Sir Herbert Baker (1937–40), the headquarters of the Canterbury Houses of Convocation, the House of Laity, the National Assembly of the Church of England, and over 50 Church societies. In 1940–44 it was used on several occasions as a meeting-place for Parliament. Later, it housed the Preparatory Commission of the United Nations, and the first sessions of the Security Council were also held here. The Assembly Hall with its fine timber roof, and the Hoare Memorial Hall are sometimes open to visitors. On the w. side is the *Abbey Choir School,* whose boys share the central green with Westminster School.

Crossing to the opposite corner of Dean's Yard, we emerge in Broad Sanctuary (Pl. 18; 2), a name recalling the sanctuary or precinct to the n. and w. of Westminster Abbey in which refugees were protected from the civil power by the sacred character of the Abbey. The privilege of sanctuary was finally abolished by James I. The *Westminster Column,* a Gothic memorial of red granite by Sir Gilbert Scott (1861) was erected in memory of Old Westminsters who fell in the Crimean War and the Indian Mutiny. At the corner of Tothill St. rises the large domed *Central Hall* (open to visitors when not in use; Rest.), built in 1912 as the headquarters of the Methodist Church and used also for popular concerts, organ recitals, and exhibitions. In January 1946, it became the first home of the General Assembly of the United Nations. Despite French Renaissance trappings it has a steel frame and is one of the earliest examples of such use in London. At the beginning of Tothill St. was the Almonry where William Caxton, the first English printer had his press from 1483.

Victoria St. leads w. to Victoria and Pimlico (see Rte 12).

2 WESTMINSTER ABBEY

Stations: *Westminster* and *St James's Park*, both on the Circle line, are respectively 3 min N.E. and 7 min w. – Buses and Car Parking, see Rte 1.

Admission and Services. The abbey is open daily from 8 a.m. to 6 p.m. (8 p.m. on Wed) except on the occasion of special services (see below). There are Sunday services at 8 (Holy Communion), 10.30 (Matins), 11.40 (Holy Communion; sung on festivals and 2nd and 4th Sun), 3 (Evensong) and 6.30. Weekday services are at 8 (Holy Communion), 9 (for Westminster School), 9.20 (Matins; sung on Tues & Fri), 12.30 (Lunch Hour service, Wed only; Holy Communion, Fri only), 5 (Evensong; choral exc. Wed), 3 (Sat & BH).

On Sun between services, only the nave and transepts may be visited; on Mon Wed, Thurs, Sat, these are open to view from 9.45, on Tues and Fri from 10.45. On certain Festivals (c. 12 days yearly) the abbey is not open for visiting until 11.30, and on Good Friday not until 4.30 p.m.

SPECIAL SERVICES are held in the Abbey on the opening of the Law Courts in Oct, and other important occasions. Biennially, on Maundy Thursday, i.e. the Thursday before Easter, the distribution of the *Royal Maundy* usually takes place here. On that day gifts of money (formerly of clothing, provisions, and money) are made to as many poor men and as many poor women as the sovereign has lived years. The Abbey is open to the public, but tickets for the reserved portions must be obtained at the Almonry Office. The name Maundy is usually connected with the first word of the text (Mandatum novum do vobis; John xiii. 34), with which the interesting ceremony begins.

The *Royal Chapels* (fee; free Wed evening) are open Mon & Thurs 9.20–4; Tues & Fri 10–4; Wed 9.20–4, 6–8; Sat 9.20–2, 3.45–5. The *Norman Undercroft* with its *Museum* (fee) is open weekdays 9.30–5 (also Sun, April–Oct); the *Chapter House* (fee) is open Oct–Feb 10.30–3.30; March–Sept 10.30–6; closed Sun 12–1 & BH.—*Abbey Garden*, see p. 63.

The usual ENTRANCE to the Abbey is by the West Door, outside which is a bookshop, but there are other entrances (not always open) in the South Transept (Poets' Corner) and the North Transept.

TIME OF VISIT. It is advisable to avoid the peak hours (especially in summer) between 10–12 and 2–3.30. The Abbey is seen to full advantage on a bright sunny day. A short prayer is said from the pulpit every hour on the hour.—The volunteer Abbey *Guides* are most helpful. Tours conducted by an Abbey verger take place Mon–Sat at 10.45 (and 2.30 exc. Sat); fee.

The figures in italics after monuments, etc., refer to the Plan on p. 55.

**Westminster Abbey (Pl. 18; 2), more officially the *Collegiate Church of St Peter in Westminster*, holds a unique position in English history as both the crowning-place and the burial-place of most English sovereigns. Though built at different periods, it is, with the exception of Henry VII's magnificent Perpendicular chapel at the E. end and the 18C W. towers, in the Early English style, of which it constitutes one of the most beautiful and best preserved examples.

According to tradition a church built on *Thorney Isle*, or Isle of Thorns, by Sebert, king of the East Saxons, was consecrated by Mellitus, first bishop of London in 616: but there is no authentic record of any earlier church than that of the Benedictine Abbey, founded here probably between 730 and 740, which was dedicated to St Peter and received the name 'West Minster', or western monastery, probably from its position to the W. of the city of London. Edward the Confessor (d. 1066; canonised 1163) rebuilt the abbey on a larger scale, and in his Norman church, consecrated in 1065, the body of the sainted builder was placed in 1163. Within this church, or its successor, every English sovereign since Harold (except Edward V and Edward VIII) has been crowned. In 1220 a Lady Chapel was added at the E. end, and in 1245 Henry III decided to honour St Edward by rebuilding the entire church in a more magnificent style, as we now see it. The architects were Henry de Reyns (1245–53), John of Gloucester (1253–60), and Robert of Beverley (1260–84). The influence of French cathedrals such as Rheims and Amiens and of the Sainte Chapelle can be seen in the height of the nave, and the arrangement of the radiating chapels around the apse. In 1269 the new church was consecrated. From this time until the reign of George III the Abbey became the royal burial-church. About 1388 Henry Yevele began to rebuild the nave for Abp Langham, and the work was continued after 1400 by William of Colchester; the design of Henry III's time was followed with even the details little changed. The nave-vault was completed by Abbot Islip in 1504–06. The new nave was hardly finished when the Lady Chapel was pulled down to make way for the magnificent Chapel of Henry VII (1503–19) attributed to Robert Vertue.

The lower part of the W. façade dates from c. 1390, but was altered by Hawksmoor; the towers (225 ft high) were added by the same architect about 1739. The whole of the exterior was restored by Wren and Wyatt in 1697–1720. In 1875–84 the façade of the N. transept was entirely remodelled by Sir Gilbert Scott and J. L. Pearson. The light and delicately shaped walls of Henry VII's Chapel remain the most pleasing part of the solemn heavily-buttressed exterior.

Elizabeth I made the church a 'Royal peculiar' under an independent Dean and Chapter, whose successors rule it today. The extant monastic buildings date mainly from the 13C and 14C, but there is Norman work in the Chamber of the Pyx and the adjoining Undercroft.

Measurements. The Abbey is 513 ft in length, including Henry VII's Chapel, 200 ft broad across the transepts, and 75 ft broad across the nave and aisles. The Chapel of Henry VII is 104½ ft long and 70 ft broad.

Entering by the West Door, we pass below a gilded teak group of Christ between St Peter and St Edward the Confessor, by Michael Clark (1967). The visitor should now allow the beautiful interior of the church to make its impact, before diverting his attention to the monuments. The architectural and sculptural details can be fully appreciated since the interior cleaning was completed in 1965. The height of the nave is at once striking; separated from the aisles by a tall arcade supported on circular columns round each of which are grouped eight slender shafts of grey Purbeck marble, it is the loftiest Gothic nave in England (102 ft; York Minster 100 ft). Above the arches runs the double triforium with exquisite tracery and diaperwork and still higher, the tall clerestory.

Nave. Burial in the nave took place only after the Reformation. Many monuments throughout the church commemorate men who are not buried in the Abbey. A few paces from the w. door in the middle of the nave a slab of green marble (*1*) is simply inscribed "Remember Winston Churchill". It was placed here "in accordance with the wishes of the Queen and Parliament" on the 25th anniversary of the Battle of Britain. *Churchill*'s body lies at Bladon. Immediately to the E., isolated by poppies, is the tomb of the *Unknown Warrior* (*2*), brought from Flanders and interred here on 11 Nov 1920, as representative of all the nameless British dead in the First World War, "the bravely dumb that did their deed and scorned to blot it with a name". He rests in earth brought from the battlefields. In contrast, a florid monument to *William Pitt* (1759–1806), by Westmacott crowns the w. door. On the s.w. pier hangs a *Portrait of *Richard II* (*3*), the oldest contemporary portrait of any English monarch.

At the foot of the w. piers are two fine bronze candelabra by Benno Elkan, representing the Old and the New Testaments (1940).

A stone N.E. of the Unknown Warrior's tomb marks the spot where the remains of *George Peabody* (1795–1869), the American philanthropist, lay for a time before being removed to Massachusetts. The *Earl of Shaftesbury* (1801–85) and *Baroness Burdett Coutts* (1814–1906), likewise benefactors of London, are commemorated nearer the w. door.—In the centre of the nave, farther E., are the graves of *David Livingstone* (1813–73; *4*), African traveller and missionary, and of *Thomas Tompion* (1639–1713; *5*), 'father of English watch-making'.

NORTH AISLE OF NAVE. Across the front of the NORTH-WEST or BELFRY TOWER (containing 10 bells, recast in 1971) is a bronze effigy of *Lord Salisbury* (1830–1903; *6*). On the w. wall are busts of *General Gordon* (1833–85), the defender of Khartoum, by Onslow Ford, and *Joseph Chamberlain* (1836–1914), by John Tweed. Among the crowded monuments is one (E. side) to *Viscount Howe* (1725?–58; *7*) by Scheemakers, erected by the Province of Massachusetts while it was a British colony.—Behind it, in the next bay, called by Dean Stanley the 'Whigs' Corner', is a large monument to *Charles James Fox* (1749–1806; *8*). Floor-slabs commemorate *Earl Attlee* (1883–1967), *Ramsay MacDonald* (1866–1937), *Ernest Bevin* (1881–1951), and *Sidney* and *Beatrice Webb* (1859–1947; 1858–1943). On the wall is a monument to *Campbell-*

Bannerman (1836–1908; *9*).—In the 3rd bay, a small stone in the pavement, inscribed 'O Rare Ben Jonson', marks the grave of the poet *Ben Jonson* (1573?–1637; *10*); the original stone may be seen at the foot of the adjoining wall, beneath the monument to *Thomas Banks* (1735–1805; *11*), the sculptor. In the 4th bay is one of the earliest monuments in the nave, of unusual design, to *Mrs Jane Hill* (d. 1631). In the 5th bay, at the foot of the window, *Spencer Perceval* (1762–1812; *12*), prime minister, who was shot by a madman in a lobby of the House of Commons; monument with a relief depicting the murder, by Westmacott.—A slab in the 7th bay marks the grave of *Sir John Herschel* (1792–1871); nearby is a memorial to *Sir William Herschel* (1738–1822; buried at Slough), like his son, an astronomer.

The choir screen (1828; re-gilded) is the work of Edward Blore. Set in to the w. side are two impressive works by Rysbrack and Kent commemorating *Sir Isaac Newton* (1642–1727; *13*) and *Earl Stanhope* (1673–1721; *14*). Beside Newton's grave is that of *Lord Kelvin* (1824–1907), mathematician and physicist.

South Aisle of Nave. Several of the bays have interesting old coats of arms. To the left, in the 7th bay, *Major John André* (1751–80; *33*), hanged by Washington as a spy during the American War; on the bas-relief Washington receiving André's vain petition for a soldier's death. Floor slabs in front of the next bay (usually covered by stalls) mark the graves of *Andrew Bonar Law* (1858–1923) and *Neville Chamberlain* (1869–1944), prime ministers. The 5th bay has unusual Morland monuments with trilingual inscriptions including Hebrew, Coptic, and Greek.—Above the w. cloister door is a dramatic monument by Roubiliac to *Field-Marshal George Wade* (1673–1748; *34*), who provided the Scottish Highlands with roads and bridges in 1720–30. In the last bay is a small gallery of oak called the *Abbot's Pew* (*35*), erected by Abbot Islip (16C), and below, *William Congreve* (1670–1729), the dramatist.

The South-West Tower, or Old Baptistery, is now the CHAPEL OF ST GEORGE, dedicated to all who gave their lives in the World Wars and containing a tablet to the million British dead. In the wrought-iron screen is the trophy sent by Verdun to the Lord Mayor. Below is a tablet to *Lord Baden-Powell* (1857–1941), founder of the Scout movement. In the floor, slabs mark the graves of *Lord Plumer* (1857–1932) and *Lord Allenby* (1871–1936), and on the south wall is an oak screen in memory of *Henry Fawcett* (1833–84), the blind statesman, and his wife, *Dame Millicent Fawcett* (1847–1929). Outside on the w. wall is a plaque in memory of *President Franklin Roosevelt* (1882–1945).

THE NORTH CHOIR AISLE has fine examples of early heraldry on the N. wall. A series of medallions under the organ (r.) commemorate famous scientists, among them *Charles Darwin* (1809–82; tomb in N. nave aisle) and *Lord Lister* (1827–1912). Three matching diamonds in the pavement honour *Elgar*, *Vaughan Williams*, and *Stanford*. In the next bay *William Wilberforce* (1759–1833; *15*), one of the chief opponents of the slave-trade, and *Sir Stamford Raffles* (1759–1833), founder of Singapore, sit pensive in effigy above the tomb of *Henry Purcell* (1659–95; *16*), composer and organist of the Abbey. Beyond, a bust of *Orlando Gibbons* (1583–1625; buried at Canterbury) faces the tomb of *John Blow* (d. 1708) and a memorial to *Dr Burney* (1726–1814), historian of music. At the entrance to the transept (r.), *William Hesketh* (d. 1605; *17*), with bright Jacobean decoration.

Sanctuary. The 18C roof of the lantern destroyed by incendiary bombs in May 1941 was replaced soon afterwards. The Sanctuary, or raised space within the altar-rails, where coronations take place, has a venerable pavement of Cosmati work laid by Master Odericus in 1268 (protected by carpets). On the left are the three most beautiful architectural *Tombs in the Abbey, dating from between c. 1298 and 1325. The nearest one is that of *Aveline, Countess of Lancaster* (d. c. 1273; *18*), first wife of Edmund Crouchback. The others commemorate *Aymer de Valence* (d. 1324; *19*), and *Edmund Crouchback, earl of Lancaster* (d. 1296; *20*), second son of Henry III and founder of the house of Lancaster. On the canopies of the two later tombs are representations of the deceased on horseback, and all three are adorned with rich painting and gilding (now much faded). The statuettes around Aymer de Valence's tomb are among the most exquisite small sculptures in England (better seen from ambulatory; see below).—On the right side of the Sanctuary are sedilia dating from the time of Edward I, with paintings (1308) of Sebert, St Peter and Ethelbert, and an ancient tapestry from Westminster School. On this is hung a Florentine triptych, by Bicci di Lorenzo (1373–1452), of the Madonna between SS. John Gualberto and Anthony of Padua (r.) and SS. John the Baptist and Catherine of Alexandria; it was given to the Abbey in 1948 by Lord Lee of Fareham. Below is the tomb of *Anne of Cleves* (d. 1557; *21*), fourth wife of Henry VIII. The 17C pulpit, replaced in 1935, is matched by a lectern (1949) in memory of William Carey (1761–1834), the missionary. The choir fittings were designed by Ed. Blore in 1830.

Transepts. The uniformity and proportions of the architecture have been upset by the host of monuments. In the N. transept the E. aisle is partially closed off, while in the S. transept the E. walk of the cloister accounts for the W. aisle. Each transept is lit by a large rose-window (the glass in the N. transept is the oldest in the Abbey, dating from 1721–22), below which are exquisitely carved censing angels, sculpted by Master John of St Alban's c. 1250; the S. transept retains also two figures below the window.

The **North Transept** is the burial-place of several eminent statesmen. In the W. aisle is a delicately carved monument to *Jonas Hanway* (1722–86; *22*), the philanthropist, and busts of *Richard Cobden* (1804–65; buried at West Lavington), the apostle of free trade, and of *Warren Hastings* (1732–1818; buried at Daylesford), Governor-General of India. On the wall behind, in the nave, is a huge monument to *William Pitt, earl of Chatham* (1708–78; *23*), and statues of *Lord Palmerston* (1784–1865) and *Lord Castlereagh* (1769–1821). In the pavement are the graves of *Henry Grattan* (1746–1820), the Irish patriot and orator, and *C. J. Fox* (1749–1806). Towards the E. wall, statues of *George Canning* (1770–1827), by Chantrey; *Benjamin Disraeli, earl of Beaconsfield* (1804–81; buried at Hughenden), by Boehm; *William Ewart Gladstone* (1809–98), by Brock; and *Sir Robert Peel* (1788–1850; buried at Drayton), by Gibson.

The three chapels (usually locked) of ST JOHN THE EVANGELIST, ST MICHAEL, and ST ANDREW occupy the E. aisle of the N. transept. At the entrance to the chapels is an overwhelming monument to *General Wolfe* (1727–59; buried at Greenwich), who fell at the capture of Quebec. To the left, as we enter, *Sir John Franklin* (1786–1847), lost in the search for the North-West Passage, with a fine inscription by Tennyson.—To the right, **Sir Francis Vere* (1560–1609), a distinguished soldier of Queen Elizabeth. This magnificent Renaissance tomb is modelled on that of Engelbert II of Nassau (d. 1504) at Breda.—*Lady Elizabeth Nightingale* (d. 1731), a skilful but theatrical sculpture by Roubiliac.—The large tomb in the next chapel is that of *Lord Norris* (1525?–1601) and his wife (neither buried here); the only one of their six sons who survived them may be distinguished by his attitude.—On the N. wall, *Sir James Young Simpson* (1811–70; buried in Edinburgh), who first used chloroform as an anaesthetic.—*Mrs Siddons* (1755–1831) as the Tragic Muse, by Chantrey after Reynolds.—*Sir Humphry Davy* (1778–1829; buried in Geneva), inventor of the safety lamp.—*John Kemble* (1757–1823), the actor, designed by Flaxman.—*Thomas Telford* (1757–1834), engineer and bridge-builder.—On the r. *Adm. Kempenfelt* (1718–82), who went down in the 'Royal George', by Bacon.

South Transept, see below.

Choir Chapels. The choir-apse is rounded and contains the Chapel of St Edward, so that the high altar is placed somewhat far forward, and the ritual choir extends into the nave. In the ambulatory are two fine brasses for *Abbot Estney* (1498; *36*) and *Sir John Harpedon* (1457; *37*). The three tombs in the Sanctuary are well seen here (see above).

The two-storied CHAPEL OF ABBOT ISLIP (lower story not shown) contains the grave of *Adm. Sir Charles Saunders* (d. 1775; *38*), who shared with Wolfe the glory of taking Quebec. On the carved screen appears the abbot's rebus: an eye with a slip of a tree or a man slipping from a branch. The upper chapel (adm. on application), with a too graphic window (1950), is now the Nurses' Memorial Chapel.

The CHAPEL OF ST JOHN THE BAPTIST is entered through the tiny Chapel of Our Lady of the Pew. Above the entrance is a delicately carved alabaster niche from the demolished Chapel of St Erasmus (15C). Traces of the painted vault remain from the late-14C; a statue of the Madonna by Sister Concordia was placed in the niche in 1971. To the right in the polygonal Chapel of St John the Baptist are several 15C tombs of abbots, notably *William de Colchester* (d. 1420; *39*). The huge tomb of *Lord Hunsdon* (d. 1596; *40*), cousin and lord chamberlain to Elizabeth I, is a masterpiece of Elizabethan bombast. The plain tomb by the N.E. wall of *Hugh* and *Mary de Bohun* (*41*), dates from 1304–05. Behind is a monument to *Col. Popham*; the inscription was removed because of his Parliamentarian activities. In the centre is a large monument to *Thomas Cecil, earl of Exeter* (1542–1623; *42*), son of Lord Burghley, with his effigy and that of his first wife; his second wife refused to accept the less honourable position on his left hand and was buried in Winchester Cathedral.

In the ambulatory opposite the chapel, the mosaics on the tomb of Henry III (p. 59) are well seen. The well-lit CHAPEL OF ST PAUL is the easternmost chapel of the North Ambulatory and contains (r.) the tomb of *Lord Bourchier* (d. 1431; *43*), recently repainted, which forms part of the screen. On the monument of *Lord Cottington* (d. 1652; *44*) is a bust of his wife (d. 1633), by Le Sueur. On the site of the altar, *Frances Sidney, countess of Sussex* (d. 1589; *45*), founder of Sidney Sussex College at Cambridge. The fine monument to *Dudley Carleton* (d. 1632; *46*) is by Nicholas Stone. Beyond good monuments to *Sir Thomas Bromley* (1530–87) and *Sir James Fullerton* (d. 1631) is one to *Sir John Puckering* (1544–96; *47*), speaker of the House of Commons. In the centre, *Sir Giles Daubeny* (d. 1508; *48*) and his lady, with fine contemporary cos-

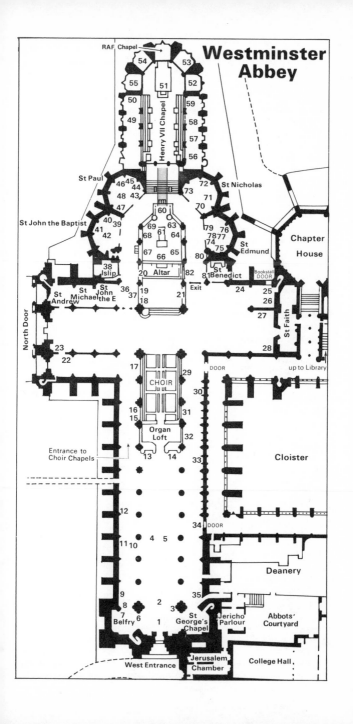

tumes. To the right of the exit, bust of *Sir Rowland Hill* (1795–1879), champion of penny postage.—In the ambulatory, opposite the exit from this chapel, we note the *Grate of Queen Eleanor's tomb, an admirable specimen of English wrought-iron work by Thomas of Leighton, 1294. Beneath are traces of paintings by Walter of Durham. Above can be seen the Chantry of Henry V, forming a bridge over the ambulatory.— We now ascend the flight of steps leading to the Lady Chapel (Chapel of Henry VII), entered appropriately through a spacious barrel-vaulted vestibule, decorated with bright panelling.

Chapel of Henry VII. Built in 1503–19, this chapel is the finest example in England of late-Perpendicular or Tudor Gothic. Henry ordered it to be "painted, garnished and adorned in as goodly and rich a manner as such work requireth and as to a king's work apperteyneth". Of its profuse decoration the culminating glory is the superb fan-tracery vaulting, hung with pendants in the nave, and stretched as a canopy to accommodate the bay windows in the aisles. The beautiful tall windows, curved in the aisles and angular in the apse, are particularly ingenious. The carving throughout is of the highest quality, and includes a series of 95 (originally 107) statues of saints popular at the time, with a frieze of angels and badges below. The chapel was begun as a shrine for Henry VI, and carved stalls of the Knights of the Bath separate the nave from the aisles, which have separate entrances at the w. end.

In 1725, when George I reconstituted the most honourable Order of the Bath, this chapel became the chapel of the Order, with the Dean of Westminster as its perpetual dean. After 1812, however, no installation of knights was held until 1913, when the ceremony was revived with all its ancient pomp and the present banners placed in position.

NORTH AISLE OF HENRY VII'S CHAPEL. The tall canopied *Tomb in the centre of the aisle was erected by James I to *Elizabeth I* (1533–1603; *49*), who rests here in the same grave as her sister *Mary I* (d. 1558): "Consorts in throne and tomb, here we sisters rest, Elizabeth and Mary, in hope of the resurrection" (epitaph). The marble figure is the work of Cornelius Cure (1605–07).

The E. end of this aisle (*50*) was called 'Innocents' Corner' by Dean Stanley, for here are commemorated two infant *Children of James I* (d. 1607), one represented in a cradle which is the actual tomb; and in a small sarcophagus by the E. wall are some bones (comp. p. 248), re-interred as those of *Edward V* and his brother *Richard, Duke of York*, the young sons of Edward IV, who were murdered in the Tower c. 1483. Edward V had been born in the Sanctuary of the Abbey.

NAVE OF HENRY VII'S CHAPEL. The beautiful oak doors plated with bronze at the entrance date from the 16C. The heraldic devices that appear on them and recur elsewhere in the decoration of the chapel refer to Henry VII's ancestry and to his claims to the throne.

The Welsh dragon indicates his Tudor father; the daisy-plant and the portcullis refer to the names of his Lancastrian mother, Margaret Beaufort; the falcon was the badge of Edward IV, father of Elizabeth of York, Henry's wife; the greyhound that of the Nevilles from whom she was descended. The crown on a bush recalls Henry's first coronation on Bosworth field; while the roses are those of Lancaster and York united by his marriage. Other emblems are the lions of England and the fleur-de-lis of France.

Within, on each side, are the beautiful carved stalls of the Knights of the Bath, each with the arms of its successive holders emblazoned on small copper plates and the banner of the current holder suspended above. The lower seats are those of the esquires (no longer used as such) with their coats-of-arms. Beneath the seats are a number of grotesquely carved misericords, one of which (8th stall on s. side) dates from thè 13C. At the w. end is the naval sword of George VI, with which he conferred the accolade of the Order. The altar (1935) is a reproduction of the original, with a 15C altarpiece by Bart. Vivarini.

Beneath the pavement between the door and the altar reposes *George II* (d. 1760; the last king buried in the Abbey), with *Queen Caroline* and numerous members of his family. Below the altar is the grave of *Edward VI* (d. 1553). Behind it is the beautiful *Tomb (*51*)* of *HenryVII* (d. 1509) and *Elizabeth of York* (d. 1503), an admirable work by Torrigiani, completed about 1518. The noble effigies of the king and queen repose on a black marble sarcophagus, with a carved frieze of white marble and adorned with gilt medallions of saints. The fine grate is the work of Thomas Ducheman. *James I* (1566–1625) is buried in the same vault as Henry VII and his queen.—The first apse-chapel on the s. is filled by Le Sueur's monument to *Ludovick Stuart, duke of Lennox and Richmond* (1574–1624; *52*) with a gilt canopy; in the next is buried *Dean Stanley* (1815–81; *53*), with a fine effigy by Boehm. Here too lies the *Duc de Montpensier* (1775–1807), brother of Louis-Philippe.

The E. chapel is now the ROYAL AIR FORCE CHAPEL. The window by Hugh Easton, commemorating the Battle of Britain (July–Oct 1940), incorporates in the design the badges of the 63 Fighter Squadrons that took part. The Chapel keeps the Roll of Honour (facsimile in adjoining chapel) of the 1497 airmen of Britain and her allies who fell in the battle. Nearby is the grave of *Lord Dowding* (1882–1970), who commanded the air defence of Great Britain, and on the s. side that of *Lord Trenchard* (1873–1956), 'father' of the R.A.F.

In this chapel were buried *Oliver Cromwell* (1599–1658; tablet), *Henry Ireton* (1611–51), *John Bradshaw* (1602–59) and *Admiral Blake* (1599–1657). At the Restoration all were removed from the Abbey; Blake was reinterred in St Margaret's churchyard, but the bodies of the others were treated with ignominy, and their heads were struck off at Tyburn and afterwards exposed on Westminster Hall.

In the next chapel is a vault (usually covered with an organ) with the graves of *Anne of Denmark* (1574–1619; *54*), queen of James I, and *Anne Mowbray*, the child wife of Richard, duke of York, reburied here in 1965. In the last chapel is the large tomb by Le Sueur, of *George, duke of Buckingham* (assassinated in 1628; *55*), the favourite of James I and Charles I, with statues by Nicholas Stone of his children. The low stone screen preserved here is in keeping with the originality of the design of the outer walls of the chapel.

SOUTH AISLE OF HENRY VII'S CHAPEL. At the end of this aisle are memorials to *Lord Cromer* (1841–1917), *Lord Curzon* (1859–1925), *Viscount Milner* (1854–1925), and *Cecil Rhodes*. In the centre, tomb of *Margaret, Countess of Lennox* (d. 1578; *56*). Her son, Henry Darnley, was husband of Mary, Queen of Scots, and father of James I of England; and his figure among the effigies of her children on the sides of the tomb may be identified by the (restored) crown over his head (as Henry I of Scotland). Next, under a tall canopy, is a recumbent *Figure of *Mary, Queen of Scots* (1542–87; *57*), whose remains were removed hither from

Peterborough Cathedral in 1612 by order of her son, James I. The work of Cornelius and William Cure (1605–10), this was the last royal tomb erected in the Abbey.

The next *Tomb is that of *Margaret Beaufort, countess of Richmond* (1443–1509; *58*), mother of Henry VII, patron of Wynkyn de Worde, and foundress of Christ's and St John's Colleges at Cambridge. The beautiful recumbent figure in gilt-bronze, the masterpiece of Pietro Torrigiani of Florence, is noted for the delicate modelling of the hands. It is surrounded by a contemporary screen. On the wall to the N., is a fine bronze bust of *Sir Thomas Lovell* (d. 1524), also by Torrigiani. The statue of a Roman matron beside it, by Valory, commemorates *Catherine Lady Walpole* (d. 1737).

The incongruous monument to *General Monk, duke of Albemarle* (1608–70; *59*), restorer of the Stuarts, covers a vault containing the remains of *Charles II* (d. 1685), *Mary II* (d. 1694), her husband *William III* (d. 1702), *Queen Anne* (d. 1714), and her husband *Prince George of Denmark* (d. 1708).

We now cross a reinforced glass bridge (1971) past the tomb and beneath the CHANTRY OF HENRY V (1387–1422). His dispoiled effigy (*60*) rests on a slab of marble and was originally covered with silver-gilt plates, stolen together with the solid silver head in the reign of Henry VIII. The head was replaced in 1971 in gilt bronze by Louisa Bolt. In the chantry (no adm.) *Katherine of Valois* (d. 1437), Henry's 'beautiful Kate', lies beneath the altar; she was originally interred in the old Lady Chapel. On a beam still higher are a shield, saddle, and helmet, probably made for Henry's funeral.

*Chapel of St Edward the Confessor, once the most gorgeous as it is the most sacred part of the church. In the middle stands the mutilated *Shrine of St Edward the Confessor* (d. 1066; *61*), erected in the late 13C for Henry III by 'Peter of Rome', probably the son of Odericus (see above), and showing traces of the original mosaics. The upper part, now of wood (1557), was originally a golden shrine decorated with jewels and gold images of saints, all of which disappeared at the Dissolution. In the recesses of the base sick persons used to spend the night in hope of cure. Roman Catholic pilgrims visit the shrine on St Edward's Day (13 Oct).—On the s. side of the shrine is the tomb of *Philippa of Hainault* (d. 1369; *63*), wife of Edward III, with the alabaster effigy of the queen by Hennequin of Liège, sculptor to the king of France. The elaborate tomb of *Edward III* (d. 1377; *64*) has niches in which were statuettes of his fourteen children, six of which remain (seen from s. ambulatory); the contemporary wooden canopy is fine. The last tomb on this side is that of *Richard II* (d. 1400; *65*) and his first wife *Anne of Bohemia* (d. 1394), which is in the same style as that of Edward III. It is profusely decorated with delicately engraved patterns, among which may be distinguished the broom-pods of the Plantagenets, the white hart, the rising sun, etc.; the beautiful paintings in the canopy represent the Trinity, the Coronation of the Virgin, and Anne of Bohemia's coat-of-arms.—At the w. end is a beautiful screen (mid-15C) with 14 scenes of the life of Edward the Confessor. In front are remains of the Cosmati pavement, and the *Coronation Chair* (*66*), made in oak by Walter of Durham c. 1300–01. It has left the Abbey only thrice—when Cromwell was installed as Lord Protector in Westminster Hall, and for safety during the two World Wars. It encloses the famous 'Stone of Scone', carried off from Scotland by Edward I in 1297, used for all subsequent coronations of English monarchs. Beside it are the *State Sword* (7 ft long) and *Shield* of Edward III.

The *Stone of Scone*, on which the Scottish kings were crowned from time immemorial down to John Baliol, was regarded as the palladium of Scottish independence, and its character is supposed to have been vindicated when James VI of Scotland became also James I of England in 1603. A long but quite mythical history attaches to this block of reddish sandstone from central Scotland. It is traditionally identified with Jacob's pillow at Bethel, afterwards the 'Lia Fail' or 'Stone of Destiny' on the sacred hill of Tara, in Ireland. Historically, it is recorded as being used for the enthronement of Macbeth's stepson at Scone in 1057, and was certainly in use there earlier. On 24 Dec, 1950, the stone was stolen by Scottish 'Nationalists' and taken to Arbroath; it was replaced on 13 April, 1951.

On the N. side is the plain altar-tomb, without effigy, of *Edward I* (d. 1307; 67); in 1744 his body (6 ft 2 in long) was found to be in good preservation, dressed in royal robes with a gilt crown. Beyond are the beautiful Gothic *Tombs of *Henry III* (1207–72; 68), and his daughter-in-law, *Eleanor of Castile* (d. 1290; 69), wife of Edward I. Henry's tomb was designed by Peter of Rome, and Eleanor's was executed by Richard Crundale with paintings by Walter of Durham; but both the beautiful bronze effigies, the earliest cast in England, are by William Torel, a goldsmith of London. The canopy over Eleanor's tomb dates from the 15C, when the old one was destroyed by the erection of Henry V's Chantry.

The CHAPEL OF ST NICHOLAS, off the s. ambulatory, has a fine stone screen. On the right of the door, *Philippa, Duchess of York* (d. 1431; 70). —In the centre is the fine tomb of *Sir George Villiers* (d. 1606; 71) and his wife (d. 1630), parents of the Duke of Buckingham.—The large monument on the s. wall, to the *Wife* and *Daughter of Lord Burghley* (c. 1588; 72), and that on the E. wall, to the *Duchess of Somerset* (d. 1587; 73), widow of the Protector, are good examples of the Renaissance period. Below this chapel is the vault of the dukes of Northumberland, the only family with right of sepulture in the Abbey. In the Ambulatory, opposite this chapel, has been placed an oaken *RETABLE, a precious example of French or English painting of c. 1255, with rich decorations.

The CHAPEL OF SS. EDMUND AND THOMAS THE MARTYR is separated from the ambulatory by an ancient oaken screen. To the right, inside *William de Valence, earl of Pembroke* (d. 1296; 74), half-brother of Henry III. This tomb consists of an oaken coffin and effigy of the deceased, which were formerly coated with Limoges enamel, remnants of which may still be seen.—*Edward Talbot, earl of Shrewsbury* (d. 1617; 75) and his wife, a handsome Jacobean tomb, to accommodate which, however, some of the arcading was destroyed.—*Sir Richard Pecksall* (1571), master of the buckhounds.—*Sir Bernard Brocas* (d. 1395), captain of Calais.—Beyond the large monument to *Lord John Russell* (d. 1584; 76), with his infant son, is the seated figure of his daughter, *Lady Elizabeth Russell* (1576–1601), the earliest non-recumbent statue in the Abbey.—In the floor, grave of *Edward Bulwer Lytton* (1803–73), the novelist.—In the centre of the chapel are the tombs of *Robert Waldeby, archbishop of York* (d. 1397; 77), the companion of the Black Prince, with a brass representing him in full eucharistic vestments, and of *Eleanor de Bohun, duchess of Gloucester* (d. 1399; 78), in conventual dress, the largest and finest brass in the Abbey.—Near the E. wall, *Frances, Duchess of Suffolk* (d. 1559), mother of Lady Jane Grey.— Adjoining are the finely modelled but mutilated effigies of two children of Edward III (1340).—Beside the door into the chapel, **John of Eltham* (1316–37; *79*), second son of Edward II; this tomb, with the earliest alabaster effigy in the Abbey, is especially interesting for the careful representation of the prince's armour.—Opposite the entrance to this chapel we see the outer side of Edward III's tomb, with beautiful little brass *Statuettes of his children, with enamelled coats of arms. Between this chapel and the next a small altar-tomb (*80*) covers the remains of four children of Henry III and four of Edward I.

Opposite is the CHAPEL OF ST BENEDICT (no adm.), best seen from the s. transept. Beside the railing on this side is the alabaster tomb of *Simon Langham* (d. 1376; *81*), abbot of Westminster and afterwards archbishop and cardinal.—In the ambulatory is the so-called tomb of *Sebert* (*82*) and his wife; then a tablet to Anne Nevill (1456–85), queen of Richard III. Above is the back of the sedilia in the sanctuary, with 14C paintings of Edward the Confessor and the Annunciation (mutilated). Outside the gate (r.) is a monument to *Dr Richard Busby* (1606–95), a famous headmaster of Westminster School.

We have now come to the **South Transept and Poets' Corner.** Poets' Corner, taking its name from the tombs of Chaucer and Spenser, is, strictly speaking, the s. end of the E. aisle of this transept; but the tombs of the poets have overflowed into the s. end of the central aisle also. On the end wall of the transept are two magnificent Wall-paintings of St Christopher and the Incredulity of St Thomas. Uncovered in 1936, they are ascribed to Walter of Durham (c. 1280) and are outstanding examples of the Westminster school of painting.

On the left side of the E. aisle as we enter is a bust of *John Dryden* (1631–1700), and on the pier opposite (r.) is a bust of *William Blake* (1757–1827), by Epstein. By the next pillar (left) is a bust of *Henry Longfellow* (1807–82), placed by the English admirers of the American poet in 1884.—Beneath the next window is the Gothic *Tomb of *Geoffrey Chaucer* (1340?–1400; *24*), the poet of the 'Canterbury Tales', erected 155 years after his death. The space at the end of the altar-tomb is perhaps a prayer recess. Farther on, *Michael Drayton* (1563–1631). Beneath the pavement in front of Chaucer's tomb is the grave of *Robert Browning* (1812–89), and memorials to *Alfred Tennyson* (1809–92), *T. S. Eliot* (1888–1965), and *Lord Byron* (1788–1824).

At the s.E. angle are two doorways. Outside that in the E. wall is an ancient pathway going straight to the Palace of Westminster, and a tablet on the left marks the approximate site of Caxton's original printing-press (1477), six years before he set up in larger premises in the Almonry (p. 49).—In the s. wall is the entrance to the *Chapter-House Crypt* (no adm.), an eight-sided undercroft (1248) with a massive central column, once used as the royal treasury.

On the s. wall, above the door to the crypt, is a medallion of *Ben Jonson* (1573?–1637; buried in the nave).—Farther on, *Edmund Spenser* (1552?–99; *25*), the poet of 'The Faerie Queene'; the present monument is a copy (1778) of the original one.—*John Milton* (1608–74; *26*; buried at St Giles, Cripplegate), a memorial delayed by political feeling for over 60 years after the poet's death.—Below, *Thomas Gray* (1716–71; grave at Stoke Poges).—On the partition-wall, the remarkable monument to

Matthew Prior (1664–1721), designed by Gibbs, executed by Rysbrack, with a bust by Coysevox.—On the next pier, beyond a bust of Tennyson, *Adam Lindsay Gordon* (1833–70), the poet of Australia, and *Thomas Campbell* (1777–1844).—In the floor a little to the N., gravestone of *Thomas Parr* (d. 1635; 'Old Parr'), said to have lived 152 years and under ten sovereigns, while farther s. are those of *Dr Samuel Johnson* (1709–84), with a bust by Nollekens above it, *David Garrick* (1717–79), and *Sir Henry Irving* (1838–1905).—On the w. side of the partition-wall. *William Wordsworth* (1770–1850; buried at Grasmere); *Samuel Taylor Coleridge* (1772–1834; buried at Highgate); and *Robert Southey* (1774–1843; buried at Crosthwaite), epitaph by Wordsworth.—*William Shakespeare* (1564–1616; *27*; buried at Stratford-on-Avon). On the monument, by Scheemakers, which was erected in 1740, are inscribed some lines from 'The Tempest', and at the corners of the pedestal are carved heads representing Elizabeth I, Henry V, and Richard III.—*John Keats* (1796–1821) and *P. B. Shelley* (1792–1822), both buried in Rome, are commemorated above.—*James Thomson* (1700–48; buried at Richmond), author of 'Rule Britannia'.—Above, *Robert Burns* (1759–96; buried at Dumfries).—Below, the *Brontë Sisters*, with a line from Emily's 'Old Stoic': "with courage to endure."—Above the door to the Chapel of St Faith, *Oliver Goldsmith* (1728–74; date of birth given wrongly in the epitaph; buried in the Temple), with an epitaph by Dr Johnson.

The *Chapel of St Faith* (restored, 1972), formerly the revestry, is reserved for private devotion.

To the right of the chapel, *Sir Walter Scott* (1771–1832; buried at Dryburgh), and above, *John Ruskin* (1819–1900; buried at Coniston), The monument to *John Campbell, Duke of Argyll* (1680–1743; *28*) is a fine work by Roubiliac. Above on the w. wall, *George Frederick Handel* (1685–1759). A slab in the floor marks his grave, and one beside it that of *Charles Dickens* (1812–70).—In the floor are a tablet commemorating *Thomas Hardy* (1840–1928) and the grave of *Rudyard Kipling* (1865–1936).—By the pier, *William Makepeace Thackeray* (1811–63; buried at Kensal Green).—*Jos. Addison* (1672–1719).—*Lord Macaulay* (1800–59).

South Choir Aisle. Opposite the E. door into the cloisters are two good monuments to *William Thynne* (d. 1584), and to *Sir Thomas Richardson* (*29*), in black marble, by Le Sueur. To the left in the next bay is an inappropriate monument to *Sir Cloudesley Shovel* (1650–1707; *30*) between memorials to *Admiral Blake* (1599–1657) and *Robert Clive* (1725–64). Above is a monument to *Sir Godfrey Kneller* (1646–1723; buried at Kneller Hall), the only painter commemorated in the Abbey.— In the 3rd bay (r.), the tomb of *Thomas Owen* (d. 1598; *31*), with a fine painted alabaster figure. On either side of it, are the tomb of *General Pasquale Paoli* (1725–1807), the Corsican patriot who died as a refugee in England, and tablet to *William Tyndale* (1490–1536), translator of the Bible. Opposite, medallions to *John Wesley* (1703–91) and *Charles Wesley* (1707–88), both buried elsewhere, *H. F. Lyte* (1793–1847), author of 'Abide with me', with *Dr Isaac Watts* (1674–1748; buried in Bunhill Fields), the hymn writer, beneath. Under the organ loft is a monument to *Thomas Thynne* (1648–82; *32*), with a bas-relief depicting his assassination.

Cloisters and Conventual Buildings. The earliest parts of the present Cloisters date from the mid-13C, the remainder from 1344–70. The cloisters are connected with the church by two doors in the s. nave aisle, affording convenient entrance and exit for conventual processions. Visitors should quit the church by the one to the E., entering the cloisters at their N.E. angle, the earliest and finest part. The external carving on the doorway should be noticed. In the *E. Walk* a tablet on the wall in the second bay bears the touching inscription "Jane Lister, dear Childe", with the date 1688. We pass the entrances to the Chapter House and to the Chamber of the Pyx, between which is the entrance to the Library and Muniment Room (comp. p. 63).—The *South Walk* (14C) was the burial-place of the abbots for nearly 200 years after the Conquest. The three effigies beneath the wall seat are of Abbots Laurence (d. 1173), Gilbert Crispin (d. 1117), and William de Humez (d. 1222). The recesses in the wall beside the old entrance to the Refectory served as towel-cupboards.—The *W. Walk* (14C) was used as the monastery school. On the wall is a memorial, by G. Ledward, to the members of the submarine branch of the Royal Navy who lost their lives in the two World Wars, and to members of the Commandos, the Airborne Forces and Special Air Service killed in 1939–45.—In the *N. Walk* (14C; being restored) is buried *General Burgoyne* (1722–92), who surrendered to General Gates at Saratoga in 1777.

The *CHAPTER HOUSE (adm. see p. 50) is entered from the East Walk. Over the entrance are sculpted figures, much mutilated, of the 13C. The vaulted vestibule has fine bosses. At the top of the stairs *James Russell Lowell* (1819–91), the American writer, and *Walter Hines Page* (1855–1918), American ambassador, are commemorated. Opposite, the coffin-lid, with a cross in relief, is perhaps the only extant relic of Sebert's church; the Roman sarcophagus was buried in the green N. of the Abbey. Visitors are provided with overshoes to avoid injury to the original tiled *Pavement. The beautiful octagonal room, 56 ft in diameter, was built c. 1245–55 above the crypt of the Confessor's chapter-house. On the left is the Roll of Honour of the Royal Army Medical Corps. The lofty roof is supported by a single central shaft, 35 ft high, and it is lit by six huge windows. These, destroyed by bombing in 1941, were reset in 1950 with some of the original glass; they show scenes from the abbey's history and the arms of benefactors. The tracery, like the roof, is modern, though copied from the blank window which escaped mutilation. The arcading on the walls is adorned with paintings (partly restored) of the life of St John and of the Apocalypse, with a frieze of animals below, presented by John of Northampton (1372–1404), a Westminster monk. The beautiful Madonna and angel above the door date from 1250–53.

The Chapter House is especially memorable as the "cradle of representative and constitutional government throughout the world", for here the early House of Commons, separated from the House of Lords in the reign of Edward III, held its meetings down to 1547, when it migrated to St Stephen's Chapel. From c. 1550 to 1865 it served as a State muniment room; and it is still in the charge of the government, not the Abbey authorities.

THE CHAMBER OF THE PYX (for adm. apply to an Abbey Guide), entered from the E. walk by a Norman archway and massive doors with seven locks, is part of the Confessor's building. Originally a chapel, it was afterwards used as the abbots' treasury and contained many sacred relics. It subsequently became the depository of the 'pyx', or chest containing the Exchequer trial-plates of gold and silver used as standards of reference at the periodical tests of the coins of the realm. The altar here is the oldest in the Abbey.

The E. walk of the cloisters is continued to the s. by the *Dark* or *Norman Cloister* (11C), whence the NORMAN UNDERCROFT (adm. see p. 50) is entered. Here is a museum illustrating the history of the abbey, and containing effigies carried at royal funerals.

It used to be the custom to show the embalmed bodies of royal persons at their funerals; the actual bodies were later replaced by life-like effigies of wood, plaster, or, at a later period, wax. Notable among the wooden effigies or heads here are those of Edward III (perhaps the oldest in Europe) and Henry VII, both death-mask portraits. The plaster head of Mary II is less successful. Anne of Bohemia, Katherine of Valois, Elizabeth of York, and Anne of Denmark represent the queens-consort. The eleven wax figures are interesting both as portraits and for their costumes. The oldest is that of Charles II, the one of Elizabeth I having been remade in 1760; others represent Lady Frances Stuart, William III, Mary II, and Queen Anne. The figures of Nelson and Chatham are not funeral effigies, but were added to attract visitors; they are outstanding as portraits.

Also displayed here are the royal writ and seal of Edward the Confessor and William I; a letter from John of Gaunt; the lease made out to Chaucer for premises in the garden of the old Lady Chapel; and the Coronation service book. A complete medieval arrow (unique), in the case opposite, was found in the top of Henry V's Chantry, possibly having been used as a pigeon scarer. Among other objects found in the Abbey are: the sword of Henry V; the ring of Bp. Courtenay of Norwich (d. 1415) found in his grave in 1953; the ring said to have been given by Elizabeth I to the Earl of Essex, and to have been intercepted by the Countess of Nottingham when Essex, on his condemnation, sent it back to the Queen in hope of pardon; a trunk thought to belong to Lady Margaret Beaufort; and the frater bell of the monastery. The building accounts of the nave also survive here, and 17C–20C plate is on display.

Farther on an arched passage on the left leads to the LITTLE CLOISTER, on the site of the monks' infirmary, a retired and picturesque spot, though modernised and restored after damage in 1940–41. In the E. walk survives the 14C doorway of *St Catherine's Chapel* (1165–70; the infirmary chapel), the ruined arcades of which may be viewed through a doorway to the left. In the s. walk a door leads to *College Garden* (open to visitors on Thurs. 12–4 or 6; entrance also from Gt. College St.) The Dark Cloister ends at the yard of Westminster School (p. 48).

From the junction of the w. and s. walks of the great cloister a corridor leads to the w. to Dean's Yard. Near its w. end, on the right, is a passage admitting to the *Abbots' Courtyard*, lying between the Deanery, formerly the Abbots' Palace, on the right, and the College Hall, on the left. The steps at the end ascend to the *Jericho Parlour*, or panelled ante-room, to the **Jerusalem Chamber** (14C), the abbots' retiring room, now used as the chapter-room and shown only by special permission of the Dean. In this chamber Henry IV died in 1413, having had a stroke while praying at the shrine of the Confessor.

The *Library and Muniment Room* (adm. by special permission only), occupying part of the monks' dormitory, above the chapter-house vestibule and the Chamber of the Pyx, is entered from the E. walk of the cloister by the original day-stairs. The library was founded c. 1623 and contains contemporary book-presses, as well as a priceless collection of books, charters, etc. For Dean's Yard, and the precinct wall, see Rte 1.

3 THE HOUSES OF PARLIAMENT

STATION: *Westminster* on the Circle line. – BUSES and CAR PARKING, see Rte 1.

ADMISSION. The Houses of Parliament and Westminster Hall are open to the public on Sat from 10 to 5 (no adm. after 4) and on Easter Mon & Tues; Spring and late Summer BH Mon & Tues; Mon, Tues, & Thurs in Aug; and Thurs in Sept, provided neither house is sitting. The entrance is adjoining the Victoria Tower; visitors are allowed to wander through the chambers unaccompanied, although guides are available at the door to conduct groups. On all other days visits must be arranged direct with a Member of Parliament. Westminster Hall is also open separately, Mon–Thurs, 10–1.30 (4 p.m. during recesses) provided neither House is sitting; 10–5 on Sat; and when the House is not sitting (but closed on Sun, Fri, Good Fri and Christmas Day). The entrance is then by the N. door.

ADMISSION to the DEBATES in the House of Commons may be obtained on application at the Admission Order Office in St Stephen's Hall (p. 68); the head of the queue is usually admitted from 4.15 p.m. (after 11.30 a.m. on Fri). If the House is sitting late (i.e. after 10 p.m.) it is not usually necessary to queue. Earlier admission can normally only be obtained by writing to a member beforehand for a ticket. The entrance then is by St Stephen's Porch. When the House of Lords is sitting as a Court of Appeal it is open to the public; but for admission to the debates a peer's order is required, or visitors can join the public queue.

The House of Commons usually meets on Mon, Tues, Wed, and Thurs at 2.30 p.m., on Fri at 11 a.m. After prayers and 'questions' addressed to ministers, public business begins about 3.30 p.m. and lasts until 10.30 p.m., unless the 10 o'clock order be suspended or the business be of a special character. On Fri, generally devoted to private members' bills, questions are not usually asked, and the House rises at 4.30 p.m. Visitors to the Galleries may obtain the 'order paper' or official programme from a doorkeeper. The House of Lords usually meets about 2.30 p.m. and rarely has protracted sittings.

The ***Houses of Parliament** (Pl. 19; 1), or *New Palace of Westminster*, a stately pile in an admirable late-Gothic style, rises close to the Thames. The rich external decoration of oriels, pinnacles, and turrets is well balanced by the imposing towers. The building, which incorporates the ancient Westminster Hall and the crypt and cloisters of St Stephen's Chapel, was designed by Sir Charles Barry, and was built in 1840–50. Augustus Pugin provided many of the detail drawings. It covers 8 acres and has 11 courtyards, 100 staircases, 1100 apartments, and 2 m. of passages. Besides the House of Commons, in the N. half, and the House of Lords, in the s. half, it contains the dwellings of various parliamentary officials (including the Speaker). The w. front is interrupted by Westminster Hall, which stands between New Palace Yard and Old Palace Yard; but the E., or river façade, extends unbroken for a length of 940 ft, and is preceded by a terrace on the river, 700 ft long. This long façade (best seen from the river) is embellished with the statues and royal arms of British sovereigns from William the Conqueror to Victoria, while figures of the earlier English kings, from the Heptarchy to the Conquest, appear on the short N. front.

Of the three towers, the tallest and the finest is the noble **Victoria Tower* (336 ft high; 75 ft square), at the s.w. angle, said to be the loftiest square tower in existence. The archway, 50 ft high, below this tower, is the royal entrance to the building. The *Central Spire* (300 ft) rises above the Central Hall and serves also as a ventilating shaft. The finial of the *Clock Tower* is 320 ft from the ground. The clock (still wound by hand), an authoritative time-keeper, has four dials, each 23 ft square; the figures are 2 ft high; and the minute-hands are 14 ft long. The hours are struck upon 'Big Ben', a bell weighing $13\frac{1}{2}$ tons, named after Sir Benjamin Hall, First Commissioner of Works when it was hung.—A flag on the Victoria

Tower by day and a light in the Clock Tower by night indicate that Parliament is sitting. M.P.s usually use the entrance in New Palace Yard (adorned with catalpa trees); beacons on the gate posts warn them of a division (comp. below). During the construction of an underground car park in 1973, successive fountains (12C & 15C) were unearthed.

HISTORY. The Houses of Parliament occupy the site of an ancient palace, and in virtue of that fact still rank as a royal palace and are in the charge of the hereditary Lord Great Chamberlain (not to be confounded with the Lord Chamberlain of the Household). This palace was the chief London residence of the sovereign from the reign of Edward the Confessor (or perhaps earlier) until Henry VIII seized Whitehall in 1529. Old Palace Yard was an inner court of the palace, and down to 1800 the House of Lords assembled in a chamber at its s. end, which, in 1605, was the scene of the Gunpowder Plot. In 1512 the palace was very seriously damaged by fire, and it was never completely rebuilt. In 1547 the House of Commons transferred its sittings from the Chapter House of Westminster Abbey to St Stepehen's Chapel; and in 1800 the House of Lords removed to the old Court of Requests. In 1834 the entire palace was burned down, with the exception of Westminster Hall, the crypt of St Stephen's Chapel, and part of the cloisters, but the rebuilding was at once begun, and the Lords removed to their new abode in 1847, the Commons to theirs in 1852. During the Second World War the buildings were damaged on more than twelve occasions. The worst attack caused the almost complete destruction of the House of Commons on 10 May, 1941, besides other damage.

The INTERIOR of the building, recently repainted and reguilded, is handsomely fitted up in a style characteristic of its period, with fine ceilings, friezes, mosaic pavements, and metal work. From the public entrance we ascend the *Royal Staircase* to the NORMAN PORCH, intended to be decorated with statues and frescoes illustrating the Norman period.

Around the QUEEN'S ROBING ROOM, used as the House of Lords in 1941–50, runs a series of carved panels, by H. H. Armstead, with episodes from the Arthurian legend, while frescoes above, by W. A. Dyce, illustrate the virtues of chivalry.

The ROYAL GALLERY is a fine hall, 110 ft long, through which the sovereign passes on the way to the House of Lords. Here are portraits of George III and Queen Charlotte, George VI and Queen Elizabeth, George V and Queen Mary (by Sir Wm. Llewellyn), Queen Victoria and Prince Albert (by Winterhalter), and Edward VII and Queen Alexandra (by Luke Fildes). The two huge mural paintings by D. Maclise represent the Death of Nelson and the Meeting of Wellington and Blücher after Waterloo. The gilt statues of English Monarchs are by B. Philip. A recess at the s. end forms a War Memorial to Peers and their sons, by John Tweed. The floor of Minton tiles is noteworthy.

The PRINCE'S CHAMBER, which follows, is decorated in a more sombre tone, with dark panelling. In the recess opposite the entrance is a white marble statue of Queen Victoria, enthroned between Justice and Mercy, by Gibson. On the walls are portraits of the Tudor kings and their consorts (1485–1603). Below bronze reliefs depict events of their reigns.

The **House of Lords,** a lavishly decorated and colourful Gothic hall by Pugin (90 ft long, 45 ft wide, and 45 ft high), was used by the House of Commons from the destruction of their own chamber in 1941 until the opening of the rebuilt House of Commons in 1950. At the s. end, beneath an elaborate canopy, is the throne of the Sovereign. In front, separated from the throne by a gilded railing, the Woolsack, a plain cushioned ottoman stuffed with wool, is occupied by the Lord Chancellor, as presiding officer of the House of Lords. It is said to have

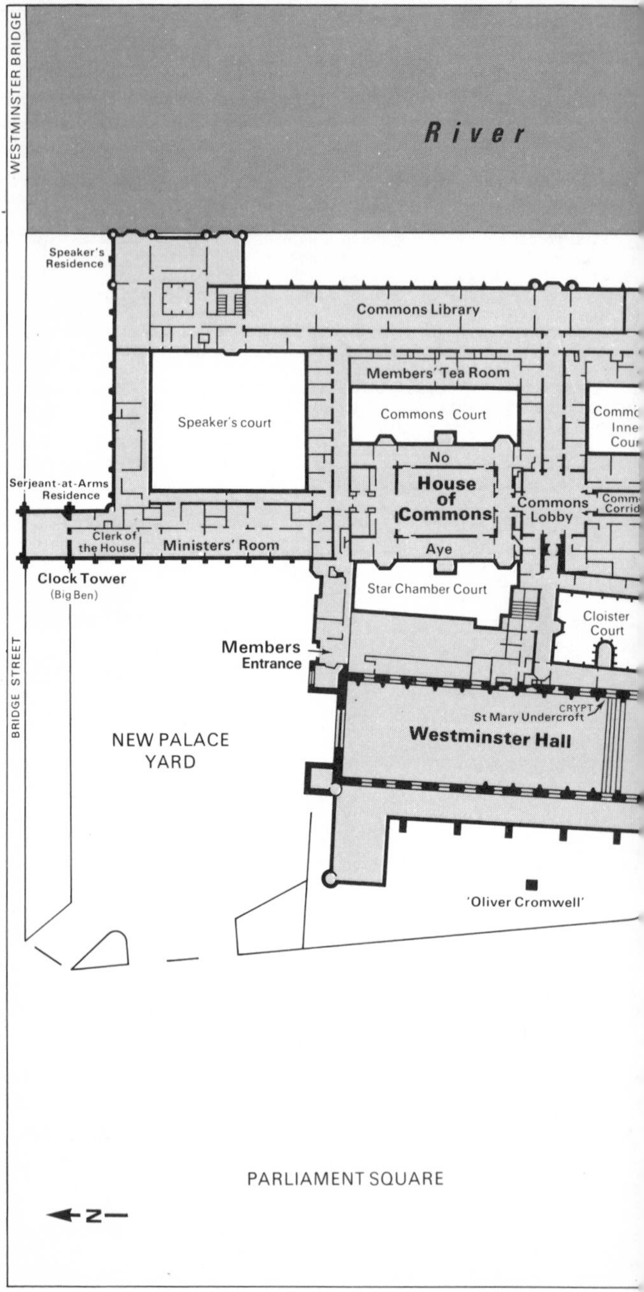

WESTMINSTER BRIDGE

River

Speaker's
Residence

Commons Library

Members' Tea Room

Commons Court

Speaker's court

Commons
Inner
Court

No

**House
of
Commons**

Commons
Lobby

Commons
Corridor

Serjeant-at-Arms
Residence

Clerk of
the House

Ministers' Room

Aye

Clock Tower
(Big Ben)

Star Chamber Court

Cloister
Court

BRIDGE STREET

**Members
Entrance**

St Mary Undercroft CRYPT

NEW PALACE
YARD

Westminster Hall

'Oliver Cromwell'

PARLIAMENT SQUARE

←N→

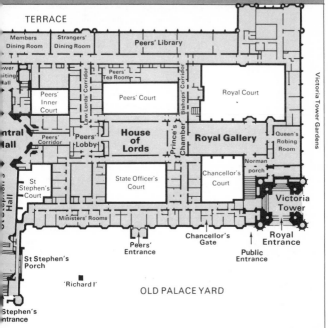

Houses of Parliament

Thames

TERRACE

Members Dining Room

Strangers' Dining Room

Peers' Library

-wer siting Hall

Peers' Inner Court

Peers' Tea Room

Peers' Court

Law Lords Corridor

Bishops Corridor

Royal Court

Victoria Tower Gardens

ntral all

Peers' Corridor

Peers' Lobby

House of Lords

Prince's Chamber

Royal Gallery

Queen's Robing Room

St Stephen's Court

State Officer's Court

Chancellor's Court

Norman porch

Victoria Tower

Ministers' Rooms

Chancellor's Gate

Royal Entrance

Peers' Entrance

Public Entrance

St Stephen's Porch

'Richard I'

OLD PALACE YARD

Stephen's ntrance

ABINGDON STREET

| 0 | | 200 feet |
| 0 | | 50 metres |

been adopted in the reign of Edward III as a reminder of the importance to England of the wool trade. At the N. end is the Bar, where the Commons, headed by their Speaker, attend at the opening of Parliament, and lawsuits on final appeal are pleaded. Above it is the *Press Gallery* with the *Strangers' Gallery* behind. The six frescoes above are by Maclise, Cope, Dyce, and Horsley.

The PEERS' LOBBY, a handsomely decorated chamber, has a fine encaustic tiled pavement and good brass gates in the S. doorway. Over the N. and S. doors are the arms of six dynasties of English rulers (Saxon, Norman, Plantagenet, Tudor, Stuart, and Hanoverian), with the initial letter of the dynastic name below each. In the PEERS' CORRIDOR, leading N. to the Central Hall, are eight paintings, by C. W. Cope (1856–66), of the Stuart and Commonwealth periods.

The CENTRAL HALL (usually called the Central Lobby), an ornate octagonal vestibule, 60 ft in diameter and 75 ft high, separates the precincts of the Lords from those of the Commons. On the floor is the text, in the Latin of the Vulgate: "Except the Lord keep the house, their labour is but lost that build it." The ceiling is inlaid, between the massive ribs of the vaulting, with Venetian glass mosaic, showing various royal badges. Over the doorways, the patron saints of Great Britain and Ireland are represented in glass mosaic by Poynter and Anning Bell. In niches around the hall are statues of English sovereigns of the Plantagenet line and their consorts; and on pedestals are statues of eminent statesmen.

When Parliament is sitting, visitors who have business with members are admitted to this hall, whence they 'send in their cards' to the House, through the medium of one of the policemen on duty.

The **House of Commons,** approached by the COMMONS' CORRIDOR and COMMONS' LOBBY, lies to the N. of the Central Hall. The original chamber was destroyed by fire on 10 May, 1941; a new chamber (130 ft long, 48 ft wide, and 43 ft high) designed by Sir Giles Gilbert Scott in a less inspired and more sombre interpretation of the late-Gothic style, was opened in Oct 1950. The structural oak and the stonework are English; many of the furnishings were gifts of the Empire. The chamber is entered from the Commons Lobby through the CHURCHILL ARCH, built of stones battered and flaked by the fire of 1941, and flanked by statues of Churchill (1966; by Oscar Nemon) and Lloyd George.

The Speaker's chair (from Australia) is at the N. end of the chamber. In front of the chair is the table of the House (from Canada), on which the mace rests during the sittings of the House. When the House is 'in Committee' the mace is placed 'under the table'. On either side are the 'front benches', the ministerial on the Speaker's right, the opposition on his left. On the floor of the House and in the side galleries are seats for 602 of the 630 members. Above the Speaker's chair is the Press Gallery, with 161 seats, and at the other end, facing the Speaker, is the gallery seating for *Distinguished and Ordinary Strangers.* The House is flanked on each side by *Division Lobbies,* into which the members file when a vote is being taken, 'Ayes to the right' (W.), 'Noes to the left' (E.).

Passing through the W. door of the Central Hall, we enter ST STEPHEN'S HALL, the walls of which roughly correspond with the ground plan of St Stephen's Chapel, founded by Edward I and completed by Edward

III, 1292–1364. In this chapel, the chapel royal of the Old Palace of Westminster, the House of Commons met from 1547 until 1834, and to this day the name 'St Stephen's' is sometimes used as equivalent to 'House of Commons'. In the angles of the hall are figures of the early Norman kings, and on pedestals by the walls are statues of British statesmen. The panels beneath the windows illustrate The Building of Britain. —We descend a few steps to St Stephen's Porch, whence we command a fine view of Westminster Hall. The beautiful large window on our left originally formed the s. end of this hall, but was moved to its present position by Sir Charles Barry. The stained glass, by Sir N. Comper (1953), and the sculpture below, by Sir B. Mackennal (1922), are war memorials to Members and Officers of both Houses of Parliament.

The venerable and beautiful *Westminster Hall (239½ ft long, 67½ ft wide, and 92 ft high), originally built by William II in 1097, received its present form, and more especially its magnificent oaken *Roof, from Richard II in 1394–1402. Entirely bare of ornament and usually quite empty, the hall is one of the finest and largest timber-roofed buildings in Europe. The mason was Henry Yevele and the carpenter Hugh Herland. From the 13C until 1882 the chief English law courts sat at Westminster Hall, at first in the hall itself, afterwards in buildings (now pulled down) erected for the purpose on the w. side. A thorough restoration of the roof was completed in 1923 and the war damage of 1941 has likewise been repaired.

Westminster Hall is perhaps specially memorable as the scene of the condemnation of Charles I in 1649. A brass tablet on the steps at the s. end marks the spot where the king sat during his trial. But it has witnessed many other historic events and grave state-trials. Here Edward II abdicated in 1327, and, by the irony of fate Richard II, the builder of the hall, was here deposed in 1399, soon after its completion. A tablet on the e. wall marks the position of the door through which Charles I passed in 1641 when he attempted to arrest the Five Members in their seats. Since then no sovereign entered the Commons until 1950, when George VI visited the rebuilt chamber. In 1653 Oliver Cromwell was here installed as Lord Protector. Among those who have been condemned to death in this hall are William Wallace (1305), Lord Cobham (1417), Sir Thomas More (1535), Sir Thomas Wyatt (1554), the Earl of Essex (1601), Guy Fawkes (1606), and Strafford (1641). The last public trial in the hall was that of Lord Melville for malversation in 1806. Since the 19C the hall has been used for the lying-in-state of monarchs and eminent statesmen.

From the s.e. angle of Westminster Hall a staircase descends to *St Stephen's Crypt, the ancient crypt of St Stephen's Chapel, now known also as the church of *St Mary Undercroft*. The crypt, with its finely groined vaulting retaining most of the original bosses, has been restored and richly decorated and is still occasionally used for christenings and marriages in the families of Members of Parliament.

A doorway on the e. side of Westminster Hall opens upon the beautiful *St Stephen's Cloisters* (not open to the public), built by Henry VIII, with a fan-tracery ceiling little inferior to that of Henry VII's Chapel in Westminster Abbey. A small oratory or chapel projecting from the w. walk is traditionally said to be the place where the death-warrant of Charles I was signed.

4 WHITEHALL

STATIONS: *Embankment*, see Rte 5; *Westminster*, on the Circle line. — BUSES, Nos. 3, 11, 12, 24, 29, 53, 88. — CAR PARKING meters in streets leading to Embankment.

The brief half-mile (now known as **Whitehall**) which separates Westminster from Charing Cross has been a thoroughfare at least since the 15C. In the 16–17C most of the region between Charing Cross and the present Westminster Bridge and between the Thames and St James's Park, was occupied by the ROYAL PALACE OF WHITEHALL, of which little now remains but the name and one building. The association of the area with government began as early as the 17C, and today it is the political centre of Great Britain, lined on the w. side of the street with public offices, which range in date from 1725, at the N. end, to 1919, at the s. end. Recent cleaning has greatly enhanced their effect.

Whitehall Palace originated in a mansion purchased by Walter de Grey, Archbishop of York in 1240, which for nearly 300 years became the London residence, known as *York Place*, of his successors. When Card. Wolsey succeeded to the Archbishopric he embellished the Palace (sited on the river side of the thoroughfare) with characteristic extravagance, and Henry VIII seized the desirable property in 1529. He renamed the palace 'Whitehall', a name then generally applied to any centre of festivities, and acquired more land towards St James's Park, on which he erected a tiltyard, cockpit, and tennis courts. Whitehall became the chief residence of the court in London. Anne Boleyn was brought here on the day of her marriage to Henry in 1533, and in 1536 it was the scene of his marriage to Jane Seymour. In 1547 Henry died in the palace, and under Elizabeth the festivities of her father's reign were revived. Masques by Ben Jonson, with sets by Inigo Jones, and by James Shirley were frequently presented at court in the time of James I and Charles I. Plans for a huge and sumptuous new palace for James I drawn up by Inigo Jones and John Webb were never carried out, although the Banqueting House was rebuilt after fire in 1622. Charles I was executed in 1649 in front of this hall, and Oliver Cromwell died in the palace in 1658. Under Charles II Whitehall became the centre of revelry and intrigue described by Pepys; and hence James II fled into exile in 1688. The offering of the Crown to William and Mary provided the last great ceremonial function here. In 1698 the palace was accidentally burned to the ground, and the royal residence transferred to St James's 'Palace. The government offices already established here, such as the Horse Guards (1663), the Paymaster-General's Office (1676), the Admiralty (1694), and the Treasury (1698) remain to the present day.

From Parliament Square we proceed up PARLIAMENT STREET (as the s. section of Whitehall is called), towards Trafalgar Square, starting on the left side. The large blocks of government offices here include the corner building (1907, by Brydon) connected by a bridge over King Charles Street with the *Foreign* and *Commonwealth Offices.* Churchill's War Room, entered from Great George St., may be visited by previous appointment at the Cabinet Office (conducted visits twice daily at approx. 11 and 2.30). At the end of King Charles St. steps descend past a statue of Lord Clive by John Tweed (1912) to St James's Park, where the façade of the *Foreign Office*, by Sir George Gilbert Scott (1873) in the style of Inigo Jones, is well seen. In the roadway rises the ***Cenotaph**, commemorating in dignified simplicity the Glorious Dead of 1914–18 and 1939–45. The monument, designed by Sir Edwin Lutyens, was first erected in plaster as a saluting point for the Allied 'Victory March' of 1919, and was rebuilt in stone and unveiled on 11 Nov 1920; the later inscription was unveiled in 1946.

The E. side of Parliament St., including the former New Scotland Yard (1891, by Norman Shaw) and Richmond Terrace (1822–25), a relic of residential Whitehall, though threatened with demolition, has so far survived. An extension to the Houses of

Parliament designed by Robin Spence and Robin Webster is planned for the area nearer Bridge St.

Beyond (l.) is the narrow **Downing Street** (Pl. 14; 6), built in 1683–86 by Sir George Downing (who was the second graduate at Harvard in 1642), and famous out of all proportion to its appearance.

On the right is the office of the *Judicial Committee of the Privy Council*, the final Court of Appeal for countries of the Commonwealth that have not set up their own Supreme Court of Appeal. Built by Soane in 1827, the Council Chamber, where cases are heard, is sometimes open to the public. The remainder of the N. side of the street was rebuilt in 1722 and 1766–74 and carefully restored in 1960–64. **No. 10** Downing Street is the official residence of the First Lord of the Treasury, and in its Cabinet Room many momentous meetings have been held. George II offered this house in 1732 as a personal gift to Sir Robert Walpole, then prime minister, but was induced by Sir Robert to annex it to his office instead, and Walpole removed to it in 1735. No. 11 is the official residence of the Chancellor of the Exchequer; No. 12 is the Government Whips's Office, beyond which steps descend to St James's Park. Boswell lodged in Downing St. on his first visit to London in 1762–63 and Smollett set up a doctor's practice here c. 1745–48.

A roadway on the right before 'No. 10' descends to *Treasury Green*, where the tall brick wall of Henry VIII's smaller tennis-court was exposed to view in 1961 (tablet). Beside it Treasury Passage leads through the building to Horse Guards Parade (comp. p. 72).

To the N. is the long dignified façade of the *Treasury*, begun by Soane in 1827, and altered and enlarged by Sir Charles Barry in 1844. The façade was restored recently when the interior was restyled. This is the office of the commissioners who now discharge the duties of the office of Lord High Treasurer (in abeyance since about 1612), viz. the First Lord of the Treasury (or Prime Minister), the Chancellor of the Exchequer, and several Junior Lords. Next door *Dover House* (now the Scottish Office), was the birthplace of Lord Melbourne (1779–1843). The delicate portico and circular hall are by Henry Holland (1787). In Whitehall is an equestrian statue of Earl Haig (1861–1928).

On the E. side of the street stands the ***Banqueting House** (adm. Tues–Sat 10–5; Sun from 2; fee), the chief relic of the Palace of Whitehall. This superb example of Palladian architecture in Portland stone was erected by Inigo Jones in 1625, on the site of a banqueting hall of 1607 burned down in 1619. The weathercock at the N. end of the roof is said to have been placed there in 1686 by James II to show whether the wind was favourable or not to the approach of the Prince of Qrange.

Through a window of this hall Charles I passed in 1649 to the scaffold erected in the roadway in front of it (tablet beneath the lower central window; in fact it was probably a window in a N. annexe since demolished). From 1698 to c. 1890 the hall was used as a Chapel Royal, and later as the museum of the United Service Institution.

We ascend to the lofty main hall (115 ft long, 60 ft wide, and 55 ft high), decorated in 1635. The nine allegorical ceiling *Paintings (restored and cleaned) were designed for Charles I in 1629–34 by Rubens, who received for them £3000 and a knighthood. The principal subject, in the large central oval, is the Apotheosis of James I; to the s., James is enthroned between Peace and Plenty; to the N., allegory of the birth and coronation of Charles I.

Behind the Banqueting House and the attractive *Gwydyr House* (1772; now the Welsh Office) to the s., rises a huge block (1935–53; by Vincent Harris), housing the *Ministry of Defence*. In front, on the lawn facing Whitehall, is a statue of Sir Walter Raleigh (1552–1618), by Wm.

McMillan (1959). The main entrance, in Horse Guards Avenue, is flanked by colossal sculptures (Earth and Water; 1949–53), by Sir Charles Wheeler. In the gardens on the river side is a statue of Gen. Gordon (1838–85), by Hamo Thornycroft; here the surviving part of *Queen Mary's Terrace*, built for Mary II in 1691, has steps descending to the 17C water-level.

Underneath the building is the *King Henry VIII Wine Cellar*, a brick-vaulted undercroft of York Place. Its preservation involved moving it bodily in 1950, 43 ft to one side and 20 ft downwards. It may be visited by special permission from the Department of the Environment.

Beyond the Banqueting House a huge building by Wm. Young (1906), formerly the War Office, continues its function as part of the *Ministry of Defence*. In front is a statue by Adrian Jones of the Duke of Cambridge (1819–1904), Commander-in-Chief of the British armies in 1856–95.

The **Horse Guards** (1760; by Kent and Vardy), a pleasant stone building with a central arch surmounted by a low clock tower, succeeds a guard house built here in 1649 in the old tiltyard of the Palace of Whitehall. It is now the office of the Commander-in-Chief of the Home Forces. Two mounted troopers of the Life Guards or Royal Horse Guards (now a mechanized cavalry regiment, officially the Blues and Royals) are posted here daily from 10 to 4 o'clock, and two dismounted sentries within the archway. The former are relieved hourly, the latter every two hours. At 11 a.m. (10 a.m. on Sun), the Guard on duty is relieved by a new Guard of 12 men who troop from the Knightsbridge Barracks viâ the Mall, accompanied (when the Queen is in residence) by the Queen's Trumpeter, a Standard Bearer, and an Officer.

The passage beneath the clock-tower leads towards St James's Park. The wide gravelled space immediately beyond the archway is known as the **Horse Guards Parade** (Pl. 14; 6), and here the ceremony of 'trooping the colour' is performed on the Queen's official birthday (in June). Frequently of late it has provided emergency car-parking space during the disruption of public transport by strikes. On the N. side is the large *New Admiralty*, built in 1894–95, now a Civil Service Department, with its old wireless installations on the roof. It is connected on the N. to Admiralty Arch, and on the W. to the Citadel (see p. 90). Looking back from the Parade we see the W. elevations of Admiralty House, the former Paymaster-General's Office (façade of c. 1755 moved from No. 37 Gt. George St. in 1910), and beyond the long rusticated façade of the *Horse Guards* (by William Kent), *Dover House* (1758, by James Paine), and on the E. side, the Portland stone façade of the *Old Treasury* building completed in 1736 by William Kent. The barrel-vaulted *Treasury Passage* leads through to Downing St. (see above). To the right, behind a statue by Tweed of Earl Kitchener (1850–1916), are the gardens of Downing St.

In front of the Horse Guards are equestrian statues of Viscount Wolseley (1833–1913), by Goscombe John, and Earl Roberts (1832–1914), by H. Bates, and a huge mortar from Cadiz presented by the Spanish government in 1814, encased in a carriage made in Woolwich. On the edge of St James's Park is the Guards' Memorial for 1914–19 by G. Ledward and H. C. Bradshaw.

Farther N., in Whitehall, beyond the former *Paymaster-General's Office* (1732–33, by John Lane; now the Parliamentary Counsel), the flank of *Admiralty House* (1786–88, by S. P. Cockerell) is set back behind a wall and railing. Beyond is the *Old Admiralty* (by Ripley; 1725–28), with a tall classical portico in a small courtyard masked from the street by an attractive stone screen designed by Robert Adam in 1759. This was the Admiralty of Nelson's time, and here his body lay in state in 1805; it is now used by the home civil service. Immediately behind, facing on to Horse Guards Parade is the New Admiralty (see above).

Across Whitehall opens *Great Scotland Yard*, the headquarters of the Metropolitan Police until 1891. The street-name is thought to originate in a mansion occupied before the 15C by the kings of Scotland and their ambassadors when in London. Stables of the Metropolitan Mounted Police (which has included women since 1970) occupy a building beyond the Army Recruiting Centre. A ramp ascends to the stables (for c.15 horses) on the first floor (adm. on request). Opposite, the *Ministry of Agriculture and Fisheries* is housed in a building by John Murray (1910). Farther N. along Whitehall *Craig's Court* (r.; opposite the Whitehall Theatre) preserves the façade of the residence of Joseph Craig, called *Harrington House* (1692). Whitehall ends at **Charing Cross.**

5 CHARING CROSS AND TRAFALGAR SQUARE

STATIONS: the new *Charing Cross* on the Fleet, Northern, and Bakerloo lines replaces both the former *Trafalgar Square* (Bakerloo) and *Strand* (Northern); *Embankment*, on the Circle, Bakerloo and Northern lines. – BUSES to and from every part of London. – CAR PARK, St Martin's St.

Charing Cross (Pl. 14; 6), the irregular open space at the top of Whitehall before Trafalgar Square, is an ancient road junction. Here in 1291 Edward I erected the last of the series of thirteen crosses that marked the stages in the funeral procession of his wife Eleanor to Westminster Abbey. It was destroyed in 1647, and since 1675 the site has been occupied by a fine equestrian *STATUE OF CHARLES I by Hubert Le Sueur (1633), on a pedestal by Joshua Marshall, from a design by Wren.

At the entrance of Charles II to London in 1660, 600 pikemen were stationed here, and later in the same year it was the scene of the execution of Harrison and seven other regicides, witnessed by Pepys, who commented, "Thus it was my chance to see the King beheaded at Whitehall and to see the first blood shed in revenge for the blood of the King at Charing Cross". In 1668 Punchinello 'ye Itallian popet player' performed here. At the pillory set up near the statue Defoe (1703) and John Middleton (1723) suffered.—On 30 Jan, the anniversary of the execution of Charles I, the statue is adorned with the wreaths by sympathetic adherents of the Jacobite tradition.

To the E., beyond Charing Cross Station, runs the Strand (Rte 17), leading to Fleet St. and the City. To the W., Admiralty Arch gives access to the Mall and St James's Park (Rte 6). The wide Northumberland Avenue descends past the *Royal Commonwealth Society* to the Thames Embankment.

Trafalgar Square (Pl. 14; 4), laid out in 1829–c. 1850 at the suggestion of Nash, is said to have been described by Sir Robert Peel as "the finest site in Europe". Since the reign of Edward I the area had been a royal mews. Except when disturbed by the periodic political or social demonstrations for which the square is a traditional rendezvous, pigeons crowd the area by day and starlings take refuge in the surrounding buildings at dusk. The NELSON MONUMENT, 185 ft high, by William Railton (1841), carries a colossal statue of Lord Nelson, victor at the Battle of Trafalgar in 1805, by E. H. Bailey (1840–43). The fluted granite column rises from a base guarded by four huge bronze couchant *Lions, beloved of children. These were modelled by Sir Edwin Landseer and cast by Marochetti in 1867. At the foot are four bronze reliefs cast from French cannon captured at the naval battles they depict. The monument is annually decorated on the anniversary of the Battle of Trafalgar (21 October).

In the square are two fountains, designed by Lutyens in 1939 with fine sculptures by Charles Wheeler and W. McMillan, often the scene of indecorous revelry at New Year's Eve and on Election nights. The statue of *Sir Henry Havelock* (1795–1857) is by Behnes, and that of *Sir Charles James Napier* (1782–1853) by G. G. Adams. At the N.E. corner an equestrian statue of *George IV*, by Chantrey, was intended to top the Marble Arch in front of Buckingham Palace (comp. p. 108). Against the N. wall are bronze busts of *Lord Cunningham* (1883–1963) by Franta Belsky, *Lord Jellicoe*, (1859–1935), by W. McMillan, and *Lord Beatty* (1871–1936) by Sir Charles Wheeler. In the centre are the former Imperial standards of length, placed here in 1876.—A Christmas tree for the square is traditionally presented by the people of Norway as a thank-offering for help in the Second World War.

Around Trafalgar Square are several large buildings: to the E., *South Africa House* (1933), designed by Sir Herbert Baker; and to the W., *Canada House*, built in 1824–27 by Sir Robert Smirke. Streets lead hence to Pall Mall and the fashionable quarter of the West End (Rte 7). Above the N. side of the square rises the National Gallery (see below). On the grass in front are a bronze statue of James II in Roman costume by Grinling Gibbons, and a copy in bronze of Houdon's marble statue of George Washington at Richmond, Virginia.

The large church of **St Martin in the Fields,** at the N.E. corner of Trafalgar Square, built in 1722–24, is perhaps the finest work of James Gibbs. The controversial combination of a steeple and classical portico has been often copied, but less successfully. In the interior, with its richly decorated ceiling by Artari and Bagutti, are a font (1689) from the previous church on this site, and a handsome 18C pulpit brought here after 1858. The side aisles, with canted walls and 'closet' pews, are particularly attractive. The *Crypt* (entered from the porch at the s.w. end), originally a burial vault, contains the old parish chest (1597) of elm, and whipping post (1751). In 1930–45 it served as a shelter for the homeless; off the s. side opens the *Dick Sheppard Chapel* (1954), a memorial to the vicar who in 1914–27 began the tradition of social service still carried on by the church. The gateway to the chapel commemorates the 'Old Contemptibles' of the First World War.

In this church Bacon, Hampden, and Charles II were christened and Tom Moore married; while the burials of George Heriot, Nell Gwynn, Farquhar, Roubiliac, Chippendale, and John Hunter are here recorded. The first broadcast religious service was celebrated here in 1924. A bust of Gibbs by Rysbrack is preserved in the Vestry Hall.—The school building to the N. is now a Youth Centre.

On the 'island' in St Martin's Place is a poignant monument by Frampton (1920) to Nurse Edith Cavell, who was shot at Brussels in 1915, and across Charing Cross Road is a statue of Sir Henry Irving (1838–1905).

The National Gallery

ADMISSION daily, exc. Christmas Eve, Christmas Day, Boxing Day, New Year's Day, and Good Fri, 10–6, Sun 2–6.

LECTURES: Oct–May, Mon–Wed at 1, Sat at 12; June–Sept, Mon, Wed, & Thurs at 1, Tues at 6.

RESTAURANT on the Ground Floor, open Mon–Sat, 10–3 & 3.30–5; Sun 2.30–5.

The ****National Gallery** (Pl. 14; 4) occupies a commanding position on a terrace extending along the whole of the N. side of Trafalgar Square. The idea of a national collection of paintings was first given effect in 1824 when Parliament voted £60,000 for the purchase of thirty-eight pictures from the collection of John Angerstein. A regular grant for purchases was first voted in 1855, and since that date the policy of successive directors has been to build up a representative selection of western European art.

The collection shown in Angerstein's house in Pall Mall, was moved in 1838 to the present buildings, constructed by William Wilkins who used some columns from the demolished Carlton House (see p. 96). Extensions were later made by E. M. Barry, and further extensions to the N.W. were opened in 1975.

The opening of 13 new rooms has heralded a new definitive display and rooms are being redecorated and relit in turn; some changes must, therefore, be expected in the E. rooms. Paintings are here listed (selectively) in each room clockwise from the door of entry; handboards explaining various schools and techniques are available in many rooms and illustrated catalogues in many languages are on sale. Special displays of a single masterpiece are mounted in the vestibule of the new wing.

The standard of the National Gallery is remarkably high and it has not been thought necessary to star individual paintings. Nevertheless some Schools are better not seen immediately after others, and a single comprehensive tour is not to be recommended.

The collection, arranged chronologically, begins up the stairs (left) with the **Italian School**.

ROOM 1. *564. Margaritone d' Arezzo*, Madonna and Child (c. 1260; the earliest picture on display in the Gallery); *6361. Master of San Francesco* (fl. 1272), Crucifix; *565.* Follower of *Duccio*, Madonna with angels. In alcove: *4451.* The *Wilton Diptych* (late 14C), probably by a French artist, shows Richard II presented to the Madonna by his patron saints, and (on the cover) the arms and badge of the King. The Diptych, once in the collection of Charles I, later hung among Lord Pembroke's pictures at Wilton House. *566. Duccio*, Triptych with Madonna and Child; *567. Segna di Bonaventura* (style of), Crucifix; *Duccio*, 1139, 1140, 1330. Panels, probably from the predella of the 'Maestà' altarpiece in Siena cathedral museum; *6386.* Madonna with four angels; *Ugolino di Nerio*, Santa Croce altarpiece.

ROOM 2. Gothic to Renaissance. *Lorenzo Monaco*, 2862, 4062. Scenes from the life of St Benedict; *1468.* Style of *Orcagna*, Crucifixion; *Lorenzo Monaco*, 215, 216, 1897. Triptych (perhaps the altarpiece of the destroyed San Benedetto fuori della Porta a Pinti, Florence); *276. Spinello Aretino*, Two Mourners (fresco fragment); *2927. Barnaba da Modena*, Four scenes; *4250. Venetian School* (late 14C), Altarpiece of the Virgin Mary; Attrib. to *Masolino*, 5962, 5963. Panels with saints and a pope (possibly by Masaccio); *3046. Masaccio*, Virgin and Child (centrepiece of a polyptych from Pisa); *569. Orcagna*, Coronation of the Virgin, probably a studio work.

ROOM 3 (not definitively arranged in 1977). 15C Florentine. *758. Alesso Baldovinetti*, Portrait of a Lady in yellow; *1138.* Attrib. to *And. del Castagno*, Crucifixion; *283. Benozzo*, Virgin and Child enthroned; *Paolo*

Uccello, 6294. St George and the Dragon, 583. Rout of San Romano (one of a series of three pictures of this battle; the others are in the Uffizi and Louvre); *Fra Filippo Lippi*, 667. Seven saints, 666. Annunication. It is probable that other works by *Fra Angelico* and *Pesellino* will be here.

ROOM 4. Late 15C Florentine. *Botticelli*, 3918, 3919, Scenes from the Life of St Zenobius; 296. *And. del Verrocchio*, Virgin and Child with angels; 292. *Piero del Pollaiuolo* (helped by his brother *Antonio*, particularly in the landscape), Martyrdom of St Sebastian; 592. *Botticelli*, Adoration of the Magi (an early work); 648. *Lorenzo di Credi*, Virgin adoring the Child; *Botticelli*, 626. Young Man (long attrib. to Masaccio), 1033. Adoration of the Magi (tondo), 1034. Mystic Nativity, 915. Venus and Mars.

ROOM 5. *Filippino Lippi*, 4904, 4905. Scenes from Exodus; 293. Virgin and Child with SS Jerome and Dominic; 1412. Virgin and Child with St John; in case below: 2902. *Dom. Ghirlandaio*, A Legend of Volterra, predella panel of an altarpiece; *Piero di Cosimo*, 698. Mythological subject, 4890. Battle between Lapiths and Centaurs; 2489. Follower of *Ghirlandaio*, Portrait of a Young Man.

ROOM 6. 1155. *Matteo di Giovanni*, Assumption; *Giovanni di Paolo*, 5451–54. Scenes from the life of St John the Baptist, four predella panels; *Sassetta*, 4757–63. Scenes from the life of St Francis (seven panels of an altarpiece of 1444 from Sansepolcro; the eighth is in the Musée Condé, Chantilly); *Piero della Francesca*, 769. St Michael (from a polyptych), 908. The Nativity (the two shepherds damaged by an early restorer); between the two, 1032. *Lo Spagna*, Agony in the garden; 703. *Pintoricchio*, Virgin and Child; 665. *Piero della Francesca*, Baptism of Christ; *Luca Signorelli*, 3929. Coriolanus, 910. Triumph of Chastity, and 911. *Pintoricchio*, Return of Odysseus, three of a series of eight frescoes (c. 1509) from the Palazzo del Magnifico, Siena; 1128. *Signorelli*, Circumcision; 181. *Perugino*, Virgin and Child with St John.

ROOM 7. 6337. **Leonardo da Vinci,** Cartoon of Madonna and Child with St Anne and St John the Baptist. This unfinished work in black chalk on buff paper is dated c. 1499. It was bought from the Royal Academy by public subscription in 1962.

ROOM 8. 1450. *Sebastiano del Piombo*, Holy Family; *Correggio*, 23. Madonna of the Basket, 15. Ecce Homo; *Parmigianino*, Portrait of a man, 6427. Mystic Marriage of St Catherine; 33. Vision of St Jerome; *Raphael*, 744. Madonna and Child with the infant Baptist, 2919. Procession to Calvary; 3943. Crucifixion (painted when Raphael was 19 years old and still under the influence of Perugino); 213, 213A. The Dream of Scipio (shown with its cartoon, pricked for transfer).

1. *Seb. del Piombo*, Raising of Lazarus (painted on panel and transferred to canvas in 1771; cleaned in 1968); Michelangelo probably helped in the design of this huge altarpiece commissioned by Card. Giuliano de' Medici for Narbonne cathedral. It is flanked by *Beccafumi*, 6369, Marcia and 6368. Tanaquil.

Raphael, 1171. Virgin and Child enthroned with the Baptist and St Nicholas of Bari (The Ansidei Madonna); 168. St Catherine of Alexandria, 27. Pope Julius II (cleaned in 1970), painted for the church of S. Maria del Popolo, Rome. 790. *Michelangelo*, The Entombment (unfinished; discovered in Rome in the mid-19C in use as the surface of a market barrow; restored 1969); 690. *Andrea del Sarto*, Portrait of a Young Man;

1035. *Franciabigio*, A Knight of Rhodes; 809. Attrib. to *Michelangelo*, The 'Manchester' Madonna.

ROOM 9. **16C Venetian.** First Bay: 294. *Paolo Veronese*, Family of Darius before Alexander; 16. *Tintoretto*, St George and the Dragon; 1041. *Veronese*, Vision of St Helena; 636. *Palma Vecchio*, Portrait of a Poet; 4452. *Titian*, The Vendramin Family, a superb group portrait; 277. *Jacopo Bassano*, The Good Samaritan; 26. *Veronese*, Consecration of St Nicholas.

Second Bay: *Veronese*, 1318. Unfaithfulness, from a ceiling decoration, 268. Adoration of the Magi, a colossal composition, 1326. Happy Union; 1324, 1325. Scorn and Respect, ceiling decorations.

Third Bay: *Titian*, 35 (on screen), Bacchus and Ariadne (1523; cleaned 1967); 4. Holy Family with a shepherd (some parts of the work may be by another hand); 6420. Death of Actaeon (bought in 1972 by public subscription for £1 ¾ million); 224. The Tribute Money; 6376. Allegory of Prudence, an emblematic painting of 1565 illustrating the inscription 'Instructed by the past the present acts prudently lest it spoil the future'. The triple portrait is composed of Titian as an old man, his son Orazio Vecellio in middle age, and (probably) his young relative Marco Vecellio. 3948. Madonna (c. 1570; in poor condition); 5385. La Schiavona; 1944. Portrait of a Man in Blue (possibly a self-portrait; once owned by Van Dyck); 270. Noli me tangere (an early work of c. 1512). *Tintoretto*, 4004. Portrait of Vinc. Morosini; 1313. Origin of the Milky Way. 635. *Titian*, Madonna and Child with the Baptist and St Catherine (c. 1530).

ROOM 10. 2493. *Sebastiano del Piombo*, Daughter of Herodias; *Giorgione*, 6307. Sunset Landscape with saints, 1160. Adoration of the Magi, 234. Warrior adoring; 4946. *Giambattista Cima*, St Sebastian. *Antonello da Messina*, 673. Salvator Mundi, 1418. St Jerome in his study, 1166. Crucifixion, 1411. Portrait of a Man, the last flanked by two portraits (2509, 3121) in a similar vein attrib. to *Jacometto. Giov. Bellini*, 726. Agony in the Garden, 3912. Pietà, 599. Madonna of the Meadow (transferred from panel to canvas in 1949), 280. Madonna of the Pomegranate, 1455. Circumcision (from the studio), 189. Doge Leonardo Loredan.

ROOM 11. Round the spiral staircase leading down to the ground floor, large altarpieces by *Francia* (179, 180); 1847. *Luca Signorelli*, Madonna with saints; and 1119. *Lor. Costa* and *G. F. de' Manieri*, Madonna with saints.

Below in 1977 were displayed the collection earmarked for transfer in 1978 to provincial galleries.

ROOM 12. **15C North Italian.** Works by *Ercole de' Roberti* and *Cosimo Tura*, including 772. Madonna enthroned, fussy with detail; 2486. *Lor. Costa*, A Concert; 1436. *Pisanello*, Vision of St Eustace (?). 768, 1284. *Ant. Vivarini* and *Giov. d' Alemagna*, Four saints; 284. *Bart. Vivarini*, Madonna; *Andrea Mantegna*, 1417. Agony in the Garden, 274. Madonna with the Magdalen and the Baptist, 1145. Samson and Delilah (monochrome on linen); 748. *Gerolamo dai Libri*, Virgin and Child with St Anne.

ROOM 13. Eight paintings by *Carlo Crivelli* include 807. Madonna enthroned; 788. The Demidoff Altarpiece; 602. Pietà; 739. Annunciation.

ROOM 14. **15C Italian.** 1665. *Ambrogio de Predis*, Fr. Archinto (?); 18. *Bernardino Luini*, Christ among the Doctors; 1093. *Leonardo da Vinci*, Virgin of the Rocks. A second version of the same subject in the Louvre, this work is attributed by most scholars to Ambr. de Predis and other assistants in the workshop of Leonardo; they also painted the angel musicians (1661, 1662, farther on) on the wings of the altarpiece. *Ant. Boltraffio*, 3916. Portrait of a man; 328. Madonna; *Ambr. Bergognone*, 1410. Virgin and Child, 298. Altarpiece, 1077A, 1077B. Agony in the Garden, Christ bearing the Cross; 729. *Vinc. Foppa*, Adoration of the Magi; *And. Solari*, 923. Man with a pink, 734. Giov. Crist.

Room 15. **16C Italian.** 5379. *Dosso Dossi*, Bacchanal; 651. *Bronzino*, Allegory with Venus and Cupid; 1131. *Iacopo da Pontormo*, Joseph in Egypt; 10. *Correggio*, School of Love (bought by Charles I in 1628); *Lor. Lotto*, 4256. Lucrezia; 1047. Family group; 1105. The protonotary apostolic Giuliano; 3939. *Palma Vecchio*, Flora; 674. *Paris Bordone*, Young lady in a red dress.

Room 16. **17C Dutch.** Small Landscapes. 2533. *Jan Wijnants*, Track by a dune; 1005. *Nicolaes Bercham*, Ploughing scene; 827. *Karel du Jardin*, Peasants at a ford; 824. *Cuyp*, Ubbergen Castle; 2562. *Jacob van Ruisdael*, Ruined castle gateway; 823. *Cuyp*, Herdsman with cows by a river; *Gerrit Berckleeyde*, 1420. Marketplace at Haarlem, 1431. Grote Kerk, Haarlem, with, between them, 866. *Jan van der Heyden*, View in Cologne (with the unfinished cathedral); 1053. *Emanuel de Witte*, Oude Kerk, Amsterdam; 1344. *Salomon van Ruysdael*, Landscape with a carriage; 849. *Paulus Potter*, Landscape.

Room 17 continues the smaller Dutch pictures: 6423. *Jan van Goyen*, Estuary scene; 1256. *Harmen Steenwyck*, Still life; 2528. *Frans Hals*, Man holding a glove; 2592. *Pieter Claesz*, Still life with drinking vessels. –
Room 18. Peep-show box, painted by *Samuel van Hoogstraten*, to resemble the interior of a Dutch house. 3714. *Karel Fabritius*, View of Delft (an exercise in deep perspective?).

Room 19. **Rembrandt.** 672, 221. Self-portraits at the ages of 34 and 63; 4930. Saskia van Ulenborch (Rembrandt's wife) as Flora; 1400. Christ presented to the people; 6350. Belshazzar's Feast. Adjacent are portraits by *Hendrick ter Bruggen*, 6347. Luteplayer, and *Van der Helst*, Lady in black; also, 4503. *Honthorst*, St Sebastian.

Room 20. **17C Flemish. Rubens.** 6379, 194. Two versions of the Judgment of Paris; 853 (studio). Drunken Silenus supported by Satyrs; 46. Peace and War (presented by the artist to Charles I); 6393. Ludovicus Nonnius, a contemporary doctor and scholar; this picture was brought to England in the latter half of the 17C by the Earl of Kent, and sold by a descendant in 1970 to the Nat. Gall., where it was cleaned and restored. 38. Rape of the Sabines; 278. Triumph of Julius Caesar; 59. The Brazen Serpent.

Room 21. 49. *Van Dyck*, Three men; *Jacob Jordaens*, 6293. Portrait of Govaert van Surpele (?) and his wife; 3215. Holy Family; 164. Holy Family. **Van Dyck,** 1172. Charles I on horseback; 5633. Wm. Feilding; 4889. Abbé Scaglia adoring the Virgin and Child; 3011. Woman and child; 6437. Lady Eliz. Thimbleby and Dorothy, Viscountess Andover (purchased 1976).

Room 22. *Rubens*, 57. St Bavo; 680. The Miraculous Draught of Fishes; 853P. A Lion Hunt; 1195. Birth of Venus; 187. Minerva and Mercury conduct the Duke of Buckingham to the Temple of Virtue (?); 66. Landscape with a view of Steen. 877B. *Van Dyck*, Carlo and Ubaldo see Rinaldo conquered by love. 157. *Rubens*, Landscape at sunset. 52. *Van Dyck*, Portrait of Van der Geest, painted when he was barely twenty. *Rubens*, 4815. The Watering Place; 2924. Landscape with a shepherd; 852.

The so-called 'Chapeau de Paille' (though it is clearly of felt), depicting his second wife's sister. Also here, 1137. *Jacob van Oost*, Portrait of a Boy; 817. *David Teniers the Younger*, View of Het Sterckshof, near Antwerp; 821. *Gonzales Coques*, A family portrait.

ROOM 23. **15-16C German.** *Master of Liesborn*, Panels from the high altarpiece (c. 1480) of Liesborn Abbey, Westphalia; 1049. *Master of the Aachen Altarpiece*, Crucifixion; 1427. *Hans Baldung*, Pietà (flanked by *Lucas Cranach*, Four saints, on loan); 1938. *Dürer* (ascr. to), The Painter's Father; 245. *Hans Baldung*, Portrait of a man. 687. *Unknown Master*, St Veronica with the Sudarium, from St Lawrence, Cologne; 707. *Master of the St Bartholomew Altarpiece*, SS Peter and Dorothy; 706. *Master of the Life of the Virgin*, Presentation in the Temple, from St Ursula's, Cologne (other panels survive in Munich).

ROOM 24. **Netherlandish.** On centre plinth: 2922. *Master of Delft*, Triptych, Scenes from the Passion; behind, 6275. *Memlinc*, Triptych. *Gerard David*, 1079. Adoration of the Magi, 1078. Deposition, probably from the same altarpiece; 2594. *Memline*, Young man at prayer; *Rogier van der Weyden*, 6394. St Ives (?); 6265. Pietà; 1433. Portrait of a lady; 654. The Magdalen reading (fragment); 747. *Memlinc*, SS John the Baptist and Lawrence; *Master of St Giles*, 1419, 4681. Two panels; 2609. *Robert Campin*, Virgin and Child; *Dirk Bouts*, 2595. Virgin and Child, 664. The Entombment, 943. Portrait of a man (1462), 774. Virgin and Child with SS Peter and Paul; 6282. *Quinten Massys*, Virgin enthroned with Angels. To be returned to this room after special display elsewhere: *Jan van Eyck*, 186. The Arnolfini Marriage; 222. Man in a Turban (self-portrait?); 290. Young man (possibly the composer Dufay); 1689. *Jan Gossaert (Mabuse)*, Elderly couple.

ROOM 25. 1314. *Hans Holbein*, The Ambassadors. Three versions of the Adoration of the Magi, by *Mabuse* (2790), *Pieter Brueghel the Elder* (3556), and Bartholomaeus Spranger (6392). 6344. *Lucas Cranach*, Cupid complaining to Venus (from Theocritus, Idyll. xix); 944. *Marinus van Reymerswaele*, Two tax gatherers; 3604. *Lucas van Leyden*, A man aged 38; 2475. *Holbein*, Christina of Denmark; 4744. *Hieronymus Bosch*, Christ mocked; 656. *Mabuse*, Man with a rosary.

ROOM 26. **17C Dutch.** *Rembrandt*, 6432. Hendrickje Stoffels, 54. Woman bathing in a stream; 830. *Hobbema*, The Avenue, Middelharnis; 4042. *Karel Fabritius*, Self-portrait; *Rembrandt*, 243. Elderly man as St Paul, 190. Man in a cap; 2285. *Frans Hals*, Family group in a landscape; 166. *Rembrandt*, Franciscan monk; 627. *Jacob van Ruisdael*, Waterfall; 965. *Jan van de Cappelle*, Shipping scene; 961. *Aelbert Cuyp*, Milking scene; 1459. *Gerbrand van den Eeckhout*, The wind contract.

ROOM 27. *Jan Steen*, 2558. Peasant family at mealtime; other genre scenes; 6442. Consequences of intemperance; 6300. *Rembrandt*, Equestrian portrait; 835. *Pieter de Hoogh*, Courtyard of a house in Delft; *Rembrandt*, 6274. Old man in a an armchair, 1674. Jacob Trip, 1675, 5282. Margaretha de Geer, Trip's wife; 1021. *Frans Hals*, Portrait; 990. *Ruisdael* and 6398. *Philips Koninck*, two typical landscapes.

ROOM 28. CENTRAL OCTAGON: 3679: *Gerrit van Honthorst*, Christ before the high priest; 1893. *Cornelis van Haarlem*, Two followers of Cadmus devoured by a dragon, signed and dated 1585 (cleaned and horrific); 6296. *Karel du Jardin*, Conversion of St Paul; 757. *Nicolaes Maes*, Christ blessing children. The wings display smaller paintings:

RIGHT: 1399. *Gerard ter Borch*, Portrait of a young man; 5225. *Gabriel*

Metsu, A woman drawing; *Emanuel de Witte*, 3682. New Fishmarket, 6402. Oude Kerk, both Amsterdam. Opposite are some famous Dutch interiors and courtyard scenes, including *Johannes Vermeer*, 1383, 2568. Young lady at the virginals; 834. *Hoogh*, Interior; 207. *N. Maes*, Sleeping maid and her servant.

LEFT: Outdoor scenes by the *Ruisdaels* and *Van Goyen*; *Hendrick Avercamp*, 1348, 1479. Winter scenes; 5416. *Jan Molenaer*, Children making music. Opposite: *Rembrandt*, 43. Deposition, 45. Woman taken in adultery, 47. Adoration of the Shepherds; 850. Philips Lucasz (?), 775. Portrait of an 83 year old woman. 896. *Borch*, Treaty of Münster (Peace of Westphalia, 1648).

ROOM 29. **17C Italian.** 48. *Domenichino*, Landscape with Tobias; 9. *Ann. Carracci*, Domine, Quo Vadis?; *Guercino*, 22. Angels weeping over the dead Christ; 3216. Incredulity of St Thomas; 6381. *Gian Lorenzo Bernini*, SS Andrew and Thomas, the earliest known painting (1637) by the great sculptor; 172. *Caravaggio*, Supper at Emmaus; 4919. *Le Valentin*, Four ages of Man; *Guido Reni*, 193. Lot and his daughters leave Sodom, 214. Coronation of the Virgin; 174. *J. F. Voet*, Card. Carlo Cerri; 6372. *Mattia Preti*, Marriage at Cana; 6327. *Luca Giordano*, Martyrdom of St Januarius; 6397. *Solimena*, Dido and Aeneas; 4680. *Salvator Rosa*, Self-portrait.

ROOM 30. Brescia School. Portraits by *Moretto* and *G. B. Moroni.* – R. 31 closed in 1977.

ROOM 32. **17C French.** The artists, well represented, are *Claude, Nicolas Poussin*, and his brother-in-law *Gaspard Dughet.* In these landscapes with figures, many painted in Italy, the particular interest lies in the quality and direction of the light and in weather effects. By contrast are *Philippe de Champaigne*, 1449, 798. Portraits of Card. Richelieu. Claude's influence appears in *Turner*, 479. Sun rising through vapour, and 498. Dido building Carthage, both hung (at the far end of the room) between Claude's 'The Mill' (12) and Seaport (14), as Turner requested in his will. 6331. *Louis le Nain*, Adoration of the Shepherds.

ROOM 33. **18C French.** Portraits and genre scenes. 5118. *La Tour*, Henry Dawkins; 201. *Claude Vernet*, Sea-shore; *Chardin*, 4078. The House of Cards, 4077. The Lesson; 6428, *Rigaud*, Antoine Paris; 3588, *Perronneau*, A Girl with a Kitten; 101–104. *Nicolas Lancret*, Four Ages of Man; 4253. *F-H. Drouais*, The Comte de Vaudreuil pointing at Santo Domingo, his birthplace, on a map.

ROOM 34. **English.** *Turner*, 521. Hero and Leander, 1984. View of Margate, 508. Ulysses deriding Polyphemus, 1991. The Evening Star (unfinished), 538. Rain, Steam, and Speed: the Great Western Railway, 524. The 'Fighting Téméraire' towed to her last berth, 472. Calais Pier; *Reynolds*, 5985. Col. Tarleton, 1259. Anne, Countess of Albemarle, 681. Capt. Robert Orme, 111. Lord Heathfield, 2077. Lady Cockburn and her children; *Gainsborough*, 6209. The Morning Walk, 683. Portrait of Mrs Siddons, 3812, 1811. The painter's daughters (both unfinished); 5984. John Plampin, 925. Cornard Wood, 6301. Mr and Mrs Robert Andrews (an early work), 684. Dr Ralph Schomberg; *Hogarth*, 1162. The Shrimp Girl (sketch), 113–118. Marriage à la Mode; *Constable*, 2651. Salisbury Cathedral, 130. The Cornfield, 1207. The Hay-Wain, 1272. The Cenotaph; 3529. *George Stubbs*, Lady and Gentleman in a phaeton; 4257. *Sir Thos. Lawrence*, Queen Charlotte.

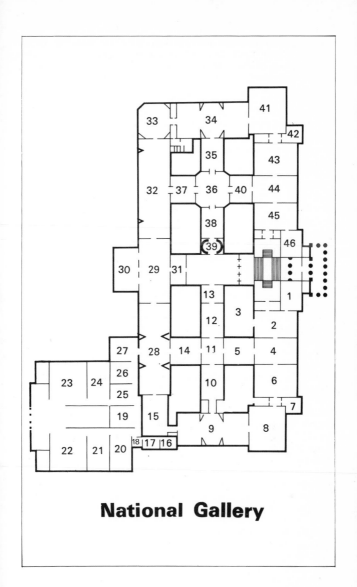

National Gallery

ROOM 35. **18C Italian,** mainly Venetian scenes. 210. *Guardi*, Piazza S. Marco; *Canaletto*, 163. Grand Canal with S. Simeone Piccolo, 937. Scuola di S. Rocco, 127. 'The Stonemason's Yard'; *Guardi*, 2098. S. Maria della Salute, 2099. Doge's Palace; *Canaletto*, 4453. Ascension Day ceremony, 4454. Regatta on Grand Canal, 942. Eton College.

ROOM 36. **19C French.** *Horace Vernet*, 2963–66. Four battle scenes painted for Louis-Philippe.

ROOM 37. **17C Italian.** 6270. *Guido Reni*, Adoration of the Shepherds dominates the work of his emotional Neapolitan contemporaries. 4778. *Bern. Cavallino*, Christ driving the Traders from the Temple; 6389. Ascr. to *Caravaggio*, Salome with the head of the Baptist; 235. *Ribera*, Pietà.

ROOM 38. **18C Italian.** 1334. *Pietro Longhi*, A Fortune-teller at Venice; 851. *Seb. Ricci*, Bacchus and Ariadne; 6279. *G. B. Pittoni*, Nativity; 2100. *G. D. Tiepolo*, Marriage of Barbarossa to Beatrice of Burgundy; 2513. *G. B. Tiepolo*, Virgin and Child with saints, hangs between two Depositions (5589, 1333) by his son, probably influenced by the Rembrandt (R. 28) then owned in Venice by Consul Smith; 1101. *P. Longhi*, Exhibition of a Rhinoceros at Venice. – ROOM 39 (not shown to advantage in 1978), *Guardi*, 2524. Venetian Lagoon, 2525. Piazza S. Marco; *Canaletto*, 2515, 2516. Piazza S. Marco.

ROOM 40. **19C French.** 1285. *Horace Vernet*, Napoleon I; 1909. *Paul Delaroche*, Execution of Lady Jane Grey, formerly in the Tate; 6436. *Gustave Moreau*, St George and the Dragon; works by *Puvis de Chavannes.*

ROOM 41. **Spanish.** *Velazquez*, 1129. Philip IV in brown and silver, 745. Philip IV, 2057. The Rokeby Venus, 6380. Abp. Fernando de Valdes; *Murillo*, 232. Adoration of the Shepherds (variously ascribed), 13. The Two Trinities, 5931. Christ at the Pool of Bethesda, 6153. Self-portrait; *Velazquez*, 1375. Kitchen scene, 6424. Immaculate Conception, 1148. Christ after the Flagellation, 6264. St John on Patmos; *El Greco*, 6260. Adoration of the Name of Jesus, 1457. Christ driving the Traders from the Temple; 74. *Murillo*, Peasant Boy; *Goya*, 6322. Duke of Wellington, 1472. Scene from a play, 1951. Don Andres del Peral, 1473. Doña Isabel de Porcel; 1930. *Francisco de Zurbaran*, St Margaret. – ROOM 42 was closed in 1977.

ROOM 43. **19C French.** Beginnings of Impressionism. 2636. *J-F. Millet*, The Whisper; 3860. *Degas*, Young Spartans; 3244. *Daumier*, Don Quixote (unfinished sketch); *Ingres*, 3291, 4821. Portraits, 3292. Scene from Orlando Furioso, 3290. Oedipus and the Sphinx; 3250. French School, A Black Woman; *Corot*, 3816. Horseman in a wood, 3285. The Roman Campagna, 6439. Peasants under the Trees at Dawn (purchased 1977); 4783. Portrait of a Woman; 3237. Avignon, 4181. The Seine near Rouen, 6340. Waggon; *Courbet*, 6396. Beach scene, 6355. Girls of the Seine banks; 4583. *Jongkind*, River scene; 4927. *Géricault*, Horse frightened by lightning; *Delacroix*, 6262. Ovid among the Scythians, 6433. Christ on the Cross, 3286. Baron Schwiter; *Boudin*, 6310, 6309. Two beach scenes, Trouville; *Daubigny*, 6324. Landscape with cattle, 2876. St Paul's from the Surrey side.

ROOM 44. Impressionists. *C. Pissarro*, 4119. Boulevard Montmartre at night, 4197. Côte des Boeufs; 3337. *Degas*, Princess Pauline de Metternich; 6351. *C. Pissarro*, Lower Norwood; 3259. *Manet*, Eva Gonzalès; 4186. *Toulouse-Lautrec*, Woman seated in a garden; 6295. *Degas*, Après le bain; 4138. *Alfred Sisley*, L'Abreuvoir de Marly; *Monet*, 3951. The Beach at Trouville, 6399. The Thames at Westminster; 4865. *Degas*, La Toilette;

Renoir, 6319. Nude, 6204. Moulin Huet Bay, Guernsey; 3294. *Manet*, The firing party, from an abandoned version of the Execution of the Emp. Maximilian (in Mannheim); *Degas*, 4121. La La at the Cirque Fernando, Paris, 4167. Elena Carafa; 3858. *Manet*, La Servante de Bocks; *Renoir*, 3268. Les Parapluies, 3859. La Première Sortie.

ROOM 45. *Vuillard*, 6373, 6388. Déjeuner à Villeneuve-sur-Yonne; *Van Gogh*, 3861. Cornfield with cypresses, 4169. Long grass with butterflies; 3908. *Seurat*, Une Baignade, Asnières; 3289. *Paul Gauguin*, Flower piece; 6421. *Henri Rousseau*, Tropical storm with a tiger. On balcony: *Cézanne*, 4135. Self-portrait, 6385. Portrait of the painter's father (probably painted at the age of 20), 4136. Montagnes en Provence, 6359. Les Grandes Baigneuses, 6195. La Vieille au Chapelet; 3863. *Van Gogh*, Sunflowers.

ROOM 46. *Monet*, 6343. Water-lilies; 6278. L'inondation, 4240. Le Bassin aux Nymphées, 6383. Irises.

The National Portrait Gallery

ADMISSION daily 10–5, Sat 10–6, Sun 2–6; closed Christmas Eve, Christmas Day, Boxing Day, New Year's Day, & Good Friday.

LECTURES some Sat & Tues, as announced. — EXHIBITIONS are held on ground floor (left of main entrance) and in Room 30. No refreshment facilities are available. W.C.s in basement.

The **National Portrait Gallery** (Pl. 14; 4), in St Martin's Place, immediately behind the National Gallery, contains a most interesting and historically valuable collection, founded in 1856, of nearly 10,000 portraits (paintings, sculptures and drawings) of men and women of significance in every walk of life. The present building, the gift of W. H. Alexander, was opened in 1896. In general no portrait of any living person is exhibited, except for members of the royal family.

The works are chosen mainly on grounds of historical significance, but many of the portraits are of artistic interest, and well-known painters and sculptors are represented in the collection. Any portrait which is not on show may usually be seen on request; a Duty Officer is available Wed & Fri 2.30–4.30. Some changes must be expected, especially in the basement.

The collection, arranged chronologically, begins on the **Top Floor** (lift). Handsheets are available in RR. 1–5. FRONT LANDING. The earliest painting from life in the collection is Henry VII (*416*), by *Michel Sittow*, dated 1505. He is also shown with his son Henry VIII, in the superb *Holbein* cartoon (*4027*), originally a working-drawing for a fresco in Whitehall Palace (now destroyed). Nearby is another portrait of Henry VIII (*157*; after *Holbein*). Other pictures here include Henry VII's wife, Elizabeth of York (*311*), and three of Henry VIII's wives: Catherine of Aragon (*163*), Anne Boleyn (*668*), and Catherine Parr (*4168*).

We ascend a few steps to ROOM 1, the **Tudor Gallery.** Here are portraits of Edward VI (*1299*; a distorted perspective portrait by *Scrots* dated 1546, formerly in Whitehall Palace; and *442*), Lady Jane Grey (*4451*; attrib. to *Master John* c. 1545). Mary I appears in a miniature (*4861*) by *Hans Eworth*, and (*428*) a portrait by *Master John*. Nearby is her husband Philip II (*347*). Among fine portraits of Tudor statesmen: *65.* William Paulet; *842.* Ant. Browne, by *Hans Eworth*; *961.* Will. Paget; *4693.* Henry Fitzalan; *2918.* Earl of Lincoln; *535.* Archbishop Cranmer, ·by *Gerlach Flicke*; *1851.* Thos. Wentworth, attrib. to

J. Bettes; *1035.* Sir Thomas Wyatt. The portraits of Sir Thomas More (*4358*) and Thomas Cromwell (*1727*) are after *Holbein*.

The second section in this room is devoted to the **Elizabethans.** Queen Elizabeth I appears in several portraits (*2082*, *4449*, *2471*) and in a fine painting (*2561*) by *M. Gheeraerts the Younger*. The portrait of Mary, Queen of Scots (*429*) is after *Nicholas Hilliard*. Elizabethan statesmen and soldiers portrayed include: *2095.* Sir Henry Lee; *7.* Sir Walter Raleigh; *107.* Robert Cecil, Earl of Salisbury (by *J. de Critz*); *2184.* William Cecil, Lord Burghley (attrib. to *A. van Brounckhorst*); *447.* Robert Dudley, Earl of Leicester; *2096.* Sir Philip Sidney; *1807.* Sir Francis Walsingham (attrib. to *J. de Critz*); *660.* Archbishop John Whitgift; *352.* Sir Thomas Gresham; *710.* Sir Henry Unton, with scenes from his life. The Chandos portrait of Shakespeare (*1*) was the first portrait acquired by the gallery in '1856; it is the only known contemporary painting of the playwright.

ROOM 2. **Early Stuart.** Some of the portraits are accompanied by engravings. On the screen (*665*), group portrait of the Somerset House Conference of 1604 which negotiated peace between England and Spain. Among soldiers of the period appear (*3914*) Sir Walter Raleigh with his son, and (*4514*) Edward Cecil, Viscount Wimbledon. The crowned heads include James I (*109*) by *Mytens*, shown in company with his wife Anne of Denmark (*4656*; attrib. to *W. Larkin*), his son, Henry Prince of Wales (*4515*; by *R. Peake*), and his favourite Buckingham (*3840*). Charles I (*1246*; by *Mytens*), and (*4444*; by *Honthorst*) is accompanied by his wife Henrietta Maria (*1247*), his sister Elizabeth (*511*), the Winter Queen, and her husband Frederick (*1973*), King of Bohemia. The portrait of the Countess of Somerset (*1955*) is attrib. to *W. Larkin*; and the Capel Family (*4759*) is a charming work by Cornelius Johnson. Poets and dramatists of the time are represented by John Donne (*1849*; after *Isaac Oliver*), and Ben Jonson (*2752*). Also here are Charles I's advisors Laud (*171*) and Strafford (*4531*). A fine portrait of the art patron and collector Thomas Howard, Earl of Arundel (*2391*; by *Rubens*) is hung close to a portrait of Inigo Jones (*603*; after *Van Dyck*). The Civil War is recalled by the portrait of Charles I in armour accompanied by his secretary (*1961*), and by pictures of his opponents, Cromwell (*536*) and Ireton (*3301*).

ROOM 3. Stuart artists, scientists, and men of letters. Writers include Sir Thomas Browne (*2062*, with his wife); *2148*, John Evelyn, by *Hendrik van der Borcht*; John Dryden (*2083*; by *Kneller*); Samuel Butler (*2468*; by *G. Soest*); Andrew Marvell (*554*), John Milton (*4222*), an unusual early portrait; and John Bunyan (*1311*). Thomas Hobbes (*225*) and John Locke (*3912*) represent philosophy; while Robert Boyle (*3930*) and Sir Isaac Newton (*2881*; by *Kneller*), are a reminder that this period saw the birth of modern science.

ROOM 4. **Restoration and late Stuart.** Decorative engravings and mezzotints, and an inlaid cabinet with charming hunting scenes are also exhibited here. Charles II (*4691*; probably his last portrait from life) is accompanied by his queen, Catherine of Braganza (*2563*); and some of his mistresses, including Louise de Kérouaille, duchess of Portsmouth (*497*), Barbara Palmer, duchess of Cleveland (*2564*), and Nell Gwynne (*3976*). Among leading statesmen of the reign are the members of the Cabal: Clifford (*204*), Arlington (*1853*), Buckingham (*279*), Shaftesbury

(*3893*), and Lauderdale (*2084*; by *Huysmans*). The portrait of Samuel Pepys (*211*) by *J. Hayls* is mentioned in Pepys' Diary. The portrait of James II (*666*) is by *Kneller*; his relatives include his nephew, the unfortunate duke of Monmouth (*151*). Judge Jeffreys (*56*) conducted the 'Bloody Assize' after Monmouth's rebellion.

The **Glorious Revolution** is recalled by portraits of William III (*1902*) and his wife Queen Mary II (*197*), James's daughter. The fine picture of Sir Christopher Wren (*113*) was painted by *Kneller*. Two leading figures of the period were A. J. van Keppel, earl of Albemarle, (*1625*; by *Kneller*), and Halifax, the 'Trimmer' (*2962*). The 17C arts are represented by the playwright (*880*) Wycherley; the composer (*1352*) Purcell; Thomas Betterton, the actor (*752*); Lely, a self-portrait (*3897*), and Vanbrugh (*1568*).

ROOM 5. **Queen Anne.** Here a portrait of the Queen (*215*) hangs near the great Duke of Marlborough (*902*), by *Kneller*, and his wife Sarah (*3634*). A bust of Marlborough (*2005*) comes from the studio of *Rysbrack*. Politicians include the Duke of Shrewsbury (*1424*) and Robert Harley, earl of Oxford (*4011*).

In the vestibule at the top of the stairs (which lead down to the First Floor, comp. p. 87) the Hanoverian succession is illustrated by a portrait (*4223*) of George I; nearby is a portrait of the son of James II, the 'Old Pretender' (*976*; with his sister Louisa Maria Theresa).

ROOMS 6 and 7. A self-portrait (*3794*) by *Kneller* precedes the unique collection of portraits by him of members of the Kit Cat club, which by 1700 included most of the leading Whigs of the day, among them Robert Walpole (*3220*), the first Prime Minister; Newcastle (*3215*); and Charles Montagu (3211), earl of Halifax, and founder of the Bank of England. Among the writers are Congreve (*3199*), Vanbrugh (*3231*), Addison (*3193*), and Steele (*3227*).

ROOM 8. **Early Georgian.** The Court of Chancery during the reign of George I is depicted by *B. Ferrers* (*798*). George II (*670*) is shown with his wife Queen Caroline (*4332* by *J. Amigoni*); his mistress (*3891*), the Countess of Suffolk; and his son Frederick (*2501* and *1556*, with his sisters; both by *P. Mercier*). Reminders of the exiled Stuarts are given by the portraits of the Young Pretender (*434*), his brother Cardinal York (*435*), and 'Butcher' Cumberland (*625*), who suppressed the '45 Rebellion. The prime minister Robert Walpole appears in a portrait (*70*). Pope (*1179* and *873*) dominates the writers of his age who include: Samuel Richardson (*1036*; by *Highmore*), Jonathan Swift (*278*), and Matthew Prior (*3682*; attrib. to *Dahl*). A full length portrait of Handel (*3970*), by *T. Hudson*, hangs close to another musician, William Boyce (*4212*). Self-portraits by artists include Hogarth (*289*), Roubiliac (*2145*; bust), Jonathan Richardson (*1693*), and Sir James Thornhill (*4688*).

18C Arts are continued in ROOM 9, together with fine portraits from the studio of *Allan Ramsay* (*223, 224*) of George III and Queen Charlotte. Artists' self-portraits include: Joseph Wright of Derby (*4090*); Angelica Kauffmann (*430*); Zoffany (*399*); Ramsay (*3311*); Stubbs (*4575*); and Gainsborough (*4446*). Architectural designs from the collection of the Royal Institute of British Architects are displayed with portraits of artists and architects: *576*. George Vertue, by *J. Richardson*; *121*. Hogarth, terracotta bust by *Roubiliac*; *3186*. Carlini,

Bartolozzi, and Cipriani, by *F. Rigaud*; *2953*. Robert Adam; *L107*. Lancelot ('Capability') Brown, by *Nathaniel Dance*. Writers include: Lawrence Sterne (*1891*; bust by *Nollekens*); Thomas Gray (*989*); Horace Walpole (*988*); Smollett (*1110*); Samuel Johnson (*L142*), and James Boswell (*4452*), Oliver Goldsmith (*130*), both fine portraits by *Reynolds*; Fanny Burney (*2634*); Edward Gibbon (*1443*); and Mrs Delany (*1030*; by *J. Opie*). Also here are the actors Garrick (*4504*) and Colley Cibber (*1045*; bust); the statesmen Lord Chesterfield (*533*; by *Allan Ramsay*); the courtesan Kitty Fisher by *N. Hone* (*2354*); Sir William Hamilton, the archaeologist (*680*); and Dr Burney, the historian of music (*3884*; by *Reynolds*).

ROOM 10. **The British overseas.** Among the founders of empire are Clive (*39*; by *N. Dance*) and Warren Hastings (*4445*), a fine portrait by *Reynolds*. The statuette (*4005*) of Joseph Collet was made during his administration in Sumatra and Madras. The defence of Gibraltar is recalled by a portrait (*170*) of Baron Heathfield (by *J. S. Copley*). Captain Cook's voyages are illustrated by plant specimens which he collected and a portrait (*26*) painted at the Cape of Good Hope in 1776. Arthur Phillip (*1462*), first governor of New South Wales, is shown in a portrait by *F. Wheatley*.

ROOM 11. British failure in the American War of Independence is personified here by Lord North (*3627*), the reluctant prime minister, and his victorious opponent George Washington (*774*). Statesmen and soldiers of the period include: the Earl of Bute, favourite of George III (*3938*) a fine portrait by *Reynolds*; Lord Amherst (*150*), by *Gainsborough*; John Burgoyne (*4158*); and the Earl of Chatham (*1050*), by *William Hoarse*. Also here are two busts by *Nollekens* of William Pitt the Younger (*120*) and Charles James Fox (*3887*).

ROOM 12. Here Nelson (*394*) is shown near his mistress Lady Hamilton (*4448*), a fine portrait by *Romney*. Leading politicians of the day include William Pitt the Younger (*697*), by *Hoppner*, Fox (*743*), and Burke (*655*). These also appear in a large painting (*745*) of Pitt addressing the House of Commons in 1793. Among other statesmen are: William Windham (*38*), and Lord Melville (*746*), both by *Lawrence*; Lord Thurlow (*249*) by *T. Phillips*; and Lord Grenville (*318*), by *Hoppner*. The military leaders of the period include Adm. St Vincent (*2026*); Sir John Moore (*1128*), the hero of Corunna, by *Lawrence*; and the Marquess of Anglesey (*1581*), by *W. Beechey*.

ROOM 13. **The Romantic Movement.** To the left, literature: Robert Burns (*46*), by *Alexander Nasmyth*; Sir Walter Scott (*391*), by *Landseer*; Charles Lamb (*507*), by *Wm. Hazlitt*; Byron (*142*; by *Thos. Phillips*) in Albanian costume; Shelley (*1234*), the only authentic portrait from life; Leigh Hunt (*2508*); Southey (*193*); Coleridge (*184*); Wordsworth (*1897*), by *Haydon*. To the right, the artists include Romney (*959*; self-portrait); R. P. Bonnington (*444*); Constable (*1786*); Opie (*47*; self-portrait); Blake (*212*; by *T. Phillips*, also 1809A, life-mask).

ROOM 14. **Science and the Industrial Revolution.** Erasmus Darwin (*88*), by *Wright of Derby*; Sir Humphrey Davy (*1794*); James Watt (*186A*) and his partner Matthew Boulton (*1532*); Marc Isambard Brunel (*89*); John Loudon Macadam (*3686*), the great road builder; John Rennie (*649*; bust by *Chantrey*); Sir Richard Arkwright (*136*), by *Wright of Derby*. The small portraits, miniatures, drawings, etc are worthy of attention.

ROOM 15. **The Regency.** On screen, the Stage: Master Betty (*1392*), by *Opie*, flanked by engravings of Kemble and Sarah Siddons. To the left, Mrs Siddons, by *Lawrence* (on loan from the Tate Gallery); Sheridan (*651*); Kean (*1829*); to the right, groups of art patrons, by *P. C. Wonder*; Sir John Soane (*701*). In the main gallery, **George IV's England:** statesmen, Liverpool (*1804*), Goderich (*4875*), Castlereagh (*891*), and Canning (*1832*), all by *Lawrence*. George IV (*123*) also appears by *Lawrence*; his unfortunate marriage to Caroline of Brunswick (*244*) is recalled by the group painting by *Hayter* (*999*) showing her trial in 1820; William IV

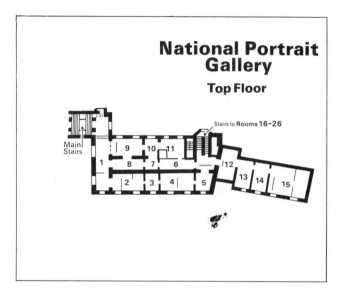

(*2199*); Mrs Fitzherbert is represented by a *Reynolds* (on loan). The far end is devoted to **Radical Reform,** a movement inspired by William Cobbett (*1549*). Earl Grey (*4137*); Baron Brougham (*3136*) and Wm. Wilberforce (*3*), by *Thos. Lawrence*; Elizabeth Fry (*898*).

Stairs descend from outside R. 12 to the **First Floor,** devoted to **Victorian England** but still in course of rearrangement in 1978; beyond R. 18 is unlikely to correspond exactly with the text below.

ROOM 16 is dominated by Queen Victoria (*1250*) in coronation robes, by *Hayter*; engravings of the event; cartoons of the Holland House and Blessington D'Orsay sets; the Duchess of Kent, Victoria's mother (*2554*), by *Winterhalter*; Lord Melbourne (*941*), her favourite Prime Minister.

ROOM 17. **Early Victorians.** Writers include Tennyson (*2460*), by *S. Lawrence*; Borrow (*1841*), C. M. Yonge (*2193*); Thackeray (*4210*); Dickens (*1172*), by *Daniel Maclise*; the Brontës, Emily (*1724*) and the three sisters (*1725*), both by *Branwell Brontë*; Macaulay (*4882*). Music is represented by Jenny Lind (*3801*), surrounded by opera bills and contemporary composers; the Theatre by posters and caricatures and a portrait of Kean (*1249*). Sir Charles Barry (*1272*) heads the Fine Arts Commissioners who decorated the new Houses of Parliament. James Sadler is the first of a group of early balloonists. The Oxford Movement found their painter in *George Richmond*, and the Scientists most prominent are Faraday (*269*), the members of the British Association, and Sir Roderick Murchison (*906*). There is also a rare section of Daguerrotypes and Calotypes, the 1840 precursors of photography.

ROOM 18, entitled 'Poverty and the People', consists mainly of politicians: Cavendish Bentinck (*1515*); Derby (*1806*); Peel (*722*); Aberdeen (*750*); Russell (*1895*), between youthful engravings of Gladstone and Disraeli; the Chartists are featured, and Ireland is represented by Daniel O'Connell (*4582*), by *Hayter.*

ROOM 19 is devoted to the **Empire Overseas,** with a group of African explorers, including David Livingstone (*386*); Sir Richard Burton (*1070*), by *Leighton*: Stanley, etching by *Herkomer.* Other foci of interest are provided by the Indian Mutiny and the Crimean War, with several portraits by *Watts*; Sir James Brooke (*1559*).

ROOM 23 (left wall) seven worthy gentlemen on either side of Ellen Terry (*5048*), all by *Watts.* Opposite, science and the arts, with a group of Pre-Raphaelites by themselves or each other.

ROOM 25, dominated by Edward VII (*1691*), by *Luke Fildes*, has suffragettes, statesmen, and soldiers: Balfour (*2947*), by *Philip de Laszlo*; Joseph Chamberlain (*4030*) and Sir Frank Swettenham (*4837*), both by *J. S. Sargent*; Kitchener (*1782*), by *H. von Herkomer.*

ROOM 24. **The Edwardians.** The writer Beatrix Potter (*3635*), creator of Peter Rabbit, is shown here in company with James Barrie (*3539*), creator of Peter Pan. Beyond a bust (*4208*) of Galsworthy, are the architect Charles Voysey (*4116*), and the artists Sir William Rothenstein (*4414*) and Aubrey Beardsley (*1991*). Writers include W. E. Henley (*1697*; bust by *Rodin*); Oscar Wilde (*3653*; by *Pellegrini*); Sir Max Beerbohm (*3850*); Jerome K. Jerome (*4492*); G. K. Chesterton, Hilaire Belloc, and Maurice Baring (*3654*); Rudyard Kipling (*1863*; by *Burne-Jones*); R. L. Stevenson (*1028*); Conrad (*4159*; bust by *Epstein*); Henry James (*1767*; by *J. S. Sargent*); Hardy (*2929*); and Meredith (*1543*; by *Watts*). The actors include Ellen Terry (*L132*) and Henry Irving (*1560*). Beyond the architect Sir Aston Webb (*2489*), the group of artists include Sickert (*3142*; by *Wilson Steer*); Wilson Steer (*3116*; by *Sickert*); Whistler (*4497* and *1700*); and a malicious group by *Orpen* showing the selecting jury of the New English Art Club in 1909 (*2556*). Here also W. S. Gilbert (*2911*) and Sir Arthur Sullivan (*1325*; by *Millais*).

The main stairs are hung with portraits of 15C kings, not contemporary but probably based on authentic portraits. In early 1978 the landings were in a state of constant change, except for King George V and Queen Mary with their children (*1745*) and a temporary showing of the newly acquired Warwick Castle portrait of Queen Elizabeth I in coronation robes.

We may now descend to the **Basement,** devoted to leading figures of the **Twentieth Century.** In the vestibule (left), Richard Hillary (*5167*; by *Eric Kennington*); Alan Cobham (*5018*; by *Frank Salisbury*); Dame Laura Knight (*4839*; self-portrait); Benjamin Britten. — Main gallery, two studies of Dame Edith Sitwell (*4464, 4465*), by *Wyndham Lewis*; W. H. Davies (*4194*), by *Wm. Nicholson*; W. H. Auden (*4677*); D. H. Lawrence (*4036*; by *Jan Juta*); Roger Fry (*3833*; self-portrait); Lytton Strachey (on loan from the Tate Gallery); James Joyce (*3883*); bust of Shaw (*4047*), by *Epstein*; Sir Alan Herbert (*4894*; by *Ruskin Spear*); Noel Coward (*4950* by *Clemence Dane*); Ralph Vaughan Williams (*4829*; by *Gerald Kelly*) also bronze (*4068*; by *David McFall*); Sir Thomas Beecham (*4221*; head and hands by *David Wynne*), and a fine group of bronze heads by *Epstein* includes Augustus John (*4295*), Somerset Maugham (loaned) and T. S. Eliot (*4440*). The farther section of the room contains a group portrait of George VI taking family tea at Royal Lodge, Windsor (*3778*); prime ministers and others include Neville Chamberlain (*4279*; by *Henry Lamb*); Ramsay Macdonald (*2959*; by *Sir J. Lavery*); Churchill (*4438*; by *Sickert*); and a loaned portrait of Montgomery, by *Frank Salisbury*.

The Ground Floor rooms are used to mount special exhibitions.

6 ST JAMES'S PARK. THE MALL AND BUCKINGHAM PALACE

STATIONS: *St James's Park*, on Circle and District line; *Victoria* and *Green Park*, on Victoria line (Green Park also on Piccadilly and Fleet lines). – BUSES in Whitehall, see Rte 4. – CAR PARKING (limited) in Birdcage Walk. The Mall is closed to cars on Sunday (8–dusk).

*St James's Park (Pl. 14; 6; 93 acres) extends from the Horse Guards Parade, on the E., to Buckingham Palace, on the W., and is bounded on the N. by the Mall, on the S. by Birdcage Walk. Charmingly laid out in an aristocratic surrounding of palaces and government offices, and commanding a famous view in the direction of Westminster, this park is one of the most attractive in London. The lake in the centre (5 acres) is frequented by ornamental waterfowl, for which Duck Island at the E. end is reserved as a breeding place. Among the "great variety of fowle" described by Pepys are six pelicans (their successors best seen at feeding time, at 4 p.m. in summer or 3 p.m. in winter, near Duck Island). The flower-beds are beautifully maintained, and the trees, some dating from the Restoration, add an oriental flavour to the views over the lake.

Henry VIII laid out the land between his palaces at Whitehall and St James's in 1532 as the first royal park in London. Under the early Stuarts it was the resort of the Court and other privileged persons, among them Milton (who lived in 1652–60 in a house in Petty France overlooking the park). In 1649 Charles I walked across it on the morning of his execution from St James's Palace to Whitehall, and here in 1660 Pepys had his first view of Charles II on his return to London: "Found the King in the parke. There walked. Gallantry great". After the Restoration Le Nôtre was employed to make "great and very noble alteracions", and the scattered ponds were united to form a 'canal'. It was then opened to the public, and remains the only large park in London which has not been enclosed by railings. It became a fashionable resort, where the king was frequently to be seen strolling unattended and feeding the waterfowl for which he established a 'volary' or aviary. The park was further altered, and the form of the lake changed by Nash in 1827–29, as an appendage to Carlton House, then occupied by George IV. During the First World War the lake was emptied and its bed occupied by temporary government buildings.

In July and Aug a band plays in the park, daily exc. Sun 12.30–2, 5.30–7; on King George VI's Steps, Sun at 3. – Since 1785 chairs have been on hire in the park.

From Charing Cross we enter St James's Park by passing under the **Admiralty Arch**, through which we enjoy a striking view down the 'triumphal avenue' of the Mall, with the Victoria Memorial and Buckingham Palace closing the vista. This massive triumphal arch was designed by Sir Aston Webb as part of the national memorial to Queen

Victoria. On the left, immediately beyond the Arch, is a statue of *Captain Cook* (1728–79), by Brock (1914); on the right a memorial to the *Royal Marines* by Adrian Jones (1903). The conspicuous and grim-looking building on the left is the 'Citadel', an extension of the Admiralty built in 1941–42. Beyond it opens Horse Guards Parade (see p. 72).

The **Mall**, the spacious avenue lined with double rows of plane trees that skirts St James's Park on the N., is so called from having been used in Charles II's time for the game of 'pail-mail' (from the Italian 'palla', meaning ball, and 'maglio', meaning mallet; a cross between croquet and golf). Overlooking it on the right is the bright *Carlton House Terrace* designed by Nash, a monumental terrace of mansions (entered from Waterloo Place, see Rte 7), with small gardens on the projecting podium below. Here are the entrances to the *Mall Galleries* of the Federation of British Artists, and, just before Duke of York's steps, at *Nash House*, to the Institute of Contemporary Arts, with galleries, an auditorium, theatre, and restaurant (open Tues–Sat 12–8; Sun 2–10). Carlton House Terrace is interrupted by the Duke of York's Column and Waterloo Place, described on p. 96. Opposite is a Royal Artillery monument (1910) in memory of the dead in South Africa 1899–1902.

A path here enters the park and descends past meteorological equipment to the *Cake House* (1970; Rfmts) and Duck Island.

At the end of the Terrace is a double flight of steps designed by De Soissons. At the top a statue of George VI by W. McMillan (1955) fronts Carlton Gardens (p. 97). The Mall now skirts the gardens of Marlborough House (see below), beyond which we may diverge on foot into Marlborough Road, to pass between (l.) St James's Palace and (r.) the Queen's Chapel and Marlborough House. The *Queen's Chapel* (open for services Easter–Aug; Sun 8.30, 11.15; Holy Days 8 a.m.) was designed by Inigo Jones in 1623.

It was built as a private chapel for the Roman Catholic Infanta Maria of Spain whom Prince Charles, later Charles I, was expected to marry, and completed for Henrietta Maria, his eventual wife. With a temple-like façade, the classical double-cube hall has a superb elliptical coffered ceiling constructed of timber. The interior retains its 17C fittings, with an altarpiece of the Holy Family, by Annibale Carracci.

Marlborough House (Pl. 14; 6), concealed behind the chapel in a pleasant garden of 4½ acres, and approached by an unassuming entrance at the w. end of Pall Mall, is the Commonwealth Centre. The former state apartments are open, when not in use, from Easter–Sept, on Sat, Sun, & BH. from 2–6 (visitors may first telephone 930 8071). The staircases have mural paintings by Laguerre (restored), and a ceiling by Orazio Gentileschi was moved from Greenwich in the 18C and inserted in the Blenheim Saloon.

Marlborough House, a good example of Wren's red brick work, was built in 1709–11 for the great Duke of Marlborough with bricks brought back as ballast from Holland after the Duke's military campaigns there. The third story was added by Sir William Chambers in the 18C, and the porte-cochère and entrance in 1860–63. Here, next door to 'Neighbour George', the great Duchess Sarah lived for 22 years after the death of her husband at Windsor. Later occupants were Leopold I of the Belgians (before his accession), Queen Adelaide, and (as Prince of Wales) Edward VII and George V (1903–10). The last was born here in 1865. On the death of Edward VII it became the residence of Queen Alexandra (1844–1925). In 1936 Queen Mary (1867–1953) returned to her former home.—On the garden wall in Marlborough Road is an elaborate, finely wrought memorial

(1932) to Queen Alexandra by Alfred Gilbert, and (on the Mall) a plaque to Queen Mary.

St James's Palace (Pl. 14; 5; no adm.), an irregular and picturesque brick building, encloses several secluded courtyards which are open to the public.

The palace stands on the site of a hospital for fourteen "maidens that were leprous" which was dedicated to St James the Less and is mentioned at least as early as 1100. Henry VIII acquired the hospital and its grounds in 1531, and built a palace here, of which only the Gatehouse, parts of the Chapel Royal, and the Old Presence Chamber (Tapestry Room) remain. Mary I died at St James's in 1558. Charles I, most of whose children were born in this palace, spent his last days here. Charles II employed Wren to provide state apartments overlooking the park, and the palace became the principal residence of the Duke of York (afterwards James II). After 1698, when Whitehall was burned down, St James's Palace became the official London residence of the sovereign, where all Court functions were held; the British Court is still officially known as the Court of St James's, and the sovereign is proclaimed from the balcony in Friary Court. Among those born in the palace are Mary II (1662), Queen Anne (1664), the Old Pretender (1688), and George IV (1762). George IV employed Nash to restore and redecorate the palace. It is now occupied by 'Grace and Favour' apartments, the Gentlemen and Yeomen-at-Arms, and the Lord Chamberlain.—Sentries guard the palace in Ambassador's Court and outside the walls (unlike those at Buckingham Palace who now stand within the forecourt).

The open *Friary Court*, on the E. side of the palace, takes its name from a Capuchin friary established by Henrietta Maria and demolished to make room for Marlborough House. The most attractive feature of the exterior is the fine 16C brick *Gatehouse, to the N., facing St James's St., with its four octagonal towers. The carving over the original doors which lead into *Colour Court* (no adm.) shows the initials of Henry VIII and Anne Boleyn. Beyond the large restored N. window of the Chapel Royal, an archway leads into the charming *Ambassador's Court* from which the Chapel is entered.

The **Chapel Royal** has been greatly altered since it was built for Henry VIII, and it was enlarged in 1837. It preserves a fine ceiling, probably designed by Holbein in 1540. The music here has always been noted for its excellence; among early organists were Orlando Gibbons and Purcell. The private choir of the sovereign is composed of 6 'Gentlemen' and 10 boys; the boys wear traditional Court costume. At the Epiphany (6 Jan) an offering of gold, frankincense, and myrrh is made on behalf of the sovereign, on which occasion the service is conducted by the Bishop of London. Several royal marriages have been celebrated in this chapel, including those of Mary, the daughter of Charles I and mother of William III (1641), William III and Mary II (1677), Queen Anne (1683), George IV (1795), Queen Victoria (1840), and George V (1893).—Visitors are admitted to the services held here when the Queen's Chapel (see above) is not in use.

An original passage-way leads to Colour Court, and, on the s. side, picturesque passages admit to Engine Court (both private). Opposite is *York House*, now the residence of the Duke and Duchess of Kent. Lord Kitchener lived here in 1915–16. The w. wing (with some fine Adam details) is being restored for use as offices of the Crown.

Farther w. lies *Stable Yard*; the former stables (1661) remain in the N. range. Facing them is the imposing entrance portico of **Lancaster House,** a massive palace built by Benj. Wyatt in 1825–27 for the Duke of York (the s. façade is well seen from the Mall). It was continued in 1827–30 for the first Duke of Sutherland, earlier Marquess of Stafford, and enlarged to Wyatt's designs by Smirke and Barry in 1833–41 for the second Duke. The third Duke entertained Garibaldi here in 1864. It is now a Government Hospitality Centre. Visitors are admitted Easter–Christmas on Sat & Sun, 2–4, when the building is not in use.

Known as *Stafford House* from 1842 to 1912, it was then presented to the nation by Lord Leverhulme (d. 1921) and named Lancaster House. It was decorated in the Louise-Quinze style and reopened in 1950. Notable among the gorgeous fittings are Barry's double staircase, and the ceiling paintings in the great first floor galley (Assumption of St Chrysogonus, by Guercino), and state anteroom (Cupid with the Graces, by Veronese).

A passageway which gives access to Green Park (see p 94), skirts *Warwick House* (1716; by Hawksmoor). On the E. side of the Court is the *Lord Chamberlain's Office* (Examiner of Plays, King's Bargemaster, Keeper of Swans, etc.), in an attractive house with fine first floor windows.

We may return to the Mall by Stable Yard Road past the bright stucco flank of *Clarence House* built in 1825 by Nash for William IV when Duke of Clarence, restored in 1949 for Princess Elizabeth (Elizabeth II) and the Duke of Edinburgh, and now the residence of the Queen Mother. A piper plays in the garden every morning at 9 a.m. when the Queen Mother is in residence. The s. façade of St James's Palace extends eastwards (seen from the Mall), built by Wren in the late 17C.

Opposite Marlborough Rd., a path, preceded by a fine wrought iron gate, leads through St James's Park and across the lake by a bridge (1957; fine view). BIRDCAGE WALK skirts the park on the s. side; the name recalls a royal aviary established here in the reign of James I. A small road across Birdcage Walk leads to QUEEN ANNE'S GATE, to the left a quiet street of delightful houses, built by Charles Shales (who lived at No. 15) in 1704. No. 50 (r.; see p. 138) shows the gulf between 18C and 20C politics.

The houses have carved masks to the keystones, and elaborately carved door cases with canopied hoods, unique in London. The statue of Queen Anne in state robes, is contemporary. Lord Palmerston (1784–1865) was born at No. 20, and Lord Haldane (1856–1929) lived at No. 28. Wm. Paterson 'founder' of the Bank of England, probably assisted Shales in building the square; he lived at No. 19 in 1705–18. At No. 40 three ornamental lead cisterns are fixed on the exterior, one dated 1745 (probably used inside the house).

Old Queen St., farther w., presents a medley of domestic architectural styles, including Nos. 9–15 dating from 1698–99. No. 14, possibly designed by Adam, was occupied by Charles Townley in 1777–1805 and here he entertained Reynolds and Zoffany at his renowned 'Sunday dinners'. The parallel Lewisham St. is a narrow alley-way of unexpectedly tall industrial buildings. The old street lighting of the area survives.

We may regain Birdcage Walk viâ Cockpit Steps between Queen Anne's Gate and Old Queen St., and return westwards, passing attractive houses with bay windows and balconies overlooking the park. Built in 1780 all are narrow in width and present pleasantly varied façades. Near the w. end of Birdcage Walk are the *Wellington Barracks* (1834–59) occupied by the Grenadier Guards, the stucco buildings spaciously laid out around the parade ground.

The **Guard's Chapel**, or *Royal Military Chapel*, is approached by a memorial cloister (1954–56), by H. S. Goodhart-Rendel, in honour of the Household Brigade in the Second World War. The chapel itself, opened in 1838 but completely transformed within in 1875–78 by G. E. Street, was wrecked by a flying bomb on 18 June 1944, during morning service, with the loss of 121 lives. The present chapel, opened in 1963, is by George, Trew, and Dunn; its austerity sets off Street's ornate apse, which survives. At the end of the narthex opposite the memorial cloister is the Household Brigade Cenotaph, while the six s. chapels are dedicated to the five regiments of Foot Guards and the Household Cavalry. The sculptured aluminium screens are by Geoffrey Clarke. The chapel is open free on weekdays 10–1, 2–4 (Mon and Sat 10–12 only) and for services on Sun, at 8 a.m., 11 a.m., and 6.30 p.m.

A small *Guards Museum* (weekdays 10–4 or 5, Sun 11.30–1.30, 2.30–5; fee) illustrates the history of the Brigade of Guards.

At the w. end of the Mall and St James's Park, a spacious circus with planted lawns surrounded by a stone balustrade opens before Buckingham Palace. In the centre rises the conspicuous **Queen Victoria Memorial** (1911) of white marble, crowned by a gilded bronze figure of victory with Courage and Constancy at her feet, and surrounded by water.

The monument designed by Sir Aston Webb, and well sculpted by Sir Thomas Brock, consists of the seated figure of Queen Victoria (E. side), and groups typifying Truth (S.), Motherhood (W.), and Justice (N.). Other allegorical groups in dark bronze decorate the podium, representing Peace and Progress (E.), Science and Art (N.), Manufactures and Agriculture (W.), and Naval and Military Power (S.).— The monument provides a good viewpoint for the changing of the guard and royal processions.

Buckingham Palace (Pl. 14; 7), the residence of the Queen, stands between St James's Park and a private garden of 40 acres. When the sovereign is in residence the royal standard is flown. The guard is changed daily at 11.30 in the forecourt.

The palace takes its name from *Buckingham House*, built on this site in 1703 by the Duke of Buckingham. George III purchased this house in 1762, and here the famous interview between him and Dr Johnson took place (1767). The building was altered and remodelled by Nash for George IV about 1825, and since that time it has been known as Buckingham Palace, although neither George IV nor his successor ever occupied it. Since the accession of Queen Victoria in 1837, however, it has been the London residence of the sovereign, and here Edward VII was born in 1841 and here he died in 1910. The w. façade towards the garden remains largely as Nash designed it; the E. wing, facing the park, was added by Blore in 1847, but in 1913 the entire E. façade was replaced by a much more dignified design by Sir Aston Webb. The interior of the palace, never open to sightseers, contains many magnificent and sumptuously decorated apartments, besides a very fine gallery of paintings and other works of art. The Throne Room, 66 ft long, has a marble frieze representing the Wars of the Roses. The royal apartments are in the N. wing.

The palace gardens, the scene in summer of royal garden parties, include a lake and one of the mulberry trees planted by James I after 1609 to encourage the silk industry. These *Mulberry Gardens* soon degenerated into a place of popular entertainment (c. 1630–90), described by Pepys as "a very silly place".

The **Changing of the Guard** takes place at Buckingham Palace daily at 11.30 a.m., and is normally carried out by the Brigade of Guards. The best vantage-point is the Queen Victoria Memorial, or near the centre gates of the palace. The ceremony involves the trooping of the Queen's colour from St James's Palace to Buckingham Palace. At approx. 11.10 a.m. one contingent of the old guard parades in Ambassador's Court, St James's (Pl. 14; 5), and then troops to Buckingham Palace. There they join the old Palace Guard at the left side of the centre gates at approx. 11.25.

The new Guard, accompanied by a band, march either from Chelsea Barracks (see p. 149) or the nearby Wellington Barracks (when the weather is bad). They form up and are inspected in their barracks before coming on duty; at Wellington Barracks they are on parade by about 10.15, and at Chelsea by about 9.30. They enter the palace by the normal 'out' gate, and form up facing the old guard, slow marching to the right side of the centre gates. The officers of the old and new guard advance and touch left hands, symbolizing the handing over of the keys, and at this point the guard is 'changed'. Eight men now peel off from the ranks to relieve sentries guarding St James's Palace, Clarence House, and Buckingham Palace. Meanwhile music is played in the forecourt of Buckingham Palace. The old guard complete with the sentries march out of the centre gates at approx. 12.10 accompanied by the massed bands, turning right to return to barracks. The new guard is dismissed to go on duty at Buckingham Palace, while a small detachment of drums (or pipes and drums) leaves the palace by the r. gate to accompany the new guard back to St James's Palace and Clarence House.

BUCKINGHAM GATE and its extension *Buckingham Palace Road* skirt the ornamental wall in front of the s. wing of the palace. Here are the entrances to the Queen's Gallery and the Royal Mews. In the **Queen's Gallery** (adm. daily exc. Mon, 11–5, Sun from 2; fee) are mounted exhibitions, changed about twice a year, of ****Treasures** selected from the splendid royal collections.

The private chapel, in the s. wing, was the part of the palace most seriously damaged in the air raids of 1940–44. It was rebuilt in 1961–62, and the w. part adapted to form the Queen's Gallery.

Beyond a conspicuous pediment (with a scene of Hercules sculpted by Wm. Theed) added by Nash to the Riding House of 1764, is the quadrangle (1824–25) and clock tower of the **Royal Mews** (Pl. 14; 7; adm. Wed & Thurs 2–4). Here may be seen the Queen's horses and the royal equipages, including the magnificent state carriage designed by Sir William Chambers in 1761, and painted by Cipriani. In the old Carriage House is a charming frieze of the Coronation of William IV by R. Barret Davis (1782–1854).

On the opposite side of Buckingham Palace Road are the headquarters of the *Girl Guides Association* (No. 17) and the *Scout Association* (No. 25). Westminster Theatre in Palace St. is described on p. 140. In *Lower Grosvenor Place*, at the s.w. angle of the palace grounds, two attractive Regency shop fronts (Nos. 5 and 6) remain, flanking an entrance to the paved Victoria Square. For Victoria and the area to the s., see Rte 12.

On the N. side of Buckingham Palace the tree-lined *Constitution Hill* (probably so named after the 'constitutionals' taken here by Charles II) leads due w. to Hyde Park Corner (see Rte 10), with a sand-track for riders skirting Green Park. Here three attempts on the life of Queen Victoria were made (in 1840, 1842, and 1849), and in 1850, Sir Robert Peel was fatally injured by a fall from his horse.

Green Park (53 acres), created in 1668 with fine expanses of grass and trees, extends N. to Piccadilly. The decorative Dominion gateway opposite the Victoria Memorial, leads into a broad walk; while the paved Queen's Walk, opened in 1730 and named after Caroline, wife of George II, skirts the E. border of the park (see p. 98). Ice houses were built here in 1660 by Charles II when the park was used for royal picnics. The only ornament is a small fountain near Hyde Park Corner (1954; by E. J. Clack). The Tyburn (comp. p. 108), now channelled underground, still crosses the park, and can be heard near the centre. The railings along Piccadilly are hung with 'art' at week-ends.

7 PALL MALL AND ST JAMES'S

STATIONS: *Green Park* on Piccadilly, Victoria, and Fleet lines; *Piccadilly Circus* on Piccadilly and Bakerloo line. BUSES in Piccadilly (see Rte 8). Meter CAR PARKING in St James's Sq., Carlton House Terrace, etc. Car Park in Arlington St.

Between St James's Park (Rte 6) and Piccadilly (Rte 8) lies the fashionable region known as **St James's.** The compact lay-out of the area remains virtually as it was planned in the 1670s by Henry Jermyn, Earl of St Albans (c. 1604–84), the 'founder' of London's West End, described by Pepys in 1660 as 'a fine civil gentleman'. Established as a largely residential district near St James's Palace and Court, St James's was famous by the late 18C for its bachelor lodgings; but since the end of the 19C many of the houses have been occupied by offices. The area became also a centre of fashionable trade, and some long-established shops survive here. From the reign of William III the coffee and chocolate houses of St James's (of which the present exclusive private clubs are the successors) were the rendezvous of the aristocratic and learned London gentleman.

London's clubs are traditionally the preserve of men, though some have added ladies' annexes in recent years. In contrast to many of the shops and businesses in the area, with their bright brass name-plates, the clubs have no name on the entrance. The elaborate flambeaux outside are lit by gas on state occasions.

Pall Mall, the chief thoroughfare of St James's, is soon reached from Trafalgar Square either viâ *Cockspur Street* with the offices of many shipping companies, running N.W. from Charing Cross or viâ Pall Mall East, which leads due W. from the National Gallery. These two streets converge at a fine statue of *George III*, by M. C. Wyatt, 'a good horse ridden by a horseman'.

In *Suffolk Street*, off Pall Mall East, among good façades designed by Nash are No. 6½ and No. 23 where Richard Cobden died in 1865.

At the E. end of Pall Mall the Haymarket brings traffic S. from Coventry Street and Piccadilly Circus. The pile supported on steel pillars at the corner, square, massive, and obtrusive, is *New Zealand House* (opened 1963), by Matthew and Johnson-Marshall. New Zealanders are admitted to the roof terrace from which there is a magnificent view. Adjoining it to the W., the charming *Royal Opera Arcade* (1816) by Nash and G. S. Repton is lit by circular skylights and hung with lamps and flower-baskets. This survives from an operatic successor to Vanbrugh's Her Majesty's Theatre of 1704–05, which opened with Dryden's 'The Indian Queen'.

The present (fourth) *Her Majesty's*, elaborately decorated and crowned by a Baroque copper dome, was founded by Sir Herbert Tree in 1897. It faces the HAYMARKET, where a market was established as early as the 16C and provided hay for the horses of London until 1830. The *Haymarket Theatre* opened in 1821 and has been associated with the names of Squire Bancroft and Beerbohm Tree, who migrated across the road. Here Wilde's 'An Ideal Husband' was first played (1895). In a former theatre on this site, built a century earlier, Aaron Hill, Theophilus Cibber, and Henry Fielding all appeared, and Charles Macklin and Samuel Foote produced plays. The massive brick columns of the present building, by Nash, extend over the pavement. The *Design Centre* of the Council of Industrial Design (open weekdays 9.30–5.30; Wed & Thurs till 9 p.m.) occupies No. 28; while at No. 34 bow-windows of a tobacconist survive in a building first occupied by Peter Fribourg (who began the present business here) in 1751.

Pall Mall (Pl. 14; 6) runs W. from George III's statue to St James's Palace. Like the Mall, it derives its name from 'pail-mail' (comp. p. 90) which was played here in the 17C, before the construction of the Mall. The S. side consists of a succession of stately clubs. The *United Service and Royal Aero Club* occupies a house built by Nash in 1827 (altered by Decimus Burton in 1842). The United Service Club, founded in 1815, was the earliest service club in London. The Royal Academy was established on part of this site in 1768–79. Across Waterloo Place stands the *Athenaeum*, founded in 1823 as a club for 'scientific and literary men, and Artists', by Sir Humphry Davy, President of the Royal Society, Lord Aberdeen (Prime Minister 1852–55), and Sir

Thomas Lawrence, President of the Royal Academy. It remains the leading club for academics, and includes many bishops among its members. Thackeray wrote some of his works in the library, and referred to the club as 'Megatherium'. The handsome building by Burton (1830) is embellished with a reproduction of the Parthenon frieze. The mounting block in Waterloo Place was erected in 1830 for the Duke of Wellington.

WATERLOO PLACE, which here intersects Pall Mall, is characterized by banks and insurance offices, and by numerous statues.

The group to the N. of Pall Mall commemorates the Crimean War (1854–55). In the centre is the *Guards' Monument* by John Bell, with three guardsmen and a trophy of Russian guns. In front are statues of *Lord Herbert of Lea* (1810–61; by Foley), secretary of war during the campaign; and *Florence Nightingale* (1820–1910), by A. G. Walker. The fine street lamp dates from c. 1830. South of Pall Mall is an equestrian statue of *Edward VII* (d. 1910), by Sir B. Mackennal. To the left (E.), *Captain Scott* (1888–1912), the Antarctic explorer, by Lady Scott (1915); *Colin Campbell, Lord Clyde* (1792–1863), the saviour of Lucknow, by Marochetti (its base damaged by a bomb in the Second World War); and *Lord Lawrence* (1811–79), Viceroy of India, by Boehm; to the right (W.) *Sir John Franklin* (1786–1847), the Arctic explorer, by Matthew Noble, and *Sir John Burgoyne* (1782–1871), the Crimean general, by Boehm. The British Crafts Centre has a Gallery at No. 12 Waterloo Place.

At the s. end of Waterloo Place rises the DUKE OF YORK'S COLUMN in Tuscan granite, 124 ft high, designed by Benj. Wyatt and erected in 1834. It bears a bronze statue, by Westmacott, of the Duke of York (d. 1827), second son of Geórge III, and Commander-in-Chief of the British Army in 1795–1827. Every officer and soldier in the Army contributed a day's pay to provide funds for the monument to 'the soldier's friend'. Beyond the column the *Waterloo* or *Duke of York's Steps*, with a fine view towards Westminster descend to the Mall (see p. 90). *Carlton House Terrace*, once one of the most aristocratic places of residence in London, overlooks the Mall.

Carlton House, which stood on the site of Waterloo Place and the York Column, was built in 1709. George IV, when Prince of Wales, set up his establishment here in 1783, and here celebrated the news of his accession. Nash laid out Regent St. to connect the house with Regent's Park to the N., but it was demolished in 1829. On the left of Waterloo Steps, No. 10 houses the *Commonwealth Secretariat*. No. 11, built in 1831, was occupied by Gladstone in 1857–75; it is now the headquarters of the *Foreign Press Association*. In Nash House are the offices of the *Association of Societies of Art and Design* (including the I.C.A.; entered from the Mall, see p. 90). Beyond the *Crown Estates Office* (No. 13), is *Crockford's* (No. 16), founded in 1827 (comp. p. 100), London's most famous gambling club recently reopened after the loss of its licence in 1970. The British Council building occupies the site of Carlton Mews and Spring Gardens, formed in the reign of Elizabeth I.

Under a tree on the right of the York Column, the tomb stone of an ambassador's terrier recalls the Prussian and later German Embassy at No. 9, from 1849 until 1939. *The Royal Society*, one of the most famous scientific bodies in the world, now occupies Nos. 6–9 (entrance at No. 6). It originated in a coterie of savants who began to meet informally in London or in Oxford in 1645. Its formal foundation dates from 1660 and its royal charter of incorporation from 1662. It now numbers about 760 fellows (F.R.S.), with about 70 foreign members. The rooms contain many busts and portraits of distinguished Fellows, and also some interesting relics; Newton's telescope, watch, and sundial; MS. of the Principia; original model of Davy's safety lamp, etc.

Beyond the Turf Club (No. 5; formerly the residence of Lady Cunard), Nos. 3 and 4 are being renovated as a conference centre. No. 2 (*The Royal College of Pathologists*) was occupied in 1906–25 by Lord Curzon, a statue of whom stands opposite. The attractive s. façades of clubs in Pall Mall are well seen across the gardens. In 1807 F. Albrecht Winzler erected 13 gas lamp-posts outside his house here, the earliest use of gas for lighting in London. By 1820 the whole parish of St James's was lit by gas; the area retains some of the oldest and most closely spaced lamp-posts in the city (temp. George IV).

Farther w. in *Carlton Gardens*, Lord Palmerston and Lord Balfour lived at No. 4 (rebuilt in 1933 by Sir Reginald Blomfield), where a tablet marks this as General de Gaulle's Free French headquarters from 18 June 1940. An attractive small square opens behind a statue of George VI (comp. p. 90), and stairs descend to the Mall. No. 3 was designed by Decimus Burton. Lord Kitchener lived at No. 2 (now the Royal Fine Art Commission) in 1914–15. No. 1 was occupied by Napoleon III (1840–41) and Lord Northcliffe (1920–22); it is now the Foreign Secretary's official residence. The well-proportioned Wool House (1967, by David Hodges) stands on the site of Nos. 5 and 6.

The Athenaeum is adjoined by the *Travellers' Club*, founded in 1819, and occupying a fine building (1829–32), in an Italian Renaissance style, the masterpiece of Barry. It draws many of its members from the Foreign Office. Next door is the imposing *Reform Club*, founded by Radicals and Whigs after the passage of the Reform Bill. It was established here in 1836 in a building also by Barry but on a larger scale, on the site of a house which contained the National Gallery from 1824 until 1834. Noted for its cuisine since the days of the chef Alexis Soyer (1837–50) who assisted in planning the kitchens, it numbers many senior civil servants among its membership. The *Royal Automobile Club*, founded in 1897, with an Egyptian swimming pool and squash courts, has a long façade of 1911. Opposite, the *Junior Carlton Club* (1966, by Norman Royce), was established in 1864 to accommodate the 'waiting list' for the Carlton Club. Benjamin Disraeli held political meetings here in 1868–74 round a circular table still owned by the club. To the w. is the new building (1963) of the *Army and Navy Club*, familiarly known as 'The Rag', a contraction for 'rag and famish', a phrase used by a dissatisfied member in 1839 to characterize his entertainment.

Behind the Junior Carlton Club lies **St James's Square** (Pl. 14; 6), laid out by Lord St Albans (who lived on the site of Chatham House in 1675–82). Nearly all the houses have since been several times rebuilt, and offices and clubs have displaced the former fashionable residences. In the garden of flowering trees in the centre are an equestrian statue of William III, by John Bacon, the Younger (1808), based on designs by his father, and a seat designed by John Nash (1822).

Norfolk House (No. 31; rebuilt in 1939), was owned by the dukes of Norfolk from 1722 until 1937. Frederick, Prince of Wales leased the property in 1737–41, and George III was born here. It was General Eisenhower's Allied Force headquarters in 1942 and again in 1944 (tablet). No. 32 was from 1771 till 1919 the town residence of the bishops of London. Across Charles II St. (with a good view of the Haymarket Theatre, p. 95), No. 4 (rebuilt by Hawksmoor in 1726–28, with an attractive garden behind), is occupied by a Crown Court. From 1912 until 1942 this was the residence of Lord and Lady (Nancy) Astor, and in 1943–45 it was the London headquarters of the Free French forces; later it was the home of the Arts Council. No. 7 has an entrance porch rebuilt by Lutyens in 1911. On this site was the showroom of Josiah Wedgwood from 1796 until 1830. No. 10, *Chatham House, The Royal Institute of International Affairs*, has been occupied by three prime ministers: Chatham (1759–62), Lord Derby (1837–54), and Gladstone (1890). Cast iron railings and lamp-holders adorn the entrance.

Beyond a façade by Robert Adam at No. 11, the *London Library*, founded in 1841 by Thomas Carlyle, occupies No. 14. One of the largest private subscription libraries in Britain (c. 167,000 vols.), it has served Dickens, Thackeray, George Eliot, T. S. Eliot, and E. M. Forster. No. 15 has a fine classical façade by James Stuart (1764); a house on this site was tenanted by the Duchess of Richmond ('La Belle Stuart') in 1678–79. The *East India and Sports Club* has absorbed Nos. 16 and 17. Queen Caroline lived at No. 17 during her trial in 1820, while Lord Castlereagh, then foreign secretary, lived next door (No. 18). No. 20 is a fine Robert Adam building (1771–74; the magnificent interior may be seen on written application to the Secretary, Winchester House Property Company). The steps and carving on the door can be enjoyed from the pavement. No. 21 which skilfully duplicates the façade of No. 20, was added in 1934–37, on the site of Winchester House.

Duke of York Street leads N. from the square past the Red Lion, with a characteristic Victorian 'Gin Palace' interior. Across Jermyn St., is **St James's Church** (Pl. 14; 3), a fine building by Wren (1676–84; rebuilt after damage in the 'blitz' of 1940–41) on a spacious site. Keystones bear the arms of Lord St Albans (see above). This was the most fashionable church in London in the early 18C, and three of its rectors became archbishops of Canterbury. The s. entrance gate and railings date from c. 1800.

The sumptuous INTERIOR has galleries supported by elegant columns, and an ingeniously designed roof. The limewood altarpiece is a magnificent work by Grinling Gibbons. The marble font, at which Lord Chatham and William Blake were baptized, is attributed to Gibbons. The organ, from a chapel in Whitehall Palace, was presented to the church by Queen Mary in 1690 when John Blow and Henry Purcell supervised its installation. It was built by Renatus Harris and the splendid case is again the work of Gibbons. William Van der Velde the Elder (c. 1610–93) and William Van der Velde the Younger (1633–1707), the marine painters, are buried here (plaque beneath the tower). The courtyard towards Piccadilly commemorates Londoners of 1939–45; the gates were designed by Sir Reginald Blomfield (1937). A neo-Georgian rectory was built by Austin Blomfield (1955–57). The pleasant open garden with a fountain by A. Hardiman is a memorial to Lord Southwood (1873–1946), journalist and newspaper owner.

JERMYN STREET, one of the first streets to be built in the area, bears the St Albans family name. Among fashionable shops here is a specialist cheesemonger (No. 93), survivor of many in the 18C, and a perfumier (No. 89). On the corner of Duke St. St James's, the Cavendish Hotel recalls its predecessor managed by the formidable Rosa Lewis, an establishment featured in the novels of Evelyn Waugh. The façade incorporates a jeweller's where security has been achieved with modern decorative skill. In the same street Benjamin Franklin lodged in 1725 as a journeyman printer.

On the s. side of Pall Mall Gainsborough lived from 1774 till his death in 1788 in the w. wing (No. 80) of *Schomberg House*, a 17C building of red brick with stone dressings (restored in 1956, when the rest of the house was rebuilt). No. 79 (rebuilt) was given to Nell Gwynn by Charles II, with whom, according to Evelyn, she used to talk over the garden wall. The cellars of the original house survive beneath the pavement. Opposite, Nos. 48–49 are the headquarters of the *Royal British Legion*, concerned with the welfare of ex-servicemen. At No. 71 the *United Oxford and Cambridge Clubs* occupy a building (being extended) by Sir Robert and Sidney Smirke (1830). At the end of Pall Mall is the entrance to **Marlborough House** (p. 90). CLEVELAND ROW continues w. past **St James's Palace** (see Rte 6) to Green Park.

Three mansions (now offices) overlook the park. The Reform Bill of 1832 was drafted in *Stornoway House* (1794–96; rebuilt in 1959), which became the residence of Lord Beaverbrook in 1924 and housed his Ministry of Aircraft Production in 1940–41. Beyond the delightful bow-front of *Selwyn House* (1895), the Italianate *Bridgewater House* (1841–49) with an elaborate two-storied hall by Barry, occupies the site of a house presented by Charles II to Barbara Villiers, duchess of Cleveland, who lived here in 1668–77.—Access to Green Park may be gained from Stable Yard (p. 91), or farther N. off St James's Place (comp. below).

St James's Street (Pl. 14; 5) ascends to Piccadilly. *Byron House* occupies the site of No. 8 where, in 1811 after the publication of the 3rd Canto of 'Childe Harold', Lord Byron "awoke one morning to find himself famous". Berry Bros. & Rudd Ltd. have traded at No. 3 since

1699; the shop-front retains a late-18C design. A passage at the side admits to the secluded *Pickering Place* (c. 1733); a plaque records that a legation from the Republic of Texas was set up here in 1842–45. Beyond, *Lock & Co. Ltd.*, hatters, were established here in 1759, with a delightful shop front dating, in part, from the previous century.

The shop window usually displays period headgear, including an original 'bowler' hat. This was designed for the Earl of Leicester's 'beaters'; the order was sub-contracted to Thomas Bowler & Co., who produced what later became, in a modified form, the fashionable London hat. Nelson's hat (on his wax effigy in Westminster Abbey, see p. 63) was made here.

On the opposite side of St James's the *Constitutional Club* (No. 86; with elaborate carving) now shares its premises with the *Savage Club*. The *Carlton Club* (No. 69) was founded by the Duke of Wellington after the defeat of the Tories in 1831 and with the Marquess of Salisbury as its chairman was used as a centre for the Tory party organization; it remains the leading Conservative Club. Beyond the lock and safe makers, Chubb, who patented a Detector Lock in 1818, the attractive *St James's Place* diverges left.

At No. 2 Edward Gibbon lodged in 1766. *Arthur's Club* founded in 1811 as the first members' (rather than proprietary) club in the area was established at Nos. 40–45; the building of 1826–27 is by Thomas Hopper. At the end the incomplete N. front of *Spencer House* by Vardy (1756–65; fine façade on Green Park, see below) faces a block of flats (1960) by Denys Lasdun. At No. 28 lived William Huskisson (plaque). On the site of Castlemaine House, Samuel Rogers, the wealthy banker-poet lived from 1802 till his death in 1855, entertaining at his famous breakfasts the most eminent literary men of his day.—A concealed narrow passage leads alongside No. 23 to Green Park. Here the attractive façades and gardens of the mansions skirting Queen's Walk are well seen. Among them is the striking Palladian front of Spencer House with graceful statues on the pediment, and a paved terrace raised on arches extending in to the garden.

In KING STREET, across St James's St., pre-eminent among the art dealers and galleries in the area, is *Christie's* (No. 8), fine art auctioneers since 1766 (in King St. since 1823). Sales (except in Aug and Sept) are held at 10.30 or 11; Porcelain on Mon, Silver on Wed, Furniture on Thurs, Pictures on Fri, etc. Viewing (usually for 1 week before the sale) takes place daily 9.30–5. Almack House at No. 26 recalls Almack's Rooms opened here c. 1759–62; admission to the exclusive assemblies and balls held here conferred the cachet of fashion. The *St James's Theatre*, now demolished, saw the first performances of 'Lady Windermere's Fan' (1892) and 'The Importance of being Ernest' (1895). *Duke Street*, the first street in London to have a pavement, runs N. from King St. to Piccadilly. In the parallel *Bury Street*, Haydn lodged at No. 1 in 1794–95, and Thos. Moore at No. 28. The 17C *Crown Passage*, linking King St. with Pall Mall, retains an unexpected 'village' atmosphere.

We continue up St James's St. past the raised white plaza of the *Economist building* (1964; by Peter and Alison Smithson). The offices on arcades varying in height, form a striking group, and art galleries use the light ground floor premises. In *Blue Ball Yard*, opposite, attractive black and white stables survive from 1741–42. In Park Place No. 14 houses *Pratt's Club*, founded here c. 1841, and the offices and club of the Royal Overseas League. *Brooks's* (No. 60), a club founded in 1764, met in Almack's former tavern (see above) until its removal here in 1778. One of the earliest members was Charles James Fox who gambled on the faro table in the fine room overlooking St James's St. It was the leading Whig club in the 18C and the rival of the Tory White's (see below). Other members included Burke, Gibbon, Hume, Garrick, Reynolds, and Palmerston. Opposite is *Boodle's* (No. 28), founded 1762–64, also patronized by Gibbon and Fox. The building, designed by John Crunden in the Adam manner in 1775–76, has been the home of the club since 1783. *White's*, the oldest club (1736) in London, which originated in White's Chocolate House (1693), was frequented by Swift, Steele, Gray, and Pope. The building, probably designed by James Wyatt (1787–88), contains a famous bow window (1811) made the 'shrine of fashion' by Beau Brummell and his set. The proprietary clubs Brooks's, Boodle's, and White's were all distinguished in the 18C for fashion and gambling. Opposite is the *Devonshire Club* (No. 50), where Crockford's (comp. p. 96)¹ was opened in 1827 by a successful fish salesman. In Arlington St. Robert Walpole lived at No. 5 in 1742–45, and Horace Walpole was born on the site of No. 22. St James's St. ends at the busy thoroughfare of **Piccadilly** (Rte 8).

8 PICCADILLY

STATIONS: *Piccadilly Circus* on the Bakerloo and Piccadilly lines; *Green Park* on Piccadilly and Victoria lines; *Hyde Park Corner* on the Piccadilly line.—BUSES, Nos. 9, 14, 19, 22, 25, 38, etc.—CAR PARKING see Rtes 7 and 9.

Piccadilly Circus (Pl. 14; 4), an irregularly shaped 'circus' at the junction of some half-dozen important streets, smart to the w. but increasingly tawdry to the E., is one of the best known centres of traffic in the West End. Various grandiose schemes have been mooted for its 'improvement'; at present undistinguished buildings covered with illuminated advertisements ring the confined space in the centre, generally a haunt of idlers. Crowds throng the area in the evening when the theatres and restaurants open. The scene is given character by its focal point, the *Shaftesbury Memorial*, by Alfred Gilbert, an elaborately sculpted bronze fountain surmounted by a winged figure of an archer with his bow, symbolizing the Angel of Christian Charity, but popularly known as 'Eros'. As a memorial to the philanthropic Earl of Shaftesbury (d. 1885), it was unveiled in 1893. Below the circus is the well-designed circular Underground Station.

For the visitor to London Piccadilly Circus is a convenient starting-place for exploring the West End. Coventry St. runs thence to the E. to Leicester Square; the broad Shaftesbury Avenue, with its numerous theatres, leads N.E. through Soho to High Holborn and New Oxford St.; Regent St., interrupted by the Circus, leads N. to Oxford St. and Regent's Park and s. to Waterloo Place and Pall Mall; while Piccadilly runs s.w. to Hyde Park.

Piccadilly (Pl. 14; 4) runs from the top of Haymarket to Hyde Park Corner (c. 1 mile). Beyond Piccadilly Circus its initial section, to the s. of which is the region of St James's, is occupied by airline offices, banks, hotels, and some distinguished shops.

The name of Piccadilly is probably derived from 'Piccadilly Hall', the popular name of a house built c. 1611 near Windmill Street by a retired tailor, Robert Baker, who had made much of his fortune by the sale of 'piccadillies', apparently a form of collar or ruff. The street was thus named by 1627–28 when building began at the E. end, and the name gradually extended westwards as building progressed along the old 'Way to Reading'.

On the N. side of Piccadilly, beyond the Circus, is the large *Piccadilly Hotel*, with a bold colonnade on the upper storey. Opposite, Simpson's was built in 1935–36 by Joseph Emberton. Beyond is the forecourt of *St James's Church*, described in Rte 7. The attractive bank (1925) adjoining the garden was designed by Edwin Lutyens. To the w. the vast plate-glass window of an airline office intrudes into the lower story of the former home of the Royal Institute of Painters in Water Colours. The inscription and roundels remain on the façade above; the busts are of Sandby, Cozens, Girtin, Turner, D. Cox, De Wint, Barret, and W. Hunt. At No. 187 *Hatchards* (opened here in 1801) is the sole survivor of the booksellers established in the area at the end of the 18C. *Fortnum and Mason*, a luxurious department store where the assistants in the grocery department wear frock coats, was founded by Charles Fortnum, a footman in the household of George III, in c. 1770. A mechanical clock (1964; by Thwaites and Reed) crowns the entrance. Beyond, the *Piccadilly Arcade* (1909–10) has tall glass shop-fronts. On the N. side of Piccadilly a secluded courtyard admits to ALBANY with suites of private chambers.

The house, designed by Sir William Chambers for Lord Melbourne in 1771–74 was the birthplace of the 2nd Viscount and future Prime Minister in 1779. Frederick, Duke of York and Albany took possession in 1791 in exchange for his own house in Whitehall (Dover House, see p. 71). Albany was converted to its present use in 1803, when Henry Holland added two rows of chambers flanking a covered passage which runs N. to Burlington Gardens. Among the occupants of these exclusive apartments have been Lord Byron (1814–15), Bulwer Lytton, Macaulay (1840–56), 'Monk' Lewis, Canning, and Gladstone, in addition to the heroes of many fashionable novels.

Beyond is the imposing **Burlington House** (Pl. 14; 3) the home of the Royal Academy. Three lofty archways of a façade in a somewhat heavy Italianate style admit to a quadrangle built for various learned societies in 1869–73 by R. R. Banks and Charles Barry. In the centre is a fine statue of Joshua Reynolds by Alfred Drury (1931). On the N. side stands *Old Burlington House*. Its façade of 1719 was remodelled by Sidney Smirke in 1872–74 when the top story was added with statues of Pheidias, Leonardo, Flaxman, Raphael, Michelangelo, Titian, Reynolds, Wren, and William of Wykeham. The large block of exhibition galleries behind were added at the same time.

Burlington House, originally built in 1665, enjoyed its chief celebrity and splendour under the art-loving third earl of Burlington (1695–1753), patron of Pope, Gay, and Arbuthnot; he redesigned the house with the aid of James Gibbs, Colen Campbell, and Kent.

Old Burlington House is now occupied by the **Royal Academy of Arts** (Pl. 14; 3), which here maintains its free School of Art. The annual *Summer Exhibition* shows contemporary works of painting, sculpture, architecture, and engraving which have not previously been exhibited. The private view of the Exhibition and the Academy Soirée, admission to both of which is by invitation, are highly fashionable functions; and still more exclusive is the Academy Dinner, held on the Wed before the opening of the Exhibition. In winter special exhibitions of great interest are held.

ADMISSION to the Summer Exhibition, and most other exhibitions: daily 10–6; fee. An annual season ticket may be purchased. A licensed RESTAURANT is open during the exhibitions.
From the entrance hall with ceiling paintings by *Angelica Kauffmann* and *Benj. West*, the main staircase decorated with the works of *Seb. Ricci* (Diana and her Nymphs, and Triumph of Galatea) ascends to the galleries used for the Summer Exhibition. The winter and special exhibitions in the fine Diploma Gallery and adjoining rooms, are usually approached by lift (r.). The permanent collections (not usually on view; shown sometimes on request) consist mainly of diploma works presented by Academicians elected since 1770, an interesting illustration of

British art. Also good examples of the work of the original members of the Academy, including: *Reynolds* (Self-portrait), *Gainsborough*, and *Richard Wilson*; and 15 landscape studies and Dedham Lock, or the Leaping Horse, by *Constable*. The few notable earlier foreign works include the exquisite tondo in low-relief by *Michelangelo* known as the 'Madonna Taddei' (c. 1505), and a full-size copy of Leonardo da Vinci's Last Supper, at Milan, by his pupil *Marco d'Oggiono*.—The Sitters' Chair, preserved here, originally belonged to Sir Joshua Reynolds.

The ROYAL ACADEMY OF ARTS, founded in 1768, with Sir Joshua Reynolds as its first president, had its abode first in Pall Mall, afterwards at Somerset House (1780–1838), and then at the National Gallery (1838–69). It consists of 40 Academicians (R.A.) and 30 Associates (A.R.A.), and vacancies in the list are filled up by vote of the whole body of members. The distinguished honorary members included Sir Winston Churchill. The fine arts *Library* is open to scholars.

Burlington House accommodates various learned societies: in the E. wing, the British Academy, the Chemical Society, and the Geological Society; in the w. wing, the Society of Antiquaries, and the Royal Astronomical Society. Visitors are admitted by Fellow's introduction only.

The BRITISH ACADEMY was founded on the initiative of the Royal Society in 1902 for the promotion of 'Historical, Philisophical, and Philological Studies'. Among its many activities, it gives support to British Schools and Institutes abroad.—The CHEMICAL SOCIETY, founded in 1841, possesses one of the finest chemical libraries in the world.—The GEOLOGICAL SOCIETY was founded in 1807 (and incorporated in 1825) for the purpose of 'investigating the Mineral Structure of the Earth'.

The SOCIETY OF ANTIQUARIES OF LONDON, founded c. 1586, but not formally reconstituted until 1717, holds a charter of 1751. From 1781 to 1874 it occupied quarters in Somerset House. The rooms contain interesting paintings, MSS., etc., and a fine archaeological library.—The ROYAL ASTRONOMICAL SOCIETY was founded in 1820.—The LINNEAN SOCIETY was founded in 1788 for "the cultivation of the Science of Natural History in all its branches". The Society possesses the collections of Carl Linnaeus (1707–78), the Swedish botanist who created the system of scientific nomenclature for plants and animals. Sir Joseph Banks, Sir Joseph Hooker, and Thos. Huxley have all been associated with the society, and it was here in 1858 that Charles Darwin and Alfred Russel Wallace read their first joint paper on evolution by natural selection.

The long *Burlington Arcade* (1818 by Sam. Ware; s. façade of 1931; N. end rebuilt 1952–54), a covered passage lined on both sides with fashionable shops, provides an "undulation conducive to the leisurely and agreeable spending of money". Near its N. end, at No. 6 Burlington Gardens, is the Italianate building originally erected in 1866–67 by Pennethorne for London University. The Civil Service Examinations were later held here, and it now houses the *Ethnographic Department of the British Museum* (adm. 10–5, Sun 2.30–6; closed BH.), renamed in 1972 the MUSEUM OF MANKIND. *Exhibitions are changed approximately every year and the collection illustrating the tribal and village cultures of the world is particularly strong in material from W. Africa, Oceania, and America. The Department issues informative handbooks and guides in conjunction with exhibitions.

At the E. end of Burlington Gardens is SAVILE ROW, a street synonymous with fashionable tailoring since the 1850s (neighbouring Cork Street was already famous for its tailors in the previous century). Sheridan lived at No. 14 (tablet) and died in 1816 in the front bedroom of No. 17 (where George Basevi lived in 1794–1845). The *British Association for the Advancement of Science*, at Fortress House, stimulates public interest in science and technology and their relation to social problems and promotes the advancement of science to the benefit of the community. An Annual Meeting is held in a different centre each year.

We may return to Piccadilly viâ **Bond Street** (Pl. 14; 3), the s. portion of which is *Old Bond Street*, while the N. portion, running to Oxford St., is known as *New Bond Street*. It was laid out by Sir Thomas Bond in 1686, and, forming the E. boundary of Mayfair, is renowned for its fashionable shops and picture-dealers' galleries. The fine art auctioneers, *Sotheby's* (No. 35), were founded in 1744 and went into partnership with the Parke-Bernet Galleries of New York in 1964. Sales (except in Aug and Sept) are usually held at 11 a.m.: books on Mon, porcelain on Tues, pictures on Wed, silver and jewellery on Thurs, furniture on Fri, etc. Viewing (usually for 1 week before) takes place daily 9–4.30. At the corner of Bruton St. is the Time-Life Building, with a sculpted screen by Henry Moore (1953).

Among noted residents of Old Bond St. have been Sterne (No. 41), Sir Thos. Lawrence (Nos. 24 and 29), and Boswell. In New Bond St. lived Dean Swift, Nelson (at No. 147), and Lady Hamilton (at No. 150).

Albemarle Street, leading (r.) from Piccadilly, occupies the site of Clarendon House, sold after 1664 to George Monk, duke of Albemarle, and pulled down about 1683. Behind a long façade of Corinthian columns at the N. end of the street lies the *Royal Institution of Great Britain*, a society founded in 1799 for the diffusion of scientific knowledge, on the initiative of the cosmopolitan Sir Benjamin Thompson (1753–1814; Count Rumford of Munich), born in Massachusetts.

Here Campbell's lectures on Poetry were delivered in 1812 and Carlyle's on Heroes in 1840. Amongst the most popular of its lectures are those for children in the Christmas holidays. The Davy-Faraday Research Laboratory here commemorates two illustrious chemists closely connected with the work of the Royal Institution.—Opposite Brown's Hotel, founded by Lord Byron's butler, is a Georgian house (No. 7), where the *National Book League* maintains its headquarters with a children's reference library. Here are held periodical exhibitions of books, printing, etc.—In *Grafton Street*, at the end of Albemarle St., Lord Brougham lived at No. 4 and Sir Henry Irving at No. 15A (tablet).

Across Piccadilly St James's St. descends to St James's Palace (comp. Rte 7).—In *Dover Street*, the next street on the N., *Ely House* (No. 37) a fine mansion built in 1772 by Sir Robert Taylor, was the town house of the Bishops of Ely until 1909. No. 40 (restored) is the *Arts Club*. On the S. side of Piccadilly rises the large *Ritz Hotel* with an arcade over the pavement; the Portland stone exterior clothes one of the first steel-framed buildings (1904–06) in London. Its name inspired an American epithet for luxurious living. Opposite, between Berkeley St. and Stratton St., a palatial block of shops and offices occupies the site of the ducal Devonshire House, one of the great Whig mansions (pulled down in 1924). The principal gateway, designed by Inigo Jones, was moved farther W. to the N. entrance of the Broad Walk in Green Park.

Berkeley Street, with the head office of Thos. Cook & Son, leads N. to Berkeley Square (Rte 9). Beyond Stratton Street the next three side-streets lead from Piccadilly to Curzon St., Mayfair (p. 105). In *Bolton Street* Henry James lived at No. 3 in 1875–86. On the corner of Piccadilly the ground floor of an office building is used for exhibitions.—*Clarges Street* was the residence of C. J. Fox (No. 46), Lord Macaulay (No. 3; on the site of the Kennel Club), Edmund Kean (No. 12), and Lady Hamilton (No. 11), the last three houses demolished.—At the end of *Half Moon Street*, where Boswell, Hazlitt, and Shelley lived, a Christian Science church (p. 106) closes the vista.

Farther on, clubs and luxurious hotels overlook Green Park which borders Piccadilly on the S. The *Naval and Military Club*, at No. 94, known also as the 'In-and-Out' from the instructions on the gate-posts,

occupies an 18C building (damaged in the War) where Lord Palmerston
lived from 1855 till his death in 1865. Beyond the *American Club*
(No. 95), White Horse Street diverges right for Shepherd Market
(p. 106). No. 105 Piccadilly is now the home of *The Arts Council*. Next
door is the *St James's Club*, a diplomatic club, in a mansion designed by
Kent. Beyond Down St., at No. 107, Blücher found a temporary home
in 1804. Opposite the *Cavalry Club* (No. 127), is a 'Porters' Rest' (1861),
an unassuming relic of the past. No. 138 was the house of the notorious
Duke of Queensberry (d. 1810), the 'Star of Piccadilly', familiarly
known as 'Old Q'. The last house in Piccadilly ('No. 1, London')
overlooking Hyde Park Corner, and now isolated by traffic, is **Apsley
House** (Pl. 13; 6), the residence of the Duke of Wellington. Acquired by the
nation in 1947, and opened in 1952 as a *Wellington Museum* (adm. 10–6,
Sun 2.30–6; free; closed Fri), it contains relics and works of art acquired by
the Iron Duke.

Built of red brick between 1771 and 1778 by Robert Adam, for the second Earl
Bathurst (Baron Apsley), this house was bought in 1805 by Marquess Wellesley
and sold by him in 1817 to his younger brother, Arthur, the famous Duke of
Wellington. In 1828–29 the mansion was faced with stone by Wyatt, who added
the Corinthian portico and the Waterloo Gallery, in which the Waterloo Banquet
was annually held until the Duke's death in 1852. The iron shutters put up in 1832
during the Reform agitation, when the windows were broken by the mob, were
removed in 1856.

In the ENTRANCE HALL are two appropriate paintings: *Turner*, Tapping the
Furnace; *Landseer*, A Dialogue at Waterloo. Marble busts of Wellington and his
contemporaries by *Nollekens* and *Chantrey* are exhibited here and in various rooms
in the house. The GROUND FLOOR rooms contain the Duke's orders and decorations and many personal relics. In the PLATE AND CHINA ROOM (l.) is part of the
Prussian Service (1816?–19) presented by Frederick William III of Prussia.—The
STAIRCASE VESTIBULE is filled with a colossal statue of Napoleon by *Canova* (1810).
On the first floor landing is the 'Mattei' Bust of Cicero (1C B.C.; the only bust of the
orator bearing an antique inscription). We turn left into the PICCADILLY DRAWING
ROOM, which, with the adjoining Portico Room, retains its Adam decoration. The
paintings here include: *Correggio*, Agony in the Garden; three works by *Jan
Brueghel the Elder*; and a seascape by *Willem van der Velde the Younger*.—In the
PORTICO ROOM are works by *David Teniers the Younger*; *Pieter de Hooch* (A
Musical Party); *Claude Joseph Vernet*; *Jan Steen* (The Dissolute Household, The
Egg Dance); and *Giov. P. Pannini* (St Paul at Athens).

The long WATERLOO GALLERY contains the ornate Portuguese Service, given to
the Duke in 1816 by the Prince Regent of Portugal (the centrepiece is on the
original banquet table). Many of the paintings here were captured after the battle
of Vitoria (1813) from Joseph Bonaparte, by whom they had been taken from the
Spanish royal collections; they were afterwards bestowed on the Duke by
Ferdinand VII. They include works by *Murillo* (portrait of an Unknown Man),
P. Wouwerman, *Ribera* (Santiago), *Claude Lorraine*. *School of Bernardino Luini*,
The Holy Family; *School of Rubens*, Hercules wrestling with Achelous in the form
of a Bull; *Cav. d'Arpino*, The Marriage of St Catherine, Expulsion from Paradise;
Goya, Equestrian portrait of Wellington; *Rubens*, Head of an Old Man; *Sasso-
ferrato*, The Holy Family.—In the YELLOW DRAWING ROOM are *Paintings by
Velazquez (The Water-seller of Seville, Spanish Gentleman, Two Young Men
eating at a Humble Table). Also *Rubens*, Portrait of a Nun; *Murillo*, Isaac blessing
Jacob; *Wouwerman*, Return from the Chase, Departure of a hawking party.—The
STRIPED DRAWING ROOM has several portraits by *Sir Thomas Lawrence*, including
one of Wellington. Part of the Saxon and Austrian services are displayed in cases.
The DINING ROOM contains Sèvres porcelain.

9 PARK LANE AND MAYFAIR

STATIONS: *Hyde Park Corner* on Piccadilly line; *Green Park* on Victoria and Piccadilly lines; *Bond Street* and *Marble Arch* on Central line. — BUSES in Piccadilly, see Rte 8; in Oxford St., see Rte 15; in Park Lane, Nos. 2, 16, 30, 36, 73, 74, and 137. — CAR PARKING: Hyde Park Underground Car Park, Carrington St., Charles St.

Sydney Smith once asserted that the parallelogram between Oxford St., Piccadilly, Regent St., and Hyde Park "enclosed more intelligence and ability, to say nothing of wealth and beauty, than the world had ever collected into such a space before". The region thus defined practically coincides with the district known as **Mayfair,** though Bond St., rather than Regent St., may now be regarded as its E. limit. It derives its name from a fair held annually in May from a very early period down to the reign of George III.

The area retains an exclusive and opulent air with some quiet residential streets of Georgian houses and broad mews. Unexpected pockets of less grand houses, often in individual architectural styles, may still be found (in Shepherd Market, Mount Row, Waverton St., Bruton Place, Pitts Head Mews, Farm St., etc.). The huge luxurious hotels (mostly on Park Lane) are among the most fashionable in London.

Park Lane (Pl. 13; 4) runs N. from near the W. end of Piccadilly to the Marble Arch. It is bordered on the W. side by Hyde Park, while on the E., the names of blocks of residential flats and large hotels recall the luxurious dwellings which made this area a centre of fashion and wealth.

From Hyde Park Corner we may avoid the initial noisy section of Park Lane by taking the parallel *Hamilton Place* or *Old Park Lane* which skirt the Inn on the Park and converge at the towering Hilton Hotel (1961–63). The houses to the S. of No. 4 Hamilton Place (Royal Aeronautical Society; occupied by the Duke of Wellington, 1814–15) were demolished for a new hotel in 1972. The premises to the N. are now clubhouses. At No. 17 Old Park Lane are the headquarters of the *Women's Royal Voluntary Service.* In *Hertford Street* (r.) Gen. John Burgoyne lived and died (1722–92) at No. 10, occupied by Sheridan in 1795–1802. No. 20 was the residence of Sir George Cayley (1773–1857), 'inventor of the aeroplane'. At No. 14 (destroyed), Edward Jenner, the champion of vaccination, made an unsuccessful attempt to establish a practice in London. In Down St. (r.) *Christ Church* dates from 1865–68.

Farther along Park Lane, Curzon St. diverges right. Park Lane continues N. past the Dorchester and Grosvenor House Hotels. Benjamin Disraeli resided at No. 93 Park Lane from his marriage in 1839 until the death of his wife (to whom the house belonged) in 1872. The charming row of bow-fronted houses with 'Chinese' balconies (Nos. 93–99) survive from the 19C.

CURZON STREET (Pl. 13; 4) with some fine houses (a few now owned by clubs) runs E. from Park Lane through Mayfair. At No. 19 Disraeli died in 1881. *Worcester House* (No. 30) contains the showrooms of the Worcester Royal Porcelain Company (adm. 9–5; closed 12.45–1.45), in a beautiful Adam house (1771). At No. 32 Lord Reading died in 1935. The *Curzon Cinema* (1933) is almost opposite *Crewe House* (now the offices of an industrial holding company), a stucco mansion set back from the road, by Ed. Shepherd (c. 1730; altered 1813). Two archways lead s. from Curzon St. beyond Trebeck St. to *Shepherd Market*, established by Ed. Shepherd, with its residential 'village' atmosphere. At the end of Half Moon St. is the large portico of the *Third Church of Christ Scientist* (1910). We now follow Queen Street, Mayfair, where lived Harriette Wilson, the courtesan whose threats prompted Wellington's famous 'Publish and be damned', and come to CHARLES STREET. Beyond its narrow w. end, is a curious house with a timbered upper story, thought to have been built by John Phillips, a carpenter who worked for Lord Berkeley in this area c. 1750. No. 16 formerly the *Guards' Club*, and to the E., the *Chesterfield Hotel* have good 18C features. The area to the N. remains quietly residential. At the E. end of Charles St. lies **Berkeley Square** (Pl. 13; 4), formerly one of the most aristocratic of London squares, built c. 1739 on part of the gardens of Berkeley House. The beautiful plane trees in the open garden in the centre (planted c. 1789) dwarf the Pump House (c. 1800) and a statue by A. Munro (1867). Rebuilding in the 20C has practically destroyed its elegant character.

In the s.w. angle of the square the *Lansdowne Club* incorporates part of a house begun in 1762 by Robert Adam, and sold in 1768, before it was finished, to the Earl of Shelburne, the prime minister who conceded the independence of the United States and was created Marquess of Lansdowne in 1784. The few remaining houses of interest in the square are situated on its w. side. No. 50 is the so-called 'haunted house'. Winston Churchill lived as a child at No. 48, and at No. 47 William Pitt resided for a time with his brother, the Earl of Chatham. No. 45 was the scene of the suicide of Lord Clive in 1774, and here Lady Dorothy Nevill received Gladstone and Disraeli and the celebrities of their day. No. 44 (now the Claremont Club, a fashionable gambling den) was designed by Kent and possesses a beautiful interior staircase.

From the N.w. angle of the square Mount St. returns due w. to Park Lane. We, however, follow Carlos St., which bears r. past the *Connaught Hotel* to reach **Grosvenor Square** (Pl. 13; 2) laid out in 1725 by Sir Richard Grosvenor on the site of Oliver's Mount, an earthwork hastily thrown up by the citizens in 1643, when Charles I was approaching London after the battle of Edgehill. It is dominated on the w. side by the *American Embassy* (1957–58) by Eero Saarinen. A memorial in the open 6-acre garden to Franklin Roosevelt, President of the United States in 1932–44, includes a statue by Reid Dick (1948). The monumental terraces which now surround the square to house the diplomatic and other offices of the United States as well as two hotels, have conformed to a uniform style.

At the building in the N.E. corner of the square (No. 9) John Adams, American ambassador and later President, lived in 1785. No. 6 was the residence of W. H. Page while American ambassador in London (1913–18). No. 1 is the Sir John A. Macdonald building of Canadian offices. No. 20 (N. side) was the headquarters of General Eisenhower in 1942 and 1944.

North Audley Street leads out of the N.w. corner of the square. Here Lord Ligonier lived in 1730–70 (No. 12). Beyond is the American church of *St Mark's* (1825–28) by J. P. Gundy with a severe Greek classical porch and vestibule. The dark interior was remodelled by Blomfield in 1878. Sydney Smith died at No. 59 Green St., opposite the church.

In Brook St. (where Handel lived at No. 25), and Grosvenor St., leading E. to Bond St., are several clubs.

South Audley Street leads due s. from the square. Across Mount St. is the pleasant exterior of the independent *Grosvenor Chapel* (1730), the burial-place of Lady Mary Wortley Montagu (d. 1762), and John Wilkes (d. 1797), styled "a friend of liberty" in the epitaph by himself. The U.S. armed forces used the chapel during the Second World War. A gate to the left admits to the quiet public *Mount St. Gardens* which we now cross to emerge in the secluded *Farm Street.* Here the Jesuit church of the Immaculate Conception (good music) by J. J. Scoles (1844–49) has a high altar by A. W. N. Pugin.

We may regain Charles St. (comp. above) by descending the pleasant Chesterfield Hill, or return w. along South Street. On the corner of South Audley St. *Thos. Goode,* china and glass specialists, occupy an elaborate building of 1875–90, and, opposite, No. 71 has a fine doorway of 1736–37. South St. continues hence to Park Lane.

10 HYDE PARK, KNIGHTSBRIDGE, AND BELGRAVIA

STATIONS: *Hyde Park Corner* and *Knightsbridge* on Piccadilly line; *Victoria* and *Sloane Square* on Circle and District line (Victoria also on Victoria line); *Marble Arch* on Central line.—BUSES: along Knightsbridge, 9, 14, 19, 22, 30, 52, 73, 74, 137, 509 (19, 22, and 137 continue down Sloane St.); along Park Lane, 2, 16 30, 36B, 73, 74, and 137; along Grosvenor Place, 2, 16, 36B, 38 and 52.

CAR PARKING: for Hyde Park, see below; Cadogan Place (Sloane St.; underground); Pavilion Rd. (parallel to Sloane St.); some meter parking in Belgravia.

Hyde Park Corner (Pl. 13; 6), the spacious area at the w. end of Piccadilly and at the s.e. angle of Hyde Park, abandons itself to motor traffic (underpass). *Wellington Arch*, the triumphal arch at the end of Constitution Hill, dominates an open green reached by a maze of pedestrian subways. Designed by Decimus Burton in 1828 and crowned by a statue of Wellington, it originally stood opposite the main entrance to Hyde Park. The present group of Peace in her quadriga, by Adrian Jones, dates from 1912. A statue of Wellington, mounted on 'Copenhagen' by Boehm (1888) faces Apsley House (p. 104). To the right an heroic figure of David by Derwent Wood (d. 1926) is the *Machine Gun Corps War Memorial.* Close by rises the *Royal Artillery War Memorial,* for both world wars, in white marble and bronze, finely sculpted by C. S. Jagger and Lionel Pearson.

To the w. is *St George's Hospital,* founded in 1719, in a building by Wilkins (1827; with later extensions). A bust of John Hunter (1728–93), a surgeon at the hospital, crowns the side entrance at the beginning of Knightsbridge (see p. 111). *Grosvenor Place* leads s. between Belgravia (see below) and the gardens of Buckingham Palace to Victoria Station (Rte 12).

On the N. side of Hyde Park Corner, a delicate screen with a triple archway by Decimus Burton (1828; reproduction of Parthenon freize by Heming) gives access to **Hyde Park* (Pl. 13; 3). Lying between Park Lane, Knightsbridge, and Bayswater Road, and marching on the w. with Kensington Gardens, the park has an area of 361 acres and measures $3\frac{1}{2}$ m. round. Together with Kensington Gardens it forms one continuous park of over 600 acres, visually sadly reduced by tower blocks protruding above a sky-line once filled only with trees.

Stretching in a curve diagonally across the centre of both Hyde Park and Kensington Gardens is the *Serpentine,* an artificial lake of 41 acres ($4\frac{1}{2}$–14 ft deep), frequented by waterfowl. The portion within Kensington Gardens is known as the *Long Water*. It was in this lake that Harriet Westbrook, Shelley's first wife, drowned herself in 1816.

MOTOR TRAFFIC. Private cars and taxicabs are admitted to the roads skirting the park, and to The Ring, which crosses it at the Serpentine bridge.

PARKING, N. of the Serpentine bridge, is restricted Mon–Fri 10–11; otherwise free when the park is open. An underground car park (fee) is entered from Park Lane and Marble Arch.

CHAIRS may be hired.

RESTAURANTS. Dell Café and Bar (E. end of Serpentine); Pergola Restaurant and Bar (by the bridge).

BOATS. Sailing dinghies and rowing skiffs may be hired; ferry service across Serpentine.

BANDS at the bandstands, Sun 3–4.30, 6.30–8, and daily in Aug and Sept.

SWIMMING. Mixed bathing May–Sept, daily from 6 a.m. (fee after 10 a.m.; season tickets available). In winter 6–9 a.m., male bathers only (free).

HISTORY. The manor of Hyde belonged to the monks of Westminster Abbey from the Conquest to the Dissolution, when Henry VIII seized it and converted it into a royal hunting-park. Under Charles I the place began to be a fashionable resort, though the deer were hunted until after the middle of the 18C and did not finally disappear until about 1840. In Charles I's reign the 'Ring', a circular drive and racecourse, was laid out, and was much frequented by fashionable carriages. Under William and Mary and Queen Anne the roads leading across the park were infested by footpads, and it became a favourite resort of duellists, but under the Georges its character improved. In 1851 the first *Great International Exhibition* was held in Hyde Park on a space of about 20 acres between Rotten Row (see below) and Knightsbridge. Sir Joseph Paxton's famous exhibition-building of glass and iron was afterwards re-erected at Sydenham as the Crystal Palace.—The park contains several 'bird sanctuaries'. Some of the fine lodges by the numerous entrance gates are by Decimus Burton.

On entering the park from Hyde Park Corner we have on our left the carriage-road running along the s. side of the park, passing the Knightsbridge Barracks (see below). Almost parallel with this is *Rotten Row*, the famous sand-track for riders (mounting blocks remain near many of the gates). From Hyde Park Corner another broad road runs N. to Marble Arch, forming a dual carriageway (northbound) with Park Lane (described in Rte 9). On the left is a colossal bronze figure known as the *Achilles Statue*, by Westmacott, erected in 1822 in honour of the Duke of Wellington and his companions-in-arms "by their country-women". The statue is a modified copy of one of the Dioscuri on the Quirinal in Rome. On the right is a poor statue of *Byron*, by Belt (1880). We pass a delightful fountain before reaching *Speakers' Corner*, at the N.E. angle of the park, where orators hold forth in the open air (especially on Sunday afternoon). Beyond, the four important thoroughfares of Park Lane, Oxford St., Edgware Road, and Bayswater Road radiate from a broad open space. Here, between two elaborate, landscaped traffic islands (1961–62), rises the **Marble Arch** (Pl. 13; 1), designed by Nash more or less after the Arch of Constantine at Rome, and originally erected in 1828 in front of Buckingham Palace. It was removed in 1850–51 to its present site, where it formed an entrance to Hyde Park until 1908. The gates are finely wrought.

At the Marble Arch the visitor is close to the site of **Tyburn**, the famous place of execution, to which during many centuries victims were dragged through the centre of the city from the Tower or from Newgate. The first recorded execution took place here in 1196, the last in 1783. From 1571 to 1759 'Tyburn Tree', a permanent triangular gallows, stood on the spot now indicated by a stone slab on the traffic island opposite the site of the Odeon Cinema.

To the w., in Hyde Park Place, is the *Shrine of the Sacred Heart and Tyburn Martyrs* where 25 nuns say mass in memory of "the glorious martyrs who laid

down their lives in defence of the Catholic faith here on Tyburn Hill 1535–1681".
The chapel was built in 1961. Just beyond, new blocks of flats are being erected
on the site of a cemetery; the body of Laurence Sterne was removed hence to
Coxwold. No. 2 Connaught Place, nearby, was the home of Lord Randolph
Churchill in 1883–92.

The walk skirting the N. bank of the Serpentine is known as the
Ladies' Mile. At the E. end is the rich vegetation of the *Dell*, watered
by the Westbourne, and, nearby, on the shore of the lake, a pleasant
open-air café. Beyond the boating pier, a road leads N. to Ranger's
Lodge, offices of the Park Superintendent, and a police station. The
undulating *Buck Hill*, to the N., retains a pump and water-trough used
when the area was pastureland (sheep still grazed here in 1937). The
Bird Sanctuary and sunken area of green-houses lies behind a memorial
'Rima' (by Epstein; 1925) to W. H. Hudson (1841–1922). The fine bridge
over the Serpentine (built in 1828 by the brothers Rennie) commands
an open view to the towers of Westminster, and (N.W.) to the thin
steeple of Christ Church (p. 114) amidst the wooded dells of Kensington
Gardens (Rte 11A). The island in the Serpentine is the home of Peter
Pan. The 'Magazine' (1764–75) at the N. end of the bridge was remodelled c. 1825 by Decimus Burton. On the S. side of the lake are a
restaurant, Lido (surrounded by pavilions in summer), and fishing area,
while farther S., the *Serpentine Gallery* holds exhibitions in summer
(open 11–7.30 or 8). The building, formerly a tea house, is by Henry
Tanner (1908).

We may now follow the long sweep of Rotten Row, and turn S. across
the site of the 1851 Exhibition (see above) to the conspicuous *Knightsbridge Barracks*. The angular buildings by Sir Basil Spence (1970)
surround a tower block (310 ft) which provides accommodation for men
of the Household Cavalry; their horses (c. 270) are stabled in the
E. wing. They exercise daily 6–8 a.m. in the park, and may often be seen
at drill on Rotten Row. The guard for Horse Guards in Whitehall
(comp. p. 72) leaves the barracks beneath the fine pedimented portico
daily at approx. 10.30 a.m.; the old guard returns just before midday.
The carriage road continues past *Bowater House* (1958–60), with the
extraordinary group 'Pan' by Jacob Epstein, his last work (1959).
We leave the park by *Albert Gate*. The two houses here were built by
Cubitt (No. 58, formerly the residence of Hudson, the Railway King, is
now the French Embassy; No. 60 is the Royal Thames Yacht Club).

Across the noisy *Knightsbridge* (Pl. 13; 5), named from a bridge over
the Westbourne, we may diverge r. into *Wilton Place* which leads S. to
Belgravia. This fashionable residential area was developed in 1825–35
by Lord Grosvenor and Thomas Cubitt. The monumental white stucco
mansions are well set off by delightful squares, and behind the spacious
streets lie charming mews and less grand Georgian terraces. Beyond the
fine light yellow stone façade of the New Berkeley Hotel (1972, by Brian
O'Rorke) is *St Paul's, Knightsbridge*, built in 1840, with an unexpected
timbered roof. A tablet on the outside wall of the church commemorates 52 members of the Women's Transport Service who died in
1939–45. At the end, the unusual *Wilton Crescent* was built in 1827 by
Seth Smith. In the mews behind are several 'pubs', and in Kinnerton
Street carriage archways admit to tiny subsidiary mews. Photographers'
studios abound here, and at the S. end, the Halkin Arcade (1971) contains antique shops and art galleries (one devoted to the theatre arts).

Motcomb St. leads w. from the Crescent past the doric columns of the Pentechnicon built in 1830 by Smith as a bazaar, and now the Victorian showrooms of Sotheby's Belgravia (auctioneers; comp. p. 103).

Beyond lies **Belgrave Square** (Pl. 13; 5) built by Basevi in 1825 and now the home of many embassies which surround the beautiful sunken garden in the centre (c. 10 acres). The philanthropic Earl of Shaftesbury died at No. 5 in 1885, and Seaford House (s.e. corner) was built by Hardwick (1842). Halkin Street leads e. out of the square past the Caledonian Club and Forbes House, set back amidst gardens. At the end (r.) No. 6 was the residence of Sir Henry Campbell-Bannerman (1836–1908), Prime Minister in 1906–08.

We follow Upper Belgrave Street out of the s.e. corner of the square, with several pretty Georgian streets leading e. to Grosvenor Place. At No. 12 Walter Bagehot lived (1826–77). Beyond, at the e. end of Eaton Square is *St Peter's*, the scene of many fashionable weddings. The stained glass of the life of the Saint is by John Hayward. The long *Eaton Square* (Pl. 13; 8) has fine gardens flanked by two uniform rows of white stucco terraces.

In Eaton Place, parallel to the n., No. 15 was the home of Lord Kelvin, and No. 29 that of Lord Avebury. On the doorstep of No. 36 Sir Henry Wilson was shot dead in 1922. Near the w. end of the square, the animated Elizabeth Street leads s. to the peaceful Chester Square, with *St Michael's*, in a retired churchyard. Matthew Arnold lived at No. 2, and Mary Shelley, widow of the poet, died at No. 24 in 1851.

In Lyall St., n. of the square, Thomas Cubitt (1788–1855) lived at No. 3 while building much of the area (comp. above). On the corner of Eaton Place here, a plaque at No. 88 records the first London recital given by Chopin (1848).

At the w. end of Eaton Square, Eaton Gate and Cliveden Place lead to *Sloane Square*, with the Royal Court Theatre, at the beginning of Chelsea (Rte 13). We turn n. up SLOANE STREET (Pl. 13; 7), a fashionable residential and shopping street, remarkably long and straight, bordered on the e. by fine gardens. Near its s. end *Holy Trinity* has an e. window by Burne-Jones, and elaborate art nouveau fittings. In Sloane Terrace (r.) is the First Church of Christ Scientist in London. No. 44 Cadogan Place (across the gardens) was the home of William Wilberforce, the campaigner against slavery. No. 76 Sloane St., just before the intersection with Pont St., was the home of Sir Herbert Tree and Sir Charles Dilke (plaques). Strikingly seen at the far end of the red Dutch terraces of *Pont Street* (l.) is the Scottish church of *St Columba's*, well sited on a corner with a fine helm roofed tower, by Sir Edward Maufe (1950–55). Inside is a memorial chapel to the London Scottish regiment.

Arnold Bennett lived for many years at No. 75 Cadogan Square, s. of Pont St. and to the n., in Hans Place, with its thickly planted oval gardens, lived Jane Austen (at No. 23), and Shelley (at No. 41; both houses demolished).

Beyond the delightful balconied houses of Cadogan Place, we regain the busy intersection of **Knightsbridge** at the top of Sloane Street (see below).

11 KENSINGTON
A Knightsbridge and Brompton to Kensington Gardens and Holland Park

STATIONS: *Knightsbridge* on the Piccadilly line; *South Kensington* on the Circle, District, and Piccadilly lines; *High Street Kensington* on Circle and District lines. *Lancaster Gate, Queensway, Notting Hill Gate,* and *Holland Park* on Central line (Notting Hill Gate also on Circle and District lines). – BUSES along Kensington Road and High St., 9 and 73; along Kensington Rd., Kensington Church St. and Kensington Park Rd., 52; along Brompton Rd., 14, 30, and 74 (only 74 continues along Cromwell Rd.). Buses 12 and 88 run from Marble Arch along Bayswater Rd., Notting Hill Gate, and Holland Park Avenue.

CAR PARKING. Trevor Place (Pl. 12; 6); Meter parking N. and S. of Cromwell Rd.; Hyde Park (N. of Rennie's Bridge, see Rte 10); Kensington Gardens (N.W. corner, approached from Bayswater Rd.); Young St. (S. of Kensington High St.); Kensington Church St.; Holland Park (approached from Abbotsbury Rd.); Earl's Court Road (corner of Kensington High St.).

Kensington was made a royal borough at the wish of Queen Victoria in 1901, and was combined in 1965 much against its will, with Chelsea. The remarkable group of museums and educational institutions between Kensington Gardens and Cromwell Road were built on land purchased out of the proceeds of the 1851 Exhibition.

The thoroughfare that continues the line of Piccadilly (Rte 8) west from Hyde Park Corner, along the s. side of Hyde Park and Kensington Gardens, is known at first as *Knightsbridge* and farther on as Kensington Road and Kensington High Street. It forms the main approach to Hammersmith and the w. suburbs.

From Knightsbridge Station (at the top of Sloane Street, comp. p. 110) BROMPTON ROAD (Pl. 13; 5), a wide and bustling thoroughfare runs s.w. towards the South Kensington museums. It passes the huge terracotta edifice of *Harrods* (1901), a superior department store where almost anything may be purchased. Beyond, opposite a stretch of raised pavement with trees, *Beauchamp Place* diverges left, its modest regency housing brightly transformed below iron balconies into fashionable boutiques and restaurants. The area to the N. of Brompton Rd. retains some quiet residential streets (including Cheval Place, Rutland St., and Montpellier St., with Bonham's, the auctioneers). Beyond Brompton Square built in 1820 (where Stéphane Mallarmé, the poet, lived at No. 6 in 1863), an avenue of limes leads to *Holy Trinity* (1827; the chancel added by Blomfield in 1879), the rural parish church of Brompton. Across an open green behind is the colourful Ennismore Gardens Mews and Street.

Brompton Oratory (Pl. 12; 8), or the *Oratory of St Philip Neri*, is served by secular priests (housed in a building of 1853 to the w. of the church) of the institute of the Oratory, founded by St Philip Neri at Rome in 1575. The institute was introduced into England by Cardinal Newman in 1848 (his statue by Chavalliaud stands to the l. of the entrance). The present church, a large and elaborate edifice in the Roman Baroque style, designed by H. Gribble, was opened in 1884, the façade and dome being completed in 1896–97. The interior, which is remarkable for the width of its nave (52 ft), is heavily decorated with marble and statuary (including a series of Apostles from Siena, by Mazzuoli, c. 1680). The huge Renaissance altar in the Lady Chapel (S. Transept) comes from Brescia.

Brompton Road now branches left through an area of attractive squares and crescents (Alexander Sq., Thurloe Sq., Pelham Place and Crescent, etc.) built in 1820–40; while CROMWELL ROAD (Pl. 12; 7) continues due west, named from a vanished house of Henry Cromwell, son of the Protector. Though mainly lined with monotonous terraces of hotels, it begins with the long imposing Renaissance façade in stone and red brick by Sir Aston Webb (1909) of the VICTORIA AND ALBERT MUSEUM, the first of the **South Kensington Museums** described in Rte 11B. Beyond Exhibition Road (with an entry to South Kensington Stn.), the NATURAL HISTORY MUSEUM stands amid plane trees.

In Cromwell Rd., opposite the Natural History Museum, is the *Institut Français du Royaume Uni*, a centre of French culture in London with a lycée. In Cromwell Place, No. 7 was the home of Millais (1862–79). At the corner of Queen's Gate is *Baden-Powell House* (1959–61), with an international hostel for Scouts, mementoes of Lord Baden-Powell (1857–1941), and historical records. Farther w. in Cromwell Rd., near Gloucester Rd. station, is the *London Air Terminal*. No. 39 Harrington Gardens (parallel to the s.) was built in 1881 for W. S. Gilbert; its terracotta decorations recall the Savoy operas. The E. wing was restored in 1972; in the w. wing are the offices of the *Society of Genealogists* (closed Mon). Non-members may use the Library on payment of a daily fee. Its collection of parish register copies is unrivalled.

EXHIBITION ROAD runs N., passing (l.) the GEOLOGICAL MUSEUM and the SCIENCE MUSEUM (Rte 11B) and (r.) a *Mormon Chapel* (1959–61) with a tapering spire covered in gold leaf. The elaborate organ is played 12.30–1 on most days. Beyond, on either side of the road, are the buildings of the IMPERIAL COLLEGE OF SCIENCE AND TECHNOLOGY, a magnificently equipped group of associated colleges, incorporated in the University of London in 1907 for advanced training and research in science, especially in its application to industry. The open Prince's Garden (r.) is gradually being surrounded by residential halls (that on the s. opened in 1963; the Sports Centre lies to the N.). On the left side of Exhibition Rd., unimaginative faculty buildings (1958–63) surround a huge *Campanile* by Thomas Collcutt (1887–93), preserved from the former Imperial Institute, erected as a national memorial to Queen Victoria's Jubilee and designed to exhibit and promote the resources of the Empire. The Chemistry block is still under construction and extensions are taking place farther w. on Queen's Gate.

We may diverge left along Prince Consort Road which skirts the Royal School of Mines to reach the *Royal College of Music*, incorporated in 1883, but occupying a building opened in 1894. It contains the Donaldson Collection of ancient musical instruments (adm. on application to the Curator, Mon & Wed in term-time, 10.30–4.30; fee). Opposite, steps lead up past a bronze statue of Prince Albert, on a memorial to the Great Exhibition of 1851, to the former entrance to the Royal Albert Hall. To the left is the Union building of Imperial College, and to the w., is the *Royal College of Organists*, with bright sgraffito decoration. The grim yet individual building of the *Royal College of Art* (1960–61) is the last of this remarkable group of institutions devoted to science and art. Here are held periodic exhibitions.

The **Royal Albert Hall** (Pl. 12; 5), originally the Hall of Arts and Sciences, a huge amphitheatre roofed over by a glass dome, was inspired by the Roman works of Provence and built in 1867–71. The exterior, with a terracotta frieze by Minton, was cleaned in 1969–70; it measures 273 ft in length, 240 ft in breadth, and 155 ft in height. The interior (admission if no rehearsals are in progress) has an arena of 103 ft by

68 ft. It is capable of containing about 8000 persons, and is used for concerts, public meetings, balls, etc., and has a celebrated Willis organ. The famous Promenade concerts founded by Sir Henry Wood, are held here in summer.

Between Exhibition Road and Queen's Gate the houses flanking the Albert Hall are known as *Kensington Gore*, from Gore House, which stood approximately on the site of the Albert Hall, and was famous for the salon held in it by Lady Blessington (1836–49). At the beginning of the 19C it was the residence of William Wilberforce.

Kensington Road runs E. to Knightsbridge (comp. p. 111). On the corner of Exhibition Road, the *Royal Geographical Society* in a building by Norman Shaw (1874) is adorned with statues of Sir Ernest Shackleton and David Livingstone. Admission to the small exhibition with relics of these and other explorers is granted by the Director. The library is available to scholars. Across Exhibition Rd., at No. 14 Prince's Gate (now the Royal College of General Practitioners), J. F. Kennedy lived while his father was ambassador to Britain (1937–40). Earl Haig (1861–1928) died at No. 21, and No. 25 is the *Royal School of Needlework* (adm. 9.30–5.30) founded in 1872, which holds evening classes and has an embroidery shop. In Ennismore Gardens, the Russian Orthodox church of *All Saints* (ring for verger, r. of entrance), in a curious mixture of architectural styles, contains sgraffito work by Heywood Sumner (1898); and on the corner of Rutland Gardens is the Westminster Synagogue. Farther on, opposite Knightsbridge Barracks (see p. 110), Knightsbridge House is fronted by a pleasant bronze group 'The Seer' by G. Ledward. The quiet streets to the s. around Trevor Square are attractive.

West of the Albert Hall, beyond the wide Queen's Gate, with its statue of Napier of Magdala (d. 1890) by Boehm, is Hyde Park Gate. Here at No. 18 Epstein had his studio and died in 1959; Sir Leslie Stephen (1832–1904) lived at No. 22, and at No. 28 Winston Churchill died in 1965. Beyond, in De Vere Gardens, lived Browning (in 1887–89) and Henry James (in 1886–1901).

Facing the Albert Hall is the Gothic spire of the ALBERT MEMORIAL, the national monument to Prince Albert of Saxe-Coburg-Gotha (1819–61), consort of Queen Victoria, designed by Sir G. Gilbert Scott (1872). The statue of the prince (with the catalogue of the Great Exhibition) is by Foley. The pedestal is decorated with admirable marble reliefs of artists and men of letters by J. B. Philip (N. and W. sides) and H. Armstead. At the angles are allegorical groups (Agriculture, by Calder Marshall; Manufactures, by Weekes; Commerce, by Thornycroft; and Engineering, by Lawlor). At the foot of the steps are groups representing Europe, Asia, Africa, and America.

We are now in **Kensington Gardens* (Pl. 12; 5), 274 acres in area, once the private gardens of Kensington Palace (see below), which adjoin Hyde Park on the w. Although the Round Pond and Broad Walk were planned by George I, their present aspect is largely due to Queen Caroline, wife of George II, under whose direction they were laid out by Charles Bridgeman in 1728–31. The beautiful avenues of trees are a special feature. These gardens are a favourite resort of children and their attendants.

At the N. end of the *Long Water*, as the upper reach of the Serpentine is called (comp. p. 109), is an attractive paved garden with a pavilion and fountains and a statue of *Jenner* by W. Calder Marshall (1858). Nearby is the charming *Queen Anne's Alcove* (originally at the s. end of the Broad Walk), probably designed by Kent. The spot on the w. bank of the water, where *Peter Pan*, the hero of Sir J. M. Barrie's fairy play, first landed his boat, is marked by a delightful statue of him by Sir G. Frampton (1912). A little to the s.w., a bronze cast of a fine equestrian figure by G. F. Watts (1903) represents *Physical Energy* (a replica forms part of the memorial to Cecil Rhodes at Groote Schuur, near Cape Town). An obelisk memorial to *Speke* (1827–64), the African explorer, lies to the N. A children's playground, with an 'elphin oak' occupies the N.W. corner of the park.

Behind the Albert Memorial we may take the charming *Flower Walk* w. to the *Broad Walk* which runs N. between Kensington Palace and the *Round Pond* (7 acres) noted for its model yachts in summer. In the private gardens on the s. side of the palace is a statue of *William III*, presented to Edward VII in 1907 by William II of Germany; and on the E. side is a statue of Queen Victoria, by Princess Louise. The approach to the palace passes between a beautiful sunk garden, surrounded on three sides by a pleached walk of lime trees, and a group of bay and thorn trees in front of the brick **Orangery*, built in 1704 by Hawksmoor and Vanbrugh, with ringed half-columns flanking the entrance. Inside (open daily 10–4 or 6) the festoons on the elaborate entablature were carved by Grinling Gibbons. The marble crater with Roman reliefs of 2C A.D. was found, according to Piranesi, in Hadrian's Villa, Tivoli in 1760.

*Kensington Palace was bought by William III from the 2nd Earl of Nottingham in 1689, and from that time until the death of George II (1760) it was a residence of the reigning sovereign. The old house of 1605 was altered and added to by Sir Christopher Wren, and the exterior is much as he and Hawksmoor left it, but considerable interior alterations were made by William Kent in 1722–24. Mary II, William III, Anne, and George II all died in Kensington Palace. Queen Victoria was born here on 24 May 1819, and continued to live at the palace until her accession in 1837. Queen Mary was likewise born in this palace (26 May 1867). It is still the residence of various members of the Royal Family.

The State Apartments, virtually abandoned in 1760, were first restored and opened to the public in 1899. They were renovated and rehung from the royal collections in 1975. Adm. weekdays 10–6 in summer, 10–4, 5 in winter; Sun from 2; fee.

In QUEEN MARY'S GALLERY the Vauxhall glass overmantels with gilded surrounds by Grinling Gibbons date from 1691. The fine portraits include *Adriaen Hanneman*, William III as a young man (1669); *William Wissing*, William and Mary as prince and princess; *Lely*, Anne Hyde; *Kneller*, Peter the Great. QUEEN'S DINING ROOM: *Lely*, Queen Mary aged 10 as Diana. DRAWING ROOM: *Kneller*, William, duke of Gloucester, and *Michael Dahl*, Prince George of Denmark, Queen Anne's son and husband; paintings by *Van Dyck* and *David Teniers.* The BEDCHAMBER, damaged in 1940 by enemy action, contains the bed belonging to James II and Mary of Modena, in which probably the 'Old Pretender' was born. The large 17C bowl in the hearth recalls Q. Mary II as a great collector of oriental porcelain. There follow two of the three rooms rebuilt in grander fashion in 1718–21 by Colen Campbell and decorated by *William Kent.* His also is the trompe l'oeil painting on the King's Staircase. The King's Gallery preserves the wind-dial made in 1694 by Robert Morden and (?) Thos. Tompion. Among the pictures, *Van Dyck*, Cupid and Psyche, and a particularly unattractive *Rubens.*

The following suite has been restored to near its appearance when occupied by the Duchess of Kent and Princess Victoria in 1834–36 with many personal mementoes. The KING'S DRAWING ROOM is hung with 17C pictures mainly acquired by Charles I or painted for Charles II. The COUNCIL CHAMBER, arranged as a memorial of the Great Exhibition of 1851 contains the ivory throne of the Maharajah of Travancore. The CUPOLA ROOM, grand but inartistic, is the third of Colen Campbell's improvements.

Hyde Park and Kensington Gardens are skirted on the N. by *Bayswater Road* s. of a residential area of monotonous white stucco terraces, with many hotels. For the region around Marble Arch, see p. 109. The Broad Walk reaches Bayswater Rd. just W. of *Queensway*, a busy street with provision shops open late at night. Farther E., in *Lancaster Gate*, the conspicuous spire of Christ Church rises behind a memorial by Hermon Cawthra (1934) to the Earl of Meath. West of Queensway, No. 1 *Orme Square* was the residence of Sir Rowland Hill, introducer of the penny postage, in 1839–45. The next turning on the r., *St Petersburgh Place*, leads N. between the tall Eastern towers of the New West End Synagogue and the tapering spire of St Matthew's Church to Moscow Rd. and the Byzantine Greek Cathedral of the Holy Wisdom, with mosaics by Boris Anrep. Sir James Barrie lived at No. 100 Bayswater Rd. in 1902–08. Beyond Kensington Palace Gardens (see below) and the Czechoslovak Centre and Embassy (1971, by Stramek, Bocon & Stepanski; No. 25), *Notting Hill Gate* continues W. Rebuilt for commercial interests in

1958–61, it now presents a chilly aspect. No. 57 Palace Gardens Terrace was the birthplace of Max Beerbohm (1872–1956).

Pembridge Road runs N. from Notting Hill Gate to the long *Portobello Road* (l.); the name commemorates the capture of Puerto Bello in the Caribbean by Adm. Vernon in 1739. Famous for its weekday vegetable and fruit market here since c. 1870, it is known locally as 'The Lane'. The popularity of the Saturday antique market in the s. section of the road has reduced the likelihood of bargains. To the w., *St John's, Ladbroke Grove* (Pl. 10; 1) was built in 1845 on the site of a grandstand; only the shape of the housing terraces and Hippodrome Place recall the racecourse here in 1837–41. Near by, Pottery Lane survives from 'The Potteries', a once notorious area of brick-making and pig-keeping, described by Dickens in 1850 as 'a plague spot scarcely equalled for its insalubrity by any other in London'.

Holland Park Avenue continues the line of Notting Hill Gate to *Shepherd's Bush*, just w. of which is Lime Grove, now synonymous with B.B.C. Television.

West of the fine Palace gateway (temp. William III), Kensington Road becomes *Kensington High Street*, a busy shopping centre running through the well-to-do residential district of Kensington proper. Here *Kensington Palace Gardens* (r.), dubbed 'Millionaires' Row', was planned by Pennethorne in 1843, and remains a private road lined with fine mansions in gardens, many of them now used as embassies. Among the architects were Decimus Burton and Sidney Smirke who used an entertaining variety of styles including the Eastern and the Italianate (best seen at N. end). No. 8 was a primary interrogation centre for German prisoners during the 'Battle of Britain'. At the top on the left is the new Czechoslovak Embassy (see above). In *Palace Green* (s. end; with an informal entrance to Kensington Palace), Thackeray died in 1863 at No. 2, a house designed by himself, and No. 1 was built by Philip Webb (1863).

The next turning on the right at the ancient centre of Kensington, is *Kensington Church Street*, the narrow main road N. to Notting Hill (see above). On the corner stands the parish church of *St Mary Abbots* (1869–81). A large church in 13C style with a conspicuous spire, it is the result of the combined efforts of Archdeacon Sinclair and Gilbert Scott. In Holland Street (a charming street of early-18C houses built for the ladies-in-waiting at Kensington Palace), tablets mark the homes of Walter Crane (No. 13; 1845–1915), the artist, and Sir C. V. Stanford (No. 50A; 1856–1924), the musician. In Pitt St., to the N., Bullingham Mansions succeed the house where Newton died in 1727.

South of Kensington High St., *Young Street* (where Thackeray lived at No. 16 from 1846–53 and wrote 'Vanity Fair') leads to KENSINGTON SQUARE, a highly fashionable quarter in the early 18C when the Court was frequently at Kensington Palace. Here Talleyrand lived after his escape from Paris in 1792. On the s. side J. R. Green lived at No. 14, Hubert Parry, the musician, at No. 17, and J. S. Mill at No. 18. In the corner is the R.C. convent of the Assumption, with a surprising façade of 1860. No. 33 (N.T.; no adm.) built in 1695, was the residence of Mrs Patrick Campbell (1865–1940), the actress. At No. 40 lived Sir John Simon, pioneer of public health, and next door, Burne-Jones.—The Armenian church of St Sarkis (1922) lies to the w. in Iverna Gardens.

We may ascend Campden Hill Road on the north side of the High St. to reach Campden Hill. On the right, beyond the *Kensington and Chelsea Public Library*, the new Town Hall by Sir Basil Spence has contrasting asymmetrical blocks. Farther up on the left is *Queen Elizabeth College* (domestic and social science), a brick building of 1915. In this road Sir Henry Newbolt, the poet, died at No. 29 in 1938, and Galsworthy lived at No. 78. Campden Hill runs w. between the science departments of the College and Holland Park School to Holland Walk (see below). Here, at Holly Lodge, died Lord Macaulay in 1859. North of the school is the West

London College of Commerce (entered from Airlei Gardens). In Peel St., which diverges r. from Campden Hill Rd., Russell Flint lived from 1929 to his death in 1969.

We follow *Aubrey Walk* w. on to **Campden Hill** which descends steeply N. to Notting Hill. It has been a favourite place of residence since the 17C and once frequented as a spa for taking the waters (the springs are still active); a few of the fine houses in spacious grounds survive, though the gardens of many were absorbed by Holland Park School. Swift, Gray, and Queen Anne (as Princess) were among its famous inhabitants. The peaceful Aubrey Walk, a colony of artists in Edwardian days, ends at the gates of Aubrey House which retains its spacious park. Formerly the residence of Evelyn Underhill, it contains the private collection of the Misses Alexander (one of whom was painted by Whistler, comp. p. 150). Aubrey Road leads into the delightful *Campden Hill Square* (Pl. 10; 1) which slopes steeply to the N. Here in the gardens while staying at Hill Lodge (on the corner of Hillsleigh Rd.), Turner painted the sunset. At No. 9 lived John McDouall Stuart (1815–66), the first explorer to cross Australia.

We may return towards Kensington High St. down *Holland Walk*, parallel to Aubrey Road (entered down the hill l. off Holland Park Avenue), a pleasant lane which skirts the park of **Holland House,** a beautiful and historic Tudor mansion, famous in the time of the third Baron Holland (1773–1840) as "the favourite resort of wits and beauties, painters and poets, scholars, philosophers, and statesmen". The house was badly damaged by incendiary bombs in 1941 and only the E. wing remains, now forming an open quadrangle with the *King George VI Memorial Hostel* (1956–58). The gateway (with piers surmounted by griffins) was designed by Inigo Jones and executed by Nicholas Stone in 1629. Plays and concerts are performed here in the summer.

Built by John Thorpe in 1607, Holland House passed by marriage to Henry Rich, created Earl of Holland (in Lincolnshire), who was executed in 1649. The house was then occupied for a time by the parliamentary generals Fairfax and Lambert, but was later restored to Lord Holland's widow. In the reign of Charles II William Penn seems to have lodged in this house, and in 1689 William III and Mary temporarily occupied it. Addison spent the last three years of his life here (d. 1719). Lord Kensington, heir of the Rich family, sold the house to Henry Fox (father of Charles James Fox), who was made Baron Holland in 1763. The brilliant literary and political (Whig) circle of which Holland House was the centre is described in Macaulay's essay on Lord Holland.

The wooded ***Holland Park** (café and restaurant; free car park on w. side, approached from Abbotsbury Rd.) surrounds the gardens, frequented by peacocks. Beyond the Flower Garden, the *Orangery* (the statues are free copies of the famous Classical 'Wrestlers' in Naples) is used for exhibitions and concerts. The Belvedere Restaurant is being restored after fire (1972). Near the car park is a children's 'Jungle'.

In *Melbury Road* at the s. end of Abbotsbury Rd., No. 2B was the residence of Sir Hamo Thornycroft (1850–1925), sculptor. To the E., Tower House (No. 29), an eccentric '13C' mansion, was designed by William Burges for himself in 1875. At No. 31 (by Norman Shaw) Sir Luke Fildes lived in 1878–1927, and Holman Hunt died in 1910 at No. 18. In *Holland Park Road* (s. of Melbury Road), LEIGHTON HOUSE (No. 12) was designed as the residence and studio of Lord Leighton (1830–96) who here spent the last thirty years of his life. The house (adm. Mon–Sat 11–5), decorated by Geo. Aitchison, is noted for its beautiful Arab Hall, and its 13–16C Persian and Saracenic tiles. Amidst the Victorian furnishings are ceramics designed by William de Morgan, and paintings by Burne-Jones and Leighton. In the charming garden (open April–Sept) is a bronze athlete by Leighton. Next door is the *British Theatre Museum* (adm. as for Leighton House).

At the s. end of the park, approached from Kensington High St., is the *Commonwealth Institute* (adm. 10–5.30, Sun 2.30–6). The ungainly copper-sheathed roof hides a superb multi-level exhibition hall built in 1960–62 by Robert Matthew, Johnson-Marshall, and partners. The instructive and colourful exhibits are provided by each Commonwealth government, and there is a free cinema, schools reception centre, and cafeteria restaurant.

On the s. side of the main road is *Earl's Terrace* where at No. 12 George du Maurier lived in 1867–70, and Walter Pater in 1866–93. Behind this long façade is the charming EDWARDES SQUARE, with small houses built in the early 19C by Changier. Here Leigh Hunt lived at No. 32 in 1840–51, and G. K. Chesterton at No. 1 in 1901. To the E., set back from the High Street, is the austere church of *Our Lady of Victories*, at one time the R.C. pro-cathedral. *Earl's Court Road*, with many restaurants, leads s. to *Earl's Court* and its Exhibition Halls.

Kensington High St. ends about ¼ m. w. of Holland Park at **Olympia,** see Rte 39.

B The South Kensington Museums

STATIONS. *South Kensington*, on the Piccadilly, District, and Circle lines, c. 300 yds s. of Victoria and Albert Museum (connected by subway). Other entrances to subway outside Science Museum (in Exhibition Rd.), and in the garden of the Natural History Museum.

BUSES, 14, 30, & 74, in Brompton Road, pass the Victoria and Albert Museum; 74 continues along Cromwell Road past the Natural History Museum; 45, 49, 207A pass South Kensington Station; see also Rte 11A.

Meter CAR PARKING in streets N. and s. of Cromwell Rd.

THE VICTORIA AND ALBERT MUSEUM

ADMISSION free daily exc. Friday (closed), weekdays 10–5.30, Sun from 2.30; closed Christmas Eve, Christmas Day, Boxing Day, and New Year's Eve. For the *Library* (weekdays only 10–5.45, Sat 10–1, 2–4.50) and *Print Room* (weekdays 10–4.30, Sat as Library) tickets are obtained on written application to the Keeper accompanied by a recommendation from a householder, or a member's card of the National Art Collections Fund (comp. p. 37) will admit.

PUBLIC LECTURES on Tues and Wed at 1.15 in the Lecture Theatre, Sat at 3 (one in the Lecture Theatre and one in the Galleries). Evening lectures in winter, Thurs at 6.30.

Self-serviced cafeteria in R. 39 on the ground floor.

An excellent 'Brief Guide' may be purchased (French, German, Italian, and Spanish translations). The *Publications Department* of the museum is outstanding, and informative reasonably priced booklets on most aspects of the collection are available. – The *Press and Information Office, Photography Dept.*, and *Slide Loan service* are located in R. 10 on the Lower Ground Floor (closed Sat & Sun).

The ****Victoria and Albert Museum** (Pl. 12; 8) with its spacious and well-lighted halls, galleries, and courts, contains perhaps the largest and finest collection of applied art in the world. The high standard of display and explanatory labels are most helpful, but repeated visits are necessary to do justice to its store of treasures.

The present Museum originated in the Museum of Manufactures (later the Museum of Ornamental Art) established by the Department of Science and Art at Marlborough House in 1852, on the initiative of Prince Albert. It was founded with the object of developing decorative design in British manufactures, by providing models and samples of applied art, ancient and modern, for study by craftsmen and others. Gifts, bequests, and Government grants rapidly extended the museum, and the present unrivalled collection fulfils far more than its primary utilitarian function and appeals to every lover of art.

The Museum is not always fully open, and the present description represents the arrangement in Summer 1977. Enquiries concerning recent alterations should be made at the Press Office. Temporary exhibitions are held in RR. 45, 48E, 38A, 70–73, and 74. The museum galleries have been arranged in two distinct groups: the Primary Galleries, showing masterieces of all the arts, brought together by style, period, or nationality; and the Study Collections, where the scholar and student can find the exhibits grouped within the various classes — sculpture, ceramics, painting, etc. In the following description the Primary Collections are given pride of place.

In front of the main entrance R. 49 is the Bookshop. R. 43, beyond, contains the Primary *Collection of **Early Medieval Art**. This gallery is divided into three sections, each of which contains textiles of the period. *Late Antique and Early Christian Art* (left wall-case): **212. Leaf of Symmachorum Diptych (4C), A 47. Miracles of Christ (diptych, A.D. 450–60), two splendid ivories; 1052. Portrait medallion in stippled gold, 2C or 3C; 272. Apostlé (ivory, 5C); (1st central case) 368, 139. Consular diptychs of ivory (Byzantine, 6C; the latter probably a Roman copy). *Byzantine and Sassanian Art*. 265. Cross-reliquary in cloisonné enamel (Byzantine, 9C); A 15, A 16, A 89. Rock crystal intaglios (late 6C) with the Emperor Marcus Tiberius, and the Nativity; M 6. Pair of gold earrings (6C or 7C); 215. Ivory relief of St John the Baptist and four Apostles (early 12C); 702. Ivory statuette of the Madonna (late 11C); A 1. Relief in serpentine of the Blessed Virgin (Byzantine, 11C); *216. Veroli casket, carved with mythological scenes (Byzantine, late 10C); 1615. Virgin and Child enthroned, gilt bronze triptych (Byzantine, 12C); 8980. St Mark from a Book of the Gospels (13C); 247. Casket with combat scenes. *Early Medieval Art in the West* (2nd central case). *7649. Gloucester Candlestick (c. 1110), and ecclesiastical ivories. The tall stone cross-shaft (A 88) from Easby, Yorkshire, dates from the 9C. (Right wall-case) 12C English objects: 816. Leaf from an illuminated Psalter; 159. Warwick Ciborium, gilt copper, engraved and enamelled; *142. Adoration of the Magi, relief in whalebone. (3rd central case) 7650. Eltenberg Reliquary in the form of a church (Rhenish, 12C); *567. Sion Gospels, cover in gold cloisonné and precious stones (French or German, c. 1000); *A 18. Basilewski Situla made at Milan (c. 980); 4757. Alton Towers Triptych, enamel on gilt copper, and other examples of metal work of the Meuse school (12–13C). Left wall-case: 138. Lorsch Gospel-cover (Carolingian, 9C). At the end of the room, 12C stone capitals, and four wooden columns from Salerno.

Rooms 22–29 are occupied by the Primary Collection illustrating **Gothic Art**. R. 23. *Northern Gothic Art of 14C*. 175. Tree of Jesse Cope (English); 17. Hildesheim Cope (German); 83. Syon Cope (English); *T 36. Butler-Bowdon Cope, embroidered with opus anglicanum. The collection of stained glass includes *4237. Winchester College Window.

Room 22. *Italian Gothic Art*. A 13. *Giov. Pisano*, Bust of the prophet Haggai, carved for the façade of Siena Cathedral; 781. *Barnaba da Modena*, Processional banner, with Crucifixion and Saints (c. 1375); 25. *Bart. Buon*, Madonna in Istrian stone (Venice, c. 1450); Embroidered altar frontal designed by *Paolo Veneziano*; 7719. *Nino Pisano*, Angel of the Annunciation (pigmented wood); 7573. Madonna from the workshop of *Ghiberti*, in terracotta (15C). Cases display 15C majolica, and 14C and 15C N. Italian ivories.

Room 24. A 10. Angel of the Annunciation, in painted oak (French, 15C); *7973. Basle Minster Altar-cross; *403. Mérode Cup (Burgundian; 15C); two charming 14C Madonnas (Ile de France); French and German ivories, including (211) Soissons Diptych (13C); A 28. Madonna and dead Christ (alabaster), by the Master of Rimini (c. 1430); 14C English work: *M1. Studley Bowl, chased and enamelled silver-gilt, *M268, 269. Ramsay Abbey Censer and Incense Boat, silver gilt; 244. Altar Cross by Hugo of Oignies; 357. Reliquary of St Boniface, from Constance (S. German, late-15C); A 89. Late-15C altarpiece (English, in alabaster); Tournai tapestry altar frontal (early-15C); A 36. Alabaster carving of Tree of Jesse (English, early-15C), with panels from a Passion altarpiece, and (37) St Anne, an English oaken statue of the same period; *1049. Altarpiece of oak (late-15C, probably from St Bavon at Ghent); 5940. Altarpiece from the workshop of Meister Betram (N. German), 15C tapestries, vestments and embroidery. – R. 25. *Spanish Gothic Art.* The great Retable of St George (Valencia, c. 1400), with scenes from his life; Spanish processional cross in silver, parcel-gilt on a wooden core (c. 1400). The stairs lead up to the Library (see p. 132). – RR. 32 and 33 contain carpets.

Room 26. *Late Gothic and Early Renaissance Art*, including examples of Spanish and Portuguese silverware: 665. St Hubert Crozier (Flemish; mid-16C); *M 249. Campion Cup, hammered and engraved silver-gilt (English; 1500); T 141. Spanish altar frontal from Toledo (c. 1530); M 60. Burghley Nef, by *Pierre le Flamand* (1482–83); A 531. The Entombment (walnut), S. Netherlandish of the late 15C; *552. Louis XII Triptych, with portraits of the king and Anne of Brittany (Limoges enamel, c. 1500); 389. Agate cup (German, c. 1500); 587. Alabaster altarpiece (S. Netherlandish, late 16C); A 31. Head of St John the Baptist in alabaster (N. German, late 15C).—R. 27. A 16, 17. Angels bearing candles (c. 1510); *110. *Tilman Riemenschneider*, St Mary Salome and Zebedee (c. 1506); A 41. Scenes from the Legend of St George, in boxwood (Franco-Flemish, late-15C); *646. *Veit Stoss*, Statuette of the Madonna in boxwood (c. 1510); 5894. Altarpiece with scenes from the Legend of St Margaret (N. German, early-16C); South German 'honestone' reliefs (16C).—R. 28. contains late-15C stained glass from Bruges and Cologne.—RR. 29, 29A. 4413. Lirey Altarpiece from near Troyes (painted and gilt stone; c. 1535); vestments from various countries (15–16C); P 19. Virgin Annunciate, a Valencian painted hanging (ink on linen; c. 1500); A 48, 49. Recumbent effigies of a Spanish grandee and his wife (late 15C).

Room 38 (r.) contains fine **Gothic Tapestries** (mainly Flemish) dating from before 1515 when Raphael's cartoons arrived in Brussels to be woven for the Vatican. To the right, Story of Troy, made in 1472 by Pasquier Grenier for the City of Bruges to present to Charles the Bold. This copy came from the castle of the Chevalier Bayard. The three large tapestries illustrating Petrarch's poem 'I Trionfi', were made in Brussels in 1507–10. Smaller tapestries depict the Story of Esther (from Brussels), and Susanna and the Elders, and the Three Fates (from Flanders); in the s.e. corner are two examples of the 'Pastoral' style. In

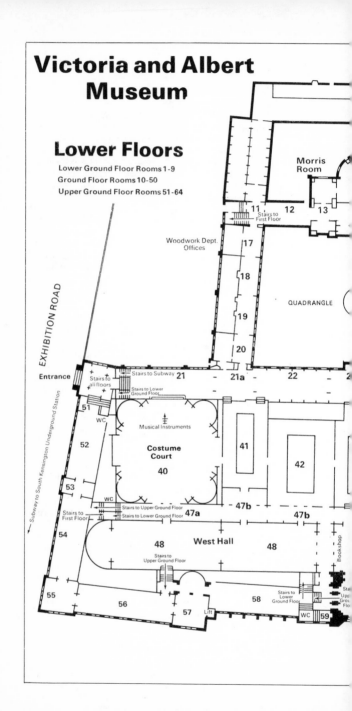

Victoria and Albert Museum

Lower Floors

Lower Ground Floor Rooms 1-9
Ground Floor Rooms 10-50
Upper Ground Floor Rooms 51-64

Morris Room

11   12   13
Stairs to First Floor

Woodwork Dept. Offices   17

18

QUADRANGLE

19

20

EXHIBITION ROAD

Entrance   Stairs to all floors   Stairs to Subway   21   21a   22

Stairs to Lower Floor

51

WC   Musical Instruments

52   Costume Court   41

40   42

53

WC   Stairs to Upper Ground Floor   47b

Stairs to First Floor   Stairs to Lower Ground Floor   47a   47b

54   48   West Hall   48

Stairs to Upper Ground Floor

Bookshop

55   Stairs to Lower Ground Floor

56   58   59

57   Lift   WC

Subway to South Kensington Underground Station

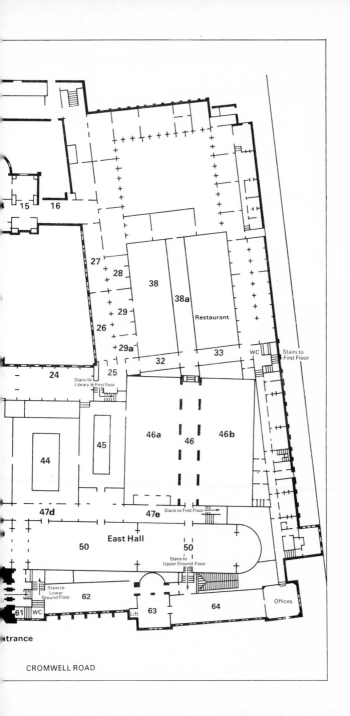

15 16

27
28
38
38a
29
26
Restaurant
29a
32 33 WC Stairs to First Floor
24 25
Stairs to Library & First floor

44 45 46a 46 46b

47d 47e Stairs to First Floor

East Hall
50 50
Stairs to Upper Ground Floor

Stairs to Lower Ground Floor 62
Lift 63 64 Offices
61 WC

Entrance

CROMWELL ROAD

the left-hand section of the room are the *Devonshire Hunting tapestries, probably from Tournai (c. 1450) associated with the marriage of
Henry VI and Margaret of Anjou.

We return through RR. 29 and 27 to reach Rooms 16–11 and 17–21, the
galleries on the N. and W. sides of the main quadrangle, which contain the
Primary *Collection of **Italian Renaissance Art**. Fine pieces of sculpture
are complemented by cases of majolica, cassoni, coffer-fronts, etc. – R. 16
contains exquisite bas-reliefs, including: 4355. *Florentine* (mid-15C),
Annunciation, diptych in ivory; **7629. *Donatello*, Ascension with Christ
giving the Keys to St Peter, a superb example of the sculptor's 'stiacciato'
technique (c. 1430); A 98. *The Impruneta Master* (mid-15C), Madonna
with angels; 66. *Desiderio da Settignano*, Madonna; 7473. *Neapolitan*
(late-15C), Madonna; 934 A. *Michaelozzo di Bartolommeo*, Adoring
Angels; *Donatello*, Virgin and Child with Four Angels, bronze roundel,
475. Winged putto, 57. Madonna (gilt terracotta), *7577. Dead Christ
tended by angels; 8522. The Lamentation; A 163. *Vecchietta*, The
Flagellation. The two doorways in grey sandstone come from the Palazzo
Ducale at Gubbio. – R. 15. 5801. *Florentine* (1441), Madonna and Child;
A 14. *Agostino di Duccio*, Madonna with angels; A 84. *Desiderio da
Settignano*, Madonna, a beautiful 'stiacciato' relief (A 3, of the same
subject, is from his workshop). – R. 14. Enamelled terracotta sculpture
associated with the *Della Robbia* family of Florence, of which the most
distinguished members were Luca (1400–82), his nephew Andrea
(1435–1525), and Andrea's son Giovanni (1469–1529). *Andrea della
Robbia*, 5633, 7630. Madonnas, 4412. Adoration of Magi; 7615. *Giov. della
Robbia*, Two Kneeling Angels; 6740. *Luca della Robbia*, Large roundel
with a garland of fruits and the arms of René of Anjou (d. 1480). The
majolica tiled pavement in the centre is from the Palazzo Petrucci at Siena
(1509). Wall-cases contain early-16C majolica from Cafaggiolo, Deruta,
and Gubbio. – R. 13. 476. *Giov. della Robbia*, Head of Christ; A 3. *Mino
da Fiesole*, Bernardo Giugni; fine series of medals by *Pisanello*, *Matteo de'
Pasti*, *Sperandio*, *Bertoldo*, and other masters. 7631. *Fr. di Simone*,
Madonna; 974. *Benedetto da Maiano*, Portrait of a man; 765, 765 A.
Vittorio Crivelli, St Jerome, St Catherine of Alexandra (paintings in
tempera). – Off this toom opens the Green Dining Room, decorated for the
museum by *William Morris* and *Philip Webb* in 1866. The stained glass and
painted panels were designed by *Edward Burne-Jones*.

Room 12. contains *Bronzes by *L'Antico* (A 27. Meleager), *Bertoldo*, *Il
Riccio* (A 88. Warrior on horseback), and *Vecchietta*. *Giul. da Sangallo*,
Step-ends from Palazzo Gondi, Florence; 7632–45. *Luca della Robbia*,
Twelve roundels depicting the Labours of the Months; 5896. *Desiderio da
Settignano*, Chimney-piece; *7671. *Ant. Rossellino*, Bust of Giov. di Ant.
Chellini. – R. 17, at the beginning of the next corridor, has a ceiling from
Cremona (c. 1500), with Apollo and the Muses, by *Ant. della Corna*. 492.
Carlo Crivelli, Madonna and Child (tempera). This and the succeeding
rooms are adorned with contemporary majolica, furniture and
embroidery. – R. 18 has some miniature bronze reliefs by *Il Riccio*, and
others. 251. *Fr. di Giorgio Martini*, Classical scene; 4495. *Ant. Rossellino*,
Madonna and laughing child; 7593. *Bened. da Maiano*, Birth of St John the
Baptist; 7599. *And. del Verrocchio*, Sketch for the Forteguerri monument
at Pistoia (1476); 240–242. *Benedetto da Maiano*, Terracotta studies (Story
of St Francis) for reliefs on the pulpit of Santa Croce in Florence (1475);

7591. *Dom. Rosselli*, Madonna. – R. 19 contains N. Italian works: 5390, 5391. *Ant. Bregno*, Virgin and anunciatory angel; bas-reliefs by Mantuan artists; 122. *Giov. Ant. Amadeo* (style of), Dead Christ tended by angels; bronze roundels by *Moderno*; A 134. *Pietro Lombardo*, The Christ Child; 450. *Giov. Ant. Amadeo*, Three Adoring angels; A. 19. *Ant. Lombardo*, Venus Anadyomene. – R. 20. 7694. Walnut mirror frame; 157. *Giov. Fr. Rustici*, St Mary Magdalene; *137. Altarpiece in pearwood from Piacenza, with the Curcifixion, and the Nativity as predella (early-16C).

This collection is continued in the s. corridor in RR. 21A and 21 (r.): 7659. *Matteo Civitali*, Tabernacle; M 61, 61A. *Valerio Belli*, Crystal altar cross and candlesticks made for Francis I of France; 362. *Perino del Vaga*, Raising of Lazarus (fragment of a fresco from the Trinità dei Monti, Rome); 6742, 6743. *Andrea Ferrucci*, Altarpiece and tabernacle from San Girolamo at Fiesole (c. 1495); 1634. Stained glass from Cortona Cathedral, and Spanish church furniture. A 14. *Cellini*, Head of Medusa; *Nicc. Tribolò*, Cosimo I; A 60. *Baccio Bandinelli*, Giov. Bandini. – R. 21. A 100. *Vinc. Danti*, Leda and the Swan; 328–330. *Giambologna*, Sketch models in red wax for the Grimaldi chapel in S. Francesco di Castelletto, Genoa; *7595. *Jacopo Sansovino*, Descent from the Cross, a gilt wax group, probably made as a model for Perugino. A case of bozzetti include works by *Giambologna* and *Michelangelo* (4117. Model in red wax of a slave for the tomb of Julius II). A 20–28. *Hubert Gerhard*, Christoph Fugger Altar; bronzes by *Roccatagliata*, *Aless. Vittoria*, etc. A 5. *Iac. Sansovino*, Story of Susanna. In the centre (A 7.) is a fine group of Samson slaying the Philistine, by *Giambologna*, and (up a flight of stairs) A 18. *Neptune and a Triton, by *Bernini*, made for a villa in Rome, and once the property of Reynolds. At the end of the room: terracotta sketch model of a river god by *Giambologna*, and Recumbent youth, by *Pietro Francavilla.* – Steps ascend to the Exhibition Road entrance to the museum; we descend left to RR. 1–7.

Rooms 1–7. **Continental Art, 1570-1800,** a magnificent Primary Collection, with masterpieces from all departments, skilfully arranged to convey an impression of the decorative ideas of the periods covered.

R. 1A. *Adriaen de Fries*, Emperor Rudolph II 1609. Limoges enamels. Silver from Augsburg. Damascened steel from Milan. Amber. Venetian glass. Ivory cabinet. Jewelled spinet by *Annibale dei Rossi.* Steel casket made for Cosimo II de' Medici. Globe by *Georg Roll* Augsburg, 1585. – R. 1B. *Hubert Le Sueur*, Henri IV. *Francois Dieussart*, Queen Elizabeth of Bohemia, 1641. Cabinet by *Master H. S.* Augsburg, 1560. German cabinet from Fonthill Abbey. Spanish cabinet. – R. 1C. Silk hangings from Tasso's 'Gerusalemme Liberata'. Busts include *Bernini*, Thomas Baker, 1638. *Algardi*, Cardinal Zacchia, *Foggini*, Cosimo III de' Medici. Ivories including *Bernhard Straus*, Tankard 1651. Cabinet of Marie de' Medici. Cabinet of John Evelyn. Spanish silver. Marble tables. – R. 2. Silver by *Van Vianen family.* Italian maiolica. Genoa ewer and basin, 1621/2. Turned ivory cups (one by *Grand Prince Ferdinando of Tuscany*, 1681). Bust of young Louis XIV. Wax relief by Zumbo. – R. 3A. Silver and tortoiseshell cabinet. Designs for ornament (*Stefano della Bella*). Engraved ornament. Old master drawings (*Carracci*, *Guercino*, *Golkius*). Baroque book-bindings. *Pieter Brueghel*, Garden of Eden. Papal mace c. 1700. – R. 3A (Annex) Torah mantle from Amsterdam. Italian silks, velvets and lace. — R. 3B. Room from château near Alençon, c. 1690. Eger cabinet. Dutch and French furniture. — R. 3Ci. Silver. Enamels. Pistols by *Lazarino Cominazzo*, Brescia. Rapier by *Gottfried Leygebe.* Italian lace alb. Glass bottle engraved by *Willem van Heemskerck*, 1674. — R. 3Cii. Florentine pietre dure panels. Gilt bronze fountain masks. Portuguese tile panels. Tin glazed earthenware from Spain, France, Holland, Germany and Italy. — R. 3Ciii. Silver clock by *Hans Breghtel.* Deposition by *Lebrun.* Italian furniture. Harpsichord by *Vaudry*, Paris, 1681. Floral marquetry cabinet by *Van Mekeren.* Nativity terracotta by *Agostino Cornacchini.* — R. 4. Continental porcelain, faience and glass of 18C, including some fine Meissen ware (service made in 1761 to the order of Frederick the Great for the Prussian General Mollendorff).

Rooms 5–7 house the Primary Galleries of **18C Continental Art**, including the *JONES COLLECTION OF FRENCH 18C ART*. — R. 5. Furniture in the style of *Andrè Charles Boulle* and *Jean Berain*, including an early commode and large cupboard; Japanese black lacquer furniture; portrait by *Boucher* of Mme. de Pompadour. The end bay contains Vincennes and early Sèvres porcelain. A room of carved panelling houses rococo furniture of c. 1750 with a 'duchesse' couch by *Tilliard.* Beyond are displayed some early neo-classical furniture, including two cupboards by *J. F. Oeben.* — R. 6. French 18C caskets; 18C guns, bronzes, and gold smiths' work. Designs for ceremonial gondalas by *Fr. Guardi.* — R. 7. Snuff-boxes; commode and secretaire designed by the royal cabinet maker *Gilles Joubert* in 1774; gilt bed by *Georges Jacob* (c. 1780); *Boudoir of Mme. de Sérilly* (Paris) outside which is furniture set with Sèvres plaques; a music-stand and work-table once belonging to Marie Antoinette; small harpsichord in the 'Chinese' style by *Pascal Taskin* (1786); table by *Martin Carlin* and furniture by *David Roentgen.* The small Italian oval room dates from 1780, beyond which is a bust of a young girl, by *J. Saly*, and of *Voltaire and the Marquess de Miromesnil, by *Houdon*. The last room contains Sèvres porcelain, and 5 lapis lazuli columns which belonged to Marie Antoinette.

The galleries above these (52–58) are devoted to the Primary Collection of **English Art from the Tudor Period to 1750**. R. 52 (near the Exhibition Road entrance to the museum). *146. Mostyn Salt, a fine standing salt-cellar (London, 1586); M273. Vyvyan Salt (London, 1592); 19. Queen Elizabeth's Virginal (c. 1570); 2011. Oak panelling, carved with Tudor devices, from a house at Waltham Abbey (c. 1520–30); *Pietro Torrigiani*, Bust of Henry VII (?). Panelled room from Sizergh Castle, Westmorland (1575), and the 'Great Bed of Ware' (12 ft by 12 ft), a famous Elizabethan bed (c. 1580), painted and carved, mentioned by Shakespeare and Ben Jonson.—R. 53 contains 16–17C English embroidery and costume, and the upholstered chair believed to have been used by Charles I at his trial. — R. 54. Oxburgh hangings, worked by Mary Queen of Scots and Bess of Hardwick. Oak panelling from the State Room of the Old Palace, Bromley-by-Bow, completed in 1606 for James I, with original plaster ceiling; W 181. *Grinling Gibbons*, Cravat carved in limewood, Stoning of St Stephen, Crucifixion (all fine examples of the sculptor's carving ability); 17C English silverware, including (M 30) a wine cooler by Ralph Leeke.

Room 55 contains **Portrait Miniatures,** arranged by dates. Miniature painting in Britain in the 16–17C excelled that of any other country. Note especially: *Nicholas Hilliard*, Young Man leaning against a tree among roses; *Hans Holbein the Younger*, Anne of Cleves, Mrs Pemberton; *Isaac Oliver*, Richard Sackville and Frances Howard; portraits by *Samuel Cooper.* In the centre of the room is the Calverley Toilet Service (1683–84).

R. 56 includes a panelled room from Clifford's Inn, London (1688), and a late 17C state bedstead. – R. 57 covers late 17C and early 18C art, and incorporates a room from Henrietta Place, London, designed by *James Gibbs*. A case of silver made by *Paul de Lamerie* includes the Walpole Salver made for Sir Robert in 1728. Beyond a display of English embroidery and Spitalfields silks, R. 57A contains 18C and 19C portrait miniatures. – R. 58 (mid-18C). Deal panelled room from Hatton Garden (c. 1730); music room from Norfolk House (1756); panelled room from Great George St., Westminster (c. 1755). At the end of the gallery is some fine contemporary furniture by *Matthias Lock*.

The corresponding rooms on the floor above (126–118) are devoted to the Primary Collection of **English Art, 1750-1900,** including furniture, textiles, china and glass, silver, and paintings.

The landing (126) exhibits a representative series of portrait busts by *Rysbrack, Nollekens, Wilton, P. Scheemakers*, and others, including (21) *Roubiliac*'s terracotta sketch for a monument. – R. 125 (mid-18C). 738. Chimney-piece from Winchester House, Putney; 'Chinese' bedstead from Badminton, probably by *Chippendale* (1754); chamber organ, in mahogany, by him (1760); Library from Croome Court, Glos. designed by Robert Adam; bookcases by Vile & Cobb, carved by Sefferin Alken, 1763; Glass Drawing Room from Old Northumberland House at Charing Cross, designed by Robert Adam; *Gainsborough*, *Queen Charlotte. Among the china, some charming Bow, Chelsea, and Derby figures. – R. 123. W. 48. Strawberry Room, from Lee Priory, Littlebourne, built 1782–90 by James Wyatt for Thomas Barrett. Collection of 18C porcelain and silver, including *M149. Newdegate centrepiece (1743) by Paul de Lamerie. – R. 122 (late 18C). Ceiling and chimney-piece from Garrick's dining-room in the Adelphi (by *Robert* and *James Adam*; 1768–72); Wedgwood 'jasper' ware; mantelpiece in the Adam style from Portman Square; portraits by *Raeburn* and *Lawrence.* – R. 121 (early 19C), with 'Regency' furniture.

Rooms 120–118 contain the Primary Collection of **Victorian Art.** R. 120. Rockingham vase (c. 1826) in the rococo style; *E. H. Baily*, Material Affection; Gothic furniture by *Pugin*; Silver gilt centre-pieces designed by Prince Albert; large and elaborate objects made for the Great Exhibition; Paintings by *Landseer* and *Mulready.* – R. 119. Works by *William Morris* and his followers, including a wardrobe designed by *Philip Webb* and painted by *Burne-Jones* as a wedding present for Morris. On the left, furniture by *E. W. Godwin.* – R. 118. Works by *William Burges*; room from a Birmingham house panelled in the late Gothic Revival style (1877); furniture by *C. R. Ashbee*, and *Charles Rennie Mackintosh*; bronzes by *Alfred Gilbert.*

Rooms 44 and 47D, near the main entrance to the museum, are devoted to **Far Eastern Art.** R. 44 contains a magnificent collection of Chinese art from c. 1550 B.C.–A.D. 1900, and a smaller section of Japanese art. We proceed first to the central part of the room where are displayed some Buddhist sculpture mainly of 6C A.D. : A 98. Head of Buddha; A 55. Apsara relief; A 6. Torso of Buddha in Ting-chou marble (7C); A 9. Stele in sandstone. In cases to the left: A 16. Head of a horse in jade (Han dynasty, 206 B.C.–A.D. 220); C 879, C 50, C 51. Bright pottery tomb figures, and bronze mirrors (on end wall), of the T'ang dynasty (A.D. 618–906); Caledon ware from Lung-ch'uan, Kuan ware with 'crackled' glaze, and (A 28) jade camel (all Sung dynasty, c. 12C). (Centre) A 7. Kuan-yin, the Bodhisattva of mercy, in carved wood (late Sung, 13C). Cases on the right contain 17–18C ware from N. China (some from the reign of Ch'ien Lung), including porcelain with iron-red glaze, jade vases, and (A 17) a buffalo in jade. The large lacquer screen representing a Taoist paradise, and the Imperial throne date from the 17C. On either side are cases of porcelain in underglaze blue and red (14C), and lacquer ware, and (behind), a display of superb robes of the Ch'ing Dynasty (A.D. 1644–1912).

Returning to the entrance, we may follow the evolution of the ceramic art of China, starting with the left wall-case. From the Shang (c. 1550–1025

B.C.), Chou (c. 1025–249 B.C.), and Han (206 B.C.–A.D. 220) dynasties come bronze vessels for ritual use and jade objects, including (r.) a Chou wine vessel (M 5) in the form of an owl, and a case of small jade pendants, etc. Tomb pottery of the Han and Six Dynasties period includes (C 12) an earthenware horse (C 809) bird-monster, and (C 814) duck. During the latter period of the Six Dynasties (A.D. 265–589) a glazed stoneware was developed in the Yueh district (C 44; jar). T'ang white stoneware (C 894; flask) is displayed before later Ting ware with moulded designs (C 39) of the Sung dynasty (960–1279). In the cases opposite: Head of a Bodhisattva (6C); T'ang dynasty earthenware figures. Beyond on the left wall, Grooms feeding Horses (ink and watercolour on silk), ascribed to Jen Jen-Fa (14C). M 1154. Square Hu of bronze inlaid with gold and silver (Sung dynasty). The chronological display of porcelain continues with the blue and white and enamelled ware of the Ming dynasty, also carved and mother-of-pearl inlaid lacquers of this period. Beyond is 17C 'Blanc de Chine' porcelain which includes (135) a fine bottle. At the end of this side of the room, A 29. A Lohan (dsciple of Buddha) in wood (?14C). The cases along the right wall of the room contain 17C and 18C porcelain, including 'famille verte' and 'famille rose' ware (note particularly, C 3, plate; and 719, dish), and 18C 'sang-de-bœuf' red glaze porcelain. Opposite are cases of objects in rock crystal, quartz, lacquer, and ivory. The Chinese section concludes with the fine throne and red lacquer jars of the Emperor Ch'ien Lung (1736–95). – JAPANESE ART. On the left wall are two fine screens: E 617. Landscape by Masunobu (d. 1694), E 3054. Battle of Uji river, by Tosa School (17-18C). Opposite (E 1477) An eagle feeding its young, by Hoyen (19C). Show-cases (r.) contain fine miniature animals (netsuke) and sword furniture. In the centre: earthenware jar of c. 500 B.C.; C 44. Seto jar with brown glaze (13–14C). On the left are vessels used for the tea ceremony; C 610. 18C tea bowl, with the mark of Kenzan. Near the door, C 130. Porcelain dish of late 17C; The Four sleepers, by Sotatsu (early 17C, ink on paper), a charming work.

The Corridor (R. 47D) continues the display of Japanese art: A 10, A 11. Two Judges of Hell in painted wood (late 15C); drawings by Hokusai, Utamaro, etc.; lacquer work, including W 49. 17C Document Box; 803. Painted folding screen c. 1600; large 17C chest which belonged to the Mazarin family; A 9. Mask of Bodhisattva, probably 14C; Amida Buddha in cyprus wood (mid-13C).

We cross the top of R. 43 (p. 118) to reach RR. 47B and 42 which house a collection of **Islamic Art** from Asia, N. Africa, and Spain. R. 47B. Abbasid pottery from E. Persia and Mesopotamia (9–10C); white earthenware with black slip decoration, and glass, from Persia (12C); lead glazed earthenware from Nishapur; 7953. Ivory horn (Siculo-Arabic, 11C or 12C); Egyptian glass, including 7904. Rock crystal ewer (Fatamid Egyptian, late 10C); C 49. Bowl with figure of a Coptic priest signed by the potter Sa'd (early 12C). Fragments of 12C silk tapestries from Syria are displayed near delicate Hispano-Arabic ivories from Cordoba (10C). Beyond Persian earthenware of 12–13C, a brass bowl (760) inlaid with silver and gold dates from A.D. 1351.

Room 42 has a fine collection of earthenware, ivories, and wood-carvings, silks and carpets. Near the door (left): Persian pottery of c. 1220. Pottery from Jurjan. A case of Kashan lustreware includes a dish (C 51) with the figure of a polo-player dated 1207, and (381) a ewer of hammered brass. Beyond, 12–13C Persian pottery with fine examples of 'minai' ware. In the centre of the room, a carved marble basin from Hama (Syria; 1277). Against the left wall, inlaid pulpit (mimbar) and lamp from a mosque in Cairo (15C). Cases of Syrian pottery, glass, and damascened work include a basin (740) with an inscription of the late 13C, and the Luck of Eden Hall, a beaker of enamelled Syrian glass (13C) brought to England in the Middle Ages. More cases continue the chronological display of Persian and Syrian pottery, with contemporary textiles and tiles displayed nearby. On the end wall is the huge 'Ardabil' carpet dated 1540, among other 16–17C Persian carpets. The Ottoman Turkish collection of the 16–18C includes pottery from Iznik, textiles, and carpets.

Rooms 41, 47B, 47A1, and 47A2 hold the Primary Collection of **Indian Antiquities and Art**, an important and varied collection. R. 47B (a continuation of R. 47B, above) contains Indian Sculpture. In the centre case: Two early bracket figures from Mathura depicting tree goddesses (2C A.D.); Two small standing figures showing a celestial beauty arranging her hair and a musician playing on a flute (Orissa, 11C). Large seated figure of a Jain saint (7C). Near the right wall: *Torso in sandstone of the Bodhisattva Avalokitesvara (one of a pair from Sānchi, c. 900 A.D.). Among sculpture in the Gandhara style (2–5C) from N.W. India, showing Roman affinities, is the Head of a Buddha, and a relief with a scene of the death of Buddha. South Indian tribal bronzes include Shiva as Lord of the Dance (Madras 10–11C), and Hanuman, another Hindu deity, from Ceylon (14C).

Room 41 illustrates the art of Mughal India. Indian miniature paintings: 16–17C examples from Rajasthan and Middle India; 16–18C Mughal paintings. White jade *Cup once belonging to the Emperor Shah Jahan (1657). On the floor in the centre, *Carpet (Lahore; 1630), presented to the Girdlers' Company of London. The centre cases display Mughal jades and crystals and Mughal and Rajput jewellery; cotton paintings are displayed around the walls.

R. 47A1, the passage beyond R. 47B, contains S.E. Asian art, including a Burmese container in the form of a goose, and puppets from Burma; Tibetan and Nepalese objects (note the carved triptych and crystal jug).—Beyond 47A2 (in course of arrangement), R. 47A3 is dominated by 'Tipoo's Tiger', a hand organ in the form of a tiger mauling a British officer, made for Tipoo Sahib of Mysore c. 1790. Around the walls are Indian bedspreads and ivory carvings.

Space does not allow the display of all the treasures. Special permission to view the Reserve Collection, housed in other parts of London, can be arranged by appointment.

Room 40 is the **Costume Court** with a fine collection of English and Continental fashionable costume from c. 1580 to the present (excellent guide-book available). Each tableau is charmingly displayed and accompanied by illustrations, fashion plates, or photographs. The cases are numbered in chronological order, beginning on N.E. side of the Court. Here also are a panelled room from Haynes Grange, Bedfordshire (1620), and part of a room painted by Paul Sandby (1793). In the centre stairs lead up to a mezzanine floor with the **Musical Instruments Gallery**. Besides the beautifully displayed collection, notable for its 16C keyboard instruments, pull-out frames store more specialist instruments, and a listening bay provides musical recordings. The cases are numbered in roughly chronological order from 1520 to 1890. The following should not be missed: 16C Italian spinets; 6007. Harpsichord by Giov. Baffo (Venice; 1574); 226. The earliest dated harpsichord in existence (1521, by Jerome of Bologna); 402. Virginal and chitarrone of the late 16C and early 17C; R. 52, earliest surviving English harpsichord and organ dated 1579. On the outer rim of the gallery are cases of clocks, watches, musical boxes, etc.

Across R. 47A, in Room 48 are hung the ****Raphael Cartoons**, seven of a famous series of ten designed by Raphael in 1515–16 for Pope Leo X, as patterns for the tapestries woven at Brussels for the decoration of the Sistine Chapel at Rome. The cartoons were bought by Charles I in 1623 and are the property of the Queen. The tapestries are still preserved in the Vatican. The subjects of the series are scenes from the Acts of the Apostles.

The **Paintings Galleries** (102–106B, and 87) are best reached via the stairs which ascend from R. 25 (see plan). R. 102, the corridor on either side of the entrance to the main rooms, contains a series of transparencies by *Gainsborough*, painted for showing in his 'Exhibition Box'; also two huge paintings: *Burne-Jones*, The Car of Love (a fine work), and *Lord Leighton*, Industrial art as applied to war. The **CONSTABLE COLLECTION* of oil paintings is displayed in RR. 8 and 9. The works, in chronological order (1806–36), include: Study for the Hay Wain, Boatbuilding near Flatford Mill, Hampstead Heath, Dedham Mill, Salisbury Cathedral, Study for Leaping Horse, etc. Also, scenes of Suffolk, Weymouth, and Brighton, Still Lifes, and three Sketchbooks. R. 106B contains a selection of watercolours by Constable.

British paintings of the 19C are exhibited in RR. 104, 104A and 104B. R. 104. 64. *John Crome*, A woody Landscape; *Geo. Fred. Watts*, Portrait of Carlyle; works by *Frith, Egg, Thos. Barker* (1769–1847), etc.—R. 104A. *Turner*, 208. Venice, 211. A stranded vessel; 261. *Peter de Wint*, Woody Landscape; *Turner*, 210. East Cowes Castle, 207. Line fishing off Hastings; *Etty*, Nudes, and works by *Landseer*; 232. *John Crome the Elder*, Mousehold Heath, Norwich, 236, On the skirts of the Forest; 258. *Peter de Wint*, A Cornfield; works by *Mulready*.

Room 104B contains 18C British works: D 12, *Sir Godfrey Kneller*, Self-portrait; 564. *James Barry*, Self-portrait; 812. *James Thornhill*, Sketch for ceiling painting at Greenwich; P 29. *Francis Hayman*, The Wapping Landlady; 247. *Julius Caesar Ibbetson*, Jack in his Glory; 246. *Richard Wilson*, Landscape; evening, Landscape composition.   Works by *Geo. Morland*.   F 9. *Gainsborough*, His daughters; *Reynolds*, *Portrait of a Lady, 496. Mary Barnardiston; D 19. *Gainsborough*, John Joshua Kirby. The IONIDES COLLECTION in R. 105, is particularly noted for works by French 19C artists. 95. *Dom. Tiepolo*, Sketch for ceiling of S. Lio, Venice; 103. *Tintoretto*, Self-portrait; 98. *N. Italian*, early 16C, Martyrdom of St Catherine; *Fantin-Latour*, Still life; 19. *Degas*, Ballet scene from 'Robert le Diable'; 67. *Ingres*. A sleeping Odalisque; 54. *Rousseau*. A tree in Fontainebleau forest; 48. *Jean François Millet*, The Shepherdess; 63. *Delacroix*, Good Samaritan; 66. *Corot*, Morning; 64. *Delacroix*, Sketch for shipwreck of Don Juan; 59. *Courbet*, L'immensité; 65. *Corot*, Twilight; 47. *Millet*, The wood sawyers; 172. Landscape; 13. *Bonington*, La Place du Molard, Geneva. Portraits of the Ionides family by *George Frederick Watts*. 8. *Edward Burne-Jones*, The Mill; 83. *Adriaan van Ostade*, The Itinerant Musician; *17. *Louis le Nain*, Landscape with figures; 99. *Pier Fr. Fiorentino*, Virgin and Child; 104. *Nardo di Cione*, Coronation of the Virgin; 100. *Botticelli*, Smeralda Bandinelli; 78. *Rembrandt*, The Departure of the Shunammite woman; 165. *Beccafumi*, Charity; 22. *Poussin*, Artists sketching amongst ruins.

RR. 106 & 106A exhibit a changing collection of water-colours, which usually includes works by John R. Cozens, Thos. Girtin, Turner, Cotman, David Cox, P. de Wint, Samuel Prout, Thos. Shotter Boys, Bonington, etc.

The Foreign Paintings are in R. 87, reached via R. 94 where the Museum's finest English and French tapestries of the 17C and 18C are displayed. R. 87. 1352. *Canaletto*, Capriccio; 854. *Pieter Neefs*, Interior of Antwerp Cathedral; 340. *Jan Brueghel the elder*, The Garden of Eden; P 143. *Carlo Dolci*, Salome with the head of John the Baptist; 667. *School of Mantua*, Two decorative profiles; *Bart. Neroni*, 426. Confidence; 425. Chastity; 766. *Bern. Fungai* (1460–1516, Sienese),

The Holy Family; *1562. *Beccafumi*, The Conversion of St Paul; Fl. *Fil. Mazzola* (attrib.), Head of a Laureated Poet; 1541. *Rousseau*, View in Les Landes; *Fantin-Latour*, Cherries, Lilies, Nasturtiums; *Master of St Ursula Legend*, The Martyrdom of St Ursula and the 11,000 Virgins.

The remaining rooms in the museum are occupied by the STUDY, or DEPARTMENTAL COLLECTIONS, in which the objects exhibited—many of the highest interest and artistic value—are grouped according to class.

The collection of **Sculpture** is housed in RR. 62–64 (on the Upper Ground Floor, reached by stairs to r. of the main entrance) and the parallel West and East Halls (R. 50) on the ground floor (connected by stairs from R. 64). R. 62. ***English Medieval Alabaster**, mainly scenes from the Passion, and Life of the Virgin, the majority of which originally served as panels for altarpieces and were painted and gilded. Cases 1 & 2 contain works of 1340–1420; Cases 3–13 cover the period 1420–1520 (note the Twelve Apostles in Case 10). The Collection of ***Ivories** embraces Egyptian examples from the Old Kingdom (2815–2294 B.C.) to Coptic work done shortly after the Arab conquest in 641; Byzantine carving; medieval Gothic work from Germany, the Rhineland, England, and Northern Italy; Near Eastern and Latin American ivories (various periods, up to 18C).—R. 63 contains small European sculptures in stone, wood, wax, and alabaster. In the narrow section of the room (at the top of the stairs): 17–19C Continental wax sculpture, and 18–19C English wax portraits.—R. 64. Italian, French, Netherlandish, and German terracottas (17–19C); Italian bronzes by Il Riccio and his school; medals by Pisanello; Spanish and German work in bronze. Stairs lead down to the huge sculpture galleries (RR. 50 West & East). The larger examples of Continental sculpture and architectural detail of the 15–18C include: 908. Doorway in volcanic stone from Clermont-Ferrand (1557); 531. Dormer window from the Château de Montal (c. 1523); 4254. Chimney-piece from Antwerp (1552). On the right wall: *61. Great doorway from Ghedi (Brescia; 1515); *191. Monument of the Marquis Spinetta Malaspina from Verona (1532). Beyond a fine *Roodscreen in marble and alabaster from Bois-le-Duc (Holland; 1613), the eastern half of the hall is devoted to the Italian Renaissance: 221, 222. Carved doorways in slate from Genoa, ascribed to *Giov. Gaggini* (d. 1517); 81. Marble doorway from Genoa (early 16C); A 9, 1842. Wellheads from Verona and Venice; etc. 655. Chimney-piece from Padua (c. 1500), carved with hunting scenes; 455. Monument of Gabriele Moro (d. 1546), from Venice; 4887. Venetian marble fountain (late 15C); A 82–84. Balcony of the Palazzo Pola at Treviso. 6738–39. Florentine chimney-pieces (16C). On the left: 5895. Raphael Cartoon Gallery. On the right: 5959. Fountain ascribed by *Bened. da Rovezzano*; 548, Arch of an altar, perhaps by *Giuliano da Maiano*; 256. Nativity of the Virgin, a large mosaic from Orvieto (late 14C). The E. apse is occupied by the tribune of the church of Santa Chiara (Florence; c. 1493).

Beyond, RR. 46, 46A & 46B house an extensive collection of PLASTER CASTS and electrotypes, some of great size, reproducing many of the most famous examples of sculpture in the world.—R. 48 (East), beyond the bookstall to the left of the main entrance, contains the collection of Woodwork used for architectural purposes. *A 8. Oak staircase from Morlaix (c. 1500). Several characteristic English examples (16–18C): front of Birch's restaurant removed from Cornhill in 1926; brick front of a school at Enfield at which Keats was a pupil; *846. Oak front of Sir Paul Pindar's house (c. 1600), removed from Bishopsgate Without; balustrade of painted and gilded wood from Ferrara (16C); and a screen from a Dutch church (17C).

The rooms of the first floor (127–130) and the second floor (133–145) are occupied by the magnificent collection of **Ceramics**, in which all schools of British, European, and Oriental pottery are copiously represented. R. 127. French earthenware, mainly 16C and 17C. – R. 128. French painted earthenware (18C); French porcelain (18–19C). – RR. 129, 130. Chinese hardstones, glass and ivory, mainly of the Ch'ing Dynasty, including snuff bottles; also some wood sculpture is included here. The collection of GLASS from 15C B.C. to the present day occupies RR. 131 & 112 (connected by stairs). R. 111 contains STAINED GLASS from England, France, Germany, Holland, and Flanders (13–19C); while RR. 116 & 117 are devoted to German stained glass. – Stairs lead up from R. 129 to the Far Eastern ceramics (RR. 143–145). R. 144. 18C and 19C Chinese export porcelain. – R. 145. Chinese pottery and porcelain, mainly 17–18C, from the Salting Bequest, and painted enamels. – R. 143. Six Dynasties, and T'ang figures; pottery and porcelain of all periods; 13–17C Siamese pottery, Japanese, and Korean works of Koryu period (918–1392). – R. 142. European porcelain and painted enamels, mainly 18C – R. 141. Dutch, German, Swiss, and English tiles of 16–18C. –

Victoria and Albert Museum

Upper Floors

First Floor Rooms 65-117
Upper First Floor Rooms 118-131
Second Floor Rooms 132-145

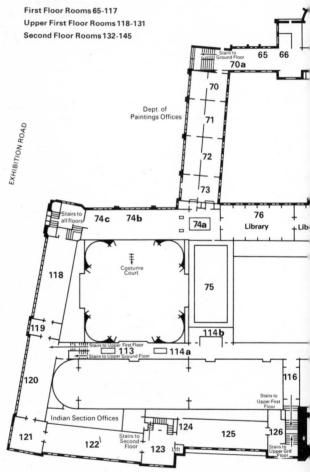

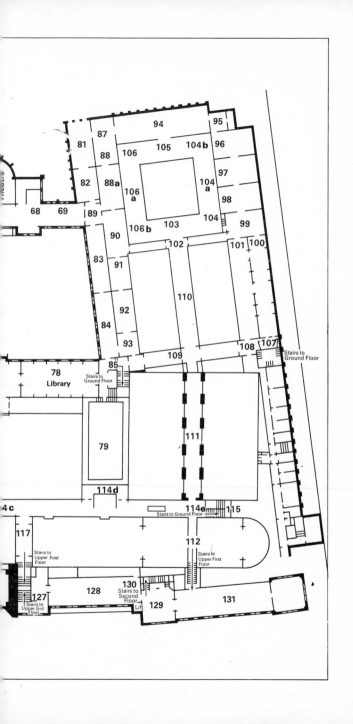

RR. 140, 139. English porcelain of 18C and 19C, including the SCHREIBER COLLECTION made by Lady Charlotte Schreiber; S. Staffordshire enamels. – R. 138. French and Italian enamels. – R. 137. English and Continental earthenware (13–20C), including a water pitcher by Picasso. – R. 136. European faience; German stoneware (15–18C). – RR. 135–133. Italian majolica (14–18C); Deruta ware from Urbino; Dutch delft; Spanish, N. African, Persian, Turkish, and Egyptian ceramics. (Best coll. of majolica outside Italy.)

From the Exhibition Road entrance we ascend to R. 74 West, with a changing exhibition of works from the Library, including Illuminated manuscripts, printed books, illustrations, etc. In R. 74 East the tools and methods used in engraving, etching, lithography, etc. are shown, together with a selection of prints. RR. 73–70 are the temporary exhibition galleries of the **Department of Prints and Drawings**. The *Print Room* (R. 71) contains over 500,000 engravings and illustrations from all periods. The **Library** (RR. 77, 78; adm. see p. 117), owns the largest collection in the world of books on fine and applied arts (over 650,000 vols.); also an important collection of Dickens novels in MS. – R. 132 is used for temporary exhibitions of **Theatre Art** including theatre models; the ENTHOVEN COLLECTION, in the adjoining room, illustrates the history of the London Theatre from the 18C to the present day (open to scholars).

The **Department of Metalwork** includes a section of *GOLDSMITHS' AND SILVER-SMITHS' WORK (RR. 65–70A) with fine examples of English and Irish domestic pieces. In R. 65 are the earliest English teapot (1670) and an early coffee-pot (1681); *M 2680. Howard Grace Cup (London, 1525); M 220. Pusey Horn (c. 1450); M 80. Romney Cup (London, 1627).—R. 68. German, Swiss, and Scandinavian work; 150. Guild Cup of the Nuremberg goldsmiths (1572–73).—R. 69. French, Italian, Dutch, Flemish, and Spanish work; 106–113. Rouen treasure of French 14C silver discovered in an old house.—R. 70A. Silver piqué and mother of pearl inlay on tortoiseshell; Spanish silver.

RR. 81–93 are occupied by the collections of METALWORK. R. 81. English and Continental pewter and lead; cutlery.—R. 82. Sheffield Plate.—R. 83 contains Limoges and other enamels of 12–13C, and Continental Church Plate.—R. 84. Brass and bronze work.—R. 88. Near Eastern metalwork.—RR. 88A & 90. European Arms and armour.—In R. 89 English Church Plate from the Middle Ages to the early 19C is displayed.—RR. 93–91 were rearranged in 1972 to house the fine collection of **Jewellery**, which includes rings and snuff-boxes. Of special interest are: 841. Darnley Ring, commemorating the marriage of Mary, Queen of Scots, to Lord Darnley in 1565; *M 81. Armada Jewel (1580), with a miniature of Elizabeth I attributed to Hilliard. This was given to Sir Thos. Heneage by Elizabeth after the defeat of the Spanish Armada. Fine 16C English work; *2697. Canning Jewel (Italian; 16C); *736. Enamelled Book-Cover of S. German workmanship; M 30. Rosary (English, 15C). The medieval jewellery includes some English 14C enamels.—R. 114, the long gallery on the First Floor, has an impressive display of ironwork and steelwork (English in RR. 114A and B; Continental in RR. 114C, D, and E).

RR. 95–101 in the E. wing, are devoted to **Textiles.**—R. 97. Carpet Study Collection. – R. 99. Near Eastern textiles (16–19C). – R. 98. Far Eastern work (mainly from China and Japan). – R. 96, 109. European and English embroideries, lace, etc. – R. 94 contains changing exhibitions of later tapestries.

THE NATURAL HISTORY MUSEUM

ADMISSION on weekdays (except Good Fri, and 3 days at Christmas) 10–6, Sun from 2.30.—CAFETERIA on First Floor; snack bar on ground floor.

GALLERY TOURS on weekdays at 3, starting from the Central Hall; LECTURES with films in the Lecture Hall. A *Children's Centre* open on Sat & in school holidays, 10.30–12.30, 2–4, provides drawing facilities, a Nature Trail, etc.

The **Natural History Museum** (Pl. 12; 7) originated in the scientific collections of Sir Hans Sloane, which were purchased for the nation in 1753 (comp. p. 176). The present building, in an elaborate Romanesque style with fine terracotta detail in keeping with the function of the building, was erected in 1873–80 by Alfred Waterhouse, and the *British Museum (Natural History)*—its official title—transferred here from Bloomsbury.

The museum contains five departments, each with its own library and study room:
Zoology, Mineralogy, Botany, Palaeontology, and Entomology. – It is becoming
increasingly biased towards biology and man. – Parties of school children crowd the
museum during term-time.

Ground Floor. The CENTRAL HALL is 170 ft long, 97 ft wide, and
72 ft high. Here is a fine display of elephants, including an African
specimen 11 ft 4 in. in height, hippopotamuses, rhinoceroses, together
with the smallest species of mammal, the pygmy white-toothed shrew
from Spain. The bays illustrate the general principles of Evolution. On
the right (E.) side Bays I–III show variation, adaptation, and selection
of species; Bay IV relates fossils to living species; Bay V demonstrates
constancy of plan in anatomy, geographical isolation, etc. On the left
Bay VI shows the principles of classification by means of lower verte-
brates and fishes (including the coelacanth); Bays VII–X, Evolution
of Man.

Behind the great staircase is the NORTH HALL, used for temporary
exhibitions (the bay to the right exhibits recent acquisitions). The two rear
cases are devoted to the giant panda, including (r.) Chi-Chi (d. 1972 in
London zoo). The passage leading to the lecture hall is lined with cases of
large reptiles (and is also used for temporary exhibitions). Beyond is an
entrance to the Science Museum (see p. 136; this access is closed on Sun).

In the W. wing, to the left of the entrance, is the fine *BIRD GALLERY.
At the end (l.) are a skeleton and model of the dodo; at the far end is
a room devoted to *British Birds*, arranged by habitat. The new *INSECT
GALLERY lies to the N. A section on British insects precedes the main
gallery which has exhibits illustrating the relationship of insects with
man, the classification of insects (l.), and the lives of insects (r.). A doorway (r.) admits to the STARFISH GALLERY which contains also molluscs,
worms, sea-urchins, etc., and a case of beautiful corals from the Great
Barrier Reef.

We may return towards the entrance along the narrow CORALS AND
SPONGES GALLERY, parallel to the Bird Gallery. Opening off this is the
HALL OF HUMAN BIOLOGY where no aspect of man's structure and functions
is not made explicit. Beyond (N.) the WHALE HALL, with models or
skeletons of the blue whale or rorqual (91 ft and 82 ft long), right whale
(60 ft), sperm whale (60 ft), and Californian grey whale (44 ft). Beyond an
exhibition gallery, the FISH GALLERY exhibits several models of large flish,
including a Whale Shark suspended from the roof. It is separated from the
main hall by the narrow *Arachnid Gallery*.

In the E. wing of the ground floor, to the right of the entrance, is the
*FOSSIL COLLECTION, arranged for the most part zoologically. The main
gallery, containing the remains of *Extinct Mammals*, is not yet completely arranged (and the W. section remains closed). It includes
mastodons, mammoths, and the Irish 'elk'; at the far end are *Extinct
Birds*, including the archæopteryx from Bavaria and wingless moas
(dinornis) from New Zealand; also the giant sloth (megatherium) and
the glyptodon, a gigantic armadillo.

The long corridor to the N. of the main gallery contains a magnificent
*Collection of *Extinct Reptiles*, including the great sea-lizards (ichthyo-
saurians and plesiosaurians), and a skeleton of a pariasaurus from
S. Africa.—The first gallery on the N. side, running at right-angles,
contains fossils of plants, the second has fossil invertebrates. The third

gallery includes the remains of dinosaurs, the largest of all land-animals, and a model of the Diplodocus Carnegii, 84 ft 9 in. long and 11 ft 5 in. high, from Wyoming, U.S.A. The skeleton of the dinosaur Tyrannosaurus (40 ft long) shows the largest flesh-eating animal. The last gallery contains fossil fishes. At the end a passage (in 1972, the only entrance) with fossil amphibians leads to the gallery of fossil mammals.

First Floor, reached by the grand staircase. The W. BALCONY contains a selection of *Mammals*, a series continued in the MAMMAL GALLERY leading off at the s. end. Among many rarities are okapi, platypus, pangolin, and Tasmanian devil. The greater part of this is occupied by offices, and (at the far end) the *Rowland Ward Pavilion* was stripped and empty in 1977. Cases on the E. BALCONY demonstrate the characteristics of Mammalia with detailed displays of their form and functions.

In the S.E. corner are cases of marbles, crystals (a crystal of Iceland spar illustrates its double refractive properties), and meteorites, including one from the Argentine weighing over half a ton.

The *MINERAL GALLERY (E.) displays part of a notable collection of c. 130,000 mineral specimens comprising about three-quarters of the known minerals in the world. The flat cases in the hall contain a systematic display of minerals (with two introductory cases l. of door, and British minerals in Cases Y & Z). In the wall cases are some notable large specimens of rocks (including fluorites). Crystal structures are demonstrated in the central cases and to the l. of the door. A case to the r. of the entrance illustrates X-ray diffraction.—At the end of the gallery the display of METEORITES is taken from the largest collection in the world, comprising specimens from more than 1270 falls. The huge Cranbourne meteor from Australia ($3\frac{1}{2}$ tons) is also displayed here.

At the top of the staircase leading to the Second Floor is a marble statue of Sir Joseph Banks (1743–1820), by Chantrey. The section of a giant sequoia from California, 15 ft in diameter, has 1335 rings of annual growth. This floor houses the BOTANICAL Department. In the *Botanical Gallery* plant ecology is the subject of a series of dioramas showing different types of habitat in the British Isles, the Arizona desert, and the Himalayas. At the far end are two large dioramas showing an African tropical rain forest, and a high altitude mountain scene in East Africa.

THE SCIENCE MUSEUM

ADMISSION on weekdays 10–6, Sun from 2.30 (closed Good Fri, and 3-day Christmas holiday). – REFRESHMENTS on 3rd Floor. *Children's Reception Centre* (with refreshment facilities; open 10.30–5). – The *Science Library* (in the S.W. part of the main Imperial College block, comp. p. 112) contains some 360,000 vols. and 18,000 periodicals (Mon–Sat, 10–5.30, closed BH.).

PUBLIC LECTURES on Mon, Wed, & Fri at 1, Sat at 3 in Large Theatre. Special lecture series (adm. by ticket on application to Publications Section) as advertised, usually recommended for children of specified age-groups. – SCIENTIFIC FILMS, Wed, Thurs, Fri & Sat at 1 (daily programme at 12.30 exc. Sun of short films for children) in Small Theatre. – Public Demonstrations of equipment take place in various galleries (Entrance Hall, Gall. 3, Gall. 66, Gall. 25, etc.).

Galleries are sometimes closed for rearrangements. The Information Office will give details of changes and closures.

The **Science Museum** (Pl. 12; 7) occupies a handsome building opened in 1928. The museum, founded in 1856, is a remarkable collection of machinery and industrial plant, working models, and apparatus of every kind for scientific research and educational purposes. Its perspicuous arrangement and its many historic and personal relics lend it great interest even for the unscientific visitor.

Ground Floor. On the left of the entrance hall is the Foucault Pendulum for demonstrating the rotation of the earth on its own axis. GALLERY 1 (r.) is devoted to temporary exhibitions. The EAST HALL and its flanking galleries illustrate the development of motive power. GALLERIES 2 and 3 (l. and r.) contain *Stationary Engines*, including

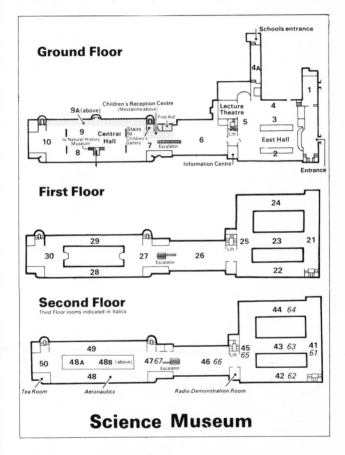

steam-engines (several beam-engines of 1777–1810), oil, turbine, wind, and atmospheric engines. GALLERY 4 to the N. is used for temporary exhibitions. GALLERY 5, at the end of the East Hall, is devoted to mechanical power transmission, hot-air, and oil engines. To the N., beyond James Watt's workshop, GALLERY 4A exhibits *Weighing and Measuring* apparatus. Behind the lift, stairs lead down to the basement with exhibits illustrating *Lighting* from the earliest times and **Mining*, including the reconstruction of a modern mine, and a wheelwright's shop.

GALLERY 6 holds an exhibition (opened in 1977 for the Silver Jubilee and designed to remain till 1980) entitled 'Exploration'. It is devoted to six topics on the fringe of present-day knowledge: *Underwater Exploration*, with a reproduction of a manned submersible; *Spaceflight*, featuring the Apollo 10 capsule (on loan) and a simulated moon-base; *The Planets and Beyond*; new developments in *Medical Science*; *Remote Sensing* and the use of non-visual wavelengths; *Climatology*. Beyond, in the new wing, Gallery 7 leads into the huge Centre Hall. GALLERY 7 has displays of steam-powered road vehicles (r.) and Underground transport (l.). Stairs lead down to the *CHILDREN'S GALLERY and Small Theatre in the basement. The gallery gives an introduction to some scientific ideas and their development, through the medium of dioramas, working models, and selected exhibits of special interest to children. The development of transport (land and water), lighting, sources of mechanical power, and measurement of time are graphically illustrated.

In the centre of the main hall is a Glasgow tram-car, and a display of *Rail Transport*, with a fine showing of locomotives and rolling-stock. Here are 'Puffing Billy', the oldest locomotive in the world (1813), the 'Rocket' and 'Caerphilly Castle'. GALLERY 9 (r.) is devoted to *Road Transport*, and GALLERY 8 (l.) displays locomotive fittings, railway models, George Stephenson memorials, etc., and, beyond stairs up to the Natural History Museum (comp. p. 133) is a display of bicycles, and motor-cycles. The Boiler House beneath the stairs is open in winter 10–12, 2–4. At the end of the Hall are Horsedrawn Vehicles, and in GALLERY 10, Fire-Fighting Appliances. A mezzanine floor (9A) in the Centre Hall accommodates an exhibition of Roads, Bridges, and Tunnels. The Children's Reception Centre is also located here.

On the **First Floor** GALLERY 21 shows a collection illustrating *Hand and Machine Tools*; 22, *Manufacture of Iron and Steel*; 23, *Glass Technology*; 24, *Textile Machinery* and *Sewing Machines*, including Arkwright's Spinning Machine (1769); 25, *Printing and Paper-making, Typewriting, etc.* Opposite the lift is a working computer portrait machine. 26 (on w.), *Agricultural Machinery*, and (l.) *Gas Manufacture and distribution*; 27, *Meteorology*; 28, *Time measurement*, including the old clock from Wells Cathedral (1392); 29, *Surveying*; 30, *Astronomy*, with a Star Dome (demonstrations weekdays 11.30, or weather permitting, in Astronomical Observatory in the roof).

Second Floor. GALLERY 41, *Biochemistry, Cinematography, Photography*; 42, *Pure Chemistry*, and the history of its study; 43, Structure of Matter; 44, *Nuclear Power*, Radio-Isotope applications, demonstration models of nuclear fission, cosmic rays, and cloud chambers, atomic physics; 45, *Industrial Chemistry*; 46, *Mathematics and Computers*; 47, *Navigation*; 48, *Marine Engineering*; 49, Models of *Ships of all kinds, including Warships, Passenger and Cargo Ships, small steam and motor craft. On the mezzanine floor are models of Sailing Ships from the earliest times and from many parts of the world (among them Oriental Craft); 50, Models of Docks, a fully equipped Ships Bridge, Diving apparatus.

Third Floor (in the course of rearrangement, 1972). 61, *Optics, Acoustics, Talking Machines*; 62, *Temperature Measurement and Control, Earth Sciences*; 63, *Physics* (18C and 19C, including the collection of George III; at the w. end is a small display of pre-1700 physics); 64, *Acoustics, Electricity*, and *Magnetism*; 65, *Electronics*, the *Discovery of the X-ray*; 66, *Telecommunications, Telegraphy, Telephony, Radar, Radio*, and *Television*. The adjacent demonstration Radio Station is usually operated Mon–Fri at 11.30 and 4, and Sun from 3; 67, *Space exploration and Rockets*, including a working model of a supersonic wind tunnel, a V2 Rocket in section, and a collection of flown air-mail covers.

The *National Aeronautical Collection* occupies GALLERY 67. Among aircraft of various types and designs imaginatively displayed with recorded histories, are Henson and Stringfellow's model for a proposed aeroplane (1843), a replica of the craft constructed in 1903 by Wilbur and Orville Wright (the first power-driven aeroplane to make a free and sustained flight), the Vickers-Vimy aeroplane in which Alcock and Brown made the first direct transatlantic flight (1919), the De Havilland 'Gipsy Moth' used by Amy Johnson on her flight to Australia (1930), and the Supermarine aircraft which won the Schneider Trophy for Britain in 1931. Craft lighter than air include a model of Montgolfier's hot-air balloon (1783). Among war exhibits are the Gloster-Whittle aircraft (1941), the first successful jet-propelled aircraft, with its engine; and a VI flying bomb, sectioned to display its mechanism. Other exhibits include aero-engines, Professor Piccard's stratosphere gondola (1932), a German rotating-wing kite (1943) and the Rolls-Royce Vertical Take-off test rig (1954), the 'Flying Bedstead'. A fine series of models shows the development of the aeroplane and airship.

THE GEOLOGICAL MUSEUM

ADMISSION to the Museum as for the Science Museum, from which it may be reached by a covered gallery. The *Library*, with 60,000 vols and thousands of geological maps and photographs of British Geology, is open free, Mon–Fri 10–4.30 (Sat closed 1–2).

LECTURES, Demonstrations, or Films Tues, Wed, Thurs, & Sat at 3.

The **Geological Museum** (Pl. 12; 7), established in 1837, occupies a handsome building (1933) by John H. Markham. Here are also the headquarters of the Geological Survey of Great Britain. The collections open to the public are exhibited in a spacious hall and in two galleries; extensions to the s. will provide a new cinema for the museum.

GROUND FLOOR. *The Story of the Earth* (in course of arrangement, 1972). A section on the London and Wealden area is at present also located here, and a *Collection of Gem Stones, with many beautiful specimens, models of famous diamonds, etc. The concave glass lids of the cases minimize unwelcome reflections. Note the vases of Siberian aventurine and of fluor-spar ('blue john'), alabaster, and serpentine.

The galleries are devoted (First Floor) to the *Regional Geology of Great Britain* (fine *Collection of British fossils) and (Second Floor) to *Economic Mineralogy*, with remarkable panoramas of mines, quarries, etc., and cases of radioactive minerals (E. end).

12 VICTORIA AND PIMLICO. TATE GALLERY

For buses and underground to Westminster, see Rte 1.—BUSES No. 11, 24, 29, 39, etc. run along Victoria St. (11 & 39 continue viâ Pimlico Rd. to Chelsea).—VICTORIA STATION is on the Circle, District, and Victoria lines.

For the *Tate Gallery*, PIMLICO STATION on Victoria line; BUSES from Victoria, Nos. 2 & 36 along Vauxhall Bridge Rd. (about 3 min. w. of the gallery); from Parliament Sq., No. 88 (or No. 77 along Millbank).—There is usually adequate meter car parking in streets near the Tate.

The long VICTORIA STREET connects Parliament Square with Victoria Station. It has been transformed at either end in clean rectilinear styles with much use of glass, though its scale was already set by the huge Artillery Mansions (1895), in gloomy Gothic, in the centre. At its E. end (l.)

are the *Department of Trade and Industry* and (r.) *New Scotland Yard*, the headquarters of the Metropolitan Police since 1967.

Broadway skirts New Scotland Yard and a solitary green with a memorial to women suffragettes (1970; by E. & L. Russell). In Caxton St. (l.) are *Caxton Hall* (1878), used for concerts, lectures (and until 1977, civil weddings), etc., and the former *Bluecoat School* (1709, with attractive brickwork), the membership office of the National Trust. At the end of Broadway are the *London Transport Headquarters* (1929), in an ingenious building by Adam, Holden & Pearson with a lofty tower and remarkable sculptures by Jacob Epstein, Henry Moore, and Eric Gill. In Petty France to the w., Queen Anne's Mansions, by Sir Basil Spence (1976), house the *Home Office*, its fortress appearance suggesting the potential violence of the age; the ugly building it replaced had sinister connections (at least in spy fiction) with military intelligence. Farther on is the *Passport Office.* — For Queen Anne's Gate and the area to the N. skirting St James's Park, see Rte 6.

The streets s. of Victoria St. beyond Strutton Ground are described on p. 140.

Farther w. rises the characterless *Westminster City Hall* (1965). Beyond, the rebuilding of Victoria St. has been more imaginative. The new *Army and Navy Stores* has stepped upper stories over arcaded pavements; the store was founded in 1871, and in 1891–1952 had branches in India. Two large blocks, beyond, were designed to frame a piazza opening before Westminster Cathedral.

*Westminster Cathedral (Pl. 18; 3), seat of the Cardinal Archbishop of Westminster, and the most important Roman Catholic church in England, was erected in 1895–1903. It was designed by J. F. Bentley (1839–1902) in an early-Christian Byzantine style, and the alternate narrow bands of red brick and grey stone of the exterior add to its exotic appearance. The church is oriented from N.W. to S.E. The square campanile is 284 ft high and commands an extensive *View (lift; fee; in the entrance vestibule). The (N.W.) façade is richly articulated in three receding stages. In the tympanum of the main entrance is a mosaic by Anning Bell (1916): Christ, St Peter, Edward the Confessor, Our Lady, and St Joseph. The detail of the dark interior is hard to see, except when lit during services.

INTERIOR. The brick walls are still partly bare, but the vast size and beautiful proportions of the church are remarkably impressive, especially when viewed from the w. end, from between the two great columns of red Norwegian granite (emblematic of the Precious Blood of Jesus, to which the cathedral is dedicated). The church has a basilican plan roofed with four domes. In the apse beyond the raised Sanctuary at the E. end is the still higher retro-choir; the Lady Chapel lies at the end of the s. aisle. When the decorative scheme is completed the walls and piers up to the height of about 30 ft will be covered with coloured marble, while the upper walls and the domes will be lined with mosaics. The total length is 342 ft; the height of the main arches is 90 ft, while the domes are 112 ft above the floor. The nave is the widest in England (60 ft; or, including the aisles and side-chapels, 149 ft). On the piers are Stations of the Cross, carved in stone in low relief by Eric Gill. The great rood hanging from the arch at the E. end of the nave is 30 ft long; it bears painted figures of Christ and (on the reverse) the Mater Dolorosa, by Christian Symons. The cosmatesque pulpit was enlarged in 1934 by Cardinal Bourne (1861–1935), in commemoration of his thirty years as archbishop here.

The lateral CHAPELS are decorated with rich marbles and mosaics. The *Baptistery*, to the right of the main entrance, is divided from the

Chapel of *SS. Gregory and Augustine* by a marble screen. The chapel was designed by J. F. Bentley, and contains mosaics referring to the conversion of England. Here is the tomb of Richard Challoner (1691–1781), bishop of Debra and Vicar-Apostolic of the London district, the most prominent Roman Catholic ecclesiastic of 18C England. The Chapel of *St Patrick and the Saints of Ireland* is a memorial to the Irishmen who fell in 1914–18. Each regiment has its own marble tablet and 'Liber Vitae'. The gilded bronze statue of the saint is by Arthur Pollen. In the pierced marble screen near the aisle appear the shamrock of St Patrick and the oakleaves of St Bridget. Next is the chapel, in a faithful Byzantine style by Robert Schultz Weir, dedicated to *St Andrew and the Saints of Scotland*. Scottish marbles and stone are largely employed in the decoration, with sculpture by Stirling Lee (lights to l. of grille). The fine inlaid ebony choir stalls (c. 1912) are the work of Ernest Gimson. The *Chapel of St Paul* has a mosaic floor based on a design by the Cosmati.

We now cross the South Transept with an early-15C Madonna in alabaster of the Nottingham School, and (above, on the pier) a bronze panel of St Teresa of Lisieux by Giac. Manzù. The apse of the LADY CHAPEL, beyond, contains a mosaic of the Madonna by Anning Bell. The mosaics of the walls and vault are by Gilbert Pownall, as are those in the sumptuous *Sanctuary*. Here the altar table, flanked by double arcades of coloured marble, consists of a solid block of Cornish granite, 12 tons in weight. Above it rises a white marble baldacchino, with eight monolithic columns of yellow Verona marble on pedestals of verde antico. The throne of the archbishop, to the left, is a reduced copy of the papal chair in St John Lateran at Rome.

On the left of the Sanctuary is the *Chapel of the Blessed Sacrament*, sumptuously decorated with mosaics (1956–62), by Boris Anrep, symbolizing the Trinity and the Blessed Sacrament. Immediately to the left of it is the small *Chapel of the Sacred Heart*, while opening off the North Transept is the chapel of *St Thomas of Canterbury*, or *Vaughan Chantry*, in which is a recumbent statue of Cardinal Vaughan (1832–1903; buried at Mill Hill), archbishop during the building of the cathedral. The chapels on this side of the nave, as we return towards the exit, are those of *St Joseph, St George and the English Martyrs*, and the *Holy Souls*. In the first is the tomb of Cardinal Hinsley (1865–1943); in the second is the shrine of the Blessed John Southworth (1592–1654), the Jesuit martyr, while figures of St John Fisher and St Thomas More are seen in the altarpiece (1946) by Eric Gill. The Chapel of Holy Souls designed by J. F. Bentley, contains mosaics by Christian Symons.

The *Crypt* may be visited on request at the Sacristy (entered from the E. end of the S. aisle of the Lady Chapel). In the S. wall of the semicircular crypt, or *Chapel of St Peter*, are four relic-chambers, in which are preserved a mitre of St Thomas Becket, some fragments of the True Cross, and other relics. A floor slab at the E. end marks the tomb of Cardinal Griffin (1899–1956), and against the N. wall is the tomb of Cardinal Godfrey (1889–1963). Off the W. side of the crypt opens the *Shrine of St Edmund*, a small chapel situated directly beneath the High Altar of the Cathedral and containing an altar under which is preserved a relic of St Edmund (displayed on 16 Nov). In this chapel are the tombs of Cardinal Wiseman (1802–65) and Cardinal Manning (1808–92), the first two archbishops of Westminster (who were originally buried at Kensal Green).

Across Victoria St. *Stag Place* on the site of the former Stag Brewery, is a precinct dominated by the well-designed Portland House (1962), cigar-shaped and raised on arches, and a colossal sculptured stag. Beyond, in Palace St., is the *Westminster Theatre and Arts Centre* (Restaurant), built in Welsh slate by John and Sylvia Reid in 1966. As a memorial to Peter Howard (1908–65), it is devoted to the cause of 'moral rearmament'.

Victoria St. ends in a confused intersection of tawdry streets serving **Victoria Station** (Pl. 18; 3), the chief West End terminus of the Southern Region of British Rail (including many of the continental boat trains). Victoria underground station, bus station (not to be confused with the coach station, see p. 141), and British Caledonian Airways terminal are located here. 'Under the clock' was a recognized meeting-place from 1860 to 1970 when the clock was sold to a San Francisco restauranteur.

The bend in the river between Lambeth Bridge and Chelsea Bridge s.e. of Victoria Station accommodates few buildings of interest to the visitor, with the notable exception of the Tate Gallery. From Victoria, this may best be reached by underground (see p. 137) or by bus along *Vauxhall Bridge Road*. This otherwise dreary street has been enhanced at its southern end by an imaginative estate of government housing, Lillington Gardens, by Darborne and Dark (1969). The well landscaped slate and brick buildings set back from the road with a pub and old peoples' home surround a Gothic church, Parish Hall and school by G. E. Street (1860). Just before VAUXHALL BRIDGE (1906) which spans the river between Pimlico and Kennington, rises (r.) the strangely coloured Rank Hovis McDougall House (1971, by Chapman Taylor), with a block of flats overlooking the river, and (l.) a pile of cantilevered Government offices (1966), with a curious air-conditioning device in the forecourt. Turning e. along *Millbank* we pass an attractive riverside garden, the setting for Henry Moore's 'Locking Piece' (1968). A plaque records the site of the steps down to the Thames used by prisoners from Millbank (the first national penitentiary built in 1812–21 on the site of the Tate Gallery) sentenced to deportation to Australia. The **Tate Gallery**, see below, is flanked on the e. by the attractive *Queen Alexandra's Military Hospital* and on the w. by the *Royal Army Medical College*. Just to the e. rises *Millbank Tower* (1959–62), the colour of the glass reflecting the changing daylight. It is the tallest occupied building in London (387 ft). We may return via Vauxhall Bridge Rd. to Victoria, or take the more circuitous route described below on foot to Victoria St.

Millbank continues e. to LAMBETH BRIDGE (1932) on the site of an ancient horse-ferry to Lambeth. *Horseferry Road* leads back to Victoria St., passing between Thames House (now government offices) and Imperial Chemical Industries House, and skirting the buildings of *Westminster Hospital* (founded 1719; present buildings of 1937). Smith Square (p. 48) lies just to the e. The cohesion of the street has not been helped by the erection of three vast connected tower blocks to house the *Ministry of the Environment*. Only after a sharp bend at its w. end do the buildings in the area become more interesting. Beyond No. 97, the *Industrial Health and Safety Centre* (adm. Mon–Thurs 10–4.30, Fri 10–4), with a permanent exhibition, Elverton St. leads s.w. to the unexpected expanse of VINCENT SQUARE, once a bear garden, and now used as playing fields by Westminster School. To the right stands the heavy exterior of the main building (1904) of the *Royal Horticultural Society* (founded 1805). Fortnightly flower shows are held here and in the second hall behind (1928; also used for exhibitions of stamps, model railways, etc.), with its curious barrel-vaulted roof lit with stepped sky-lights. In contrast is the neighbouring No. 86, with art nouveau details, and the nearby Maunsel St., a secluded terrace of early 19C cottages. Almshouses of the 19C survive off the n. side of the square. At the end of Horseferry Rd. in Greycoat Place are the pleasant buildings of the *Grey Coat Hospital* (1698, cupola added 1735; restored 1955), now a school for girls. From here Strutton Ground, which retains its street market, leads back to Victoria St. (see p. 138).

North of Victoria Station GROSVENOR GARDENS forms a double triangle of trees. The equestrian statue here of Marshal Foch (1851–1921) is by G. Malissard, a copy of one at Cassel. Between the two gardens, No. 32, now the *Commonwealth War Graves Commission*, was the site of Lord Birkenhead's death in 1930. Nos. 42–44 are the headquarters of the *Royal National Lifeboat Institution*, the oldest organization of its kind in the world, founded in 1824, and still an entirely voluntary service. Farther N. is the Riflemans' War Memorial.

. *Buckingham Palace Road*, which skirts Victoria Station, the coach station, and conspicuous British and Pan American Airways terminals, runs S.W. to Pimlico Road. *Ebury Street*, parallel to the N., is a more pleasant approach to Pimlico, crossing a series of attractive residential streets on the southern border of Belgravia (Rte 10), many connected by mews. At No. 22 is the doric portico (1830) of the former Pimlico Literary Institute. George Moore (1852–1933) died at No. 121, and Mozart composed his first symphony at No. 180 in 1764 at the age of 8. Opposite, Coleshill Flats, with an outside stair and balconies above shops, are amusing examples of 19C building.

We join *Pimlico Road*, with its attractive shops, at a small 'square' of plane trees. Here is the well-sited church of *St Barnabas*, built in rusticated stone by Cundy and Butterfield in 1846. One of the earliest 'Ritualistic' churches, it was the first in London to open with all its seats free.

We may continue W. to Chelsea (Rte 13), or turn N. into Sloane St. for Knightsbridge (Rte 10).

The Tate Gallery

The ***Tate Gallery** (Pl. 18; 6), in Millbank, overlooking the Thames, houses the National collection of British painting, and of modern foreign and British painting and sculpture, from the Impressionits to the present day. The building, in a free classical style by Sidney R. J. Smith, was opened in 1897 and three times enlarged. Opening of a further extension to the N.E., has been postponed at least until the autumn of 1978. At present only a quarter of the collection can be shown at one time, so that the paintings on exhibition are frequently changed. Galleries will often be found closed during the building extensions, and our description gives only a general idea of the collection. Any picture may be seen on application giving 48 hours' notice.

ADMISSION weekdays 10–6, Sun 2–6, except on Good Friday, Christmas Eve, Christmas Day, Boxing Day, and New Year's Day.

Good RESTAURANT with attractive murals by Rex Whistler, and COFFEE BAR in the basement.

The small GARDEN is pleasant and open to visitors.

Excellent PUBLIC LECTURES are given on Tuesdays (1 p.m.), Thursdays (1 p.m. and 3 p.m.), Saturdays (3 p.m.), and Sundays (3 p.m.).

The FRIENDS OF THE TATE GALLERY is a society which aims to help buy works of art for the Gallery. Subscribing members are entitled to extended visiting hours, free admission and private views of special exhibitions, use of a members' room and reference library, etc.

The Gallery owes its origin to the generosity of Sir Henry Tate (d. 1899). The Turner Bequest, which consisted of 100 finished paintings, 182 unfinished, and over 19,000 drawings and sketches by J. M. W. Turner (d. 1851) is partly housed in the Turner Wing, presented by Sir Joseph Duveen (d. 1908). The Tate Gallery is the repository of the works annually purchased by the Chantrey Bequest, a fund bequeathed by Sir Francis Chantrey (d. 1841), the sculptor.—Exhibitions are held in the Great Hall.

The arrangement of the British Collection in Jan 1978 was as follows: Room 3, 16–17C; R. 2, Hogarth; R. 4, 18C: Stubbs, Wilson, and Gainsborough; R. 17, Reynolds and Neo-Classicism; R. 16, Painters of the Sublime and the Exotic; R. 5, Lawrence, Raeburn, and the Picturesque; R R. 6, 7, 11, Turner; R. 8, Constable; R. 9, Landscape, early 19C; R. 10, Blake and his followers; R. 12, Martin, Danby, and Dadd; R. 14, Late Victorian and Edwardian Painting; Staircase to lower floor, Stanley Spencer; R. 28 (downstairs), Pre-Raphaelites.

Post-Reformation painting (1545–c. 1630) starts appropriately with the close follower of Holbein, *John Bettes,I*, 1496. Man in a Black Cap (1545); T606. *Hans Eworth*, Portrait of a Lady (1557); T400. *Master of the Countess of Warwick* (attrib.), Unknown Girl (1569), remarkable for the fine detail of the dress; 6090, 6091. *George Gower*, Sir Thomas and Lady Kytson; T69. *Anon*, the Cholmondeley sisters, an amusing portrait showing the closeness of the sisters; *Nicholas Hilliard*, *Queen Elizabeth I, one of two known portraits by this artist; T68. *Robert Peake* (attrib.), Lady Anne Pope, where the background has been used to heighten the charm of the subject; *3474. *Daniel Mytens*, 1st Duke of Hamilton as a boy (?), a splendid work anticipating Van Dyck; T398. *Paul van Somer*, Lady Elizabeth Grey, in a less naïve style than the earlier works; *Marcus Gheeraerts the Younger*, Lady Scudamore; two small exquisite portraits of a Lady and Gentleman by *Cornelius Johnson* (T744, T745; dated 1629). Works of the subsequent period in British art influenced by Van Dyck's arrival here in 1631. *William Dobson*, 1249. Endymion Porter, an early portrait of an English Sportsman, 4619. Sir Charles Lucas; T56. *Isaac Fuller*, Portrait falsely inscribed as John Cleveland; *Anon*, 2878. Lady of the Horton family (c. 1665).

Works of 1650–1730, including early landscapes and conversation pieces, begin with the decorative works of Sir Peter Lely and his followers. *Lely*, *3583. Frans Mercurius van Helmont, T885. Man playing a Pipe; T884. Boy playing a Jew's Harp, T70. Elizabeth, Countess of Kildare, T452. Susanna and the Elders, T58. Two Ladies of the Lake family; T247, T248, T620, T621. *Francis le Piper*, Illustrations to 'Hudibras'; *Peter Monomy*, T807. Ships in Distress; *Michael Wright*, Sketch for ceiling of Charles II's bedroom in Whitehall Palace, T132. Sir Neill O'Neill, an extravagant work; T901. *Jacob Huysmans*, Margaret Blagge as Diana (?). Also works by *Gerard Soest* (T746. Henry Howard, Duke of Norfolk. Portrait of a Lady as a Shepherdess, c. 1670), and *Laroon* (T911. Knight and Beggar Woman, 4420. Interior with figures). Kneller and the English Baroque are represented by *James Thornhill*, T814. Venus giving arms to Aeneas, 6200. Sketch for ceiling; T894. *Louis Cheron*, Apollo; 4500. *Joseph van Aken*, An English family at tea; T789. *Peter Angelles*, Conversation Piece; *Michael Dahl*, Self-portrait (1691); early landscapes by *Jan Siberechts* (landscape with rainbow), and *Jan Griffier the Elder*; *Kneller*, *273. John Smith, the engraver, 3272. 1st Marquess of Tweeddale.

*Works by *Hogarth*: 1153. The Strode family; 2437. Scene from 'The Beggar's Opera'; 1161. Lavinia Fenton as 'Polly Peachum'; 2736. Bp Hoadly; 1663. Mrs Salter; 112. Self-portrait with Pug; 1464. Calais Gate; 4756. The Graham children; 1374. The Artist's six servants; 5359. The Staymaker.

The 18C represents the great age of British painting, dominated by Allan Ramsay, Reynolds (first President of the Royal Academy founded in 1769), Gainsborough, Richard Wilson, and Stubbs. Portraiture is no longer exclusively aristocratic, the genre and conversation piece become popular, and landscapes and seascapes reach a luminous perfection. *Joseph Highmore*, 5864. Mr Oldham and his guests, 4107. Gentleman in a brown velvet coat; *Allan Ramsay*, *T1049. Alexander Boswell, *Lady Robert Manners (particularly fine colouring), 4083. Portrait of a man (1743), Lady Inglis of Gramond; T52 *Francis Hayman*, Thomas Nuthall and Hambleton Custance; 143. *Reynolds*, Lord Ligonier; 3573, 3576. *Highmore*, Illustrations to 'Pamela'; 5281. *Arthur Devis*, The James Family (a charming work); *Reynolds*, *5799, *5798. Suzanna and Francis Beckford; *Gainsborough*, Mr and Mrs Kirby (an early work), *4777. John Viscount Kilmorey, 1283. View of Dedham (?), 5845. Landscape with Gipsies, 310. Sunset: carthorses drinking at a stream; T642. Officer of 16th Light Dragoons, 308. Musidora, *T727. Edward Richard Gardiner, 5803. Gipsy encampment, 1482. The Painter's Daughter, Margaret, 2284. The Bridge, 2928. Mrs Graham as the Housemaid (unfinished).

George Lambert, T2111. Classical Landscape, 5981. Landscape near Woburn Abbey (?); *Richard Wilson*, *4874. The Thames near Marble Hill, 4458. On Hounslow Heath, *6196. Holt Bridge on river Dee, 5596. Llyn-y-Cau, Cader Idris, 303, 302. Hadrian's Villa and Maecenas' Villa, Tivoli, 3727. Portrait of Fr. Zuccarelli; *Francis Holman*, Shore scene with shipping; *Zoffany*, Mrs Catherine Wodhull; *Samuel Scott*, T1235. Sunset, with a view of Nine Elms, *T1193. Arch of Westminster Bridge, 5450. Cuckold's Point; *Charles Brooking*, 4003, 1475. Seascapes; 4679. *Wootton*, Members of the Beaufort Hunt; *Stubbs*, *T1192. Lion devouring a horse (enamel on copper), Lion and snarling lioness, *T295. Mares and Foals in a landscape. 1452. Grey hack, dog, and groom; T1115. *James Seymour*, A kill at Ashdown Park (a naïve work).

Further examples of British art in 18C, some in a neo-classicist style. *Reynolds*, 886. Adm. Viscount Keppel, 307. The Age of Innocence, 79. Three ladies adorning a Term of Hymen, 182. 'Angels' heads', 889, 306, 4505. *Self-portraits; 6005. *Zoffany*, Charles Macklin as Shylock; *Francis Wheatley*, 4654. Man with a Dog, The Bradshaw family; *Henry Morland*, 5471. Girl singing Ballads, 1403. Laundry maid ironing; 3400. *Romney*, The Beaumont family; *Wright of Derby*, 725. An experiment with the Air-Pump, 4132. Sir Brooke Boothby (an engaging work), 11278. Catania and Mount Etna (with a striking use of colour); 1943. *Fr. Cotes*, Paul Sandby; 5796. *George Morland*, Higglers preparing for market; (on screen) 142. *Lawrence*, Kemble as Hamlet; *Benjamin West*, St Paul shaking off the Viper; *J. H. Mortimer*, 5837, 5838. The Progress of Virtue; 1068. *Romney*, 'The Parson's daughter'; T930. *William Marlow*, View on Thames; 2870. *Henry Walton*, Girl plucking a Turkey (finely coloured); 217. *Gilbert Stuart*, William Woollet, engraver; *Gavin Hamilton*, Priam pleading with Achilles; *J. S. Copley*, sketch for the death of Earl of Chatham; *James Barry*, Self-portrait, T556. King Lear weeping over Cordelia; 229. *Gilbert Stuart*, Self-portrait; *Benjamin West*, T945. The Golden Age, 3510. View from Windsor, 5264. Sir Thomas Beauchamp-Proctor; T925. *John Inigo Richards*, Landscape with bridge; *Francis Towne*, Haldon Hall, near Exeter; 733. *J. S. Copley*, The death of Major Peirson.

Works by Henry Fuseli (1741–1825) and Philip James de Loutherbourg (1740–1812), painters of the 'Sublime and Picturesque'. They offer an appropriate introduction to the works of Turner. *Fuseli*, T876. The Shepherd's Dream, from 'Paradise Lost', T733. Lady Macbeth seizing the Daggers, 1228. Titania and Bottom, 5304. Percival delivering Belisane; *De Loutherbourg*, 1451. Battle of Camperdown, 1452. Battle of the Nile, T772. An avalanche in the Alps, Vision of the White Horse, T921, Travellers attacked by Banditti, 316. Lake scene in Cumberland: evening.

The *Turner Collection is the finest and most representative collection of works by J. M. W. Turner (1775–1851) in existence. It is presented chronologically.

Works painted in 1797–1815. 461. Morning amongst Coniston Fells, 496. Fishing upon the Blythe-Sand, 460. Buttermere Lake, 480. Battle of Trafalgar from mizen starboard, The Shipwreck (1805), 497. Crossing the Brook.

There is a series of sketchy landscapes, including 492. Frosty Morning, 483. London from Greenwich; also water-colours, and a self-portrait of c. 1798.

Works painted during two visits to Italy made by Turner in 1819, and 1828–29. 505. The Bay of Baiae, 5498. Venus reclining, 5506. Southern landscape with an Aqueduct and Waterfall, 2990. Ariccia (?)–sunset; fine small Italian landscapes, including (5527) Coast Scene, near Naples.

Later, more impressionistic period in the artist's work (1830–40). 5539. A vaulted hall, 2064. Old Chain Pier at Brighton, *560. Chichester Canal, 559. Petworth Park: Tillington Church in the distance; and two earlier works: 1997. Regatta at Cowes, and 2858. George IV at a Banquet in Edinburgh. Further works painted after 1830, as well as relics from, the artists studio. 2424. Ponte delle Torri, Spoleto, 1981. Norham Castle Sunrise, 1985. Sunrise: a castle on a bay. Also a series of Venetian scenes. 1987. Breakers on a flat beach, 5515. Seascape, 4658. Stormy sea with blazing wreck.

Constable and landscapes by artists living in the early 19C. *Constable*, portrait of Maria Bicknell (2655), Flatford Mill (1273), 2649. Near Stoke by Nayland, 2650. Yarmouth Jetty, 1813. View on Hampstead Heath, 2656. Sea near Brighton, 1815. Summer, afternoon after a shower. – 4785. *John Sell Cotman*, *Seashore with boats; *John Crome*, 2674. The Poringland Oak, 1645. Moon rise on the Yare (?); *R. P. Bonington*, 6326. Pont des Arts, Paris, 2664. Landscape in Normandy; *Francis Danby*, Clifton from Leigh Woods; *Constable*, 4237. Branch Hill Pond, Hampstead Heath, 1275. Hampstead Heath with rainbow.

William Blake and his followers. *Blake*: T.1128. Allegory of the Bible; 5192, 5060. House of Death; illustrations to the Visions of the Daughters of Albion; 5055. Elohim creating Adam; 5063. God judging Adam; 5058. Newton; 5059. Nebuchadnezzar; *Illustrations to Dante's 'Divina Commedia'; Woodcuts illustrating the Pastorals of Virgil; 5062. Pity; 5056. Hecate; 5875, 1164, 5896. Scenes of the Passion; 5887. The River of Life; 5188. Mrs Blake. Among the series of visionary heads are: 5187. The man who taught Blake painting; 5184. Ghost of a Flea; 5185. The man who built the pyramids. – Among works by his followers: *Samuel Palmer*, 5923. A dream in the Apennines; T1008. The Colosseum and Arch of Constantine from the Palatine; T1069.The Waterfalls, Pistil Mawddach; 4842. The Gleaning Field; 3699, 3700. Moonlit landscapes; 5805. A Hilly scene. *George Richmond*, 1492. Christ and the woman of Samaria, 5858. Abel and the Shepherd; engravings by *Ed. Calvert*. The fine detail and light effect characteristic of the Pre-Raphaelites is illustrated by (1407) *Will. Dyce*, Pegwell Bay, and (5665) *Holman Hunt*, Strayed Sheep.

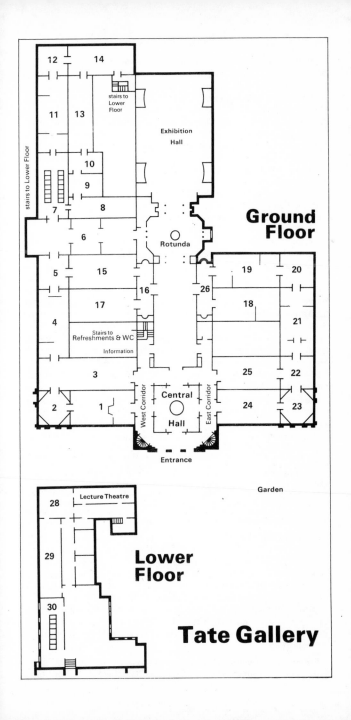

The **Pre-Raphaelite** collection. The Brotherhood was formed in 1848 by D. G. Rossetti, Millais, Holman Hunt, and others. Their choice of title illustrated their revolt against the Academy's assertion that Raphael's work was the criterion of perfection. The group ceased to exist in 1853, when Millais was elected to the Academy (of which he later became President). *Rossetti*, 1210. The Annunication, *4872. Girlhood of Mary; 1279. **Beata Beatrix** (portrait of Mrs Rossetti), 5064. Proserpine; *Millais*, *3584. Christ in the house of His Parents ('The Carpenter's Shop', painted at the age of 20), much criticized by his contemporaries for the crudity of its detail, 1657. Order of Release (showing the artist's later conformity to the sentimentality of the age), *1506. Ophelia; *Holman Hunt*, Fanny Holman Hunt, 4624. F. G. Stephens; 3597. *Will L. Windus*, Too Late; 2476. *A. Hughes*, April Love; *Madox Brown*, 3064. The Last of England, 2063. Chaucer at the Court of Edward III, 1394. Jesus washing Peter's feet; 4999. *Will. Morris*, Queen Guinevere.

English Impressionists. *Walter Greaves*, 3643. Hammersmith Bridge on Boat-race Day; 6246. Self-portrait, 4564. Walter and Alice Greaves on the Embankment; *Wilson Steer*, 5351. Beach at Walberswick, 5256. The Bridge, 4422. Mrs Cyprian Williams and her children; *Augustus John*, 4653. Llyn Treweryn, 3731. Head of a Girl (Dorelia), 3730. Washing Day; *Walter Sickert*, T221, T222. Sir Alec and Lady Martin, T259. The Servant of Abraham, 5313. L'armoire à Glace, 3846. Ennui, 4655. Aubrey Beardsley, 3182. Café des Tribunaux, Dieppe; *Harold Gilman*, 5783. French interior, T96. Edwardian interior, 4273. Leeds Market; *Spencer Gore*, 3558. View from window in Cambrian Rd., 4675. Letchworth; *Malcolm Drummond*, Girl with Palmette; *Rex Whistler*, 1905. Old Battersea Bridge, 3418. The Little White Girl, No. 2. – Sculptures by *Epstein*: Jacob Kramer, The Visitation, and Kathleen.

Sentimental Victorian and Edwardian painting. 1543. *John William Waterhouse*, The Lady of Shalott; *Alfred Stephens*, 2213. Portrait of a Man c. 1839, 3805. Self-portrait at the age of 14, 1923. King Alfred and his mother, 1775. May Ann Collmann; *George Frederick Watts*, 1634. Russell Gurney, *1561. Self-portrait (1864), etc. *John Singer Sargent*, 3706. Mrs Wertheimer, 5052. Sir Philip Sassoon, 3044. Lord Ribblesdale, 4787. Vernon Lee, 4791. Val d'Aosta; *Stanhope Forbes*, 1544. The Health of the Bride; 1522. *Sir Luke Fildes*, The Doctor; 1627. *Frank Bramley*, A Hopeless Dawn. – Sculpture: 4176. *Sir Alfred Gilbert*, Model for 'Eros'; Busts by *Alfred Stevens.*

20C British Art. 5125. *Ben Nicholson*, Guitar; *L. S. Lowry*, 5003. Dwellings, 6032. The Pond; *Gaudier Brzeska*, Horace Brodzky (bust); *Wyndham Lewis*, 5039. La Suerte, 5768. Siege of Barcelona, 5042. Ezra Pound; 5660. *Frank Dobson*, Sir Osbert Sitwell (head). Examples of the painters of the Euston Road School, founded in 1937 by *Sir William Coldstream, Victor Pasmore*, and others. 5718. *John Piper*, St Mary le Port, Bristol; works by *Paul Nash;* works by *Stanley Spencer*, including (6138) Self-portrait.

Modern Collection. The works in rooms 18–26 are changed every few months. Critics have questioned whether recent displays have not provided rather a record of outré avant-garde experiments than a show of representative masterpieces from the mainstream of art. For many reasons, not least artistic malaise in the face of the possibilities of photography, art in the 20C has tended toward obscure forms. Its fringes appear to many to degenerate into hoax, impudent cover for lack of talent or inspiration, or intellectual absurdity. The description below therefore gives merely an indication of the main artists and Schools represented in the collection.

French Impressionist Paintings. Among the most notable works in this superb collection are: *C. Pissarro*, 5576. La Charcutière, 4671. The Louvre (snow scene), 4592. Portrait of the artist; *Sisley*, 4138. L'abreuvoir, 4249. Bridge at Sèvres; 1952. *Fantin-Latour*, Mr and Mrs Edwards; *3295. *Manet*, Mme Manet; *Degas*, 3157. Carlos Pellegrini ('Ape' of 'Vanity Fair'), 4711. La Toilette, 4710. Miss Lala, 3833. Head of a Woman; *Cézanne*, 4135. 'Cézanne chauve', 4724. The gardener, 4725. Still-life; *Monet*, 6182. Seine at Port-Villez, 4184. In the park, 4183. Les Peupliers; *Gauguin*, 3289. Flowers, 3470, and other studies of Tahiti and Brittany; *Forain*, 4789. Le Prétoire, 5294. Girl Bathing; *Bonnard*, 4494. The Window, 4495. The Bath, 5414. Afternoon Tea; *Van Gogh*, 4169. Field at Arles, 3862. Yellow chair, 4713. View at Auvers; *Seurat*, 6067. Le Bed du Hoc, 3908. La Baignade; *Vuillard*, 4436. Seated Woman, 4612. The Red Roof; *Utrillo*, 4139. Place du Tertre, 4780. Porte St-Martin, 5143. Montmartre; 5142. *Toulouse-Lautrec*, Les deux amies; *Modigliani*, 4723. Portrait of a girl, 5269. Peasant boy. There are small sculptures by *Degas*, *Dalou*, *Renoir* and *Modigliani.*

A selection of the following (and other) sculpture is usually on view: *Degas*, *La Petite Danseuse; *Rodin*, *Le Baiser (marble), *St John the Baptist, and *The Age of Bronze (bronzes); *Maillol*, *Venus with a Necklace, Torso, Three Nymphs; *Renoir*, La Laveuse, Venus Victrix; *Eric Gill*, Mankind; *Zadkine*, Venus; *Marino Marini*, Cavaliere; *Emilio Greco*, Seated Figure, Bather; and works by *Hepworth* and *Noguchi.* Works by *Henry Moore*: 5387. Recumbent figure, 228. King and Queen, 389. Mother and Child, 6078. Girl, and 6004. Family Group.

Henri Matisse and the Fauves. 6241. *Matisse*, André Derain; *Andrè Derain*, T165. Matisse, 6030. The Pool of London; *Matisse*, 4717. Tree near Trivaux Pond, 4924. Woman reading with Parasol, T306. Draped Nude; The four reliefs in bronze of 'The Back' by Matisse are dated c. 1909, 1913, 1914, and 1929. 4718, Nude Study in Blue. The colourful L'Escargot is a late work (1953) by Matisse, using shapes cut from paper.

Works by Picasso and the Cubists and artists experimenting with collage; by Delauney showing a development of Cubism into colour, and works by the Futurists concerned to capture an element of dynamism in painting. *Picasso*, 5915. Bust of a Woman (1909), 5904. Seated Nude; *Georges Braque*, T445. Still Life with fish, T833. Mandolin; *Jean Metzinger*, Woman with a coffee pot; T414. *Picasso*, Guitar, Glass and Bottle (1913); *Juan Gris*, The Sunblind; works by *Giac. Balla,* *Gino Severini*, and *Carrà*; T913. *David Bomberg*, In the Hold (a work in which the process has been turned into the painting); *Robert Delaunay*, *Windows open simultaneously, 1912. Sculpture by *Jacques Lipchitz* (Head, 1915), and *Constantin Brancusi* (Danaide).

Works by artists of schools after Cubism. *Picasso* is well represented in his Blue and Pink periods, the monumental neo-Classical phase, and by later works (after 1925): (r.) Seated Woman with Hat, T729. Nude Horseman, *Three Dancers (presented by the artist), T145. Goat's Skull, Bottle, and Candle (the only post-war painting by Picasso in the Gallery), 4719. Seated Woman, T341. Dora Maar seated (both l. on screen). *Dufy* (5943. Deauville, Drying the Sails), and two fantastical paintings by *Marc Chagall* (5390. The Poet Reclining, 5758. The Green Donkey). *Braque*, *4416. Guitar and Jug, 4722. Nude; *Fernand Leger*, 5991, 5990. Still Lifes, 5907. Leaves and Shell (works showing how the object may be removed from any form of realistic context). T297. *Balthus*, Sleeping Girl. The Surrealists are well represented by *Max Ernst* (T548. Forest and Dove, Le

Ville Entiere, Bottled Moon), *Salvador Dali* (Impressions of Africa, Metamorphosis of Narcissus; both lent) and by *Magritte* and *Miro*.

The Russian Constructivists and pioneers in abstract art. The cold architectural style is represented by *Friedrich Vordemberge-Gildewart*, Composition No. 15, *Laszlo Moholy-Nagy*, KVII, and *El Lissitzky*, Proun P. 23 No. 6; and the logical development into sculpture using transparent materials is well illustrated by *Naum Gabo* and his brother *Antoine Pevsner*. Composition with Red, Yellow, and Blue by *Piet Mondrian* who reduced abstraction to the use of vertical and horizontal lines and the three primary colours. Linear Construction No. 2 by *Gabo*. The works of *Ben Nicholson* (Painting 1937, White Relief 1939) represent his pursuit of pure form and fascination with planes. *Jean Dubuffet*, The Busy Life 1953; *Francis Bacon*, Study for a Portrait of Picasso; *Graham Sutherland*, Entrance to a lane; *John Piper*, Abstract I, 1935. *Giacometti* (sculptures dating from 1949–64, and paintings including 5909. Seated Man, T781, T782. Caroline) and *Mark Rothko*.

13 CHELSEA

STATION: *Sloane Square* on the Circle and District lines. BUSES Nos. 11 and 39 (from Victoria), 19, 22, 137 (from Hyde Park Corner), 31, 45, and 49 (from Kensington). No. 39 passes the National Army Museum.—Meter CAR PARKING in streets between King's Road and the Embankment; Car Park for visitors to the National Army Museum.

Chelsea, a pleasant residential district, with many interesting old mansions and many more or less picturesque modern houses of red brick, extends for about $1\frac{1}{2}$ m. along the N. bank of the Thames, W. of Pimlico and S. of Fulham Road. From the 16C onward it has been the residence of many eminent persons, and to this day it is the home of numerous artists, and plumes itself upon its artistic and bohemian atmosphere.

About 1520 Sir Thomas More settled here with his large household in a mansion afterwards known as Beaufort House, and here he was visited by Erasmus and Holbein. In 1536 Henry VIII acquired the manor of Chelsea and built a palatial new manor-house. In this new house Princess (afterwards Queen) Elizabeth seems to have spent the interval between her mother's death and her father's (1536–47), and here Anne of Cleves, Henry's fourth wife, died in 1557. After the Restoration Chelsea became a gay and fashionable resort much patronized by Charles II and his court. Sir Hans Sloane (1660–1753), the physician whose collections were the nucleus of the British Museum, bought the manor in 1712, though he did not take up his abode in Chelsea until about 1742. Thomas Carlyle 1795–1881), the 'Sage of Chelsea', lived in Cheyne Row from 1834 till his death. Turner (b. 1775), the great landscape painter, died in Chelsea in 1851, but its vogue as a painters' quarter is connected with names of a later date, such as D. G. Rossetti (1828–82), J. McN. Whistler (1834–1903), J. S. Sargent (1856–1925), P. Wilson Steer (1860–1942), and Augustus John. Ellen Terry (1847–1928) occupied No. 215 King's Rd. in 1904–21. Smollett lived in 1750–62 in part of a house at No. 16 Lawrence St., where the celebrated Chelsea China Factory was active from c. 1740 to 1784.

The busy SLOANE SQUARE (Pl. 17; 1), with a fountain by Gilbert Ledward (1953) beneath plane trees, is the home of the avant-garde *Royal Court Theatre*. Many of G. B. Shaw's plays had their first performance here, and John Osborne's 'Look Back in Anger' was staged here in 1956. On the opposite corner stands Peter Jones, a department store in a building of 1936, by William Crabtree. KING'S ROAD, a private royal way from Hampton Court to St James's until 1829, is now the haunt of young shoppers, especially on Saturday. Antique shops abound at its W. end. It leads S.W. through Chelsea past the *Duke of York's Headquarters*, built in 1801, *Chelsea Town Hall*, and *Chelsea College of Science and Technology* (1964), and *School of Art* (1965).

From Sloane Sq., Lower Sloane Street leads s. to Chelsea Bridge Road which passes between Ranelagh Gardens and the *Chelsea Barracks* (1960–62). Just before *Chelsea Bridge* (700 ft long; opened in 1858 and rebuilt in 1937), the Lister Institute of Preventative Medicine has been embellished by the Wolfson wing opened in 1971.

The CHELSEA EMBANKMENT (Pl. 17; 4), built in 1872, extends from Chelsea Bridge to Battersea Bridge, a distance of over a mile. This picturesque reach of the river is bordered on the s. by Battersea gardens (p. 273). Just E. of Chelsea Bridge the Grosvenor Canal passes under the embankment, near a Pumping Station and tall chimney. Turning w., past a memorial to the Carabiniers of the South African War, we soon reach an entrance to the *Gardens of the Chelsea Hospital* (open on weekdays; scene of the Chelsea Flower Show in May), which command a fine view of the beautiful brick buildings of *Chelsea Hospital (Pl. 17; 3), built by *Sir Christopher Wren* in 1682–92. This refuge for old and disabled soldiers occupies the site of an unsuccessful theological college, founded about 1618. The foundation stone of the hospital was laid by Charles II; the real originator of the scheme was Sir Stephen Fox (1627–1716), and not Nell Gwynn. The central portion of the building, containing the Hall and the Chapel (see below), has a Doric portico flanked by a low colonnade with coupled columns, and is surmounted by a small tower and cupola. In the projecting wings, each enclosing a court, are the pensioners' dormitories and, at the s. ends, the houses of the Governor (E. wing) and Lieutenant-Governor (w. wing).

It was damaged several times in 1940–45, and there were a number of fatal casualties including one centenarian pensioner.

Visitors are admitted to the Hospital daily 10–12 and 2–4, and on Sun may attend the services in the chapel at 8.30, 11, and 12 (seats not very numerous; doors open ½ hr before the service begins).—The in-pensioners, about 420 in number, are boarded, lodged, clothed, nursed when ill, and receive a small weekly allowance. In summer (from 29 May, Oak Apple Day) they wear long scarlet coats, exchanged in winter for dark blue ones.

From the colonnade of the *Centre Court* we enter the vestibule off which open the Chapel (E.) and Hall (w.), in each of which a pensioner acts as guide (gratuities). The *Chapel*, on the right, is almost as Wren left it, with elaborate oak carving. The painting of the Resurrection, in the apse, is by Seb. Ricci (restored 1948).—Over the dais at the w. end of the *Hall* is a huge equestrian portrait of Charles II, by Verrio. Among the flags are some captured from the Americans in 1812–15; the portraits represent military heroes.—In the middle of the Centre Court is a statue of Charles II, by Grinling Gibbons, which is wreathed with oak on 29 May, when the pensioners receive double rations in honour of Founder's Day. The grounds are beautifully maintained and adorned with early-18C lead flower tubs.

In the Secretary's Office Block, beyond Centre Court to the E., is the *Museum* (10–12, 2–5, Sun 2–5; free), inaugurated in 1960. Here are photographs, prints, uniforms, medals, pewter, arms, etc., and the portrait of the pensioner William Hiseland, who served 80 years in the army and died in 1732 at the age of 112.

Immediately to the E. lie the delightful RANELAGH GARDENS, which now form part of the grounds of the Hospital and are entered from the E. walk (open daily, 10–dusk, Sun from 2). Nothing now remains of the spacious Rotunda which was erected here in 1742 and speedily made Ranelagh the most fashionable and fre-quented place of amusement in London.

The East Walk emerges in *Royal Hospital Road* beside the graveyard (closed in 1854), where Dr Charles Burney, organist at the Hospital, is buried (d. 1814). We turn l. to reach the *National Army Museum (Pl. 17; 3; Adm. daily 10–5.30, Sun from 2; Car Park), opened in 1971 to demonstrate the history of the British Army from 1485 to 1914. The collections have been moved from Sandhurst and augmented by loans. A vestibule with embroidered regimental colours leads up to the MAIN FLOOR, arranged chronologically to show phase by phase and campaign by campaign by contemporary objects the developing function of the army, together with the changing nature of command, service, and conditions. This is achieved by personal relics, accoutrements, illustrations, and captured trophies, cleverly selected to fill 93 cases, with excellent explanatory labels and maps.

SECOND FLOOR. In the *Uniform Gallery*, army dress is displayed by periods in conjunction with furniture and pictures in contemporary surroundings. On a long wall are the orders and decorations of Field Marshals (Gough, Wolseley, Kitchener, and Roberts). Beyond in the *Art Gallery* portraits and battle scenes form a representative collection of British painting in the 18–19C, including works by Wootton, Reynolds, Romney, Beechey, Raeburn, and Lawrence.

The *Reading Room* (apply in writing to the director) has 20,000 books, the archives of many famous commanders, and the Col. Crookshank collection of battle prints (from the British Museum).—A BASEMENT FLOOR will display weapons and equipment.

Tite Street, which intersects Royal Hospital Road beyond the Museum, was the residence for 24 years of J. S. Sargent (1856–1925) who died at No. 31. No. 34 was the home of Oscar Wilde from 1884 to 1895. The wilderness opposite is the site of the White House, built for Whistler but occupied by him for a few months only in 1878–79; he lived also at No. 13 (in 1881–85) and No. 46 (in 1888). A tablet at No. 23 Tedworth Square, to the N., marks the London residence of Mark Twain (1835–1910). Farther on, we pass the walls of the picturesque old-world CHELSEA PHYSIC GARDEN (no adm.), established by the Apothecaries' Society (1673).

Sir Hans Sloane, whose statue by Rysbrack (1733) stands in the garden, presented the site to the Society in 1722, on condition that 2000 specimens of distinct plants grown in the garden should be sent to the Royal Society, "well dried and preserved", in annual instalments of 50, a condition that has been amply fulfilled. Access is granted only to specialists by previous written application to the Clerk to the Trustees, 10 Fleet Street, E.C.4; entrance in Swan Walk, opposite a fine 18C house.

We emerge on the Embankment, here separated by narrow public gardens from CHEYNE WALK (Pl. 16; 6; pron. 'chainy'), an attractive row of red brick Georgian houses, each with its own character. Original wrought-iron railings and gates precede many of the gardens. No. 4 was occupied by George Eliot (d. 1880) during the last three weeks of her life. No. 16, the *Queen's House*, erroneously connected with the name of Catherine of Braganza (d. 1705), Charles II's queen, was built only in 1717. The fine railings are by Thos. Robinson. Rossetti lived here in 1862–82 and kept his menagerie in the garden. A memorial to him in the Embankment gardens by Ford Madox Brown, faces the house. In the gardens near the N. end of *Albert Bridge* (1873; closed for repairs in 1972), a statue of The Boy David by Ed. Bainbridge Copnall replaces one by Derwent Wood, stolen in 1969. A statue on the other side of the bridge is a memorial to Wood, its sculptor, placed here by members of the Chelsea Arts Club. Captain R. F. Scott, the polar explorer, lived at No. 56 Oakley St. (tablet), leading N. from Albert Bridge.

In the gardens on the Embankment to the W. of the bridge is a fine statue of *Carlyle* (1882, by Boehm). In *Cheyne Row* (Pl. 16; 6), the quiet and unpretentious little street built in 1708 and running N. from the river, behind Carlyle's statue, is the house (No. 24; formerly No. 5) in which Thomas Carlyle (1795–1881) and his wife (1801–66) lived from 1834 to the end of their lives. *Carlyle's House (N.T.; adm. daily exc. Mon & Tues, but incl. BH., 11–1, 2–6, Sun from 2. Closes 3.30 Jan, Feb & Nov. Closed Good Fri, and in Dec; fee)* is preserved in the quiet and dignified simplicity impressed upon it by its famous tenants. The little rooms contain furniture used by the Carlyles; on the walls hang portraits of them and sketches and photographs of scenes and places connected with them; and in glass cases are exhibited books and MSS. belonging to Carlyle and many interesting personal relics. On the top floor is the famous Attic Study with its double walls, added by Carlyle in 1853 at a cost of £169 in a vain attempt to ensure quiet. In the Kitchen in the basement (not always shown), Carlyle and Tennyson smoked together, and in the Garden 'Nero', Mrs Carlyle's dog is buried.

To the E. in Cheyne Walk, Shrewsbury House flats occupy the site of a house built c. 1519, and demolished in 1813. The original garden walls surround the flats. At No. 21 Carlyle Mansions Henry James died in 1916 (tablet in the church).

Chelsea Old Church, dedicated to *All Saints,* on the Embankment, was probably founded in the middle of the 12C. Severely damaged by a landmine on 16 April 1941, it has been beautifully rebuilt by W. H. Godfrey, and was rededicated in 1958.

INTERIOR. By the first window on the right are several old *Chained Books,* given to the church by Sir Hans Sloane, including 2 vols. of a fine edition of Foxe's 'Book of Martyrs' (1684). Close by is the large monument to *Lord and Lady Dacre,* erected in 1595. The *More Chapel,* almost undamaged by the mine, dates from 1325, and was restored by Sir Thomas More in 1528. In the corner, on the right, is the mutilated tomb of the *Duchess of Northumberland* (d. 1555), mother of Robert Dudley, earl of Leicester, mother-in-law of Lady Jane Grey, and grandmother of Sir Philip Sidney. The tomb, which resembles Chaucer's in Westminster Abbey, is probably not in its original position. The archway between the More Chapel and the *Chancel* dates from the 14C, but the capitals were recarved in Sir Thomas More's time, probably by French craftsmen. Near the W. pillar is the finely carved pulpit (c. 1679). To the right of the chancel is the *More Monument* (1532), designed by Sir Thomas More while still in royal favour, with a long epitaph composed by himself. On the left is the early 16C tomb of the *Brays,* the oldest in the church, now set into the wall under an arch. Above it is the late 16C monument of *Thomas Hungerford* and his family. To the N. of the Chancel is the rebuilt *Lawrence Chapel* (1325), entered by an archway of 1563, an early example of the classic revival and a monument to *Richard Gervoise.* Henry VIII is said to have been secretly married here to Jane Seymour, some days before their public marriage. To the right is the unusual effigy of *Sara Colville* (d. 1631), daughter of Sir Thomas Lawrence, and at the E. end is the elaborate tomb of *Sir Robert Stanley* and two of his children (1632). To the right of this is the monument to *Sir Thomas Lawrence* and his family (1593). On the N. wall of the nave *Jane Cheyne, Lady Newhaven* (1621–69), benefactress of church and neighbourhood, is commemorated in a large monument by Paolo Bernini (son of the great Gian Lorenzo).

The new tower, with clock and sundial, contains a small historical museum.—In the graveyard are buried Jean Cavalier (1680–1740), leader of the Camisards in the Cévennes in 1702–04. Thomas Shadwell (1640–92), poet laureate, and Sir Hans Sloane (1660–1753).—Near the top of Old Church St. is the old *Rectory* (No. 56), where Charles (1819–75) and Henry Kingsley (1830–76) spent part of their youth, when their father was rector.—In *St Luke's* (1820–24), an early example of the Gothic revival, in Sydney St., N. of King's Road, Charles Dickens was married in 1836.

Outside the church is a statue of Sir Thomas More (1969; by L. Cubitt Bevis). Across Roper's Gardens (see below), with an unfinished bas-relief by Epstein on the site of his studio in 1909–14, and Awakening, by Gilbert Ledward, stands **Crosby Hall**. Brought from Bishopsgate in 1910 and re-erected so far as possible with the careful retention of its most beautiful features, it is now a college-hall of the British Federation of University Women (entrance from Cheyne Walk; ring for admission).

Crosby Hall was the great hall of Crosby Place, a mansion built in Bishopsgate in 1466 by Sir John Crosby, a London grocer and alderman, and occupied by the Duke of Gloucester (1483), later Richard III. Sir Thomas More, whose Chelsea garden once included the site on which the hall now stands, seems to have bought the house in 1523, and his son-in-law William Roper occupied it. Roper's Gardens are now laid out on the site of Sir Thomas More's orchard. In the 16C the mansion was considered sumptuous enough to be the abode of various ambassadors. When Crosby Place was burned in the 17C the hall escaped to meet a chequered fate, finally becoming a restaurant before its purchase in 1908 by the University and City Association of London. It was used as a reception centre by the Chelsea War Refugees Committee during the First World War. The hall retains a fine oriel window and the original roof, and contains a copy of Holbein's lost group of Sir Thomas More's family, c. 1527. — At 20A Danvers St. died Sir Alexander Fleming (1881–1955), discoverer of penicillin; in the 30s the unrelated Peter Fleming, explorer-writer, occupied the flat above.

Battersea Bridge, an iron structure (1890) crossing the river at the end of Beaufort Street, replaces the picturesque old wooden bridge of 1771–72, which was a favourite subject with Whistler and other artists. The river, lined with warehouses and docks, here bends s., and offers moorings for house-boats.

To the w. of the bridge are several interesting old houses in *Cheyne Walk*. Mrs Gaskell (1810–65) was born at No. 93 (tablet). Whistler lived at No. 96 in 1866–78, and No. 101 was his first abode in Chelsea (1863–66). *Lindsey House* (N.T.), named after the Earl of Lindsey, the only 17C mansion in Chelsea, is divided into Nos. 97–100; a tablet on No. 98 marks the home of the Brunels, father and son, both engineers. P. Wilson Steer died at No. 109 in 1942. At No. 118 (damaged) J. M. W. Turner lived in anonymous retirement from 1846, and died here in 1851. George Meredith wrote 'The Ordeal of Richard Feverel' at No. 7 Hobury St., a little to the N., and Henry Tonks (1862–1937) died at No. 1 The Vale, farther E.

At the end of Cheyne Walk is Lots Road, with a huge electric power-station. Cremorne Rd., crossing the site of the old *Cremorne Gardens* (1845–77), leads on the right to *King's Road*, the approach to Fulham (see Rte 39A).

14 SHAFTESBURY AVENUE AND SOHO

STATIONS: *Piccadilly* on Bakerloo and Piccadilly lines; *Leicester Square* on Northern and Piccadilly lines; *Tottenham Court Road* on Central and Northern lines.—BUSES: Nos. 14, 19, 22, 38, etc. in Shaftesbury Avenue; Nos. 1, 24, 29 & 176 in Charing Cross Rd.—CAR PARKS: Poland St., Broadwick Garage, Gerrard St., Wardour St., Leicester St. (crowded in the evening).

Shaftesbury Avenue (Pl. 14; 4), a centre of entertainment runs N.E. from Piccadilly Circus through the area known as **Soho**. The name, first recorded in 1636, derives from an ancient hunting cry used when the area w. of Wardour St. was parkland.

This congested, sometimes squalid district of narrow streets dating from the end of the 17C, is given character by its cosmopolitan elements. French refugees settled in Bateman St. soon after the Revocation of the Edict of Nantes in 1685. It is now renowned as a centre of gastronomy and of dubious entertainment. The restaurants of Soho, not all of them inexpensive, have long enjoyed a considerable vogue. Most of the houses with historical associations, or of architectural merit, have been brutally altered or destroyed in the commercial interest. Carnival processions with dragons are held at Chinese New Year.

Wardour Street, home of the cinema industry, crosses Shaftesbury Ave. In *Gerrard Street*, now almost entirely given over to Chinese trading, Dryden lived from 1687 till his death in 1700 (No. 44, rebuilt; tablet on No. 43). In 1900 G. K. Chesterton and Hilaire Belloc first met at a French restaurant here. To the N. of Shaftesbury Ave., beneath the heavy steeple (1801–03, by S. P. Cockerell) of *St Anne's*, is the monument of William Hazlitt (1778–1830). The body of the church (1685, partly by Wren) was destroyed in 1940.

Old Compton Street, with many foreign provision shops, lies to the N., near *Berwick Street*, the scene of an animated produce market. Broadwick Street was the birthplace of William Blake (1757–1828) who lived at No. 74 (demolished; inscription in Marshall St.) till 1771, returning in 1772 till his marriage in 1782 when he moved next door. Shelley took lodgings at No. 15 Poland St., near by, in 1811 after his expulsion from Oxford.

In *Dean Street*, the next turning left from Shaftesbury Ave., Nollekens the sculptor, was born in 1737 at No. 28, and Karl Marx lived at No. 26 from 1851–56 (both houses built c. 1734, now a restaurant). Clubs and restaurants abound in the parallel *Frith Street* where Hazlitt died at No. 6 (1718, partly rebuilt) in 1830, and at No. 22 (Bianchi's Rest; plaque in upstairs room) J. L. Baird staged his first television demonstration in 1926.

To the N. lies **Soho Square**, laid out in 1681 (though only one 18C house survives), and now a centre of the music trade. In 1764 Mozart (then lodging at No. 20 Frith St.) taught music in the house (No. 22) of Lord Mayor William Beckford, brother of Richard (see below). The statue of Charles II is by Cibber (1681). On the E. side of the square, the Italianate *St Patrick's* church (R.C.) was opened in 1793 (rebuilt, 1891–93). The French Protestant church (ring for adm. at door on r.) dates from 1893.

The square was first surrounded with large mansions, including one belonging to the Duke of Monmouth, whose chose 'Soho' as his password at the Battle of Sedgemoor (1685). It soon became a fashionable area, and Sir Roger de Coverley had his town quarters here. In the 18C it was a favourite residence of ambassadors. No. 32 (rebuilt), where Sir Joseph Banks came to live in 1777, was the centre in London for the scientists of the time (Cavendish, Priestley, and others) and the inaugural meeting of the Royal Institution was held there.

In the s.e. corner of the square the House of ST BARNABAS-IN-SOHO (adm. Mon 10.30–12, Thurs 2.30–4.30; donations welcome), a mansion built in the late 1740s, has been occupied by a charity for the destitute (founded by Dr Henry Monroe in 1846) since 1862. It was the home of Richard Beckford in 1754, and he was probably responsible for the fine rococo plasterwork, wood carving, and ironwork in the interior. The chapel dates from 1862. The meeting between Dr Manette and Sidney Carton in Dickens' 'Tale of Two Cities' occurred in the rear courtyard (comp. Manette St., entered by an archway in Greek St.). *Greek Street* is named after a colony of Greeks from Melos whose church founded c. 1680 was in Charing Cross Road, parallel to the e.

Charing Cross Road (Pl. 14; 4), still a market for second-hand books though the trade is less flourishing than formerly, has many theatres. The *Phoenix Theatre*, to the n., opened in 1930 with Coward's 'Private Lives'. In *Cambridge Circus*, the junction with Shaftesbury Avenue, is the terracotta *Palace Theatre* (1888, by T. E. Colcutt). It opened as the English Opera House in 1891 with Sir Arthur Sullivan's 'Ivanhoe', and Anna Pavlova made her first London appearance here. To the s., is the octagonal lantern of the Welsh Presbyterian Chapel (1887, by James Cubitt). In Gt. Newport St. is the Photographers' Gallery (Tues–Sat, 11–7; Sun 12–6).

Cranbourn St. leads w. to **Leicester Square** (Pl. 14; 4), already notorious by 1700 as a scandalous centre of entertainment. Laid out in the 1670s, it was named from Leicester House, which stood on the n. side in 1631–35. In the centre is a statue of Shakespeare, and at the four corners are busts of distinguished residents. It is now partly closed to traffic.

In the 18C the area was much frequented by artists. From 1753 until his death in 1764 Hogarth had his town house at the s.e. corner (No. 30). Sir Joshua Reynolds lived at No. 47, on the w. side, from 1760 till his death in 1792; this was the first house to acquire an official commemorative plaque (1875). Charles d'Agar lived at Nos. 22 and 29, Philip Mercier at No. 40, and Michael Dahl at No. 49. Swift had rooms here in 1711. At No. 28 John Hunter built a museum for the famous Hunterian collection, later moved to the College of Surgeons.

Here three famous 19C music halls gave place to 'super-cinemas' presenting first runs of Hollywood films. First to change in 1920 was the *Empire* (rebuilt 1927) which had shown moving pictures as early as 1891. Later the *Warner* succeeded *Daly's*, where the Carl Rosa Opera had introduced 'Hansel and Gretel' to England and later musical successes included 'The Merry Widow' and 'Maid of the Mountains'. The *Odeon* occupies the site of the *Alhambra* (1854–1936), where the eclectic entertainment ranged from the 'Bing Boys' to the distinguished Diaghilev season of 1921.

In St Martin's St., leading out of the square on the s. side, the admirable *Westminster Reference Library* (open free weekdays) replaces the house occupied by Sir Isaac Newton (1710–27) and Dr Burney (1774–94). Here Fanny Burney wrote 'Evelina' – In Leicester Place, on the n. side, the French church of *Notre-Dame de France*, burned in 1940, was completely rebuilt in 1955 save for its circular wall (a relic of Burford's 'Panorama' established in 1793). In the interior is a mural by Jean Cocteau (1960), and over the altar an Aubusson tapestry.

More theatres are located in **St Martin's Lane** (Pl. 14; 4), farther e. The *Coliseum Theatre*, with its prominent globe, became in 1968 the new home of Sadler's Wells now English National Opera Company. It was built (1904) as a Music Hall by Sir Oswald Stoll, and Ellen Terry, Lily Langtry, and Sarah Bernhardt all appeared on its elaborate stage. The *Duke of York's* (1892) saw the first performance of Barrie's 'Peter Pan'. A tablet on No. 6 marks the site of Chippendale's workshop from 1753; in 1764 Mozart lodged in *Cecil Court* (l.), now lined with print and book shops; while *Goodwin's Court* (r.) preserves some charming 18C shop-fronts. The

Albery Theatre was named after Sir Bronson Albery, theatre manager in the Thirties. Formerly the New Theatre, it presented the first performance of Shaw's 'St Joan' (1924).

St Martin's Lane is continued N. by Monmouth Street, through Seven Dials, once a notorious thieves' quarter, towards St Giles and New Oxford St. *Seven Dials* proper (Pl. 14; 2), a circular space at the junction of seven streets, derived its name from a column (comp. p. 291) bearing six or seven arms which stood here until 1773.

15 REGENT STREET TO REGENT'S PARK.
MARYLEBONE AND PADDINGTON

STATIONS: *Piccadilly Circus* on Piccadilly and Bakerloo lines; *Oxford Circus* on Victoria, Central and Bakerloo lines; *Warren Street* (for Post Office Tower) on Northern and Victoria lines; *Regent's Park* on Bakerloo line; *Great Portland Street* on Metropolitan and Central lines.—*Baker Street* (for Mme. Tussaud's) on Bakerloo, Metropolitan, and Circle lines; *Marble Arch* (for Wallace Collection) on Central line.—*Paddington* and *Warwick Avenue* (for 'Little Venice') on Bakerloo line.

BUSES: Nos 3, 6, 12, 15, 53, etc. in Regent St.; No. 3 & 53 continue up Portland Place (one-way N.; Gt. Portland St., one-way s.) and Albany St. No. 137 runs along Oxford St. and up Portland Place. For the Zoo, No. 74 runs N. along Gloucester Place to Prince Albert Road.—In Marylebone Rd., Nos. 27 & 30.—For the Wallace Collection, Nos. 2, 30, & 74 in Gloucester Place (one-way N.) and Baker St. (one-way s.).—From Marble Arch, No. 6 runs N. along Edgware Rd. (and left into Clifton Rd. for 'Little Venice').

CAR PARKING prohibited in all the main thoroughfares; meter parking in side-streets extremely limited. Car parks in Cavendish Square, Marylebone Lane, and Queen Anne St. (Harley Garage). For Regent's Park, see p. 157.

Regent Street (Pl. 6; 7), 1 m. in length, the main thoroughfare from s. to N. in the West End and essentially a street of shops, begins on the s. at Waterloo Place (comp. p. 96), crosses Piccadilly Circus and Oxford Circus, and ends on the N. at Langham Place. It was laid out about 1813–20 by Nash to unite Carlton House with Regent's Park, but has since been entirely rebuilt.

Above Piccadilly Circus is the curved portion of Regent St. known as the *Quadrant*, the façades in which were rebuilt in 1925–26 from the designs of Sir R. Blomfield. Beyond, the *Café Royal* was frequented by aspiring literary figures and artists in the early part of this century, including Aubrey Beardsley, Max Beerbohm, and Augustus John (comp. the painting inside of c. 1916 by Adrian Allinson).

GOLDEN SQUARE, to the E., is now a centre of the woollen cloth trade. Angelica Kauffmann lived at No. 16, Cardinal Wiseman at No. 35, and John Hunter, the surgeon, at No. 31 (all rebuilt). The statue in antique costume, in the centre of the square, represents George II. In Warwick St., near by, a R.C. church survives from 1789.

On the w. side of Regent Street, Conduit St., and Maddox St., with many fashionable milliners and tailors, lead to New Bond St. On the E. side, in Tenison Court is *St Thomas's* (closed), built for Abp. Tenison in 1702 and partly rebuilt in 1860. Beyond Hamley's renowned toy shop, Liberty's, noted for fabric design, has a mock Tudor building of 1924 in Great Marlborough St. Behind, *Carnaby Street*, a byword for the eccentric fashionable in young people's clothes, has been made a pedestrian precinct (closed to motor traffic Mon-Sat, 11–8).

West of Regent St. lies **Hanover Square**, with a bronze statue of

William Pitt (1759–1806). No. 21 was occupied by Talleyrand in 1835. *St George's, Hanover Square*, to the s., was built in 1713–24, and three of the E. windows contain 16C stained glass from Malines placed here c. 1843. The two cast-iron dogs in the porch are said to be by Landseer.

The registers contain entries of the marriages of Sir Wm. Hamilton and Emma Lyon or Hart (1791), Benjamin Disraeli and Mrs Wyndham Lewis (1839), 'George Eliot' and Mr J. W. Cross (1880), Theodore Roosevelt and Edith Carow (1886), and H. H. Asquith and Margaret Tennant (1894); also of the remarriage of Shelley and Harriet Westbrook in 1814 confirming the Scottish marriage of 1811.

Oxford Circus marks the junction of Oxford St. and Regent St. On the line of a Roman road, Oxford Street, with Selfridge's and other clothing and department stores, is always crowded with shoppers (partially closed to cars from 11 a.m. to 9 p.m. exc. Sun). In Regent St. N. of Oxford Circus is the *Polytechnic of Central London* founded in 1882, for the mental, moral, and physical development of youth. The line of Regent St. is prolonged to the N. by the curving *Langham Place* where the tower and needle-like spire of *All Souls' Church* were built by Nash in 1823–24 and almost detached from the church in order to close the vista up Regent St. In the portico is a bust by Behnes of the architect.

Langham Place is continued northward towards the green expanse of Regent's Park (p. 157) by PORTLAND PLACE, one of the broadest streets in London. At its foot (r.) rises *Broadcasting House*, the headquarters of the B.B.C., a huge edifice by Val Myer and Watson Hart (1931), with a sculptured group of Prospero and Ariel by Eric Gill. The Corporation has spread to other buildings across the road.

The Adam houses in Portland Place (1776–80) are gradually yielding to larger modern structures. At No. 28 is the *Royal Institute of Public Health and Hygiene*. No. 66 is the *Royal Institute of British Architects*, in a striking building by G. G. Wornum (1934). Monuments in the roadway commemorate *Quintin Hogg* (1845–1903), founder of the Polytechnic (see above); *Sir George White* (1835–1912), defender of Ladysmith (opposite No. 47, once the house of Lord Roberts); and *Lord Lister* (1827–1912), the surgeon.

The attractive and fashionable physicians quarter to the w. of Portland Place is famed for its consulting rooms of many medical and surgical specialists, occulists, and dentists. **Cavendish Square** (Pl. 6; 5; underground car park) dates from about 1717; the columned facades of two of the houses on the N. side are relics of a great mansion begun in 1720 for the Duke of Chandos. The archway connecting the two wings is adorned with a Madonna by Epstein. Nelson lived at No. 5 in 1787. No. 20 is the *Cowdray Club* for nurses, formerly the house of H. H. Asquith (1852–1928), Prime Minister. Dr Brown-Séquard (1817–94; born in Mauritius), a pioneer in many fields of medicine, was also a resident in the square. In the garden is a statue of Lord George Bentinck (1802–48).—In *Holles St.* (s.) Lord Byron (1788–1824) was born at No. 21, now the site of a department store, with a sculpture by Barbara Hepworth on the s.w. wall. At the end of Chandos St. (N.E. corner of the square), the fine *Chandos House* built by Robert Adam in 1771 is part of the Royal Society of Medicine.

WIGMORE STREET, a fashionable shopping street with restaurants and coffee shops, and Henrietta Place lead hence to the w. Chamber music recitals are held in *Wigmore Hall*. At the end of Henrietta Place is the *Royal Society of Medicine*, with its famous library. Opposite *St Peter*, *Vere Street*, a neat little church by Gibbs (1721–23) has unusual capitals inside. To the w. of Oxford St., the attractive *Stratford Place* (1773–75) retains Stratford House, now the Oriental Club. In WELBECK ST., leading N. from Wigmore St., Anthony Trollope died at a house on the site of No. 34 in 1884. Thos. Woolner lived at No. 29 and Thos. Young at No. 48 (tablets). Edward Gibbon published the first volumes of his great history while living at No. 7 Bentinck St. (leading hence to Manchester Sq.) in 1772–83 and Sir James Mackenzie lived at No. 17 (plaques). Berlioz stayed at No. 58 Queen Anne St. (on the E. side of Welbeck St.) in 1851 when he was a judge at the Great Exhibition competition for makers of musical instruments.

Henry Hallam lived in 1819–40 at No. 67 WIMPOLE STREET, "the long unlovely street" of 'In Memoriam' written in commemoration of A. H. Hallam (1811–33). From No. 50 (rebuilt), her home since 1836, Elizabeth Barrett stole secretly in 1846 to be married to Robert Browning in Marylebone church and again a few weeks later to accompany him to Italy. Wilkie Collins, who died at No. 82 in 1889, was born in 1824 at No. 11 (demolished) New Cavendish Street which leads E. to Great Portland St. and W. to Marylebone High St. Turner, the landscape-painter, lived for many years at No. 64 HARLEY ST., and was also the eccentric tenant of a house in Queen Anne St. (close by) from 1812–51 (house rebuilt; tablet on No. 23). No. 73 Harley St. was occupied by Gladstone from 1876–82 (rebuilt). *Queen's College* (43 Harley St.), founded in 1848, is the oldest college for women in England.

An unattractive area N.E. of Oxford Circus contains the shops of textile wholesalers. In *Great Portland Street*, the main thoroughfare of this quarter with many motor-dealers, Boswell died at No. 122 (rebuilt). The *Central Synagogue* (l.), N. of New Cavendish St., was rebuilt in 1958. Margaret St. runs E. to *All Saints Church*, a brick building by Butterfield (1849–59), with a fine tower and spire, important to the development of Gothic revival architecture.

Mortimer Street, where (at No. 44) Nollekens, the sculptor, lived for fifty years, leads to the *Middlesex Hospital*, a noted teaching hospital founded in 1755. Here Kipling died in 1936. Behind the hospital is Foley St. where lived Sir Edwin Landseer (No. 33) and Henry Fuseli (No. 37). At 82 Great Tichfield St. (demolished), parallel with Gt. Portland St., Samuel Morse, the American pioneer of electric telegraphy, and C. R. Leslie, the Philadelphia artist, had rooms, in 1811, before moving to No. 8 Buckingham Place, now No. 141 Cleveland St., near by. The huge new glass science building of the London Polytechnic dominates New Cavendish St. to the N. In *Charlotte Street*, the main axis of a 'Bohemian' quarter to the E. (Greek restaurants, and produce shops in Goodge St.), No. 76 was leased by Constable in 1822 until his death in 1837, and the Rossettis lived at No. 50 in 1847 (both houses demolished). In Scala St. (r.) *Pollocks' Toy Museum* is open daily 10–5 (Punch and Judy shows 12.30 and 2.30). In Fitzroy St. (which continues N. to Fitzroy Square) Richard Wilson, Sickert, and Whistler lived. The central headquarters of The Post Office stand below the tallest building in London, the **Post Office Tower** for television and radio-telephony (1964; 619 ft. Lift to viewing platform. Revolving Restaurant, not cheap). The compact FITZROY SQUARE was begun (E. and S. sides) by the Adam brothers in 1792. Bernard Shaw lived at No. 29 in 1887–98.

Portland Place emerges in *PARK CRESCENT, a fine composition (1812–22) by John Nash. Outside the International Students' House (No. 1) is a bust of President Kennedy by J. Lipchitz. We cross Marylebone Rd. (see below) and skirt Park Square Gardens to reach **Regent's Park** (Pl. 5; 4). Roughly circular in shape, the park has an area of 472 acres, and within its precincts are the Zoological Gardens.

CARS are admitted to the Outer Circle, and (viâ Chester Road and York Bridge) to the Inner Circle. Unlimited free parking on all these roads after 10.30 a.m.

RESTAURANT and Cafeteria in Queen Mary's Gardens; Snack bar on Broad Walk.

An open-air THEATRE in Queen Mary's Gardens holds performances of Shakespeare plays in summer.

BANDS play on Sun in Aug.

BOATS may be hired at the boat house near Hanover Gate (N.E. end of lake). Children's boating pond.—For boats along Regent's Canal, see p. 174.

Marylebone Park was claimed by Henry VIII as a royal hunting ground, and continued as such until Cromwell's day. It was laid out in its present style as an aristocratic 'garden suburb' after 1812 by Nash, and named after the Prince Regent, who contemplated building a country house here.

The park is encircled by a carriage-road known as the *Outer Circle*, the S. half of which is flanked by fine monumental Regency *Terraces in the classical style, mainly by Nash. From S. to N., across the E. half of the park, runs the *Broad Walk* (1 m.) leading straight to the Zoological Gardens. In the S.W. portion of the park is an artificial lake of 22 acres (with many wildfowl), while to the N. runs the Regent's Canal laid out by Nash in the 1820s. Near the S. end of the Broad Walk are beautifully kept flower-gardens, but the fine greensward covering the greater part of the park is used for cricket and other games.

From York Gate on the s. a road leads to the N. to the drive known as the Inner Circle. On the left, beyond the bridge, stands **Bedford College,** a School of London University, founded in 1849 to provide for women a liberal education in secular subjects, and removed here in 1913. The buildings were rebuilt in 1948–50 after war damage. Men have been admitted since 1965. The circular *Queen Mary's Gardens* (18 acres; entered by elaborate gates of 1933–35), within the Inner Circle, occupied from 1840 to 1932 by the Royal Botanic Society, is now one of the prettiest little public parks in London, with a rosery, a lily-pond, the Mermaid fountain (by W. McMillan, 1950), and an open-air theatre.

St John's Lodge, with a secluded rose-garden on the N. side of the Inner Circle, is part of Bedford College. It was enlarged by Barry in 1846–47 (and altered in the 90s by Robert Weir Schulz).—*Winfield House*, on the Outer Circle, was built for Barbara Hutton in 1936, and is now the residence of the American Ambassador. Residents of Nash's *Hanover Lodge* (c. 1827), across the road, include Thos. Cochrane, Joseph Bonaparte, king of Naples, and Adm. Earl Beatty. Lutyens's additions were swept away in 1961–64 when the building became a hall of residence for Bedford College. *Regent's Lodge*, by Hanover Gate, houses the Islamic Cultural Centre next to the *Central Mosque*, built 1954–77. H. G. Wells (1866–1940) died at No. 13 Hanover Terrace, and Ralph Vaughan Williams (1872–1958), the composer, died at No. 11. The last home of Sir Edmund Gosse (1849–1928), the critic, was No. 17. In Sussex Place, beyond the new building of the Royal College of Obstetricians and Gynaecologists, the *London Graduate School of Business Studies* (founded in 1965; c. 250 students) occupies a pleasant new building in yellow stone (1970, by Westwood, Piet, & Ptnrs.) concealed behind the fine Nash façade on the park. *St Cyprian*, in Glentworth St. to the s., has a light interior by Ninian Comper (1903). *York Terrace West* (now entered from the pleasant road to the s.) has been faithfully rebuilt to Nash's design.

On the E. side of the park the monumental terraces by Nash (Chester and Cumberland Terrace, 1825–26) facing the Outer Circle have their backs to the long ALBANY STREET. At the s. end is the *Royal College of Physicians* (1962–64), a fine building by Denys Lasdun. *St Katharine's Church*, at the N. end, formerly the chapel of the St Katharine's Royal Foundation (comp. p. 276), was built in 1823. Restored (after war damage) in 1950–52, it is now the church of the Danish community in London. It has fine carving on the ceiling, two wooden figures of saints (by C. G. Cibber, 1696) from the old Danish church at Limehouse, and, above the windows, 39 shields of arms of the Queens of England from Matilda to Queen Mary. In Albany St. are territorial barracks, the White House, and *Christ Church* (1837, by Pennethorne) where the Rev. William Dodsworth was the first vicar. At the s. end *Holy Trinity* church, built by Soane in 1826–27, is now the headquarters of the S.P.C.K.

The ****Zoological Gardens** (Pl. 5; 1; 36 acres), familiarly known as 'the *Zoo*', are officially the Gardens of the *Zoological Society of London*, founded by Sir Stamford Raffles and Sir Humphry Davy (1826). Situated at the N. end of Regent's Park, they are bounded on the N. by Prince Albert Road and on the E. by the Broad Walk, and are intersected by the Regent's Canal and by the Outer Circle. The three divisions thus formed are united by three bridges over the canal and by two tunnels beneath the roadway.

There are three entrances to the gardens: the Main Entrance in the Outer Circle, the North Entrance in Prince Albert Road (closed Oct–March), and the South Entrance in the Broad Walk. The Gardens are most conveniently reached by taxi, or by No. 74 bus, to the N. entrance, from *Camden Town* (Northern line) or *Baker Street* (Bakerloo line). In summer they may be pleasantly reached on foot through Regent's Park from *Gt Portland St.* (Circle line) or *Regent's Park* (Bakerloo line); or by WATERBUS from Little Venice along Regent's Canal (daily, every hour; see p. 170).
The Gardens are open daily (except Christmas Day), March–Oct from 9, Nov–Feb

from 10 to sunset or 7 p.m. whichever is earlier. The Aquarium opens at 10, and the Children's Zoo at 10.30 throughout the year. — ADMISSION £1·50. First Sat every month half price. For the Aquarium, and for the Children's Zoo, 20p extra. Children always half-price. — Push-chairs, and invalid chairs may be hired. — Restaurant, Cafeterias, and Bar.

The FEEDING TIMES of the animals are as follows: pelicans and penguins 2.45; penguins (Penguin Pool) 2.30; sea lions 12 and 3.30, winter 2.30, exc. Fri; eagles and vultures 3.15, exc. Thurs; reptiles 2.30, Fri only. — Elephants' bathtime, 11.30. — In the Childrens Zoo: Donkey rides 1.15, exc. Sun. — Llama trap, pony trap, and camel rides in summer (1.45). — Feeding of animals by visitors is forbidden for dietary reasons.

The Gardens are in course of complete redevelopment, begun in 1959 to a plan by Sir Hugh Casson, which is now nearly completed. In the following directions only the most popular exhibits are mentioned. Some of the animals will be moved from time to time. Excellent Official Guide available.

From the Main Entrance we take the right-hand path to the high *Mappin Terraces* built of reinforced concrete in 1913–14, an early example of simulating natural conditions and using safety ditches and undercut rockwork in place of bars. Here are sheep and goats, bears (good polars), pigs, and, below, penguins and pelicans. Beneath the terraces is a large **Aquarium* (fee). At the back (no adm.) are service blocks, the *Wellcome Institute of Comparative Physiology* (1964), and an *Animal Hospital* and prosectorium.—Just to the E. the **Reptile House* contains crocodiles, alligators, monitors, salamanders, pythons, boas, vipers, etc.; among smaller exhibits are geckos, chameleons, and skinks. To the S.E. is the *Sea Lions' Pond*, especially popular at feeding-time, with wild dogs on the terrace above. Near by is an aviary, and the Stork and Ostrich House.

In the flower-planted broad walk are the *Michael Sobell Pavilions* (1972) where the monkeys and great apes (gorilla, orang-utan) are always a centre of attraction. Here also are the giant pandas. Farther on are baboons and gibbons. Opposite rises the fortress-like **Elephant and Rhinoceros Pavilion* (1965). The *New Lion Terraces* (1976) are occupied by tigers, leopards, pumas, and jaguars as well as lions.

In the *Children's Zoo*, to the S., visitors are afforded the opportunity of handling young and tame animals. A nocturnal house and the chimpanzee den are among the attractions, as well as pony and donkey rides. In front are the attractive *Penguin Pool*; (1934, by Lubetkin and Tecton), seals, and racoons.

In the extreme S.W. angle of the gardens a fine group of bird houses includes the *Small Bird House*, with **Birds* of paradise, talking mynahs, tanagers, toucans, etc., and a *Tropical House* with humming-birds. *Wolf Wood* is on the terrace above. Beyond the S. entrance we skirt the *Birds of Prey Aviaries* (r.) and *Three Island Pond* (l.) to reach the colourful but noisy *Parrot House* (macaws, lovebirds). Beyond (r.) are British crows and flamingos. Facing the main concourse with its fine trees are a Cafeteria and Restaurant. To the S. are the *Cockatoo Aviary* and *Gibbon Enclosure*. Beyond the *Children's Playground* the 'Old Camel House', with its clock, and the *Raven's Cage* (inside the Members' Lawn), both by Decimus Burton, have been preserved.

The old or E. tunnel leads beneath the *Nuffield Institute of Comparative Medicine* to the canal bank. To the right are the *Society's Offices* with a lecture hall and a superb library of 100,000 volumes. To the left, beyond the *Caird Insect House* are the *Otter Pool* and Great Apes breeding colony. The **Charles Clore Pavilion for Mammals* (1967) houses more than 200 burrowing, jumping, flying, climbing and aquatic animals. Reversed lighting systems allow study of nocturnal creatures.

Beyond the waterbus landing-stage and the New Bridge, extend the COTTON TERRACES (1961–63) with moated paddocks. In succession are the *Camel House* (alpaca, vicuña, llamas, etc.), the *Giraffe House*, by D. Burton (1826; altered 1963), and the *Cattle and Zebra House* (bison, Przewalski horse). Along the bank below are other ungulates. On the far side of the bridge rises the *Northern Aviary*, a modernistic structure designed by Lord Snowdon in association with Cedric Price and Frank Newby. We may return to the main gate by the New Bridge and W. tunnel (adorned with copies of the Lascaux and Altamira cave-paintings), or along the N. canal walks past various aviaries (pheasantry, geese, owls) and by the *Old Bridge*; or we may leave by the North Entrance.

To the N. of Regent's Park, separated from the Zoological Gardens by

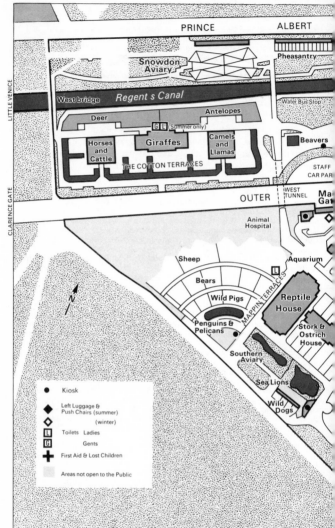

Zoological Gardens (Regent's Park)

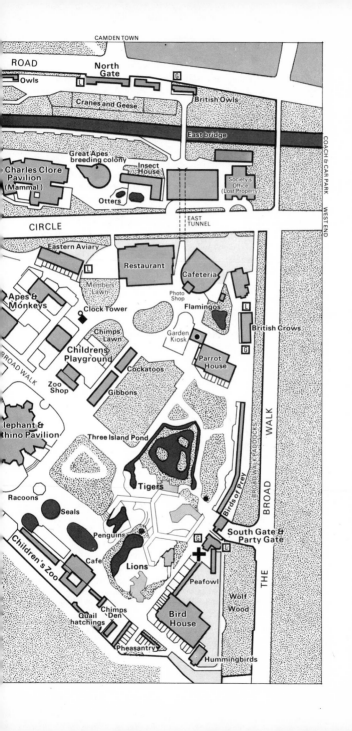

Prince Albert Road (where in 1855 Wagner lodged and completed 'Die Walküre'), rises *Primrose Hill*, a park of 61 acres. The top of the hill (219 ft) commands a fine view. To the w. of it is **St John's Wood,** a residential district extending to Maida Vale, and a favourite quarter with artists and bohemians since it was first built early in the 19C. Many of its attractive villas standing in large gardens have been replaced by massive blocks of flats. Among its many distinguished residents were Sir Edwin Landseer, George Eliot, Thomas Hood, Charles Bradlaugh, Thomas Huxley, and Herbert Spencer. At the junction of several thoroughfares quite close to Regent's Park is the church of *St John*, in which Joanna Southcott (1750–1814) is buried (under the name of Goddard). J. S. Cotman (1782–1842), the painter, is buried in the churchyard. *Grove House*, opposite, built by Decimus Burton in 1823–24, is now the seat of the Nuffield Foundation. Wellington Road leads N.W. to *St John's Wood Station* and Finchley Road. To the E., the Riding School (1825) of the R.H.A. barracks (rebuilt) has been restored to use. St John's Wood Road runs s.w. from the church to Maida Vale, passing **Lord's Cricket Ground,** property of the Marylebone Cricket Club (the 'M.C.C.') and headquarters of the English national game.

Here is *Lord's Cricket Museum* (adm. weekdays, 10.30 to close of play; in winter Mon.–Fri 10–4), with mementoes of the game including the original urn that contained the 'Ashes' (1882–83).

To the s. of the park the **Marylebone Road** (Pl. 5; 5; comp. p. 157) runs through the old borough of St Marylebone. The name is derived from the church of 'St Mary on the Bourne', or stream, i.e. Tyburn. Opposite York Gate is *St Marylebone* (1813–17), by Thos. Hardwick, the church in which Robert Browning was married in 1846 (a Browning Room here contains relics of the poet). The Schulze swell organ was formerly in Charterhouse School. In a chapel in the N. aisle is a painting of the Holy Family, by Benjamin West.

The site of the 18C parish church (demolished in 1949), a successor to that in which Francis Bacon was married (1606) is now laid out as a Garden of Rest in Marylebone High St. (a winding relic of the old village). Lord Byron (1788) and Nelson's daughter Horatia (1801) were baptized in this church; Sheridan was here married to Miss Linley (1773). The graves of Charles and Samuel Wesley (d. 1788 and 1837), James Gibbs (d. 1754), John Rysbrack (1770), Allan Ramsay (1784) and George Stubbs (1806) remain in the Garden.

On the corner of Marylebone High St., to the E., a carved panel (1960, by E. J. Clack) shows Dickens and characters from six of his works written in 1839–51 when he lived in a house on this site. Opposite is the *Royal Academy of Music*, founded in 1822. To the w., are the conspicuous buildings of MADAME TUSSAUD'S WAXWORKS and the LONDON PLANETARIUM.

Adm. to Mme. Tussaud's daily 10–6 in winter (until 7 on Sat and Sun), and 10–7 in summer; to the Planetarium daily 11–6: presentations given hourly on the hour. An inclusive entrance ticket may be purchased. Restaurant in Mme. Tussaud's. The waxworks are crowded in summer.

Madame Tussaud (1761–1850) was employed at the court of Louis XVI to make wax-figures. She was imprisoned during the Revolution and took models from the heads of guillotine victims (the original moulds are now in the Chamber of Horrors). She fled to London in 1802, and later exhibited her collection here. The museum now exhibits historical tableaux, great figures of the day, 'Heroes' (melted down c. every four years), etc. It also contains Mme. Tussaud's self-portrait at the age of 81.

Opposite are the huge buildings (1971, by Kinner) of the architecture and town planning departments, etc. of the London Polytechnic (comp. p. 156). BAKER STREET (Pl. 5; 5), a busy thoroughfare which runs N. to s., links Marylebone Rd. and Oxford St. Bulwer Lytton was born at No. 68 in 1803. No. 82 was the headquarters of Special Operations Executive (S.O.E.) in 1940–45. Sherlock Holmes had rooms at '221B' Baker St. North of Marylebone Rd., Arnold Bennett died in 1931 at Chiltern Court (No. 97). In *Gloucester Place*, parallel with Baker St. on the w., Wilkie Collins lived at No. 90 (now No. 65) in 1863–76 and 1883–88. George St. crosses Baker St. near its s. end. To the r., at No. 85, Thos. Moore had his first lodgings in London, and to the l. is the large R.C. church of *St James's, Spanish Place* in a pure E.E. style (by Goldie, 1885–90). Spanish Place (where a tablet at No. 3 marks the house of Capt. Marryat) leads hence s. to the secluded **Manchester Square**, built about 1770–88, and retaining some pleasant houses. At No. 2 lived Sir Julius Benedict, No. 3 was the home of John Hughlings Jackson, the neurologist, and No. 14 the residence of Lord Milner (plaques). In Duke St., just out of the s. side of the square, Simon Bolivar stayed in 1810 (No. 4).

Hertford House, once the residence of the marquesses of Hertford and afterwards that of Sir Richard Wallace (d. 1890) and of Lady Wallace (d. 1897), lies on the N. side. The ****Wallace Collection** (Pl. 5; 7) is the most important single collection in London for the lover of art in its various manifestations; in the choiceness and variety of its contents it resembles and rivals the Château of Chantilly in France. Not its least charm is its arrangement, the beautiful furniture, porcelain, sculptures, and innumerable small works of ornamental art being admirably exhibited in the rooms containing the paintings. It is notable especially for its French paintings, furniture, and porcelain and for its European arms and armour.

ADMISSION daily 10–5, Sun from 2 (closed Good Fri, Christmas Eve, and Christmas Day).—Public lectures on Wed and Fri.—The National Art Collections Fund uses part of the house as offices.

The collection was formed mainly by the fourth Marquess of Hertford (1800–70) who resided chiefly in Paris. His father, the third Marquess, figures as Lord Steyne in Thackeray's 'Vanity Fair', and as Lord Monmouth in Disraeli's 'Coningsby'. The fourth Marquess bequeathed the collection to his natural son, Sir Richard Wallace (1818–90), who removed it to London, added to it the collection of arms and armour, besides many pictures and Renaissance works of art, and changed the name of the house to Hertford House. In 1897 the priceless collection was bequeathed to the nation by Lady Wallace. The present gallery was opened in 1900.

From the ENTRANCE HALL, which has portraits by *Lawrence* (George IV) and *Van Dyck*, and busts by *Roubiliac* (Charles I) and *Rysbrack* (Queen Caroline), the Grand Staircase ascends to the first floor, on which is exhibited the most important part of the collection. Visitors with limited time should therefore ascend thither at once. In the following description, however, the rooms are taken in their numerical order (comp. the Plan). From the entrance hall we turn first to the right.

GROUND FLOOR. ROOMS I and II (combined) contain French furniture in the style of Louis XVI, covered with Beauvais tapestry with designs by *Casanova*; portraits by *Lawrence* (558. Countess of Blessington, 39. Miss Siddons), *Hoppner* (563. George IV as Prince of Wales), *Largillière* (122. Louis XIV and his heirs), and *Van Loo* (477. Louis XV in robes of state), and a series of paintings by *Boilly*; and cases of Sèvres porcelain. The furniture includes a chest of drawers attributed to *Boulle*, and two fine chandeliers (French 18C).

ROOMS III and IV illustrate the Renaissance. ROOM III. Large *Wall*

Cases contain a choice *Collection of Italian majolica from the most famous factories, including the *Bath of the Maidens, by *Maestro Giorgio Andreoli* (1525). Above (4, 5) are two old squeezes from the marble pulpit at Prato by *Donatello* and *Michelozzo*. Three central cases contain bronzes of the 15–17C (chiefly Italian); reliquaries; enamels; and ivory and boxwood carvings. Notable among the last are: *279. Elaborately carved tabernacle (Flemish c. 1500), and *273. *Fr. da Sant'Agata* of Padua, Statuette of Hercules swinging his club. In the lower part of the third case are beautiful illuminations on vellum, including (M342) a miniature of the Duke of Milan praying for victory by *Cristoforo de Predis* (1475). On the end wall (7) French ecclesiastical seat in walnut (16C).—On the W. Wall, *Head of Christ in marble, by *Torrigiani*.—On the E. Wall: Alabaster reliefs (Danish 16C and English 15C). The chimney-piece at the N. end of the gallery (Italian c. 1500) is flanked by two malachite columns surmounted by figures of the Lion of St Mark (Russian 19C). Among the paintings are: 555. *Bronzino*, Eleonora di Toledo; 548. *Flemish School* (early 16C), Madonna and Child; 539. *Bonsignori*, An Italian Gentleman; 26. *Frans Pourbus the Elder*, Portrait of a Gentleman; P541. *Bart. Veneto* (attrib.), Man in a black dress; *541. *Memlinc*, St Michael; 527. *Crivelli*, St Roch; 536. *Ferrarese School*, Annunciation.

ROOM IV. The wall case (r. on entering) contains a beautiful *Collection of Limoges enamels (15–16C) including a series of twenty-four plaques showing scenes of the Passion after woodcuts by Dürer. The 1st centre case displays bronze medals; French 13–16C ivories; 499. Horn of St Hubert (15C); 498. Bell of St Mura (Irish, 7C); woodcarving and metalwork.—2nd case: Goldsmiths' and silversmiths' work; 110–1. Portuguese embossed silver salver and ewer (late 16C); 107. Astronomical clock of gilt copper made at Augsburg (late 16C); 195. Steeple cup of silver gilt formerly belonging to Serjeants' Inn (English, 1606–13); 104. Salt-cellar and cover (1578).—3rd case: 15–17C Italian drawings; French and Italian bronze reliefs; 508. Official collar of the 'king' of a guild of archers in Holland, with pendant plaques dated 1499–1826. Paintings: 533. *German School* (16C), Boy with a nosegay; 129. *Ph. de Champaigne*, Adoration of the Shepherds, one of his finest works; 530. Mary, Queen of Scots, in mourning, after *Clouet*; 130. *Rigaud*, Card. Fleury. Bronze busts of Turenne and Condé, by *Jérome Derbais*, and of Charles le Brun, by *A. Coysevox*. On the right, French, Italian and German earthenware (16–17C); Venetian glassware (16C); Arabian mosque lamp (15C), etc.—A flight of steps ascends from this room to R. XV on the first floor. We, however, pass through the back corridor, with its collection of 17C Dutch and Flemish paintings and 16C Italian majolica, and proceed to inspect the collection of *EUROPEAN ARMS AND ARMOUR (RR. V–VII) which is unsurpassed in England and will repay unhurried examination. The arms and armour are arranged in chronological order, beginning in R. VII. Note, especially in R. V the fine suit of equestrian armour (29) made in the 1530s and bearing the arms of the Palatinate; the three upright cases (14, 15, and 16) which contain a valuable collection of early firearms; and case 23, with its cuirassier armour (63) made in N. Italy in the early 17C and bearing emblems of the House of Savoy. In R. VI, an Italian bronze cannon (1245) dated 1688; a remarkable Gothic war harness (21), made in S. Germany in the late 15C; and the

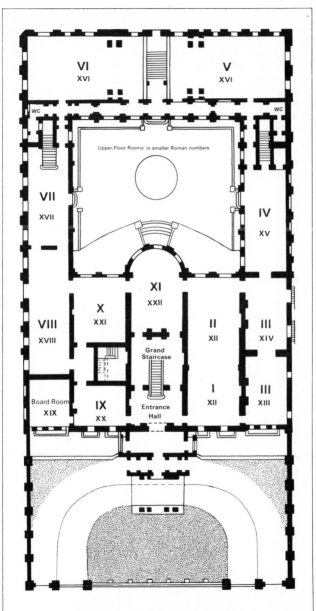

Wallace Collection

embossed and damascened shield with the monogram of Diane de Poitiers (325). The English armour (62) made c. 1590 for Thomas Sackville, later earl of Dorset is outstanding. In Room VII, the N. Italian bascinet (69) made c. 1390, one of the few surviving examples; the beautiful Renaissance parade casques (105–9) in case 4; and in case 5 the serving-knife (881) bearing the arms of Philip the Good, duke of Burgundy and a remarkable cross-bow (1032) decorated in carved horn. In a case on the west wall is tilting armour (23) made in Augsburg in the early 16C. ROOM VIII is devoted to Oriental arms and armour. Near the entrance is the figure of a Rajput warrior (1791–94); case 1 has an interesting collection of miscellaneous weapons; case 4 a fine shield of decorated hide; and case 6 a figure òf a Chinese mandarin (1701) dressed for battle. On the walls are paintings of Oriental subjects by French 19C artists.

The FOUNDER'S ROOM OR OLD BOARD ROOM contains busts of Sir Richard Wallace, Lady Wallace, and the fourth Marquess of Hertford, and the following portraits: *Reynolds*, 561. Fourth Duke of Queensberry ('Old Q'), 31. Lady Elizabeth Seymour-Conway, 33. Countess of Lincoln; 564. *Sully*, Queen Victoria in robes of state.

ROOM IX contains *Venetian scenes by *Canaletto* and *Guardi*; and 560. *Allan Ramsay*, George III. The furniture includes a superb cylinder-top desk, attrib., to Riesener. In the passage connecting R. IX with R. X is a collection of water-colours by *Bonington* and *Turner*.

ROOM X has more French furniture, including a fine large ebony and marquetry wardrobe attributed to Boulle; terracottas, mainly Italian, including *Rossellino*, Bust of a boy; and an unusual collection of waxes, with many portrait miniatures. Paintings: *538. *Foppa*, A boy reading (fresco from the Banco Mediceo, Milan); 646. *Sassoferrato*, Marriage of St Catherine; 19. *Titian* (?), Venus disarming Cupid; *B. Luini*, 537. Head of a girl (fresco fragment), 8, *10. Madonnas; 9. *And. del Sarto*, Madonna and St John; 534. Portrait of Robert Dudley, earl of Leicester, by an unknown Flemish artist; and 535. *Hans Eworth*, English nobleman; 525. *Beccafumi*, Judith; *1. *Cima*, St Catherine; P2. *Fr. Bianchi-Ferrari*, Daphnis and Chloe.

ROOM XI has a number of important paintings by *Murillo*, including 34. The Adoration of the Shepherds; 46. Joseph and his Brethren; and 14. Marriage of the Virgin. 126. *Sassoferrato*, Madonna and Child. The octagonal show-case contains miniatures of Napoleon and those connected with him. The main collection of miniatures, however, is in the two upright cases. Case A includes a very fine Self-portrait (203) by *Hans Holbein the Younger* dated 1543. Case B is given up to French miniatures. Among the furniture in the room are two sets of wall-lights of high quality, one made for the Château of Compiègne and the other for Fontainebleau.

FIRST FLOOR. The GRAND STAIRCASE has a *Balustrade of forged iron and gilt bronze, made for Louis XV, and originally in the Bibliothèque Nationale in Paris. Half-way up are three marble busts of exceptional quality; 21. Louis XIV, by *Coysevox;* 25. Madame Victoire and 26. Madame de Serilly, both by *Houdon*. On the top landing are French sculptures in marble (18C) and French and Italian bronzes, including several after *Giov. da Bologna*. On the walls are large paintings by *François Boucher* (1703–70), *The Rising and the Setting of the Sun, etc.

The southern half of Room XII has fine views of Venice by *Guardi*, including 503. Santa Maria del Salute, 491. San Giorgio Maggiore, and four small works (504, 494, 502, and 647). 457. *Le Brun*, Mme. Perregaux. Among the furnishings are an unusual rococo cartel clock (92) and a bronze bust (165) of Louis XIV by *Coysevox*. In the other half of the room are views of Venice by *Canaletto*, including 497 and 499. The Bacino di San Marco, and 500. Fête on the Piazzetta; a large library-cabinet (390) by *Levasseur*; a chest of drawers (88) made by Marchband in 1755 for Queen Marie Leczinska's bedroom at Fontainebleau; and a 'régulateur' clock (98) dating from the mid-18C. The centre showcases contain a magnificent collection of Sèvres porcelain.

Rooms XIII and XIV. Dutch and Flemish paintings of the 17C. In R. XIII: *Rubens*, 71. Christ on the Cross, and five small but important studies including 519. Adoration of the Magi; 61. *Wilhelm Drost*, Young Woman; 89. *J. A. Backer*, Portrait of an old woman; *66. *M. J. Mierevelt*, Dutch lady; 20, 96. *J. van Noordt*, Boys with hawks; 189. *P. Potter*, Herdsmen with their cattle; *A. van der Neer*, 217. Skating scene, 159. Winter scene; *Rembrandt*, 777, 203. Good Samaritan, 201. Portrait of a boy; 74. *Ferd. Bol*, The Toper; 78. *Govert Flinck*, Young woman; 170. *Gerard Dou*, A Hermit; 219. *Potter*, Milkmaid.—R. XIV, *Emanuel de Witte*, Interior of a Protestant church; 251. *Gabriel Metsu*, Sleeping sportsman; 227. *D. Teniers the Younger*, Boors carousing; *236. Gerard *Terborch*, Lady reading a letter; *Jan Steen*, 154. Harpsichord lesson, 158. Merrymaking in a tavern, 150. Lute-player; *G. Metsu*, 240. Letter-writer surprised, 234. Old woman selling fish; 166. *Esaias Boursse*, A woman cooking; *Van der Heyden*, 225. View of Amsterdam, 230. Exterior of a church; 202. *A. van Ostade*, Buying fish; *N. Maes*, 239. Housewife at work; 224. Listening housewife; 209. *Jan Steen*, The village alchemist; 237. *Caspar Netscher*, The Lace-maker; 231. *D. Teniers the Younger*, Gambling at an inn; 242. *Metsu*, Old woman asleep.

Room XV. Dutch Landscapes and Seascapes (17C). 197. *Ruisdael*, Landscape and farm; *W. van de Velde the Younger*, *145, 215. 143, 221. Ships; 247. *Ruisdael*, Sunset in a wood; 80. *Adriaen van de Velde*, Migration of Jacob; 60. *Hobbema*, Landscape with ruin; *Cuyp*, 51. Avenue at Meerdervoort, *54. Ferry boats on the Maes; 229. *Rembrandt*, Landscape with a coach; *207. *Jan van Huysum*, Fruit and flowers.

Room XVI contains the gems of the picture gallery. 139. *Poussin*, Falls of Tivoli; *Reynolds*, 48. St John in the Wilderness, P38. Nelly O'Brian; 85. *Van Dyck*, The Artist as the shepherd Paris; *P11. *Titian*, Perseus and Andromeda; *Rubens*, 30. Isabella Brant, the artist's first wife, P81. Holy Family, P93. Christ's charge to Peter, P63. The Rainbow landscape; *Velasquez*, P6 (attrib.), Don Balthasar Carlos in the riding school, P88, Lady with fan, P12. Don Balthasar Carlos; *Rembrandt*, P90. Susanna van Collen and her daughter, 52. Self-portrait, P29. The Artist's son, Titus, P86, The Centurion Cornelius (attrib.); 138. *Cuyp*, River scene; P35. *Reynolds*, Mrs Carnac; P27. *Pieter de Hooch* Boy bringing pomegranates; *Van Dyck*, P79. Marie de Raet, P94. Philippe le Roy; P84. *Franz Hals*, Laughing Cavalier; Portraits of Mrs 'Perdita' Robinson by *Reynolds* (P45, P42) and *Romney* (P37); P111. *Jan Steen*, The Christening Feast; P58. *Murillo*, Holy Family and St John the Baptist; P134. *Ph. de Champaigne*, Annunciation. The *Roll-top desk (102) by Riesener, made in the 1760s for King Stanislas

Leczinski of Poland, father-in-law of Louis XV; two chests of drawers (86, made for Versailles, and 85); and the vases and candelabrum (late 18C), should also be noted.

ROOM XVII. French School (19C). The series of small paintings by *Meissonier* (1815–91) is elsewhere unsurpassed. *Decamps* and *Vernet* are well represented. Among others are 282. *Delacroix*, Execution of Marino Faliero; 348. *Proudhon*, Sleep of Psyche; 281. *Corot*, Macbeth and the witches; 267. *Decamps*, Villa Doria Pamphili; 283. *Rousseau*, Fontainebleau forest.

ROOM XVIII. French School (18C). In this and the following rooms the objects exhibited with the paintings are of the same period, and are in admirable keeping with the dainty scenes of sophisticated romance on the walls. In these rooms *Watteau* (1684–1721), *Lancret* (1690–1743), *Pater* (1696–1736), *Boucher* (1703–70), and *Fragonard* (1732–1806) are represented by a charming series of conversations galantes, fêtes champêtres, scenes from the Italian Comedy, and romantic pastoral scenes. *Watteau*, 439. Lady at her toilet, 410. Music party, 381. Gilles and his family, 389. Les Champs Elysées; *Lancret*, 422. Conversation galante, 448. Fête in a wood, 450. La Belle Grecque, and 393. Mlle. Camargo dancing; *Fragonard*, 430. The swing, 412. Boy as Pierrot, 382. The Souvenir, 411. The Schoolmistress, 379. Gardens of the Villa d'Este; 385, 399. *Boucher*, Shepherd and shepherdess, 390. The Modiste; 449. *Mme. Vigée Le Brun*, the Comte d'Espagnac, 453. *Nattier*, Comtesse de Tillières; *J.-B. Greuze*, 403. Mlle. Sophie Arnold, 428. Girl with Doves; 427. Girl in white dress. Cases contain a remarkable collection of *Snuff Boxes and Bonbonnières. The furniture in this room, all of exceptionally high quality, includes three secretaires (300–302) and two chests of drawers (247, 248), made by *Riesener* for *Marie-Antoinette*.

ROOM XIX. *Boucher*, 418. Portrait of Mme. de Pompadour; and four pictures (429, 432, 438, 444), painted by him for her boudoir, also 446. Diana and Callisto; 442. *Greuze*, The broken mirror. The fine chest of drawers (245) made by *Dubois*, is surmounted by a beautiful jasper perfume-burner (292), from the personal collection of Marie-Antoinette.

ROOM XX. P47. *Reynolds*, Mrs Braddyll. The many *Paintings by *Bonington* form the largest public collection of this artist. They include 273. Seapiece, 341. Coast of Picardy, 362. Landscape with timber-wagon, and 375. Piazza San Marco.—The 'cartonnier' (178) and writing-table (330) in green lacquer and bronze, by *Dubois*, belonged to Catherine II of Russia, and Napoleon is believed to have signed the Treaty of Tilsit on the table. In the corridor leading to ROOM XXI, watercolours by *Bonington* and a German 18C travelling canteen of silver-gilt plate.

ROOM XXI contains two still-lifes by *Desportes* (594, 628), on either side of the fireplace; 625. Hawk attacking wild duck, by *J.-B. Oudry*; 461. Mlle. de Châteaurenaud, by *Nattier*, and 465. The Italian Comedians, by *Lancret*.—The marquetry cabinet (16) may be by *Boulle* himself, and the wardrobe (63) and pedestal clock (42) come from his workshop. The showcase contains Sèvres porcelain. ROOM XXII. Over the chimneypiece is 441. Votive-offering to Cupid, by *Greuze*, who also painted the two portraits, 415 and 419. The 'conversations galantes' (406, 424, 460) are by *Pater*. The octagonal showcase contains French miniatures, and the two window cases Sèvres porcelain, including a remarkable casket (51) dated 1754–55 and a toilet-service (40–47).—Furniture includes a set of six chairs (233–8), made for the royal card-room at Fontainebleau by *Boulard*, dated 1786, anu upholstered in Beauvais tapestry; a secretaire (306) attrib. to *Riesener*; a fine mantel-clock (268) and four wall-lights (374–7) made for Marie-Antoinette. The large marble vase in front of the middle window is by *Clodion*, and in front of it is a knee-hole Carlton writing-table, on top of which stands a despatch-box stamped with the cypher of Charles II and containing a necklace and other articles connected with Marie-Antoinette.

The doorway opposite the entrance to Room XXI leads back to Room XII and the landing, and from there to the staircase and entrance hall.

On the w. side of Baker St. lies the fashionable quarter built in the 1760s round *Portman Square*. *HOME HOUSE (No. 20) is the best surviving example of a Robert Adam town house (c. 1773–76). The delightfully shaped rooms and staircase are decorated with paintings by *Zucchi*. Also here is a painting (unfinished) of the Holy Family by *Perino del Vaga*. The house belongs to the *Courtauld Institute of Art* of the University of London, founded by Samuel Courtauld in 1931, which owns the Witt Library of c. 950,000 reproductions of European paintings and drawings from the Renaissance to the present day. Visitors are shown the house (during the University vacation, or by previous appointment during term-time), and may use the Witt Library on weekdays. The Institute has spread into 21 Portman Square, a house designed by James Adam in 1772, and since 1972 the art department of the Royal Institute of British Architects. The *Heinz Gallery* (adm. Mon–Fri, 11–5) contains a changing exhibition of architects drawings, while the library consists of over 200,000 European architectural drawings (adm. Mon–Fri 2–5; comprehensive photographic service).

In *Seymour Street*, to the w., a tablet at No. 30 marks the house of Edward Lear. New Quebec Street, with some pleasant shops, leads N. to the attractive *Montagu Square* where Anthony Trollope lived (at No. 39) in 1873–80. In the N.w. corner is the Jews College (1955–57).—In Robert Adam Street, N.E. of Portman Sq., the luxurious church of *St Paul's, Portman Square* was opened in 1970.

Portman St. leads s. from the square to Oxford Street which runs w. to Marble Arch (comp. p. 108).

The Edgware Road (Pl. 4; 8) runs through an unattractive area N. from Marble Arch in a practically straight line towards Edgware (7 m.), following ancient Roman *Watling Street*. Off Harrowby St. (the sixth turning on the right), an archway leads into the narrow *Cato Street*, once notorious as the meeting-place of the 'Cato Street Conspirators' (hanged at Newgate in 1820), whose object was the wholesale murder of the ministers of the Crown at a Cabinet dinner in Grosvenor Square. To the N., in Marylebone Road, the R.C. *Church of the Holy Rosary* makes interesting use of the arch. PADDINGTON STATION (approached by Praed St.) lies to the w. The Metropolitan Railway Company opened the first underground railway in the world in 1863 from Paddington to Farringdon. The Marylebone Flyover takes the Oxford Road (here motorway) across Edgware Rd. to forge w. through an area of new building (including the Police Station, 1971). On the edge *Paddington Green* (reached by sub-way) survives around the church of *St Mary* (1791, being restored in 1972), the successor of the church in which Hogarth was secretly married in 1729. Thomas Banks (d. 1805) and Joseph Nollekens (d. 1823), sculptors, and Benj. Haydon (d. 1847), painter, have their tombs here. Mrs Siddons is buried at the N. end of the churchyard (now a recreation ground). In 1829 the first London omnibus service pulled by three horses started from the Green on its journey to the Bank of England along the Marylebone Road.

Edgware Road ends at the REGENT'S CANAL in a tranquil green oasis (l.) named 'Little Venice' by Browning. House-boats and bright Victorian houses line the canal. In *Blomfield Road* (No. 60) is the starting-point of Jason's canal cruises which, in summer, make trips through Regent's Park to Camden Town, and then back to Little Venice, with 'Browning's Island'. Water-buses (British Waterways Board) to the zoo depart every hour on the hour (daily in March–Oct 10–5, Sun & BH 10–6; reduced fee on Mon) from Warwick Crescent. Opposite the station a bas-relief by D. Thackway (1965) commemorates Browning. The tow-path from Lisson Grove (Pl. 4; 3) to Regent's Park and Camden Town has been opened for walkers (March–Oct). A permit may be obtained at the Canal Office, Delamere Terrace for the tow-path w. to Kensal Green Cemetery.

For about a mile beyond the Regent's Canal the Edgware Road is known as MAIDA VALE, and is flanked by pleasant dwellings and large blocks of flats. The name (the pronunciation of which time and gentility have corrupted) recalls the battle of Máida, by which the British under Sir John Stuart expelled the French from Calabria in 1806. On the right extends St John's Wood (comp. p. 162).

16 BLOOMSBURY AND THE BRITISH MUSEUM

STATIONS: *Tottenham Court Road* and *Holborn* on the Central line. From s. to N. this region is traversed by the Northern line, with the stations of *Tottenham Court Road*, *Goodge Street*, *Warren Street*, and *Euston*, and by the Piccadilly line, with the stations of *Holborn*, *Russell Square*, and *King's Cross*. *Euston Square* and *King's Cross* on the Circle line serve its N. portion.—BUSES in Tottenham Court Road, Nos. 14, 24, 29, 73, 176; in Southampton Row, Nos. 68, 77, 188, 196; in Theobald's Road, Nos. 19, 38, 172; in Euston Road, Nos. 14, 18, 30, 73, 77.

CAR PARKS: Bloomsbury Square (underground), West Central St., Brunswick Square, Endsleigh Gardens, Euston Station. Meter parking in the squares.

For the BRITISH MUSEUM: *Holborn* and *Tottenham Court Rd.* stations; Buses in Bloomsbury Way (E. bound) and High Holborn (w. bound), Nos. 7, 8, 19, 22, 25, 30, etc; and in Tottenham Court Rd. (N. bound) and Gower St. (s. bound). Car parking in Museum forecourt (limited) and meters in surrounding streets; underground car park in Bloomsbury Square.

A The Squares of Bloomsbury and the districts to the North

The beautifully-planted squares of **Bloomsbury** (Pl. 7; 3) date mainly from the 18C and early 19C. Their modest well-proportioned terraced houses are gradually disappearing as extensions to London University, hospitals, and new hotels encroach on the area. Many private hotels and boarding-houses occupy small houses in the formal streets. Bloomsbury is linked with the names of Virginia and Leonard Woolf, Clive and Vanessa Bell, Lytton Strachey, etc. who began here, before the First World War, an eccentric association of intellectual and artistic interests later known as 'The Bloomsbury Group'.

ST GILES CIRCUS (Pl. 6; 6), dominated by the notorious empty Centre Point tower block (1960–64) is a busy intersection at the top of Charing Cross Road (comp. p. 154). *Tottenham Court Road*, noted for its furniture dealers, leads hence N. towards Camden Town and Hampstead (see Rte 46). On the corner of Gt Russell St. (comp. below) stands the *Y Hotel* (1976), with a splendid recreation and sports club (annual membership fee) of the YMCA. Oxford Street (p. 156) is here continued E. by *New Oxford Street*.

Before New Oxford St. was constructed in 1849 through the poverty-stricken and congested region known as the 'rookery of St Giles' the main thoroughfare E. followed the shallow curve on the s. (now one-way w.), viâ St Giles High St. to High Holborn. A hospital for lepers (named for their patron saint St Giles) was founded here in 1101 by Matilda, Queen of Henry I: Shaftesbury Ave. and St Giles High St. follow the line of the walls. One of the first cases of the Great Plague in London occurred among Flemish weavers in the parish in 1664.

In High St. the church of **St Giles in the Fields**, built in 1731–33 by Flitcroft, and well restored in 1954, still preserves a rural setting. Above the w. gate is an oak relief of the Resurrection carved in 1687. Inside, the Father Smith organ (1671; partly remodelled), and the pulpit (1676) survive from an earlier church. In the s. aisle the upper part of a pulpit used by John and Charles Wesley in 1743–91 is preserved (formerly in West Street Chapel). In the s. porch is the tombstone of Richard Penderel (d. 1671), the woodman who guarded the 'royal' oak and thus secured the escape of Charles II after the Battle of Worcester. In the N. aisle George Chapman (d. 1634), translator of Homer, has an appropriate tomb said to be designed by Inigo Jones, and Andrew Marvell (d. 1678), the poet, is commemorated. The recumbent effigy of Lady Frances Kniveton was carved by Joshua Marshall. A memorial to Flaxman (carved by the sculptor) was placed in the porch in 1930. In the churchyard is an architectural monument to Sir John Soane. The baptism is recorded in the parish register of Milton's daughter Mary in 1648, and in 1818 of Allegra, daughter of Byron, and of Shelley's children, William and Clara.

Bloomsbury Street and Bloomsbury Way branch N. from New Oxford Street. In *Bloomsbury Way* the church of *St George's, Bloomsbury* (open weekdays 8–noon) was built by Hawksmoor in 1716–31. The Corinthian portico is impressive, and the steeple is surmounted by a statue of George I. Anthony Trollope was baptized in the church, which was the scene of the 'Bloomsbury Christening' in Dickens' 'Sketches by Boz'.

BLOOMSBURY STREET (or the parallel Museum and Coptic Streets with bookshops and antique dealers) lead to the **British Museum** (see p. 176). At the corner of Great Russell St. is the home of the *Trades Union Congress* (1958). Bloomsbury St. runs through the E. side of BEDFORD SQUARE, built around 1776, and presenting some characteristic examples of the style of the Adam brothers.

The *Architectural Association* is housed in Nos. 34–36; Lord Eldon (1751–1838), the reactionary Lord Chancellor lived at No. 6; and Henry Cavendish, the natural philosopher, died in 1810 at No. 11.

North of the square, in Store St., is the *Building Centre* (No. 26), founded in 1930 "to provide a permanent exhibition and information service for the free use of all interested in good building" (open Mon–Wed 9.30–5.30, Thurs till 7, Fri till 5). – Across Tottenham Court Rd., the *Whitefield Memorial Church* (by E. C. Butler; 1956–58) was built on the site of the chapel erected for George Whitefield (1714–70), the famous preacher.

The severe and rectilinear *Gower Street* continues N. past the *Royal Academy of Dramatic Art*, founded by Sir H. Beerbohm Tree (d. 1917), to University College (see below), and Euston Road.

At No. 2 a tablet commemorates Millicent Fawcett (1847–1929), a pioneer of women's rights. On the right, at the corner of Keppel St., is the *London School of Hygiene and Tropical Medicine*, established in 1922. At No. 69 William de Morgan (1839–1917) was born, and George Dance the Younger (1741–1825) lived and died at No. 91. No. 105 is the Royal National Institute for the Deaf. The Biological Department of London University (E. side) occupies the site of a house where Charles Darwin lived in 1838–42. Giuseppe Mazzini's home was at No. 183 (N. of Euston Rd.) in 1837–40.

We turn E. along Montague Place between the N. façade of the British Museum and the Senate House of the **University of London.** Many of the administrative buildings here dominated by the central tower of the Senate House, begun in 1933, are by Charles Holden. Much of the University's work of instruction and research is carried on in institutions far removed from the administrative centre; but an increasing number of departments and dependencies are being concentrated in the area in new buildings or in the terraced houses in neighbouring squares. The fine Senate House Library is accessible to visiting scholars.

London was the last of the great European capitals to found a university. In 1836 a charter was granted constituting a University of London, with the power of granting academic degrees, without religious tests, to students of University College,

King's College, and certain other affiliated institutions. In 1858 the examinations were thrown open to all students without restriction, and twenty years later (in 1878) the University of London became the first academic body in the United Kingdom to admit women as candidates for degrees on equal terms with men. Hitherto a purely examining body, it was reconstituted in 1898–1900 as a teaching university, instruction being given in existing colleges and schools. University College and King's College were incorporated as 'integral parts' of the University; these and other institutions are 'Schools of the University', each controlled by its own governing body; while others have teachers 'recognized by the University'. Students attending these colleges are known as 'internal students'; those presenting themselves for examination only are 'external students'.

Birkbeck College, founded in 1823 as a scientific and technical institute, entered its new building, facing Malet St., in 1951. The first part of the building of the *Students' Union*, adjoining on the N., was opened in 1955, while on the E. side are the *School of Oriental and African Studies* and the *Institute of Historical Research*. Other institutes occupy temporary quarters in Russell Sq., to the S.E. Between Russell Sq. and Woburn Sq. new buildings by Denys Lasdun will house the *Institutes of Education and Law* and an extension to the *School of Oriental and African Studies*.

RUSSELL SQUARE (Pl. 7; 3) laid out in 1801, is the largest square in central London, with the exception of Lincoln's Inn Fields. On the s. side of the garden is a statue of the 5th Duke of Bedford (1765–1805) by Westmacott. The *Royal Institute of Chemistry* (by Sir J. J. Burnet) is at No. 30. Over the entrance is a seated figure of Priestley. The attractive *Bedford Place* connects the square with BLOOMSBURY SQUARE (Pl. 7; 5; Underground car park), one of the earliest squares in London (c. 1665). The statue of Charles James Fox (1749–1806) in its garden is by Westmacott. No. 17, occupied and refaced by Nash in 1782–83, has been the home of the *Pharmaceutical Society* since 1841. It contains an interesting *Museum of Pharmacy* (adm. by arrangement). At No. 2 is the College of Preceptors.

To the N.W. of Russell Square new buildings for the University of London intrude into WOBURN SQUARE. In *Christ Church* Christina Rossetti (d. 1894) is commemorated by a reredos with paintings by Burne-Jones.

On the w. side of the square are the *Courtauld Institute Galleries (adm. 10–5, Sun from 2; excellent catalogue), a delightful small museum attached to the University of London (comp. p. 171). Here are housed the Collection of French Impressionist and Post-Impressionist paintings bequeathed by Samuel Courtauld (1865–1949); the Collection made by Lord Lee of Fareham (1868–1947) of 14–18C art; the Roger Fry Collection; the Witt Collection of Old Master Drawings; and the Mark Gambier-Parry Bequest (1966), which includes many early Italian paintings.

ROOM IA. 2. *Barnaba da Modena*, Madonna and Child; 3. *Simone Martini* (attrib.), Crucifixion; 5. *Ant. Vivarini*, Birth of St Augustine; 7. *Florentine School* (mid-15C), Madonna and Child; 9. '*Master of Baroncelli Portraits*', St Catherine of Bologna.—R. 1B. 1. '*Master of the Gambier-Parry Nativity*', Nativity and Adoration of the Magi; 2. *Sienese School*, c. 1340, St Peter; 5. *Agnolo Gaddi* (attrib.), Madonna of Humility with Adoring Angels; 21. *Florentine School* (c. 1430), Annunciation; *24. *Fr. Pesellino*, Annunciation; 25. '*Master of the Lathrop Tondo*', Adoration of the Kings; 97. '*Master of the Fiesole Nativity*', Madonna and Child with Saints. Also, a case of 14C French *Ivories, and majolica ware.—R. 1C. 30. *Lor. di Niccolò*, Annunciation; 31. *Fra Angelico* (follower of), Dead Christ with Saints; 32. *Lor. Monaco*, Visitation, Adoration of the Kings; 33. *Fr. Botticini*, Crucifixion; 34. '*Master of SS. Quiricus and Julitta*', Story of SS. Quiricus and Julitta.

ROOM II. 37. *Bernardo Daddi*, Polyptych; 38. *Sienese School* (c. 1340), St Julian;

69. *After Andrea del Verrocchio*, Madonna and Child; *70. *Lor. Monaco*, Coronation of the Virgin; 71. *Mino da Fiesole*, Madonna and Child with angels; 102. Attrib. to *And. del Verrocchio*, Madonna and Child; *Giampetrino* (attrib.), 118. Madonna and Child with St Jerome, 119. Madonna and Child with lily; 120. *Mariotto Albertinelli*, The Creation.—R. III. *16. *Rubens*, Descent from the Cross (study for the altarpiece in Antwerp Cathedral here illustrated in a copy by *Gainsborough*); *And. del Sarto*, Madonna of Humility (on loan from Petworth); 19. *Paolo Veronese*, Baptism of Christ; *Nicolas Poussin*, Eliezer and Rebecca at the well; 23. *Van Dyck*, Christ on the Cross; 25. *Hans Eworth*, Sir John Luttrell; 26. *Florentine School*, Morelli–Nerli Cassoni (1472); *27. *Botticelli*, The Holy Trinity; 31. *G. F. de'Maineri*, Lamentation over the Dead Christ; 32. *Giov. Bellini* (with assistants), Assassination of St Peter Martyr; 29. *Marco Palmezzano*, Lamentation over the Dead Christ; 34. *Bern. Luini*, Madonna and Child with Saints; 35. *L'Ortolano*, Woman taken in adultery; 39. *Giorgione* (attrib.), Moses and the Burning Bush; 41. *Lucas Cranach the Elder*, Adam and Eve; 42. *And. della Robbia*, Madonna and Child.—R. IV. 43. *Sir Peter Lely*, Sir Thomas Thynne; 44. *The Master A.W.* (1536), Portrait of a Lady; 45. *George Romney*, Georgiana, Lady Greville; 46. *Goya*, Don Francisco de Saavedra; 50. *Gainsborough*, Charles Tudway; 54. *Jacques van Oost the Elder*, Young woman.

ROOM V. 2. *Edgar Degas*, Two dancers on the stage; 5. *Camille Pissarro*, The Quays at Rouen; *6. *Edouard Manet*, Bar at the Folies-Bergère; 7. *Alfred Sisley*, Snow at Louveciennes; *11. *Renoir*, 'La Loge'; 20. *Edouard Manet*, 'Le Déjeuner sur l'Herbe' (a smaller version of the painting in the Louvre). Among eight fine works by *Cézanne* are (14) Card-players.—R. VI. 22. *Georges Seurat*, Bridge at Courbevoie; 8. *Renoir*, Washerwoman (sculpture); 29. *Eugène Boudin*, Beach at Trouville; *Van Gogh*, 32. Portrait of the artist with bandaged ear, 33. Peach trees in blossom; 34. *Gauguin*, 'Te Rerioa'; 35. *Claude Monet*, Autumn at Argenteuil; 37. *Modigliani*, Nude.—R. VII houses the Fry Collection of 19C art, which includes works by the Bloomsbury Group. Room VIII contains the Witt Collection of drawings (changed periodically).

The *Warburg Institute*, beyond the Courtauld Galleries, faces GORDON SQUARE and the *University Church of Christ the King* (1853) with a fine interior. Adjoining in a 'Gothic' building, is *Dr Williams's Library* of theological books founded in 1716 (Mon–Fri 10–5, Tues and Thurs till 6.30). On the N. side of the square is the building of the *Institute of Archaeology*. At No. 53 (S.E. corner) the PERCIVAL DAVID FOUNDATION OF CHINESE ART (Mon 2–5, Tues–Fri 10.30–5, Sat 10.30–1) contains a magnificent collection of *Chinese ceramics of the Sung, Yuan, Ming, and Ch'ing Dynasties (A.D. 960–1912). They were given, with a rich library, to the University by Sir Percival David in 1950. No. 46 saw the beginnings of the 'Bloomsbury Group' as the home of Virginia Woolf before her marriage. Lytton Strachey and Clive Bell were also residents in the square.

Backing on to Gordon St. are the buildings of **University College** (main entrance in Gower Street). It was founded in 1826 and opened in 1828, with the title of University of London, by Lord Brougham, Thomas Campbell, James Mill, and other friends of religious liberty, with the object of affording, on undenominational lines, and "at a moderate expense the means of education in literature, science, and art". In 1900 it became a 'school' of the University of London, with which it was incorporated in 1907. The central building with its Corinthian portico and fine dome was designed by W. Wilkins; on all sides are extensions and additions. In the hall beneath the dome is the *Flaxman Gallery*, containing original models and drawings by John Flaxman (1755–1826). In the cloisters below is the 'Marmor Homericum', with Homeric subjects in marble niello, by Baron Triqueti, presented by Grote, the historian.

Both the Flaxman Gallery and the Marmor Homericum, together with the embalmed body of Jeremy Bentham, the *Flinders Petrie Egyptology Collection*, and the *Mocatta Museum* and *Gustave Tuck Theatre* of the Jewish Historical Society, are shown on previous application to the secretary.

The central *Collegiate Building*, *Union*, and *Theatre* and the *Department of Chemistry* are in new buildings in Gordon St. The college contains also the *Slade School of Art*, established under the will of Felix Slade (1790–1868), the art collector, the *Bartlett School of Architecture*, and other University departments. In Gower Street are *University College Hospital*, rebuilt in 1906 by the munificence of Sir Blundell Maple, and its *Medical School*. The hospital opened in 1834, and the first major operation performed in this country under an anaesthetic took place here in 1846.—To the s. of University College, in Malet Place, is the *National Central Library* (1933), set up as a clearing-house for exchange among public and official libraries throughout the country, and now a department of the British Library.

East of Goidon Sq. lies Tavistock Square (Pl. 6; 4) with a statue (1968) of Mahatma Gandhi (1869–1948). Off the N.E. corner of the square the *British Medical Association* stands near the site of Tavistock House, occupied by Dickens in 1850–60. Here 'Bleak House' and 'Little Dorrit' were written. Opposite is *Woburn House*, a Jewish centre, containing the Jewish Museum (first floor; adm. Mon–Thurs 2.30–5, Fri & Sun 10.30–12.45), an interesting collection of Jewish antiquities and ritual art.

Tavistock Place leads E. to Hunter St. where the house (No. 54) in which John Ruskin (1819–1900) was born was demolished in 1969.

Endsleigh Street, with the first headquarters (1922) of the National Union of Students (No. 3), leads out of the N.W. corner of the square to Endsleigh Gardens. Here we turn left to reach the *Wellcome Foundation Building* (entrance on Euston Rd.), an important scientific foundation established in 1913 by Sir Henry Wellcome (1853–1936). Here is the **Wellcome Historical Medical Museum** (adm. Mon–Sat 10–5, closed BH), a unique collection (200,000 items, 800 pictures, and 80,000 prints) illustrative of the history of medicine and the allied sciences from the earliest times. A large library and a museum are open to members of the medical profession for research, while a second museum including among its permanent exhibits a series of dioramas illustrating stages in the growth of modern medicine, with informative recorded commentaries, is open to the general public. Special exhibitions are also arranged.

Euston Road (Pl. 6; 2), the N. boundary of Bloomsbury, continues the line of Marylebone Rd. (comp. p. 166) E. to King's Cross. It forms part of the 'New Road' laid out in 1754–56 to connect Islington with Paddington, and now bears the heavy traffic of the Inner Ring Road. *Friend's House* (1926, by H. Lidbetter), the headquarters of the Society of Friends, contains documents relating to William Penn and the foundation of Pennslyvania. To the N. of *Euston Square* is **Euston Station** (Pl. 6; 2; Restaurants), rebuilt in 1963–68, when, against considerable opposition, the old classical entrance arch was demolished. The statue in the forecourt is of Robert Stephenson who, with Philip Hardwick, designed the original station in 1836. Opposite rises *St Pancras Church*, built in 1819–22 by Inwood (restored in 1951–53) in a 'Grecian' style, a pastiche of various buildings in Athens. To the s., *Duke's Road* and *Woburn Walk* preserve quaint 18C shop-fronts. W. B. Yeats lived at No. 5 Woburn Walk in 1895–1919. On the N. side of Euston Rd. huge new office buildings (1968–70) tower above the *Elizabeth Garrett Anderson Hospital* and the *St Pancras Library* and *Shaw Theatre* (1971; Rfmts), used by the

National Youth Theatre. The new British Library (comp. Rte. 16B) will occupy the former L.M.S. railway goods depot. Beyond are **St Pancras Station,** a Gothic work by Gilbert Scott (opposite which is Camden Town Hall), and, in contrasting bold simplicity, **King's Cross Station,** an avant-garde work by Lewis Cubitt (1852).

In *Pancras Road,* which leads N.W., is ($\frac{1}{2}$ m.) OLD ST PANCRAS CHURCH, of very ancient foundation, but practically rebuilt in 1848. The church is kept locked because of vandalism; the attractive interior may be seen at the service on Wed and Sun (9.30 a.m.). In the old graveyard, now a public garden entered through elaborate gates, Mary Godwin is said to have first met Shelley in 1813 beside the grave of her mother, Mary Wollstonecraft (d. 1797), whose remains were transferred to Bournemouth in 1851. John Flaxman (d. 1826), and John Christian Bach (d. 1782) are buried here, and Sir John Soane (d. 1837), with his wife, in the mausoleum he designed for her in 1815. An ash tree offers protection to a curious mass of gravestones.—To the E. the GRAND UNION CANAL (with private moorings) flows behind King's Cross Station.

PENTONVILLE ROAD ascends E. towards the Angel (Rte 25), passing on the left ($\frac{1}{2}$ m.) *St James's Churchyard* where Richard Bonington (1801–28), the painter, and Joseph Grimaldi (1779–1837; grave on E. side of church), the famous clown, are buried. In *Percy Circus* (to the S.; reached viâ Penton Rise and Vernon Rise) a plaque marks the site of the residence of Lenin when a political exile in 1902–03 (temporarily covered in 1972 because of public protest).

GRAY'S INN ROAD, a long and uninteresting commercial thoroughfare, leads S. from King's Cross to Holborn, past the *Royal Free Hospital,* founded in 1828. Here also are the new offices of Thomson Newspapers, and of 'The Times' (established 1788). A more pleasant route S. diverges r. opposite St Pancras into Judd St. whence Hunter St. continues down to BRUNSWICK SQUARE, now overpowered by the harsh Brunswick Centre of flats and shops. At No. 40 are the headquarters of the **Thomas Coram Foundation for Children** (formerly the *Foundling Hospital*), founded in 1739 by Capt. Thomas Coram (d. 1751), which still cares for unfortunate children, though it no longer maintains its own schoolhouse. The Foundling Hospital occupied the site of Coram's Fields (see below) from 1724–1926.

The present house (adm. Mon & Fri 10–12, 2–4 exc. BH) contains many relics of the old building, including part of the oak staircase and the beautiful Court Room, re-erected here with the original woodwork, ceiling, and plaster decoration; also interesting paintings by *Hogarth* (*March to Finchley; Portrait of Coram), *Kneller* (Portrait of Handel), *Gainsborough,* etc.; sculptures by *Rysbrack* and *Roubiliac;* and a cartoon by *Raphael.* Other mementoes include a MS. score of 'Messiah' and other Handelian relics, and a number of 'tokens' formerly left with abandoned infants. Handel and Hogarth both took a great interest in the hospital and its children, and readers of 'Little Dorrit' will remember that Tattycoram was a 'Foundling'.—Adjoining is the *School of Pharmacy of London University.*

To the S.E. extend CORAM'S FIELDS, a playground with Georgian colonnades, owned by the Foundation and open to children under 18 years (9–dusk); and to the N. the delightful *St George's Gardens* occupy a disused cemetery. Across the Fields at the corner of Guilford St. and Doughty St. stands *London House,* a hostel and centre of collegiate life for men students from overseas, by Sir Herbert Baker. In the undulating *Doughty Street,* with the vista at each end closed by trees, Sydney Smith lived at No. 14 in 1803–06. **Dickens House** (No. 48), the home of Charles Dickens in 1837–39, the period of 'Oliver Twist' and 'Nicholas Nickleby', is now a museum of great interest (open Mon–Sat 10–5, exc. BH; fee). Besides the most comprehensive Dickens library in the world, it contains numerous portraits, illustrations, autograph letters, and personal relics.

The Suzannet Gift (1971) includes parts of the MSS. of 'Pickwick Papers' and 'Nicholas Nickleby', Dickens' correspondence, illustrations for the novels, etc. In the basement is a reproduction of the 'Dingley Dell' kitchen.

Lamb's Conduit Street leads s. from Coram's Fields and crosses *Great Ormond Street*, which retains several attractive houses of the Queen Anne period. At its w. end are the *Hospital for Sick Children* founded in 1851, and the *Royal London Homœopathic Hospital*. No. 23 was the home of John Howard (1726–90), the philanthropist.

In the retired QUEEN SQUARE, with a statue that may represent Queen Charlotte, Queen Anne, or Mary II, William Morris had his residence and workshops in 1865–81 at No. 26 (rebuilt, now the *National Hospital*). Near by is the *Ospedale Italiano*, and the church of *St George the Martyr*, founded in 1706, which once provided annual Christmas dinners for 100 apprentice sweeps.

Beyond Theobald's Road (where, at No. 22, Benjamin Disraeli was born in 1804), Lamb's Conduit passage continues into RED LION SQUARE, built in 1684 on the fields where the bodies of Cromwell, Ireton, and Bradshaw are said to have been exposed after their exhumation from Westminster Abbey. The w. side is occupied by the Languages and Law Department of the Central London Polytechnic. On the s. side is No. 17, in which D. G. Rossetti lodged in 1851 and in which Morris and Burne-Jones lived together in 1856–59. John Harrison (1693–1776), inventor of the chronometer, and Jonas Hanway (1712–86), who has the reputation of being the first habitual user of an umbrella in London, also lived in the square. At the N.E. corner is *Conway Hall* (1929) the seat of the South Place Ethical Society, a pioneer of religious–humanist thought (chamber concerts in Oct–April).

In SOUTHAMPTON ROW, to the w., the *Central School of Art and Design* uses the theatre named in honour of Jeannetta Cochrane who taught at the school from 1914 to 1957. Many productions for children are staged here. On the corner of Catton St., to the s., the Baptist Church House has a statue of Bunyan.

The streets leading s. from the square run into **High Holborn** (comp. p. 216).

B. The British Museum and British Library

The ****BRITISH MUSEUM** (Pl. 6; 5), unrivalled in the world for the richness and variety of its contents, is entered from Great Russell St. in Bloomsbury, a few yards N. of New Oxford Street, or from Montague Place, on the N. In the pediment of the colonnaded main façade (s.) are allegorical sculptures by Westmacott.

HISTORY. The British Museum was founded in 1753, its nucleus being the Cottonian and Harleian MSS. and Sir Hans Sloane's collections. These, with subsequent additions, including the Egyptian Antiquities, the Elgin Marbles, and the King's Library (i.e. George III's), were contained until 1852 in *Montagu House* built by Robert Hooke in 1686 on the site of the existing edifice and opened as the first public secular national museum in the world in 1759. In 1823 the main building was begun by Robert and Sydney Smirke, and in 1852 Montagu House was demolished and the present s. front completed; the monumental neo-classical screen was built in the 1840s. The Reading Room (by Sydney Smirke) and Library were opened in 1857, the S.E. wing in 1884, and the King Edward VII Building in 1914.

In 1973 the **British Library**, formed from the library departments of the British Museum and various other national libraries, became a separate institution. Until the library moves to a future home (a site near Euston), its constituent parts still occupy their former quarters. For the visiting sightseer it is hardly yet necessary to consider its display rooms in isolation. Readers' facilities, see p. 192.

ADMISSION daily, except on Good Friday, Christmas Eve, Christmas Day, and Boxing Day, weekdays 10–5, Sun 2.30–6.

GUIDE LECTURES on weekdays at 11.30 and 3; short lunch-time lectures at 1.—Tea and Coffee Room in Basement (stairs from Room 2 of Greek and Roman Antiquities).

The Museum is administratively somewhat rigidly divided into Departments, most of which have both a Ground Floor and an Upper Floor section. Each Department has its own facilities for serious students. Our description, designed more for the casual interested visitor, is concerned rather with suggesting a way towards a general appraisal expending the least physical effort, than with following each Department round the endless ramifications of a complex building. In the main display collections each individual object is chosen from a large corpus for its excellence. The text is designed only as an aid to general location, since the display is already provided with an abundance of explanation and commentary. The Official Guide (1976, illustrated in colour; £2·25) makes also a fine souvenir.

MAIN BUILDING: GROUND FLOOR, ENTRANCE HALL. Immediately on our left as we enter from the forecourt is the Publication Sales Counter, through which we reach the principal sculpture-rooms.—On the right, opposite the principal staircase, is the Grenville Library (p. 184); while straight in front, beyond the square piers, is the entrance to the Reading Room.

The ****Collection of Greek and Roman Antiquities** is arranged in the w. wing in chronological order from the Early Bronze Age to the Roman Imperial period. ROOM 1 is entered by a scale reproduction of the entrance to the so-called Treasury of Atreus at Myœnae (actually a royal tomb of the 13C B.C.), incorporating fragments of column. Within, marble idols and marble and clay vases from the Cycladic islands (3000–1000 B.C.).—ROOM 2. Minoan and Mycenean vases and bronzes. Among typical and superb items: Jewellery from the Aegina Treasure; clay bath from Palaikastro (Crete); Bowl from Enkomi (Cyprus); gypsum reliefs from the Treasury of Atreus (comp. above).

ROOM 3. EARLY GREEK ROOM. Wall cases (l.). Domestic bronzes from tombs near Potidaia; Attic Protogeometric and Geometric *Vases; Boeotian engraved bronze brooches; later provincial Geometric, with small bronze animals flanked by a bowl from Thebes, depicting a bireme, and an amphora with a frieze of charioteers; Rhodian plate showing a Trojan battle scene.—Attic bowl (dinos) and stand by Sophilos (black-figure; c. 580 B.C.).—Sculpture from the Lion Tomb at Xanthos and the Sacred Way at Didyma, showing the progression from the Daedalic to Archaic style (c. 600–510 B.C.).—Centre cases: 1. Orientalizing *Vases and bronzes mostly from Kameiros, Rhodes (note the figurework on the alabastron and the olpe). 2. Black-figure vases by individual masters: **Neck amphora by Exekias; Oinochoe by the Amasis painter; bronze Horse and rider from Magna Graecia; Tanagra figurines. 3. Greek work from Magna Graecia: Greaves in bronze; *Reliefs in amber; hydria by Phintias (Attic; c. 510 B.C.). Side wall: Reliefs and gold jewellery from Ephesus and elsewhere in Asia Minor.

ROOM 4. Two early Kouroi (Boeotian c. 560 B.C., r.; Cypriot c. 520 B.C., l.).—R. 5. LATE ARCHAIC AND EARLY CLASSICAL ART of the 5C B.C. Sculptures from Xanthos in Lycia (5C B.C.) including the so-called Harpy Tomb and the remarkable frieze of cocks and hens; kore; *Kouros (c. 490 B.C.; the 'Strangford Apollo'). Attic red-figured pottery and polychrome lekythoi of 490–440 B.C. (works by Epiktetos, the Berlin Painter, Myson, Douris, including some of the finest individually signed

**Vases known); bronze mirrors, helmet, and vessels; bronze head of Apollo (the 'Chatsworth' head) from Cyprus (c. 460 B.C.). — If strict chronology is required, R. 8 should be taken before RR. 6 & 7. — R. 6. The *Frieze from the temple of Apollo at Bassae, depicting a battle between Lapiths and Centaurs (1–11) and between Greeks and Amazons (12–27). — R. 7. The E. façade (reconstructed) of the *Nereid Monument at Xanthos; its four friezes and statuary.

ROOM 8, the **Duveen Gallery** contains the famous sculptures from the Parthenon which form part of the collection known as the ****Elgin Marbles,** so named after Thomas Bruce, 7th earl of Elgin, Ambassador to the Porte, who in 1801–03 collected numerous sculptures which he saw being daily destroyed at Athens, and in 1816 sold them to the British Government for £35,000, i.e. half what they had cost him to remove. The collection includes other sculptures from the Erechtheion and elsewhere, and casts from marbles which were left in situ. The most important of the Elgin Marbles are the sculptures of the PARTHENON or temple of Athena Parthenos (the Virgin), the patron goddess of Athens, which stood on the Acropolis, and was dedicated in 438 B.C.

The sculptures were carved between 447 and 432 B.C., when Pericles was leader of Athens. Pheidias, the sculptor, supervised his great building schemes, Ictinus was the principal architect of the Parthenon, and Callicrates was the second architect or perhaps the contractor. The gold and ivory (chryselephantine) statue of Athena, 40 ft high, which stood in the temple, was made by Pheidias, and is believed to have been finished in 439 B.C. and dedicated at the Panathenaic Festival the following year. The Parthenon remained a temple of Athena for the next nine centuries, after which it became a Christian church. The E. Pediment was ruined by the builders of the Byzantine apse. At the fall of Athens to the Turks it was converted into a mosque. In 1674 a draughtsman, probably Jacques Carrey of Troyes, made drawings of the architectural and sculptural remains of the Parthenon. These form an invaluable record, as in 1687, during the siege of Athens by the Venetians, the centre of the temple (then used as a powder magazine by the Turks) was destroyed through an explosion caused by a shell from the besiegers' army. The W. Pediment was shattered in falling during its attempted removal by Morosini.—The South Slip Room, l. of entrance to the Duveen Gallery, contains models, drawings and photographs illustrating the structure, sculptures, and history of the Parthenon. 'Sound guide' commentaries are available.

The sculptures of the Parthenon are generally held to be the greatest ever executed. In London are preserved 15 Metopes from the S. side, major fragments of both Pediments, and 247 ft (rather under half) of the Frieze. What survives of the remainder is in the Acropolis Museum in Athens, that part hitherto in situ on the Parthenon itself having been removed in 1976 to prevent further deterioration.

The Central Room displays the ****FRIEZE** alone at eye level. It represents in low relief the Panathenaic procession up to the Acropolis, the greatest Athenian festival, which culminated in the investiture of the image of Athena in a sacred violet 'peplos' or robe. This frieze ran above the porches and around the outside of the cella wall, and must have been curiously difficult to see. Its condition varies greatly.

The W. FRIEZE (r. of door) shows horsemen preparing to take part in the Panathenaic procession. As the procession, which started at the S.W. corner, approaches the N.W. corner it gathers speed, and the two leading horsemen (2, 3) on the last slab are already cantering. N. FRIEZE (turning left and passing the N.W. angle). The procession moves forward at a trot, the number of horses increases; the fine leading *Horsemen are seen on slab XXIV (N.E. angle). On the left of the slab is the inside of the rim of a shield and an arm holding it (belonging to chariot on opposite wall which continues the N. frieze) which indicates that chariots have now joined the procession, followed by citizens and animals being led to sacrifice. E. Frieze. Girls carrying vessels for use in the sacrifices, magistrates, and the ceremony of the sacred peplos in the presence of deities and attendants. The S. Frieze is much more fragmentary, but the rendering of cattle and galloping horses on slabs XXXVIII and XXX (s.w. end of wall) is especially noteworthy (s. frieze continued on s.e. end of opposite wall).

In the North Transept in the centre is the **East Pediment Group. These sculptures are in the round and had a correspondingly projecting architectural frame. The subject represented was the birth of Athena, fabled to have sprung fully armed from the brain of Zeus.

The central group probably consisted of Zeus with Athena and Hephaistos on either side. At the left (s.) end is Helios (A), the sun-god, driving his chariot out of the sea at daybreak; in front are two heads of horses from his team (B, C). Facing Helios is a male figure (D) of wonderful power and grace seated on the skin of a lion or panther, thought to be Heracles, or to personify Mount Olympus, or to be Dionysos, the wine god. The head (the only remaining one in the group), though damaged, heightens the noble impression of the figure and justifies the fame of the Pheidian School. Two draped and seated female goddesses (E, F) are Demeter and her daughter Persephone. The young girl running towards them (G) is Iris or Hebe, the cup-bearer, who starts back in alarm at the miraculous event which has just taken place. The identity of the group of three figures (K, L, M) is doubtful; the Clouds, Thalassa (the sea) in the lap of Gaia (the earth), Aphrodite in the lap of her mother Dione, or the three Hesperid nymphs, are suggestions that have been made. The sculpture in the extreme right angle is one of the horses of Selene, goddess of the moon, descending into the waves.

On the walls are Metopes XXVI—XXXII (see below).

In the South Transept in the centre are fragments from the **West Pediment Group, which represents the contest between Athena and Poseidon for the land of Attica.

According to the myth, Poseidon with his trident made a salt spring gush from the rock of the Acropolis; Athena caused the first olive to grow and was awarded the victory. The olive tree probably filled the centre of the pediment. Athena and Poseidon have been conducted to it by Hermes and Iris, the two torsos (H, N) to the left and right of the centre. Iris is identified by holes for the wings and by the short robe. The figure (A) in the N. (left) angle of the pediment is a river god of Athens, either Kephisos or Ilissos; it has suffered less damage and is one of the most beautiful of the sculptures. The torso to the right of Iris (O) is the driver of Poseidon's chariot (as may be seen from Carrey's drawing), perhaps Amphitrite, his wife. The figure (Q) to the right may have been a sea nymph.

On the walls are *Metopes (II–IX), square panels carved in high relief, which alternated with the triglyphs above the architrave all round the building. The fifteen originals (8 here and 7 in the N. Transept) together with forty-one still remaining (much decayed) in Athens and one in Paris, are all that remains of the original series of ninety-two. The metopes represent the battle of the Lapiths (a Thessalian people) and the Centaurs, one of whom tried to carry off the bride of Peirithoös, the Lapith king.

We pass behind the Nereid Monument (comp. above). Room 9. High Classical Art (late 5C-mid 4C). *Caryatid and column from the Erechtheion on the Athenian Acropolis (421–409 B.C.); *Frieze from the Temple of Athena Nike; 5C Tomb reliefs; votive reliefs of a Panathenaic chariot and a relay team; marble head of (?) Herakles; recumbent bull from a tomb in the Kerameikos cemetery. Jewellery and seal-stones (5–4C B.C.).—In the centre: marble head of Pan, from Koropì; chased bronze helmet; bronze repoussé reliefs: acanthus-leaf finial from Eleusis; toilet bottles and mirrors; *Silver libation dish (4C B.C.) from Eze, France; polychrome terracottas and toilet boxes (pyxis).

British Museum
Ground Floor

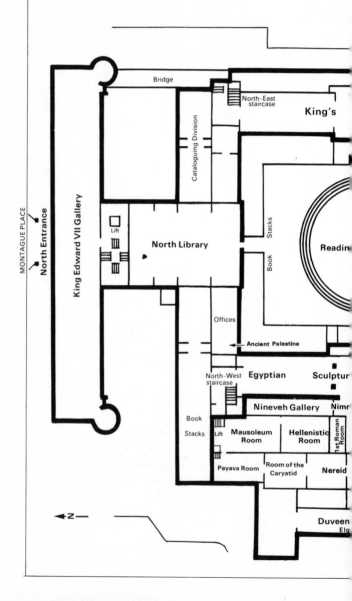

MONTAGUE PLACE

North Entrance

Bridge

North-East staircase

King's

Cataloguing Division

King Edward VII Gallery

Lift

North Library

Stacks

Book

Reading

Offices

Ancient Palestine

North-West staircase

Egyptian

Sculptur

Nineveh Gallery

Nimr

Book

Stacks

Lift

Mausoleum Room

Hellenistic Room

1st Roman Room

Payava Room

Room of the Caryatid

Nereid

←N—

Duveen

Elg

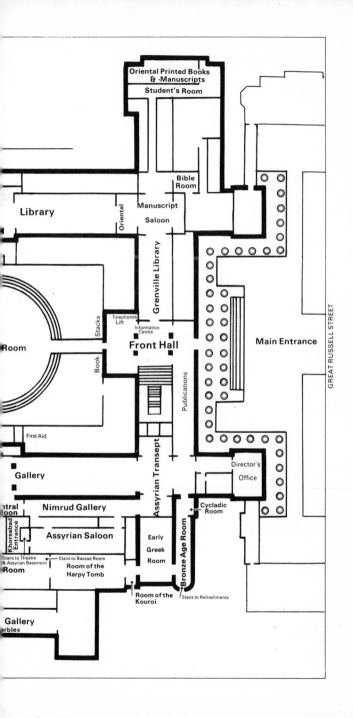

Oriental Printed Books
& Manuscripts

Student's Room

Bible
Room

Library

Oriental

Manuscript

Saloon

Grenville Library

Room

Library

Stacks

Telephones
Lift

Information
Centre

Front Hall

Main Entrance

Book

Publications

GREAT RUSSELL STREET

First Aid

Gallery

Assyrian Transept

Director's

Office

ntral
loon

Nimrud Gallery

Cycladic
Room

Khorsabad
Entrance

Assyrian Saloon

Early

Greek

Room

Bronze Age Room

Stairs to Theatre
& Assyrian Basement
Room

Stairs to Bassae Room

Room of the
Harpy Tomb

Room of the
Kouroi

Stairs to Refreshments

Gallery
rbles

Gallery

Room 10. Simple Grave-reliefs on one wall contrast with ornate volute-craters and florid objects in terracotta and bronze (in cases) mainly from S. Italy. *Head from a bronze statue of a Libyan, from Cyrene (mid-4C). In the centre, Tomb of Payava from Xanthos, with coarse reliefs and Lycian inscription; the quadriga reliefs on the curved roof and on the similar Tomb of Merehi are seen from the gallery, in which and R. 11 (above R. 9) are displayed *ETRUSCAN ANTIQUITIES of the 7–2C B.C. Two early statues flank the doorway. Remarkable are painted wall panels, a polychrome terracotta sarcophagus with a reclining figure of the dead woman, and a sculptured sarcophagus lid. In central cases, portrait heads in bronze and terracotta; bronze cists decorated with incised scenes.

Room 12. Sculptures from the *Mausoleum, the tomb built at Hali-carnassus for Mausolus (d. 353 B.C.), Prince of Caria (Asia Minor) by his wife Artemisia. They consist mainly of a frieze depicting a battle of Greeks and Amazons, and figures of Mausolus and his (?) wife; a fine lion and a magnificent horse's head with bridle and bit in bronze. The room also contains a sculptured column drum from the famous temple of Artemis at Ephesus (the temple of 'Diana of the Ephesians' of the Acts of the Apostles), like the Mausoleum one of the Seven Wonders of the World. The temple was rebuilt (comp. R. 3) at the time of Alexander the Great. Colossal lion, the crowning decoration of a tomb from Cnidus (2C B.C.), a Dorian city on the s.w. coast of Asia Minor.

From R. 12 stairs descend to a basement set out to show the orders of Classical architecture by important original fragments. All four of the buildings on the Athenian acropolis are represented, together with the Mausoleum, Temples at Ephesos, Priene, etc.

Room 13. HELLENISTIC ART. The Demeter of Knidos (c. 330 B.C.); Statue of Dionysos from the Choregic Monument of Thrasyllos in Athens (c. 320 B.C.); Torso of a Charioteer from Priene (c. 300 B.C.); Head of Asklepios, from Melos; *The Apotheosis of Homer, marble relief signed by Archelaos of Priene (150–120 B.C.) but found near Rome; Bronze head of a Goddess, from Turkey (2–1C); bronze head from a Statue of (?) Sophocles. Of the objects in cases, the glass bowls and the filigree *Jewellery show artistry as well as high technical skill.

Room 14. FIRST ROMAN ROOM. In the entrance is the famous *Port-land Vase, a work of the early Roman empire. It is made of glass in two layers, white on blue, the white being cut away cameo-wise to show the design in relief. The vase was deliberately shattered by a madman in 1845, but was skilfully pieced together again. Mosaic colossal head and mural paintings from Boscoreale, Pompeii, etc. In cases: Glassware, cameo and jewellery, fluor-spar cup; *Silverware from the Chaourse Treasure; bronze statuettes. Behind the screen: marble portrait head (Antonia?); bronze head of Hyphos (Roman copy of a 4C Greek original); Head of a statue of Augustus, with inlaid eyes, from Sudan.

Room 15 arranged as a Roman atrium, with an impluvium mosaic (from St Romain-en-Gal), and Graeco-Roman statuary. Apollo, copy of a Greek bronze of 460 B.C.; Tondo, Apollo and Artemis slaying the children of Niobe; the 'Westmacott Athlete', the Farnese Diadumenos (Roman marble copies of bronze originals of c. 440 B.C.); Panel of a rider, from Hadrian's Villa at Tivoli, in style of the 5C B.C.; Porphyry head of a tetrarch (? Constantius Chlorus); Relief of a Bacchic procession (c.

A.D. 100, of Attic inspiration); Marble portrait bust of the Antonine period, original work (by an Athenian?).

We now come to the ***Western Asiatic Collections,** where room numbering and chronology do not coincide. ROOM 26 (nearest the main entrance) is the so-called Assyrian Transept. On the E. side: sculptures from the temples of Nimrud, including a huge lion from the entrance to the Temple of Ishtarbelitmati (c. 880 B.C.). Centre: Black Obelisk of Shalmaneser III (858–824 B.C.) showing surrender of Jehu, king of Israel; two human-headed lions from doorways of the palace of Ashurnasirpal II (883–859 B.C.). W. side: bronze *Gates of Ashurnasirpal and Shalmaneser III from a temple at Balawat. The NIMRUD GALLERY (R. 19) contains sculptured reliefs from the Palace of Ashurnasirpal II at Calah (the modern Nimroud or Nimrud). Also, seated figure in basalt of Shalmaneser III. The collection is continued in the NIMRUD CENTRAL SALOON (R. 20) with sculpture from the Palace of Tiglath-Pileser III (745–727 B.C.). To the side, ROOM 16 is dominated by two winged human-headed bulls from the Palace of Sargon II (722–705 B.C.), father of Sennacherib, at Khorsabad. The gallery (R. 17B) behind is filled with a frieze from the palace built at Nineveh by Sennacherib showing the siege of Lachish; a case displays objects found around the main city gate showing traces of the war.

The ASSYRIAN SALOON (R. 17A) displays hunting *Reliefs from the Palace at Nineveh of Ashurbanipal (668–626 B.C.), grandson of Sennacherib, and the last great Assyrian king. Stairs lead down to the ASSYRIAN BASEMENT (9–7C B.C.), with more reliefs from the Nineveh palaces depicting military campaigns. Also, spacious displays of arms and armour (including helmets and shields) from Assyria and Urartu; Urartian art; Assyrian furniture (including a bronze bath, bronze weights, etc.) – The LECTURE THEATRE is located here.

Stairs re-ascend to R. 16 whence we pass to the NINEVEH GALLERY (R. 21), which contains reliefs from the Palace of Sennacherib (705–681 B.C.) at Nineveh, some of them illustrating the construction of the palace.

We may cross the long Egyptian Gallery to its N.E. corner for the ANCIENT PALESTINE ROOM (24). Here Biblical events are recalled by a reconstructed rock-cut tomb from Jericho; Mycenean imports; the Lachish letters (Babylonian period); Jewish ossuary chests from the time of Christ; Dead Sea scrolls.

*Egyptian Collections. The large objects displayed on this floor were formerly arranged chronologically from N. to S. This order is in course of being reversed with modern features of display, a labour of some years. (Mummies and smaller objects are on the first floor.)

NORTH EGYPTIAN GALLERY. The exhibits here, besides some remains from the *4–12th Dynasties*, mostly represent the accomplished art of the *18th Dynasty* (1600–1320 B.C.), when after a period of foreign rule the Egyptians reached a high level of prosperity and even invaded Asia. They are largely from Thebes, the capital of the *New Kingdom*. In the middle, arm of a colossal statue of Tuthmosis III (c. 1500 B.C.); the head (9 ft high) was removed to the landing on the main stair in 1972 on the occasion of the exhibition of the treasures of Tutankhamen. Amenhetep III (Amenophis or Memnon) is represented in two seated statues (4, 5), three colossal heads (3, 7, 6), and a pair of dignified lions inscribed with his name (1, 2).

The EGYPTIAN CENTRAL SALOON is filled with monuments of the *New Kingdom* (1600–1000 B.C.). The black granite sarcophagus of Merimes, viceroy of Ethiopia under Amenhetep III (c. 1380 B.C.), is a good example of sculpture of the period. 19 and 61. Granite statues of Ramesses II (c. 1250 B.C.; sometimes regarded as the oppressor of Israel); two large granite columns bear his names and titles. A huge green granite scarab (c. 200 B.C.), emblem of the sun-god, is a symbol of creative power.

The SOUTH EGYPTIAN GALLERY contains the monuments of the later dynasties, down to the incorporation of Egypt as a province of the Roman Empire in 30 B.C. In the centre is the *Rosetta Stone*, named from a town at the mouth of the Nile near which it is was found by the French in 1797.

It bears a priestly decree, inscribed twice in Egyptian (first in hieroglyphs, the writing of the priests, and second in demotic, or ordinary secular characters) and once in a Greek translation with Greek characters. This triple inscription and especially the names of kings enclosed in cartouches, or oval frames, gave scholars the key to the Egyptian language and scripts.

Before ascending to the first floor we return to the Entrance Hall and enter the exhibition of *Manuscripts, on the E. side. In the GRENVILLE LIBRARY, which is lined with books bequeathed by the Rt. Hon. Thomas Grenville (d. 1846) is a selection of *Illuminated MSS.* (9–16C). On the left are MSS. of English origin, on the right MSS. of Continental origin. Among the English MSS. will be found: in CASE 1, the **Benedictional of St Ethelwold* (963–984); in CASE 4, the *Evesham Psalter* (mid-13C); in CASE 5, the Oscott Psalter (c. 1270); in CASE 6, the *Queen Mary Psalter* (c. 1310–20), and the *De Lisle Psalter* (early 14C); in CASE 7, the *Gorleston Psalter* (early 14C); in CASE 8, the *Luttrell Psalter* (c. 1335–40); in CASE 10, the *Bedford Hours and Psalter*, made for John, Duke of Bedford, brother of King Henry V, c. 1420–22. Among the MSS. from the Continent are: in CASE 1, a MS. of the Gospels, probably executed at the court of the Emperor Charlemagne c. 800; in CASE 6, the *Bedford Hours*, written and illuminated in Paris c. 1423 for the same Duke of Bedford mentioned above; in CASE 8, the *Breviary of Queen Isabella of Spain*, probably executed at Bruges c. 1490, and a Book of Hours with miniatures probably painted c. 1520–30 by the Flemish artist Simon Bening. Also in the Grenville Library is a case containing a selection of the important illuminated MSS. bequeathed by Mrs Yates Thompson in 1941.

The **Manuscript Saloon** is devoted mainly to historical and literary MSS. The Magna Carta Room to the S. is closed, and its treasures are also on display in this room for the present. *British Literary Autographs* (Cases I–IX) are displayed near *Foreign Literary Autographs*, which include leaves from the sketch-book of Dürer (Case I). In Case I of the *Musical Autographs* is Bach's Fugue in A flat from 'Das Wohltemperirte Klavier'. On the left, the **Lindisfarne Gospels*, the masterpiece of Early English book production, written and illuminated c. 698; and the *Codex Sinaiticus* (mid-4C) and *Codex Alexandrinus* (5C), two of the three earliest authorities for the text of the Greek Bible. On either side of the door into King's Library are displayed *Bibles:* (Case II) the *Bosworth Psalter* (mid-10C) and an 8C Psalter, both probably written at Canterbury; (Case V) the *Wycliffe Bible*, a copy, made at the end of the 14C of the first complete Bible in the English language; (Case I) *Greek and Latin Biblical MSS.*, including papyrus fragments of an Unknown Gospel (c. 100–150), and the *Ceolfrid Bible* (7–8C). Among *English MSS.* (Case I) is the unique MS. of 'Beowulf' (c. A.D. 1000), and (Case II) an early 15C MS. of the 'Canterbury Tales'.

In the E. section of the room is the *Nelson Memorandum* of 1805, and a case contains Nelson's sketch-plan of the Battle of the Nile and his last letter to Lady Hamilton, written on the eve of Trafalgar, and two log-books from H.M.S. 'Victory'; also the records of the *Scott Polar Expedition* of 1910–12, including Captain Scott's last Diary. The other side of the case has *Medieval Music*, including the unique MS. of the celebrated mid-13C musical composition 'Sumer is Icumen In'; the *Royal Books* include a Manual of Prayers believed to have been used by Lady Jane Grey on the scaffold. Among the MSS. of the *Men of Science* is the sketch-book of Leonardo da Vinci; in the same case are displayed *Chronicles of England*: the autograph MS. of the 'Historia Anglorum' of Matthew Paris, monk of St Albans (d. 1259); the Anglo-Saxon Chronicle and the Ecclesiastical History of the English People by the Venerable Bede. Behind is the *Death Warrant of the Earl of Essex*, 1601.—On the E. wall cases display *Seals* and *Monastic Records* and in the S.E. corner the BIBLE ROOM (sometimes used for exhibitions) contains Byzantine MSS. including (2) *Queen Melisende's Psalter* (1131–43); Greek and Latin classical authors; Heraldic manuscripts and bindings. Also, the *Alcuin Bible*, a copy (c. 825–50) of the Bible, as revised by Alcuin for presentation to Charlemagne on Christmas Day 800.

The large case to the S. of the room contains an exhibition concerning the granting of *Magna Carta* by King John, including two of the four extant original copies of **MAGNA CARTA itself. In a small case is a MS. written and illuminated at Santo Domingo de Silos in Spain (1109) of Beatus' *Commentary on the Apocalypse*. Beyond, cases show *Historical Autographs* from the 14C onwards; (Case I) part of the Diary of Edward VI; (Case II) description of the execution of Mary, Queen of Scots; (Case III) Oliver Cromwell's report on the Battle of Naseby; (Case IV) Wellington's list of the cavalry under his command at the Battle of Waterloo. Near by, a case displays the *Shakespeare Deed, a mortgage bearing one of the few known signatures of the dramatist, and the 'Booke of Sir Thomas More', claimed to be partly in Shakespeare's handwriting.

King's Library. This noble hall is flanked with bookcases containing the great and choice library of George III, presented to the nation by George IV. The library is frequently used for temporary exhibitions. At other times the cases contain a selection of *Early Printed Books*, both English and foreign, including the 42-line or Gutenberg Bible (c. 1455–6). Among the English works are editions of the 'Canterbury Tales' (c. 1478) and Aesop's Fables (1483) from Caxton's press; the first edition of the Authorized Version of the English Bible (1611); and a first folio Shakespeare (1623). At the S. end six cases contain MSS. and printed books from Asia and N. Africa. Among them are fine illuminated manuscripts written in Arabic, Persian, Hebrew, and other languages of the Near East, many of them illustrated with miniature paintings of superb quality. One case is devoted to Indian manuscripts in a variety of scripts, and another to the history of printing in China and Japan; notable is the Diamond Sutra printed in Chinese from wooden blocks in A.D. 868. This is the oldest dated printed document in the world. At the far end are the *Tapling Collection of Postage Stamps* of the world (1840–90), and (opposite) the *Fitzgerald Air-Mail Collection*, the *Mosely Collection of African Stamps*, and the *Bojanowicz Collection* of Polish postal history (1939–49).

Beyond the King's Library is the *N.E. Staircase*, ascending past the bridge leading to the King Edward VII Gallery, to the Upper Egyptian Galleries. The *Bridge* usually holds a temporary exhibition. If we approach from Montague Place by the N. entrance, we leave the Japanese Room (75) to the left, and ascend the *North Staircase* (or take the lift), passing the Official Publications Library (formerly State Paper Room), and enter the centre door of the King Edward VII Gallery.

King Edward VII Gallery (34), **Oriental Antiquities.** The collection of ****CHINESE ANTIQUITIES** is arranged in chronological sequence in the bays to the right (E.) of the main entrance, starting on the s. side and proceeding round the Gallery in anti-clockwise direction. Outstanding are the ritual bronze vessels of Shang (1523–1027 B.C.) and Chou (1027–221 B.C.) dynasties, and jade carvings, bronze weapons and chariot fittings of the same periods in the table cases. In the fourth bay are shown the arts of the Han dynasty (206 B.C.–A.D. 220) with fine examples of painted lacquer, glazed pottery and bronze. The next bay contains a splendid series of pottery tomb figures and furniture of the Six Dynasties (A.D. 220–589) and T'ang (618–906) periods, together with decorated bronze mirrors. T'ang porcelain and stoneware is next displayed, including a magnificent porcelain ewer with a phoenix head (10C A.D.). Opposite the seventh bay, 9–10C silver hoard from Pei Huang Shan. In the following bays and continuing on the N. side are exhibited the Chinese ceramics of the Sung (960–1279), Yuan (1280–1368), and Ming (1368–1644) dynasties. The Museum collection of these fine wares is unrivalled in the West, and includes many world-famous pieces. Following the Ming porcelain, the arts of the Ch'ing dynasty (1644–1912), including carved lacquer, glass enamels, ivory, jade and horn carvings, as well as porcelain. The bays in the centre of the gallery contain wood carving, paintings, and Buddhist sculpture from Central Asia. Near by is a case of Japanese long swords.

The W. half of the gallery is devoted to INDIAN ANTIQUITIES, mainly sculpture and bronzes from temples in the sub-continent and South East Asia. The arrangement is regional, clockwise from the main door, beginning with North India and including in the latter bays Thailand, Cambodia, and Java. Particularly striking are sculpture from Central and South India of the Pallava (7–9C) and Cola (9–13C) dynasties, including a bronze statue of Siva Vishāpahavana (c. 950 A.D.); Sculpture from Orissa and East India (8–13C); 7–10C carving from Kashmir; and the Buddhist collections from Tibet and Nepal, including several fine bronzes (12–16C).

At the end of the Gallery is a fine display devoted to the decorative arts of the LANDS OF ISLAM, with pottery, cut and enamelled glass, and engraved and inlaid metalwork. Especially notable: 13C silver and gold objects, including astronomical instruments and astrolabes; 13C Mesopotamian bronze inlaid with silver and copper; 16–18C Turkish armour; Persian mosque lamps (14–19C); and 16C Isnik pottery from Turkey.

The *North Staircase* ascends from outside the centre of the gallery to the Prints and Drawings (p. 188), and the Upper Egyptian Rooms (p. 187); or we may return by the bridge (see above) to the main building.

FIRST FLOOR. We ascend the Main Staircase on the w. side of the Entrance Hall to the first-floor galleries of the Greek and Roman Department. On the right is the **Room of Terracottas and Bronzes** (68). The left wall cases have a fine display of Greek terracottas (2000 B.C.–50 B.C.), mainly figurines from Greece and Magna Graecia; Roman terracottas, 50 B.C.–A.D. 100.—On the right wall: Greek bronzes of 1200 B.C.–150 B.C., including a series of animals (6C B.C.) found at Çeşme, Asia Minor, and a statuette of Aphrodite (late 3C B.C.); Etruscan bronze heads (athlete, 300–250 B.C., and youth, c. 350 B.C.); Roman bronzes (50 B.C.–A.D. 220). In the centre cases: Etruscan bronze mirrors; Greek repoussé reliefs; moulds for making terracottas from Tarentum (330 B.C.–A.D. 50). Also, Etruscan dinos, tripods, cistae, etc.

We now enter (R. 69) the beautifully arranged collections illustrating ****Greek and Roman Life.** In wall cases beginning r. of entrance are Greek armour, including an Etruscan helmet from Cumae (474 B.C.) dedicated by Hiero at Olympia; Roman silver including part of the 2C A.D. **Chaourse Treasure* (comp. p. 182), Mycenean, Greek, and Etruscan silverware. Roman water-wheel. Articles to illustrate home life; food and agriculture; athletics; a magnificent collection of *Glass from the earliest sand-core glass (6–1C B.C., pre-Roman) to the blown glass of the 1–4C A.D., and cases devoted to music and drama. In the centre of the gallery are cases devoted to Greek, Mycenean, and Roman weapons; Roman religion and magic; Greek and Roman weights and measures; spinning and weaving; lamps and lighting; Roman locks and plumbing; games and toys; writing; toilet articles; dress; and transport. In the gallery are beautiful collections of *Jewellery: Minoan and Mycenean including part of the Aegina Treasure (comp. p. 177): Greek, Roman and Etruscan jewellery, and *Coins and medallions including some of the finest examples of late Roman numismatic art and the Bredgar Treasure Trove. Paintings adorn the staircase.

The GREEK AND ROMAN CORRIDOR (70) contains a *Display of works of art illustrating the gods and myths of the classical world. It leads to the THIRD VASE ROOM (71) which temporarily houses a collection of *Cypriot Antiquities* (2500 B.C.–A.D. 330), and a secondary exhibition of South Italian red-figured pottery which may be seen on request. The two **Vase Rooms** beyond contain a surfeit of superb examples of all periods. In the FIRST VASE ROOM (73; farthest from the door) are examples of Geometric vases from 1000–700 B.C. (Attic and non-Attic); Corinthian and East Greek pottery with animal motifs; early Iron Age examples from Etruria and Latium; 7–6C Italian imitations; Etruscan bucchero ware. The w. wall has a magnificent display of Attic black-figured pottery.—THE SECOND VASE ROOM (72) contains Attic pottery of 530–350 B.C. with scenes of everyday life or of gods and heroes.

Beyond the First Vase Room we cross the Landing (see below) to enter the smaller *Egyptian Rooms, in the N. wing of the main building, which contain the large collection of mummies and other objects found in tombs, from which our knowledge of the life and ideas of the ancient Egyptians is mainly derived.

FIRST EGYPTIAN ROOM (l.; 60). Mummy-cases, elaborately decorated; mummies of sacred animals (Cases 2–4), including numerous cats, dogs, fishes, insects, a bull, an ibex, an ape, and crocodiles.—SECOND EGYPTIAN ROOM (61). In Case A, Mummy of a man of the prehistoric period (c. 3300 B.C.), and of a woman of the 1st Dynasty; the other centre cases contain wooden coffins. The wall cases contain fine mummy-cases and coffins. – In the THIRD EGYPTIAN ROOM (62) the left compartment contains shabti figures and other funerary furnishings, papyri of Books of the Dead and other writings; the right compartment contains legal and literary papyri, wall-paintings, etc. – FOURTH EGYPTIAN ROOM (63) illustrates daily life in Egypt with fine displays of basketry and rope, toilet articles and cosmetics, clothing and footwear, spinning and weaving, musical instruments, magic, servants, dolls, toys and games, food and drink, navigation, agriculture, weapons and hunting, domestic equipment, weights and measures, trade and currency, scribes and artists, tools, and furniture. – FIFTH EGYPTIAN ROOM (65). Small sculptures in stone, metal, wood and terracotta; figures of gods. The SIXTH EGYPTIAN ROOM (64, entered from R. 63) illustrates pottery from earliest times to the Coptic period. Table and wall cases contain the pre-dynastic and early dynastic collections, scarabs and jewellery, faience and glass.

In the CORRIDOR leading from the Fourth Egyptian Room to the King Edward VII Building (comp. below) are shown Coptic sculptures and textiles, and painted portraits of the Roman period.

This forms the approach to the KING EDWARD VII BUILDING (comp. above). The *Upper Gallery* contains in the w. half, a changing exhibition of ***Prints and Drawings,** including European prints and drawings (15–20C), and Oriental works.

The N. Staircase (or the lift) descends past the Map Room and the King Edward VII Gallery to the N. Museum Entrance in Montague Place.

The smaller rooms flanking the Egyptian collections are devoted to Western Asiatic Antiquities. To the s. of Room 66 are (R. 55) the *Prehistoric Room* with typed and stratified finds from Persia, Palestine, Mesopotamia, Syria, and Asia Minor (7000–2800 B.C.); and the *Room of Writing*, with documents in cuneiform and alphabetic scripts. Beyond (w. of) R. 64 are Room 57 (being rearranged 1978) showing antiquities of Syria, Phoenicia, and Carthage; Room 58, the Nimrud *Ivories; and the Landing (R. 59) at the top of the N.W. staircase, devoted to South Arabian antiquities, including limestone and calcite sculpture from the land of the Queen of Sheba and inscriptions in Sabaean.

Across the landing at the top of the N.E. Staircase (with relief slabs from Carchemish) we enter Room 54 with ***Sumerian Antiquities from Ur,** mainly excavated in 1919–34, and dating from c. 3500 to 1500 B.C. Two *Lyres and a harp, the latter reconstructed by pouring plaster into the holes left by the perished parts; inlaid ornaments of shell and limestone in bitumen; statuette of a royal personage; *Bust of a governor of Lagash; *Statuette of a goat and a tree in gold, shell, copper, and lapis lazuli; copper relief of a lion-headed eagle; *Shell and lapis lazuli mosaic, depicting the life of a prince in peace and war; game board with pieces.

Running s. from the landing, the ANATOLIAN AND IRANIAN ROOMS (52, 51) form an interconnected display with large maps and photographs of Hittite sites. In cases: Hittite cuneiform tablet from Bogazköy; statuettes of gods and gold grave goods from Carchemish; Urartu bronzes, including a model castle façade with three stories; bronze shield (7C B.C.) with repoussé lions from Toprak Kale. Beyond a polychrome relief of an archer in glazed brick from the Palace of Darius at Susa, earlier Elamite antiquities and horse bronzes from Luristan; in the centre, the *Oxus Treasure, with an exquisitely detailed gold model chariot. Periods following Alexander's conquests: Parthian gold masks; glazed clay coffin, Sassanian silver dish (5C A.D.).

Room 50 displays COINS OF THE BRITISH ISLES from Celtic times to Victoria. From it can be reached the Medieval Antiquities, better approached from the main staircase (see below).

Prehistoric and Romano-British Antiquities begin at the top of the main stair in the *Central Saloon* (R. 35). Here is a large 4C mosaic pavement from St Mary, Dorset; one medallion has a representation of Christ. Cases contain British gold work (1500–500 B.C.), including the great cape from Mold; the 'Lorraine Flagons', bronze La Tène vessels (c. 400 B.C.) from Basse-Yutz on the Moselle; and Belgic wrought-iron burial objects from Welwyn, Herts. (50–10 B.C.). – The upper gallery (R. 36; l.) has the theme MAN BEFORE METALS, assembled from a rich quaternary collection spanning over two million years. The everyday use of flint and obsidian and painted pre-wheel pottery have as much prominence as the occasional mature work of art. Outstanding in interest are stone artefacts from Olduvai Gorge (Tanzania), carvings on mammoth and walrus tusk (France), stone idols from Grime's Graves, and the mysterious 'Folkton Drums'.

Across the Central Saloon, the SECOND PREHISTORY ROOM (37) exhibits European objects from 2000–1000 B.C., some found in Wessex; gold work from Wilsford, Wiltshire; examples of British and European 'Beakers'; finds from cemeteries of the El Argar culture in Southern Spain; British Bronze Age pottery; daggers and axes in copper from the Únětice culture. – The THIRD PREHISTORY ROOM (38) illustrates various North European Bronze Age cultures of 1400–650 B.C., with pottery and weapons in Britain culminating in the Hallstatt period.

IRON AGE ROOM (39). Wall cases: Objects from the Ticino valley cemeteries (c. 500 B.C.–A.D. 37); early Celtic art in N.W. Europe; the Somme-Bionne chariot burial; finds from the Aylesford cemetery (50–10 B.C.) including a situla with embossed bronze mounts; a chariot burial from the Lady's Barrow, Arras, Yorks.; finds from Early Iron Age sites in Wiltshire. Central cases: Gold *Torc from Snettisham (1C B.C.); bronze disk from Ireland, and bronze armlets from Scotland (2C A.D.); decorated bronze *Shield from Battersea (early 1C A.D.); mirror from Holcombe, East Devon; decorated bronze scabbards, hoards of decorated bronze harness trappings from Stanwick, Yorks. and Polden Mill, Somerset; decorated bronze mirror from Desborough (early 1C A.D.); 6 gold torcs (1C B.C.) found in Ipswich in 1968 and 1970; decorated bronze shield from the River Witham (c. 200 B.C.).

The ROMANO-BRITISH ROOM (40), to the N., displays objects from the 1–4C A.D. In the first case (left): statuette in bronze of an archer, and porphyry cinerary urn (1–2C A.D.; both found in London). The 2nd (wall) case contains the Saxmundham Claudius, a bronze head of the mid-1C A.D. 3rd Case: pewter ware from Appleshaw, Hampshire, and a colour coated jar with hunting scenes (3C A.D.). The following cases contain Samian pottery and glass, jewellery and the Backworth treasure, and silver and bronze plate. At the end of the room, large leaden vessel (probably a font) fron Icklingham; and a mosaic pavement from Thruxton. A case contains the Capheaton treasure (including intricate skillet handles), a statuette of Nero in the guise of Alexander, from Baylham Mill (1C), and a hoard of 3C bronzes from Felmingham. A group of funerary monuments occupies the centre of the room. The wall case here contains the **Mildenhall Treasure* of Roman silver (4C), including a large embossed dish of superb workmanship, disocvered in 1942. Marble heads from Broadbridge and Lullingstone are displayed below painted wall plaster from Lullingstone and St Albans. – In the gallery above, objects relating to the army in Roman Britain include a bronze helmet from Guisborough, and a parade-helmet (with visor mask) from Ribchester (late 1C A.D.). Also: bronze goose-head from Richborough, and a bronze head of Hadrian found in the Thames. On the stair, mosaic of a chariot race from Horkstow.

The rooms to the E. display **Medieval and Later Antiquities.** THE EARLY MEDIEVAL ROOM (41) takes the form of a cross, appropriately since the art of the Early Christian period is shown in relation to its classical pagan models and its influence on both pagan conquerors in the west and on the Eastern church. In the first arm: the *Lycurgus Cup* (4C); the silver treasure of the Esquiline Hill in Rome (note the *Marriage casket); Byzantine ivory plaques; bird panels in Coptic tapestry; and the Carthage, Cyprus, and Lampsacus treasures. Material from Anglo-Saxon cemeteries in Dover (left arm) and evidences of the Anglo-Saxon incursions on the Continent (right arm) add archaeological point to the central **SUTTON HOO TREASURE, a 7C royal ship burial, probably that of King Redwald of the East Angles, excavated in Suffolk in 1939. Relics of gold, silver, bronze, and enamel include exquisite jewellery, swords, a helmet (restored in 1971) and a lyre. Farther on are the remarkable contents of the Taplow barrow.

The long MEDIEVAL ROOM (42) is arranged in rough sequence from c. 800 to 1500. All the arts of the middle ages are represented in ecclesiastical or secular form: enamelling, gilding, metalwork, painting, sculpture. Outstanding among innumerable *Treasures are (l.) the Carolingian *Crystal of Lothar* engraved with the story of Susanna and the Elders; the Townley Brooch; early 13C Reliquary of St Eustace from Basel; (r.) the 'Franks' Casket from 8C Northumbria showing classical influences; South Italian ivory horns (oliphants). In the centre, set of 12C *Chessmen* in walrus ivory from the Isle of Lewis. Left, English alabasters; wall paintings from St Stephen's Chapel, Palace of Westminster (c. 1360); right, Gothic astrolabes; the Savernake Horn. At the far end (l.), the *Lacock Cup* (English; c. 1400); (r.), *Royal Cup* of the Duc de Berri (1391), enamelled gold; end wall, Sword of state of a Prince of Wales (? Edward V or Edward, son of Richard III); Shield of Parade (late 15C).

To the left is the MEDIEVAL TILE AND POTTERY ROOM (43). To the right in the GALLERY OF CLOCKS AND WATCHES (44) a splendid array of working timepieces, divided into three sections: clocks before and after the invention of the pendulum in 1657, and watches. The mechanical side is fully apparent; artistically outstanding is the Emp. Rudolf II's ship-clock, attrib. to Schlottheim of Augsburg (c. 1580).

ROOM 45 displays the **WADDESDON BEQUEST, amassed by Baron Ferdinand de Rothschild in the tradition of the Renaissance merchant-princes. Exquisite and often exotic objets d'art of the 14–17C include silver plate, cups and caskets, Limoges enamels, a Mantuan damascened shield of 1554, and a magnificent collection of gold and jewelled pendants, outstandingly the Lyte Jewel.

A long gallery (46) shows outstanding items of **RENAISSANCE AND LATER ARTS in relation to rich patronage, English to the right, Continental to the left. Among the priceless objects (l.), Pisanello's portrait medal of John VIII Palaeologus; Limoges triptych (c. 1510); Nautilus shell cup; (r.), Henry VIII's astrolabe; the Rochester mazer; communion plate; the Goodricke Cup. In the centre, overhead, Swiss birdcage clock; the historical and personal relics include the 'magic mirror' (of Mexican

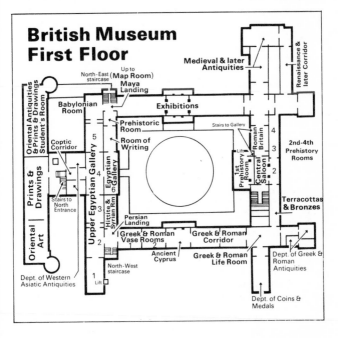

obsidian) used by Dr John Dee, the Elizabethan alchemist, astrologer, and mathematician.—The WILDING BEQUEST of Huguenot silver made in England (c. 1690–1723) is displayed opposite English pottery, including Lambeth Delft, Fulham stoneware (note the bust of Prince Rupert by John Dwight, 1670–75), and 17–18C silver.

ROOM 47 contains *EUROPEAN GLASS AND PORCELAIN and a carillon clock by Isaac Harbrecht (1589).

The **British Library** contains over 8,000,000 volumes, though some 200,000 were lost by enemy action during the last war; and its shelves, if placed end to end, would stretch for about 85 miles. Though now surpassed in size by the library of Congress at Washington and the Lenin State Library, it still ranks as one of the most important libraries in the world, and it is especially rich in books in foreign languages. These and older books are provided from a Treasury grant and by donation, while, by law, a copy of every book, newspaper, and so forth published in the United Kingdom must be deposited at the British Museum, where it must be accepted and preserved. The University libraries at Oxford and Cambridge, and Dublin, and the national Libraries of Scotland and Wales have the right to demand copies of books, etc., without the statutory duty to preserve them.

On the N. side of the Main Entrance Hall is the circular **Reading Room,** tickets of admission to which are granted for purposes of research and, reference which cannot be carried out elsewhere. The dome (140 ft in diameter and 106 ft high), is, next to that of the Pantheon in Rome (142 ft), the widest in the world. The superintendent's raised desk occupies the centre, and from it a service passage leads into the library; it is ringed round with desks holding the General Catalogue, which, including the Maps and Music Catalogues, is in well over 2000 volumes. The ground-floor shelves are occupied by a large library of reference books, which may be consulted directly by readers; other books are requisitioned by filling up forms.

The *Reading Room* (9–5 or 9) and the *Students' Rooms*, Manuscripts (10–4.45), Oriental Printed Books and Manuscripts (10–5, Sat 10–1), and Prints and Drawings (10–4, Sat 10–1) are open on weekdays to holders of tickets (gratis) for which a written application, accompanied by a letter of recommendation from a person of recognized position, should be made to the Director at least two days in advance. The Reading Room is closed for cleaning during the week including the first Monday in May.

Besides the main Reading Room, there are the *Map Room* (open to students, weekdays 9.30–4.30), the *State Paper Room* (open to students 9.30–4.45 or 8.45), and the *North Library*, for the study of rare books. Newspapers are stored in the Newspaper Library at Colindale, N.W.9 (week-days, 10–5).

17 THE STRAND AND COVENT GARDEN

STATIONS: *Charing Cross*, see Rte 5; *Covent Garden* and *Aldwych* on Piccadilly line (Aldwych open Mon–Fri rush hr. only).—BUSES in the Strand, Nos. 1, 6, 9, 11, 15, 77, 170, 176, 505, etc.—Limited meter CAR PARKING in congested streets N. and S. of the Strand.

The **Strand** (Pl. 14; 4), c. ¾ m. long, running N.E. from Trafalgar Square, is one of the busiest and most congested streets in London, with several hotels and theatres. An ancient thoroughfare (with its prolongation Fleet Street) linking the City and Westminster, it has been the scene of many historic processions. The name recalls the former proximity of the Thames, now artificially constricted and concealed by intervening buildings.

Charing Cross Station (Pl. 15; 3), near its W. end, was erected in 1863 on the site of *Hungerford Market*. The town house of Walter (1st Baron) Hungerford was erected here in 1422–23, and a descendant opened the market (later destroyed by fire) in 1682. The Gothic Cross (by E. M. Barry; 1865) in the station forecourt is a memorial, but not a copy, of Eleanor's Cross (p. 73). On the N. side of the Strand, the façade and eccentric turrets of the Coutts's Bank building by Smirke have been 'saved' at disproportionate cost. Behind is the old *Charing Cross Hospital* (moved in 1973 to Fulham), and, on the corner of Agar St., are allegorical sculptures (1907; weathered) by Epstein.

Craven Street skirts the W. side of Charing Cross Station and descends towards the Victoria Embankment (with The Playhouse, used by the B.B.C. for television recordings). Benjamin Franklin lived at No. 36, now the headquarters of the British Society for International Understanding, and a centre for Anglo-American Co-operation. On the left, in Craven Passage, we may pass under *The Arches* of the station (made famous by Flanagan and Allen), where recent attempts at rehabilitation have been various and short lived, to reach *Villiers Street*. On the site between

Villiers St. and the parallel Buckingham St., George Villiers, duke of Buckingham, partly rebuilt (in 1624) *York House*, the birthplace in 1561 of Francis Bacon. The old **Water-Gate* survives at the end of Buckingham St.; built by Nicholas Stone in 1626, it shows where the Thames reached at that time. Victoria Embankment Gardens descend to the river (comp. Rte 26). Sir Richard Steele lived in Villiers St. from 1721 to 1724, and Rudyard Kipling's first London home (in 1889–91) was at No. 19 (now No. 43). Pepys occupied No. 12 Buckingham St. in 1679–88; while No. 14 bears a tablet recording its tenancy, in its various transitions, by Pepys (in 1688–1700), Robert Harley, earl of Oxford, William Etty, the painter, and Clarkson Stanfield, the marine painter. Burdett House opposite (rebuilt as the headquarters of the Royal National Pension Fund for Nurses) was occupied by Peter the Great in 1697–98. The names of David Hume, Rousseau, and Henry Fielding were also associated with this house.

John Adam Street, parallel to the Strand on the s., runs through the region known as THE ADELPHI, named after the four Scottish brothers Adam who planned a residential area on the land sloping down to the river in 1768. The ambitious scheme involved the erection of streets, houses and terraces supported on an embankment of arches and subterranean vaults. The main brick terrace overlooking the Thames was directly inspired by the Palace of Diocletian at Split. A lottery was authorized by Parliament in 1773 to rescue the enterprise from financial disaster. A few fine Adam houses survive.

Among artists and writers who came to live here were David Garrick, Thos. Rowlandson, Tom Hood, Charles Dickens (whose youthful experiences in this quarter are described in 'David Copperfield'), Bernard Shaw, Sir James Barrie, H. G. Wells, and John Galsworthy. Robert Adam himself lived at No. 10 Adam St. (built in 1772; signboard).—The ROYAL SOCIETY OF ARTS occupies a fine Adam building in John Adam Street. The Society was established in 1754 to foster art, manufacture, and trade. The hall (adm. on application; closed Sun) contains mural paintings by James Barry (1777–83), illustrating (not very perspicuously) the benefits of civilization.—The 'Gilbert and Sullivan' public house contains relics of the composers; W. S. Gilbert was born in Southampton St. on the N. side of the Strand, and Richard d'Oyly Carte lived at No. 4 Adelphi Terrace while producing the Gilbert and Sullivan comic operas at the Savoy Theatre (1881 et seq.; see below).

Beyond the *Savoy Hotel* and *Theatre* (the first public building in the world to be lit by electricity in 1881), Savoy Street leads s. to the Thames Embankment past the garden of the **Chapel of the Savoy,** erected in the late-Perpendicular style in 1505, on part of the site of Savoy Palace. Entered from Savoy Hill, it is open on Tues–Fri, 9.30–4, and for services on Sunday.

Savoy Palace built in 1246, was given by Henry III to his wife's uncle, Peter, earl of Savoy and Richmond (d. 1268), and afterwards passed into the possession of John of Gaunt. King John of France, taken prisoner at the Battle of Poitiers (1356) died in the palace in 1364. Geoffrey Chaucer and John Wyclif here enjoyed the patronage of John of Gaunt. The palace was burned down by Wat Tyler in 1381, and the manor made over to the Crown in 1399 by Henry IV. It was rebuilt as a hospital and chapel by Henry VII in 1505. Here in 1661 took place the famous Savoy Conference for the revision of the Prayer Book.

The chapel was restored by Queen Victoria after a destructive fire in 1864. It is the Chapel of the Royal Victorian Order, and the stalls of the knights are marked by small copper plates emblazoned with the arms of the holder. A stained glass window commemorates Richard d'Oyly Carte (1844–1901; see above).—The studio of the B.B.C. in 1923–31 (comp. below) was on the other side of Savoy Hill.

Just in Wellington St., off the N. side of the Strand, the former *Lyceum Theatre* has a portico of 1834; here Irving was manager in 1878–98 and played in 'The Bells'.

The busy *Lancaster Place*, on the right, forms the approach to Waterloo Bridge, passing the w. façade of Somerset House. Beyond, Aldwych, taking the eastbound traffic, forms a wide crescent to the N. (see below).

Continuing along the Strand, we soon reach the N. façade of **Somerset House** (Pl. 15; 3), a Palladian building erected by Sir William Chambers in 1776–86. The E. wing (King's College) was added by Sir R. Smirke in 1829–34, the W. wing by Sir James Pennethorne in 1852–56. The chief *Façade, nearly 600 ft long, fronting the Thames, stands on a terrace 50 ft above the Victoria Embankment. Its basement arcade originally rose straight from the river, and the great central arch was the water-gate. The present building occupies the site of a palace begun by the Lord Protector Somerset c. 1547, but left unfinished at his execution in 1552. The palace then passed into the hands of the Crown. Elizabeth I lived here for a time during the reign of her sister Mary. Oliver Cromwell lay in state here in 1658.

Somerset House is mainly occupied by Government Offices. In the W. wing is the *Board of Inland Revenue*, which deals with stamps, taxes, death duties, and land values duties. The *Principal Probate Registry* (in the S. wing), which formerly housed also Prerogative Court of Canterbury (PCC) wills from 1382 (transferred to the Public Record Office), now holds only wills and testaments registered in England since 1858. A copy of any will can be seen for a fee (Mon–Fri, 10–4.30). Other wills (pre-1858) are preserved elsewhere. The *State Rooms* in the N. wing (good staircase and ceilings) are open for occasional exhibitions.

To the E. of Somerset House is the new building (1972; with a fine theatre) of **King's College,** one of the incorporated colleges of the University of London. Following a public meeting in 1828 with the Prime Minister (the Duke of Wellington) in the Chair and the Abps. of Canterbury and York in attendance, it was opened in 1831.

The names of the next series of streets leading from the Strand to the Embankment commemorate the sites of the town houses of Thomas Howard earl of Arundel, Surrey, and Norfolk (c. 1585–1646), and of Robert Devereux, earl of Essex (1567–1601). The street layout has been altered by recent demolition. Off Surrey St. is an alleged *Roman Bath*, fed by a rivulet (N.T.; adm. 10–12.30 exc. Sun); the bricks used are small and non-porous, of an unusual kind, the Roman origin of which is by no means certain. Adjacent are the remains of an Elizabethan bath, said to date from 1588.—Rising on neighbouring sites are a hotel, and an extension to King's. During building in 1973 part of a Roman frieze from Pergamon was found, having been shipped to England in 1627 by the Earl of Arundel, and abandoned in his garden.

In the middle of the Strand stands the finely proportioned church of **St Mary-le-Strand,** with an Ionic portico and graceful steeple, built by James Gibbs in 1714, and consecrated in 1724. The barrel vault has fine plasterwork, and the pulpit is usually attributed to Gibbons. The fabric of the church is to be restored. The space in front was the site of the famous Maypole where the first hackney carriage rank stood in 1634; it was removed in 1718 and bought by Sir Isaac Newton as the stand for a telescope at Wanstead House. Thomas Becket was once lay-rector of the parish and Charles Dickens's parents were married in the church in 1809.

Farther E., the church of **St Clement Danes** forms another island in the Strand. Designed by Wren and built in 1680–82 on the site of a much earlier building, it is traditionally believed to be the burial-place of Harold Harefoot and other Danes. The tower, added by James Gibbs in 1719–20, is 115 ft high and contains a famous and tuneful peal of bells ("Oranges and lemons, say the bells of St Clement's"). In 1941 the church was gutted by fire and it has been beautifully restored as the headquarters church of the Royal Air Force.

The interior has bright white and gilt stucco decoration, and a Father Smith organ (restored). The floor is inlaid with unit and squadron badges, and Books of Remembrance line the aisles. The altarpiece is by Ruskin Spear. A fine staircase descends to the crypt which is decorated with ancient tomb slabs. William Webb Ellis, the inventor of Rugby Football in 1823, was rector here (memorial tablet). Dr Johnson was a worshipper in this church and is commemorated by a statue by Percy Fitzgerald outside the choir.—A *Gladstone Memorial*, by Hamo Thornycroft (1905), stands opposite the w. front of the church.

The Strand is continued by Fleet Street towards the City (see Rte 19). We turn N.W. into **Aldwych**, which takes its name from an old colony (ald-wych) of Danes in this vicinity before the Conquest. On the s. corner is AUSTRALIA HOUSE built in 1911–18 as the office of the Commonwealth of Australia. The groups flanking the entrance represent Exploration, and Shearing and Reaping; high above are the Horses of the Sun. Across Melbourne Place, BUSH HOUSE, a massive pile of offices, begun in 1920 by Harvey Corbett, occupies the greater part of the area between Aldwych and the Strand. Here are located the External Services of the B.B.C. The entrance facing Kingsway is a huge archway surmounted by a colossal group, by Malvina Hoffmann (1925; damaged by a flying bomb), symbolizing the friendship of Britain and the United States. Across Aldwych, in Houghton Street, are the premises of the *London School of Economics and Political Science*. Sidney and Beatrice Webb participated in its establishment in 1895, and Harold Laski when Professor of Political Science here in 1926, instilled some of the left-wing views for which it is celebrated. Clare Market to the N. was once a slum district associated with the names of Jack Sheppard and Dick Turpin. KINGSWAY (Pl. 15; 1) runs N. to High Holborn (comp. p. 216). On the corner stands *St Catherine's House*, the Office of Population Censuses and Surveys (General Register Office), whither the records of Births, Marriages, and Deaths in England since 1837 have been removed from Somerset House.

Beyond Bush House, INDIA HOUSE (1930) designed by Sir Herbert Baker, is the office of the High Commissioner for India. The fine interior is decorated in the Indian style and largely by Indian artists. There are occasional exhibitions of Indian arts and crafts, and the Reading Room is open to the public (Mon–Fri, 9.45–6). On the last building on the island (now a bank) tablets record the site of the Gaiety Theatre, home of musical comedy in London in 1903–39, and the Broadcasting Station of Marconi's Wireless Telegraph Company from 11 May to 15 Nov 1922, when it became the first station of the B.B.C.

On the N.W. side of the crescent, the *Aldwych Theatre* stands at the corner of Drury Lane. It gave name to the farces of Ben Travers, played here in 1920–33, but since 1950 has been the London home of the Stratford Memorial Theatre Company (and used in spring by foreign companies).

A mainly residential and local shopping street, DRURY LANE (Pl. 15; 1) runs N.W. to High Holborn. John Sainsbury opened his first shop here in 1869. The huge entrance portico (1820) of the **Theatre Royal, Drury Lane,** is in Catherine St. (parallel to the w.). The site has been in continuous use as a theatre for more than three centuries. The present building, with its gracious foyers, was built by Benjamin Wyatt in 1812, though the auditorium (2283 seats) was remodelled in 1922. It specialized in romantic musicals and is now celebrated more for spectacles of a popular nature than for any serious dramatic contribution.

The first theatre was erected through letters patent granted by Charles II in 1663, and used by Killigrew's 'King's Company', who for some years were the only players allowed to perform in London. By 1690 the theatre was known by its present name. Burned down in 1671, it was rebuilt in 1674, probably to designs by Wren. Riots in the building were not uncommon, from causes ranging from leakage of rain in the pit (1668) to the inclusion of 'Papists and Frenchmen' among the performers (1754). Garrick's management began in 1747 with a prologue by Dr Johnson, containing the famous line, "We that live to please must please to live". Sheridan, manager in 1776–1816, here produced his brilliant comedies; John Kemble played 'Hamlet' in 1783: and his sister Mrs Siddons triumphed in many Shakespearian parts. The theatre was rebuilt in 1791–94 by Henry Holland for Sheridan, and burned again in 1809. The prologue for the opening of the present building in 1812 was written by Byron.—The interior contains statues, busts, and paintings of famous players, and in the vestibule is a statue of Shakespeare by John Cheere.

Farther N. Drury Lane crosses the junction of Long Acre and *Great Queen Street*, named after Queen Henrietta Maria, in which is the huge *Freemason's Hall*, built in 1931–33, the English headquarters of the Masonic craft.

Lord Herbert of Cherbury died in Great Queen St. in 1648; Sir Godfrey Kneller (1646–1723), Sir Charles Sedley (1658), and Richard Wilson (1714–82) had houses here; and here Sir Joshua Reynolds was apprentice (1740–43) to Hudson, and William Blake to the engraver Basire. Sheridan is said to have written 'The School for Scandal' at No. 55 (rebuilt). Boswell and Mrs Robinson ('Perdita') are among other famous inhabitants.

Drury Lane continues past the *Winter Garden Centre*, with the New London theatre (Restaurant and Car Park), rebuilt in 1972 by Paul Tvrtković and Michael Percival to a design determined by the possibilities of mechanical diversity within (movable proscenium, etc.). We turn S.W. along LONG ACRE, from c. 1695 the chief street of coachbuilders, where a few fruiterers survive from the old Covent Garden. In BOW STREET, so named 'as running in shape of a bent bow', stands the massive Corinthian portico of the **Royal Opera House, Covent Garden** (Pl. 15; 1), home of the Royal Ballet and Opera. It was built by E. M. Barry in 1857–58 and incorporates a sculptured frieze by Flaxman from an older building by Sir Robert Smirke which was destroyed in a fire. The foyer, grand staircase, and 'crush bar' are celebrated for their atmosphere of sumptuous occasion, and the *Auditorium, a fine horse-shoe which seats 2158 people, for its acoustics. The stage, of vast proportions, is closed by red velvet curtains embroidered in gold with the Royal Cypher.

The first theatre constructed by Edward Shepherd in 1731–32 opened with Congreve's 'The Way of the World', and here in 1773 was given the first performance of Goldsmith's 'She Stoops to Conquer', and in 1775 of Sheridan's 'The Rivals'. When, after fire, the second theatre was opened, riots broke out over the increased price of seats, and continued for several months until the old prices were restored.

Opposite is *Bow Street Police Court* (1879–80) the chief of London's fourteen Metropolitan police courts. The first courthouse here was established in 1739. The 'Bow Street Runners' (called 'Robin Redbreasts' from the colour of their waist-coats), were the precursors of the Criminal Investigation Department. The *Metropolitan Police Historical Museum* of policemen's clothing and equipment since 1829 (adm. by appointment, exc. Sun) is in the adjacent Police Station.

Among former residents of Bow St. were Henry Fielding (1707–54); Grinling Gibbons, from 1678 till his death in 1721; Peg Woffington, the actress (1720–60); Garrick (1717–79); and Wycherley, whose scandalous second marriage took place in his lodgings here, eleven days before his death in 1715.

Russell St. crosses Bow St. The bookshop of Tom Davies, in which Boswell first met Johnson (1763), was at No. 8 Russell St. On the left the Ionic colonnade (1831; by Sam. Beazley) of the Theatre Royal, Drury Lane (see above) faces the Fortune Theatre. We turn right to skirt the *Floral Hall* (1860; by Barry) on the E. side of **Covent Garden** (Pl. 15; 3).

The name of Covent Garden goes back to the 13C *Convent Garden* of the monks of Westminster which extended from the Strand to Long Acre. After the dissolution of the monasteries, the land reverted to the Crown, and in 1552 it was granted to John Russell, first earl of Bedford, who built his town house in the Strand. In 1610–13 the central 20 acres were walled in for pastureland, and here in 1631–39 Francis Russell, the fourth earl, planned with Inigo Jones the first and most important of the squares which began the expansion of London westwards from the City. The plan of the grand estate had the form of an Italian piazza, with houses on three sides above tall arcaded walks, and a church on the fourth side. Although shops and stalls appeared almost at once beneath the porticoes, a licence for a market in the piazza was not granted until 1670. In 1700 Bedford House was demolished and the market expanded, so that by the end of the 18C it was the most important fruit and flower market in England. The names of the adjoining streets (such as Bedford, Russell, and Tavistock) indicate the long connection of the district with the Bedford family, which ended in 1914, when the Duke of Bedford sold the Covent Garden estate. The market (where Eliza Dolittle sold flowers in Shaw's 'Pygmalion') remained in private hands until 1962. In 1974 it moved to Nine Elms (p. 273) since when plans for the area have caused controversy. So far most of the activities (street markets, amateur theatre, etc.) are of a temporary nature.

The old *Central Market Hall*, erected in 1825-30 by Charles Fowler, has been restored. The old *Flower Market Hall* may become the home of the London Transport Museum (comp. Rte 42). The *Floral Hall* may house a theatrical museum.

Nothing remains of the 17C piazza except the rebuilt church; the arcaded Bedford Chambers (1877–79) on the N.W. side of the square, are loosely modelled on the original arcades. On the W. side of the market stands **St Paul's, Covent Garden,** the 'actor's church', begun in 1631 and consecrated in 1638 and thus one of the first Anglican churches to be built in London after the Reformation. It was designed by Inigo Jones and rebuilt by Thomas Hardwicke in the original style after a fire in 1795.

The Tuscan portico, planned as the focal climax of the piazza, was never used as the altar was moved to the E. end, probably at the instigation of Bishop William Laud. The church is therefore approached from Bedford St. (or passages from King St. and Henrietta St.) through a pleasantly overgrown churchyard. Those buried here include Samuel Butler (1612–80), Sir Peter Lely (1618–80), William Wycherley (c. 1640–1715), Grinling Gibbons (1648–1721), Dr Thomas Arne (1710–78), and Thomas Rowlandson (1756–1827).

Inside, on the S. wall, a silver casket holds the ashes of Dame Ellen Terry (1847–1928). On the W. screen plaques commemorate famous actors and actresses, including Marie Lloyd, Clemence Dane, Ivor Novello, and Vivien Leigh. Here too is an exquisite llmewood wreath carved by Grinling Gibbons for St Paul's, and removed here in 1965. J. M. W. Turner was baptized in the church in 1775, and W. S. Gilbert in 1837. In the portico a plaque commemorates the first recorded performance of 'Punch and Judy' witnessed by Pepys in May 1662.

In the second half of the 18C and in the 19C the Covent Garden area abounded in coffee-houses, the rendezvous of writers and artists of the day. In Garrick Street (branching N.W. from King St.) the *Garrick Club* (No. 15) has been frequented by actors since 1831, and the Ivy in West St. is a restaurant traditionally frequented by actors and singers.

Among the artists who resided in the piazza were Samuel Cooper, Sir Peter Lely,

Sir Godfrey Kneller, Sir James Thornhill, William Hogarth, Samuel Scott, and Richard Wilson. In Maiden Lane, s. of Henrietta St., lived Andrew Marvell (1621–78). Voltaire also lodged here for about three years (1726–29), and J. M. W. Turner (1775–1851), born in his father's barber's shop (No. 26; demolished in 1861), lived here until 1800.

Bedford St. or Southampton St. leads s. to the Strand and Charing Cross.

II THE CITY, NORTH-EAST, AND EAST END

The CITY OF LONDON, one of the most important commercial square miles in the world, extending from Temple Bar to Aldgate and from Southwark to City Road, has definite limits but no natural boundaries. Nearly one third of the City was destroyed during the Second World War; rebuilding continues slowly. The surviving City churches and livery company halls still contain much interest for the visitor, but the intimate alley-ways and courts once characteristic of City life are disappearing in the shadow of huge tower blocks. The demolition of houses and realinement of streets is taking place in the interest of traffic flow though the medieval line of many thoroughfares is still apparent.

On a weekday, when the population increases eightyfold, the hustle of business gives life to the City; to explore the area at week-ends offers peace from noisy traffic and congested pavements. An attempt has been made to open small gardens (often on the site of a bombed church) which provide attractive refuges for the City worker and the visitor.

The *City Information Centre* (open Mon–Fri, 9.30–5, Sat 9.30–12.30, or 4 in April–Sept) in St Paul's Churchyard, supplies much useful help to the visitor in the form of literature about various aspects of City life, and advice on opening times, etc.

The City churches are usually open Mon–Fri 11–3, often for longer hours; on Sat they are usually closed. In many, concerts as well as services are held for the day-time population.

The Livery companies' halls can be seen only by appointment at the City Information Centre, where information can be obtained about the days (usually c. 4 a year) on which each hall is open to the public.

18 THE INNS OF COURT AND LEGAL LONDON

STATIONS: *Chancery Lane* on Central Line; *Temple* on Circle and District line.—BUSES in Fleet Street (see Rte 19) and Holborn (see Rte 21); No. 171 connects Fleet St. and High Holborn (running N. along Chancery Lane, and S. down Fetter Lane). —Cars are not allowed into the Inns (except on business); restricted meter parking in Lincoln's Inn Fields.

The district between the Thames on the S. and Theobald's Road on the N., bounded (roughly) on the E. and W. by lines running through Fetter Lane and Lincoln's Inn Fields, may be fairly described as 'Legal London', including as it does the Royal Courts of Justice, the four great Inns of Court, and the chambers of the leading solicitors and barristers.

Where the Strand and Fleet Street meet (comp. p. 195) rise the **Royal Courts of Justice** (Pl. 15; 2) or **Law Courts,** an imposing Gothic pile, erected in 1874–82 for the Supreme Court of Judicature, established in 1873. The architect was G. E. Street (1825–81), who died about a year before the completion of his work, and it was finished by Sir Arthur Blomfield and A. E. Street. The main feature of the interior is the fine Central Hall, 238 ft long by 38 ft wide, and 80 ft high, with a mosaic pavement designed by Street (adm. daily 8–dusk). A small exhibition of legal costume is displayed in a room off the hall. The public entrances to the courts and to the galleries of the hall are in the towers flanking the main entrance.

The four great **Inns of Court** (*Lincoln's Inn, Inner Temple, Middle Temple,* and *Gray's Inn*) have the exclusive right of calling persons to the English Bar. They originated in the 13C, when the clergy ceased to practise in the courts of justice, giving place to professional students of law. The members of the Inns comprise Benchers, Barristers, and Students. Barristers of the leading order are Queen's Counsel, who wear silk gowns; others wear 'stuff' gowns. Each Inn has a dining-hall, library, and chapel, the Temple Church (see below) serving in the last capacity for both the Temple Inns. The Inns provide lectures for law students and examine candidates for admission to the Bar. The students may pursue their legal studies elsewhere, but to become a member of an Inn they must 'keep term' or 'commons' by dining so many times in hall.

Visitors are practically always admitted freely to the quaint and quiet precincts of the Inns of Court (closed on Ascension Day), among which only Lincoln's Inn survived the Second World War without extensive damage.

We skirt the s. side of the Law Courts and turn N. into Bell Yard. Across Carey Street, synonymous in England for bankruptcy proceedings which centre on the street, attractive archways admit to the dignified 17C quadrangle of *New Square*, part of **Lincoln's Inn** (Pl. 15; 2). It probably takes its name from Henry de Lacy, earl of Lincoln (d. 1311), adviser to Edward I in matters of law and a great proponent of legal education; though the Inn is not on the site of his London mansion, which lay E. of Barnard's Inn. A body of lawyers is known to have occupied the present site about 1292, though no formal records exist earlier than 1424. Visitors should call at the Porter's Lodge (11A New Square) for admission to the halls and chapel (daily, exc. Sun; Sat 9–3 only).

Between New Square and the *Old Buildings* to the E. is the *Old Hall* (c. 1492; s. bay of 1624), with good exterior brickwork and fine open roof, well restored in 1926–28. It served as the Court of Chancery from 1733 to 1873, within which period falls the famous fictional case of Jarndyce v. Jarndyce (in 'Bleak House'). The *Chapel*, probably by John Clarke (1620–23), has been restored and enlarged; the crypt used to serve, like the Temple Church, as a rendezvous for the barristers and their clients, and more recently acted as a shelter from air raids. The side windows contain glass by Bernard van Linge (1632–34). The *Gatehouse* into Chancery Lane (comp. p. 202) was built in 1518 by Sir Thomas Lovell (whose arms it bears). To the N. are the classical range of *Stone Buildings* (1774–80) and the attractive Gardens (adm. 12–2.30 Mon–Fri).—The imposing *New Hall and Library* (to the w.) is a successful red-brick edifice in the Tudor style, by Philip and P. C. Hardwick (1843–45). The hall contains a large mural painting by G. F. Watts ('Justice—a Hemicycle of Lawgivers'; 1853–59), and many legal portraits. The brilliant heraldic glass dates from 1954. The Benchers' Rooms also contain fine paintings, incl. a small work by Holbein, and the library is the oldest in London (1497), and contains the most complete collection of law books in England (70,000 vols.); but these may be visited only with a member of the Inn.

Among the eminent names associated with Lincoln's Inn are those of Sir Thomas More, Donne, Penn, Pitt, Horace Walpole, Newman, Macaulay, Canning, Disraeli, Gladstone, Morley, Asquith, Galsworthy, and Newbolt.

We pass through an archway at the N.W. corner of New Square into **Lincoln's Inn Fields** (Pl. 15; 2; fine plane trees), the largest square in central London, the old houses surrounding which are mainly occupied as solicitors' offices. It was laid out in 1618 by Inigo Jones, who is said also to have built some houses on the w. and s. sides (now practically all gone). On the s. side, beyond the *Land Registry Office* and *Nuffield College of Surgical Sciences*, the **Royal College of Surgeons** occupies a large building with an Ionic portico, erected in 1806–13 by G. Dance, Junior. It was modified with great skill by Sir Charles Barry (1835–37), but has been marred since by extensions and alterations.

The College contained the greatest medical museum in the world, but many of the specimens were destroyed by enemy action in 1941. Now the surviving exhibits of the Hunterian Collection prepared by the celebrated surgeon John Hunter (1728–93) may be seen on written application to the Secretary. Part of the Wellcome Medical Museum here is available to members of the medical profession.

Next door is the large new building of the *Imperial Cancer Research Fund* which extends into Portsmouth Street, where an old shop survives, claiming to be Dickens' 'Old Curiosity Shop'; the original of the novel, however, really stood about the site of Irving's statue in Charing Cross Road.

On the w. side of Lincoln's Inn Fields beyond the office of the *Public Trustee* (to be closed), *Lindsey House* (Nos. 59, 60) is attributed to Inigo Jones (c. 1640); Nos. 57–58 are imitations built in 1730, and altered by Soane. *Powis House*, at the N.W. corner, is a fine brick building of 1684–89 (restored).

Among famous residents were Lord Brougham (1778–1868), Spencer Perceval (1762–1812; No. 60), John Milton, Lord Tennyson (1809–92), John Forster (1812–76; No. 58), and Nell Gwynn (1650–87).—Before their enclosure the gardens were a favourite duelling-ground and a great haunt of thieves. The pillory was often erected here. Lord William Russell was executed in Lincoln's Inn Fields in 1683. Memorials on the N. side of the garden commemorate Mrs Ramsay MacDonald (d. 1911), who lived at No. 3 Lincoln's Inn Fields, and Lord Hambleden (1868–1928) head of the book-distributing organization of W. H. Smith & Son.

The N. walk of the gardens has been named *Canada Walk*, to commemorate the establishment here of the headquarters of the Royal Canadian Air Force in 1940–45 (tablet beside a memorial maple tree).

In the middle of the N. side of the square (where most of the fine houses have been demolished) No. 13 survives as ***Sir John Soane's Museum**, founded by Sir John Soane (1753–1837), architect of the Bank of England. Owing to the stipulation of the founder that his collections should not be augmented nor disturbed, the museum has the unusual interest of retaining the character of a private house of the period (1813). The arrangements to make the most of the room available are exceedingly ingenious; and the effect of space is enhanced by a clever use of mirrors. The museum includes some objects that no visitor to London should miss, pre-eminently the paintings by William Hogarth and the sarcophagus of Seti I.

The Museum is open from 10–5, Tues–Sat, except on BH. Lecture tours on Sat at 2.30. Excellent short guide available.

The PICTURE ROOM (shown by a custodian), on the ground floor, contains two admirable series of paintings by *William Hogarth* (1697–1764), the *Rake's Progress (8 scenes; 1735) and the *Election (4 scenes; 1754–57), excellent examples of his satirical humour, harmonious colouring, and able composition. Here also are The Passage Point by *Callcott*, and a Design for the Ceiling of the Queen's State Bedchamber at Hampton Court, by *Thornhill*. We descend to the SEPULCHRAL CHAMBER with the *Sarcophagus of Seti I*, King of Egypt c. 1370 B.C. and father of Ramesses the Great.—Re-ascending to the ground floor we visit the first room past the plaster casts, in which are *Turner's* *Admiral Tromp's barge entering the Texel after his defeat of Blake in 1652, and *Canaletto's* *View of the Grand Canal. We ascend to the FIRST FLOOR (renovated in 1970) where a connecting door admits to the adjoining house (No. 12) built by Soane for himself in 1792, and now used as a library for students. The numerous small works of art, antiquities, casts, and furniture, etc., throughout the Museum include many objects of great interest. The fine doors of mahogany and ebony deserve notice, and many of the windows are filled with old stained glass.

We leave the square by Newman's Row (at the N.E. corner) and emerge in High Holborn (see p. 216). We turn E., cross, and turn N. into Fulwood Place to reach **Gray's Inn** (Pl. 7; 6). Originally in the buildings of the manor of Portpool, it is known to have been occupied by lawyers before 1370 and takes its name from the former owners of the site, the Lords Grey de Wilton. The Inn was very seriously damaged by enemy action in 1941, the Hall, the Chapel, and the Library being burned out. It has been restored in a harmonious style. Both the Chapel and Hall are open when not in use. We pass through an archway (r.) to the squares either side of the *Hall* (1560), rebuilt in 1951, with a second oriel presented by the American Bar Association. It preserves its stained glass and much of the fine carved screen. Shakespeare's 'Comedy of Errors' had its first performance here in 1594, and the Court of Exchequer was held in this hall in the 18C. The *Chapel* was reconsecrated on the 19th anniversary of the fire; it preserves a stoup from the 14C manor chapel. The *Library*, in South Square, is a harmonious building by Sir Edward Maufe (1956). The *Gardens* (entered from Field Court through a gate of 1723), with their ancient catalpas, were supposed to have been laid out by Francis Bacon (whose statue stands in South Square). They are open to the public in Aug and Sept, Mon–Fri 8.15–5. *Raymond Buildings* (1825) and *Verulam Buildings* (1811) skirt the gardens on the w. and E. in long terraces.

The great name of Gray's Inn is Francis Bacon, who became Treasurer of the Inn and retained his chambers here from 1577 till his death in 1626. Among other members were Sir William Gascoigne, the judge traditionally reported to have committed the Prince of Wales (Henry V) to prison, Sir Thomas Gresham, Thomas Cromwell, Nicholas Bacon, Burghley, Abp. Laud, and Lord Birkenhead. The Council of Legal Education occupies a building in Gray's Inn Place where Sun Yat-Sen, the 'Father of the Chinese Republic', lived during his political exile from his country (tablet to be replaced).

We return across High Holborn to **Chancery Lane** (Pl. 7; 6) which runs s. to Fleet St.

The nine **Inns of Chancery** differed from the Inns of Court in being of minor importance and subordinate character. It was long the custom for students of law to enter first an Inn of Chancery and then graduate to an Inn of Court, but this practice had become obsolete at the beginning of the 17C. The Inns of Chancery were thenceforward abandoned to the attorneys, and by the middle of the 18C they had practically ceased to have any legal character.
Clement's Inn, Clifford's Inn (the oldest and most important of the Inns of Chancery), *Thavie's Inn*, and *Furnival's Inn* now exist merely as names of modern buildings. *Lyon's Inn, New Inn*, and *Strand Inn* have completely disappeared. The legal history of *Staple Inn* goes back to the reign of Henry V (1413–22), that of *Barnard's Inn* to the time of Henry VI (1422–61).—The two *Serjeants' Inns* were independent bodies, composed solely of serjeants-at-law ('servientes ad legem'), an order of the highest rank of barristers. The society was dissolved in 1877, but the buildings of one of their inns survived until 1941.

Chancery Lane skirts the E. side of Lincoln's Inn (p. 200). To the left diverges Southampton Buildings, with the entrance to the *London Silver Vaults* (Mon–Fri, 9–5.30; Sat 9–12.30), storing a copious stock of antique silver, etc. Farther on (r.) is the PATENT OFFICE. The former *Patent Office Library* (318,600 vols; Mon–Fri 9.30–9, Sat 10–1), now Holborn Division of the British Library (British Science Library), is the finest collection of technical and scientific works in England. It is adjoined on the N. by the small garden of Staple Inn.

Farther s. rises the **Public Record Office,** one section of the chief repository of the state archives of England (open Mon–Fri 9.30–5, Sat till 1), a fortress-like building in a Tudor style (1851–66, by Pennethorne, and 1891–96, by Sir John Taylor), very reminiscent of the 19C parts of the Tower of London from which many of the archives were removed. Here are the legal and judicial records from the Conquest; 16–18C papers of Secretaries of State; and 19C census returns (see also Kew, p. 298). A Reader's Ticket is necessary.

The *Record Office Museum (open 1–4; closed on Sat and Sun; parties at other times by arrangement) occupies the exact site and area of the old Rolls Chapel. Three of the monuments, erected in the old chapel, are still in their original positions on the N. wall. Adjacent is the most important object in the museum, *Domesday Book* (2 vellum vols.), containing the results of the statistical survey of England made by order of William the Conqueror in 1086. The so-called *Domesday Chest*, with its triple lock, is likewise shown. The glass cases contain a remarkable series of famous and interesting historical documents and records.

Cases in the centre are in alphabetical order; those on the wall in numerical order. Case D. Letters patent of John Baliol signifying that he had sworn fealty to Edward I, as suzerain of Scotland (1292). Case H. Wooden tallies for keeping accounts. Case P. Log of the 'Victory', recording the battle of Trafalgar. Case Q. Despatch from the battle of Waterloo, with Wellington's signature. Case T. 'Scrap of paper' guaranteeing the neutrality of Belgium (1839). Case U. Letter of c. 1220, interesting as one of the earliest extant examples of the use of paper in Europe; Abingdon Indulgence (1476), the oldest document printed in England. Case W. Shakespeare's signature (1612); Bunyan's preaching licence. Case Y. Memorials of Shelley. Case IV. Anonymous letter to Lord Monteagle warning him of the Gunpowder Plot (1605); signatures of Guy Fawkes (Guido Faukes), the latter supposed to have been written after torture. Case XI. Shakespeare's Will (transferred from Somerset House as were those of Pitt, Burke, Dr Johnson, and Newton). Case XII. 'Olive Branch Petition' to George III from Congress (1775), with the signatures of John Adams, Stephen Hopkins, Benjamin Franklin, and others; interesting autographs, including a letter from Washington to his "great and good friend", George III (1795).

Almost opposite the Record Office, are the massive offices of the *Law Society*, which controls the education, admission, and discipline of the solicitors' branch of the legal profession. At the foot of Chancery Lane we cross Fleet Street to enter the **Temple** (Pl. 7; 8) by Wren's fine *Gatehouse* (1684), which opens from Fleet St. near Temple Bar. The general name covers two Inns of Court, the *Middle* and the *Inner Temple*, extending from Fleet St. to the Thames, and named from their topographical relations to the City proper and the Outer Temple. The last, merely a piece of ground belonging to the Templars, was absorbed at an early date by private owners.

The Temple was originally the seat in England of the famous Order of Knights Templars. On the dissolution of the Order in 1312 the Temple passed to the Crown and later into the possession of the Knights Hospitallers of St John, who leased it in the reign of Edward III (c. 1338) to certain professors of the common law. The first trustworthy mention of the Temple as an Inn of Court is found in 1449. The church (see below), and the crypt and buttery of the Inner Temple Hall are the only edifices going back to the Middle Ages, the other old buildings dating mainly from the reign of Elizabeth I or just after the Great Fire of 1666. Widespread destruction in 1940–41 has been repaired, and new buildings in traditional style have been erected by *Sir Edward Maufe, Sir Hubert Worthington,* and *T. W. Sutcliffe.* Buildings belonging to the Inner Temple bear the device of the Winged Horse, those of the Middle Temple the Lamb and Flag.

Among famous members of the Inner Temple may be mentioned Grenville, Hampden, Jeffreys, Lyndhurst, Thurlow, and Hallam: of the Middle Temple, Clarendon, Raleigh, Pym, Congreve, Wycherley, Sheridan, Blackstone, Fielding,

Thos. Moore, De Quincey, Burke, Dickens, Blackmore, Eldon, Havelock, and Birkett.

The *Temple Church, or *Church of St Mary the Virgin*, belonging to the Middle and Inner Temple in common, is the most important of the five remaining round churches in England. It is a 'peculiar', i.e. exempt from episcopal jurisdiction. The round part of the church was consecrated in 1185, and is in the transition-Norman style, with handsome ornamentation. The Norman w. doorway survives. The chancel ('oblong'), an admirable example of Early English, was added in 1240. The whole building was very seriously damaged by enemy action in 1941, but the final touches of restoration were completed in 1961.

The chancel, entered by a new s. porch, is borne by clustered piers of Purbeck marble, from the same quarry as the originals. The reredos, designed by Wren in 1682, was removed at a restoration in 1840, and so escaped damage. The stained glass of the beautiful E. windows, given by the Glaziers' Company, the Middle Temple (N.), and the Inner Temple (S.), is by Carl Edwards. On the s. is a noble effigy of a 13C ecclesiastic, and near the s. door (beneath a glass slab) is the gravestone of John Selden (1584–1654), the jurist. In the round church are nine *Monuments of Associates of the Temple* of the 12–13C, with recumbent marble figures (damaged) in full armour. The two arresting coloured *Monuments* are to Richard Martin (1618; s. side) and Edmund Plowden (1585; N. side).

The lawyers used to await their clients in 'the Round', just as the serjeants-at-law did in St Paul's Cathedral. The *Master's House*, the home of the incumbent of the Temple Church, N.E. of the church, was re-erected after the Great Fire and totally destroyed in 1941 but has been rebuilt in its 17C form.—In the churchyard, N. of the choir, is a slab (now covered) marking the whereabouts of the grave of Oliver Goldsmith (1728–74).

To the s. of the church is a cloister built, by Maufe, in accordance with Wren's original design. Beyond is the **Inner Temple Hall** and *Library*, by Worthington (1952–56) replacing the 19C range destroyed in 1941. The refaced buttery at the w. end and the crypt below it date from the 14C. To the E. is *King's Bench Walk*, with two houses ascribed to Wren (Nos. 4 and 5). Towards the river lie the *Inner Temple Gardens* (no adm.); and on the other side of Middle Temple Lane are the *Middle Temple Gardens* (no adm.). In one of these, according to a well-known scene in 'Henry VI' (Pt. I, ii, 4), were plucked the white and red roses, assumed as badges in the Wars of the Roses.

On the w. side of Middle Temple Lane is *Middle Temple Hall (open daily 10–12 & 3–4.30; closed Sun), a stately Elizabethan chamber of 1562–73 (100 ft long, 42 ft wide, 47 ft high), the interior of which, heavily damaged in 1941–44, is now rebuilt and restored (inscription on the E. gable). Shakespeare is said to have taken part in a performance of 'Twelfth Night' in this hall on 2 Feb 1601–02.—The *Middle Temple Library*, which lost some 65,000 volumes, is housed in Middle Temple Lane, below the hall.

At No. 2 Brick Court, Middle Temple Lane (destroyed), Oliver Goldsmith died. Blackstone, the celebrated jurist, occupied the rooms below Goldsmith, and complained of the noise made by his 'revelling neighbour'. Thackeray (1853–59) and Praed also had chambers in this building. Crown Office Row, where Charles Lamb was born (1775) and spent his first seven years (at No. 2), has been rebuilt. Later he lived with his sister within the Temple from 1801 to 1817, first at 16 Mitre Court Buildings and (after 1808) at 4 Inner Temple Lane (both houses pulled down). Dr Johnson occupied rooms at 1 Inner Temple Lane, replaced by Johnson's Buildings. Thackeray had rooms at 10 Crown Office Row from 1848–50. Fountain Court, to the N. of Middle Temple Hall is indissolubly associated with Ruth Pinch's tryst with her brother Tom ('Martin Chuzzlewit'). The fountain, dating from 1681, was restored in 1919 to its original condition.

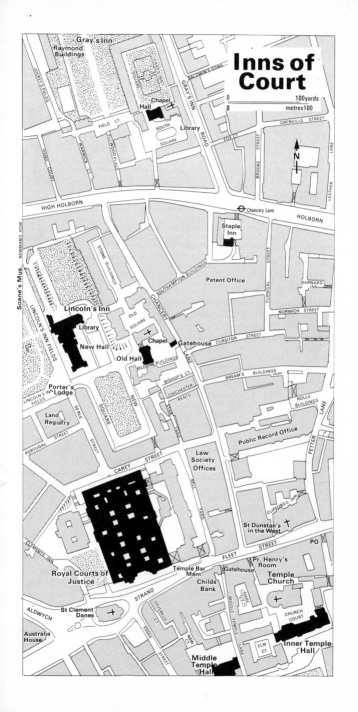

19 FLEET STREET TO ST PAUL'S

BUSES: Nos. 4, 6, 9, 11, 15, 502 and 513 run along Fleet St., up Ludgate Hill to St Paul's.

Where the Strand ends (comp. p. 195) and Fleet Street and the City begin stands the feeble *Temple Bar Memorial*. It was erected in 1880 on the site of old Temple Bar, and has statues of Queen Victoria and Edward VII (as Prince of Wales) by Boehm. The bronze 'griffin' is by C. B. Birch.

Temple Bar was erected by Wren in 1672, after the Great Fire, but its wooden predecessor is known to have stood here in 1502, and some kind of a bar or chain, on the boundary between Westminster and the City proper, seems to have existed as far back as the 12C. From the top of the gate projected a number of iron spikes, on which were exhibited the heads of felons and traitors (e.g. those of the rebels of 1745). The gate was removed to Plumstead Marshes in 1878, and ten years later was re-erected by Sir Henry Meux as an entrance to Theobalds Park, near Waltham Cross. Plans are periodically mooted to rescue it from its rural decay. When the sovereign of England visits the City on state occasions, the ancient custom of obtaining permission from the Lord Mayor 'to pass Temple Bar' is still observed.

The *Wig and Pen Club* (members only), just w. of Temple Bar (230 Strand), occupies a quaint building of 1625; it provides at an appropriate locality a meeting-place for journalists and jurists.

Fleet Street (Pl. 7; 8), the busy continuation of the Strand, leads from Temple Bar to Ludgate Circus. 'The Street' is still the centre of newspaper production despite recent moves to Grays Inn Rd., and vast newsprint lorries congest the area. The name is derived from the *Fleet River* or *Fleet Ditch* (now a sewer), which rises amid the heights of Hampstead, flows through the Holborn Valley, and joins the Thames near Blackfriars Bridge.

Newspapers, even if published in Fleet St. itself, are generally printed in the streets, squares, and courts on either side. The neighbourhood is especially animated between 9 p.m. and midnight, when the daily journals go to press with their first editions, which are carried to the great railway termini to catch the 'newspaper trains'. 'Late London editions' continue to be printed until 3 a.m., when the whirr of machinery subsides. Soon after this, however, the early editions of the evening papers call for a revival of activity, which continues until 6 p.m. or later.

Immediately below the Temple Bar Memorial, on the right, No. 1 Fleet St. is *Child's Bank*, one of the oldest in London (founded 1671), now amalgamated with Williams and Glyn's Bank. On its books occur the names of many royal personages, of Oliver Cromwell, Marlborough, Nell Gwynn, Prince Rupert, Pepys, and Dryden. At the *Devil Tavern*, on this site, Ben Jonson reigned supreme in the 'Apollo Club'.

Middle Temple Lane, beyond Child's Bank on the same side, leads through Wren's gateway to the *Temple* (Rte 18), and just beyond is another passage (Inner Temple Lane) leading to the Temple Church. No. 17 Fleet Street, above this latter archway, is an interesting specimen of a timbered house of 1610, with a projecting upper story. On the first floor is *Prince Henry's Room* (open weekdays, 1.45–5, Sat to 4.30), with a decorated ceiling, referring to Prince Henry, elder son of James I. The *Cock Tavern*, at No. 22, preserves some internal fittings and other interesting relics of the old tavern, which stood till 1887 on the other side of the way, and is well known from Tennyson's reference to the "plump head-waiter at the Cock". The original sign carved by Grinling Gibbons is preserved in the bar on the first floor.

On the N. side of Fleet St., beyond a branch of the Bank of England, *Chancery Lane* (comp. p. 202) runs N. to Holborn. Beyond, *Clifford's Inn*

Passage leads through the old gatehouse of the Inn of Chancery to a block of flats which has appropriated the name. The octagonal church of **St Dunstan in the West,** by John Shaw (1831–33) was well restored in 1950; it stands on the site of an earlier building. The fine tower ends in an open-work lantern. The figure of Queen Elizabeth I (1586) over the E. (vestry) porch, and the statues of King Lud and his sons within it, came from the Ludgate, which stood half-way up Ludgate Hill and was pulled down in 1760. The fine clock (1671) with 'striking Jacks', from the old church, was returned from St Dunstan's Lodge in Regent's Park in 1936.

On the s. front are a bust of Lord Northcliffe (1865–1922), and a tablet to J. L. Garvin (1868–1947), journalist and editor. Inside, the chapel on the left contains a quaint brass to Henry Dacres, 'merchant taylor and alderman of the City of London', and his wife (1530). The chapel to the left of the altar is now closed by an iconostasis from Autim monastery, Bucharest, dedicated in 1966 to mark the chapel's second use by the Roumanian orthodox congregation. A stained glass window in the chapel, and a tablet to the r. of the entrance porch, commemorate Izaak Walton, a vestryman of the parish. On the wall beneath are plaques to George Calvert, Lord Baltimore (1580?–1632), founder of Maryland, who was buried in the old church, and to Daniel Brown of Connecticut, the first Anglican clergyman to be ordained for America (1723). The communion rail was carved by Grinling Gibbons while John Donne was vicar here (1624–31).

Hoare's Bank, No. 37 Fleet St., on the s. side, founded in 1672 by Richard Hoare, a goldsmith and the son of a successful horse-dealer, moved to Fleet St. in 1690. It is the only remaining 'private' bank in London. *El Vino's* wine bar, haunt of generations of newspaper men, is still fussy about dress. FETTER LANE, diverging to the N. (l.) beyond St Dunstan's and leading to Holborn, derives its name either from the 'faitours' (i.e. beggars) with which it used to swarm, or from a colony of 'feutriers' (felt-makers). Swift assigned residence and property in Fetter Lane to Captain Lemuel Gulliver.

A little farther on a bend in Fleet St. reveals a celebrated view of St Paul's. On the N. side a series of small courts and alleys (dating from the late 17C and probably originating as gardens), all redolent of literary and historical associations, are now noisy with printing machines. *Crane Court* was the home of the Royal Society from 1710–80. In *Johnson's Court* Dr Johnson lived from 1765–76; in allusion to his residence here he jokingly called himself, when in Scotland, 'Johnson of that ilk'. From 1776 till his death in 1784 he lived in *Bolt Court* (both houses demolished). —*Wine Office Court* was another resort of Dr Johnson and the old 'Cheshire Cheese' restaurant (rebuilt in 1667; entr. 145 Fleet St.), in which he, Goldsmith, and Boswell are said to have foregathered (though Boswell makes no mention of it), is still extant. The authenticity of the chair here shown as Johnson's is not beyond cavil. Ladies are not admitted to the front bar.—Johnson's Court and Bolt Court both lead into *Gough Square*, containing **Dr Johnson's House** (No. 17), where he lived from 1749 to 1758, engaged in the production of 'The Rambler' and of his famous 'Dictionary'. His wife died here in 1752.

The house, built c. 1700 and restored in 1948, is open Mon–Sat (10.30–4.30 or 5, visitors ring; fee). Among relics of Dr Johnson are an early edition of the 'Dictionary' and autograph letters. The portraits include Dr Johnson by J. Opie, and James Boswell by Joshua Reynolds. The most notable room is the large attic in which Johnson and his six amanuenses worked at the 'Dictionary'.

On the s. side of Fleet St., behind No. 49, a pleasant brick quadrangle (1956) is entered by the old iron gates of *Serjeants' Inn.* Here an archway through Mitre Court Buildings admits to the Inner Temple (comp. p. 203). Beyond *Bouverie Street*, invariably blocked by newsprint lorries, *Whitefriars Street* perpetuates the name of the Carmelite monastery founded about 1241 and dissolved in 1538. A crypt may still be seen (usually on request) at No. 30 Bouverie Street.

The fact that the privilege of sanctuary attached to the precincts of the monastery was not abolished till 1697 apparently explains the appropriation of this quarter, under the name of *Alsatia*, by debtors, criminals, and lawless characters of all kinds (comp. 'The Fortunes of Nigel'; name apparently taken from the province forming a debatable ground between France and Germany). Alsatia is now predominantly a journalistic region containing the offices of 'Punch' and many other well-known papers. At the corner of Whitefriars St. tablets mark the site of the home of Tompion and Graham, the clockmakers, and of the offices of the anti-Corn Law League, managed by Cobden and Bright. Hanging Sword Alley, a sordid crack opening off Whitefriars St., was the home of the rascally Jerry Cruncher of 'Tellson's Bank'.

On the N. side of Fleet St. are the massive office of the 'Daily Telegraph' and the glass house of the 'Daily Express' (1931); and opposite is the former 'News Chronicle' office, with a bust of T. P. O'Connor (1848–1929), journalist and parliamentarian. No. 85 (s. side) is the headquarters of Reuter's and the Press Association. Just behind the s. side of Fleet St. is the church of **St Bride**, rebuilt by Wren in 1671–75, and seriously damaged in 1940. The *Spire (1703), called by Henley "a madrigal in stone", was originally 234 ft high, but was struck by lightning in 1764 and rebuilt 8 ft shorter. It is still, however, the tallest of Wren's steeples and has survived the damage to the rest of the church. Restoration, by Godfrey Allen, was carried out in 1953–57, with woodwork (stalls and reredos) in the style of Wren and Grinling Gibbons, by Alfred Banks. The reredos is a memorial to Edward Winslow, the Pilgrim Father, a parishioner. At the w. end are statues of St Bride and St Paul, by D. MacFall, while the E. end has been painted by Glyn Jones, in a trompe-l'œil manner, to create the effect of an apsidal ending.

The old church was the burial-place of Weelkes (1623), the madrigalist, and of Lovelace (1658), the Cavalier poet. The parish registers include entries of the baptism of Samuel Pepys (1633; born in Salisbury Court, overlooking the churchyard, where his father was a tailor). The UNDERCROFT of the much-rebuilt medieval church which Wren incorporated into his own church is open to the public. Excavations have revealed a Roman ditch (15–16 ft wide) and the pavement of a Roman building, the first recorded outside the wall of London. Evidence of a Late Saxon cemetery was found, and remains of earlier churches on the site (the first built in the mid-11C). The coffin of Samuel Richardson (d. 1761), author of 'Clarissa Harlowe', who carried on his business as printer in the adjacent Salisbury Square, is preserved here. A small exhibition illustrates the development of printing in Fleet St.

Bride Lane, passing St Bride's Church, contains (r.) the *St Bride Foundation Institute* (1894), an educational club for printers and others. Fleet St. ends at *Ludgate Circus*, formed by its junction with Farringdon St., Ludgate Hill, and New Bridge St. On the N.W. side is a tablet with a relief portrait of Edgar Wallace (1875–1932), novelist and journalist.

FARRINGDON STREET, a wide thoroughfare, leads N. (l.) from Ludgate Circus to Charterhouse St. On the right, beyond Seacoal Lane, is the site of the historic Fleet Prison, which stood on the E. side of the Fleet River, and was used for persons committed by the Star Chamber and for debtors. The prison was twice rebuilt, after its destruction in the Great Fire (1666) and in the Gordon Riots (1780), and it was finally pulled down in 1844–46. This was the prison in which Mr Pickwick was confined. The so-called 'Fleet Marriages' arose out of the fact that clergymen imprisoned for debt in the Fleet were not deterred from celebrating clandestine marriages by the financial penalties they nominally incurred. Such marriages were legal down to 1753.

Beyond Ludgate Circus **Ludgate Hill,** (Pl. 8; 5), rises towards St Paul's Cathedral. To the N. diverges the *Old Bailey*, which leads to Newgate St. and the Central Criminal Court (see Rte 21). Farther up Ludgate Hill, to the left, is the church of ST MARTIN LUDGATE, the slender spire of which shows up well against the dome of St Paul's. This church was rebuilt by Wren in 1677–87 and has fine oaken *Woodwork, and a Father Smith organ. Captain (later Adm. Sir) William Penn, father of the founder of Pennsylvania, was married in the former church in 1643. The old church stood just within the Roman wall close to Lud Gate, the first curfew gate in London to be closed at night (comp. p. 225).

At No. 3 Ludgate Hill lived William Rich (1755–1811) a pastry cook who modelled his wedding cakes on the steeple of St Bride seen from his window, starting a fashion still followed. *Ave Maria Lane* diverges left just before St Paul's. Here is the STATIONERS' HALL, the guildhouse of the Stationers' Company, the members of which (unlike those of most City Guilds) have some actual connection with their nominal trade.

The Hall (adm. see p. 199) was built soon after the first Great Fire of London in 1666, but was stone-faced in 1800, and a wing was added in 1887. It was severely damaged by enemy action in 1940, but the hall has now been restored. It contains a fine screen and panelling of the late 17C, the work of Stephen Colledge.

The Stationers' Company, founded c. 1402, was incorporated by royal charter in 1557, and for a time it preserved the sole right of printing in England (apart from the presses at Oxford and Cambridge), while it had a monopoly of the publishing of almanacks down to 1771. Until the passing of the Copyright Act of 1911 every work published in Great Britain had to be registered for copyright at Stationers' Hall. In 1933 the company was amalgamated with that of the Newspaper Makers. A plane tree in the court behind the Hall marks the spot where seditious books used to be burnt.

Among the buildings spared by the war in this area is *Amen Court*, a curiously quiet little nook in the heart of London, entered from Ave Maria Lane. It contains the dwellings of the Canons Residentiary of St Paul's, which Wren is supposed to have built.

Beyond the projecting Juxon House (1964) at the top of Ludgate Hill we reach the w. façade of St Paul's. In front stands a poor statue of *Queen Anne*, in whose reign the cathedral was finished; the present statue is a replica of the original by Francis Bird (1712).

20 ST PAUL'S CATHEDRAL

STATIONS: *St Paul's*, on the Central line; *Mansion House* and *Blackfriars*, on the Circle line.—BUSES plying along the Strand and Fleet St. (Nos. 6, 9, 11, 15) run past the Cathedral; others viâ Oxford St. and Holborn to the City (Nos. 8, 25) pass close by on the N. From the s. side of the river Nos. 17, 45, 63, 76, cross Blackfriars Bridge, a few minutes' walk s.w. of St Paul's.—CAR PARK in Ave Maria Lane.

ADMISSION. St Paul's is open daily from 8 to 6 or 7, and visitors may freely inspect the nave and choir except on Sun and during services. The *Crypt* (entered from the South Transept) is open daily 10.45–3.30, exc. Sun (15p.). The *Library*, *Galleries*, and *Dome* (entered from the E. end of the s. aisle) are open daily 10.45–3.30 (also 4.45–5.30 or 6.30, May–Sept), exc. on Sun and during big services. The Library closes at 3, and is also closed on Mon. Inclusive ticket 20p.

SERVICES on weekdays at 8 and 10 a.m., 12.30 (Wed and Fri) and 4 p.m.; on Sun at 8, 10.30, 11.30, 3.15, and 6.30. Mattins and Evensong daily and the services at 12.30 on Wed and Fri, and at 11.30 on Sun are choral.—'Son et Lumière' performances June–Oct (exc. Sun & Mon).

*St Paul's Cathedral (Pl. 8; 6), the largest and most famous church in the City, stands at the top of Ludgate Hill. The cathedral of the Bishop of London, it is the masterpiece of Sir Christopher Wren, a dignified edifice in a Renaissance style, dominated by the famous dome. The Portland stone of which it is built was picturesquely bleached and stained by the London climate and London smoke, until cleaning in the 1960s disclosed its golden colour and the beautiful detail of the carved stone work. An urgent programme of repairwork to the fabric of the cathedral was begun in 1972; the foundations are to be strengthened and the nave roof repaired.

HISTORY. The tradition that a Roman temple dedicated to Diana stood on the commanding site now occupied by St Paul's was repudiated by Wren, and is supported by no evidence. A Christian church, said to have been founded here in the 7C by Bp. Mellitus and endowed by Ethelbert, King of Kent, was burned down in 1087 and its Norman successor was partly destroyed by fire in 1136 but immediately restored. In the 13C the steeple was rebuilt and the choir extended eastwards. This was the noble church of *Old St Paul's*, in which John Wyclif was tried for heresy in 1377, and Tyndale's New Testament publicly burned in 1527. It was the longest cathedral in England (600 ft). The central tower was surmounted by a steeple, which, at the lowest estimate, was 460 ft high, but was destroyed by lightning in 1561 and never re-erected. For a long period the church was sadly neglected, but restorations were begun under Charles I. Inigo Jones added a classical portico to the w. front, one of his objects being to divert from the church the secular rabble that for over a century had used the middle aisle of the nave ('Paul's Walk') as a place of business and intrigue. In 1666 the cathedral was practically burned down in the Great Fire. Sir Christopher Wren planned an entirely new cathedral; building was begun in 1675; the first service was held in the choir in 1697; and the last stone was placed in position in 1710. (A model of Old St Paul's is in the crypt and Wren's models in the triforium.) Between 1666 and 1723 the amount spent on the cathedral was about £748,000, most of which was raised by a tax on sea-borne coal entering London. Wren's original ground plan, designed in the form of a Greek cross, was modified at the demand of the Court party, some of whom may have looked forward to the restoration of the old religion, for the ceremonies of which a long nave and side-chapels were required. In 1941 the E. end and the N. transept received direct hits from high-explosive bombs; another, which did not explode, was dug out, with great heroism, from beneath the E. end; and the building, throughout the war, was guarded from fire by the coolness and efficiency of its Night Watch.

MEASUREMENTS. The exterior length of the cathedral is 515 ft; its w. front, with two towers each 212½ ft high, is 180 ft wide. Internally it is 479 ft long and 227½ ft wide across the transepts. The nave, 125 ft across (including the aisles), is 92½ ft high. The dome is 122 ft in diameter, and the total height from the pavement of the church to the top of the cross above the ball is 365 ft. The area of St Paul's is 87,400 sq. ft; that of St Peter's in Rome 163,181 sq. ft.

The **Exterior** of St Paul's consists throughout of two orders, the lower Corinthian, the upper Composite. On the N. and S. sides the upper order is merely a curtain-wall, not corresponding with the height of the aisles and concealing the flying buttresses that support the clerestory of the nave. The balustrade along the top was added against the wishes of Wren, who cynically remarked of it that "ladies think nothing well without an edging". The *West Front*, approached by a broad flight of steps, and flanked by towers, has a lower colonnade of twelve columns and an upper one of eight columns. In the N.W. tower is a peal of bells, and in the S.W. tower are the clock and 'Great Paul', a bell weighing nearly 17 tons (hung in 1882), which is rung daily for 5 minutes at 1 p.m. In the pediment of the *South Front* is a Phœnix, typifying the rise of new St Paul's from the ashes of the old, and recalling also the incident when Wren sought a stone from the ruins to mark the centre of the new dome-space a fragment of an old tombstone was brought to him bearing the word 'Resurgam' ('I shall rise again'). The sculpture in the West Pediment and Portico and the statutes above the North Pediment are by Francis Bird.—The famous **Dome* lifts its Cross 365 ft above the City below. The outer dome is of wood covered with lead, and does not bear the weight of the elegant lantern on the top, which rests upon a cone of brick rising between an inner brick dome and the outer dome. The Ball and Cross date from 1721.

The **Interior**, though 'classical' in detail, has the general ground plan of a Gothic church: nave and aisles with triforium and clerestory, transepts, and choir, with, however, the great dome-space at the crossing. Against the massive piers rise Corinthian pilasters, and stone enrichments relieve the wall-spaces. Wren no doubt contemplated the use of colour in the decoration, but, though Thornhill's paintings in the dome were finished in 1720, nothing more was done until the dome and choir mosaics were added in 1863–97.

The visitor on entering St Paul's should first walk up the centre of the NAVE to the great space beneath the dome, where the huge proportions of the church are especially impressive. The candelabra at the w. end are by Henry Pegram. On the last piers are paintings by G. F. Watts; 'Time, Death, and Judgment' on the N., 'Peace and Goodwill' on the S.

The DOME, the inner cupola of which is 218 ft above our heads, rests upon twelve massive supports, of which the four chief ones, at the angles, afford room in their interiors for the vestries and the library staircase. In the spandrels of the dome are mosaics executed by Salviati of Venice. Those on the w., designed by Alfred Stevens and partly executed by W. E. F. Britten, represent (from s. to N.) Isaiah, Jeremiah, Ezekiel, and Daniel; the others represent SS. Matthew and John (by G. F. Watts) and SS. Mark and Luke (by Britten). In the quarter-domes, at a lower level, are more recent mosaics by Sir W. B. Richmond (d. 1921).—Above the arches is the Whispering Gallery, above which again are recesses with marble statues of the Fathers of the Church. The cupola, above, was decorated by Sir James Thornhill with eight scenes in monochrome from the life of St Paul.

We now begin to inspect the monuments in the church, eloquent of the nation's history, returning to the w. end by the NORTH NAVE AISLE. In the first recess, Two Angels at the Gate of Death (by Marochetti), in memory of *Viscount Melbourne* (1779–1848) and his brother. On the wall, *Lord Roberts* (1833–1914), bust, by Tweed. In the next recess, *General Gordon* (1833–85); in the last recess, *Lord Leighton* (1830–96), the painter. Beneath the arch opposite Gordon's monument is a dignified *Monument to the *Duke of Wellington* (1769–1852), by Alfred Stevens. Above the pediments at either end are groups representing Truth plucking out the tongue of Falsehood, and Valour thrusting down Cowardice. The equestrian statue on the top was executed by Tweed in 1912 from a sketch-model by Stevens.—At the w. end of this aisle beyond *St Dunstan's Chapel* is *All Souls' Chapel* now the *Kitchener Memorial Chapel*, with a recumbent figure of Field-Marshal Lord Kitchener (1850–1916) by Reid Dick, and a roll of honour of the Royal Engineers.

SOUTH NAVE AISLE. The chapel at the w. end has been since 1906 the *Chapel of the Most Distinguished Order of St Michael and St George*, with the banners of the Knights Grand Cross (G.C.M.G.). The order (instituted in 1818) is conferred for distinguished services in colonial or foreign affairs. The prelate's throne is a memorial of Lord Forrest (d. 1918) of Bunbury, Western Australia, the first Australian peer. On the fourth pier in the s. aisle hangs 'The Light of the World', a painting by

Holman Hunt. At the E. end of the aisle is the ticket-office for the upper part of the church.

SOUTH TRANSEPT. In the W. aisle are monuments to *Sir Ralph Aber-cromby* (1734–1801) and to *Sir John Moore* (1761–1809), who died at Corunna. To the left, above, is a memorial by Princess Louise, to the *Colonial Troops* who fell in the South African War. On the W. wall of the transept, *Monument of *Lord Nelson* (1758–1805), by Flaxman; the reliefs on the pedestal represent the Arctic Ocean, the North Sea, the Nile, and the Mediterranean. On the S. wall of the E. transept aisle, *J. M. W. Turner* (1775–1851), the painter, and *Lord Collingwood* (1750–1810), Nelson's successor. On the E. wall, *Lord Howe* (1726–99), by Flaxman. On the left, farther on, *Sir Henry Lawrence* (1806–57). Opposite is the entrance to the Crypt, beyond which, at the angle of the dome-space, is a statue of *John Howard* (1726–90), the prison reformer, the first monument admitted to new St Paul's.

We now enter the CHOIR, at the end of the S. choir aisle, with fine iron gates by Jean Tijou. On the right side of this aisle, beyond the monument of *Dean Milman* (1791–1868), is the figure (clad in a shroud) of *Dr John Donne* (1573–1631), poet and Dean of St Paul's. This is the only comparatively uninjured monument that survived the destruction of Old St Paul's, and it still shows traces of fire.—We now enter the choir proper. Above the High Altar is a carved and gilded baldacchino of marble and oak, by Godfrey Allen and S. E. Dykes Bower, replacing the reredos damaged in 1941 and serving as a memorial to the Common-wealth people of all creeds and races who lost their lives in the two World Wars. The tall bronze *Candlesticks* in front are copied from four now in St Bavon's, in Ghent, which were made by Benedetto da Rovezzano for the tomb of Henry VIII at Windsor, but were sold under the Common-wealth.—The beautiful carved *Choir Stalls* and the *Organ Case* are by Grinling Gibbons. The organ was originally built in 1695 by Father Smith to John Blow's direction, and Jeremiah Clarke played for its inauguration. Although a bomb struck the east end of the choir, bringing down tons of masonry on to the Sanctuary, the priceless carvings escaped almost undamaged.—The *Jesus Chapel*, which occupies the apse of the cathedral, is the memorial to America's fallen in the Second World War, with a roll of honour containing 28,000 names of those who fell in operations based on Britain.

The *Mosaics* with which the vaulting of the choir is decorated were designed by Sir W. B. Richmond and were executed in 1891–1912. The stained glass windows are by the same artist.

In the central panel of the great apse is Christ in majesty, seated upon the rain-bow. In the shallow cupolas above the choir proper are (from W. to E.) the Creation of the Beasts, of the Birds, and of the Fishes.

In the N. choir aisle is the Altar of the Modern Martyrs. We leave it through another set of gates by Tijou and see, on our right, a statue of *Dr Johnson* (1709–84) in a Roman toga, by Bacon. The choir-screen, formed of the original altar rails, is also by Tijou. On the right is a carved wooden pulpit (1964), designed by Lord Mottistone.

NORTH TRANSEPT. This transept was severely damaged by a heavy bomb in April 1941, when the transept dome and the whole of the North Porch, with the famous inscription from Wren's tomb: "Si monumen-

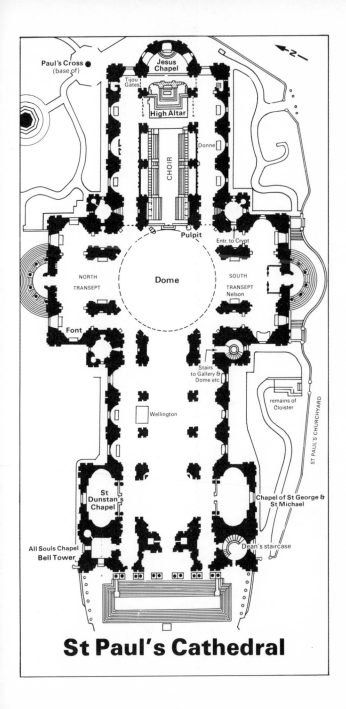

St Paul's Cathedral

tum requiris, circumspice" ("If you would see his monument, look around you"),. fell into the crypt below. Here are commemorated *Sir Arthur Sullivan* (1842–1900), the composer, *Lord Rodney* (1718–92), and *Sir Joshua Reynolds* (1723–92), the last by Flaxman. The w. aisle of this transept is now the *Baptistery*.

The *Crypt (entrance in the s. transept) corresponds in size with the upper church. Here are the graves of many of those whose monuments we have already seen, as well as many additional monuments and graves.

We first reach the crypt below the s. choir-aisle. At the foot of the staircase is (r.) a bust of *Sir John Macdonald* (1815–91), premier of Canada. In the second bay (r.) monuments to *Sir Edwin Landseer* (1802–73) and *Reginald Heber* (1783–1826), by Chantrey. In the pavement is the tomb of *Sir Lawrence Alma-Tadema* (1836–1912). In the next bay is the tombstone of *Sir Christopher Wren* (1632–1723), above which is the original tablet with its famous epitaph (see above). This bay, and the one to the N., are known as 'Painters' Corner', for here rest *Lord Leighton* (1830–96), *Benjamin West* (1738–1820), *Sir Thomas Lawrence* (1769–1830), *Landseer* (1802–73), *Millais* (1829–96), *Turner* (1775–1851), *Reynolds* (1723–92), *Opie* (1761–1807), and *Holman Hunt* (1827–1910), while on the walls are memorials to *Randolph Caldecott* (1846–86), *William Blake* (1757–1827), *Van Dyck* (1599–1641), *Constable* (1776–1837), *Wilson Steer* (1860–1942), *Lutyens* (1869–1944), and *Muirhead Bone* (1876–1953). *J. S. Sargent* (1856–1925), buried elsewhere, is commemorated by a relief-group of the Redemption, designed by himself.— The Chapel at the E. end of the crypt, formerly called *St Faith's*, was dedicated in 1960 as the Chapel of the Order of the British Empire. Farther w. a wall-tablet marks the grave of *Sir Alexander Fleming* (1881–1955), discoverer of penicillin.

We pass through the gates to the w. portion of the crypt, and find ourselves in front of the colossal porphyry sarcophagus of the *Duke of Wellington* (see p. 215). On the left, farther on, is a memorial to *Florence Nightingale* (1820–1910). Below the centre of the dome *Lord Nelson* rests in a coffin made from the mainmast of the French ship 'L'Orient', enclosed in a sarcophagus of black and white marble originally designed for Cardinal Wolsey. In recesses to the s., *Lord Beatty* (1871–1936), *Lord Jellicoe* (1859–1935), *Lord Keyes* (1872–1945) and his son, *Lt.-Col. Keyes*, *V.C.* (1917–41), and *Lord Napier of Magdala* (1810–90). To the N., *Lord Wolseley* (1833–1913), *Lord Roberts* (1832–1914), and a bust of *Lawrence of Arabia* (1888–1935). A plaque commemorates 5746 men of the garrison of Kut (Iraq) who died in 1916. In the adjoining recess: *R. J. Seddon* (1845–1906) and *W. M. Hughes* (1864–1952), prime ministers of New Zealand; *Sir Stafford Cripps* (1889–1952; fine bust by Epstein). Opposite: bust of *George Washington* near a tablet to P/O William Fiske, R.A.F., who lost his life in the Battle of Britain, "an American citizen who died that England might live". Here too are memorials to *George Cruikshank* (1792–1878), the caricaturist and *W. E. Henley* (1849–1903; *Bust by Rodin), the poet and critic. In the nave: *Wilson Carlile* (1847–1942), founder of the Church Army; *R. H. Barham* (1788–1845), of the 'Ingoldsby Legends'; *Sir W. Besant* (1836–1901) and *Charles Reade* (1814–84), the novelists; and *Sir Alfred Duff Cooper* (1890–1954), the statesman.

Farther w. (1st bay N. side) are memorials to the brothers *Sir Charles* (1782–1853) and *Sir William Napier* (1784–1860). By contrast, the next bay contains five mutilated monuments from Old St Paul's. Next a monument to the historian *Henry Hallam* (1777–1859); opposite is one to *Lord St Vincent* (1735–1823).

At the extreme w. end of the crypt is the *Funeral Car* of the Duke of Wellington, made from cannon captured by him and inscribed with the names of his victories.

The **Upper Parts** of the cathedral are reached by a staircase from the s. aisle (adm. see p. 209). An easy ascent of 143 steps leads to the *South Triforium Gallery*, in which are plans and sketches illustrating the history of the site. At the end is the *Library*, in which the floor and the carved woodwork should be noticed. It contains a good collection of MSS., books, and relics. Farther on, we cross the *West Gallery* (*View of the interior), and reach the *Trophy Room*, off the North Triforium, with models and drawings by Wren, including the 'Great Model' (1674), and paintings, drawings, and relics recording the history of the cathedral.

Returning to the staircase, we continue the ascent to the WHISPERING GALLERY, 112 ft in diameter, within the lower dome, where words whispered near the wall on one side can be distinctly heard at the other side. This gallery is the best point from which to see Thornhill's paintings on the dome.—The STONE GALLERY, the exterior gallery round the base of the dome, commands a fine *View of London, which is still more extensive from the *Golden Gallery*, at the base of the lantern above the dome. An ascent (quite safe) leads thence to the *Ball* on the top of the lantern, which, however, has no view. The total ascent to the Ball involves 727 steps.

The churchyard (now a public garden) surrounding the cathedral is enclosed by massive railings, usually regarded as among the latest examples of charcoal-smelted iron work from the Weald. In the N.E. angle are the foundations of *Paul's Cross*, an open-air pulpit where sermons were regularly preached. On the s. side of the church are a few fragments of the cloisters and chapter house, destroyed in 1666.

The street skirting the s. side of the cathedral is likewise called *St Paul's Churchyard*. In Dean's Court, leading s., is the *Deanery*, built by Wren c. 1670, and adjoining it, in Carter Lane, is the Choir House, with the old Choristers' School (see below; now a Youth Hostel). A tablet in Carter Lane, a few paces to the E., records Shakespeare's connection with the Bell Tavern which stood here. Farther E., beyond the *City Information Centre*, extends *Old Change Court*, now flanked by modern offices. The stepped *St Peter's Hill* reveals a view of the Thames across Queen Victoria St.

Across Cannon St. the pleasant *St Paul's Garden* is adorned with a fountain, and a statue by Georg Ehrlich. To the N. the tower (and restored spire) of *St Augustine's* has been incorporated in the new *Cathedral Choir School*, designed in 1962 by Leo de Syllas and built after his death, with four linked buildings. The church was rebuilt by Wren in 1683 and destroyed in 1941.

The area to the N. of the cathedral was devastated by fire in 1940; only the *Chapter House* by Wren (reopened in 1957) survived. New buildings with clean lines, effectively grouped but lacking individual distinction, now tower above the chapter house to form *Cathedral Place* and *Paternoster Square*. The raised piazzas (underground car park) with shops, restaurants, and pubs, afford good views of St Paul's. The ecclesiastical character of the district survives only in some street and place-names. Panyer Alley, so named from having formerly been largely occupied by basket-makers, has been replaced by *Panyer Alley Steps* which lead down to Newgate St. (N.; comp. p. 218). The old relief (1688) of a boy seated on a 'panier', marking the highest ground in the City, has been placed on the steps.

21 ALONG HOLBORN AND CHEAPSIDE TO THE BANK OF ENGLAND

STATIONS: *Chancery Lane*, *St Paul's* and *Bank* on Central line (Bank also on Northern line).—BUSES: Nos. 8, 22, 25, & 501 follow the route.

Holborn (Pl. 8; 5), beginning at the s. end of Gray's Inn Road, continues the line of Oxford St. and High Holborn to the City. The w. limits of the City (Holborn Bars) are indicated by stone obelisks near Chancery Lane Tube station and opposite Staple Inn. In the roadway stands the *War Memorial of the Royal Fusiliers* (City of London Regiment), by Albert Toft. Holborn derives its name from the fact that the Fleet River flowed through the valley here and was known as the 'Hole-Bourne', or stream in the hollow.

On the right, opposite Gray's Inn Road, is ***Staple Inn,** the picturesque gabled and timbered façade of which, dating from 1586 (last restored in 1950), is a unique survival of its kind in a London street. The inn, which seems to have been a hostel of the wool-staplers in the 14C, was an Inn of Chancery from the reign of Henry V until 1884. It consisted of two little quadrangles, with houses dating mainly from the 18C, but was severely damaged by a flying bomb in 1944, when the fine 16C hall was demolished. This has now been rebuilt (with much of the old material) and is occupied by the *Institute of Actuaries* (adm. on application at the porter's lodge, preferably in morning). Dr Johnson lived for a time in a house here in 1759–60, and here he is said to have written 'Rasselas' in the evenings of a single week, to pay for his mother's funeral. The second court now contains a pleasant garden.

In Brooke St., on the left, Thomas Chatterton (1752–70) poisoned himself at No. 39. Just beyond Brooke St. rises the *Prudential Assurance Co.*, a huge Gothic edifice of red brick (by A. Waterhouse 1879–1906, altered in 1932). It occupies the site of *Furnival's Inn*, in which Charles Dickens was lodging when he wrote the first part of the 'Pickwick Papers' (memorial tablet and bust in the court). A passage down its E. flank leads to Leather Lane market. On the other (s.) side of Holborn, near the corner of Fetter Lane, is the entrance to *Barnard's Inn.* The old *Hall (late 14C), the oldest surviving secular building in the City, has 16C panelling and good heraldic glass. It is sometimes shown on request at the main offices of the Prudential across Holborn.

In 1894–1959 the inn, mainly rebuilt, was occupied by the *Mercer's School.* The school, founded about 1450, had Dean Colet and Sir Thomas Gresham among its pupils. The device of the Mercers' Company still survives above the gateway.

Beyond Fetter Lane, where the corner bank's elegant cupola emphasizes the brash, obtrusive mass of the 'Daily Mirror' building (1958–61), Holborn reaches HOLBORN CIRCUS. In the middle is an equestrian statue of *Prince Albert*.

Hatton Garden, to the N.W., now occupied largely by diamond merchants, takes its name from the garden belonging to the house of Sir Christopher Hatton, Lord Chancellor to Queen Elizabeth. A tablet with a bas-relief portrait and a device of clasped hands commemorates the residence at No. 5 of Giuseppe Mazzini, who while living in this house inspired Young Italy to struggle for freedom.

At the beginning of Charterhouse St. (l.) opens *Ely Place* (1772), occupying the site of the town house of the bishops of Ely, where John of Gaunt died in 1399. The garden was famous, and is mentioned in 'Richard III' (iii, 4). When forced to cede these grounds to Sir Christopher Hatton (at the picturesque yearly 'rent' of a red rose, ten loads of háy, and ten pounds), the Bishop reserved in perpetuity the right to walk in the gardens and to gather yearly twenty bushels of roses. The Mitre Inn in Ely Court (the quaint passageway on the left) was built in the 18C on the site of a 16C tavern. The sign probably comes from the bishop's gatehouse. Ely Place is guarded at night by a watchman of its own, who used to call the hours from 10 p.m to 5 a.m.

The only relic of the bishop's house is the beautiful little *Ely Chapel (St Etheldreda's)*, a gem of 13C Gothic (1290), with an old chestnut roof. The tracery of the E. and W. windows, and the arcaded statue-niches are superb. The notable glass and statues of English martyrs are by Charles and May Blakeman (1952–64), who also adorned the vaulted *Crypt* (1252) which stands on Roman foundations. In the entrance is a fine carved escutcheon from the time of Charles I which, until 1874, hung over the communion table. St Etheldreda's was the first pre-Reformation church in the country to return to the Roman Catholics (purchased 1874). It is always open.

In Saffron Hill, parallel to the E., was Fagin's Thieves' Kitchen in 'Oliver Twist', while the name of Bleeding Heart Yard, off Greville St. (l.) is familiar to readers of 'Little Dorrit'. Some cobbled corners with gloomy warehouses preserve a Dickensian air.

To the right, just beyond Holborn Circus, is the church of *St Andrew*, built by Wren in 1684–87, ruined in 1940–41, and restored in 1960–61. The interior of the medieval tower, dating from 1446 and unaltered by Wren, survives. The church is closed at week-ends.

The tomb of Capt. Thomas Coram was designed by Lord Mottistone (1962); the organ was originally presented by Handel to the Foundling Hospital (p. 175). In this church William Hazlitt was married to Sarah Stoddart in 1808 (Mary Lamb being bridesmaid and Charles Lamb the best man). Benjamin Disraeli (at the age of 12) was here (in 1817) received into the Christian Church.—In Shoe Lane (r.) is *Fleet House* with a Telephone Museum (adm. Mon–Fri, 10–4.30).

Beyond St Andrew's is the *City Temple* (Congregational), opened in 1874, under Dr Joseph Parker, for a congregation founded in 1640. Burnt out in 1941, it was rebuilt (apart from the façade) by Seely and Paget in 1956–58. *Atlantic House* (1951), opposite, is the headquarters of *H.M. Stationery Office* and the *Central Office of Information.*—We have now reached HOLBORN VIADUCT, 1400 ft long and 80 ft wide, constructed at the cost of over 4000 dwellings in 1867–69, by William Haywood to carry the thoroughfare over the depression of the 'Hole-Bourne'. Beyond the bridge is *Holborn Viaduct Station*.

At the end of Holborn Viaduct, to the left, at the corner of Giltspur St. (leading to Smithfield) is the church of **St Sepulchre**, the history of which goes back to the days of the Crusaders (12C), though it was rebuilt in the 15C, altered within by Wren in 1670–77, over-restored in the 19C, and more carefully repaired in 1950. Down to 1890 the bells of St Sepulchre were tolled on the occasion of an execution at Newgate, and before 1774 it was the custom to present a nosegay here to each condemned criminal on his way to Tyburn.

INTERIOR (open Mon–Fri, 9–4). In the *Musicians' Chapel* in the N. aisle windows commemorate Sir Henry Wood (d. 1943) who, at the age of 12, deputised for the organist here, Dame Nellie Melba (d. 1931), and Dr John Ireland (d. 1962). The organ

(1670) is by Renatus Harris. A musical service is held on St Cecilia's Day (22 Nov; admission by ticket). In the same chapel an Easter sepulchre is thought to mark the tomb of Roger Ascham (1515–68), tutor to Queen Elizabeth I. Capt. John Smith (1580–1631), "sometime Governor of Virginia and Admiral of New England" is buried in the s. aisle. On a pillar near by is displayed a handbell which it was the duty of the bellman of St Sepulchre's to ring outside the condemned cell at Newgate at midnight preceding an execution, at the same time reciting the inscribed verses. The s. aisle and chapel and the garden serve as a memorial to the Royal Fusiliers.

Adjoining in Giltspur St. is the rebuilt Watch House (1791; 1962), with a bust (1935) of Charles Lamb moved from near the site of Christ's Hospital School in Newgate St. (see below), where Lamb was educated.

Opposite St Sepulchre's, at the corner of the *Old Bailey*, rises the curved façade of the **Central Criminal Court** (1905). This occupies the site of Newgate Prison, some of the stones of which have been used in the rustic work of the lowest story.

The *Central Criminal Court*, or *Old Bailey Court*, is the chief criminal court for Greater London, and parts of Surrey, Kent, and Essex. An extension (by McMorran and Whitby), with an impressive exterior in Old Bailey, was opened in 1970. This stood up well to a terrorist bomb in 1973. The public are admitted to trials; the 12 courts in the new building are entered from Old Bailey, and the 6 courts in the old building from Newgate St.

Tours of the building, which incorporates a large section of the medieval wall of London, and includes a Great Hall, are no longer given. Visitors may, however, see part of the wall in *Warwick Slip* which connects Old Bailey and Warwick Lane (parallel to the E.). Milton's writings justifying the execution of Charles I were burned by the common hangman in the Old Bailey in 1660.

NEWGATE PRISON, long the chief prison of London, was begun in 1770 and completed in 1782, after having been partly destroyed by the Gordon Rioters in 1780. It was finally demolished in 1902. Public executions, previously carried out at Tyburn, took place in front of Newgate from 1783 to 1868, and then within the prison down to 1901. Among the prisoners confined here were Anne Askew, Daniel Defoe, Jack Sheppard, Jonathan Wild, Titus Oates, William Penn, and Lord George Gordon (who died of gaol fever in 1793). Mrs Elizabeth Fry's successful efforts to improve the conditions of prison life in Newgate (1817) laid the foundation of prison reform throughout Europe.

Newgate Street (Pl. 8; 6) continues the general line of Holborn towards the heart of the City. To the right diverges Warwick Lane, in which stands *Cutlers' Hall*, with terracotta reliefs by Benj. Creswick (1887). Opposite Warwick Lane is the first block of the General Post Office, the buildings of which adjoin *Christ Church*, built by Wren in 1667–91 (steeple added in 1704) on part of the site of the great church of the Grey Friars. The church was burnt out during the 'blitz' of 1940–41 and remains a hollow shell. The steeple was re-erected in 1960 from the original stonework. Lawrence Sheriff (d. 1567), founder of Rugby School, was buried in Christ Church.

To the N. of the church formerly stood CHRIST'S HOSPITAL, the famous 'Blue Coat School', founded by Edward VI in 1552. In 1902, however, the school was removed to the country (near Horsham in Sussex), and its site is now occupied by buildings of the Post Office and St Bartholomew's Hospital.

A great part of the block bounded by Newgate St., Giltspur St., St Bartholomew's Hospital, and St Martin's-le-Grand is occupied by **The Post Office** (Pl. 8; 6). In King Edward St., on the left beyond Christ Church, is the KING EDWARD BUILDING, in which ordinary postal business is transacted with the public. Outside is a statue of Rowland Hill. The **National Postal Museum** (open Mon–Fri, 10–4.30, Sat till 4) was established in 1965 when Reginald M. Phillips donated to the nation his unique collection of artists' drawings, proofs, and stamps of the Queen Victoria issues of Great Britain. This collection and the comprehensive range of specimen stamps of the world, received by the Post Office through the Universal Postal Union since 1878, are displayed; temporary exhibitions of specialized material from the postal archives are mounted; and a reference library is available.

The *Post Office North*, opposite, contains the offices of Postal Headquarters including the library. Applications to visit the departments of the post office should be made in writing to the Public Relations Officer. Marconi made the first public transmission of wireless signals from the roof in 1896.

Until 1913 the General Post Office proper stood on the E. side of St Martin's-le-Grand, a street commemorating the church, college, and sanctuary of St Martin, dissolved in 1548. The name St Martin's-le-Grand is still often used as a synonym for the chief postal authorities, which, since 1969 has been rested in a corporate public body, under a Minister of Posts and Telecommunications.—The former burial-ground of Christchurch, Newgate St., has been laid out as Postman's Park.

On the S. side of Newgate St. are the new buildings in the precinct of St Paul's (see p. 215). Beyond St Martin's-le-Grand, Newgate St. is continued towards the E. by **Cheapside** (Pl. 8; 6), a short and busy thoroughfare formerly known as the *Chepe* (from O.E. 'ceap', a bargain). The names of the cross-streets probably indicate the position of the different classes of traders' booths at this early period. The 'prentices of Chepe were long notorious for their turbulence. The street is lined with new buildings, the most prominent of which is the curving neo-Georgian block of offices for the Bank of England, extending S. to Watling St.

In Foster Lane stands the church of St Vedast (p. 224), and in Gutter Lane, the next turning left from Cheapside, is the entrance to the new *Saddlers' Hall* (1958; adm. see p. 199). The Saddlers' Guild is thought to have its origin in Anglo-Saxon times. On the same side, at the corner of Wood St., a plane tree grows on the site of the church of St Peter; it is protected by special clauses in the leases of adjoining buildings.

In Cheapside (r.), near the corner of Bread St. stood the *Mermaid Tavern*, famous for the club founded by Ben Jonson in 1603 and frequented by Shakespeare, Raleigh, Donne, Beaumont, and Fletcher.— John Milton (1608–74) was born in *Bread Street*, to the right, and Sir Thomas More (1478–1535) in *Milk Street*, nearly opposite. Milton is commemorated by a tablet (with Dryden's famous lines) on the exterior w. wall of Bow Church.

*Bow Church, or *St Mary-le-Bow*, in Cheapside, was begun by Wren in 1670 and completed with the steeple in 1683, but was badly damaged by enemy action in May 1941. It succeeds the older church of 'St Marie de Arcubus', "the first in this city built on arches (bows) of stone". Saxon finds indicate that a church must have existed on this site before the crypt was built. The beautiful *Steeple, a very fine Renaissance campanile, is 222 ft high.

The restoration by Laurence King was completed in 1971. The exterior has been restored to its original design, but the interior has been redesigned to suit the needs of 20C worship. The beautiful E. windows are the work of John Hayward. The N.E. window represents the bombed city churches grouped round Mary who holds the church of St Mary-le-Bow in her arms. There are two pulpits, both used in the service. Seating is provided according to need. In the churchyard outside is a statue of Capt. John Smith, founder of Virginia, a copy of the statue in Jamestown.

The Norman *CRYPT, built about 1090, is the oldest ecclesiastical structure in the City. Also restored, it has an etched glass entrance screen by John Hayward. It contains the chapel of the Holy Spirit built in the part formerly used as a burying place, and is once again the meeting-place of the ecclesiastical *Court of Arches.*

In 1914 an ancient stone from the crypt of Bow Church was placed in Trinity Church, New York, in reference to the fact that William III granted to the vestry of that church, the same privileges as those of St Mary-le-Bow.

Anyone born within the sound of Bow Bells is a 'cockney', i.e. a Londoner pure and simple. The bells that (according to the old story) called back Dick Whittington to be three times Mayor of London perished in the Great Fire; their successors were destroyed in 1941; but new ones have been recast from those salved after enemy action.

A Roman public bath (c. A.D. 100) was found in 1955 on the other side of Cheapside.

Beyond Bow Church *King Street* and *Queen Street* diverge to the left and right, the former leading to the Guildhall, the latter to Southwark Bridge. At the corner of Ironmonger Lane, just beyond King St., stands MERCERS' HALL (adm. see p. 199), the guildhouse of the Mercers, one of the richest of the City companies and first in order of civic precedence. It has been rebuilt (1954–56) after its destruction.

In Ironmonger Lane is the tower of *St Olave's*, a relic of a Wren church demolished in 1888, now used as offices. The Roman mosaic pavement beneath No. 11 may usually be seen on request.

Old Jewry diverging to the left beyond Mercers' Hall, was the ghetto before the expulsion of the Jews in 1290. The *Headquarters of the City Police* are at No. 26. The continuation of Cheapside is known as the POULTRY, from its early occupation by the shops of poulterers. It is dominated by the Midland Bank headquarters by Lutyens. Mansion House St., its continuation, runs into the busy junction outside the **Bank of England** (Rte 24).

22 SMITHFIELD AND CLERKENWELL

STATIONS: *Farringdon* and *Barbican* on the Circle line; *St Paul's* on the Central line.—BUSES: Nos. 63, 221, 259 in Farringdon Road; No. 4 in Aldersgate Street; Nos. 19, 38, 171, 172 in Rosebery Avenue.—CAR PARK in Smithfield, and off Clerkenwell Green.

From St Sepulchre's Church, at the E. end of Holborn Viaduct, *Giltspur Street* runs N. to Smithfield, passing (r.) the loading yard of the G.P.O., below which is a well-preserved bastion of the Roman Wall (apply to the Post Master Controller). A small gilt figure of a naked boy on the corner-house of *Cock Lane*, on the left, marks *Pye Corner*, where the Great Fire of 1666, which started at Pudding Lane, near the Monument, is generally but erroneously said to have stopped.

Smithfield (Pl. 8; 3), more particularly known as West Smithfield to distinguish it from the less important East Smithfield near Tower Hill, is a place of great historic interest, though now noted mainly as the site of the principal London meat market. Originally a spacious 'smoothfield' or grassy expanse just outside the City Walls, it was the scene of various famous tournaments, and from 1150 to 1855 it was the chief horse and cattle market of London.

From an early period until the reign of Henry IV it was a usual place of execution, and here Sir William Wallace, the Scottish patriot, suffered in 1305. In 1381 the rebel Wat Tyler was slain here by Sir William Walworth, the Mayor, in the presence of Richard II. Under the Tudors many persons were burned at Smithfield for their religious convictions. Anne Askew perished here in 1546. Memorials on the exterior wall of St Bartholomew's Hospital commemorate Wallace and the Protestant martyrs of the reign of Mary I. From 1133 till 1840 Smithfield was the scene of Bartholomew Fair, held every year for several days about the Feast of St Bartholomew (24 Aug), and the Royal Smithfield Show (now held at Earl's Court) had its origins at Wooton's Livery Stables here in 1799.

On the s.e. side of Smithfield is **St Bartholomew's Hospital,** which, together with a priory for Augustinian canons, was founded in 1123 by Rahere, a favourite courtier of Henry I, in fulfilment of a vow made by him when lying sick at Rome. It is the oldest charitable institution in London that retains its original site. Whittington, the famous mayor, bequeathed money for its repair in 1423. At the Dissolution the hospital was spared by Henry VIII, who is regarded as its second founder. The fine gateway (1702) is by Edward Strong the Younger. The buildings in the great quadrangle were built by James Gibbs in 1730–70. Inside the gates to the left is the small octagonal church of *St Bartholomew the Less*, rebuilt (except for the striking 15C tower) in 1823–25 and well restored in 1950. Inigo Jones (1573–1652) was baptized here.

Harvey, who discovered the circulation of the blood, was chief physician of the hospital in 1609–43; Abernethy, the famous surgeon, was a lecturer from 1791 to 1827 at its famous medical school ('Bart's').

By far the most interesting building at Smithfield is the church of ***St Bartholomew the Great,** which belonged to the priory founded in 1123 by Rahere, and is, next to the chapel in the White Tower, the oldest church in London. It is approached from the e. corner of Smithfield (to the n. of the hospital), through a small gateway, once the w. entrance to the s. nave-aisle. Above the gateway is a house, with an Elizabethan half-timbered façade, brought to light by a zeppelin bomb explosion in 1915 through the loosening of the tiles that long concealed it. The site of the nave, which was completed in the 13C, is now occupied by the church-yard. We enter the church by a modern porch beneath a brick tower built in 1628 to take the place of the tower over the crossing. The five bells date from 1510. The church, noted for its music, is open from 7.45 to dusk; Sun services at 9, 11, and 6.30.

At the Dissolution the conventual buildings and much of the church were pulled down or alienated, and of the original priory-church there stands only the choir, built by Rahere, with the crossing and one bay of the nave, added before 1170 by his successor. The restoration of the church, begun in 1863, was resumed in 1886, with Sir Aston Webb as architect.

On Good Friday, in accordance with a custom dating from 1686, twenty-one poor widows each received an old 'sixpence', which is laid on a flat tombstone in the churchyard. The sixpence is now supplemented by a hot cross bun and a share in the proceeds of the collection.

The INTERIOR of the church, the choir of Rahere's priory-church, is most impressive, with its heavy columns, piers, and round arches in the pure Norman style. The clerestory was rebuilt early in the 15C, and the Norman triforium is interrupted on the s. side by *Prior Bolton's Window*, a beautiful oriel (once communicating with the prior's house) added by

Prior Bolton (1506–32), whose rebus, a bolt and a tun, it bears. The apsidal ending of the choir, with its stilted arches, was built in 1886 by Sir Aston Webb in place of the previous square ending, which is supposed itself to have been an innovation of the 15C. On the N. side of the sanctuary is the *Tomb of Rahere* (d. 1143), with a coloured effigy, beneath a rich canopy (c. 1400; perhaps by Yevele).—In the *South Transept* stands the 15C font at which Hogarth was baptized in 1697. In the *South Ambulatory* is the alabaster tomb of Sir Walter Mildmay (d. 1589), founder of Emmanuel College, Cambridge. The *Lady Chapel*, rebuilt in 1896 and retaining little of the original fabric of the 14C, is separated from the E. end of the choir by a beautiful modern iron screen. It was at one time used as a printing office, and then as a fringe factory; it now serves as the chapel of the Imperial Society of Knights Bachelor. The *North Transept* was at one time occupied by a blacksmith's forge. The stone screen at its w. end dates from the beginning of the 15C. The screen beneath the organ has painted panels (1932) illustrating the life of Rahere.

A Norman doorway, with the original 15C oaken doors, at the w. end of the South Ambulatory, admits to the E. walk of the old *Cloister*, built c. 1405 and reconstructed in 1905–28. The arches in the wall mark the entrance to the former chapter-house. A few ancient fragments and relics are exhibited here.

To the s. of the church is *Bartholomew Close*, in which Milton sought hiding after the Restoration in 1660. Hogarth was born here in 1697, and here Benjamin Franklin lived while working in the printing office in the Lady Chapel. Washington Irving also lodged here. At Nos. 87–88 is *Butchers' Hall* (1959).

Cloth Fair, skirting the N. side of the church, marks the site once occupied by the booths of drapers and clothiers at Bartholomew Fair. A Jacobean house (1614) here has been well preserved and restored.

The N. side of the square is filled with the elaborate building of the **Central Meat Market** (built in 1867 by Sir Horace Jones); the *Poultry Market* (1963) with a vast barrel vault, lies to the w. The largest dead meat, poultry and provision market in the world, it covers 10 acres, and has a 'shop frontage' of nearly two miles. 'Pitchers' arrive at about 11 p.m. to unload the carcases which are then prepared by 'cutters' ready for selling at 5 a.m. The scene remains animated until midday when the wholesale market closes.

Charterhouse Street, skirting the N. side of the market, leads E. to the quiet *Charterhouse Square*. Here is the 16–18C gatehouse of the *Charterhouse, founded in the 14C as a monastery, but since 1611 a hostel for poor gentlemen. The buildings, dating mainly from the 16C, were badly damaged in 1941. Their restoration is now complete, much intrusive 19C work having been removed in the process. Visitors are not admitted, except by arrangement with the master or registrar, or usually at 2.45 on Wed in April–July.

In 1371 the Carthusian priory of the Salutation of the Mother of God was founded here by Sir Walter de Manny, a distinguished soldier under Edward III, on a burial-ground where 50,000 victims of the Black Death had been interred. This was the fourth English house of the Carthusians; the name Charterhouse is a corruption of the French name Chartreuse. Sir Edward North, afterwards Lord North, to whom the property was granted in 1545, built a mansion on the site of the Little Cloister. This passed later to that Duke of Northumberland who was executed in 1553 for his attempt to put Lady Jane Grey (his daughter-in-law) on the throne. The property was considerably altered by a later owner, the fourth Duke of Norfolk, who was executed for complicity in a plot to put Mary, Queen of Scots, on the throne. Elizabeth I paid four visits to the mansion (then known as Howard House), and

James I was entertained here prior to his coronation in 1603 by Thomas Howard, later earl of Suffolk, to whom the property had passed in 1601. In 1611 the Charterhouse was bought for £13,000 by Thomas Sutton, a shrewd Elizabethan soldier, probably also a merchant-adventurer, who here founded the 'Hospital of King James in Charterhouse', including a hospital for 80 poor brethren and a free school for 40 poor boys.

Owing to a decline in the revenues, the normal number of brethren is now 40. Pensioners must be bachelors or widowers, members of the Church of England, and over sixty years of age; and they must have been officers in the Army or Navy, clergymen, doctors, lawyers, artists, or professional men. They occupy chambers in Master's Court and Wash-House Court. The *British Records Association* also has offices here.

The *Charterhouse School* rapidly developed into one of the chief public schools of England, and in 1872 it was transferred to Godalming in Surrey. Thackeray, a former pupil, in 'The Newcomes' describes the Charterhouse under the name of 'Greyfriars'; Col. Newcome is represented as both an ex-pupil of the school and a poor brother, a coincidence that has almost never occurred in fact.—From 1875 to 1933 the site of the school, mainly around the Great Cloister, was occupied by the *Merchant Taylors' School*, founded in 1561 in Suffolk Lane, Upper Thames Street, where Spenser, Lancelot Andrewes, Clive, and Gilbert Murray were pupils. This school is now at Moor Park (see the 'Blue Guide to England'), and the buildings here, with large new extensions, are occupied by St Bartholomew's medical school.

The *Chapel* was perhaps originally the chapter house of the monastery, and portions of the s. and e. walls belong to the 14C structure. The ante-chapel was built in 1512. The n. arcade, the n. aisle, the pulpit, communion table, and seats in the middle of the church date from about 1614. The elaborate tomb of Thomas Sutton (d. 1611), with a recumbent effigy, was designed by Nicholas Stone and Bernard Jansen. Above rises a low tower containing a vaulted chamber (perhaps the monks' treasury). This is provided with a round squint affording a view of the high altar of the original church (to the s.), which was demolished by Lord North to build his hall, and the site of the tomb of the founder, Sir Walter de Manny (d. 1372), was located in 1947, in front of this now vanished altar. The *Chapel Cloisters* (1613) contain memorials to famous 'Carthusians', including John Wesley. On the n. side of the *Master's Court* are the *Great Hall*, and (on the first floor) the *Great Chamber*, both of the 16C, with 17C alterations, restored to something very near their original splendour by Lord Mottistone and Paul Paget (1956). To the w. is the *Wash-House Court*, the best preserved part of the monastic buildings as rebuilt in the 16C and to the n. are two courts of 1826–39. The *Great Cloister*, with traces of the monks' cells, lay to the e.

From Charterhouse St., opposite the Central Meat Market, *St John Street* runs n. to the Angel at Islington. To the left diverges St John's Lane, spanned by **St John's Gate** (erected in 1504), the s. gate of the once famous and wealthy priory of the Knights Hospitallers of the Order of St John of Jerusalem, which was founded about 1130 and was suppressed by Elizabeth I.

The priory was later the residence of Edmund Tilney (d. 1610), Master of the Revels, who licensed thirty of Shakespeare's plays. In 1731–81 the gatehouse was the printing office of the 'Gentleman's Magazine', conducted by Edward Cave, to which Dr Johnson used to contribute. The premises are now occupied as the Grand Priory in the British Realm of the *Venerable Order of the Hospital of St John of Jerusalem*, revived in 1831, which devotes itself to ambulance and hospital work. An entirely voluntary organization 'in the service of mankind', it is supported by public donation. Visitors are usually admitted to the gatehouse, museum, library, and church by appointment with the curator.

In St John's Square, across Clerkenwell Road, lies **St John's Church,** built about 1720 and incorporating the choir-walls of the ancient priory church, probably destroyed c. 1381 when Wat Tyler burned the priory. The area of the original circular nave is indicated by a line in the road. In 1930 this again became the priory church of the order, and it has been sympathetically restored after its destruction in 1941. The altarpiece consists of two wings of a Flemish triptych (15C) probably removed at the Dissolution and recovered in 1932. Lion head handles on the church doors were found in the ruins of the Muristan, the site of the original hospice of the order in Jerusalem. Below is an interesting and well-preserved **Crypt*, the three w. bays of which date from about 1140; the two E. bays and the side-chapels were added about 1185. Monuments here include a 'memento mori' from the tomb of Sir William Weston (d. 1540), last Prior of the Order, and a fine alabaster effigy (16C) of a knight of the Order, brought from Valladolid.

We are now in **Clerkenwell** (Pl. 8; 3), noted especially as the quarter of watchmakers, jewellers, and opticians. Among former residents in Clerkenwell were Izaak Walton (1650–61), John Wilkes (born here in 1727), Christopher Pinchbeck, inventor of the alloy that bears his name (1721), and Emanuel Swedenborg (d. 1772). The old 'Clerks' Well' (on the site of 14–16 Farringdon Rd.) mentioned as early as 1174, where the parish clerks of London used to perform miracle plays, gave name to the district.

CLERKENWELL ROAD, its s. boundary, leads from Gray's Inn Road (p. 175) to Old Street, passing (l.) the old *Sessions House* (1779–82), with reliefs by Nollekens, in Clerkenwell Green, with the graceful steeple of *St James's Church* (by James Carr; 1788–92) behind. In Clerkenwell Green Nos. 37 and 38, a house of 1738, contain the *Marx Memorial Library*, a pointer to the place's radical history.

Farringdon Road, with some second-hand bookstalls, leads back towards Holborn.

23   LONDON WALL, THE BARBICAN, AND GUILDHALL

STATIONS: *Barbican* and *Moorgate* on Circle and Metropolitan lines, Moorgate also on Northern line. *Bank* on Central and Northern lines.—BUSES: Nos. 141 & 502 traverse London Wall; No. 4 in Aldersgate St.; Nos. 21, 43, & 76 in Moorgate; Nos. 8, 22, & 25 in Cheapside (for Guildhall).—CAR PARKS near the Barbican.

From the w. end of Cheapside (comp. Rte 21) Foster Lane leads N. past the church of *St Vedast*, rebuilt by Wren in 1670–73, and restored in 1962. Within is a richly decorated ceiling, fine carving, and a splendid sounding organ, built by Renatus Harris in 1731 and now restored. Robert Herrick was christened here. Farther on, on the corner of Gresham St., stands the GOLDSMITHS' HALL (adm. see p. 199), a handsome Renaissance edifice (1835) rebuilt by Philip Hardwick, containing some interesting portraits and a fine collection of plate. The Goldsmiths' Company, which was incorporated in 1327, has the duty of assaying and stamping gold and silver plate. Its hall-mark is the leopard's head.

Across Gresham St. (l.) *St Anne and St Agnes*, a Wren church (1680), restored in 1963–68, was rehallowed for Lutheran congregations in 1966 (open for services on Sun). At the end of Noble Street a new *Plaisterers' Hall* (1971) faces London Wall.

It is slightly longer but more interesting to turn E. along Gresham St., passing Staining Lane with the entrances to the *Haberdashers' Hall*, and (in Oat Lane) to the neo-Georgian *Pewterers' Hall* (1961; the original hall was built in 1496), and turn N. up Wood Street. Here stands the tower of *St Alban* built by Wren in 1682–98. Beyond the police station (1965) we may cross London Wall by walkway.

LONDON WALL (Pl. 8; 6), though here realined, still follows more or less closely the site of the old **City Wall.** Parts of the wall have been exposed in this area, especially since the clearance of bomb damage.

The **Roman Wall** around the city was 2 m. long, usually 8 ft thick, and probably 20–25 ft high. The best preserved section is exposed near the Tower (comp. p. 252). It was built c. A.D. 190–225 with stone shipped along the river Medway from Maidstone; one of the ships sank near Blackfriars and has been excavated (comp. p. 239). The five gates were Aldgate, Bishopsgate, Cripplegate, Newgate, and Ludgate. A sixth, Aldersgate, was added later. The fragments of wall now visible show the Roman substructure with its characteristic bands of tiles, and, above, additions made to these foundations in the succeeding centuries.

Preceding the City Wall in date was a **Roman Fort,** built A.D. 120–30, and discovered in 1950. Its N. and W. boundaries were later strengthened and incorporated into the city defensive wall. Cripplegate was on the site of the N. gate of the fort.

Sometime after the 13C a system of semicircular bastions was constructed outside the walls; a number of these are now visible.

Beyond lies the **Barbican** (Pl. 8; 4) where a 60-acre area, heavily bombed in the last War, has been rebuilt to provide accommodation for over 6000 people who work in the City, and an arts centre. Designed in massive concrete in derivative styles in which medieval fortification and Le Corbusier seemingly predominate, the residential blocks are linked by raised walkways. The shapeless unusable corners left by ramps and open stairways and the rectangular expanses of open water are alike untidy and unsuited to London's fickle climate. The building of a theatre for the Royal Shakespeare Company, a concert hall for the London Symphony Orchestra, new premises for the Guildhall School of Music and Drama, the City Lending Library, and a students' hostel, will help to make the area less isolated.

Walkways cross London Wall to podium level at the s.w. corner. Here the ****Museum of London,** opened by Queen Elizabeth II on 2 December 1976, presents the history, the social and domestic life, and the manners of the capital from the earliest habitation to the most recent past. It combines the former Guildhall and London Museums.

The Guildhall Museum was founded in 1826 as an adjunct to the Guildhall Library by the Corporation of the City of London. The London Museum was a national museum formed in 1911. Before 1939 it had been in Lancaster House. After 1945 both museums had temporary quarters: the Guildhall Museum in the Royal Exchange and the London Museum in Kensington Palace.

The new building, by Powell, Moya, and Partners, with inteior by Higgins, Ney, and Partners, surrounds a central court and is on two levels connected by a glazed ramp.

ADMISSION: Free. Tues–Sat 10.00–18.00, Sun 14.00–18.00. Closed Monday, Christmas Day and Boxing Day. For Public Holiday opening telephone 01-600 3699. Special arrangements for invalid visitors. All School Parties and adult parties of more than 20 people must be booked in advance.

The exhibition, on the continuous open plan, consists of chronological tableaux incorporating 'bygones' of every kind, presented as an illustrated social history of some brilliance. Later centuries are accompanied by discreetly recorded period music. Costume is particularly well represented. Exhibits come from all social levels, inevitably with some imbalance, since Tudor relics tend to survive from court and church circles, while for the 19C, equally a period of high material progress and endeavour, poverty and trivia are perhaps too preponderant, and the early 20C appears quaint rather than innovatory.

The arrangement is in general anti-clockwise and from the walls to the centre. Displays are numbered consecutively (our italics) and well documented; our description only picks out particular objects (individual descriptive labels are often unhelpfully grouped low down).

A relief model of the Thames Valley faces an imaginary section through a City cellar to demonstrate archaeological levels.

PREHISTORIC. Flint and bone tools from riverine gravel terraces (*2, 5*); Neolithic bowl from Heathrow (*9*); leaf-shaped swords of the Bronze Age (*10*); finds from a temple site (6C B.C.) found at Heathrow during airfield construction; early British coins (*11*); iron dagger; the Brentford Tankard (1C), of bronze-mounted oak with an ornamental handle (*12*).

ROMAN from A.D. 43 (when Claudius's soldiers crossed the Thames). Stone figure of a legionary; soldiers' accoutrements (*14*); imports from Italy; commercial wax letter tablet addressed Londinio (*15*); inscribed gravestones; tile from state tile works stamped P.P. BR. LON; head of Hadrian and other fragments of bronze statues (*18*).

A vantage window overlooks ill-kept remains of the 2C Roman fort; opposite, Roman tools, little changed in type in 2000 years (*21–25*). House reconstruction comprising 1C and 4C dining-rooms and kitchen grouped round a 3C tessellated pavement from Bucklersbury; cases (*32, 33*) contain writing materials; leather 'bikini' trunks (one from a well in Queen St.), probably worn by dancing girls; board games; sandals; articles of toilet.

Small cult and votive statues (*41, 42*); marble sculpture (mainly 2C–3C) found on the Mithraic temple site, including *Heads of Mithras and Serapis, a colossal hand, and a 3C Bacchic group; note also the late-Roman decorated silver box containing a strainer (*43*); clay jug inscribed Londini (*44*); sarcophagus from Lower Clapton (*39*); architectural fragments found in the city wall.

SAXON AND VIKING. Scramasaxes, the large knives from which the Saxons are supposed to have taken their names (*49*); brooches from Saxon cemetery at Mitcham; Celtic bell (? 8C) found in the Thames at Mortlake (*50*); spear-heads, axes, and other Viking weapons (*53, 56*); Viking grave slab (11C) with runes, from St Paul's churchyard (*58*).

MEDIEVAL. Models of William the Conqueror's White Tower (*60*) and Old St Paul's (*61*); 15C City chest of solid iron; chain-mail hauberk; sculptured panel in elm (from a chest) with Chaucerian scene; huge 13C storage jar (*65*). A corner window overlooks a medieval bastion. Heraldic fragments of the Cheapside Eleanor Cross (*71*); earliest known swinging cradle (15C) (*73*); coin hoard (temp. Edward III) from Upper Norwood (*79*); costrels, tallybag in leather with inscription of the Calais garrison (*84*). A 15C carved door frame from the church of St Ethelburga-within-Bishopsgate (*98*), flanked by the four Civic Virtues from the medieval Guildhall (*95*), leads to:

TUDOR. Italian bronze head reliquary found in the Thames (*104*); 16C armour from Greenwich (*106, 109*); the *Cheapside Hoard, probably part of the stock-in-trade of a 16C jeweller (*110*); Brewers' Company pall, below a painting of Jonah and the Whale from a Waltham Abbey house (*111*). In wall-cases: leather clothing preserved from a Moorfields rubbish dump (*112*); *Copper plate engraved with part of the earliest known survey of London (c. 1558); characteristic flat cap with ear pieces; Ming bowl mounted on silver-gilt stand, said to have belonged to Mary, Queen of Scots (*115*); Sir Thos. Gresham's *Steelyard; fashionable *Gloves and leather hat; lace shirt; cups and apostle spoons (*116*); 'Ballarmines' or 'greybeards', earthenware flasks named after Card. Bellarmine (d. 1621).

EARLY STUART AND COMMONWEALTH. The transition from Tudor to Stuart is marked by scale models of Tudor London and Whitehall Palace. Fragment of Classical frieze, perhaps from Didyma (Asia Minor), typifying Jacobean antiquarian collecting. Relics of Charles I (vest worn on scaffold) and Cromwell (death mask); swords from a factory at Hounslow; *Armour made at Greenwich c. 1630 and worn by John Dymoke as hereditary King's Champion at George III's coronation. Panelled room from Wandsworth with embroidered hangings (*134*); builder's sacrifice; Mercers' Company silver flagon (*135*); plague relics; 'Great Fire Experience', an audio-visual reconstruction of the Great Fire of 1666.

A ramp leads down to the **Lower Floor.**

LATE STUART. Continuity is given by the lying 'Popish Plot' slab removed from the Monument (*152*); Pepys' chess set (*154*); communion plate from Wren churches. Shop and tavern signs: Gerard the Giant, Ape and Apple, etc. Trumpet of 1666; silver tankard of Sir E. Berry Godfrey, murdered on Primrose Hill; playing cards illustrating the murder and other facets of the 'Popish Plot' (*158*); scientific instruments; imports from the East Indies (*172, 173*); panelled room with a pair of virginals by James White, 1656; sedan chair (*179*).

GEORGIAN. In the rotunda, enclosed by bow-fronted shop windows, printing press (*192*); bust of James Thomson, by Roubiliac; box of Reeves' paints used by Isaac Smith on Cook's voyage (*194*); Lambeth Delft pottery; Chelsea and Bow porcelain; Battersea enamels; debtor's cell from Wellclose Square Lockup (visited and described by John Howard, the penal reformer); Debtor's Door and cell from Newgate Prison. The 'Bull and Mouth' sign (c. 1810) from St Martin's-le-Grand marks the entrance to the:

NINETEENTH CENTURY HALL. Grimaldi and Kean's costumes (*220*); the Woolsack from the old House of Lords; Dickens's chair; relics from Coal Exchange and Great Exhibition (*241*); Hodges' fire engine of 1862 (*242*); Board school room; Victorian kitchen; Valentines and early Christmas cards; railway and postal relics.

IMPERIAL LONDON. Toys; public house bar; barber's shop; the Music Hall (*280*); 'Popularity', a panorama of stage artists by W. H. Lambert; cooper's, haberdasher's, grocer's (*302*); chemist's, and tailor's shop interiors; Hansom cab (*305*).

THE TWENTIETH CENTURY (*306–338*) ranges from cigarette cards to an early broadcasting studio; Woolworth's 3d and 6d counter; lifts from Selfridge's; art nouveau clocks; model Y Ford car.

CEREMONIAL LONDON. The Lord Mayor's *State Coach, built in 1757 and used in the annual Lord Mayor's Show; it is decorated with allegorical scenes having a London setting, reputedly by Cipriani. Model of the last Lord Mayor's barge (1807). – In the TREASURY, opposite, reminders of the coronation ceremony: Pursuivant's tabard; George IV's surcoat and doublet; part of William IV's canopy; gloves, coronets, stoles, etc. worn at the last seven coronations; robes worn by Her Majesty in 1953 (on loan); coronation souvenirs since 1831.

ALDERSGATE STREET, which skirts the Barbican on the w., takes its name from the old

N. city gate (pulled down in 1761). The road follows a Roman alinement; recent excavations revealed a sequence of eleven subsequent roads on its course. The decorative *Ironmongers' Hall*, hidden behind the new buildings, is the successor (1925) of the old hall in Fenchurch St., destroyed by enemy aircraft in 1917. *St Botolph without Aldersgate* (open 12–3), slightly injured by the Great Fire, was entirely rebuilt in 1790.

From the museum a walkway (l.) runs above London Wall to Wood St., then turns left to 'The Postern' through which a descent is made to the paved piazza around the church of **St Giles without Cripplegate** (open Mon–Thurs 9.30–2, Fri till 12, Sat 2.30–5, and on Sun).

The stone tower (with a brick top story added in 1682 by John Bridges), and the nave, belong to the church built in 1390. After a fire in 1545 and alterations in the 17–18C, the edifice received a direct hit during the first enemy air attack on the City on the night of 24 Aug 1940, and was even more badly damaged during the great fire of 29 Dec of the same year. In 1960 it was restored; the E. and W. windows were renewed in 1967–68, and the fine organ (incorporating an 18C case) installed in 1969.

In this church Shakespeare attended the baptism of his nephew in 1604 while lodging near by in Silver St. with Christopher Montjoy, a Huguenot and 'tire maker' whom he had known "for the space of tenne yeres or thereaboutes". Oliver Cromwell was married here in 1620.

In the S. aisle is a monument (restored in 1971) over the burial-place of John Speed (1552–1629), topographer, and an epitaph to Thamas Stagg (1772) ending with the curt phrase "That is all". At the W. end of this aisle a plaque records the burial here of John Milton, who died in Bunhill Row in 1674, in the same grave as his father. The bust is by John Bacon (1793). 'Paradise Lost' was sold by Milton to an Aldersgate printer; the poet occupied several houses in the region from 1643–47, and after the Restoration. A plaque to the r. of the entrance door recalls other 'Men of Mark' connected with the parish, who include Sir Martin Frobisher (d. 1594), seaman and explorer, John Foxe (d. 1587), martyrologist, John Bunyan (d. 1688), and Daniel Defoe (d. 1731; the parish register records his burial in Bunhill Fields). The Great Plague was at its worst in the parish of St Giles, and plague burials fill nearly a folio volume of the parish register (1665). The documents are now in the Guildhall Library (p. 229).

Outside, tombstones have been set in to the paving, including some curious mummy-shaped tombs dating from the early 19C. A bastion built outside the city wall sometime after the 13C is prominent to the s. The *City of London School for Girls*, founded in Carmelite St. in 1894, was moved here in 1964.—Farther s., in Monkwell Square is the new *Barber Surgeons' Hall*. The West Gate of the Roman Fort (comp. above) is entered from London Wall (Mon–Fri 12.30–2; other times by arrangement at Guildhall Museum). On view are remains of the N. guardroom, a gravelled roadway, and the central piers of the gate.

Off the E. side of Wood St., in the sunken garden of *St Alphage*, another fine section of the city wall has been exposed. Above the Roman level (part of the N. wall of the early fort), the additions in grey stone date from c. 1350, and the red brick top was added c. 1477. Near by are the remains of the N. porch of *Elsing Spital*, a priory church founded in 1329 "for the sustentation of a hundred blind men".

We should now recross London Wall. To the E. of *Brewers' Hall*, on this site since 1420 and rebuilt in 1960 after its destruction in 1940, is the *City Business Library* (formed from the Commercial Reference Room and the Newspaper Room of the Guildhall Library). In front is a charming statue 'The Gardener' by Karin Jonzen (1971). Here steps lead up to the Bassishaw Highwalk, with a view (l.) of *Girdlers' Hall* (1961) in Basinghall

Avenue. We descend a wide flight of steps past the pleasant new pavilion-like building of the *Guildhall Exhibition Hall* used for varied exhibitions relating to the City. On the w. is the *Chartered Insurance Institute* (1934), with its museum of fire-marks and fire-fighting equipment.

Beyond a sculptural group by K. Jonzen, a flight of steps descends right to a coloured glass fountain by Allen David. Across *Aldermanbury* a pleasant garden surrounds the site of the Wren church of *St Mary* bombed in 1940 and removed in 1968 to the campus of Westminster College, Fulton, U.S.A. as a memorial to Winston Churchill (who made his famous Iron Curtain speech at the College). The memorial to the editors of Shakespeare's First Folio, Heminge and Cøndell, church-wardens, remains. Judge Jeffreys was buried here, having died in the Tower in 1689. The registers recording Milton's second marriage (1656) are now in the Guildhall library.

Aldermanbury leads past the new Guildhall Library (see below) to **Guildhall** (Pl. 9; 5) which is entered viâ Guildhall Buildings in Guildhall Yard. As the *Hall of the Corporation of the City of London* it dates from c. 1411–35, though its external appearance is substantially due to the design of George Dance, Jr. (1788–89). Over the porch is the City coat-of-arms, with the motto 'Domine dirige nos'. The lower part of the great hall, the porch, and the crypt are medieval; much damage was caused by fire in 1666 and 1940; and the interior was beautifully restored by Sir Giles Scott in 1952–54. The Hall and Crypt are open Mon–Sat 10–5, Sun in summer and BH 2–5.

The GREAT HALL ($151\frac{1}{2}$ ft long, 48 ft wide, and 89 ft high) was restored in 1668–71 and in 1866–70, but its 19C timber roof was destroyed in 1940 and has been replaced by stone arches with a panelled ceiling (1954). The hall (open 10–5, Sat to 4) is now used for municipal meetings, public meetings, the election of the Lord Mayor and Sheriffs, and the state banquets of the Corporation. The most important of these last is the banquet given c. 9 Nov, by the new Lord Mayor and Sheriffs, to the members of the Cabinet and other important citizens. At an earlier period the hall was used also for important trials (recorded on a panel). Against the walls are a statue of *Churchill*, by Oscar Nemon, and monuments to *Nelson* (inscription by Sheridan), *Wellington*, *Chatham* (inscription by Burke), *William Pitt* (inscription by Canning) and *Lord Mayor Beckford*; the popular wooden figures of *Gog and Magog*, by David Evans (w. end), replace those burned in 1940.

The **Guildhall Library** (open weekdays, 9.30–5; founded in 1425), is reached either by a corridor running w. from the porch of the Guildhall or from an entrance in Aldermanbury. It contains about 140,000 printed volumes and pamphlets and over 30,000 MSS. It is especially rich in works on London and Middlesex, and includes several important special collections. The Commercial Reference, and Newspaper Libraries now form the City Business Library (p. 228). The *Whittington Room* (closed Sat) contains a collection of old clocks, watches and chronometers belonging to the Clockmakers' Company. A small Exhibition Hall, opposite, is used for displays from the collections.

The CORPORATION ART GALLERY (to be rebuilt), entered from the E. side of Guildhall Yard, was established in 1886, and is devoted to British 19C art with a basis of historical portraits. About nine exhibitions a year of various Art Societies are held here. The former main library hall (1870–72 in a Tudor style) is used for receptions, etc.

The CRYPT is a very interesting survival of the building of 1411–35. The *Eastern Crypt* is borne by six clustered columns of Purbeck marble, restored in 1961.

In *Gresham Street* stands the church of ST LAWRENCE JEWRY, built by Wren in 1671–77 and effectively restored by Cecil Brown (1956–57; after heavy war damage) as the official church of the City Corporation. The painting in the heavy Renaissance-style reredos is by the architect. In the N. aisle is the Commonwealth Transept.

Pepys records a visit to the church "for curiosity", and his disappointment with the sermon. Sir Thomas More delivered a series of lectures here. Among the rectors were Grocyn and Seth Ward.

To the E. GRESHAM COLLEGE was founded by Sir Thomas Gresham in 1579 for the delivery of lectures in Latin and English on "divynitye, astronomy, musicke, geometry, law, physicke, and rethoricke" by seven professors. It is now the Graduate Business Centre of The City University. The lectures (adm. free) are now all given in English. The present building dates from 1913.

At the end of Gresham St., Prince's Street, skirting the huge wall of the Bank of England (see below) leads s. to the Mansion House. Opposite the bank a driveway admits to *Grocers' Hall*, virtually destroyed by fire in 1965. A new hall was completed in 1970, the fifth to be built on this site; it preserves part of the 17C ironwork from the second hall, and the oldest bell in the city (1458; recast since the fire). The Grocers or 'Pepperers' was first mentioned as a guild in 1180 and incorporated in 1428. Extensions have necessitated its temporary closure to the public; apply to the City Information Centre for admission.

Prince's Street emerges at the Mansion House, see below.

24 BANK OF ENGLAND, MANSION HOUSE, AND STOCK EXCHANGE

STATION: *Bank* on Central and Northern line.—BUSES: Nos. 8, 22, 25, 11, 15, 6, etc.

The triangular space overlooked by the Bank, the Royal Exchange, and the Mansion House may fairly claim to be the heart of the City; from it radiate eight important streets. Near by are the headquarters of all the big banks.

The **Bank of England** (Pl. 9; 5) covers about three acres between Lothbury, Bartholomew Lane, Threadneedle St., and Princes St. In 1694–1734 the bank operated in Grocers' Hall. Its first building was erected by George Sampson in 1732–34, but the bank's later aspect (one-storied in appearance) was due to Sir John Soane, who built the massive external wall (windowless in the interests of security) with its Corinthian columns, from 1788 onwards. The present building, facing Threadneedle St., was rebuilt by Sir Herbert Baker in 1925–39. It rises seven stories above ground within Soane's original outer wall and has three floors below ground. The sculptures are by Charles Wheeler; in the pediment appears the 'Old Lady of Threadneedle Street'. The public are not admitted.

The Bank of England was projected by William Paterson (whose connection with it was, however, brief) and incorporated in 1694 by Royal Charter, under which, and another of 1946, it now operates. The first joint stock bank in England, it had an original capital of £1,200,000 later increased to £14,553,000 which is held by the Treasury. Its affairs are managed by a Court consisting of a Governor, a Deputy Governor and 16 Directors appointed by the Crown. The Bank is the Government's banker and, on its behalf, administers the Exchange Control Regulations and manages the National Debt and the Note Issue of which it has the sole right in England and Wales. It is also the bankers' bank and the central bank of the country. All important overseas central banks have accounts in its books but for many years it has not undertaken new commercial banking business. After the Gordon Riots (1780) the Bank was protected nightly by a picket mounted by the Brigade of Guards until 1973.

Opposite the Bank, in the angle formed by Threadneedle Street and Cornhill, stands the **Royal Exchange**, erected by Tite in 1842–44. It is the third building of its kind on this spot; the first Exchange, erected by Sir Thomas Gresham in 1564–70, was burned down in 1666, and the second in 1838. The tympanum group above the Corinthian portico represents Commerce holding the charter of the Exchange and attended by the Lord Mayor, British merchants, and natives of various foreign nations. The campanile, 180 ft high, with a peal of bells, has a statue of Gresham on its E. face and a gilded vane in the form of a grasshopper (Gresham's crest). The rooms in the building are now occupied by the Royal Exchange Assurance Co. and no exchange business is transacted.

In front of the Exchange are an equestrian statue of *Wellington*, by Chantrey (1844), and a *War Memorial* (1920), by Aston Webb and Alfred Drury. Behind it is a seated figure of *George Peabody* (d. 1869), facing a charming little fountain-group by Dalou (1878).

INTERIOR (usually open; it is at present being used for temporary exhibitions). The glass-roofed courtyard preserves the pavement of Turkey stone from the original Exchange. The wall-panels are adorned with large and clearly-labelled historical paintings; in the farther corners are statues of Elizabeth I, by M. Watson, and Charles II, by John Spiller.

The **Mansion House**, the official residence of the Lord Mayor, faces the s. corner of the Bank. It is a Renaissance edifice, with an imposing Corinthian portico, erected by George Dance the Elder in 1739–53, with a pediment sculptured by Sir Robt. Taylor.

The chief feature of the interior (visitors usually admitted on Sat, 10.30–11.30, on written application to the Invitations Officer) is the *Egyptian Hall*, the scene of banquets, balls, and other functions, as well as numerous public meetings. Dance modelled it after the so-called Egyptian Hall of Vitruvius, which, however, bore no resemblance to Egyptian architecture. It contains some 19C sculptures. The *Long Parlour*, with a remarkable ceiling, the *Saloon*, adorned with tapestry and sculpture, the *State Drawing Room*, etc., are shown also. Visitors enter by the door in Walbrook.

The colourful *Lord Mayor's Show* is held on the second Sat in Nov, when the new Lord Mayor is led by coach through the streets of the City preceded by a procession with a theme chosen by the Lord Mayor, but always tranditionally including the defence services, and made especially spectacular by the presence of the Hon. Company of Men at Arms and the Household Cavalry.

In Walbrook, just behind the Mansion House, is the church of ST STEPHEN, rebuilt by Wren in 1672–79. The noble *Interior, with its circular dome (63 ft high) supported on eight arches, is one of the architect's masterpieces, and has been carefully restored since its partial destruction in 1941. The dome represents, on a smaller scale, Wren's original design for St Paul's. The font is by Thomas Strong, with a fine cover by William

Newman, and the rich pulpit is by Thos. Creecher. On the left wall is a large Burial of St Stephen, by Benj. West. To the left a tablet commemorates Dr Nathaniel Hodges, appointed by the Lord Mayor in 1665 to combat the spread of the Plague, which had started in Mansion House Place. The fine sword rest dates from 1710, and the organ (by Hill) from 1906. A glass mosaic in the s. wall commemorates John Dunstable (d. 1453), 'the father of English harmony', and a tablet serves as memorial to John Lilburne (d. 1657), the political agitator. In the vaults lies Sir John Vanbrugh (1664–1726), playwright and architect.

In 1964–67 the Crypt and Vestries were converted for use as the headquarters of the London Branch of the Samaritans, a world-wide organization 'to befriend the suicidal and desperate', founded by the present Rector.

In Lothbury, on the N. side of the Bank, is the church of *St Margaret Lothbury*, rebuilt by Wren in 1686–90. It contains an exquisite carved font, pulpit, and canopy ascribed to Grinling Gibbons, and a fine chancel screen from All Hallows the Great, probably English work of c. 1689. The elaborate sword-rests date from the late-18C. The bust of Sir Peter le Maire (d. 1631), at the w. end of the nave, is perhaps by H. le Sueur.— Opposite, in an alcove in the wall of the Bank, is a statue of Sir John Soane.

To the E. of the Bank, beyond Bartholomew Lane, the **Stock Exchange**, the headquarters of the dealers in negotiable securities, occupies a tall tower and new buildings at its foot. The site, part of which has been occupied by the Exchange since 1802 extends to the post office where Throgmorton St. and Old Broad St. meet, and s. to Threadneedle St. The public are admitted to the Visitors' Gallery (Mon–Fri 10–3.15) and to a cinema where films explaining the working of the Stock Exchange are shown.

A special feature of the London Stock Exchange is the differentiation of its members into *Stock-Jobbers* and *Stock-Brokers*. The jobber, or dealer, does business only with other members, 'making prices' and dealing in certain classes of securities selected by himself. The broker acts as intermediary between the jobbers and the general public. Speculators on a rise in prices are known as 'bulls', those who speculate on a fall as 'bears'. Bargains are made 'on the nod'; defaulters are 'hammered'. Members, who are elected, buy a 'nomination' or 'seat' from a retiring member and must be nominated by two members. They pay an entrance fee of £1050, and an annual subscription of £262 50p, and must normally have been employed for at least three years with a member firm of the Stock Exchange.

Much business is now carried out by an automatic telephone and paging system. This has reduced the activity in the members' 'Street' market in Throgmorton St. and the adjacent courts, where securities used to be dealt in after closing hours, especially during a 'boom'. 'Outside brokers', or non-members of the Stock Exchange, include some old-established firms and others of a less stable character ('bucket-shops').

In Throgmorton St., just N. of the Stock Exchange, is DRAPERS' HALL, dating in part from 1667 but practically rebuilt in 1866–70 (restored 1949; adm. see p. 199; entrance in Throgmorton Avenue). It contains a handsome staircase, and a famous mulberry still flourishes in the garden. —In Austin Friars, close to Drapers' Hall, stands the DUTCH CHURCH, by Arthur Bailey (1950–54). This lofty church (open Mon–Thurs and Sun 11–3), with its graceful flèche, replaces the 13C building—originally the nave of a priory of Augustinian friars—that was assigned by Edward VI in 1550 to Protestant refugees and was ultimately left exclusively to the Dutch. The old church was completely destroyed in 1941, and the great w. window, by Max Nauta, shows Edward VI and Princess Irene of the Netherlands, who laid the foundation stone of the new church. Beneath the Communion table is the altar-stone of the priory church (1253).

Old Broad Street, diverging on the left from Threadneedle St., leads to Liverpool St. and Broad St. stations. On its E. side the elegant City of London Club, by Philip Hardwick (1834), is near the focus of the icy swirling draughts caused by its skyscraper neighbours. Farther E. in Threadneedle St. (No. 30) is MERCHANT TAYLORS' HALL, the largest of the livery company halls, incorporated in 1327, damaged by the Great Fire of 1666, gutted by fire in 1941, and reopened in 1959. A 14C crypt survives. The company, incorporated in 1327, maintains a large public school for boys. The activity of the Merchant Taylors and the needlemakers (whose hall was near by) probably gave name to 'Threadneedle' Street. At the end of Threadneedle St. (N. side), behind the present *South Sea House*, stood the old South Sea House, built in 1711 for the South Sea Company, where Lamb was a clerk in 1789–92. Threadneedle St. ends at Bishopsgate.

25 BANK TO THE ANGEL. ISLINGTON

STATIONS: *Bank, Moorgate, Old Street*, and *Angel* on Northern line; *Highbury and Islington* on Victoria line.—BUSES: No. 43 follows the route to the Angel; Nos. 4, 19, 30, 43, and 104 traverse Upper Street.

From the junction of Princes St. and Lothbury, near the s.w. corner of the Bank of England, MOORGATE (Pl. 9; 5) runs N. On the right, in Great Swan Alley, is the *Chartered Accountants' Hall*, a Renaissance-style building by John Belcher (1890–93; extended 1930), with sculptures by Hamo Thornycroft and H. Bates. The Moorgate, built in 1415, and pulled down in 1761, stood at the junction with London Wall. To the left in London Wall stands *Armourers' Hall* (1841), founded 1453. The Barbican beyond is described in Rte 23. In its right (E.) section is *Carpenters' Hall*, rebuilt 1956–60 (adm. see p. 199), and, farther on, the church of *All Hallows on the Wall*, by the younger Dance (1765–67), with a fine plaster ceiling and blue and gold decorations, well restored in 1962. The monumental pulpit is entered through steps from the vestry. Part of the medieval city wall may be seen in the churchyard.

Moorgate continues beyond London Wall; parallel to the w., Moorfields preserves the memory of the marshy district outside the old Moorgate, once the resort of archers, washerwomen, and (later) of booksellers. John Keats was born in 1795, the son of a livery stable keeper, on the site of No. 85 (public house; tablet). Opposite is the School of Business Studies of the City of London Polytechnic. On the right opens *Finsbury Circus* (bowling green), with Britannic House by Lutyens. In Ropemaker St. (l.) Daniel Defoe died in 1731. From here the line of Moorgate is continued by *Finsbury Pavement* to the unexpected expanse (reminiscent of Continental cities) of *Finsbury Square* (underground car park) laid out by George Dance the Younger. To the w. runs Chiswell St., at the end of which is *Whitbread's Brewery*, on this site since 1750. The stables (on two floors) may be seen on previous written application. North of the square begins the long CITY ROAD. Here is the entrance to the drill-ground and headquarters (*Armoury House*, 1737) of the **Honourable Artillery Company** of the City of London, the oldest military body in the country, having been incorporated by Henry VIII in 1537 under the title of the Guild or Fraternity of St George. It has been established at its present home since 1642, and since 1660 the captain-general has usually been the Sovereign or the Prince of Wales. Officers for the Trained Bands of London were supplied by this company, in whose ranks Milton, Wren, and Pepys served. The H.A.C. has the rare privilege of marching through the City of London with fixed bayonets.

Admission only when accompanied by member of H.A.C. or on written application. Visitors should note the Long Room; and the Court Room with a fine suit of armour (Greenwich; c. 1555) and a unique leading-staff of 1693.—In 1638 Robert Keayne, a member of the London company, founded the Ancient and Honourable Artillery Company of Boston, in the United States, the oldest military body in America.

On 15 Sept 1784, Lunardi made a balloon ascent from the H.A.C. ground and became the first aerial traveller in the English atmosphere.

The adjoining castellated building is a Territorial Force headquarters. Immediately to the N., between the City Road and Bunhill Row (formerly Artillery Walk), lie *Bunhill Fields*, the famous cemetery of the Non-conformists, disused since 1852, the earliest burial on record being 1623.

Possibly this is the site of a Saxon burial-ground which gave these two fields the name of Bon or Bone-Hill Fields.

Here are the graves of *John Bunyan* (d. 1688; recumbent effigy; restored 1950), in the second turning of the s. from the main walk; *Daniel Defoe* (d. 1731; obelisk erected in 1870 by boys and girls of England), to the N. of the main walk, close by (renovated 1949); *Dr Isaac Watts*, the hymn-writer (d. 1748; altar-tomb), to the E. of Defoe (renovated 1951); William Blake (d. 1828), 25 yds N.W. of Defoe; and *Susannah Wesley* (d. 1742), mother of John Wesley (renovated 1957).

Milton wrote 'Paradise Regained' and died in 1674 at a house (No. 125; demolished) in Bunhill Row. In the *Friends' Burial Ground*, across Bunhill Row, laid out as a garden in 1952 and surrounded by new flats, is the grave of George Fox (1624–91), founder of the Society of Friends.

On the opposite side of City Road stands *Wesley's Chapel* (closed for restoration 1972–74), built in 1777, with a statue of John Wesley (1703–91), the founder of Methodism, in front of it and his grave behind. The chapel still retains Wesley's pulpit. **Wesley's House** (tablet; adjoining the chapel), where he moved in 1779, contains the simple room in which he died 12 years later. Here also are mementoes of his brother, Charles Wesley. It is open weekdays 10–1, 2–4, exc. Fri afternoon, and Tues in winter. The Foundry, near by, used by Wesley as a headquarters in 1739–78 before he built the chapel, is commemorated by a plaque in Tabernacle St. (No. 21), just to the E.—A little farther on City Road crosses *Old Street* (busy roundabout) which leads right (E.) to Shoreditch and left (w.) to Clerkenwell, passing the partly demolished church of *St Luke* with its obelisk steeple by Hawksmoor and John James (1727–33). Here Wm. Caslon (1692–1766), the type-founder, is buried.

City Road continues past *Moorfields Eye Hospital* to (1 m.; Buses 104, 43) the *Angel*, a busy road junction named after a long-demolished but once famous old coaching tavern. It was the birthplace of James Pollard (1792–1867), the artist.

To the s.w. extends *Finsbury* with some attractive 19C housing (e.g. Lloyd Baker St.). St John St. leads s. from the Angel towards **Sadler's Wells Theatre** (in Rosebery Avenue), rebuilt in 1931, and now an opera and ballet centre. The building incorporates parts of the old theatre where Grimaldi played in 1781–1805, and where Samuel Phelps produced 34 of Shakespeare's plays in 1844–64. The 'well', discovered by Mr Sadler in 1684 and developed as a pleasure resort, still survives. Just beyond is *New River Head* the original end of the water-supply brought to London by Sir Hugh Myddelton in 1613. The office of the *Metropolitan Water Board* (1920) contains a room from the Water House of 1693.—Farther s.e., at *Mount Pleasant*, is the largest letter and parcel sorting office in the United Kingdom, built in 1900 on the site of the Coldbath House of Correction, a prison from 1794 to 1877.

The populous district of **Islington,** formerly noted for its dairy produce, lies mainly to the north of the Angel. It is again rapidly becoming a fashionable district and should be visited on account of its well-restored and elegant terraces and squares built from c. 1770 to c. 1830. *High Street* which leads due N., soon splits into the long, still drab *Liverpool Road* and *Upper Street*. Liverpool Rd. runs N.W. past Chapel Market (closed Mon) to Holloway. To the W. among interesting terraces and squares is Cloudesley Square with *Holy Trinity Church* in the centre, built by Barry in 1826 and inspired by King's College Chapel, Cambridge, To the N. is the collegiate-style Lonsdale Square by R. C. Carpenter (c. 1842–45). Parallel to Upper Street, where Kate Greenaway lived between c. 1851 and c. 1884, is *Camden Passage* (r.), the entrance to a flourishing antique furniture market (Wed and Sat) and an area of antique shops and good restaurants. Farther E. are the attractive Colebrooke Row and Duncan Terrace. Charles Lamb came to live at No. 64 Duncan Terrace in 1823 "never having had a house before". It was on leaving this house that his friend George Dyer walked into the New River and nearly drowned. The New River (comp. above) is now covered at this point; its course is indicated by the garden in front of Duncan Terrace. It is carried across Regent's Canal (also underground). The canal tunnel-mouth is seen from Noel Road (towpath to the E. to be opened to walkers).

At Islington Green Essex Road diverges N.E. On the Green is a statue of Sir Hugh Myddelton (d. 1631) who projected the New River scheme for supplying London with water (comp. above). We continue N. along Upper St. passing (r.) *St Mary's Church* with a tall tower and spire which remains from the previous church begun in 1754. The church was restored in 1962 and contains striking mural paintings. Behind the church, with entrance from Dagmar Passage off Cross St., is the *Little Angel Theatre*, the only permanent puppet theatre in England. On the other side of Upper St. is the King's Head (with a theatre which gives lunchtime and evening performances).

Beyond the Town Hall Canonbury Lane diverges right into the fashionable district of CANONBURY, with the charming Canonbury Square, begun in 1790. Farther on, fronting Canonbury Place (with stuccoed houses of c. 1770) is **Canonbury Tower,** a red brick tower 66 ft high and 17 ft square, the chief relic of a 16C house of the priors of St Bartholomew's. On the W. side are two old three-storied buildings, in the first of which are the beautiful oak-panelled Spencer Room and Compton Room. The house came into the possession of Sir John Spencer, Lord Mayor of London, in 1594–95, and in 1616–25 Sir Francis Bacon was the lessee of 'Canbury House'. In the 18C the buildings were let out in lodgings and among the noted people who stayed here was Oliver Goldsmith (in the Compton Room). The tower commands an extensive view, and behind it is a pleasant garden. The buildings (with the modern hall adjoining) are occupied by the Tower Theatre; visitors are admitted to the panelled rooms on application to the Warden. The old octagonal garden-houses that marked the s.e. and s.w. corners of the garden of the 16C house are still to be seen in Alwyne Villas (1824) and Alwyne Place (mostly late Georgian), to the s. From Alwyne Road the pleasant New River Walk leads to St Paul's Road.

Continuing along Upper St. past handsome Compton Terrace with the incongruous Victorian *Union Chapel* (it contains a piece of the rock upon which the Pilgrim Fathers landed from the 'Mayflower'), we come to *Highbury*. In Highbury Place (with fine terraces of c. 1774–79), on the s.e. side of Highbury Fields, Sickert had a studio at No. 1 and No. 25 was the frequent lodging of Wesley and was the residence of Joseph Chamberlain in 1845–54 (tablet). The attractive Highbury Terrace (1789) skirts the n. side of the Fields. Off Highbury Hill is the *Arsenal Football Ground*, removed here in 1913 from Woolwich, where it had been founded at the Royal Arsenal Factory in 1884 (whence the sobriquet, "the gunners").

From *Highbury and Islington Station* the wide Holloway Road leads to the n.w. through *Holloway*, with a well-known women's prison. It was built in 1852 by James Bunning as a House of Correction for the City. The 20 ft perimeter walls were demolished in 1971 at the beginning of a rebuilding scheme. To the w., in Caledonian Road, is *Pentonville Prison* built in 1840. Within this prison Roger Casement was hanged for high treason on 3 Aug 1916, the first person hanged in England for this offence since the execution of the Cato Street Conspirators in 1820. —On the opposite side of the road is the *Metropolitan Cattle Market* (closed) transferred hither from Smithfield in 1855, and occupying 50 acres in what was formerly Copenhagen Fields.

Buses 172 and 271 run along the Holloway Road to Highgate (Rte 46).

26 THE THAMES EMBANKMENT BETWEEN WESTMINSTER AND BLACKFRIARS

STATIONS: *Westminster, Charing Cross, Temple,* and *Blackfriars* on the Circle line; *Charing Cross* on the Bakerloo and Northern lines.—BUSES: Nos. 109, 155, 168, 172, 184 along the Embankment.

The **Victoria Embankment** (Pl. 15; 5, 4 & 8; 7) extends along the left bank of the Thames from Westminster Bridge to ($1\frac{1}{2}$ m.) Blackfriars Bridge. The first suggestion to embank the Thames here came from Sir Christopher Wren, but this notable improvement was made only in 1864–70 under the supervision of Sir Joseph Bazalgette (1819–91). The broad roadway, planted with trees and lined with gardens, affords a pleasant route for those driving or walking from Westminster to the City. The elaborate lamp-posts should be noted, and the benches are raised to provide a view of the activity on the river.

*Westminster Bridge, 810 ft long, a graceful structure built in 1862 by Thomas Page, spans the Thames from Westminster to Lambeth and commands beautiful views of the river, which here runs n. and s. At its w. end is a colossal group of Boadicea (Boudicca, queen of the Iceni) in her war-chariot, by Thomas Thornycroft (1902).

The bridge replaces an older stone bridge constructed in 1739–50, the view from which inspired Wordsworth's well-known sonnet (1802).—Just above the bridge are the Houses of Parliament (left bank), with their famous terrace, and the new St Thomas's Hospital, on the Albert Embankment (right bank). Just below the bridge, on the right bank, is the London County Hall.

From *Westminster Pier* (river launches, see p. 28), as we begin our walk along the Victoria Embankment, the wide curve of the Thames provides a fine view to the E. with the dome of St Paul's in the distance between the County Hall and the Festival Hall. On the left is the former NEW SCOTLAND YARD, saved from demolition in 1972, and beyond this, and backed by the huge Ministry of Defence building, is a garden containing 'Queen Mary's Terrace' (see p. 72), marking the 17C water-level of the Thames.

Here also is a statue of Lord Trenchard (d. 1956). On the right, the *Royal Air Force Memorial* (1923), by Sir Reginald Blomfield and Sir W. Reid Dick, is crowned by a golden eagle; and in the gardens beyond Horse Guards Avenue are statues of *William Tyndale* (c. 1484–1536), reformer and translator of the New Testament, and of *General Sir James Outram* (1803–63). Outside is a memorial to *Samuel Plimsoll* (1824–98), 'the seamen's friend'. The huge Renaissance pile behind these gardens includes *Whitehall Court* and the *National Liberal Club*, its pinnacles an integral part of any river view.

Beyond the gardens Northumberland Avenue comes in on the left and the railway (S.R.) is carried across the Thames by the *Charing Cross Railway Bridge* (1860–64), alongside which runs a separate footway, the 'Hungerford Foot Bridge' (built to provide access to the old Hungerford Market, comp. p. 192; now much used by concert-goers to the Festival Hall). On the river wall is a bust of Sir J. Bazalgette (see above). The Thames now bends round till it again flows from w. to E. Opposite Embankment Underground Station in the Embankment wall is a bronze medallion of *W. S. Gilbert* (1836–1911). To the left is the entrance to another section of the Embankment Gardens in which is the old Water Gate of York House (see p. 193).

The garden (café and 'amphitheatre') contains also statues or memorials of the *Imperial Camel Corps*; *Robert Burns* (1759–96); *Sir Wilfrid Lawson* (1829–1906), a noted temperance advocate; *Lord Cheylesmore* (1848–1925), another philanthropist; *Robert Raikes* (1735–1811), the founder of Sunday schools; and (outside the Savoy) *Sir Arthur Sullivan* (1842–1900), the composer. A tree was planted here to commemorate the coronation of Elizabeth II (1953).

On the left rises the massive river front of the Adelphi, while on the river side, opposite the middle of the gardens, stands **Cleopatra's Needle,** a monolith of pink granite (now cleaned of its coat of grime), 68½ ft in height and 180 tons in weight, erected here in 1878.

The obelisk, which has no connection with Cleopatra, was one of two erected at Heliopolis by Thothmes III, a sovereign of the 18th Dynasty (c. 1500 B.C.), and dedicated to Tum of Heliopolis. It was presented to the British nation by Mohammed Ali in 1819, but was not brought to England and erected on its present site until 1878. The inscriptions on the grey granite pedestal relate its history. The bronz sphinxes at its base, scarred by a bomb in 1917, were designed by G. Vulliamy. Companion obelisks are in Central Park, New York, and in the Place de la Concorde, Paris.

Opposite Cleopatra's Needle is the *Monument of Belgium's Gratitude* for British aid in 1914–18, designed by Sir R. Blomfield (1920), with sculptures by V. Rousseau (1919). Behind tower the many-windowed Shell-Mex House (1932), with a huge clock, and the Savoy Hotel.

We pass under ***Waterloo Bridge,** leading S.E. to Waterloo Station and the 'Elephant'. The original bridge, built by John Rennie in 1811–17, began to show signs of weakening in 1923; in 1934 the demolition of the old bridge began. The new bridge, by Sir Giles Scott, after having been in use for some time, was officially opened in November 1945. Near by a plaque commemorates Sir Walter Besant (1836–1901), historian of London. The 'Old Caledonia', a paddle steamer built in 1934, is moored here as a bar and restaurant.

Just below Waterloo Bridge are (r.) the floating Thames Police Station, and (l.) the *River Façade of *Somerset House* (restored), with its water-gate and fine terrace supported by arches. At the corner of Temple Place is a statue of *Isambard K. Brunel* (1805–59), engineer of the Thames Tunnel. In the river is moored 'Discovery', Scott's polar research ship, now a Royal Navy and Royal Marines recruiting vessel, and training ship for the Sea Cadet Corps (adm. daily 1–4.30). On the left, beyond *Temple Station*, a Tudor style (restored) mansion, built by J. L. Pearson (1895) for Lord Astor (d. 1919), now houses the International Telegraph office of the Post Office, and the Sheriff of London's office.

The gardens beyond the Temple Station contain a statue of *W. E. Forster* (1818–86), the statesman, and the feet of a stolen statue erected by the children of the Loyal Temperance Legion to Lady Henry Somerset. At the end stands *John Stuart Mill* (1806–73), the philosopher and economist.

On the river parapet opposite the E. end of the gardens are a memorial of *W. T. Stead* (1849–1912), the journalist; a tablet commemorating the naming (1935) of *King's Reach*, the stretch of the Thames between Westminster and London; and the *Submarine War Memorial* (1914–18).

On the left are the Temple Gardens (comp. p. 204), outside which two heraldic dragons (from the demolished Coal Exchange) mark the boundary of the 'City'. In the river are moored three ships: first the 'Wellington', serving as the livery hall of the Master Mariners' Company, then two training ships, the 'Chrysanthemum' and the 'President'. Farther on, near the bridge, the Gothic buildings of **Sion College and Library,** were designed by Sir Arthur Blomfield (1886) who incorporated the original timber roof from London Wall.

Sion College (adm. on application), founded in the City in 1624, exists for the benefit of the Anglican clergy. Its chief glory is the Library (300,000 vols.), which possesses many rarities, but suffered considerable war damage.—The City Livery Club is also accommodated here.—The Guildhall School of Music and Drama, in John Carpenter St., is to move to the Barbican.

The next large building is the *City of London School for Boys* (to be moved to the other side of Blackfriars Bridge), opened in 1837 in Milk St., and removed hither in 1883. Lord Asquith, Sir J. R. Seeley, and Sir F. Gowland Hopkins were educated at this school.—At the curved corner of the Embankment and New Bridge St. is the huge *Unilever House* (1932). The Embankment is continued by an underpass below Blackfriars Bridge into Upper Thames St. (see Rte 27B); beyond the bridges a spur (l.) joins Queen Victoria St. (Rte 27A).

Blackfriars Bridge (Pl. 8; 7), built in 1865–69 from the designs of J. Cubitt (on the site of an earlier structure of 1760–69), is 1270 ft in length. The huge cast-iron coats-of-arms of the South-Eastern and Chatham Railway on the adjacent railway bridge are impressive. At its N. end is a statue of Queen Victoria. New Bridge St. leads N. to Ludgate Circus (see p. 208) past the site of the notorious old prison of *Bridewell.*

Some kind of castle, taking its name from the holy well of St Bride (p. 208), and occasionally occupied by English sovereigns, stood here in early Norman times. Henry VIII restored it so as to form the 'stately and beautiful house' which was the residence of himself and Queen Catherine during the latter's trial. Edward VI granted it to the City of London, and in 1556 it became a prison for vagrants and immoral women. Partly destroyed in the Great Fire, it was rebuilt in 1668. New Bridewell, built in 1829, was pulled down in 1864.

27 BLACKFRIARS BRIDGE TO THE TOWER OF LONDON

A Viâ Queen Victoria Street, Cannon Street, and Eastcheap

STATIONS: *Blackfriars, Mansion House, Cannon Street* (closed at week-ends), and *Monument* on Circle and District line. BUSES: No. 76 in Queen Victoria St.; 513 past Cannon St. Station; 9A (Sun only) along Cannon St. to the Tower.—Car Parks, see Rte 27B.

QUEEN VICTORIA STREET (Pl. 8; 7), a wide thoroughfare about $\frac{3}{4}$ m. in length, leads E. from Blackfriars Bridge (p. 238) to the Mansion House. On the left beyond the railway bridge leading to Holborn Viaduct Stn. diverges Blackfriars Lane, in which stands the charming APOTHECARIES HALL, dating partly from 1670, partly from 1786, with portraits of James I, Charles I, John Keats (a licentiate of the Hall), and others.

The district of **Blackfriars**, N.E. of the bridge, was so called from the Dominicans who settled here in the 13C and erected extensive monastic buildings, of which there are now no visible vestiges. In the monastery, in 1382, an assembly condemned as heretical twenty-four Articles deduced from the teachings of Wyclif. It was here that a decree of divorce was pronounced against Queen Catherine of Aragon (1529; 'Henry VIII', ii. 4). In 1596 James Burbage established here the first covered theatre in London, in which Shakespeare (who owned a house in the district) in all probability acted. The name of *Playhouse Yard* commemorates its existence.

On the N. side of Queen Victoria St., in *Printing House Square*, so named from the King's Printing House erected here in 1667, 'The Times' newspaper was formerly printed. Just below the road (r.), in Puddle Dock, is the *Mermaid Theatre* (to be rebuilt). Here, by the river in 1963 a 2C Roman boat was uncovered. It had sunk with its cargo of building stone brought via the Medway from Maidstone to build the city walls (comp. p. 225).

Beyond Printing House Sq., on the N. side, is *St Andrew by the Wardrobe*, rebuilt by Wren in 1685–95, and restored in 1961 after serious war damage. It took its name from the proximity of the King's Great Wardrobe, used as an office for the keepers of the king's state apparel. At No. 146 is the house of the BRITISH AND FOREIGN BIBLE SOCIETY, founded in 1804 "to encourage a wider circulation of the Holy Scriptures, without note or comment". Visitors are admitted daily (except Sat), 10–4.30. The *Library*, perhaps the most polyglot room in the world, contains a priceless *Collection of versions of the Scriptures, in 1400 different tongues, including rare editions and copies of historic interest. – Next door is the *Faraday Building* (1933), the headquarters of the long-distance telephone service, the first building in the City allowed to go higher than the London Building Act then normally allowed, and thus the first obtrusive precursor of many into the city townscape. *Baynard House*, opposite, complements the work.

Across Godliman St. is the **College of Arms,** the seat of the official heraldic authority for England, Ireland, and the Commonwealth. The Heralds of the kings of England were first incorporated by Richard III in 1484, and in 1555 Queen Mary I gave them a new charter and the site of the present College.

The original building was burnt down in the Great Fire of 1666; the present one, by Maurice Emmett (1672–88), is a good example of the period. Splendid 19C wrought iron gates, apparently made for Goodrich Court, Herefordshire, were given to the College in 1956.

The Officers of Arms, who are members of the Royal Household, are still appointed directly by the Crown, by letters patent under the great seal, on the advice of the Duke of Norfolk as hereditary Earl Marshal. They consist of three kings of Arms (Garter, Clarenceux, and Norroy and Ulster), six heralds (Windsor, Lancaster, Somerset, York, Chester, and Richmond), and four pursuivants (Bluemantle, Portcullis, Rouge Croix, and Rouge Dragon). The titles of the heralds are taken from Royal duchies, earldoms and castles, while those of the pursuivants are taken from national badges (Rouge Croix), royal badges (Portcullis and Rouge Dragon), and the blue mantle of the Order of the Garter. For many centuries the kings of arms have been authorized by the sovereigns to grant arms to eminent men, subject to the approval of the earl marshal.

The heraldic and genealogical records and collections are unique, and the registers of recorded pedigrees include many pedigrees of families who have settled in the Commonwealth and America.—The College, not being supported by public funds, is open to visitors by appointment only (Mon–Fri, 10–4) with the Officer in waiting. Fees may be charged for work undertaken.—A *Museum of Heraldry*, to be built to the E. of the College, will exhibit some of its treasures. Here a processional way has been opened up to St Paul's (comp. p. 215).

In Bennet's Hill, to the s. (footpath), is the now isolated brick church of *St Benet* (restored after damage by arson in 1971). It was rebuilt by Wren in 1677–83, and is now used by a Welsh congregation. Henry Fielding was married here in 1748 and Inigo Jones (1573–1652) was buried in the earlier church.

On the s. side of Queen Victoria St. is the international headquarters (1962) of the *Salvation Army*, founded by William Booth, a methodist, in 1865. A Christian movement organized in a quasi-military style, it is concerned with all in need. Beyond, on the left, is the church of *St Nicholas Cole Abbey* (originally 'Cold Abbey'), rebuilt by Wren in 1671–77 and reopened in 1963 after being burnt out in 1941. A striking feature of the interior is the richly coloured glass of the E. windows, by Keith New. The font and the ornamental woodwork were saved; and behind a panel on the s. wall is a sculptured head from the medieval church.

In Bread St., to the E., the tower of *St Mildred's* was recently demolished. The church (1677–83, by Wren), where Shelley and Mary Godwin were married in 1816, had been destroyed in the last war. A memorial to Adm. Phillip (1738–1814), governor of the first colony of British settlers in Australia (1788), who was born in Bread Street, has been moved farther N. to Gateway House in Cannon St.

Queen Victoria St. now intersects the wide Cannon St. (view left to St Paul's) close to Beaver House (Rte 27B). To the N. is the church of *St Mary Aldermary*, so called, says Stow, because "elder than any church of St Marie in the City". It was rebuilt by Wren after 1681 (tower 1704). The plaster fan-vaulting is especially noteworthy. Milton married his third wife, Elizabeth Minshull, in the old church (1663). Beyond Queen St. is the huge *Bucklersbury House* (1958) occupying most of the triangle (r.) between Queen Victoria St., Cannon St., and Walbrook. In the forecourt of Temple House on a platform are the remains of a TEMPLE OF MITHRAS, unearthed in 1954 beneath the foundations of Bucklersbury House, about 80 yds to the S.E., adjoining Walbrook. Built shortly before A.D. 200, it is 58½ ft long and 26 ft wide and has the triple w. end characteristic of Mithraic temples; the bases of two rows of pillars and the walls supporting them have survived. The important sculptural finds from the site are now in the Museum of London.

CANNON STREET (Pl. 8; 8) continues E. through an area once occupied by wax-chandlers; its name is a corruption of Candlewick Street. The *London Chamber of Commerce* (1934; l.) stands at the corner of Queen Street. In Dowgate Hill, just before Cannon St. Station, are the decorative entrances to the halls of the *Tallow Chandlers* (No. 4), the *Skinners* (No. 8), and the *Dyers* (No. 10), the first two rebuilt soon after the Great Fire.

Cannon Street Station (Pl. 9; 7) has been rebuilt except for its decorative riverside turrets. Beneath Bush Lane House excavations in 1965 revealed traces of a Governor's Palace built c. A.D. 80–100 beside the mouth of the Walbrook stream, overlooking the Thames. At a lower level timber foundation suggested this was the earlier site of a Roman fort. Opposite is the *Bank of China*, built on the site of *St Swithin's*, a church rebuilt by Wren and destroyed in 1940–41 (the churchyard is now a garden in Salters' Hall court). Immured in the wall of the bank is LONDON STONE, generally believed to have been the Milliarium of Roman London, from which the distances on the Roman high roads were measured. This is the stone which Jack Cade struck with his staff, exclaiming, "Now is Mortimer Lord of this City". In St Swithin's Lane is *Founders' Hall* (No. 13).

In Abchurch Yard, off Abchurch Lane, the next side-street to the left, stands *St Mary Abchurch* (i.e. 'up' church, from its high site), rebuilt by Wren in 1681–86, containing wood carvings by Grinling Gibbons (open 10–4, Mon–Fri). The dome, with its paintings by William Snow (1708), is an architectural tour de force; considerably damaged in Sept 1940, it has been finely restored (1948–53). The 14C crypt is plain and vaulted. To the S., in Laurence Pountney Hill, two houses (Nos. 1 and 2) survive from 1703.

Cannon St. ends at a busy crossroads where King William St. converges with Gracechurch St. and Eastcheap, on a site believed to have been occupied by the 'Boar's Head Tavern' where Falstaff and Prince Hal caroused. *St Clement Eastcheap*, to the N., was rebuilt by Wren in 1683–87. It contains a handsome carved pulpit, possibly by Grinling Gibbons, and font-cover, and a fine organ of 1695.

We continue E. along Eastcheap past the church of *St Margaret Pattens* (restored 1956), built by Wren in 1684–87, with a fine tall spire. It is thought to be named from the pattens (shoes with iron rings attached to the soles to protect the wearer from muddy roads) once made and sold in the lane. The font and the reredos are fine works; the altarpiece is by Carlo Maratti. The two canopied pews are unique in London.

The S. pew has on its ceiling the engraved monogram C.W.; possibly Christopher Wren himself occupied this pew. North of the altar is the original Beadle's pew and a punishment bench. The church is a Christian Study Centre, with conference rooms in the gallery.

Great Tower Street continues E. to Tower Place (Rte 28).

B Viâ Thames Street

STATIONS and BUSES, see Rte 27A; CAR PARKS in Queen St. (Southwark Bridge), and Upper Thames St. (near London Br.).

UPPER THAMES STREET, realined as a dual carriageway extension of the Embankment, passes in a covered cutting through a complex of large buildings still in construction, which for c. 300 yds cut off the river from the scarp that rises steeply to St Paul's. Among these buildings will be the new City of London School for Boys.

On foot, the pleasantest way on a fine day is by an embanked walk fashioned along the Thames since 1967. Though the most imposing building on the opposite bank is Bankside Power Station (p. 266), the open river ahead to Tower Bridge is not without charm and the dome of St Paul's rides high on the left. The principal feature of interest will, it is hoped, be the remains of *Baynard's Castle* fronting the river.

During reconstruction in 1972, part of the castle was temporarily exposed. The castle was first built by William the Conqueror, and named after a follower. When the Dominicans took over the area (now Blackfriars) in 1278, a second castle was built a little to the E. A 15C successor to this castle was uncovered including the prominent towers and wall along the old line of the river (shown in Hollar's 'View of London'). The castle, which extended to the N. of Thames St., was destroyed in the Great Fire, and warehouses (often following the line of the old walls) were built on the site. It is hoped that the castle will be exposed permanently in the precinct of the school.

The footway ends at the whitewashed *Sunlight Wharf*, whence High Timber St. joins Upper Thames St. on its ancient line just E. of the tower of *St Mary Somerset*. The rest of the church, built by Wren in 1695, was taken down in 1871.

Although warehouses have been pulled down and many of the wharves are disused, some narrow lanes bearing historic names still run down to steps into the Thames, and the road is busy with lorries coming from the docks farther down the river. In a lane (r.) the quaint Samuel Pepys Tavern occupies a 19C warehouse. Queensbridge House and Queen's Quay (flats) have superseded *Queenhithe Dock*, once an important harbour for the City, the property of Isabella of Angoulême, and the earliest fish market in London. From the evocative cobbled lane to the E. its shape and extent are still apparent. VINTNERS' HALL, near the corner of Queen St., was rebuilt in 1671, after the Great Fire, though the Court Room (1446; panelled in 1576) was preserved. The company, incorporated in 1437, owns valuable tapestries and a painting of St Martin, by the School of Rubens (adm. see p. 199). In Vintners Lane a statue of a Vintry Ward school boy (1840), in Coade stone, survives.

The picturesque Garlick Hill (N.), devoted to the fur trade, affords a view of the tower of St Mary le Bow. Here the church of *St James Garlickhithe* (open Mon–Fri 10–3, and for services) is so called, according to Stow, because garlick was sold on the Thames near by. The attractive steeple, attributed to Hawksmoor, dates from 1714–17. The interior, by Wren (1676–83), with good wood-carving and ironwork, and an organ attributed to Father Smith (1697), has been pleasingly restored. Between the two lanes to the w. lies the *Hall of the Painter-Stainers* (adm. see p. 199), rebuilt after the Great Fire of 1666, restored after damage in 1941, and extended in 1961. A stone's throw N. is *Beaver House* of the Hudson's Bay Company.

Queen St. (r.) forms the approach to SOUTHWARK BRIDGE (Pl. 8; 8), originally the work of John Rennie in 1813–19 but entirely rebuilt in 1913–21 (good view of the river). Beyond Queen St., on the N. side of Upper Thames St., Whittington Gardens commemorate Richard ('Dick') Whittington (d. 1423), three times Mayor of London, who lived in College Hill (named from a college he founded), to the N. He rebuilt and was buried in *St Michael Paternoster Royal* (closed at weekends), again rebuilt by Wren in 1686–94, with a steeple of 1713. It was beautifully restored (with fine windows by John Hayward) and rededicated in 1968 as the chapel and headquarters (offices in the tower) of the Missions to Seamen, a society "ministering to the needs of seamen throughout the world".

We now pass under Cannon St. railway bridge. Beyond Mondial House, the new International Telephone Centre, Angel Passage or Swan Lane lead (r.) to a terrace overlooking the Thames. Here, opposite the graceful pinnacles of Southwark Cathedral, the moored paddle steamer 'Princess Elizabeth', now a tavern, affords a fine view of London Bridge. **London Bridge** (Pl. 9; 7) was rebuilt in 1967–73 by Harold Knox King, remaining open to traffic throughout the operation. Borne on three arches of pre-stressed concrete faced with granite, it is 105 ft wide. The former bridge, designed by John Rennie, begun in 1825 by his sons John and George

Rennie, and completed in 1831, was sold for £1,025,000. It was dismantled into 10,000 granite slabs which were numbered and shipped to Lake Havasu City, Arizona, where it was re-erected over an artificial lake.

A wooden bridge across the Thames existed by the 1C A.D. This probably survived until 1176, having been repaired by the Saxons. The popular rhyme 'London Bridge is broken down' may date from this time, when it was resolved to 'Build it up with stone so strong'. The new bridge, about 100 ft w. of the old, was begun in 1176 by Peter of Colechurch, at the instance of Henry II, but it was not completed till 1209 in the reign of King John. It stood close to the w. end of the church of St Mary Magnus. Rows of wooden houses sprang up on each side, and in the middle was a chapel dedicated to St Thomas Becket. At each end stood a fortified gate, on the spikes of which the heads of traitors were exposed. It was notoriously difficult to navigate because of the narrow passage between the starlings and the force of the ebb tide. After a fire in 1758 the houses were demolished and the bridge partly reconstructed and opened in 1763. This bridge, the only bridge over the Thames until 1729, was removed after the completion of Rennie's bridge 100 ft upstream.

London Bridge divides the Thames into 'above' and 'below' bridge. Downstream is the Port of London, the reach immediately adjacent to the bridge being known as the *Pool*, while upstream is the *King's Reach*.

FISHMONGERS HALL stands at the N. end of London Bridge (entrance from the viaduct across Upper Thames St. which carries King William St. on to London Bridge). With a fine classical façade on the river, it was erected in 1831–34 by Henry Roberts and Gilbert Scott. It was badly damaged in September 1940, when it was the first of the City Halls to catch fire; similarly, a previous Fishmongers' Hall on this site was the first to burn during the Great Fire of 1666.

The Fishmongers' Company is one of the richest as well as one of the oldest of the twelve great livery companies. Its origin is lost in remote antiquity, but it is unquestionable that the Company existed before the reign of Henry II. The fine interior (adm. see p. 199) has been restored in its former style. It contains the Annigoni portrait (1955) of Queen Elizabeth II (the model for stamps and bank-notes), a painted wooden figure of Sir William Walworth, the Mayor who killed Wat Tyler in 1381, and a fine dagger he is supposed to have used; also a richly embroidered pall of the Tudor period.

On the other side of London Bridge we enter LOWER THAMES STREET, which retains its cobbled surface and is redolent of fish from end to end. Geoffrey Chaucer is said to have lived in this street from 1379 to 1385, during part of which period he was Comptroller of the Petty Customs in the Port of London. On the right is *St Magnus Martyr* (open Tues–Fri 10.30–4, Sat 2–4, Sun 10.30–12.30), rebuilt by Wren in 1671–76. The *Steeple, 185 ft high, one of Wren's masterpieces, was not completed till 1705. The passage beneath the tower was from 1763 to 1832 part of the footpath of Old London Bridge. Miles Coverdale (d. 1569), author of the first complete English version of the Bible (1535), was rector of St Magnus in 1563–66 and is buried in the church.

To the N., at the top of Fish Street Hill, rises the **Monument,** a fluted Doric column, 202 ft high, erected from the designs of Wren in 1671–77, to commemorate the Great Fire of London, which broke out on 2 Sept 1666, in Pudding Lane, at a point alleged to be exactly 202 ft from the Monument. A winding staircase of 311 steps (open weekdays 9–4 or 6, Sun in summer 2–6) ascends to the upper gallery, which commands a wide and striking view. The flaming gilt urn surmounting the Monument is 42 ft high. The cage enclosing the gallery was added to prevent suicides. The allegorical relief by C. G. Cibber shows Charles II and the Duke of York encouraging the stricken city.

The falsehood of the inscription of 1681 (removed in 1831), attributing the fire to the 'Popish faction', gave rise to Pope's familiar lines:

> 'Where London's column, pointing at the skies,
> Like a tall bully, lifts the head and lies'.

A little farther on is **Billingsgate Market**, the chief fish-market of London, taking its name from an old gate, supposed to be called after Belin, a legendary king of the Britons. It claims to be the only market in which every variety of fish is sold—'wet, dried, and shell'.

Billingsgate Wharf, said to be the oldest on the river, was used from very early times (perhaps from the 9C) as a landing-place for fishing boats and other small vessels; fish are no longer brought to market by water. The daily market, beginning at 6 a.m., presents a very busy and interesting scene, when up to 300 tons of fish are handled in c. 3 hrs. The curious leathern hats of the fish-porters should be noticed. The word 'Billingsgate' as a synonym for coarse language is an aspersion on the fish-porters that is alleged to have passed long since into the domain of pointless slander.

The narrow Lovat Lane, opposite Billingsgate leads N. to the church of *St Mary at Hill* built by Wren in 1670–76. The woodwork is noteworthy, and the church is filled with box pews. The sword rests are exceptionally fine, and the organ by William Hill was rebuilt in 1971. The ceiling dates from 1849. The Dickensian atmosphere of the neighbouring passages is being conserved. A narrow passage (with a quaint warning to fishmongers) skirts the church on the s. and emerges beneath a grim gateway surmounted by a skull and crossbones in St Mary at Hill. Here (r.) is the attractive *Hall of the Watermen and Lightermen* (1776–80). At the corner of St Mary at Hill and Lower Thames St. a *Roman Bath* was discovered in 1969 which belonged to a private house of c. A.D. 200. Finds on the site showed the house to have been occupied until the second half of the 5C (adm. on application to the Director of the Guildhall Museum).

Beyond Billingsgate is the **Custom House**, a large classical edifice (1814–26), the fine river façade of which is well seen from London Bridge. St Dunstan's Hill, opposite, leads up to the church of *St Dunstan in the East*, rebuilt in 1671 by Wren, who added the fine square lantern tower in 1698. The body of the church was severely damaged in 1941; the shell remains and has been beautifully planted by the Worshipful Company of Gardeners as a public garden. A fig tree commemorating the coronation of George VI in 1937 survives outside the s. wall. In Idol Lane (N.) a wine merchant occupies a fine Georgian house. Harp Lane, a little farther on, contains the new *Bakers' Hall* (No. 9; 1963) with windows by John Piper commemorating the burning of the former halls.

The wide Tower Place diverges N., while pedestrians may continue along Lower Thames St. which ends at Tower Hill.

28   THE TOWER AND TOWER HILL

STATION: *Tower Hill* on Circle and District line.—On Sun BUS 9A runs from the West End through the City to the Tower.—CAR PARK in Tower Hill (Royal Mint St.).

MOTOR LAUNCHES on the Thames in summer run between *Westminster Pier* and *Tower Pier* (in 20 min; 50p return). The service, every 20 min., begins at 11.20 a.m. From 1 March–31 Oct a skeleton service is maintained.

The ****Tower of London** (Pl. 21; 2), a fortress of surpassing interest from its intimate connection with English history, the excellent preservation of its Norman and medieval buildings, and the many illustrious persons who have suffered within its walls, occupies a site astride the old city wall and covers an area of nearly 18 acres. The outer wall is surrounded by a deep *Moat* (drained in 1843; now beautifully planted as a public garden). Between the outer wall and the inner wall lies the narrow *Outer Ward*, and near the centre of the spacious *Inner Ward* rises the massive square *White Tower*. The entrance is near the s.w. corner, at the foot of Tower Hill.

ADMISSION. The Tower is open Mon–Sat in March–Oct, 9.30–5, and in Nov–Feb, 9.30–4. It is open on Sun in March–Oct, 2–5. It remains closed on Sun in winter, Christmas Day, Boxing Day, and Good Friday. Admission, including the White Tower, Beauchamp Tower, Bloody Tower, and New Armouries (winter 1977), 20p; for the Jewel House, 10p, for Regimental Museum, 5p; children always half price. Summer charges will be considerably higher in 1978.

Long queues for admission may be experienced in summer (especially on Sun). Yeoman Warders give frequent guided tours on fine days which begin at the Bell Tower, and include the Chapel Royal of St Peter ad Vincula (otherwise kept locked; but the Sun services at 9.30 and 11 are open to the public). The *Ceremony of the Keys*, when the main gates of the Tower are locked, takes place nightly at 9.40 p.m. For admission, apply in writing to the Resident Governor.

The Tower, in its day a fortress, a royal residence, and a state-prison, is still maintained as an arsenal, with a garrison, and during the World Wars its former use as a prison was revived. The Constable of the Tower, always an officer of high dignity, is assisted by the Lieutenant; the duties of governor are now performed by the Major of the Tower, who is Resident Governor. Quite distinct from the garrison are the *Yeoman Warders* ('honorary members of the Queen's Bodyguard of the Yeomen of the Guard'), a body of about 40 men chosen from time-expired warrant and non-commissioned officers of the army. They wear historic costume, said to date from the time of Henry VII or Edward VI and are familiarly known as 'Beefeaters', a sobriquet probably derived from the rations anciently served to them.

HISTORY. The White Tower, the oldest part of the fortress, dates from the reign of the Conqueror, when the Roman Wall formed the E. boundary of the precinct. Of Richard I's additions only some work in the Bell Tower remains, and it was in the reign of Henry III (1216–72) that the 'small castle' was turned into a great concentric fortress. The outer curtain and the moat were added in 1275–85 by Edward I.

Built by William to overawe the citizens of London, the Tower has never been seriously assaulted, and its gloomy history is more that of a state-prison than of a fortress. Sir William Wallace (executed in 1305), King David II of Scotland (1346–57), and King John of France (1356–60) were confined here under Edward I and Edward III. James I of Scotland spent part of his long imprisonment in England (1406–24) at the Tower. In the same century the Tower witnessed the secret murders of Henry VI (1471), of the Duke of Clarence, brother of Edward IV (1478), and of Edward V and his brother, 'the little Princes in the Tower' (?1483). Henry VIII (1509–47) was here married to Catherine of Aragon and to Anne Boleyn; and here Anne Boleyn, after a trial in the Great Hall of the palace, was beheaded in 1536. Other victims in this reign were Bishop Fisher and Sir Thomas More (both beheaded 1535) and Queen Catherine Howard (beheaded 1542). Among the many prisoners of Mary's reign (1553–58) were Lady Jane Grey and her husband, Lord Guildford Dudley (both beheaded 1554), Elizabeth (afterwards queen), who was rigidly confined for two months; Cranmer and Sir Thomas Wyatt (beheaded 1554), by whose followers the Tower had been attacked, for the last time in its history. In Elizabeth's reign the Duke of Norfolk, who was beheaded in 1572 for intriguing in favour of Mary Queen of Scots, and the Earl of Essex (beheaded 1601) were imprisoned here. James I (1603–25) was the last monarch who resided in the Tower. Sir Walter Raleigh was thrice confined in the Tower—in 1592, in 1603–16, and again in 1618, just before his execution. In 1605–06 Guy Fawkes and his companions were tortured in the dungeons of the White Tower. The Earl of Strafford and Abp. Laud both passed through the Tower to the scaffold (in 1641 and 1645), followed, after the Restoration, by Viscount Stafford (1680), Lord William Russell (1683), and the Duke of Monmouth (1685). Charles II (1660–85), who here passed the night before his coronation in 1661, was the last monarch to sleep at the Tower. Lord Lovat, one of the prisoners brought to the Tower after the Jacobite risings of

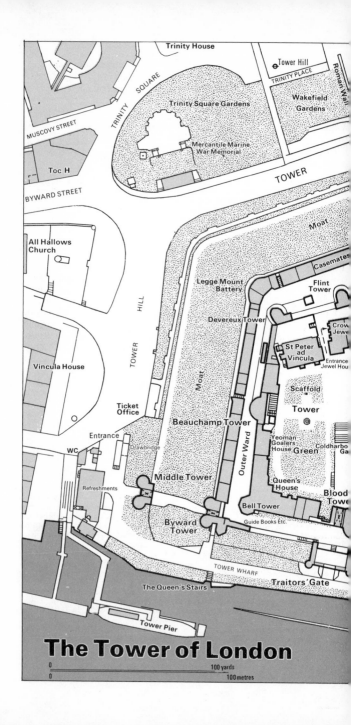

Trinity House

Tower Hill

TRINITY PLACE

Roman Wall

TRINITY SQUARE

Trinity Square Gardens

Wakefield Gardens

MUSCOVY STREET

Mercantile Marine War Memorial

Toc H

TOWER

BYWARD STREET

Moat

Casemates

All Hallows Church

Legge Mount Battery

Flint Tower

Devereux Tower

Crown Jewels

St Peter ad Vincula

Entrance Jewel House

TOWER HILL

Vincula House

Scaffold

Tower

Ticket Office

Beauchamp Tower

Outer Ward

Yeoman Goalers House

Coldharbour Gate

Green

Entrance

Drawbridge

WC

Middle Tower

Queen's House

Refreshments

Bell Tower

Blood Tower

Byward Tower

Guide Books Etc.

TOWER WHARF

Traitors' Gate

The Queen's Stairs

Tower Pier

The Tower of London

0   100 yards

0   100 metres

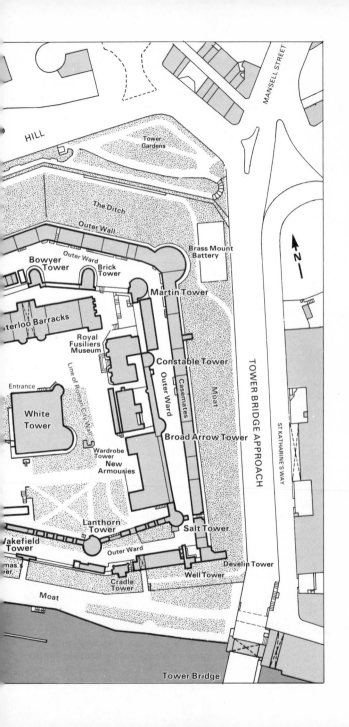

MANSELL STREET

HILL

Tower Gardens

The Ditch

Outer Wall

Outer Ward

Bowyer Tower

Brick Tower

Brass Mount Battery

Martin Tower

Waterloo Barracks

Royal Fusiliers Museum

Constable Tower

Outer Ward

Casemates

Moat

TOWER BRIDGE APPROACH

ST KATHARINE'S WAY

N

Entrance

Line of Roman City Wall

White Tower

Broad Arrow Tower

Wardrobe Tower

New Armouries

Lanthorn Tower

Salt Tower

Wakefield Tower

Outer Ward

Develin Tower

Thomas's Tower

Cradle Tower

Well Tower

Moat

Tower Bridge

1715 and 1745, was the last person beheaded in England (1747). Later prisoners in the Tower were John Wilkes (1763), Lord George Gordon (1780), Sir Francis Burdett (1810), and the Cato Street conspirators (1820). During the two World Wars several spies met their doom within its walls.

The modern entrance bridge passes over the pit of the *Drawbridge* built by Edward I. On the right is a café-restaurant, on the site of the former Lion Tower, where the King's menagerie was kept until 1834. Started by a gift of leopards from Frederick of Hohenstaufen to Henry III, and augmented in 1255 by an elephant from St Louis of France, the collection finally formed the nucleus of the London Zoo. The tame ravens which haunt the inner ward are perhaps a relic of this collection. Beyond is Tower Wharf (comp. p. 251) with alternative entrances to the Tower through the walls (tickets must first be purchased outside the railings on Tower Hill). We pass through the *Middle Tower* (also built by Edward I) and cross over the *Moat* to the *Byward Tower* (late 13C; 14C additions). Opposite us rises the *Bell Tower* (late 12C), the prison of Fisher, More, and Monmouth, where curfew is still rung at sunset. We follow the *Outer Ward* or *Outer Bail* (comp. the Plan) to the E. On our right, farther on, is *St Thomas's Tower*, above the *Traitors' Gate*, the old water-gate, through which many illustrious prisoners little deserving the name of traitor have entered the Tower. Both tower and gateway date from Edward I's reign. Opposite are the Bloody Tower and the *Wake-field Tower* (c. 1225; closed), traditionally thought to be the murdering place of Henry VI in 1471. We pass under the Bloody Tower (p. 250) into the *Inner Ward*, dominated by the White Tower. On the right of the ascent is a portion of the medieval wall of the Inner Bailey, and part of Coldharbour Gate (1240).

The *White Tower, the oldest part of the whole fortress, was begun about 1078 for William the Conqueror, by Gundulf, the builder also of Rochester Cathedral. It stands on a slope and rises to a height of 90 ft on the s. side. It measures 118 ft from E. to w., 107 ft from N. to s., and has walls 12–15 ft thick. The exterior was restored by Wren, who altered all the windows but four on the s. side; but the interior is still very much as it was in Norman times. Beneath an external staircase on the s. side, removed during the restoration, the bones of the Little Princes (see p. 56) were found 1674.

We ascend the external staircase at the N.E. corner to the FIRST FLOOR. The interior contains a magnificent *Collection of arms and armour started by Henry VIII and first concentrated here for display by Charles II.

The first gallery shows *Hunting and Sporting Weapons* from the cross-bow to the elephant gun. – The *Tournament Gallery* contains superbly displayed and labelled exhibits which include: armour made for the Court of Emperor Maximilian I (Innsbruck, c. 1490); a suit made in Augsburg, c. 1590; great wood saddle covered in rawhide (German, late 15C); half-armour made for the Elector Christian I of Saxony (1591). Most of the arms and armour for jousting was made at Greenwich (c. 1610–25), and at Augsburg (16–17C). To the s. the *Crypt* of St John's Chapel houses fascinating relics of exhibitions mounted in the past: Wooden heads and horses (one carved by Grinling Gibbons) used for the 'line of Kings' set up in armour in 1680; supposed trophies from the Armada; Jacobite trophies from Culloden; case of Victorian 'medieval' forgeries. Near the E. end is the small cell in which Raleigh is said to have spent his final term of imprisonment.

We ascend to the BANQUETING FLOOR, and enter *St John's Chapel, the oldest church in London and a splendid example of pure Norman architecture. Henry IV created 46 Knights here in 1399, and the institution of the Order of the Bath remains closely connected with the Chapel. The further gallery displays arms and armour from Anglo-Saxon times to the 15C. Also displayed here is a MS. volume on the Making of Gunpowder and its use in the late Middle Ages (German, c. 1450). At the end of the room is one of about 5 surviving examples of complete Gothic armour for the horse (German, c. 1480). The adjoining gallery displays 16C armour, a superb array including an astonishing suit for a giant.

On the third or COUNCIL FLOOR are the *Armouries, a collection from the English Royal Armour Workshop founded by Henry VIII at Greenwich, which operated from 1511 to 1642.

On the r. of the entrance, Grotesque helmet presented to Henry VIII by Maximilian I (1514, Innsbruck); horse armour traditionally thought to be a present from Maximilian to Henry (1515, Flemish); armour, including magnificent horse armour, made for Henry at Greenwich (1520–35); the suits of Robert Dudley, Earl of Leicester, and of William Somerset, 3rd Earl of Worcester, both made at Greenwich (1575); and a German suit with English decoration (c. 1580) made for Sir John Smythe. – The adjoining room displays infantry arms and armour of the 17C (including fabric and leather buff coats). Also, two suits probably made for Charles II (1640, and 1643, ?French); and armour belonging to James II.

From the Council Floor 114 steps descend to the DUNGEONS, where 16–19C weapons are displayed, including bronze mortars and cannon. In the Cannon Room, with a well 40 ft deep, are bronze guns cast for Henry VIII, and many others, some of which are trophies of war.

The *Sub-Crypt* of St John's Chapel, is entered by a doorway traditionally regarded as the cell called 'Little Ease', where Guy Fawkes was confined, tied by his ankles and wrists to a ring in the floor.

To the N. of the White Tower is the long range of *Waterloo Barracks*, built by the Duke of Wellington (1845); in the w. wing ***Crown Jewels** have been displayed since 1967. The ancient regalia were dispersed during the Commonwealth, and in consequence the present regalia date mostly from the Restoration when they were first publicly exhibited for a fee. The first room contains 19C banqueting *Plate*; silver gilt *Maces*; the *Great Sword of State* (1678; used at the opening of Parliament); insignia of the various *Orders of Knighthood*; silver State *Trumpets*; and the robes worn at Coronations since 1821.

We descend to the vaults protecting the CROWN JEWELS. The *Sword of Spiritual Justice*; *Sovereign's Sceptre with Dove*, called also the Rod of Equity and Mercy; the *Sword of Temporal Justice*.—The *Exeter Salt* and the *Plymouth Wine Fountain* were accession gifts to Charles II.—Orbs made for Charles II and Mary II are displayed near the *Crown of Queen Elizabeth*, consort of George VI, with the famous Koh-i-Noor diamond, a spoil from the fall of Lahore presented to Queen Victoria in 1850 by the East India Company. – The *Queen Elizabeth Salt* dates from 1572–73; the font (1660) was first used for George IV's christening. – Jewelled *State Sword*, made for George IV; *St Edward's Crown*, made for Charles II. – The *Imperial State Crown*, made for Queen Victoria's coronation, set with innumerable gems, including the large uncut ruby given to the Black Prince by Pedro the Cruel in 1367 and worn by Henry V at Agincourt, and one of the 'Stars of Africa' (317 carats), cut from the 'Cullinan' diamond, and worn by Queen Elizabeth II at her Coronation; *Sovereign's Sceptre with Cross*, containing the largest of the 'Stars of Africa' (530 carats), the largest cut diamond in the world; the *Coronation Ring* made for William IV. – The *Anointing Spoon*, of the late 12C, and the *Ampulla*, in the shape of an eagle, which dates probably from Henry IV (both restored for Charles

II), are the only relics of the ancient regalia. – The *Maundy Dish* holds the Maundy money distributed by the sovereign on Thurs in Holy Week. – The display ends with the *Curtana* or point-less *Sword of Mercy*.

Outside Waterloo Barracks, to the w., lies Tower Green. A brass plate marks the *Site of the Scaffold.* Here suffered Anne Boleyn (1536), Catherine Howard (1542), Lady Jane Grey (1554), and the Earl of Essex (1601). – To the n. is the *Chapel Royal of St Peter ad Vincula* (adm. see above), rebuilt by 1307 and restored in 1512, and again in 1971.

Within the altar rails are buried Anne Boleyn, Catherine Howard, Lady Jane Grey, Essex, Monmouth, and other illustrious victims. In the crypt lie St John Fisher, Sir Thomas More (bust by Raphael Maklouf, 1970), and the Jacobite lords executed in 1746–47; and there are many more recent memorials to distinguished soldiers. In the n. aisle is the sumptuous monument of the Duke of Exeter (1447), formerly in St Katharine's, Regent's Park.

Across Tower Green is the semicircular *Beauchamp Tower* (1281). The walls are covered with inscriptions and carvings by former prisoners, many brought here from other parts of the Tower. On the first floor are displayed some Roman tiles, etc. and medieval pottery found in the Tower. In the adjoining *Yeoman Gaoler's House* Lady Jane Grey was imprisoned; more recently Rudolf Hess was incarcerated here (May 1941). The top of the wall behind is *Princess Elizabeth's Walk.*

In the s.w. corner of the Green is the unpretentious Tudor *Queen's House* (no adm.), the residence of the Governor, incorporating the Bell Tower. In the council chamber of this house Guy Fawkes and his accomplices were examined in 1605. Adacent is the *Bloody Tower* (begun probably by Henry III as a water-gate and completed by Edward I). Its portcullis is still in working order. This tower was the prison of Cranmer, Raleigh, and Laud, and of Judge Jeffreys, who died here of delirium tremens in 1689. Instruments of torture are displayed on the ground floor. The winding staircase ascends to the room in which the Little Princes are said to have been smothered by order of Sir James Tyrrell at the instigation of Richard III. From the passage outside this room we emerge on *Raleigh's Walk*, where Sir Walter, during his second imprisonment, was permitted to take the air.

On the opposite side of the Inner Bailey is the *Regimental Museum of the Royal Fusiliers* (the City of London Regiment), containing uniforms, medals, equipment and relics relating to the history of the Regiment from 1685 to the present day (hand-sheet in entrance hall).

We skirt the e side of the White Tower, passing the scanty remains of the *Wardrobe Tower* (late-12C), built against the Roman city wall, of which a fragment adjoins. Beyond, in an attractive late 17C building are the New Armouries (closed in 1977). These comprise armour and weapons from oriental sources (splendid Indian elephant's armour), as well as weapons of primitive peoples. – Opposite, a new History Gallery was opened in 1978.

The tour of the Outer Ward towers (at present closed for repairs; normally application should be made to the Resident Governor) starts at the *Byward Tower*, on the second floor of which an early 14C wall-painting of the Last Judgment was discovered in 1953, then proceeds to the n.e. part of the ward, where several German spies were shot. In the *Bowyer Tower* the duke of Clarence is said to have been drowned in a butt of malmsey in 1478. Entering the interesting *Martin Tower*, the scene of Col. Blood's bold and nearly successful attempt to carry off the state crown (1671), the visit traverses the bailey wall and the *Constable, Broad Arrow,* and *Salt Towers* (the last with interesting inscriptions by prisoners), and ends at the Lanthorn Tower.

Tower Wharf (open daily), between the Tower and the river, with some old cannon, affords a good view of the river and its shipping. Here royal salutes are fired by the H.A.C. (see p. 234) on state occasions. The foreshore has been arranged as a play-beach for children. H.M.S. 'Belfast' (p. 279) is prominent.

A visit to the other buildings on Tower Hill is at present hampered by the intrusion of busy traffic thoroughfares and much rebuilding. As we leave the tower, we may avoid the lifeless raised piazza on our left, and cross instead a small area beyond, often used by a Londoner to 'air a grievance', and so reach the church of **All Hallows by the Tower,** the successor of a church founded in the 7C and committed to the care of the Abbess of Barking. Most of the main fabric of the church (15C; with 12C portions) was destroyed by enemy action in the last war, but the brick tower from which Pepys surveyed the progress of the Great Fire, the only example of Cromwellian church architecture in London, has survived. It is now surmounted by a beautiful spire, in the Wren manner, by Lord Mottistone and Paul Paget (1958), who have successfully re-built the church. Saxon work is visible in the lower portion of the tower and the clearance of bomb damage has revealed an important Saxon arch. This is set in the N. wall of the approach from the nave to the new baptistery (1960), which contains a font hewn from the rock of Gibraltar, with the beautiful, elaborately carved wooden font-cover by Grinling Gibbons (1682). The tombs and the fine series of brasses in the sanctuary survived. In 1922 All Hallows became the guild church of Toc H (p. 255); and in the sanctuary, with a 15C Antwerp painting, probably by Jan Provost, is the tomb of Alderman John Croke, with a casket containing the parent Lamp of Maintenance from which are lit all Toc H lamps around the world. In front of the sanctuary is a memorial bronze, by Cecil Thomas, to elder brethren of Toc H. In the S. aisle is the *Mariners' Chapel,* with a 16C Spanish ivory crucifix. Stairs descend to the *Chapel of St Clare,* a 17C vault, and a mid-14C crypt chapel.

The *Undercroft* (shown Mon & Wed 10.30–5, Sat 2–6; closed 12–2.15) is of the greatest interest. Entering from the W. end we see fragments of Roman remains, including some of two pavements, pottery and ashes of Roman London burned by Boudicca in A.D. 61, and a model of Roman London. There are also fragments of Saxon crosses, of one unusual type, later than the Danish occupation (c. 1025–50). At the E. end is a memorial chapel containing the ashes of members of Toc H. The plain crusading altar is from Richard I's castle at Athlit in Palestine; in front of it is the tomb in which the remains of Abp. Laud rested (1645–63) before they were re-moved to St John's College, Oxford. William Penn (1644–1718), born on Tower Hill, was baptized in All Hallows; and here John Quincy Adams, sixth president of the United States, was married to Louisa Johnson in 1797.—Kitchener's Omdurman sword is preserved in the Vestry.

Across Byward St. in TRINITY SQUARE GARDENS, a small square pavement at the W. end marks the site of the *Scaffold* where so many prisoners in the Tower met their fate in the 16C and 17C. Close by is the *Mercantile Marine War Memorial,* by Lutyens (1928), extended by Maufe with sculptures by Wheeler (1955). Beyond the gardens rises a massive building by Sir Edwin Cooper (1922; until 1972 the offices of the Port of London Authority). **Trinity House,** adjacent, was erected by Samuel Wyatt in 1793–95 for the 'Guild, Fraternity or Brotherhood of the most Glorious and Undivided Trinity', the first charter of which was granted by Henry VIII in 1514.

The corporation consists of a Master (at present the Duke of Edinburgh), a Deputy Master, Wardens, Assistants, and Elder Brethren, besides a large number of Younger Brethren, and its object is the safety of navigation and the relief of poor mariners. Pepys was Master here in 1676 and 1685. The building, badly damaged in the Second World War, was restored by Sir A. E. Richardson and reopened in 1953 (adm. on Sat on written application to the Corporate Dept.). In the main hall are statues of Capt. Maples, by Jasper Latham (1683; the first lead statue known to have been made by a British sculptor), and of Capt. Sandes, by Scheemakers (1746), both formerly in the courtyards of Trinity Almshouses (p. 260).

A large section of the Roman and medieval wall of London (with a reproduction of a Roman funerary inscription found near by and a Roman bronze statue) can be seen in *Wakefield Gardens*, beyond the Underground station. A further, and very fine portion, with its Roman substructure, is visible in the basement of the Toc H hostel at 42 Trinity Sq. (adm. usually granted by courtesy, on application to the Warden's office; not Sat or Sun, or after 6 p.m.); yet another stretch may be seen s. of Midland House in *Cooper's Row* (explanatory tablet). It is here 30 ft high; the upper part, pierced with windows and with a sentry walk along the top, was built in the 12C.

To the N.E. of the Tower is the building which used to house the ROYAL MINT (Pl. 21; 2), built in 1810–12 by Sir R. Smirke, but since then considerably extended, and damaged (1941). The Mint, first established within the Tower in 1275–85, has been moved to Llantrisant, near Cardiff, but its former building has an *Exhibition of Minting* (adm. 10p; Mon–Sat 10–4.30) with a shop (closed Sat) for the sale of coins and medals. – Across East Smithfield is the World Trade Centre (see Rte 34).

*Tower Bridge spans the Thames immediately below the Tower. The bridge, about 800 ft long between the abutment towers, was designed by Sir Horace Jones and Sir John Wolfe Barry, and was built in 1886–94 at a cost of £800,000 (including the approaches £1,500,000). The tall towers rising from massive piers in the stream are connected with each other near the top by lattice-work footbridges (which may be reopened to the public). The carriageway is formed by two bascules or drawbridges, $29\frac{1}{2}$ ft above high-water, each weighing about 1000 tons and raised in $1\frac{1}{2}$ min to permit the passage of vessels through the bridge. The original steam pumping engines used to provide hydraulic power were replaced in 1975 by electric motors.

London Docks (Rte 34), N of Tower Bridge, a little farther down the river, are reached by East Smithfield.

29 THE BANK TO ALDGATE

A   Viâ Lombard Street and Fenchurch Street

STATIONS: *Bank* on Central and Northern lines; *Aldate* on Central, Circle, and Metropolitan lines. – BUSES: see Rte 29B. – CAR PARKS: see Rtes 27 and 28.

LOMBARD STREET (Pl. 9; 5) has for centuries been one of the chief banking and financial centres of London; it is hung with decorative bank signs. It derives its name from the 'Lombard' money-lenders from Genoa and Florence, who during the 13–16C took the place of the Jews in this profession. On the right the church of *St Mary Woolnoth* forms a monumental bastion between King William St. and Lombard St. A building of great originality, it was erected by Nicholas Hawksmoor in 1716–24 and altered in 1875. It was the only City church to remain intact throughout the air raids of 1940–45. It is the church of London's German-speaking Swiss community.

The interior contains an elaborate reredos, and ornamental woodwork. From the pulpit John Newton (1725–1807; tablet on N. wall) helped to inspire William Wilberforce, Claudius Buchanan, and Hannah More to their philanthropic pursuits. On the s. wall is a memorial to Edward Lloyd (p. 255); and (end of the s. aisle) the armour of Sir Martin Bowes (d. 1566), a Lord Mayor of London, is preserved. The 'Spital Sermon' (comp. p. 258) is preached here in Easter week, attended by the Lord Mayor and aldermen in state.

The adjacent post office occupies the site of the General Post Office from 1678 till the move to St Martin's in 1829. Post Office Court also houses the *Bankers' Clearing House*, in which, four times daily, the mutual claims of the various banks against each other in the form of cheques and bills are compared and settled by cheques on the Bank of England. To the left is the church of *St Edmund the King and Martyr*, completed by Wren in 1679 (steeple, 1708). In George Yard, behind, a pleasant Neptune fountain in bronze fronts the George and Vulture, a tavern known to all readers of 'Pickwick'. Beyond (r.) is the striking grey *Lombard Bank* building, and, on the corner of Gracechurch St. are the headquarters of *Barclay's Bank* (1959) with sculptures by Sir Charles Wheeler.

The line of Lombard St. is continued beyond *Gracechurch St.* by FENCHURCH STREET (Pl. 9; 7). The *Midland Bank* (1962; r.) has a sculpture by W. H. Chattaway. Before Rood Lane (r.) is the first of the tower buildings in the City to be built with a concrete core with the floors suspended from a cantilever at the top.

Mincing Lane, named from the 'Minchens' or nuns of St Helen's, is the headquarters of the wholesale tea and colonial trade. The *Hall of the Clothworkers* (adm. see p. 199), rebuilt in 1958 on the E. side after its destruction in 1941, is the sixth hall on this site since 1456. The archives and the plate, among which is a loving cup presented by Samuel Pepys, Master of the Company in 1677, were saved. – A pleasant oasis of green (l.) marks the churchyard of St Gabriel Fenchurch (destroyed 1666). At the corner of *Mark Lane* (i.e. Mart Lane) is the war-memorial building of the Institute of Marine Engineers. Near by is the 15C tower of *All Hallows Staining*, adjoining which is a 12C crypt chapel brought from a bastion of the city wall, near Cripplegate, and rebuilt here by the Clothworkers in 1872. Near the s. end of the Lane is the principal seat of the grain trade, with the *Corn Exchange* established here in the mid-18C; the new building was opened in 1953 (chief market on Mon, 10–4.30).

In Hart St., leading E. from Mark Lane, the 'Ship' has a painted stucco façade. Here is the church of *St Olave, one of the few churches that escaped the Great Fire of 1666. Seriously damaged in 1941 it was sensitively restored in 1951–54, when Haakon VII of Norway laid the 'King's Stone' in front of the sanctuary recalling the Norwegian birth of the patron saint, and incorporating a stone from Trondheim Cathedral. Samuel Pepys (1633–1703) the diarist, who lived in the adjacent Seething Lane, was a regular attendant at this church (the entrance to his Navy Office Pew may be seen in the churchyard; a plaque was erected within the church in 1883). Mrs Pepys (1640–69) is commemorated with a charming bust, attributed to John Bushnell (N. side of the chancel) erected by her husband. Both are buried beneath the high altar.

Below the monument to Mrs Pepys is a fine monument to the Bayning brothers (d. 1610 and 1616). Over one of the pillars on the s. side of the nave is a plaque to John Watts (1780), "President of the Council of New York". Other fine monuments include: (s. aisle) Sir James Deane (d. 1608); (N. aisle) Peter Capponi (d.

1582), a Florentine merchant who died of the Plague; and Andrew Riccard (d. 1672). The pulpit and altar rails are noteworthy. From the w. end of the s. aisle (light on left) narrow steps descend to a small *Crypt* (probably late 12C), with an ancient well. Here are displayed finds from the churchyard and well, and sculptural fragments of 15–18C. The skulls over the churchyard gate in Seething Lane (Dickens's 'St Ghastly Grim') are supposed (somewhat doubtfully) to refer to the burials during the Plague in 1665.

When Pepys was Secretary of the Admiralty the Navy Office stood in *Crutched Friars* (i.e. 'Crossed Friars', from an old monastery), the prolongation of Hart St. to the E. Crutched Friars House (No. 42) is one of the few surviving City residences of the early 18C. It is now the residence of the Director of Toc H, the brotherhood established to perpetuate the memory and devoted spirit of the Talbot Houses of Poperinghe and Ypres. The first Toc H (i.e. T.H. in the army signaller's alphabet), opened at Poperinghe in 1915, was named in honour of Lieut. Gilbert Talbot.

To the right, in Railway Place, is **Fenchurch Street Station** (1840), the first to be built in the City. At the corner of Fenchurch St. and Lloyd's Avenue is **Lloyd's Register** of Shipping, a society (distinct from Lloyd's, see below) founded in 1760 and reconstituted in 1834. The roof is surmounted by an appropriate gilt weathervane.

Its primary object is to secure an accurate classification of merchant shipping, but it now discharges many other important functions for which 'surveyors' are maintained in the chief ports of the world. The Register Book contains full particulars of all sea-going merchant vessels of 100 tons and upwards. The highest class for steel and iron vessels is 100 A1, and for wooden vessels A1, the letter A referring to the hull and the figure 1 to the equipment.

Fenchurch St. ends at Aldgate Pump (Rte 29B).

B   Viâ Cornhill and Leadenhall Street

STATIONS, see Rte 29A. – BUSES: Nos. 15 and 25 follow the route – CAR PARKING, see Rte 27 and 28.

CORNHILL (Pl. 9; 5), skirting the Royal Exchange, is a busy street, named from a long extinct grain-market; a Roman building for storing grain has even been discovered here. *Change Alley*, on the right, was the scene of wild speculations during the South Sea Bubble excitement in 1720. A restored pump of 1799 (l.) recalls a predecessor of 1282; and drinking water still flows from a fountain of classical inspiration (1859) a few paces away. No. 39 Cornhill occupies the site of the house (burned down in 1748) in which Thomas Gray (1716–71), the poet, was born. Beyond, St Michael's Alley reveals the unexpectedly tall tower of *St Michael's*, rebuilt by Wren and Hawksmoor in 1670–1724, and restored by Sir G. G. Scott in an incongruous Gothic style in 1857–60. At the end of the Alley a tablet on the Jamaica Wine House recalls the opening of the first London coffee house in 1657.

St Peter's, farther on, stands on a high point of the City, occupied in Roman times by the administrative Basilica (comp. below), wrongly supposed by later tradition to have been the earliest Christian church in London. The existing structure, rebuilt by Wren in 1677–81, contains a carved wooden choir-screen, one of the only two known to be by Wren himself. The organ is by Father Smith (1681); Mendelssohn (1840 and 1842) played on the former keyboard (now in the vestry). The old bread-shelf (w. wall) and the illuminated MS. of the Vulgate made for the church in 1290 are interesting, and there is a monument to the Fifth Army. A Players company attached to the church performs Mystery Plays. Cornhill ends at the point whence Bishopsgate runs N. and Gracechurch St. s.

LEADENHALL STREET continues the line of Cornhill eastward. To the right Whittington Avenue leads to *Leadenhall Market* (meat, game, etc.; in 1663 Pepys bought "a leg of beef, a good one, for sixpence" here). The medieval street plan was retained when the elaborate arcaded buildings were erected in 1881 by Sir Horace Jones. The small area remains congested and lively. The buildings were built over part of a Roman Basilica and Forum erected in A.D. 80–100, one of the largest buildings of its kind in the whole Roman Empire. Farther E. is the palatial building of **Lloyd's of London** (Pl. 9; 6, by Sir Edwin Cooper, 1928). A larger building by Terence Heysham is on the other side of Lime St. (1952–58). Here are the handsomely decorated *Underwriting Room* ('The Room'), with the 'caller's' rostrum in the centre; the *Nelson Room*, with mementoes of the great admiral, etc. The *Adam Committee Room*, designed by Robert Adam, was brought from Bowood, the Wiltshire mansion of the Marquess of Lansdowne.

Lloyd's Underwriting Rooms, an association of underwriters and insurance brokers transacting most kinds of insurance, arose from a gathering of merchants (1688) in Edward Lloyd's coffee-house in Tower St. (later in Lombard St. and in the Royal Exchange), whose original business was marine insurance. It is still the centre of shipping intelligence. Reports are sent by Lloyd's 1500 agents and sub-agents from ports throughout the world.

On the site of Lloyd's stood (till 1862) EAST INDIA HOUSE, where Charles Lamb (1792–1825), James Mill (1819–36), and John Stuart Mill (1822–58) were clerks in the service of the East India Company. The two Mills each became head of the office, but Lamb's policy of "making up for coming late by going away early" did not lead to similar promotion.

On the N. side of Leadenhall St. opens a spacious piazza beneath two mercantile office blocks; in contrast, at the corner of St Mary Axe, stands the church of *St Andrew Undershaft*, built in 1520–32. The name is derived from the ancient practice (discounted in 1517) of erecting a 'shaft' or maypole, taller than the tower, in front of the s. door.

At the E. end of the N. aisle is the alabaster monument of *John Stow* (1526–1605); the antiquary. The pen in Stow's hand is annually renewed on the Sun nearest 5 April. On the same wall, farther to the w., is the monument of *Sir Hugh Hamersley*, Lord Mayor in 1627, notable for the fine figures of the two attendants. In the s. aisle is a tablet recording that Holbein (1497–1543) was once a resident of this parish. The font, by Nich. Stone, dates from 1631, and the organ (restored in 1969) was built by Renatus Harris in 1696. The spandrels are adorned with 18C paintings, and the roof was restored with its 16C bosses in 1950.

In St Mary Axe (in an area with the offices of many shipping companies) is the **Baltic Mercantile and Shipping Exchange**, the headquarters of a body of merchants and brokers who deal in floating cargoes, consisting of grain, timber, oil, coal, and other commodities. This institution is an amalgamation of the old Baltic (which sprang from an old coffee-house, 'The Virginia & Baltick Coffee House') and the Shipping Exchange (the modern representative of the old 'Jerusalem Coffee House'). The name 'Baltic' is now misleading.

Farther on in Leadenhall St., to the left, is the church of *St Katherine Cree* (i.e. Christchurch, from a priory founded by Maud, queen of Henry I in 1108) rebuilt in 1628–30, with a mixture of Gothic and Renaissance detail.

This church was consecrated by Laud, then bishop of London. The cover of his prayer book is kept in the vestry. The chapel in the s.E. commemorates both Laud and Charles and contains the tomb of Sir Nicholas Throckmorton (d. 1570). The E. window, with stained glass of 1630?, is in the form of a catherine-wheel. The font dates from c. 1640. The organ was built by Father Smith (1686). At the s.w. angle a pillar of the old church projects 3 ft above the floor, the level of which is said to have risen 15 ft. An unverified tradition has it that Holbein (d. 1543) was buried in the earlier church. The annual 'Lion Sermon' (on 16 Oct) commemorates the escape from a lion of Lord Mayor Gayer, who held office in Charles I's time. The church was restored in 1962; the Industrial Christian Fellowship has offices in the N. and s. aisles.

Leadenhall St. now converges with Fenchurch St., and is prolonged by ALDGATE, a short street taking its name from one of the old City gates. A draught (draft) on *Aldgate Pump* (still standing at beginning of street) was once a cant expression for a worthless bill. Geoffrey Chaucer leased the house above the Aldgate from the City of London in 1374 (tablet). Across Mitre St. is the Sir John Cass Foundation School founded in 1710 by a charitable alderman (d. 1718; buried in St Botolph's) and rebuilt in 1909 (playground on the roof).

Jewry St., to the s., reminds that we are here, as the names over the shops betoken, in the great Jewish district of London, which extends eastwards to Whitechapel and Mile End. In Duke's Place, just N. of Aldgate, stood the 18C GREAT SYNAGOGUE, the Jewish cathedral of London. Off Bevis Marks, in Heneage Lane, is the handsome *Spanish and Portuguese Synagogue* removed hither in 1701 from Creechurch Lane and the oldest in use in England. Here, too, was the office of Sampson Brass, the scene of Dick Swiveller's idyll.

Aldgate High St., continuing Aldgate, forms part of a complicated traffic system round large modern buildings, where only the 'Hoop and Grapes', on the s., shows the former scale. Beyond Houndsditch is *St Botolph Aldgate*, built by George Dance the Elder in 1741–44, and restored in 1966–71, after a fire. In the octagonal vestibule beneath the tower is a handsome font and cover. Here have been placed a memorial to Sir John Cass (1661–1718), and the monuments of Robert Dow (d. 1612; with an anxious portrait bust), and Thomas Darcy and Sir Nicholas Carew, beheaded on Tower Hill in 1538. The organ, a gift from Thos. Whiting in 1676 (plaque), was built by Renatus Harris. Thomas Bray, founder of the S.P.C.K. and S.P.G. was vicar from 1708 to 1722. William Symington (1763–1831), pioneer of steam navigation, is buried here (tablet on w. wall). In the s. aisle is a finely carved panel of David playing the harp which, together with the lectern, dates from the early 18C. Daniel Defoe was married here in 1683, and Jeremy Bentham christened in the church in 1747. During the week the Crypt becomes a refuge for about 150 homeless men, the 'Down-and-Outs'.

HOUNDSDITCH, running N.W. from Aldgate to Bishopsgate (see below) and forming the E. boundary of this part of the City, is the headquarters of Jewish brokers and dealers. The Sun morning activity here and in *Middlesex Street* (formerly 'Petticoat Lane'), a little E., is animated and curious. The Cutler St. warehouses (1782) of the East India Company rise in towering brick cliffs.

The MINORIES, running s. from Aldgate to the Tower, was formerly famous for its gun-makers. Its name is derived from an old convent of Minoresses ('Sorores Minores'), or nuns of St Clare. Off St Clare St., within the convent precincts, was found (1964) the tomb of Anne Mowbray (d. 1481; aged 8), wife of Richard, duke of York (comp. p. 56). – In America Square, just w. of the Minories, was the home of Nathan Meyer Rothschild (1777–1836), founder of the English branch of the family. No. 100 (rebuilt in 1969) houses the *School of Navigation* of the City of London Polytechnic (which incorporates the Sir John Cass College).

Aldgate High Street is continued E. to Whitechapel (see Rte 31).

30 BISHOPSGATE AND SHOREDITCH

STATIONS: *Liverpool St.* on Central, Circle and Metropolitan lines. — BUSES: Nos. 22 and 48 follow the route.

BISHOPSGATE (Pl. 9; 5), beginning at the junction of Cornhill and Leadenhall St., runs N. to Shoreditch. To the left rises London's late imitation of Manhattan, where the National Westminster Bank (600 ft), by Richard Seifert (1978) is reputedly the tallest occupied building in Europe. On the right is Great St Helen's, leading to *St Helen's, one of the largest and most interesting of the City churches, shaded by huge plane trees. The church is dedicated to the Empress Helena, and legend asserts that the Emperor Constantine himself erected the original edifice in honour of his mother.

The present church belonged to a priory for Benedictine nuns, founded c. 1210. It has two parallel naves (one the 'nuns' choir'; N.), a S. transept, and two chapels added about 1374.

The chief interest of the wide INTERIOR is in the monuments of City worthies. N. Aisle: John Robinson (d. 1599) with his nine sons and seven daughters; altar tomb of Hugh Pemberton (d. 1500); (beneath nave arches) William Kirwin (d. 1594); altar tomb of Sir Thomas Gresham (d. 1579); Sir Andrew Judd (d. 1558), founder of Tonbridge School; and the elaborate marble monument of Sir William Pickering (d. 1574). In the N. wall may be seen the nuns' night staircase, and an Easter Sepulchre incorporating a 'squint'. In the chancel are some fine 15C stalls brought from the Nuns' choir (the front stalls are mid-17C), and a rare wooden sword-rest (1665). Beyond the tomb of Sir John Crosby (d. 1475), the Chapel of the Holy Ghost contains 15C glass. The monument to John de Oteswich and his wife here probably dates from the early 15C.

The eleven fine brasses in the church (15–16C) include a Lady in a heraldic mantle (c. 1535); permission must be sought to rub the brasses (fee). Among several monuments removed from the demolished church of St Martin Outwich is one to Richard Staper (d. 1608; S. wall of the nave). Beside the S. entrance is the fine monument of *Sir John Spencer (d. 1609). The Jacobean font, pulpit, poor box, and doorcases (W. end) are noteworthy.

In St Helen's Place, farther N., is the elaborate entrance-way to the hall of the *Leathersellers' Company*, rebuilt 1949–59, and incorporated in the 14C (adm. see p. 199). Just beyond is the ragstone façade with an 18C turret surmounted by a weathervane (1671) of *St Ethelburga*, one of the smallest and most ancient churches in London. It escaped the Great Fire and dates in its present form from c. 1400. Henry Hudson (d. 1611), commemorated by three stained-glass windows, made his Communion here before starting on his first voyage in search of the North-West Passage. A shrine honours Bl. John Larke (1504–42), rector of the parish, executed by Henry VIII. Above the altar is a mural painting by Hans Feibusch (1962). The fine 17C font cover came from St Swithin's. The tiny garden with loggia and fountain is charming, and has become a refuge for birds.

The old Bishopsgate (pulled down in 1760) stood at the point where Camomile St. leads E. and Wormwood St. W. It is commemorated by a bishop's mitre in the wall. Beyond, on the left, opens a garden surrounding the pleasant church of *St Botolph Bishopsgate* (1728). The light interior has an unusual design. Keats was baptized here in 1795. Adjacent is the church hall (1861) with two charming statues (1821) of charity children. The garden contains a tennis court.

Across Liverpool St. is the Great Eastern Hotel and the huge **Liverpool Street Station,** a tour de force of Victorian Gothic. Constructed of cast-iron and brick, it withstood all the shocks of the Blitz. In the booking-hall is a memorial to Capt. Fryatt, master of the railway steamer 'Brussels' who was shot by the Germans at Brussels in 1916. The site was occupied by the Hospital of St Mary of Bethlem, for centuries London's chief hospital for lunatics or 'Bedlam'. Adjoining on the w. is BROAD STREET STATION (N. London railway). In Bishopsgate, opposite the flank of the station, a former fire station echoes its elaborate style. Off the E. side of Bishopsgate are a series of narrow courts, including Swedeland Court with a bar and restaurant. Beyond Middlesex St. (comp. p. 256), Artillery Lane leads into an area of alley-ways, including Artillery Passage, a centre of Indian trading. The *Bishopsgate Institute* (No. 230) was opened in 1894. The Library (open Mon–Fri 9.30–5.30) contains a highly interesting collection of prints of old London. Concerts, organized by the City Music Society, are given here on Tues at 1 p.m.

At the end of Brushfield Street (r.), which leads past SPITALFIELDS MARKET, is *Christ Church* (closed) a good example of Hawksmoor's work (1714–29). The *Market*, established by Charles II, deals in fruit and vegetables; trading begins at 5.30 a.m. Beneath the covered market buildings of 1887 (by Robert Horner) the colourful activity is similar to that at Covent Garden (although the market area here is considerably less). A small Flower Market (1934) adjoins to the N. In Brushfield St. the *London Fruit and Wool Exchange* (1929) holds sales on Mon and Wed.

The district of SPITALFIELDS, to the S.E., once largely occupied by silk-weavers, partly descended from Huguenot refugees, takes its name from the priory of St Mary Spital, founded in 1197, where the 'Spital Sermon' (now delivered at St Mary Woolnoth, p. 253) was first preached. Some furniture manufacturers survive here. Off Spital Square, which skirts the N. side of the market buildings, Spital Yard contains the house (No. 7) where John Wesley's mother was born in 1669. In Fort St. was the childhood home of Samuel Gompers (1850–1924), founder of the American Federation of Labour.

Bishopsgate is continued N. by *Norton Folgate*. Here a griffin marks the City boundary. *High Street Shoreditch* leads N. past Bethnal Green Road (comp. p. 261) through an area once famous for its boot-makers, to (¼ m.) a busy intersection outside **Shoreditch Church** (*St. Leonard's*). This large church, rebuilt c. 1740, was restored in 1930. James and Richard Burbage (see below) are buried here. The stocks and whipping-post are preserved in the churchyard.

Near *Curtain Road*, parallel with High St. on the w., *The Theatre* (tablet on Nos. 86–88), the first theatre in London, was erected in 1576 by James Burbage (d. 1597), father of Shakespeare's friend Richard. In 1598, owing to a dispute about the lease, the wooden structure was hurriedly pulled down at night by Burbage's sons, and the materials transported to construct the Globe Theatre in Southwark. In the vicinity stood also the *Curtain Theatre*, built in 1577.

The densely populated manufacturing district of HOXTON lies to the N.W., where new housing is being built on a modest scale. West of *Hoxton St.*, with its open market, is the attractive Waterloo church of *St John*. In *Pitfield Street* new buildings for Walbrook College have incorporated the façade of almshouses of 1825.

We continue N. up *Kingsland Road* to (c. ¼ m.) the **Geffrye Museum,** an interesting collection, well worth a visit, of woodwork, furniture, and domestic craftsmanship (adm. 10–5; Sun 2–5; closed Mon except BH; library and coffee bar). The museum occupies the old *Geffrye* or *Iron-mongers' Almshouses* (1715), a group of fourteen one-story houses ranged round a forecourt. The entrance-hall occupies the old almshouse chapel and the whole is most attractively arranged. A series of period rooms in chronological order from 1600 to the present day provide a background not only to the history of English furniture styles, but also to the history of England and English family life. Pamphlets and charts on display provide additional information. There is also a room in which temporary art exhibitions are held.

To the N. of Hoxton lie the relatively uninteresting quarters of *Haggerston, Kingsland* and *Dalston*. Holy Trinity, Dalston, is now the clowns' official church and contains portraits of famous clowns and the statuette of Grimaldi formerly in St James's, Pentonville Rd. (p. 175).

Bus No. 22 returns along Kingsland Road and Bishopsgate to the Bank (and hence to the West End).

31 THE EAST END: WHITECHAPEL AND BETHNAL GREEN

STATIONS: *Aldgate East, Whitechapel, Stepney Green,* and *Mile End* on District and Metropolitan lines; *Mile End* and *Bethnal Green* on Central line. – BUSES: Nos. 10, 25, 253 along Whitechapel Rd.; No. 8 along Bethnal Green Rd.

Whitechapel, immediately E. of the City of London, is included in Stepney (which amalgamated in 1965 with Poplar and Bethnal Green to form the London Borough of Tower Hamlets), and constitutes the beginning of the 'East End'. It has a predominantly Jewish community. WHITECHAPEL ROAD (at first called *Whitechapel High Street*) is prolonged E. by Mile End Road. The thoroughfare, with a characteristic juxtaposition of warehouses, breweries, and hostels for the poor, runs through a densely populated area. Attractive, if eccentric terraces of Georgian and Victorian buildings survive above tawdry shop-fronts, and street barrows decorate the pavements. The character of the traditional London 'cockney' may here still be appreciated. To the right and left intimate cobbled streets and lanes redolent of the 19C have now mostly been abandoned by residents and shopkeepers alike for the tower blocks which are rising behind. Beyond Aldgate East Station, to the left, diverges *Commercial Street*.

At 28 Commercial St. is TOYNBEE HALL, the first 'University Settlement' founded in 1884 and named after Arnold Toynbee (1852–83). *Attlee House* settlement was built by public subscription in 1971 (in memory of Earl Attlee, 1883–1967). The Curtain Theatre forms part of the community centre here. Behind, in contrast, the housing in Wentworth Street was provided by the East End Dwellings Company in 1890. 'The Lane' street market flourishes here. To the N.W., in Cobb St., is a kosher poultry slaughterhouse.

The archway of Gunthorpe Street, the next turning left from the High Street, reveals an evocative vista of Victorian warehouses and tenements. Here local tradition asserts 'Jack the Ripper' killed his first victim in 1888. Beyond a popular Jewish restaurant, is the *Whitechapel Art Gallery*, built in 1901 by Harrison Townsend. It has acquired a European reputation with its exhibitions mainly of the work of artists of the last fifty years. There is no permanent collection but exhibitions are held frequently (for details see press; the gallery is closed on Monday but open week days 11–6, Sun 2–6). Adjacent is the Passmore Edwards Library with a decorative frieze.

On the right Adler St. leads to the church of *St Boniface* (German R.C.; 1959) with a tall concrete bell tower. Within, the florid decoration includes plants tumbling down from the choir loft. At the next turning r. off Whitechapel Road is the *Whitechapel Bell Foundry*, established in 1570. It moved here in 1738, and still occupies part of an inn building of c. 1670. Here have been made the bells for Westminster Abbey since 1583, and for many churches in the City, Britain, and America. A small historical museum is housed in the front office. The foundry (partially rebuilt in 1970) may usually be seen by appointment. Across Whitechapel Rd. some silversmiths' shops survive in Black Lion Yard, filled with the noise of a wholesale poulterers near by.

A little farther on, across Davenant St. (l.) *Booth House* was built in 1968 by the Salvation Army (it includes a Bail Hostel, the first of its kind in Britain). A quarter of a mile farther on the pavement widens and on the s. rise the buildings of the LONDON HOSPITAL, founded in 1759, and one of the largest general hospitals in England. Behind is a colossal bronze statue of Queen Alexandra, by Wade. Opposite is a memorial to Edward VII, erected by the Jews of East London. Beyond Whitechapel Station, Brady St. diverges left.

North of the small abandoned terraces of Winthrop St. (note the carved relief on the corner) and the colonnades of Watney's Brewery (1902), gloomy dwellings of 1890 give way to imaginative new (or renovated) housing blocks. The disused Jewish Cemetery by Heathpool Court is usually open (exc. 12–2).

We pass the impressive main entrance to the Mann Brewery. Farther on *Cambridge Heath Road* leads N. towards Victoria Park (comp. below). Immediately opposite is Sidney St., notorious for the 'seige' of 1911 of a cornered gang of anarchists against whom Winston Churchill, then Home Secretary, had called out the army. We now enter MILE END ROAD, beginning 1 m. from the old City Wall. On the left a bronze bust commemorates William Booth (1829–1912), from whose open-air services in this neighbourhood in 1865 sprang the Salvation Army. The picturesque *Trinity Almshouses* were established in 1696 for master mariners and mates and their wives or widows. Damaged during the last war, they have been restored and are now houses for G.L.C. tenants. The attractive chapel, known as Capt. Cook's Church, is now a welfare centre. Opposite, No. 88 was the residence of Capt. Cook after 1764 (plaque erected on site in 1970). Beyond Cleveland Way the ungainly upper story of the former Empire Music Hall survives above shops; it is recalled in the cobbled Assembly Passage opposite. On the right diverges *Stepney Green*, with charming houses (c. 1700) on the left. Roland House (No. 29; visitors welcome) is a centre of the Scout Movement. Beyond a particularly attractive house (no. 37) is the London Jewish Hospital. The Green ends at the large churchyard of *St Dunstan's* (restored 1946–52), mostly 15C, with early 16C tombs. A Saxon *Rood-panel (early 11C) decorates the 13C chancel. In the wall of the s. aisle is a stone with an inscription (1663) stating it to have been brought from Carthage. Any child baptized at sea is entered in the church register.

On the N. side of Mile End Rd., before Stepney Green Station, we pass Charrington's Brewery and the Mile End Municipal Baths. No. 253, formerly the Spanish and Portuguese Jews' Hospital, is now an old people's home. Behind is a small disused Jewish cemetery, granted to the Jews by Oliver Cromwell in 1656 and the oldest Jewish cemetery left in Britain. Beyond Queen Mary College, is a larger Jewish cemetery opened in 1725.

We skirt the new buildings of **Queen Mary College,** a school of London University. Beyond Bancroft Road its great hall occupies the building of the *People's Palace*, opened in 1887 and intended as a realization of the 'Palace of Delights' in Sir Walter Besant's novel 'All Sorts and Conditions of Men' (1882). It was rebuilt after a fire in 1936 and again in 1953–56, with sculptures by Eric Gill. Just beyond is the beautifully simple University of London chapel of *St Benedict.*

Mile End Road is prolonged by the slightly more attractive Bow Road to Bow and **Stratford.** *Bow*, or *Stratford-le-Bow*, noted for china in the 18C, took its name from a 12C arched bridge over the Lea. Chaucer's Prioresse probably caught her accent from Elizabeth of Hainault, who died (1375) in the Benedictine nunnery of St Leonard's at 'Stratford-atte-Bowe'. The church of St Mary Stratford Bow dates from the early 14C (tower rebuilt after 1948), and stands on an island site. To the N.W. extend vast railway marshalling yards. To the s. lies *Bromley-by-Bow.*

BETHNAL GREEN, E. of Shoreditch and N. of Stepney, is a crowded district engaged in the furniture and leather trades. A. busy Sunday morning market for dogs, birds, musical instruments, etc., is held at the w. end of Bethnal Green Rd. and in Club Row. At the E. end of the same road on the green itself is *St John's,* a church built by Soane in 1824–28.

South of Bethnal Green Rd. is *St Matthew's,* built by Geo. Dance the Elder (1743–46), altered in the 19C, and rebuilt in 1961 after bomb damage.

Bethnal Green Museum of Childhood, in Cambridge Heath Rd., was opened in 1872 as a branch of the Victoria and Albert Museum (adm. weekdays, exc. Fri, 10–6, Sun 2.30–6). The fine Victorian hall of prefabricated iron and glass with open galleries is devoted mainly to decorative art, with special reference to local products. In the Central Court, where temporary exhibitions are held, is a display of board-games for children. At the E. end, a collection of sculpture by Rodin (most of which was given by the artist). It includes his first major statue, the Age of Bronze (1875), the Prodigal Son (1885–87), and two busts of Balzac. Wall cases display British ceramics, glass, and silver. On the upper floors are displayed a large collection of female costume (18C–c. 1930); Spitalfields silks and other textiles; 19C Continental sculpture and decorative arts; and Japanese arms and armour. There is also an excellent *Collection of dolls' houses and toys (including marionettes and puppets) newly arranged in 1978.

Behind the Museum is the 17C *Netteswell House*; thence *Old Ford Road* leads (½ m. r.), to *Victoria Park (217 acres), the principal playground of East London and a haunt of Sunday lecturers.

III THE SOUTH BANK

32 SOUTHWARK AND BANKSIDE

UNDERGROUND: *London Bridge* and *Borough* on Northern Line (City branch)
—*Waterloo* on Northern Line (West End branch).

BUSES: Nos. 35 and 133 cross London Bridge and follow Borough High St; No.
70 traverses Southwark St. and Stamford St.

CAR PARKING: George Inn (for patrons only); and streets off Borough High St.
Car Parks in Park St., Hopton St., and Upper Ground.

At the s. end of London Bridge (p. 242) stands London Bridge Station,
the capital's first terminus (1836). Nearby, at 28–34 Tooley St., is **The
London Dungeon** (adm. daily 10–4.30) an horrific exhibition of scenes of
medieval torture and murder, atmospherically sited in a suitably slimy
vault. Only for those with strong stomachs. BOROUGH HIGH STREET (Pl. 21;
1) runs through **Southwark** (pron. 'Suthark'). Here was the site of a Roman
settlement, and in the Middle Ages it was a borough of some importance. It
is still known as the 'Borough' par excellence. Since 1531 Southwark has
been included in the City of London, but it elects neither aldermen nor
councillors, being represented in the common council by the senior
alderman of the time.

The High Street has from earliest times been the great highway to the
s.e. of England and the Continent. It was the scene of countless processions and pageants in the Middle Ages, and was trodden by the feet of
many pilgrims to the shrine of St Thomas Becket at Canterbury. It
abounded in hostelries, the old buildings of which, however, have almost
entirely disappeared. Much rebuilding and demolition is at present
taking place here. On the left as we leave the bridge is the approach to
London Bridge Station, on the right is Southwark Cathedral. St Thomas's
St. skirts the s. side of the station.

The s. wing (1842) of the original ST THOMAS'S HOSPITAL which stood here from
1225 to 1865 is occupied by telephone engineers (behind post office façade). The
church of *St Thomas* (1702–03), now Southwark Chapter House, in St Thomas's St.,
is another relic of the hospital. In the roof space is the old *Female Operating
Theatre* of 1821, rediscovered in 1956 and restored (adm. Mon, Wed, & Fri 12.30–4).
In this vicinity lived Robert Harvard, the father of John Harvard (1607–38), who
attended St Olave's Grammar School, of which his father was a governor. A little
farther on in St Thomas's St. stands **Guy's Hospital**, founded in 1725 by Thomas
Guy, a City bookseller, who made a fortune by his speculations in South Sea stock.
The hospital contains one of the largest medical schools in England. John Keats
studied here in 1815–16. In the courtyard is a statue of Guy, by Scheemakers, and in
an inner quadrangle is another of Lord Nuffield, by Maurice Lambert (1949). New
building is taking place to the east.

*Southwark Cathedral (Pl. 21; 1) now lies hemmed in between the
railway and Borough Market. Officially the *Cathedral and Collegiate
Church of St Saviour and St Mary Overie, Southwark*, it has been the seat
of a bishop since 1905. Often rebuilt and repaired it remains the finest
Gothic building in London after Westminster Abbey.

Services on Sun at 9, 11, 4 (choral); Mon at 5.30 p.m.; Tues–Thurs at 8 a.m.; Fri
at 1.10 & 5.30 p.m.; Sat at 12 noon. Choral evensong on Tues (6 p.m.), Fri, & Sat
(4 p.m.). Organ recital at 1.10 on Mon. In the last week of April Shakespeare
Birthday celebrations are centred on the cathedral.

HISTORY. According to the legend, a nunnery was founded on this site by a
ferryman's daughter called Mary, whence is derived the former title of the church,
St Mary Overy, which is explained as 'St Mary of the Ferry' or 'St Mary over the

Ie' (water). In 852–862 this nunnery was changed by St Swithin, Bp of Winchester, into a house for canons regular of the Augustinian order. In 1106 a church was erected, of which few traces survive. The present choir and retro-choir were built by Peter des Roches, Bp of Winchester, in 1207; the transepts were remodelled in the 15C. The nave, which had collapsed about 1838 and been replaced by a temporary erection, was entirely rebuilt by Sir Arthur Blomfield in 1890–96. Over the crossing rises a noble 15C tower, 164 ft high.

Interior (open all day). NAVE. In the s.w. corner is a portion of 13C arcading; in the N.W. corner a case of splendid bosses from the 15C roof. The stained glass, mostly destroyed in 1941, is modern. Under the 6th window is the *Tomb of John Gower* (1330–1408), the friend of Chaucer. Behind the door into the Vestry may be seen the jambs of a Norman door and an ancient holy-water stoup.

TRANSEPTS. In the North Transept has been placed a dresser given to the church in 1588. The monuments here include one to John Lockyer (d. 1672), pill-maker, with an amusing hyperbolical inscription. To the E. of this transept is the *Harvard Chapel*, restored and decorated in 1907 in memory of John Harvard, founder of Harvard University, Mass., who was born in the parish and baptized in this church (1607). During the restoration a Norman shaft (l. of the altar) was disclosed. The stained glass window (restored 1948) was presented in 1905 by Joseph H. Choate (d. 1917). On the right a tablet commemorates the playwright and lyricist, Oscar Hammerstein (1895–1960).

CHOIR. This and the retro-choir represent perhaps the earliest Gothic work in London. The *Altar-screen, erected by Bp Fox in 1520, is a magnificent piece of work, though much mutilated and restored. The statues in the niches date from 1912. The fine tombs in the choir aisles include: (N. Aisle) two handsome Jacobite monuments to John Trehearne (d. 1618), gentleman-porter to James I, and Richard Humble (d. 1616), Alderman, and the wooden effigy of a Knight (1280–1300; restored); S. Aisle: fine tomb of Lancelot Andrewes (1555–1626).

The beautiful aisled *RETRO CHOIR is now used as the parish church. The Lady Chapel, which extended to the E., was pulled down in 1830. Here Gardiner and Bonner held the consistorial courts in the reign of Queen Mary, and condemned Hooper, Rogers, Bradford, Saunders, Ferrar, and Taylor to the stake. Bishop Bonner later died for his own beliefs at Marshalsea (see above) in 1569.

The SOUTH TRANSEPT was rebuilt in the 15C by Cardinal Beaufort, whose niece, Joan Beaufort, was married to James I of Scotland in this church (1423). On the w. wall is a monument in miniature to William Emerson (d. 1575), a supposed ancestor of Ralph Waldo Emerson. Above, John Bingham (d. 1625), sadler to Queen Elizabeth and King James. Nearby is a touching inscription to Mistress Margaret Maynard (d. 1653, aged 13 years).

In the s. aisle of the nave, beneath a memorial window to Shakespeare (by C. Webb, 1954), is a recumbent alabaster figure of the playwright (1911).

John Fletcher and Philip Massinger, the playwrights; Edmund Shakespeare (d. 1607), the younger brother of the poet; and Henry Sacheverell (chaplain in 1705–09), are buried in St Saviour's, but their graves are unidentified.

The buildings of *Borough Market*, founded by Edward VI and removed from the High Street in 1757, provide a stylistic contrast to the

Cathedral. In the fruit, vegetable, and flower market (wholesale only; daily exc. Sat), activity begins at about 3 a.m. and is at its height around 6.30 a.m. Little selling takes place after mid-morning. The railway is carried across the market buildings.

On the E. side of Borough High Street once rose a series of famous inns. Opposite Southwark St. the *King's Head* was called Pope's Head before 1540. Next door stood the White Hart, Jack Cade's headquarters in 1450 (Shakespeare, 'Henry VI', Part II, V. iv. 8: "Hath my sword therefore broke through London Gates that you should leave me at the White Hart in Southwark?"), and where Mr Pickwick first met Sam Weller. In a courtyard beside George House is the *George Inn* (N.T.), the last surviving galleried inn in London. It is still a public house and restaurant, and preserves a rare 'inn-keeper's' clock inside; the façade dates from c. 1676. Warehouses in the courtyard recall the hop trade for which Southwark was long a centre. Shakespeare plays are performed here in summer. On the site of Talbot Yard stood the most celebrated hostelry of all, the Tabard Inn, the "gentil hostelrye that highte the Tabard, faste by the Belle", the starting-point of Chaucer's Canterbury pilgrims. It survived (as the Talbot Inn) until 1875–76.

Beyond an old wine bar, a shop front carries a plaque recording the site of the *Queen's Head Inn* owned by the family of John Harvard (see above). The sale of this property before his emigration to America in 1637 augmented his fortune, half of which (with his library) he left to Harvard University when he died the following year. In Newcomen Street, off the High St., the *King's Arms* (rebuilt 1890) appropriated the sign from the Great Stone Gate (1728) on London Bridge when it was demolished in 1760.

A tablet in the High Street recalls the original old prison of the **Marshalsea**, first mentioned in 1377 and abandoned in 1813, when the name was transferred to the New Marshalsea (see below). Here Ben Jonson was imprisoned for sedition in 1597. Adjoining the Marshalsea on the s. stood the old **King's Bench**, the prison to which Judge Gascoigne is said to have committed Prince Henry (afterwards Henry V). Tobias Smollett was imprisoned here in 1739 for libel. In 1758 this prison was superseded by the new King's Bench, at the corner of Newington Causeway. Here John Wilkes was held for libel in 1768–70, and many debtors were imprisoned, though they were often allowed to live in lodgings near by, "within the rules of King's Bench" (comp. Dickens's 'Nicholas Nickleby'). Mr Micawber found a "temporary haven of domestic tranquility and peace of mind" at the King's Bench. The prison was partially burned in the Gordon Riots (1780; see Dickens's 'Barnaby Rudge'), disused in 1860, when imprisonment for debt was abolished, and finally pulled down.

At 207 Borough High St. a small part of the walls survive of the *White Lion* or *Borough Gaol*, a 16C prison; to a later building on this site the name of the Marshalsea was transferred. Here Dickens's father was confined in 1824, and Little Dorrit, 'the child of the Marshalsea' was born and brought up. In St George's Church (first mentioned in 1122, rebuilt 1734–36 by John Price, and since restored) Little Dorrit was christened and married. Marshalsea Road, running w. from the church, leads to *Mint Street*, in which was St George's Workhouse, usually accepted as the workhouse in which Oliver Twist asked for more (though that was not in London). The workhouse copper is preserved in the Cuming Museum (see p. 285). In *Lant Street*, the next turning on the right out of the High St., Charles Dickens lodged as a boy, while his father was in the Marshalsea and he himself worked at Hungerford Market. Here, too, lodged Bob Sawyer, the medical student in 'Pickwick'.—*Horsemonger Lane Gaol*, in which Leigh Hunt was confined for two years for libelling the Prince Regent as "a fat Adonis of 50" (1812), stood in Union Road, off the Borough High Street.

Great Dover Street branches left from the High Street to join the Old Kent Road (p. 279). At No. 75 lived C. H. Spurgeon (see below) in 1854–56. Here is the Pilgrim Fathers Memorial Church (1956), the second successor to the oldest Congregational church in London (1616). In the area, Dickens Square, Merrick Square, and Trinity Church Square date from the early 19C; in the latter is a statue of a king (?14C) said to come from Westminster Hall.

The Borough High Street is continued to the s. by Newington Causeway, in which is London Sessions House. Beyond is the **Elephant and Castle** (Pl. 20; 6), a busy traffic centre (named after a former tavern) redesigned in 1957–64 as two roundabouts linked by Newington Butts, with a shopping precinct. Facing this are the London College of Printing and the Baptists' *Metropolitan Tabernacle* (rebuilt with a modified façade 1959), the successor of the tabernacle (burned down in 1898) in which C. H. Spurgeon preached from 1861 until his death in 1892, living at No. 217 New Kent Road.

We may now approach the wharves and river front by the narrow winding *Cathedral Street* (usually congested with lorries; best attempted only when on foot). A plaque on St Mary Overy Dock (16C) reminds parishioners of St Saviours that they are entitled to free landing here. After several bends we enter CLINK STREET, a narrow canyon between huge warehouses. On the left the remains of a great hall (14C; including a rose window) of Winchester House have been incorporated in a warehouse.

Winchester House built in the 12C was the town residence of the bishops of Winchester down to 1626; it is recalled in the names of the streets to the s. It was burned down in 1814. *Clink Street* was named after the manor or park of 70 acres attached to Winchester House and known as the '*Liberty of the Clink*', where a pleasure-quarter sprang up outside the jurisdiction of the City. In the undercroft of the service block, the *Clink prison* was used by the bishops as a place of detention for heretics. It was housed across the street in the 17C, and burned in the Gordon Riots of 1780. 'In the clink' survives as a slang expression for imprisonment.

Beyond Stoney St., we pass under Cannon Street railway bridge. The magnificent arched vaults beneath are used as warehouses. The *Anchor Inn* (luncheons) was built in 1775. Bank End leads into **Bankside** (Pl. 20; 2) which skirts the river almost to Blackfriars Bridge. East of Southwark Bridge it is lined with derelict warehouses; to the w. it runs through a district of great interest as the site of the early theatres where Shakespeare's genius found expression. Here, too, in the Liberty of the Clink, were the 'stews', largely inhabited by Dutch or Flemish women, and numerous bear-gardens, used also for prize-fights. A huge electric power-station now dominates the landscape. Bankside commands a view of St Paul's, especially fine at sunset, seen over a foreground of wharves; an inscription on a 17C house (being restored) on Cardinal's Wharf marks the house whence Wren used to watch the building of his cathedral. Across the narrow Cardinal Cap Alley dating from the 17C with a secluded garden, the Cathedral Provost's Lodgings have occupied a building of 1712 (restored) since 1958.

In Bear Gardens (l.) the BEAR GARDENS MUSEUM (adm. Tues–Fri 10–4; 15 April–15 Sept 10–8; Sat, Sun & BH. 2–5; 15 April–15 Sept 11–6) occupies a 19C warehouse with its old machine driving gear. Here is a permanent exhibition relating to the Elizabethan Theatre, and a model of the frost fairs which used to be held on the frozen Thames in Southwark. Periodic exhibitions are also held relating to the history of the district.

This was the site of the *Hope Theatre* (1614–56) where Ben Jonson's 'Bartholomew Fair' was first performed. Bear-baiting began on the site before 1550 and continued in the theatre. Performances in Davies' Amphitheatre here from 1662 to

1682 were visited by Evelyn and Pepys ("After dinner, with my wife and Mercer to the Bear Garden where. . . . I saw some good sport of the bull's tossing of the dogs, one into the very boxes. But it is a rude and nasty pleasure", Diary, 14 Aug, 1666).

At the foot of this street Park Street runs E. past Courage's Brewery. This was owned in the 18C by Henry Thrale, the friend of Dr Johnson who (as an executor) remarked at the sale "we are not here to sell a parcel of boilers and vats, but the potentiality of growing rich beyond the dreams of avarice". A plaque on the wall marks the approximate site of the famous *Globe Theatre*, erected by the Burbages in 1599. Shakespeare was a shareholder and acted here for many years. Fifteen of his plays were produced at the theatre, which was a small but lofty circular building ("this wooden O"). It burned in 1613, and the second theatre was demolished in 1644. Rose Alley recalls the *Rose Theatre* put up by Philip Henslowe in 1587. The plays of Shakespeare, Marlowe, and Kyd were performed here until 1603, and Edward Alleyn was a leading actor.

In Emerson Street is the headquarters of the *Globe Playhouse Trust*, set up in 1971 to foster interest in Shakespeare and the theatrical history of the area. The World Centre for Shakespeare Studies, affiliated to King's College, runs a summer school here. Ambitious plans to reclaim much of Bankside, include the building (by 1976) of a third Globe Theatre, modelled closely on the second theatre (see above). At present a Festival is held from mid-June to the end of August with performances of Shakespearian and Elizabethan plays in a temporary theatre, and films shown in the cinema on Bankside.

The *Power Station* built in 1963 by Sir Giles Gilbert Scott stands on the site of Great Pike Gardens which supplied fish to ecclesiastic houses in the area in the 14C. Hopton Street (with the attractive almshouses of Hopton's charity; 1752) leads inland to Southwark St. The Falcon Inn occupies the site of the Swan Theatre (1596–c. 1621), the successor of a bull ring. We turn r. to reach BLACKFRIARS ROAD. In this street is *Christ Church* (1960), the industrial mission centre of Marshall's Charity (founded 1627); replacing a predecessor ruined in 1941, it occupies the site of the manor house of Robert de Paris (temp. Richard II). As Paris Garden, the manor was in the 16–17C one of the amusement centres of London, patronised by gay society and even by the Court. Farther s. in Blackfriars Road is Orbit House with the *India Office Library* (over 300,000 vols; MSS. and letters).

Across Blackfriars Road we enter STAMFORD STREET where the portico (1823) of the demolished Unitarian Chapel forms a ceremonial entrance to the parade-ground of the *London Nautical College*. In Upper Ground, parallel to the N., much rebuilding is taking place. Beyond the white headquarters of London Weekend Television (1972), is the **National Theatre** (by Denys Lasdun). This forms part of the South Bank arts centre which has been built w. of Waterloo Bridge (see Rte 33).

33 WATERLOO AND LAMBETH. BATTERSEA

UNDERGROUND: For the South Bank arts centre, *Waterloo* on the Northern and Bakerloo line, and *Charing Cross* on Circle line (Hungerford footbridge across the river).—For North Lambeth convenient stations are *Westminster* on the Circle line, *Waterloo* and *Lambeth North* on Bakerloo and Northern line.—*South Lambeth* and *Kennington* are served by the Northern line.—For the Imperial War Museum, *Lambeth North*, and *Elephant and Castle* on Bakerloo line. *Vauxhall* now has a station on the Victoria line.

BUSES: Over Westminster Bridge: Nos. 12, 53, 76, 109, 170, 172.—Over Lambeth Bridge: Nos. 3, 10, 77, 149, 159, 507.—Over Vauxhall Bridge: 2, 36, 88, 181, 185.—Over Chelsea Bridge: No. 137.—Over Battersea Bridge: Nos. 19, 39, 45, 49.—No. 507 runs from Waterloo along York Road and Lambeth Palace Rd. to Lambeth Bridge; No. 44 (from Lambeth Bridge) and No. 170 (from Westminster Bridge) run along the s. bank to Battersea Park.—For the Imperial War Museum: No. 10 from Victoria, No. 12, 53 from Westminster, No. 171 from the City across Waterloo Bridge.

Lambeth (Pl. 19; 6) is an old borough on the right bank of the Thames, opposite Westminster and between Southwark and Battersea; its more interesting parts are all near the river. At the s. end of *Waterloo Bridge* (comp. Rte 32) is the area usually referred to as 'the South Bank', a brutal concrete jungle interlaced with heavy and windswept overhead walkways and 'relieved' by sculpture in cast-iron. Amidst the confusion the visitor is rewarded with fine panoramas of the river. The site, between the County Hall (see below) and Waterloo Bridge was cleared for the Festival of Britain, an exhibition celebrating recovery after war in 1951.

The ROYAL FESTIVAL HALL (Pl. 15; 6) by R. H. Matthew and J. L. Martin was completed in 1964–65. The auditorium seats 3000; the platform will accommodate a choir of 250. The building contains a Recital Room (holding c. 200), two restaurants, and many original features (concerts, see p. 31). To the N.E. have been added the stark *Queen Elizabeth Hall* (1967) by G. Horsfall (with seating for 1100) and the *Purcell Room* (with seating for 372). The *Hayward Gallery* (1968), leased to the Arts Council for loan exhibitions, and the *National Film Theatre*, near by, complete the group of buildings w. of the bridge. To the E. is rising the National Theatre (comp. above).

WATERLOO ROAD continues s. across a roundabout. Here the church of *St John*, by Francis Bedford (1823–35), was well restored in 1951 to serve as the 'Festival Church'. Opposite is **Waterloo Station** (S.R.; rebuilt 1912–22). Farther s., on the corner of The Cut, is the OLD VIC, or Royal Victoria Hall. This was built in 1817 as the Coburg Theatre, and in 1833 renamed the Victoria (hence when the New Victoria opened, the 'old' Vic). It saw Kean and the violinist Paganini before becoming a home of lurid melodrama, and was acquired in 1880 by Emma Cons (1837–1912), who changed its character and made it a popular home for grand opera and classic plays at popular prices. The work, in conjunction with Sadler's Wells Theatre, was admirably carried on by Lilian Baylis (1874–1937), niece of Miss Cons.

Although obliged to leave the Old Vic Theatre because of bomb damage to the theatre in the Second World War, the Old Vic Company continued to perform elsewhere under the same name, and reoccupied its original home in 1950–64. The theatre was then the temporary home of the National Theatre company until their new theatre was opened (comp. above). The *Young Vic*, in The Cut, occupies an octagonal building (1970) which incorporates a former butcher's shop in the foyer. To the w., The Cut is extended by *Lower Marsh*, noted for its characteristic street market.

Waterloo Road ends at the Royal Eye Hospital and *St George's Circus* (Pl. 20; 5), the bold focal point of George Dance's development plan of 1769, where six roads converge. Here Blackfriars Rd. leads N. to Blackfriars Bridge (p. 238), passing the site of the Surrey Theatre, owned in its days as the 'Royal Circus' by Charles Dibdin, author of 'Tom Bowling'; and farther on that of the old round Surrey Chapel, famous under the Rev. Rowland Hill (1744–1833). Westminster Bridge Road runs w. from St George's Circus past *Morley College*, founded in 1885 (noted for the high standard of its courses). *Christ Church* at the corner of Kennington Road, has been rebuilt into an office block. The tower of 1876, which survived the bombing and on which appear the Stars and Stripes, was erected by subscription from Americans as a memorial to President Lincoln.

Returning to the river, we continue s. along BELVEDERE ROAD (Pl. 15; 6). Hereabouts was the factory for artificial stoneware started by Eleanor Coade (1733–1821) in 1759. The factory closed in 1840 and the secret of manufacture was lost. A lion, sculptured in the stone (1837), which formerly adorned the Lion Brewery, demolished in 1950, stood outside Waterloo Station in 1951–66 before being moved to its present site (comp. below). On the left rise the two massive blocks of the *Shell Centre* (1957–62) linked by a tunnel and one of the largest office blocks in Europe ($7\frac{1}{2}$ acres). An observation gallery (temporarily closed in 1978; adm. usually on weekdays 10–5, Thurs to 8; fee) on the 25th floor (317 ft) affords a superb *View of the whole county of London.

Beyond the *Jubilee Gardens* rises **London County Hall** begun as the headquarters of the London County Council in 1912 and now that of the Greater London Council. This huge Renaissance edifice, by Ralph Knott and W. E. Riley, has a river-façade (1932) 750 ft long. The sculptures on the exterior are by Ernest Cole and A. F. Hardiman. The meetings of the Council (alternate Tues, 2.30 p.m.) are open to the public; and visitors may inspect the interior of the building on Sat and on summer Bank Holidays (10.30–12.30 and 1.30–3.30). The *Library*, which is open to students daily on application (9.15–5.15; Sat by appointment, 9.15–12.15), is devoted to local government in general and to the history and topography of London, with large collections of photographs, prints and drawings, and maps. The *Record Office* (Mon–Fri, 9.45–4.45) contains c. 200 parish registers. The *Middlesex Record Office* (Mon–Fri, 9.30–5.30, Thurs till 7.30) is now housed in Queen Anne Buildings, Dartmouth St. (Westminster). A striking extension to the County Hall has been built on the 'island' at the end of Westminster Bridge.

The **Greater London Council** was constituted in 1964 when some 70 local authorities were combined into 32 new boroughs, and the boundaries of the County of London extended deep into Essex and Surrey and incorporating Middlesex. It is the ruling authority for the County of London (saving the jurisdiction within the City of the City of London Corporation) in such matters as main drainage, ambulance and fire services, overall planning, major roads, etc. Local administration of libraries, parks, personal health and welfare services, is in the hands of the 32 *Borough Councils*. Responsibility for education is shared.

The E. end of *Westminster Bridge* (Pl. 15; 7) has been guarded since 1966 by a colossal Lion (comp. above). The riverside promenade is continued by the *Albert Embankment*, 1 m. long, completed in 1869, and adorned with delightful dolphin lamp posts. Here, opposite the Houses of Parliament, is the new **St Thomas's Hospital,** begun in 1960. The hospital founded in 1213, was removed hither from Southwark (comp.

p. 262) in 1868 and built on the 'pavilion' plan devised by Florence Nightingale, who had established the first English school of nursing at St Thomas's in 1860. The pavilions were demolished after being damaged in the Second World War.

Following the Embankment past St Thomas's Medical School we reach *Lambeth Palace, the London residence for seven centuries of the archbishops of Canterbury. The building was begun by Abp. Langton (1207–29), but few of his successors failed to add to or alter it; the residential part was built in 1829–38. The palace was damaged in 1941. Erasmus, Thomas More, and Cranmer (who here wrote the English Prayer Book) are known to have visited the Palace. Admission is by previous arrangement with the Secretary, Lambeth Palace (conducted parties, usually on Sat afternoon).

The entrance is by *Morton's Tower*, a noble red brick gatehouse erected c. 1490. In the courtyard is a memorial to Abp. Lord Davidson (1848–1930).—The *Great Hall*, rebuilt in medieval style by Abp. Juxon in 1663, has a roof, 70 ft in height, resembling that of Westminster Hall. It now houses the *Library*, the nucleus of which was bequeathed to the see by Abp. Bancroft in 1610. It is thought to be the oldest free public library in the country. It is open to readers 10.30–4.30, weekdays (exhibitions), and contains nearly 1500 MSS., many finely illuminated, letters of Francis Bacon, Gladstone's diaries, six Caxtons, Edward VI's Latin grammar and Elizabeth I's prayer book.—The *Guard Chamber*, with a 14C roof (reconstructed), contains a fine series of portraits of the archbishops since 1503, by Holbein, Van Dyck, Hogarth, Reynolds, Romney, Lawrence, and others.—The beautiful *Crypt* beneath the chapel is the oldest part of the building, dating possibly from c. 1200. From the *Post Room* (1435) we pass through a beautiful Early English double doorway into the small *Chapel* (c. 1230), rededicated in 1955, preserving stalls and other fittings provided by Abp. Laud (1634). From 1273 down to the present day many English bishops have been consecrated in this chapel, and in 1787 Bp. White of Pennsylvania and Bp. Provost of New York were consecrated here by Abp. Moore. The chapel was the scene of the second trial of Wyclif in 1378.—The picturesque *Lollards' Tower* (1434–45) derives its name from the belief that the Lollards, followers of Wyclif, were imprisoned in it. In the stair-turret is the 'Lollards' Prison.'

Archbishop's Park, a portion of the palace grounds thrown open to the public in 1900 extends to the N.

At the gate of the palace is the closed church of *St Mary, Lambeth,* rebuilt in 1851, with the exception of the 15C tower. At the E. end of the S. aisle is the 'Pedlar's Window', commemorating the bequest to the parish of the 'Pedlar's Acre,' a piece of ground which, at first worth but 2s. 8d. a year, fetched £81,000 when it was sold to the L.C.C. as site for County Hall. This window was renewed in 1956, replacing the original destroyed, together with much of the glass in the church, in 1939–45. In the churchyard are the tombs of John Tradescant (d. 1638), the naturalist; Admiral Bligh (d. 1817) of the 'Bounty,' who lived at 100 Lambeth Road; and Patrick Nasmyth (d. 1831), the painter; here also lies Jeanne de La Motte Valois, who achieved notoriety in the Diamond Necklace Scandal in France in 1785–86. Opposite is *Lambeth Bridge House*, used by the Department of the Environment.

From Lambeth Bridge LAMBETH ROAD runs E. to St George's Circus passing (r.) *Lambeth Walk*, popularized by song and dance. At No. 124 is Morton Place, where a tablet on No. 6 marks the residence of Miss Cons and Miss Baylis (see above). In Hercules Rd. (l.) the Central Office of Information building has a huge mosaic mural of the Labours of Hercules. We cross Kennington Road where Charles Chaplin lived as a boy (at Nos. 261 and 287 and at No. 3 Pownall Terrace; in one of these he may have been born in 1889). Beyond is the building occupied from 1815 to 1930 by Bethlem Hospital ('Bedlam'; now near Croydon). The central portion of the old hospital (by Lewis, 1812; dome by Smirke, 1846, restored after fire) now houses the ***Imperial War Museum** (Pl. 19; 4). Opened in 1920 at the Crystal Palace, it was housed in 1924–36 in the Imperial Institute. It is concerned with all aspects of the two World Wars and with other British military operations since 1914.

ADMISSION. The Museum is open daily, except Christmas Eve–Boxing Day, New Year's Day, and Good Friday; on weekdays from 10–6, Sun from 2. Library and Photographic Records Dept., weekdays 10–5. Film Shows normally Tues–Fri at 12, Sat & Sun at 2.30. Refreshments on ground floor.

The museum buildings were severely damaged during air-raids. The arrangement of exhibits is liable to change. The exhibition galleries are concerned mainly with the Royal Navy and Merchant Navy, Army, Air Services, Dominion and Colonial Forces, and the Home Front. The museum possesses about 9000 works of art depicting the events of 1914–18, and a large number of the works of the 1939–45 period commissioned or purchased by the War Artists' Advisory Committee. Arrangements to see pictures not on view may be made with the Keeper of Pictures.

On the lawn in front of the entrance are two 15-inch naval guns cast in 1915–16, with a range of over 16 miles. Within, the present arrangement, in part at least subject to change, is anti-clockwise on both floors. We use the numbering of the official plan though in 1978 the galleries themselves were not numbered and their limits, especially downstairs, were ill-defined.

Upper Floor (r.). GALLERY 1 is devoted to winners of the Victoria Cross and George Cross, the two highest awards for valour and self-sacrifice. Among personal relics are Boy Cornwell's VC and medals; Albert Ball's Royal Flying Corps uniform; naval uniform of Captain A. W. S. Agar; Insall's letter smuggled from prison camp and the reversible jacket in which he made his escape in 1917; Group Captain Cheshire's flying helmet; W/Cdr Yeo-Thomas's forged papers ('the White Rabbit') in the resistance. – The CORRIDOR contains relics of Lawrence of Arabia, including his rifle; uniforms of F. M. Earl Alexander of Tunis, and of other high-ranking officers.

In the DOCUMENTS ROOM (2) are one of the four copies of Hitler's testament dictated in his Berlin bunker on 28 April 1945; the Munich declaration of 30 September 1938; combat reports of First World War pilots who became Marshals of the Royal Air Force in the Second (Harris, Tedder, Portal, Douglas, Slessor); Kitchener's instructions before the Dardanelles campaign. A Corridor of posters leads to Galleries 3–8 where are displayed a selection of the numerous paintings and drawings in the possession of the museum.

1914–18 War. Works by *Sir William Orpen, John S. Sargent, Henry Tonks, Norman Wilkinson, Paul Nash, Francis Dodd, C. R. W. Nevinson,* and *Henry Lamb*; bust of T. E. Lawrence, by *Derwent Wood.* **1939–45 War.** Works by *Charles Cundall, Ardizzone, Henry Carr, Dame Laura Knight, Richard Eurich, Paul Nash, John Nash, Anthony Gross, Stafford-Baker, John Worsley, William Coldstream,* and *John Piper.* *Head of . M. Maisky, Russian Ambassador to Britain in 1932–43, by *Epstein,* and head of Mussolini, by *Bertelli.* *Head of Sir Winston Churchill and bust of Lord Fisher, by *Epstein*; paintings of Peace Conferences of 1919; panels depicting Shipbuilding on the Clyde, by *Stanley Spencer.*

From R. 6 the lower floor may be reached by the main staircase. Off R. 7 a balcony overlooking Gallery 15 displays recent acquisitions.

The long GALLERY 9, in many sections, displays uniforms, insignia, badges, awards and medals, British, allied and enemy from before the First

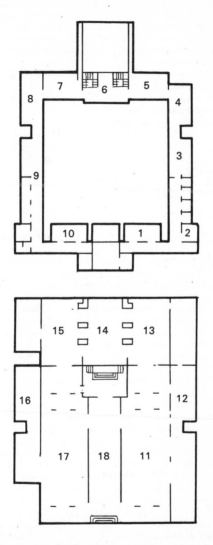

Imperial War Museum

World War to recent United Nations involvements; among exotic foreign and full-dress uniforms are some from the Indian Empire. Many are identified with individual heroes who wore them. – GALLERY 10 is devoted to a century of naval service by the Mountbatten family: their uniforms, decorations, and orders are displayed. In the CORRIDOR outside are a roll of signatures of 'The Few'; Edith Cavell's dog Jack; and the uniforms of Lord Douglas of Kirtleside.

The main display is on the **Lower Floor.** A corridor (r.) continuing into GALLERY 11 shows 'the Road to War' from 1870 to 1914 by photographs, posters, and maps. A diorama of a troop train at Waterloo with contemporary timetables and notices, and 'Ole Bill', an open-top London 'B' type bus which carried troops to the front, recall the makeshift transport of 1914. The remainder of this crowded gallery is devoted mainly to artillery, fighting vehicles, and early aircraft used for artillery 'spotting'. German and British howitzers compared; observation gondola of Zeppelin LZ 90; the gun fired by Boy Cornwell at Jutland; the 4-inch gun from H.M.S. 'Lance' that fired the first British round at sea in 1914; cumbersome Mark V tank, of 1916; above, Sopwith 'Camel' aircraft. Also, above later tanks and anti-tank weapons in GALLERY 13 are a BE2C and a Bristol F2B.

By the doorway to Gallery 12, Mau Mau weapons from the Kenya emergency. G. 12 gives a claustrophobic insight into trench warfare.

GALLERY 14 is devoted to the Royal Naval Air Service (Fleet Air Arm), centring on a Fairey 'Swordfish' torpedo bomber, which first flew in 1932 and was in service longer than any other aircraft in the history of naval aviation.

GALLERY 15 contains the caravans that constituted Montgomery's mobile headquarters in the Western Desert and from Normandy to the German surrender at Lüneburg Heath; the operational maps of the final campaign and· the document of surrender are on view, also Monty's uniforms. A supporting display of 21 Army Group equipment includes a Sherman tank.

Part of GALLERY 17 (under camouflage netting) holds sad relics of the Far East campaigns, including the fighting in Burma and the Siamese railway. The main hall is devoted to air warfare: front fuselage section of a 'Lancaster' bomber of an Australian squadron; in the centre, Focke-Wulf 190, perhaps the best German aircraft of the war; above, Heinkel 162 jet fighter, and a Spitfire Mk 1 that was flown in the defence of London throughout the Battle of Britain. (Many of the museum's aircraft are kept at Duxford, a former operational airfield near Cambridge.) Briefing models and reconnaissance photographs of precision bombing raids (Amiens prison, Gestapo H.Q. in Copenhagen, Mohne Dam). At the far end are torpedoes and one-man submarines, used with success by the Italians in the Mediterranean. In a side room (r.), German V2 rocket and V1 flying-bomb and launcher.

Off this, Gallery 16 is sumptuously arranged to trace the life of service of the late Duke of Gloucester. School blazers lead to his complete later military wardrobe, orders, etc. – The central GALLERY 18 was empty in Feb 1978.

The Reference Library of books, periodicals, pamphlets, etc., deals with all aspects of both wars, and includes a department containing c. 4 million photographs, from both official and unofficial sources, illustrating many phases of both wars throughout the world. Other reference sections deal with cinematograph films, maps, war currency and stamps, and posters.

The grounds were acquired in 1926 by Lord Rothermere and converted into the public *Geraldine Mary Harmsworth Park* in memory of his mother. The obelisk in the N. angle, erected in 1771 in St George's Circus in honour of Lord Mayor Crosby, was removed hither in 1907.

At the corner of St George's Road, on the very spot where the 'No Popery' rioters assembled in 1780, stands *St George's Cathedral*, of the R.C. diocese of Southwark, built by Augustus Pugin in 1840–48, wrecked by bombs in 1941, and freely rebuilt by Romilly Croze using the original designs. A spacious edifice, brick outside and stone within, it mixes a profusion of Gothic styles without loss of dignity.

From Lambeth Bridge we continue to follow Albert Embankment to the S. Here from 1815 to 1956 stood the Doulton pottery works of which only the London office remains. The headquarters of the London FIRE BRIGADE were transferred in 1936 to a new building on the Embankment. The Brigade, which maintains 60 fire stations and about 200 appliances and vehicles, is administered by the G.L.C. Here too is the new London headquarters of the *United Nations*. Black Prince Rd., on the left, leads to Lambeth Walk, in a turning out of which (8 Bolwell St.) the composer Sir Arthur Sullivan (1842–1900) was born.—We are here traversing the site of the *Vauxhall Gardens*, the most celebrated of the pleasure-gardens that existed on the Surrey side in the 17–19C.

From *Vauxhall Station*, near Vauxhall Bridge, *Nine Elms Lane*, realined at first and continued by the very long Battersea Park Road, leads to **Battersea** (Pl. 18; 8), a mainly industrial district opposite Chelsea. On the left is the huge new *Vegetable Market* opened in 1974 to replace the old 'Covent Garden' (p. 197). It occupies the site of the original terminus (1838) of the Southampton Railway; after the extension to Waterloo in 1848, NINE ELMS became the Southern's main goods yard with facilities kept for occasional exceptional passengers (including Queens Adelaide and Victoria, and Garibaldi; also cavalry embarking for the Boer War).

At No. 4 Battersea Park Rd. is the *Battersea Dogs' Home*, the chief collecting centre for lost dogs in London (visitors admitted; donation expected), and on the right is the huge Power Station.

Battersea Park extends along the Thames from Chelsea Bridge to Albert Bridge and is more pleasantly approached from Pimlico or Chelsea (Rte 13). It was laid out in 1852–58 on Battersea Fields, the scene of a duel in 1829 between the Duke of Wellington and the Earl of Winchilsea. The marshy ground was reinforced with earth removed from Blackwall during the building of the Victoria Docks. The *Sub-Tropical Garden*, W. of the boating-lake, is at its best at midsummer, and modern sculpture (H. Moore, etc.) ornaments the lawns.

A portion of the park, at the N.E. corner overlooking the river, has been laid out as the *Festival Pleasure Gardens.* Designed by John Piper and Osbert Lancaster, these include an ornamental lake, a theatre, an amphitheatre (concerts, etc.), several restaurants, and am amusement section (closed Sun).

From Battersea Bridge Road, Battersea Church Road leads to *St Mary's*, the old parish church, by the river. Though rebuilt in 1776, St Mary's contains monuments and stained glass from the earlier church. In the N. gallery is the monument by Roubiliac of Henry St John, the famous Lord Bolingbroke (1678–1751), who was born in the vanished manor house. Blake was married in the church, and from the bow window in the vestry, Turner painted sunsets over the Thames.

Beyond the church Vicarage Crescent leads past two good 18C houses (on the *Vicarage*, tablet to E. A. Wilson, 1872–1912, Antarctic explorer) to *Old Battersea House*, built c. 1699 and containing a collection of *Pottery and paintings by Wm. de Morgan (1839–1917), the novelist, and his wife (closed for restoration).

From Vauxhall Station (see above), the long and dull WANDSWORTH ROAD, continued by LAVENDER HILL, runs s.w. to *Clapham Junction* (S.R.), an important station, and to **Wandsworth,** a wide-spreading industrial borough with an extensive common and the Thames-side *Wandsworth Park* (20 acres).

IV THE THAMES AND
SOUTHERN ENVIRONS

34 THE PORT OF LONDON

The PORT OF LONDON extends for a distance of 94 m. on the tidal Thames, from a point 265 yards below Teddington Lock, to the Thames estuary. For sea-going ships generally the port begins below London Bridge. It includes three large dock systems: the India and Millwall Docks, the Royal Docks, and Tilbury. The change from conventional cargo to containers has led to the closure of several dock systems in the Pool of London (where, since 1968, dock berths have been reduced by one third). Development schemes are now concentrated at Tilbury, and a deepwater seaport at Maplin Sands on the outer Thames estuary. At present none of the dock systems is open to the public, and plans for the recently closed dock areas (which include 391 acres of the former Surrey Commercial Docks on the s. bank) have yet to be realized.

Though they had become inadequate some time before, quays remained the only mooring places until at the end of the 18C the provision of docks was agreed against City opposition during the Napoleonic Wars: even this was principally to counter pilfering.

In 1909 the port was placed under the *Port of London Authority* (headquarters at the World Trade Centre, East Smithfield), which has 15–16 appointed members. The total net registered tonnage of vessels using the port in 1970 was 85 million tons, and 56½ million tons of goods passed through the port in 1971. It remains the leading port in the United Kingdom.

Although the St Katharine and London Docks (100 acres; begun in 1802), immediately E. of the Tower, have been closed, the riverside districts of Wapping and Shadwell described in Rte 34A are still accessible to the visitor on foot (or in a car). Beyond Limehouse begin the major inland docks, access to which is restricted. For this area, Bus 277 which makes a circuit of the Isle of Dogs (India and Millwall Docks), and Bus 69 which runs through Silvertown (Royal Docks; see Rte 34C) are recommended in winter; in summer the motor launches between the Tower and Greenwich offer the best view of the river and its activity (see Rte 34B).

A Wapping and Shadwell. Stepney

STATIONS: *Tower Hill* on Circle line; *Shadwell* and *Wapping* on Metropolitan line.—BUSES: No. 67 runs viâ The Highway to Wapping Sta. (exc. Sun); Nos. 5 15, & 23 traverse Commercial Rd.

From Tower Hill we may take East Smithfield past the *World Trade Centre* to the gate (adorned with elephants) of ST KATHARINE DOCKS, a speculative enterprise of 1827–28 for which 11,000 people were dispossessed, built by Thos. Telford (his only project in the capital). Three basins now form a marina for large yachts and there is a 'jetfoil' ferry service to Zeebrugge. The former *Ivory House* (1854) has been attractively restored; the *Dockmaster's House*, by Philip Hardwick, survives; the *Dickens Tavern* is picturesque; and a *Rotunda* was opened by Queen Elizabeth in 1977. A growing floating museum of unusual craft includes a

Thames Barge, the Nore Lightship, the training ship 'Larvik', and the 'Dame of Sark'. Near the Bridge rises the *Tower Hotel* (1973).

In Dock St., to the N., a Sailors' Home succeeds one in which Joseph Conrad (1857–1924) often lodged.

We turn s. down Thomas More Street to reach WAPPING HIGH STREET with its picturesque warehouses along the river. Here Judge Jeffreys was arrested in 1688 in the disguise of a sailor. Opposite the attractive tower of *St John* (1760; church destroyed in the Second World War) Wapping Pierhead is flanked by fine terraces. The 'Wapping Old Stairs' of the ballad still exist (now seldom used). Beside the Tunnel Pier, beyond, is the site of Execution Dock, where Captain Kidd (d. 1701) and other notorious pirates were hanged. At Wapping Station, a plaque commemorates the tunnel, the first for public traffic ever to be driven beneath a river, designed by Marc Isambard Brunel and completed in 1843. It was used by pedestrians until 1865 when its present use as a railway tunnel began. To the N. are the Garnet Street bulk wine vats. Wapping Wall continues the line of the High St. E., past the 'Prospect of Whitby', a well-patronized drinking resort with a balcony overlooking the river.

We turn N. beside the *King Edward Memorial Park* (1922), the site of the old Shadwell fish market on the river, with a memorial to Willoughby, Frobisher, and other 16C navigators, and join *The Highway*. Once notorious as Ratcliff Highway, it ran through a lawless region abounding in drinking-dens for sailors. To the left, on Shadwell Basin, *St Paul's* was built in 1820 by John Walters. Here Captain Cook's son James and Walter Pater were baptized. We proceed E. along The Highway and turn r. at Butcher Row to meet Narrow St. In Butcher Row are the buildings of the ST KATHARINE'S ROYAL FOUNDATION, completed in 1952 (adm. by appointment).

St Katharine's Royal Hospital was originally founded near the Tower in 1148 by Queen Matilda; in 1273 Queen Eleanor, wife of Henry III, took the wardenship into her own hands and reserved the patronage for ever for the queens of England personally. The foundation was removed to Regent's Park in 1825, when the St Katharine's Docks were excavated; it returned in 1950. The funds are now administered for social welfare work near the docks. A cloister, with monuments from the Regent's Park chapel (comp. p. 158), admits to the plain but effective *Chapel* (1952), containing *Stalls, with misericords (c. 1370), and other woodwork (15C and 17C), including the Jacobean pulpit. The 18C *Warden's House* occupies the former rectory of St James's church, which was destroyed in the Second World War.

Narrow St., which skirts the Thames, retains its warehouses and crosses the end of the Regent's Canal (comp. p. 170). The 'Grapes' (No. 76) passes for the original of the 'Six Jolly Fellowship Porters' in 'Our Mutual Friend'. Limehouse Causeway, once a notorious Chinese quarter, continues E. to meet West India Dock Road. To the s., beyond 'Charlie Brown's', on the corner of Garford St. (a well-known sailors' resort, with a remarkable collection of quaint and artistic curios) is the entrance to the **India and Millwall Docks** (see Rte 34c).

We may now turn inland to return w. along COMMERCIAL ROAD, cut in 1805 to join Aldgate to the West India Dock. This runs through **Stepney**, a region of poor streets which suffered severely during the bombing of 1940–41, inhabited largely by a 'marine' population. The remarkable church of *St Anne* by Hawksmoor (1714–30; note the view of the tower from the eccentric entrance at the w. end) is surrounded by a characteristic medley of buildings. Some way farther on, just before the railway bridge, is the unusually shaped plain brick *Danish Seamen's Church* and mission by Holger Jensen (1959).

The interior, in wood and brick, with an attractive glass mosaic, contains two wooden figures (from an earlier church) of SS. Peter and Paul, by G. G. Cibber (d. 1700), father of Colley Cibber.—In Branch Road, opposite, begins the N. approach to Rotherhithe Tunnel, c. 1¼ m. long, which passes beneath the Thames to Rotherhithe.

Beyond Stepney East Station is the *London Opera Centre* used for rehearsals and training. Nearly a mile farther w. (buses, see p. 275) we cross Cannon Street Road, in which, s. of Cable St., is *St George-in-the-East* (1714–29), by Hawksmoor. Gutted in 1941, it has been ingeniously rebuilt by Arthur Bailey (1960–64). Close by, in Swedenborg Square, stood the Swedish Church, in which the body of Emanuel Swedenborg (1688–1722) rested until it was removed to Sweden in 1908.

Commercial Road ends at Whitechapel High Street (comp. Rte 31).

B From the Tower to Greenwich by River

STEAMERS: in summer only, from Westminster, and from the Tower. From *Westminster*, every 20 min., from 10.20 a.m. to dusk (in 50 min.; 70p return). From the *Tower*, every 30 min., from 11.30 a.m. to dusk (in 30 min.; 60p return).—A HYDROFOIL service operates throughout the year between the Tower and Greenwich (in 8 min.; 80p return).

The points of interest mentioned on either bank of the Thames are described in greater detail in Rtes 28, 34A, and 35 (comp. the Index). Mileages are taken from London Bridge.

Tower Pier (Pl. 21; 2) lies on the *Pool of London*, the name given to the reach, thronged with shipping, between London Bridge and Limehouse. As we leave the pier we have a magnificent view of the *Tower*, with the Traitors' Gate in front. H.M.S. 'Belfast' is moored to the opposite bank; launched in 1938, she was the largest cruiser built for the Royal Navy (see p. 279). Beyond *Tower Bridge*, the lowest bridge on the Thames, both banks of the river are lined with wharves and warehouses (many now disused). On the left are the entrances to *St Katharine's Docks*, being rebuilt as a residential area, and the London Docks (closed). Opposite lies *Bermondsey*, with the ancient St Saviour's Dock.

Farther on we have *Wapping* on our left, opposite *Cherry Garden Pier*, on the site of the cherry-gardens frequented by Pepys. On the left are the headquarters of the Thames Division of the Metropolitan Police, and the 'Prospect of Whitby', an old riverside tavern. *Tunnel Pier* adjoins the site of the old *Execution Dock*. Opposite is *Rotherhithe*, with its parish church and picturesque old riverside houses, a little short of the w. entrance to the enormous (2 m.) *Surrey Commercial Docks* (closed in 1970; no adm.). Plans include waterside housing served by a new underground line. *Shadwell*, with its park, *Ratcliff*, opposite Globe Pier, and *Limehouse*, with the entrance to the *Regent's Canal Dock* (closed), succeed each other on the left bank. Overlooking the foreshore, to the left of the tower of Limehouse Church, the quaint little river-front of 'The Grapes' may be identified. Beyond *Cuckold's Point* (r.) the river bends sharply to the s. (Limehouse Reach) and describes a wide loop round the *Isle of Dogs* (l.)

past (3 m.) *West India Dock Pier*. The **India and Millwall Docks** occupy a connected area of 454 acres on the Isle of Dogs. The West India Docks by Wm. Jessop and John Rennie were opened in 1802, the East India Dock in 1806, and the Millwall Dock in 1868. The chief articles handled here are hard woods, wine, fruit, and grain. A modern terminal has been built at Millwall to handle palletized goods. Brunel's 'Great Eastern' was built and launched (broadside) from Millwall in 1858 (site marked by black and yellow sign).

On the right bank, beyond the s. entrance to the Surrey Commercial Docks, lies *Deptford*, with the flagstaff and rum warehouses of the former Victoria Yard. Deptford Creek used to mark the boundary between Surrey and Kent. As we approach (5 m.) **Greenwich** (r.) we have a superb view of its famous hospital. Behind the tower of St Alfege appears the cupola of the Observatory. On the opposite side of Greenwich Reach lies *North Greenwich*, with its trees, at the s. extremity of the Isle of Dogs. Greenwich Tunnel, a subway for foot passengers, passes under the Thames (approached by rotundas on each bank). For Greenwich, see Rte 35.

C Poplar and the Royal Docks. Tilbury

BUSES: Nos. 5, 15, 23 in Commercial Rd. and E. India Dock Rd; No. 69 viâ Silvertown Way and North Woolwich Rd. to the Woolwich ferry.

EAST INDIA DOCK ROAD (which continues Commercial Rd. E., comp. Rte 34A) traverses **Poplar,** which includes Blackwall and the Isle of Dogs on the s. It passes *Lansbury* (l.), named after the Labour leader George Lansbury (1859–1940), the first part of a large housing estate (over 3 sq. m.) planned by the G.L.C. on a bombed area in Stepney and Poplar. The estate includes *Trinity Church* (1951), by C. C. Handisyde and D. R. Stark, a market-place, several schools, etc., of modern design. Beyond *All Saints* (1821, by Charles Hollis), in a handsome Greek style, opens the N. entrance to **Blackwall Tunnel** which passes below the Thames to East Greenwich. A second tunnel (s. bound traffic) was opened in 1967. It was from Blackwall that 105 'Adventurers' sailed in 1606 to found the first permanent British colony at Jamestown in Virginia under Capt. John Smith and others. The *Virginia Settlers Memorial*, at the entrance to E. India Dock, was unveiled in 1951.

Beyond the river Lea are the **Royal Docks,** which include the ROYAL ALBERT DOCK and the KING GEORGE V DOCK (1921). The ROYAL VICTORIA DOCK (no longer used) was opened in 1855, the first dock to be equipped with hydraulic machinery, to be designed expressly for steamships, and to be connected directly with the country's railway system. The Royal Albert Dock (230 acres) was the largest sheet of impounded water in the world when it was opened in 1880. Frozen meat, butter, cheese, fruit, tobacco, and wool are some of the chief imports here. Exports include motor vehicles, machinery, spirits, and manufactured goods. A marina has been opened in the Royal Albert Dock, from the s. end of which a passenger tunnel and free car ferry connect the N. and s. bank of the Thames at **Woolwich.** A flood barrier is under construction at Silvertown in the Woolwich Reach and is expected to be finished by 1982.

Tilbury Docks, which conclude the series, lie considerably farther down the river, 26 m. below London Bridge by water, and 21½ m. by rail from Fenchurch St. Station. Opened in 1886, it is now the largest grain importing port in the United Kingdom. It also handles forest products, and is an international container port. All passenger liners for London now dock at Tilbury.

A steam ferry plies every ½ hr. across the Thames from Tilbury to Gravesend. Original rights for the ferry were granted by Henry IV to Gravesend as compensation for damage done there by a French pirate. *Tilbury Fort,* to the E., was constructed by Henry VIII in 1539. In anticipation of the arrival of the Spanish Armada a great camp was established at Tilbury in 1588 under the command of the Earl of Leicester. Elizabeth I, mounted on a horse and wearing armour, reviewed her troops here, addressing them in the stirring words: "I know that I have the body of a weak, feeble woman, but I have the heart and stomach of a king, and of a king of England too."

Replacing the Henrician fort is a superb example of military engineering, built for Charles II by Bernard de Gomme in 1670–83. Until the middle of the 19C it provided the first line of defence for the Thames and London. Its decline ensured its escape from major alteration. In the chapel are early plans of the fort.

35 GREENWICH AND WOOLWICH

RAILWAYS. S.R. (N. Kent line) half-hourly service from Charing Cross (viâ Waterloo and London Bridge) to *Greenwich,* 5½ m. in 17 min., to *Maze Hill,* 6½ m. (for the Nat. Maritime Mus.) in 20 min., to *Woolwich Arsenal* (also from Cannon St.), 9½ m. in 29 min.

BUSES. To *Greenwich,* Nos. 70, 188, viâ *Deptford* (followed thither also by No. 47); 53, 177, viâ New Cross, continuing to *Woolwich.* Many others from S. London.—MOTOR LAUNCHES, see Rte 34B.

PLAN OF GREENWICH, see Atlas 26.

The route from the West End viâ the Old Kent Rd. (A2) and New Cross has few features of interest.—From the S. end of London Bridge Tooley St. leads E. After the disastrous fire here in 1861, in which James Braidwood, first chief of the 'London Fire Engine Establishment', lost his life, the service was reorganized as the Metropolitan Fire Brigade. To the left Vine Lane leads to the wharf (car park, 20p; Rfmts), off which lies **H.M.S. Belfast,** a Southampton class cruiser (1936–38), saved from the scrapyard and opened to the public here in 1971 (adm. daily 11–6, 30p, children 20p). We board the Quarterdeck, whence the tour of the ship (some confined spaces and steep ladders) is indicated by arrows. This can be made in c. 1 hr. The highlights are the main gun turrets, the navigation bridge, the Cruiser Exhibition, detailing the ship's fighting history (Battle of the North Cape, Normandy 'D-day', Korea, etc.), the mess decks, bakery, and machine shop. The Junior Ratings' Dining Hall has been adapted to showing a 10-minute film of the Normandy landings (addit. fee).

The former borough of **Bermondsey** (which included Rotherhithe and now forms part of Southwark) is the traditional quarter of tanners and saddlers, and has a huge biscuit factory. On the left the 19C buildings of St Olave's Grammar School form the Tower Bridge Branch of Norwood Technical College; St Olave's, founded in 1560 (a fact recalled by Queen Elizabeth St. in which it stands), occupied this site from 1855 to 1967 when it moved to Orpington. *Tower Bridge Road,* which Tooley St. next crosses, leads S. beneath the great brick arches of London's earliest railway (1836) to *St Mary Magdalene,* the ugly parish church (usually locked). The interior (restored in 1973 after a fire) has woodwork of c. 1680 and preserves some 12C capitals from *Bermondsey Abbey,* a large and powerful house founded in 1087, in which the widows of Henry V

and Edward IV died. In Bermondsey Square, opposite, the New Caledonian Market for antiques operates every Fri, 7–2.

At the E. end of Tooley St. is *St Saviour's Dock*, to the E. of which lay
the squalid 'Jacob's Island,' scene of Bill Sykes's death in 'Oliver Twist.'
Jamaica Road and Lower Road continue through **Rotherhithe**, inhabited
mainly by dock-labourers and seamen. Lemuel Gulliver is described as
a native of Rotherhithe, and here in exile (Orchard House, Lower Road)
in 1969 died Mutesa II ('King Freddie') of Uganda. With the closure of
the vast *Surrey Commercial Docks*, whose future is still uncertain, the
character of the area will change. To our right extends *Southwark Park*.
On the left, also, the growing *King's Stairs Gardens* extend to the river by
the Angel tavern (restaurant), affording a fine view of Tower Bridge. To
the N.E. just off the one-way system at the mouth of the Rotherhithe
Tunnel, stands the church of *St Mary* (1714) in whose predecessor was
buried Christopher Jones, master of the 'Mayflower' (tablet). The
church has an unaltered organ of 1764. The charity school, opposite,
still bears its statues, and the Mayflower, behind, is another riverside
'pub' sandwiched between warehouses. We pass the Norwegian Church,
the Finnish Seamen's Church, and farther on a Swedish mission.

Beyond (2¼ m.) *Surrey Docks Station* we enter **Deptford** by the long
Evelyn Street. To the left (best approached by Grove St.) the Pepys
Estate (1962–68), imaginatively planned if somewhat stark in style,
occupies the site of the *Royal Victoria Yard*, a naval victualling yard
established in 1742 and closed in 1961. A colonnaded terrace within the
old gates, and the superintendent's office, beyond, have been restored;
and on the fine riverside promenade, two handsome 18C rum warehouses
with an arcaded ground floor incorporate the Pepys Library and Deptford Sailing Centre. The view extends upstream to Limehouse Reach
and downstream to Greenwich. Henry VIII's dockyard of 1513, where
Elizabeth I knighted Francis Drake on board the 'Golden Hind,' lay to
the S.E.; some relics of the 'Great Storehouse,' removed to the custody of
the Hammersmith School of Building, may eventually be restored to the
site.

At *Sayes Court* (now represented by a small park), the residence of John Evelyn
(1620–1706), occurred in 1671 the memorable dinner given by the diarist to Pepys
and Wren, after which the last was introduced to Grinling Gibbons, who lived near
by. Peter the Great was a tenant here while working in the dockyard (1698).

Just beyond the High Street (which leads to the Town Hall and A2)
are (l.) *St Nicholas*, the old parish church of Deptford (1697, restored
after bomb damage; tower c. 1500), where Christopher Marlowe, killed
in a tavern brawl in 1593, lies buried in the churchyard; and (r.) *St Paul*,
the present parish church, a notable work by Archer, with the tomb of
Dr Charles Burney, historian of music (d. 1817). Near by in the cobbled
Albury St. are some good 18C houses. We cross Deptford Creek.

4½ m. **Greenwich**, on the S. bank of the Thames, is famous for its Hospital, Park, and Maritime Museum (Son et lumière in July–Sept). The
Observatory, as a working institution, has moved to Sussex, but its old
buildings remain with their historic instruments as an astronomical
museum. The church of *St Alfege* takes name from a Saxon Abp. of
Canterbury martyred here by the Danes, who had mounted a raid in
1012 from Greenwich roads. Rebuilt by Hawksmoor in 1712–14, it was
restored (1953) after heavy war damage. The monument to Gen. Wolfe

(d. 1759) survived the bombing. Henry VIII and Gen. Gordon were baptized here, and Lavinia Fenton, duchess of Bolton (1708–60), the original 'Polly Peachum' in Gay's 'Beggar's Opera,' and Thomas Tallis (1505–85), the 'father' of English church music, are buried here. A manual from the organ of his day is preserved, and a choral commemoration service is held on 23 November.

Here we meet Greenwich High Road, which, coming from Deptford Town Hall, passes *Queen Elizabeth's College*, an almshouse of 1819 (at its foundation in 1576 perhaps the first Anglican charitable institution), and Greenwich *Town Hall* (1939).

Greenwich Church St. or King William Walk, passing either side of the old covered *Market*, lead (l.) to *Greenwich Pier*. A concrete berth next to the pier is the permanent home of the **'Cutty Sark,'** the last of the sailing clippers (1870), brought here from Greenhithe in 1954 to serve as an educational centre for the Merchant Marine. She houses a fine collection of figureheads and other items of maritime interest (adm. 11–6, Sun & hol. from 2.30; fee). A pedestrian subway links Greenwich with the Isle of Dogs (comp. p. 278). Beyond its circular entrance is exhibited '*Gipsy Moth IV*,' the yacht in which Sir Francis Chichester made his single-handed circumnavigation in 1968. This is well seen externally; visit on board, fee, times as 'Cutty Sark'. The whole area is being improved and landscaped in 1973.

A fine riverside walk affords good views of the Hospital backed by the Park, and of shipping in the river. Hereabouts the Court in 1553 saluted Willoughby and Chancellor, setting off in search of the North East Passage; here Raleigh was arrested on his return from Guiana; and here George I landed from Holland on his way from Hanover to claim the crown of the United Kingdom. At the river end of Park Row is the attractive *Trafalgar Tavern* (1837).

In King William Walk is the entrance to ***Greenwich Hospital**, now the *Royal Naval College*, which occupies the site of Bella Court, built in 1426–34 by Humfrey, duke of Gloucester, which, as the Palace of Placentia, became a favourite residence of the Tudor sovereigns. In this palace Henry VIII and his daughters, Mary and Elizabeth, were born and Edward VI died.

Excavations in 1970–71 beneath the riverside lawns located the 15C manor house, with its many subsequent alterations and enlargements, and part of the palace that superseded it. Here the papal legate dubbed Henry VIII 'Defender of the Faith' and here Henry received the Emp. Charles V in 1522; here also began the liaison with Anne Boleyn that led to the breach with Rome.

The present building was begun for Charles II by Webb (part of N.W. block only). After 1692 it was decided to complete the palace as a home for disabled seamen, and the new buildings by Wren and Hawksmoor were opened in 1705. In 1873 the hospital was abandoned in favour of pensions, and the buildings assigned to a college for the higher education of naval officers.

The grounds are open at certain times and afford an interesting close view of the fine buildings. Of these only the *Chapel*, rebuilt after a fire by James 'Athenian' Stuart in 1779–89, with statues and an altarpiece by Benjamin West, and the *Painted Hall*, the dining hall of the college, with its ceiling paintings by Sir James Thornhill, are open to the public (adm. free 2.30–5, weekdays exc. Thurs; also Sun in May–Sept; chapel also on Sun for service at 11). The statue of George II in the Grand Square is by Rysbrack.—Facing Romney Road, w. of the College, is the *Dreadnaught Seamen's Hospital* in a building of 1763.

Behind Greenwich Hospital, on the other side of Romney Road, is the

Queen's House, designed by Inigo Jones, begun c. 1617 for Anne of Denmark and finished in 1635 for Henrietta Maria, after whom it is named. Badly damaged by enemy action, it was restored in 1949. With the adjacent buildings (1807–16; occupied until its removal to Holbrook in 1933 by the Royal Hospital School), it now houses the **National Maritime Museum** (open Mon–Fri 10–5 or 6, Sat to 6, Sun 2.30–6; free) splendidly arranged for the illustration and study of the maritime history of Great Britain in its widest sense. The arrangement of the museum is, where possible, strictly chronological, objects dating from the 17C or earlier being displayed in the Queen's House, those of succeeding periods up to 1815 in the West Wings, and later exhibits in the E. Wing. The Navigation Room and Restaurant form an annexe of the w. wings. The museum's publications are of a very high order.

From Maze Hill station visitors coming by train reach the E. wing entrance viâ Park Vista. The w. wing, with improved display and many *paintings, was reopened in Nov 1977, except for the basement galleries.

The QUEEN'S HOUSE marks the introduction into England of the Palladian style by Inigo Jones; the building was enlarged by Webb in 1662. In the entrance hall, a perfect cube, a ceiling painting by Thornhill replaces the Gentileschi original (comp. p. 90). Rooms 1–5 (Ground Floor), Elizabethan and Jacobean period; the naval scenes by *Adam Willarts* are the earliest of the remarkable succession of maritime paintings.—Here are also a fine portrait of Drake (R. 2), a collection of 17C scale-model ships, and, in the Great Hall, the original 'Chatham Chest' which held the funds for disabled seamen started by Drake and Hawkins.—RR. 6–21 (First Floor), Stuart and Cromwellian Period to 1685; portraits of Blake, Tromp, and De Ruyter; of Pepys, by *Kneller*; Sir Wm. Penn and Gen. Monk, by *Lely*; naval scenes by the *Van de Veldes*.—RR. 22–29 (Ground Floor) continue naval history up to 1702, and illustrate the foundation of Greenwich Hospital.

Traversing the w. colonnade we enter the WEST WING. To the right, beyond the *Bookstall*, opens the Caird Rotunda, in which is a bust of Sir James Caird, a notable benefactor of the museum. On either side are Seal and Medal rooms, and beyond is the LIBRARY (adm. by ticket only). —From the vestibule a staircase made of old ships' timbers ascends to Galleries 3, 4, and 5 (splendidly renewed 1974–77), illustrating the 18C. R. 3 covers the period of William III and Anne; R. 4, the naval times of Anson and Vernon; R. 5, the Seven Years' War and 18C dockyards. Displayed are seascapes by *Abr. Storck, Brooking, Samuel Scott*, and *Dominic Serres*, and portraits by *Kneller, M. Dahl, Hogarth*, etc. Beyond is the PRINT ROOM (adm. on application, weekdays, 10–5).

On the Ground Floor *Room 6 is devoted to the achievements of Capt. Cook, with fascinating drawings, paintings by Wm. Hodges, and scientific observations made on the circumnavigation of 1775–80 and other voyages.—R. 7 continues with the American War of Independence, and R. 8 with the French Revolutionary Wars; these contain fine portraits by *Romney, Copley, Reynolds*, etc.

On the right is the *NAVIGATION ROOM, a splendidly arranged collection of naval instruments, globes, portulans, and charts. At the end, four *Chronometers made by John Harrison, the last of which won him in 1764 the government prize of £20,000 offered for a reliable method of determining longitude.

Galleries 9 and 10 are occupied by the *NELSON COLLECTION. Well-known portraits of Nelson (by *Rigaud*) and his captains (*Copley*, etc.) and battles (Trafalgar, by *Turner*); autographs of Nelson and Lady Hamilton; personal relics, including the uniform worn at Trafalgar; and Nelson's Bible, grog-jug, and purse; Napoleon on the 'Bellerophon', by *Sir Chas. Eastlake*.

From the bookstall we descend to the *NEW NEPTUNE HALL, a museum within a museum, reopened in 1972 to illustrate the development of boat-and shipbuilding, and many ancillary subjects. The huge hall has as centrepiece the steam paddle tug 'Reliant' (1907), round which is built the main display showing the development of the steam ship. Chronologically however the story begins on the left wall, proceeding clockwise, first below the water-line of the tug and then above it. The development of wooden boats from prehistory to modern pleasure craft is demonstrated by more than 25 boats as well as scale models, from a Severn coracle to ceremonial barges: the BARGE HOUSE (opening left) contains Mary II's shallop of 1689, a state barge built for the Prince of Wales in 1732, and examples of Doggett's coat and badge (comp. p. 34). Farther on are Miss England III; a working model showing the pilot's use of radar; and superb naval figureheads. Above, the 'Donola', a 60 ft Thames steam yacht, is in full working order.—A basement gallery illustrates the techniques of marine and submarine archaeology.

The East Wing illustrates British maritime development from the close of the Napoleonic wars to the present day, in particular the heyday of British sea power and commerce, and Polar exploration.

To the s. lies *Greenwich Park, first enclosed by Duke Humphrey (existing wall 1619–24) and laid out by Sir Wm. Boreman to a plan by Le Nôtre under Charles II. The chestnut avenues are especially fine. A Roman villa (site marked) near Vanbrugh Gate and various unexcavated mounds attest to the existence of the Roman town of Noviomagus. On a hill in the centre are the former buildings of GREENWICH OBSERVATORY, founded in 1675. Owing to the difficulty of obtaining satisfactory astronomical observations in the then smoke-laden atmosphere of London, the Royal Observatory was moved in stages to Herstmonceux Castle, Sussex; but the zero meridian of longitude (marked on the path in front of the Observatory) passes through Greenwich, and 'Greenwich time' is still the official mean time for Great Britain. Daily at 1 p.m. a time-ball (1833) falls on a mast on the roof of *Flamsteed House*. This was built by Wren as the house of the first Astronomer Royal and, with the adjoining *Meridian Building*, an 18C expansion of Flamsteed's garden observatory, forms an astronomical annexe of the National Maritime Museum.

The fine *Octagon Room*, unaltered since Wren designed it, has been refurnished with replicas, and it and other galleries display historic instruments used by Halley, Airy, Bradley, and Herschel father and son. Flamsteed's angle-clock was made by Thos. Tompion in 1691.—The Victorian *South Building* houses a Planetarium (performances in summer).

The adjoining terrace commands an extensive *View of London. The statue of Gen. Wolfe, by Tait Mackenzie, was presented by the Canadian nation. On the w. side of the park are *Ranger's House* (music recitals in Sept), once occupied by Lord Chesterfield, *Macartney House*, the home of Wolfe's parents, and, lower down, Croom's Hill, with good 17–18C houses and the *Greenwich Theatre*. The statue of King William IV, in the N.W. corner of the park, came from King William St. in the City.

At the top of Maze Hill, on the E. side of the park, *Vanbrugh Castle* (1717–26), built for himself by Sir John Vanbrugh, is now a R.A.F. memorial school; while a nunnery, a little to the E., occupies the house built in 1772–74 by John Julius Angerstein, 'founder' of the National Gallery (d. 1823; buried in St Alfege).—Charlton Road (53 bus) leads E. in c. 2½ m. viâ Charlton (comp. below) to Woolwich.

Greenwich Park is adjoined on the S. by **Blackheath** (stations on an alternative line to Woolwich), a beautiful common 267 acres in area, once notorious for its highwaymen. The Kentish rebels under Wat Tyler in 1381, and again under Jack Cade in 1450, made Blackheath their headquarters in their attacks on London. Blackheath Golf Club, founded in 1608, is the oldest in the world, but its course is now at Eltham. Near the S.E. angle of the common is the fine crescent of houses called the *Paragon*, by Michael Searles (c. 1800; rebuilt after war damage), now associated with the charming brick almshouses known as *Morden College* (1695), almost certainly by Wren (no adm.; seen from footpath N. of the grounds).

The dreary Woolwich Road (buses), follows the railway, but keeps nearer the Thames.—6½ m. **Charlton**, birthplace of Walter de la Mare (1873–1956), stands S. of its station, nearly 1 m. from the river. From Woolwich Rd. an unexpectedly delightful walk ascends through the wooded Maryon parks in 20 min. to the Jacobean *Charlton House* (1607–12; open weekdays). *St Luke's Church* (c. 1630) preserves contemporary glass and good monuments, including one by Chantrey to Spencer Perceval, assassinated in 1812.

8 m. **Woolwich** has its shopping centre, imaginatively replanned, on low ground next the Thames, sandwiched between the former Royal Dockyard to the W. and the Arsenal to the E. and fringed with extensive military buildings on the rising ground to the S. The *Free Ferry*, established for vehicles in 1889, now links the E. ends of the North and South Circular Roads. *Woolwich Arsenal* is the oldest and largest establishment of its kind in England. Up to 40,000 workers (including a large number of women) were employed here during the war in 1939–45.

The *Royal Dockyard* was founded in the 15C. Here the 'Great Harry' was built in 1512 and the 'Royal Sovereign' in 1637. Superseded by Devonport, the yard closed in 1869 and has since been put to a variety of military and industrial uses. The 19C Record Office, with its clock tower, will be preserved; little earlier than the 19C remains intact above ground. The local council sponsored an archaeological survey in 1973 before commencing a housing estate.

From the Dockyard Frances St. (with an interesting modern estate) ascends past *Cambridge Barracks* (1847), the depot of the Royal Artillery, to their *Barracks* (1776), with an imposing frontage over 1000 ft long including a central triumphal arch. Repository Road leads to the *Rotunda* (open free, 10–12.45 and 2–4 or 5, Sun from 2), a pavilion erected by Nash in St James's Park in 1814 and removed here in 1819, which contains an important museum of the Royal Artillery.

BUS No. 161 runs S. from Woolwich, skirting the E. side of Woolwich Common, where stand the former buildings of the *Royal Military Academy*, known among military personnel as 'The Shop.' Built in 1805 for the training of cadets studying for the Royal Artillery or Royal Engineers, it was merged in 1946 with the Royal Military College, Sandhurst. Just beyond, our route crosses the old Dover Road (the Roman Watling Street) at *Shooters Hill*. On the left rises the tower of *Severndroog Castle*, commemorating the capture of Severndroog on the Malabar coast in 1755.—We traverse *Well Hall*, a suburb taking name from a Tudor building whose moat survives in the pretty park surrounding its Tudor Barn (restored 1936; restaurant and art gallery). Here in a later house (demolished) E. Nesbit lived in

1899–1922.—We reach (3 m.) **Eltham** (station ½ m. N. on the line from Charing Cross to Welling), principally interesting for the remains of *Eltham Palace*, a favourite Christmas residence of the English sovereigns from Henry III to Henry VIII. Chaucer was clerk of the works to Richard II, and Henry IV here entertained Manuel II Palaeologus, the Byzantine emperor. The Palace is now the headquarters of the Institute of Army Education; it is approached by a medieval bridge over the moat, outside which a fine restored half-timbered range survives from an outer court. The chief relic is the *Banqueting Hall (1480), noted for its fine hammer-beam roof (adm. Apr–Oct, Thurs–Mon 10.30–12, 1–6; winter Thurs & Sat, 10.30–12, 1–4).

FROM WOOLWICH TO DARTFORD, 5 m. Bus No. 99 to Erith; No. 96 (viâ Bexleyheath) to Dartford. The most interesting road, beyond Woolwich Arsenal, traverses *Plumstead*, which possesses a series of pleasant commons to the S., and a wide expanse of marshes to the N., then climbs Bostall Hill through *Bostall Woods*, a sylvan public park.

From the crossroads at the end of the woods (2½ m. from Woolwich) Knee Hill descends to *Abbey Wood* (¼ m.). Here on the right, in a park below the wood that gives this suburb its name, are the ruins of *Lessness Abbey*, an Augustinian foundation dating from 1178. Though unimpressive in height, they have been skilfully cleared (1956–59) to show the complete plan of the monastery, with its church, cloister, and domestic buildings: note the stairway to the reader's pulpit in the refectory.—To the N. Erith marshes are the site of the new town of *Thamesmead*.

3¾ m. *Belvedere* takes its name from a mansion of 1764–74, by James 'Athenian' Stuart, now the *Royal Alfred Institution* for aged seamen.—5 m. *Erith* is an ancient riverside town affording a fine view of the Thames and its shipping. At its w. end is the parish church, largely rebuilt, but retaining a 13C s. door and, in the S.E. chapel, several brasses and the alabaster tomb of the Countess of Shrewsbury (d. 1368).—9 m. *Dartford*, see the 'Blue Guide to England'.

36   DULWICH AND CRYSTAL PALACE

STATIONS: *Elephant and Castle, Loughborough*, and *Herne Hill* from Holborn Viaduct; *West Dulwich* (⅓ m. s. of Picture Gallery) from Victoria or Blackfriars; *North Dulwich* on S. London line from Victoria to London Bridge is ½ m. N. of the Picture Gallery.—For the Horniman Museum, *Forest Hill* from London Bridge. *Crystal Palace* station is served by trains from Victoria and London Bridge.

BUSES: Nos. 12, 176 from Elephant and Castle viâ Walworth Rd. to Camberwell Green.—No. 3 (from Piccadilly) passes near West Dulwich Station.—Nos. 12, 176, 185 pass the Horniman Museum.—Nos. 2, 3, 63, 108, and 137 serve the Crystal Palace grounds.

To (1¼ m.) Elephant and Castle, see p. 266. *Walworth Road* runs S.E. through Walworth past (1½ m.) Southwark Central Library and the CUMING MUSEUM (adm. Mon–Fri 10–5.30, Thurs till 7; Sat 10–5). It illustrates the history and antiquities of Southwark, and includes memorials of Michael Faraday (1791–1867), the scientist, born in the neighbourhood.—At (2¾ m.) *Camberwell Green*, with its fine trees, Camberwell Church St. runs E. In Peckham Road, the continuation of Camberwell Church St., is (No. 63; on the left) the SOUTH LONDON ART GALLERY (open weekdays 10–6, Sun from 3, when an exhibition is mounted). A reference collection of 20C prints is on display, and a small collection of paintings, including some of local interest, may usually be seen on request. About ten exhibitions are held each year.

Robert Browning (1812–89) was born in Southampton Way, the next turning on the left. Joseph Chamberlain (1836–1914) was born at 188 Camberwell Grove. In Meeting House Lane, running N. from Peckham High St., the continuation of Peckham Rd., stood the Meeting House (No. 180) used by William Penn before his imprisonment in the Tower (1668). This was completely destroyed during the Second World War.

From Camberwell Green *Denmark Hill* runs s., passing *King's College*

Hospital, to *Herne Hill.* In Champion Park (l.) is the *William Booth Memorial Training College* (1929) of the Salvation Army. *Ruskin Park* (36 acres), on the right, commemorates the long residence in this neighbourhood of John Ruskin, from 1823 to 1871.—4 m. Junction with Red Post Hill. Herne Hill continues to the attractive *Brockwell Park* (127 acres), with its fine old garden and large swimming pool; we turn left down Red Post Hill into **Dulwich Village,** a pleasant residential suburb, especially noted for its picture gallery.—5 m. ***Dulwich College Picture Gallery,** in College Road, was built by Sir John Soane and opened in 1814. It was partially destroyed by a flying bomb in 1944 and was reopened in 1953. It is open free daily on weekdays (exc. Mon) 10–4, 5, or 6, and on Sun (Apr–Sept only) from 2.—The finest paintings belonged to Noel Desenfans, a French picture-dealer, who left them in 1807 to his friend Sir P. F. Bourgeois, R.A. (d. 1811), who in turn bequeathed them to the College.

Dulwich Gallery is especially rich in Dutch paintings, and contains no less than 10 examples of the work of *Aelbert Cuyp* (especially Nos. 4, 96, and 124). There are three good paintings by *Rembrandt* (99, 163, 221), and a large number by the two *Teniers.* About 11 works are assigned to *Rubens.* The collection also contains works by *Wouwerman* (especially 97, 182), *Ruysdael* (168), *Hobbema* (87), *Gerard Dou* (56), *Adriaen van Ostade, Jan Both, Johannes Wynants, Gerard van Honthorst* (571), and *Jan van Huysum* (120). The Italian paintings are fewer in number, but include two fine works by *Canaletto* (600, 599), designs by *Tiepolo,* a good *Paolo Veronese* (270), and *Guercino* (282). Also: *Guido Reni* (262), *Seb. Ricci* (195), *Ann. Carracci* (265), and *Piero di Cosimo* (258). Of the French School, *Nicholas Poussin* is represented by 7 paintings, and *Watteau* and *Lancret* by one each (156, 167). To the Spanish School belong four delightful works by *Murillo.* In the British School there are portraits by *Cornelius Johnson* (564) and *Gheeraerts* (548); and works by *Gainsborough* (331, 140, 302, 320, 66), *Reynolds* (104, 598), *Lawrence* (178), and *Van Dyck* (170, 194, 173). Also a *Romney* (590), an *Allan Ramsay* (596), and a *Richard Wilson* (561).

The *Old College Buildings,* beside the gallery, contain the offices of the trust which administers Dulwich College, Alleyn's School, James Allen's Girls' School, etc. Edward Alleyn (1566–1626), actor-manager and keeper of the King's wild beasts, who founded the charity, is buried in the chapel.

From the old college buildings College Road leads to the Crystal Palace (see below), passing the last surviving toll-gate in the County of London and ($\frac{1}{2}$ m.) the handsome red brick buildings of **Dulwich College,** built in 1866, which is attended by about 1000 boys. The old boys include C. S. Forester and Sir Ernest Shackleton. The 'James Laird' in which he sailed in the Antarctic in 1916 is kept in the College.

Opposite the old college buildings is an entrance to *Dulwich Park* (fine azaleas and rhododendrons; aviary with talking parrots), on the other side of which Lordship Lane leads s. in $\frac{1}{2}$ m. to the HORNIMAN MUSEUM (open free daily 10.30–6, Sun from 2; lecture at 3.30 on Sat; tea room). Founded by Frederick J. Horniman, the museum was constructed for his collection in 1901 by C. Harrison Townsend. It is noted for its *Ethnographical collection, notably musical instruments, and has a good display of natural history and a fine library. A pleasant park surrounds the museum.

6$\frac{3}{4}$ m. **Crystal Palace,** on the summit of a steep hill with wide views, is now the site of the NATIONAL SPORTS CENTRE. Although building is still in progress, the centre already includes fine swimming baths, running tracks, a large exhibition hall, etc. The public may make use of facilities for swimming, tennis, badminton, squash, athletics, ski-training, etc.

(annual subscription fee £2.50). A television transmitting station crowns the hill-top, and in the park (aviary) beyond the Stadium, Waterhouse Hawkins' models of prehistoric reptilia ('Paxton's monsters') still inhabit their artificial islands. — Symphony concerts are held at the Concert Bowl (June–Aug).

The *Crystal Palace*, a huge edifice of glass and iron, was opened in 1854, but was almost entirely destroyed by fire on 30 Nov 1936. The original palace, a reconstruction of the large hall designed by Sir Joseph Paxton for the Great Exhibition of 1851 in Hyde Park, consisted of a great central hall, about 1600 ft in length, with aisles and two transepts. The water-towers, 282 ft high, at either end, survived the fire, but were removed in 1940.

37 GREENWICH TO WINDSOR VIÂ CROYDON

GREEN LINE COACH No. 725 from Gravesend to Windsor follows the route.

From *Blackheath* (p. 282) Lee Park Road (bus No. 75) and its continuation Burnt Ash Road (bus No. 94) and College Road run s. to (5 m.) **Bromley** (304,400 inhab.). Although now a London Borough, it retains the features of a town with a market square. *Bromley College*, founded by Bp. John Warner in 1666, was built in 1670. In London Lane Quernmore School occupies a fine late-18C house. *Sundridge Park*, to the N., was designed by John Nash. The park, by Repton, is now a golf course.

To the w. (2 m; bus 227) lies **Chislehurst**, a spacious well-to-do suburb planted with trees and shrubs. The chalk *Caves*, N. of the station, may be visited daily (tours 11–5; fee). *Petts Wood*, to the s., is owned by the N.T.

Beckenham Lane and Bromley Road run through *Beckenham*, where (7 m.) Croydon Road diverges s. towards (11½ m.) **Croydon** (331,900 inhab.), until 1964 the largest town in Surrey, but now absorbed in Greater London. The centre is being transformed in the most thoroughgoing Civic rebuilding undertaken since 1945 in England. Though few buildings merit individual mention, in their grouping they form an interesting exercise in the modern manner, preserving an urban rather than a suburban atmosphere. The *Fairfield Halls and Ashcroft Theatre* face the huge Technical College across a piazza. At the corner of North End and George St. is **Whitgift Hospital*, founded by Abp. Whitgift in•1596 for 16 poor brothers and 16 poor sisters. The chapel (closed 10.30–11 on Thurs, 10–10.30 on Sun), the hall, and the common room are shown daily. The *Trinity School* of John Whitgift has moved to Shirley Park; its site is now occupied by a vast shopping precinct. *Whitgift School* lies c. 1 m. s. The church of *St John* (rebuilt in 1867) has the tombs of Whitgift (d. 1604) and of J. S. Copley (1737–1815), the painter. The *Old Palace of the archbishops (now a girls' school), a reputed foundation of Lanfranc (11C), is shown by appointment, normally after school hours. The first public railway in the world was opened in 1803 in the Wandle valley between Croydon and Wandsworth; the wagons of the Surrey Iron Railway were drawn by horses.

Croydon Airport, to the s.w., had military beginnings in 1915; here in 1919 George VI (then Prince Albert) gained his 'wings'. It became the first London airport in 1920, and from 1924 to 1939 it was the base of Imperial Airways. Many pioneer British civil flights were made from here, including the Cape and Australia air races. The airfield is now the site of a huge housing estate.—At *Shirley*, c. 1½ m E. of Croydon, are the buildings (1930) of *Bethlem Royal Hospital*, the oldest hospital in the world for the treatment of the insane, once popularly known as Bedlam. Founded in Bishopsgate in 1247, it was removed to Moorgate in 1675, and thence to Lambeth in 1815. A little farther s., across Addington Park, *Addington Palace*, a former property of the archbishops of Canterbury, now houses the Royal School of Church Music.—*Mitcham*, N.W. of Croydon, is noted for its breezy common (480 acres).

Croydon stands on the old Brighton Road now taken w. of the centre by the Purley Way. As the A23, it leaves London at **Kennington**, once a royal manor with a palace granted to the Black Prince by Edward III. The Common was used in 1848 by the Chartists as an assembly place before an abortive attempt to march on Parliament with their petition. The gathering was watched by Berlioz who commented in his 'Memoirs', "My poor friends, you know as much about starting a riot as the Italians about writing a symphony". *Kennington Oval* is the ground of the Surrey Cricket Club. Thence the road traverses **Stockwell, Brixton**, and **Streatham**. Van Gogh stayed in Brixton in 1872 at the age of 19 and fell in love with his landlady's daughter, Eugenie Loyer. *Streatham Park* (pulled down in 1863), on the s. side of *Tooting Bec Common*, was the country residence of Henry Thrale (d. 1781), at which Dr Johnson was a frequent guest.

We continue w. towards Sutton and Cheam and turn N. along Malden Road skirting (17½ m.) *Nonsuch Park* where Henry VIII built an elaborate palace in 1538 (demolished in 1682–88).—18 m. We cross the old Roman Stane Street (London to Chichester road) which retains its Roman alinement from London Bridge.

From the *Elephant and Castle* (p. 265) it runs s. as the A24 through **Clapham**, a suburb with a fine common of 220 acres. Samuel Pepys died in 1703 in a house (described by Evelyn as 'a very noble House and sweet place') which he built here on the N. side of the Common. A tablet (1919) on the outside wall of the pleasant Georgian parish church (1775) commemorates the 'Clapham Sect' as Sydney Smith called the evangelical Anglican group of friends who lived in the big houses around the Common at the end of the 18C. Beyond the *South London Hospital*, managed by women for women, the thoroughfare traverses **Balham** and **Tooting**. Daniel Defoe is said to have founded the first 'Independent Meeting' at Tooting. —*Epsom*, where the Derby is run in May, lies c. 3 m. s. of Nonsuch (comp. 'Blue Guide to England').

We continue N.W. through Malden to (22½ m.) **Kingston upon Thames** (p. 297). We cross the Thames and pass **Hampton Court Palace** (Rte 41).—27 m. *Kempton Park Racecourse* (closed for rebuilding in 1973). At *Sunbury*, to the s., is Sunbury Court (now a Salvation Army conference centre) where the hall (c. 1770–80) is painted by Elias Martin, a Swedish artist. We skirt (29 m.) the N. bank of *Queen Mary Reservoir* through *Ashford*. The charming little church of *Littleton* is situated on the s. side of the lake.—31 m. **Staines** is said to derive its name from the ancient *London Stone* (on the river ¼ m. w. of the church; see p. 292). — We skirt the level meadow of *Runnymede* (p. 292), and at *Old Windsor* the road recedes from the river.—37 m. **Windsor** (Rte 43).

38 THE THAMES

A From Westminster to Hampton Court

STEAMERS: Easter–Sept only. From *Westminster Pier* to Putney, Kew, Richmond, and Hampton Court. Departures for Hampton Court at 10, 10.30, 11 &
12; for Richmond also at 2.30 and 3; for Putney and Kew every half hour from 10
to 4.30. A service also runs from Richmond to Hampton Court at 11.30 and 3, and
from Hampton Court to Richmond at 2 and 5.30.—Return from Hampton Court
at 3, 4, & 5; from Richmond at 4.30, 5.30, 6, 6.30, and 6.45; from Kew and Putney
at 2, 3, 5, 5.30, 6, 6.30, 7, and 7.15.—To Putney in 30 min; to Kew in 1 hr 30 min;
to Richmond in 2 hr 30 min; to Hampton Court in 3 hr 45 min.—A frequent
summer service connects Westminster Pier and Battersea Pleasure Grounds from
10 a.m. to dusk.

All services are subject to weather conditions; times are approx. exc. for services
commencing at Westminster and Richmond. Extra services are run when necessary, and there are later sailings on evenings in the high summer.

FARES: Westminster to Battersea, 30p, 50p return; to Putney, 40p, 60p return; to
Kew 50p, 70p return; to Richmond 70p, £1 return; to Hampton Court £1, £1 50p
return. Children half price.

Enquiries and confirmation of sailing times at *Thames Passenger Services
Federation*, Charing Cross Pier (Tel. No. 892 5255). For other river excursions,
see p. 28.

Places of interest mentioned below are described in greater detail in other routes
(comp. the Index). The area between Westminster and Battersea Reach appears on
Atlas 14, 15, 16, and 17.

In the following description the words 'right' and 'left' (r. and l.) refer to the
journey upstream.

Opposite **Westminster Pier** (Pl. 19; 1; p. 236) rises the large building
of *County Hall*. Just above Westminster Bridge is the terrace of the
Houses of Parliament on the right; opposite is the huge new *St Thomas's
Hospital*, beyond which rise the old walls and towers of *Lambeth Palace*,
with *St Mary's Church*. On the right are Victoria Tower Gardens. Passing
beneath *Lambeth Bridge*, we have the Imperial Chemical Industries
building and the tall Millbank Tower on the right. Opposite, the
headquarters of the London *Fire Brigade* are marked by their fire-floats.
Farther on is the colonnaded façade of the *Tate Gallery*.

Above (1 m.) *Vauxhall Bridge* the banks are fringed with factories and
wharves, off which lie strings of barges. On the left is passed the new
'*Covent Garden*' market at Nine Elms. Beyond *Battersea Power Station*
(l.) and the residential *Dolphin Square* (r.) we pass beneath (2 m.) the
wide *Victoria Railway Bridge* and *Chelsea Suspension Bridge*. On the left
appear the trees of *Battersea Park* (**Battersea Pier**; 2 m. from Westminster), and on the right are the *Chelsea Embankment* and the grounds
of *Royal Chelsea Hospital*, which is visible through the trees. Then, on
the right, begin the red-brick houses of *Cheyne Walk*. We pass *Cadogan
Pier* on the right, just below *Albert Suspension Bridge*. The square tower
of *Chelsea Old Church* now comes into view. Beyond (3 m.) *Battersea
Bridge* lies the picturesque part of Cheyne Walk, ending at *Lot's Road
Power Station* of the underground railways, a prominent landmark with
its four tall chimneys. The river is now flanked on either side by factories; we obtain a view of the distant Surrey hills. On the left is *Battersea Church*. We pass beneath a railway bridge near Fulham Power
Station (N. bank) and then beneath (4 m.) *Wandsworth Bridge*. On the
left is the mouth of the *Wandle*. On the right lies *Fulham*, with the leafy
grounds of Hurlingham Club opposite (5 m.) *Wandsworth Park*, beyond

which begin the houses of *Putney*. Next comes the iron lattice-bridge of the District Railway (with a footway) and the handsome stone *Putney Bridge*, flanked by the parish churches of Fulham (r.) and Putney (l.). A wooden bridge between Putney and Fulham built here in 1729 was the first to be built across the Thames after London Bridge. On the left is **Putney Pier** (30 min. from Westminster). Opposite lies *Fulham Palace*, hidden by the trees. The public Bishop's Park skirts the river for ½ m., ending at the Craven Cottage (Fulham) football ground. Meanwhile, on the left, we pass the boathouses of several rowing clubs. The University Boat Race (p. 39) begins here, and various points on the river between Putney and Mortlake acquire a temporary fame as stages in the famous race.

To the left, hidden by trees, is (6 m.) *Barn Elms*, now a public park. Between this point and Barnes the s. bank of the river, which describes a great curve, is occupied by reservoirs of the Metropolitan Water Board. We pass *Hammersmith Pier* (7 m.) on the right, close to *Hammersmith Suspension Bridge*. On the left are the new buildings of *St Paul's School*; on the right is *Hammersmith Mall*, with its attractive houses and the Doves Inn (a boat-race mark). *Chiswick Eyot* (8 m.) masks *Chiswick Mall*, except the w. end of it, where *Chiswick Church* is seen. We now enter *Corney Reach*. On the left lies *Barnes*, with another terrace of 18C houses facing the river. Beyond *Barnes Railway Bridge* (9 m.) comes *Mortlake*, on the left. The University Boat Race ends near the Ship Inn. We pass beneath *Chiswick Bridge* (by Sir Herbert Baker; 1933), and then a railway bridge, beyond which, on the right, lies the charming water-side hamlet of *Strand-on-the-Green*. Immediately afterwards we reach **Kew** (p. 298), which lies to the left. The pier (11 m.; 1 hr 30 min. from Westminster) lies just short of *Kew Bridge*. A pleasant walk along the tow-path leads hence to Richmond. On the right is *Brentford*, with Brentford Eyot in front. On the left are the *Royal Botanic Gardens*, with their fine trees, and *Kew Palace*, half hidden among the foliage. Opposite open the mouth of the river *Brent* and (12 m.) *Brentford Dock*.

The succeeding reach is a pretty stretch of wooded river scenery. *Syon House*, a seat of the Duke of Northumberland, appears four-square on the right, in the middle of a fine park, beyond an attractive boat house. Then, on the left, is the *Old Deer Park*, with the yellowish-green observatory. Opposite, behind the eyot (13 m.), lies *Isleworth*, with its quaint little quay, or 'hard'. A little higher up we reach *Richmond Lock*, the lowest lock on the Thames, constructed in 1894, beside an elevated footbridge. On the right lies St Margaret's. We pass under *Twickenham Bridge* (by Maxwell Ayrton; 1933) and a rail bridge. On the left is the recently restored *Asgill House*, and the river façade of *Trumpeter's House*. Approaching the charming *Richmond Bridge* we see **Richmond** (p. 295); rising picturesquely behind it on the hill. The pier is on the left (14 m.; 2½ hrs from Westminster). Richmond is the chief boating centre for this section of the Upper Thames, and launches ply thence upstream to Hampton Court, Staines, and Windsor.

As we leave Richmond *Richmond Hill* rises on the left, with its terrace-gardens and the *Star and Garter Home* for disabled soldiers. Farther on, to the left, lies *Petersham*, with its quaint red-brick church. Opposite Hammerton's Ferry we catch a glimpse through the trees of *Ham House*, a fine red-brick mansion close to the river. Meanwhile, we are passing

Twickenham, on the north bank, with its historic riverside mansions (in summer mostly hidden by trees): *Marble Hill*, in a public park (15 m.), *Orleans House*, and *York House*. Opposite the picturesque village is *Eel-Pie Island* (footbridge). A little farther on (16 m.) we pass the site of Pope's Villa; then, after ½ m., comes Strawberry Hill, in a secluded park about 300 yds from the river. To the right lies *Teddington*, the highest point of the tidal Thames, with a lock and footbridge across the river (17 m.). Another pleasant reach, with pretty houses on the right and *Canbury Gardens* on the left, farther on, brings us to (18 m.) a railway bridge and to *Kingston Bridge*, which unites **Kingston**, on the left with Hampton Wick on the right. Kingston is another important boating centre; steamers to Windsor, Henley, and Oxford.

We proceed, with Hampton Court Park on our right and *Surbiton* and *Thames Ditton* (20 m.) on our left. We soon come in sight of **Hampton Court Palace** on our right; opposite is the mouth of the river *Mole*. The steamer stops just beyond the bridge, on the left, not far from Molesey Lock (21 m.; 3 hrs 45 min. from Westminster).

B From Kingston upon Thames to Windsor

A STEAMER service is run from 19 May to 16 Sept by Salter Bros. of Oxford. From Kingston steamers call at *Molesey* (Hampton Court), *Sunbury*, *Walton*, *Shepperton*, *Chertsey*, *Penton Hook*, *Staines*, *Bell Weir*, *Runnymede*, *Old Windsor*, and *Windsor Bridge*. The through journey can be made only with an overnight stop at Chertsey. The service continues upstream to Oxford (comp. the 'Blue Guide to England'). For full details of timetable and 'Handbook', apply to Salter Bros., Folly Bridge, Oxford (Tel: Oxford 43421).—In the following description the words 'right' and 'left' (r. and l.) refer to the journey upstream.

From Kingston to (3 m.) **Hampton Court**, see Rte 38A. Above Tagg's Island we pass *Hampton*, with Garrick's Villa. In Roy Grove survives the gun barrel (plaque) that formed the s. end of the original Ordnance Survey base line (1784). Beyond a series of reservoirs we reach (6 m.) **Sunbury Lock**. Sunbury lies on the N. bank. — 7½ m. **Walton Bridge**. *Walton-on-Thames* is on the s. side, where also rises *St George's Hill*. At the bend in the river we pass *Cowey Stakes*, which disputes with Brentford the claim to be where Julius Caesar crossed the Thames in 54 B.C. The straight Desborough Channel here cuts off c. 1 m., but the river runs more pleasantly by *Lower Halliford* (T. L. Peacock, 1785–1866, is buried in Halliford churchyard) and *Shepperton* (r.) with a pleasing 17–18C village centre. Beyond *D'Oyly Carte Island*, once the home of Richard d'Oyly Carte, we reach (9½ m.) **Shepperton Lock**.

On the left, at the mouth of the Wey, is **Weybridge**, which preserves on its green the Seven Dials column (1794) from London. *Oatlands Park*, now a hotel, on the Walton road, was built in 1827 and succeeds a royal palace (destroyed in the Civil War) where Henry VIII married Catherine Howard.

Between Weybridge and Guildford (15 m.) the WEY NAVIGATION (N.T.) is available to pleasure-boats. It passes through a charming stretch of country at *Pyrford*, near Newark Priory and Old Woking, and skirts the grounds of Sutton Place.

Beyond *Chertsey Bridge* (1780–85) is (11½ m.) **Chertsey Lock**. *Chertsey* where the poet Cowley died in 1667, lies on the left bank. Abbey Mead recalls the famous Benedictine abbey of Chertsey, founded in the 7C and refounded in 1110, of which almost nothing survives. It was known especially for its floor-tiles, which adorn many English churches. At (r.) *Laleham* Matthew Arnold (1822–88) was born and is buried beside the part-Norman church. Laleham Abbey was the home of Lord Lucan of Crimean War fame.—13½ m. **Penton Hook Lock,** with a marina.

15½ m. **Staines Bridge,** begun in 1829 by John Rennie. Staines is on the right. The *London Stone* here marked the w. limit of the jurisdiction over the Thames of the City of London from 1285 to 1857. Just short of **Bell Weir Lock** we pass under the Staines by-pass; the Colne enters the Thames on the right. From here almost to Henley the N. bank belongs to Buckinghamshire. On the left lies *Egham,* and upstream is the meadow of **Runnymede** (N.T.) with (18 m.) *Magna Carta Island.* This is probably the actual place where King John 'sealed' Magna Carta in 1215. The entrance pavilions were designed by Lutyens. Above, on *Cooper's Hill* (celebrated in a poem by Denham) rises the *Commonwealth Air Forces Memorial* (1953), by Maufe, commanding a superb view; and just beyond is the national memorial to President Kennedy (1917–63), by Geoffrey Jellicoe (1965; damaged in 1968). The s. bank of the river now belongs to Berkshire. Just within the boundary is *Beaumont College,* a Roman Catholic public school, founded in 1861, in a house once occupied by Warren Hastings.—19½ m. **Old Windsor Lock.**

Beyond *Albert Bridge* (1925) *Windsor Home Park* reaches the river bank. On the right is *Datchet,* where Falstaff was ducked in the Thames. We pass under Victoria Bridge and Black Potts Bridge, where Izaak Walton fished, and reach (22½ m.) *Romney Lock.* On the right is *Eton College* and its playing fields, seen to great advantage from the river.— 23 m. **Windsor Bridge.**

39 RICHMOND, PETERSHAM, AND KINGSTON

A Viâ Putney and Wimbledon

UNDERGROUND: *Putney Bridge, East Putney, Southfields, Wimbledon Park,* and *Wimbledon* on District line. For RAILWAY, see Rte 39B.

BUSES: No. 22 along King's Rd. across Putney Bridge. No. 85 from Fulham Palace direct to Kingston; No. 93 from Fulham Palace to Wimbledon Common.

From Chelsea (Rte 13) King's Road leads w. to join (2¾ m.) New King's Road, lined with antique shops and 'junk' shops.—4 m. *Fulham High Road.* On the left are the grounds of the fashionable Hurlingham Club, part of which has been converted into a public park.

An alternative route from South Kensington follows Fulham Road which skirts the huge *Brompton Cemetery* with its exotic tombs, to join Fulham High Road just N. of New King's Road.

FULHAM PALACE (approached viâ Fulham Palace Road and Bishop's Avenue to the N.) is the residence of the Bishops of London, and the manor of Fulham has belonged to the See since 631. The entrance courtyard was built by Bp Fitzjames in the reign of Henry VII, but the rest of the building dates from the 18C and 19C. The grounds, 37 acres in area, are of remarkable beauty. Between them and the river extends the public *Bishop's Park,* with an open-air theatre by E. A. H. Macdonald (1960).

Just before PUTNEY BRIDGE is *Fulham Parish Church* by Blomfield (1880–81). The early-15C tower was restored in the 19C. Inside are 16–19C monuments. Across the bridge *Putney Parish Church* preserves its

15C tower. Within is a 16C Lady Chapel with a fan vault, and interesting monuments. Thomas Cromwell (?1458–1540), chancellor of Henry VIII, and Edward Gibbon (1737–94) were natives of **Putney** and Swinburne (1837–1909), the poet, died on Putney Hill. The *Embankment* (r.; often partially flooded at high tide) is lined with picturesque boat houses beyond the Star and Garter. At weekends the river here is the scene of much sailing and skulling activity.

Putney High Street leads s.—4½ m. Junction with *Upper Richmond Road*. We turn right.

Putney Hill continues to climb s. to *Putney Heath*, once famous for duels, where William Pitt died in 1806 at Bowling Green House (replaced by a modern 'close'). The heath is prolonged by *Wimbledon Common (l., with Putney Lower Common, c. 1100 acres) with Rushmere and King's Mere ponds (model boats). A Golf Course, sports area, and horse riding facilities are located here. On its s. border is the Rounds or '*Caesar's Camp*' (14 acres), thought to be an earthwork of the New Stone Age. The *Windmill* (near Queen's Mere; approached by Windmill Road) is the successor to a mill here in 1780. It is a combined smock and post mill (restored 1957). The earliest recorded duel on the heath took place in 1652. In 1798 the Prime Minister, William Pitt fought George Tierney (M.P.), and in 1809 Lord Castlereagh and George Canning fought. The last duel took place in 1840 when Lord Cardigan wounded Capt. Harvey Tuckett. To the E. the suburb of *Wimbledon* is best known for the All-England Lawn Tennis Courts in Wimbledon Park (comp. p. 34). Richmond Park (see below) may be entered at Robin Hood Gate from Roehampton Vale which skirts the N.W. side of the Common.

5¾ m. *Roehampton Lane* leads s. passing a sports and recreation centre and Roehampton Golf Course.—6½ m. *Queen Mary's Hospital*, originally Roehampton House (by Archer, 1710–12, enlarged by Lutyens). The former village of *Roehampton*, once girdled by 18C mansions, is now more obviously notable for its huge blocks of flats, which have almost engulfed *Mount Clare*, a charming mansion (1772) in the style of Henry Holland, overlooking Richmond Park. We follow the narrow Clarence Lane w. to reach the Roehampton Gate of **Richmond Park** (see Rte 39B).

B Viâ Barnes and Mortlake

RAILWAY: frequent trains (S.R.) from Waterloo viâ Putney, Barnes, North Sheen and Mortlake to Richmond.

BUSES: Nos 9 and 73 from Kensington cross Hammersmith Bridge; No. 9 continues to Mortlake High St. No. 72 from Hammersmith Bridge crosses Barnes Common to Roehampton Vale.

FOR RICHMOND: *Richmond Station* on District line and S.R. (see above; bus 65 connects the Station with Richmond Hill). — *Buses* to Richmond Bridge: No. 33 (exc. Sun) and 73 (on Sun) from Kensington viâ Upper Richmond Rd.; No. 37 from Putney. – *Green Line Coach* No. 714 from Hyde Park Corner crosses Hammersmith Bridge viâ Barnes and East Sheen to Richmond, Petersham, Ham, and Kingston.

FOR PETERSHAM AND KINGSTON: *Bus* 65 connects Richmond viâ Petersham with Kingston. – *Kingston Station* on S.R. from Waterloo. – Frequent buses from Kingston along Hampton Court Rd. to Hampton Court Palace.

CAR PARKING: Car Parks in Richmond Park; Friar's Lane (Richmond Green); and Ham House.

RIVER LAUNCHES for Richmond, see Rte 38.

To (3 m.) Hammersmith Broadway, see Rte 40.—Hammersmith Bridge Road leads s. across (3½ m.) *Hammersmith Bridge*, an impressive iron suspension bridge. On the right 45 acres of river bank provide the site for *St Paul's School*, moved here in 1968 from Hammersmith Road. The architects are Feilden and Mawson. The school (675 boys), founded by Dean Colet was removed from St Paul's Churchyard in

1884. Among its famous pupils are Milton, Pepys, Marlborough, Judge Jeffreys, Major André, Jowett, Compton Mackenzie, and 'Tubby' Clayton.—Castlenau continues s. to (4½ m.) *Barn Elms Park*.

This occupies the grounds of the former estate of Barn Elms, a house given to Sir Francis Walsingham by Elizabeth I. In 1884 it became the home of the fashionable Ranelagh Club (closed in 1939), and is now a sports centre. Another house in the park was occupied by Jacob Tonson, the publisher (d. 1736), who built a room for the meetings of the Kit-Cat Club (comp. p. 85). Kit (or Christopher) Cat was the man who supplied mutton-pies to the club. Wm. Cobbett had a farm on the estate in 1821 after his imprisonment for 'sedition'. Francis T. Palgrave (1824–97), compiler of 'The Golden Treasury', is buried in Barnes Cemetery. Rocks Lane traverses *Barnes Common* (126 acres; attractive houses in Mill Hill), to join Upper Richmond Road, whence Roehampton Lane leads s. towards Richmond Park (comp. Rte 39A).

The attractive riverside districts of **Barnes** and **Mortlake** lie to the w. Mortlake was famous for tapestries, made here from 1619 until the works expired for want of patronage after the death of Charles I. It is the finishing point of the Boat Race (see p. 290), rowed from Putney. We turn w. along Church Road. *St Mary's Church* stands in a picturesque churchyard with some fine houses nearby. The tower was encased in red brick in Elizabethan times. Parts of the Lady Chapel date from the 13C church. The brasses include one to the sisters Edith and Elizabeth Wylde (1508).—5 m. *Barnes Green* and pond. On the w. side is Milbourne House, a part-Tudor building, redesigned in the 17C and 18C. Henry Fielding lived here c. 1750. Barnes High Street continues to the river. Here *Barnes Terrace* has some interesting houses (built c. 1740). Gustav Holst, the composer, lived at No. 10 from 1908 to 1913. Beyond (5½ m.) Barnes Bridge we follow the Broadway into *Mortlake High Street*. On the right, from the garden of the Limes (18C), Turner painted two views of the Thames. Farther on (l.) is the church of *St Mary* which dates from 1543 (rebuilt by Sir Arthur Blomfield).

Within are monuments to Lord Sidmouth, Prime Minister in 1801–04, and to Sir Philip Francis (d. 1818) reputedly the author of the 'Letters of Junius'. Here, too, is buried Dr Dee (d. 1608), Elizabeth I's favourite astrologer. A fragment of Mortlake tapestry is preserved in the Choir. Sir Richard Burton (d. 1890), translator of the 'Arabian Nights', lies under a stone tent in the Roman Catholic graveyard, to the s., near the grave of J. F. Bentley (d. 1902), the architect.

We soon reach Watney's Brewery (thought to be the successor of a 15C brewery on this site) and (6 m.)*Mortlake Green*. Ship Lane leads to the river front (Inn) with a tow-path and some attractive houses (on one of which Tudor chimneys survive). Here is a good view of *Chiswick Bridge* (1933, by Sir Herbert Baker). The University Boat Race (comp. p. 290) finishes near the bridge. *Sheen Lane* skirts the E. side of the Green, and crosses Richmond Road West. On the corner of Shrewsbury Avenue, the old stables and clock tower survive of *Sheen House*, built in 1786, where Lord Grey lived in 1830. The winding Lane continues s. to (6¾ m.) *East Sheen Gate* in to Richmond Park.

To the w. lies a residential area with attractive shrubs planted along the roads. The fine houses include Percy Lodge (c. 1740) in Christ Church Road. Sheen Common is owned by the National Trust.

*Richmond Park (2350 acres) is a beautiful and undulating plain, well wooded with thickets and avenues of venerable trees. Enclosed in 1637 by Charles I, it has preserved its indigenous natural state unspoiled by alien prettifying or exotic flora. It is stocked with red and fallow deer.

Its main gates are Richmond (Star and Garter), Roehampton, East Sheen, Robin Hood, and Ladderstile, all connected by roads (closed at dusk), and most provided with car parks. The park contains several private residences, one of which, *White Lodge*, built by the Earl of Pembroke and Roger Morris in 1727–29 for George II, was the birthplace of Edward VIII in 1894. It was the residence of George VI when Duke of York. Since 1955 it has been occupied by the Royal Ballet School and is open occasionally. *Pembroke Lodge* (c. 1800) on the w. side of the Park, is now a restaurant (open daily exc. Nov & Dec, when Sat & Sun only). It was granted by Queen Victoria to her Prime Minister Lord John Russell, whose grandson, Bertrand Russell, spent much of his boyhood here. From the prehistoric barrow (*View) in its garden, Henry VIII is said to have watched for the rocket announcing Anne Boleyn's execution. *Thatched House Lodge*, near the s. end, was originally built by Sir Robert Walpole. *Isabella's Plantation*, nearby, encloses a delightful woodland garden (best in spring and early summer).

On the w. side of the park, the large *Star and Garter Home* (1924, by Sir Edwin Cooper) for totally disabled soldiers and sailors occupies the site of the famous Star and Garter Inn. This was a favourite resort of London society in the 18C and early 19C (comp. Thackeray's 'Vanity Fair'). Here Dickens held a dinner in 1850 to celebrate the publication of 'David Copperfield', attended by W. M. Thackeray and Alfred Lord Tennyson.

Leaving the park by the Star and Garter Gate, we turn right down (7 m.) RICHMOND HILL which affords a famous *View up the Thames valley, preserved in 1901 by the purchase of Marble Hill on the opposite bank. On the slope below lies **Richmond upon Thames** (173,592 inhab.), long a famous residential town, and still containing many fine old houses. Among the 18C mansions near the top of the hill, The Wick was built in 1775 by Robert Mylne. Next door Wick House was built for Sir Joshua Reynolds by Sir William Chambers in 1772, and here the painter died in 1792. Sheridan was a resident of Downe House from 1806 to 1815.

Just beyond *Terrace Gardens* (left), with an open-air theatre, we turn r. into *Friars Stile Road*. The town centre below is reached by a complicated one-way system; a more pleasant approach is described below. At *St Matthias Church* (by Sir George Gilbert Scott, 1858) we keep left down Mount Ararat Road and take the second turning left into *The Vineyard* (a reminder of the famous Richmond vineyards in the 17C and 18C). The almshouses here were founded in the 17C. At the end we emerge on to the attractive *Hill Rise*, and turn first right up the narrow *Ormond Road* with its fine Queen Anne terrace. We turn left into Paradise Road where in 1915 Virginia and Leonard Woolf moved to *Hogarth House*. In 1917 they set up the Hogarth Press here, and, in 1922, published 'Jacob's Room' and T. S. Eliot's 'The Waste Land'. The Press remained here until 1924. We cross George Street and Sheen Road, where, at No. 36, his family's home, Sir John Moore recovered from his wounds in 1799. Beyond the busy shopping streets is (8 m.) ***Richmond Green**, the scene of tournaments in Tudor times, one of which was attended by the Emperor Charles V.

Several Courts and passages off the Green contain antique shops. On the E. side the Cricketers' Inn recalls the sport played here since the 17C. Beyond, on the Little Green, is the *Richmond Theatre*, opened in 1899.

At its predecessor, on the other side of the Green, Edmund Kean and
Sarah Siddons often performed.

Beyond the *Public Library*, Parkshot leads N. over a railway bridge past the new
Richmond Court House, on the site of a house (No. 8) occupied by George Eliot in
1855–59 while she was writing 'Adam Bede'.

At the s. end of the Green, *Old Palace Terrace* preserves a row of fine
Queen Anne houses. Old Friars was built in the late 17C on the site of a
convent of Observant Friars attached to Richmond Palace. *Maids of
Honour Row* was built c. 1724 for Queen Caroline's ladies. At the end a
huge umbrella pine stands in the garden of old RICHMOND PALACE, of
which the old Gateway and Wardrobe (reconstructed in the 18C) survive.

The former *Palace of Shene* was first occupied by Henry I in 1125, and Edward
III died here in 1377. Richard II spent much time at the palace with his wife Anne
of Bohemia, and at her death in 1394, he ordered its demolition. Although rebuilding was begun by Henry V and his successors, it was destroyed by fire in 1499.
Henry VII built a new Palace on the site, naming it *Richmond* in honour of his title
of Earl of Richmond (in Yorkshire), and he died here in 1509. Wolsey occupied
the palace for a time after surrendering Hampton Court to Henry VIII. Elizabeth
died here in 1603, and Charles I held court at Richmond during the Plague years in
London. The 'Old Pretender' was the last royal resident of the Palace.

Within the Courtyard, *Trumpeter's House* dates from the early 18C.
Here Metternich stayed and was visited by Disraeli. The residential
Trumpeter's Inn (1954–56) harmonizes with the surrounding buildings.
Old Palace Lane (Inn) leads down to the river, past the grounds of *Asgill
House*, on the site of the watergate of Richmond Palace. This fine mansion
designed by Sir Robert Taylor c. 1760 was restored in 1970. Cholmondeley
Walk skirts the bank of the river (to the right is the Richmond Railway
Bridge, erected in 1848). Beyond Asgill House is seen the garden front of
Trumpeter's House. Walkers may continue across Water Lane to
Richmond Bridge.

Beyond ($8\frac{1}{2}$ m.) *Richmond Bridge* (p. 300) PETERSHAM ROAD clings to
the lower slope of Richmond Hill (past an entrance to the attractive
Terrace Gardens) and traverses Petersham Meadows. The herd of cows
here are milked at the dairy at the end of River Lane at 3 p.m.—$9\frac{1}{2}$ m.
Petersham, an old-world riverside village. Outside its charming little
church (16C, with 19C alterations) is the grave of Captain Vancouver
(d. 1798), the explorer, who lived in River Lane during his retirement.
Here, too, are many fine 17–18C mansions. John Gay, author of 'The
Beggar's Opera', lived at Douglas House from 1720; and Dickens first
rented Elm Lodge in the summer of 1839. *Sudbrook Park* (open Mon
3–5) was built for the 2nd Duke of Argyll by James Gibbs in 1726. It is
now used by the Richmond Golf Club. To the right on Petersham Road
is the pedestrian entrance to **Ham House;** motorists should follow the
signs for the car park (viâ Sandy Lane and Ham Street).

Admission Apr–Sept 2–6, Oct–Mar 12–4; closed Mon unless BH; fee. Excellent
Guide Book available.
Ham House was built in 1610 by Sir Thomas Vavasour, Knight Marshal to
James I. It was the home of the Earls of Dysart from 1637 to 1935. The Cabal
Ministry may have met here during the occupation of the Duke of Lauderdale who
married the Countess of Dysart in 1672. William Cowper, poet and author of
'John Gilpin', spent some time here while it was the home of his uncle General
Spencer Cowper, who died at Ham in 1797. It was presented to the Nat. Trust by
Sir Lyonel Tollemache in 1948.

Within, the Baroque decoration and magnificent furnishings date mainly from the time of the Countess of Dysart (d. 1697). In the Duchess's Bed-Chamber are four marine paintings by Willem van de Velde the Younger, commissioned for the house. The delightful Chapel retains its original furnishings, and the Great Staircase dates from 1637–38. One room contains a fine display of textiles and embroidery. The paintings include works by Cornelius Johnson, Sir Peter Lely, John Michael Wright, John Constable (who was a visitor to Ham), Sir Godfrey Knellér, and Sir Joshua Reynolds. A collection of miniatures includes works by Nicholas Hilliard (portrait of Queen Elizabeth), Isaac Oliver, and Samuel Cooper. Many of the ceilings were painted by Ant. Verrio. The fine English tapestries are the work of the Mortlake weavers (1699–1719), and Bradshaw (1730–50).—The pleasant grounds include a walled garden, and fine trees along the river.

Petersham Road continues to (10½ m.) *Ham Common*, surrounded by dignified houses.—12 m. **Kingston upon Thames,** an ancient market-town and royal borough (140,210 inhab.), and the assize town of Surrey. It was the coronation place of the Saxon kings from 925 (or possibly 902) to 978 (traditional coronation-stone near the *Guildhall*). The *Church* (over-restored) contains some 14–15C work. *Clattern Bridge* crossing the Hogsmill River, a small tributary of the Thames, dates substantially from the 12C.—13 m. *Kingston Bridge* (1825–28) crosses the river to Hampton Wick. A footpath (l.) leads to Hampton Court Palace, or Hampton Court Road continues to (14½ m.) **Hampton Court** (Rte 41).

40 KEW AND TWICKENHAM

UNDERGROUND: *Kew Gardens* (5 min. walk from Victoria Gate) and *Richmond* on District line.

RAILWAY from Waterloo to *Kew Bridge*; and to *Richmond, St Margaret's, Twickenham, Strawberry Hill*, and *Teddington*; from Broad Street to *Kew Gardens* and *Richmond*

BUSES: No. 27 from Kensington Church St. follows the car route described below across Kew Bridge to Kew. On week-ends it continues along Kew Rd. through Twickenham and Teddington and terminates at Bushy Park. No. 15 runs from the City through the West End to Richmond on Sun in summer. No. 65 (and 270 Mon–Fri) traverse Kew Rd. and serve the surrounding areas of Teddington, Kingston, Richmond, Twickenham, etc. Frequent buses connect Kew and Richmond (comp. Rte 39B).

RIVER LAUNCHES, see Rte 38.

CAR PARKING. For Kew Gardens: Kew Green, Brentford Ferry Gate Car Park, or side streets off Kew Road (car park in Princess Rd., approached by Kew Gardens Rd.).—Car parks at Marble Hill, Orleans House, and Church Row, Twickenham; and in Bushy Park.

The Great West Road may be approached either by Cromwell Road or by *Kensington Road* and *High Street* (comp. Rte 11A). Beyond (2 m.) *Holland Park* (p. 116), Kensington High Street is continued w. by *Hammersmith Road* past (2½ m.) OLYMPIA. This huge exhibition building was opened in 1866 and extended to the main road in 1929. The annual exhibitions held here include the Ideal Home Exhibition in March. Coleridge lived in 1811–12 at No. 7 Addison Bridge Place, opposite. Hammersmith Road terminates at (3 m.) *Hammersmith Broadway* an important road junction, now half covered by a fly-over.

Shepherd's Bush Road runs N. Thence Wood Lane goes on, passing the ungainly *B.B.C. Television Centre* (1955 onwards) and *White City Stadium*, an athletic and sports arena.

We branch left towards the Hammersmith Flyover and join the busy GREAT WEST ROAD which skirts Chiswick (Rte 42).—4¼ m. Hogarth Roundabout.—5½ m. *Chiswick Flyover.* Chiswick High Road diverges left from the M4 elevated motorway which continues w. to Heathrow, etc. (comp. p. 330). We branch left across *Kew Bridge* and into KEW ROAD which traverses (6 m.) the attractive *Kew Green* in the suburb famous for its botanic gardens and Hanoverian associations. Some houses built to accommodate members of George III's family remain, and in the churchyard of *St Anne's* (1710–14), Gainsborough (d. 1788) and Zoffany (d. 1810), the painters, and Sir William Hooker (d. 1865; comp. below), are buried.

At the end of Kew Green Mortlake Rd. diverges left. Off this, in Ruskin Ave., is the headquarters building of the **Public Record Office**, opened 1977. Here, splendidly housed and readily accessible (reader's ticket, see p. 203), are stored the non-current records (some from 16C) of existing and defunct government departments.

The main entrance to ****Kew Gardens,** officially the *Royal Botanic Gardens*, is at the w. end of Kew Green. There are two entrances on the river (Brentford Ferry Gate, with car park; and Isleworth Ferry Gate) and three in Kew Road.

The gardens are open (adm. 1p) daily (except Christmas Day) from 10 to sunset (4 p.m. in mid-winter–8 p.m. in mid-summer). The Museums open at 10; the glass-houses at 1 p.m. (and close at c. 4.50 p.m., 5.50 on Sun).—REFRESHMENTS from Pavilion (summer only) near s.w. corner of Gardens, and the Kiosk near the main entrance. Also at 'Maids of Honour' in Kew Road, and on Kew Green.—The excellent Official Guide and useful key Plan may be purchased in the Orangery. No dogs are admitted.

Kew Gardens, now 288 acres in area, has a great variety of plants. Many are nurtured in glass-houses, while others are arranged botanically by genus throughout the grounds. The gardens are rich in bird-life; many of the migrant warblers may be heard here, besides robins, wrens, thrushes, and blackbirds. In 1759 Princess Augusta, mother of George III began a small botanic garden to the s. of the Orangery, with Sir William Aiton as her head gardener. She employed Sir William Chambers to design several buildings in the grounds (the Pagoda, Orangery, and some small temples survive).

From 1772 to 1819 the gardens were under the care of Sir Joseph Banks (1743–1820) who accompanied Captain Cook on his first voyage around the world. Gardeners were sent to South Africa, Australia, and the Pacific to collect plants. William Cobbett was employed as a gardener about 1775. After the National Botanic Institute was founded here in 1838, Sir William Hooker took over as Director in 1841. Among the great services which the gardens have rendered to civilization is the introduction of the bread-fruit tree to the West Indies in 1791 (the purpose of the 'Bounty' voyage), quinine to India in 1860, and of rubber to the Malay Peninsula in 1875.

The gardens occupy the site of the grounds of two royal residences, both of modest size. Holly Walk which traverses the area marks the approximate boundary between the two estates: Richmond House lay to the w., the grounds bordering the river, and Kew House to the E. along Kew Road. The two properties were amalgamated by George III after the death of Princess Augusta in 1772. The *White House, Kew* (later known as *Kew House*) was occupied by Frederick, Prince of Wales, and his wife Augusta from 1731, and Princess Augusta remained here after his death in 1751. Their son George III and Queen Charlotte used the house frequently until it was pulled down c. 1802. The site of its E. wing is marked by the sundial on the lawn in front of the present *Kew Palace* (formally known as the *Dutch House*) which served as an annexe, and later as the residence of George III and Queen Charlotte (see below). *Richmond Lodge* was owned by George II and Queen Caroline before it was pulled down by George III and an Observatory built to the s.w. in the Old Deer Park (see p. 300).

Outside the main entrance on the N. side of Kew Green is the *Herbarium* and *Library*, open to students. The collection of dried plants (c. 7 million) is the largest in the world. We pass through fine wrought-iron entrance gates designed by Decimus Burton (1845). On the right is the *Aroid House*, designed by John Nash, which contains tropical plants of the arum lily family as well as ginger, banana, etc. Beyond is a statue of The Sower by Sir Hamo Thornycroft. At the end of this walk (r.) is KEW PALACE, a red brick building erected by Samuel Fortrey, the son of a Dutch refugee, in 1631. It became the principal royal residence at Kew after Kew House was pulled down. George IV lived here as Prince of Wales. In June 1818 two sons of George III were married at the house, and in Nov of the same year Queen Charlotte died here. Fanny Burney, author of 'Evelina' lived here while serving as Keeper of the Robes to Queen Charlotte. It contains souvenirs of George III and his family (adm. April–Sept, 11–6; Sun 1–6). On the N. side of the Palace the *Queen's Garden* was laid out in 1969 as a 17C garden. A 'mount' and a handsome Italian well-head are incorporated into the design.

The Broad Walk leads s. past the ORANGERY built of brick covered with rusticated stucco in 1761 by Sir William Chambers. The interior was restored in 1971 and is used as an exhibition centre for the scientific and botanical work carried out at Kew. The bookstall is also situated here. The two statues by Pietro Francavilla from Rovezzano were brought here in 1752 by Frederick, Prince of Wales. Close to the Orangery is the *Filmy Fern House*, built to protect delicate plants, some of which are only one cell thick.

At the end of the Broad Walk is the *Pond* and great *PALM HOUSE built by Decimus Burton and Richard Taylor in 1844–48. Among the tropical plants here are almost every known variety of palm. Screw pines or Pandanus may be seen in the N. wing. Coffee-plants, breadfruit, balsa, bamboos, etc. also flourish here (a gallery 30 ft about the floor provides a fine viewpoint). The Queen's Beasts, on the lawn, were designed by James Woodford as an heraldic embellishment to Westminster Abbey at the Coronation of Elizabeth II. The *Water-lily House* (closed in winter), to the N. of the Palm House, usually contains the Giant Waterlily (Victoria amazonica; grown annually), lotus-plants, papyrus, hibiscus, etc. Across the Pond is the *Museum* of general botany. The conspicuous tower to the s., designed as a water-tower and chimney, is connected by tunnel to the Palm House.

The N.E. corner of the gardens is filled with glass-houses. Beside the *Tropical* and *Temperate Fern Houses*, the *Conservatory* is devoted to a display of flowers in season. The *Succulent House*, close by, contains cacti and desert plants. To the E. of the *Iris Garden* and *Aquatic Garden*, on the perimeter wall, is the *Wood Museum*. Across the Aquatic Garden are the new buildings (1965) of the *Jodrell Laboratory*, where plants are identified and research is carried out on plant anatomy. It was first opened in 1876 and named after its benefactor, T. J. Phillips Jodrell. The *Alpine House*, near by, is open in spring and early summer. Across the *Rock Garden* is the *T-Range* of houses which include the Sherman Hoyt Cactus House; plants from South Africa; begonias; tropical 'stove-plants'; the Giant Waterlily (comp. above), with insectivorous plants in the s. porch; and *Orchids.

Behind the Palm House and across the *Rose Garden*, the Pagoda Vista leads towards the Temperate House. On the left towers the *Flagstaff* (225 ft high) made from a single Douglas Fir spar from British Columbia (1959). The *TEMPERATE HOUSE* was designed by Decimus Burton. The N. wing houses rhododendrons and camellias; the central portion, tree-ferns, palms, araucarias, etc.; the S. portion, sub-tropical plants, some from Mexico. Behind is the *Australian House*. To the E., near Kew Road, is the *Marianne North Gallery*, named after the artist whose paintings within were executed between 1871 and 1884. Nearby is the refreshment *Pavilion* (open in summer), and, at the end of the Avenue, the *Pagoda* (no adm.) erected by Chambers in 1761.

In the S.W. corner of the gardens is the *Queen's Cottage* (open on summer weekends and BH). The surrounding woods are noted for their bluebells. Returning towards the centre of the gardens we pass the *Water-lily Pond* and *Nursery* to reach the beautiful *Lake* (4½ acres; excavated in 1857–61). We may return to the main entrance either through the *Rhododendron Dell* (planted c. 1773 by 'Capability' Brown), near the Thames, or past the *Azalea Garden*, farther E.

Kew Road continues S. skirting the long wall of the Gardens and *Old Deer Park* (now a sports ground). The *Kew Observatory* (1769) here was built for George III by Sir William Chambers. It is now used by the Meteorological Office. The three obelisks in the Park were set up as meridian marks; calculations here were used to provide London's official time before Greenwich mean time was adopted (comp. p. 283).

A Georgian terrace of three houses (fine carved doorways) survives in *Kew Foot Road* (approached by Jocelyn Road). Also here the *Royal Hospital* occupies the site of a cottage where the poet James Thomson lived from 1736 until his death in 1748.

7½ m. We cross a roundabout into the *Quadrant* which leads into **Richmond** (Rte 39B). To the right is Richmond Green (p. 295). In the confusing one-way system, signs for Richmond Bridge should be followed.—8 m. *Richmond Bridge* (1774–77, by James Paine; widened in 1937) offers a fine view of activity on the river.

Across the bridge (l.) a pleasant walk follows the tow-path to Marble Hill and Orleans House (comp. below). A passenger ferry (operating times, see p. 301) may be taken across the river to Ham House and a return to the bridge made through Petersham Meadows (p. 296).

We follow Richmond Road which bears left towards **Twickenham,** and passes the N. border of (8½ m.) *Marble Hill Park* (66 acres), purchased for the public in 1903 to preserve the view from Richmond Hill (comp. p. 295). In Sandycombe Road (r.) Turner lived at Sandycombe Lodge (which he built) in 1813–25. Here is a fine prospect of *Marble Hill House* (adm. Tues–Sat 10–5, Sun from 2; rfmts). The house was built in a Palladian style in 1723–29 by Roger Morris for Henrietta Howard, mistress of George II. Her friends Horace Walpole and Alexander Pope helped plan the gardens. The interior contains period furniture.

Montpelier Row (where Chapel House was Tennyson's home in 1851–53, and South End House the home of Walter de la Mare from c. 1950 until his death in 1956), skirting the W. side of the Park, preserves an unspoilt terrace of early 18C houses. Beyond Orleans Park, Lebanon Park (l.) leads to **Orleans House** (adm. Tues–Sat 1–4 or 5.30; Sun & BH 2–4 or 5), near the river. The house was built in 1710 by John James, and the Octagon in 1720 by James Gibbs. It is named after Louis-Philippe, Duc d'Orléans, later King of France, who lived here in 1815–17. Most of the house was demolished in 1926, but the **Octagon* survives. The stucco decoration inside was executed by Giuseppe Artari and Giov. Bagutti. The s.w. wing now houses an *Art Gallery* which holds changing exhibitions, mostly drawn from the Ionides Bequest, and relating to Twickenham. A woodland garden surrounds the house (open daily 9–sunset).

Riverside (often flooded at high tide) continues w. past the *Twickenham Ferry* (for Ham House; 7–12, 2–sunset, weather permitting), and the attractive Syon Row, built in 1721. The grounds of *York House* (now used as municipal offices) are open to the public. A bridge passes over the road to a 'Grotto' on the river bank, built by Sir Ratan J. Tata, an Indian merchant prince, who owned the house in 1906–18. York House was owned by the Comte de Paris (1864) and by the Duc d'Orléans (1899–1906). *Eel Pie Island* in the Thames may be reached by a footbridge a little farther upstream. The parish church of *St Mary* has recently been restored (the nave was rebuilt in the 18C by John James). Alexander Pope (1688–1744) is buried here (monument "to one who would not be buried in Westminster Abbey").

Church Street winds away from the river to join the busy *King Street*. *All Hallows* in Chertsey Road (reached viâ London Rd.), c. 1 m. N., is an attractive church (1939), with the tower, woodwork, and memorials from Wren's church of All Hallows, Lombard St. (1694), taken down in 1938. —9½ m. *Cross Deep* diverges left past the site of the riverside villa where Pope lived in 1719 until his death in 1744. The famous Grotto remains in the grounds of St Catherine's Convent (adm. on Sat).—10 m. *Strawberry Vale* passes close to the park (r.) of *Strawberry Hill*, now St Mary's Training College. The house was rebuilt in 1754–1776 in an elaborate 'Gothick' style by Horace Walpole, who here wrote the 'Castle of Otranto'. Adm. by prior appointment with the Principal on Wed or Sat afternoon.

10¾ m. Twickenham Road ends at Ferry Road. To the left is *Teddington Lock and Weir* (the first weir on this site was built in 1345), which mark the highest tidal point on the Thames. We turn right between two churches; the ivy-clad *St Mary's* (partly 16C) has a brick tower of 1754. Buried here are Peg Woffington (d. 1760), actress, Henry Flitcroft (d. 1769), architect, and John Walter (d. 1812), 'founder' of 'The Times' who lived on the site of Grove Gardens to the N. Opposite, *St Alban the Martyr* was built to accommodate the growing number of parishioners in 1889–96. The surprising French Gothic design was devised by W. Niven (usually open 10–11 a.m.). Beyond St Mary's a group of old cottages date from the 18C (one now a tea-shop and restaurant).

At the w. end of *Teddington High Street*, Elmfield House survives from the 18C. Street names off the High Street (l.) recall Gomer House, home from 1860 of Richard Blackmore (d. 1900), author of 'Lorna Doone'. —11¼ m. We bear left down Park Road to enter (11½ m.) **Bushy Park.** To the right the *National Physical Laboratory* occupies the site of Bushy House (see p. 306). We traverse Bushy Park to reach (13 m.) **Hampton Court** (Rte 41).

41 HAMPTON COURT PALACE

For approaches by road from London, see Rtes 39 and 40.—CAR PARK (fee) left of entrance.

RAILWAY: *Hampton Court Station* on S.R. from Waterloo.

GREEN LINE COACHES: No. 716 from Hyde Park Corner viâ Richmond; Nos. 718, 725 from Victoria viâ Kingston.

RIVER LAUNCHES, see Rte 38.

BUSES: No. 27 from Kensington viâ Kew and Twickenham to Teddington (N. side of Bushy Park); No. 267 from Hammersmith Broadway viâ Syon and Twickenham; frequent buses from Richmond (comp. Rte 39B).

Admission. To State Apartments, Great Kitchens, Cellars, and Vine: May–Sept daily 9.30–6, Sun from 11; Oct, March, and April 9.30–5, Sun from 2; Nov–Feb 9.30–4, Sun from 2. The Royal Tennis Court and Banqueting House are open in summer only. The Palace is closed Christmas Day, Boxing Day, and Good Friday. —*Lecture Tours* in summer: Mon–Sat, 11 and 3; Sun at 4.30. *Cafeteria* in Tilt Yard w. of the Gardens; restaurants in Hampton Court Road.

**Hampton Court Palace, with its stately buildings and famous picture-gallery, its charming gardens and park, and its delightful river-scenery, is one of the most attractive points in the neighbourhood of London.

The palace was begun in 1514 by Card. Wolsey, who intended a building surpassing in splendour every other private residence. In 1529, however, the Cardinal was obliged to surrender his palace to Henry VIII, who added the great hall and the chapel. From that time for over two centuries Hampton Court was a favourite royal residence, and Edward VI was born here in 1537. William III, who died in 1702 in consequence of a fall from his horse in the Home Park, employed Sir Christopher Wren to substitute the present E. and S. wings for three of Wolsey's courtyards. Since the death of George II the palace has ceased to be the abode of royalty, but the 'grace and favour' apartments surrounding the smaller courts are still the residence of aristocratic pensioners of the Crown, etc.

In the mellow red brick front of the palace rises the *Great Gatehouse*, with oriel windows of Wolsey's time, terracotta medallions of Roman emperors attributed to Giov. da Maiano, and the arms of Henry VIII. The moat in front of it is crossed by a fine bridge, built by Henry VIII, and guarded by the 'King's Beasts'. The *Base Court*, beyond the gatehouse, is the largest court and survives from Wolsey's palace. To the left of it are several smaller courts affording an excellent idea of Tudor domestic architecture.—*Anne Boleyn's Gateway* leads to the *Clock Court*, so-called from the curious astronomical clock made for Henry VIII on the inner side of the gateway. The graceful but incongruous colonnade on the right was built by Wren. The entrance to the state apartments is at its farther end.

The **State Apartments,** in the E and S. wings, contain c. 500 pictures, among which the Italian school is best represented, and much of the original furniture and decorations.

We ascend the KING'S STAIRCASE, with walls and ceiling by Verrio to the GUARD CHAMBER, which contains more than 3000 pieces of arms. Opening off this are the panelled WOLSEY ROOMS, used by members of his household, which command a charming view of the Knot and Pond Gardens, and contain fine ceilings. The portraits here include: *William Scrots* (attrib.), Edward VI; *Gheeraedts*, Portrait of a Lady; and *Mytens*, Charles I and Henrietta Maria.—The FIRST PRESENCE CHAMBER contains portraits of William III and the 'Hampton Court Beauties, all by *Kneller*. In the SECOND PRESENCE CHAMBER are paintings by *Titian* (*Portrait of a Man, called 'Jacopo Sannazaro'), *Giorgione*, and *Dosso*

Dossi.—AUDIENCE CHAMBER. *Tintoretto*, Knight of Malta, Nine Muses; *Dosso Dossi*, Portrait of a Man; *Lotto*, Andrea Odoni.—KING'S DRAW-ING ROOM. *Lotto*, Portrait of a bearded man; *Titian*, Lucretia; *Tintoretto*, Head of an Old Man, Venetian Senator. In WILLIAM III'S BEDROOM, with a ceiling by *Verrio*, are the King's bed and a clock that goes for a year without winding. The KING'S DRESSING ROOM contains works by *Mabuse* (Adam and Eve) and *Holbein* (Noli me tangere).—The KING'S WRITING ROOM. *Giulio Romano*, Isabella d'Este; *Pontormo* (School of), Madonna and Child; *Parmigianino*, Portrait of a Boy; *Andrea del Sarto*, Madonna and Child with St John; *Berruguete* (attrib.), Federico da Montefeltro; *Lor. Costa*, Portrait of a Girl; *Franciabigio*, Portrait of a Man.

We enter the Queen's Rooms. The QUEEN'S CLOSET. *Pieter Brueghel the Elder*, Massacre of the Innocents; works by *Lucas Cranach*.—The QUEEN'S GALLERY, completed for Queen Anne, has Brussels tapestries depicting the story of Alexander the Great and a mantelpiece by *Nost*. In the QUEEN'S BEDROOM is George II's bed; the ceiling is by *Thornhill*. The walls and ceiling of the DRAWING ROOM were painted by *Verrio*, and the bed was made for Queen Anne; the windows command a fine view of the gardens.—In the AUDIENCE CHAMBER are Dutch and Flemish por-traits (*Mytens*, Sir Jeffrey Hudson, the dwarf; and *Paul van Somer*, Anne of Denmark). The PUBLIC DINING ROOM, decorated by Wm. Kent, con-tains paintings by *Sebastiano* and *Marco Ricci*.

The three small rooms to the N. form a suite once occupied by Frederick, son of George II. The PRINCE OF WALES PRESENCE CHAMBER contains some fine Italian paintings: *Jacopo di Cione* (School of), Trip-tych; *Gentile da Fabriano*, Madonna and Child with Angels; *Duccio*, *Triptych; *Bernardo Daddi*, Marriage of the Virgin; *Sano di Pietro*, *Madonna with Saints and Angels; *Fra Filippo Lippi* (School of), Madonna and St John; *Bernardino* and *Fr. Zaganelli*, Christ at the Column; *Giov. Bellini*, Portrait of a Young Man; *Orcagna*, Madonna enthroned; *Benozzo Gozzoli*, Death of Simon Magus.—The PRINCE OF WALES DRAWING ROOM is at present hung with one of the tempera paint-ings of the *Triumph of Julius Caesar by *Mantegna*, removed from the Orangery after restoration (see below).—The PRINCE OF WALES BED-ROOM contains Queen Charlotte's bed designed by Robert Adam.

We now cross the PRINCE OF WALES STAIRCASE with an elaborate bal-cony and Mortlake tapestries depicting the Battle of Solebay (1672), and enter a lobby with a charming portrait of Henry, Prince of Wales, with the Earl of Essex (c. 1605). Beyond the QUEEN'S PRESENCE CHAMBER (r.; often closed) we enter the QUEEN'S PRIVATE CHAPEL (l.) where the paint-ings include: *Luini* (School of), Flora, and *Georges de la Tour*, St Jerome. —The PRIVATE DINING ROOM contains portraits of Saints by *Feti*, and works by *Salomon van Ruysdael*, and *Pieter de Hooch*.—The QUEEN'S PRIVATE CHAMBER. Works by *Willem van der Velde II* and *Jan Brueghel the Elder*.—A series of small rooms lead to the CARTOON GALLERY de-signed by Wren for the Raphael Cartoons now in the Victoria and Albert Museum. It contains 17C Brussels tapestries copied from the cartoons, below which are paintings illustrating the life of Henry VIII, and a view of Hampton Court (temp. George I), by *Knyff*. The COMMUNICATION GALLERY contains the *'Windsor Beauties' by *Sir Peter Lely*, portraits of the ladies of Charles II's court.—The gallery leads to three small rooms,

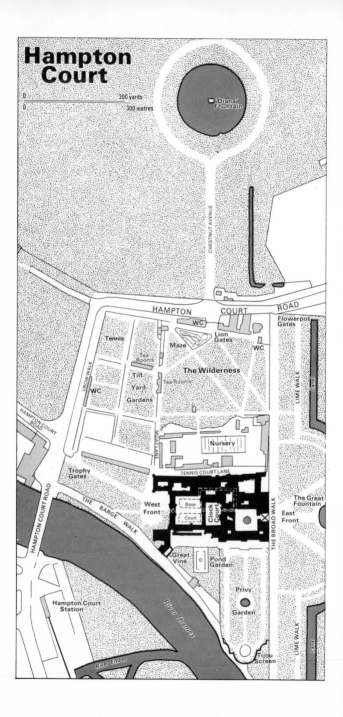

Hampton Court

0 — 300 yards
0 — 300 metres

"Diana" Fountain

CHESTNUT AVENUE

HAMPTON COURT ROAD

WC

Flowerpot Gates

Tennis

Maze

Lion Gates

WC

Tea Rooms

The Wilderness

LIME WALK

Tilt

Tea Rooms

VROW WALK

WC

Yard

Gardens

HAMPTON COURT ROAD

MOAT LANE

Nursery

HAMPTON COURT ROAD

TENNIS COURT LANE

Trophy Gates

West Front

Base Court

Clock Court

The Great Fountain

East Front

THE BROAD WALK

THE BARGE WALK

Great Vine

Pond Garden

Privy Garden

Hampton Court Station

River Thames

Garden

LIME WALK

River Ember

Tijou Screen

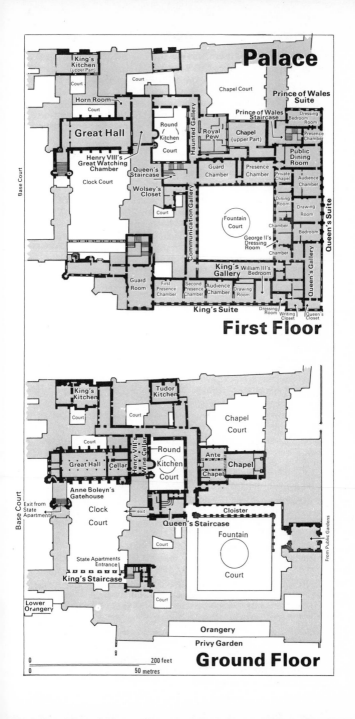

Palace

First Floor

King's Kitchen (upper Part)

Court

Horn Room

Court

Court

Chapel Court

Prince of Wales Suite

Prince of Wales Staircase

Dressing Bedroom Room

Great Hall

Round Kitchen Court

Royal Pew

Haunted Gallery

Chapel (upper Part)

Presence Chamber

Henry VIII's Great Watching Chamber

Clock Court

Queen's Staircase

Guard Chamber

Presence Chamber

Public Dining Room

Wolsey's Closet

Communication Gallery

Private Chapel

Audience Chamber

Court

Dining Room

Drawing Room

Fountain Court

Chamber

George II's Dressing Room

Bedroom

Chamber

Queen's Suite

Chamber

King's Gallery

William III's Bedroom

Queen's Gallery

Guard Room

First Presence Chamber

Second Presence Chamber

Audience Chamber

Drawing Room

King's Suite

Dressing Room

Writing Closet

Queen's Closet

Queen's Gallery

Base Court

Ground Floor

King's Kitchen

Court

Tudor Kitchen

Court

Chapel Court

Great Hall

Cellar

Henry VIII's Wine Cellar

Round Kitchen Court

Ante Chapel

Chapel

Chapel

Anne Boleyn's Gatehouse

Exit from State Apartments

Clock Court

exit

Cloister

Queen's Staircase

Fountain

Court

From Public Gardens

State Apartments Entrance

Court

King's Staircase

Court

Base Court

Lower Orangery

Orangery

Privy Garden

0   200 feet

0   50 metres

including WOLSEY'S CLOSET, with good linen-scroll panelling and vivid
painted decoration including 16C panel paintings overlying 15C work.
The CUMBERLAND SUITE was designed by Wm. Kent in 1732.

We cross the upper landing of the QUEEN'S STAIRCASE which has fine
ironwork by *Tijou* and a brilliant allegorical painting, by *Honthorst*, of
Charles I and his queen as Apollo and Diana. We next enter the
HAUNTED GALLERY, built by Wolsey, where the ghost of Queen Catherine Howard is said to walk. The tapestries probably belonged to Elizabeth I. Off it opens the *Holy Day Closet*, leading to the upper part of the
CHAPEL (fine ceiling and woodwork), which may be viewed (Mon–Fri)
from *Queen Anne's Pew*.

From the end of the Haunted Gallery we enter HENRY VIII's GREAT
WATCHING CHAMBER, which is hung with Flemish tapestries (that once
belonged to Wolsey), then pass through the *Horn Room* to enter the
*GREAT HALL (106 ft by 40 ft and 60 ft high), built by Henry VIII in
1531–36, with one of the finest hammer-beam roofs in existence. The
walls are hung with beautiful Brussels tapestries. From its farther end a
flight of steps descends to Anne Boleyn's Gateway, where we turn to the
right.

In the right-hand corner of the Base Court is the entrance to the *King's
Beer Cellar* and Henry VIII's '*New Wyne Sellar*'. On quitting the cellars
we turn to the left, then to the right, to reach the Serving Place and the
Tudor Kitchens, with huge fireplaces and some ancient utensils. From
the Serving Place dark corridors (first to the left, then to the right) bring
us to the cloistered *Fountain Court*, designed by Wren, who occupied
the rooms off the w. walk. To the N. is the *Chapel*, open for service on Sun
(11 and 3.30).

The *Gardens*, entered from the E. walk of the cloister, were laid out in their
present formal style under William III. At right angles to the *Broad Walk*, which
skirts the E. front of the palace, is the *Long Water* bisecting the *Home Park*. To the
left is the entrance to the old *Tennis Court* (open Apr–Sept; play occasionally), rebuilt by William III on the site of the court built by Henry VIII in 1529. On the S.
side of the palace are the *Privy Garden*, at the end of which (near the river) is a fine
screen by Jean Tijou, the Elizabethan *Knot Garden* of aromatic herbs, the *Pond
Garden*, a sunk garden laid out by Henry VIII, and a new *Sunk Garden* in a formal
17C style. Beyond is the *Great Vine* planted in 1768, and producing an annual crop
of c. 600 bunches of the finest Black Hamburgh grapes.

To the right is the *Orangery*, and farther on is the LOWER ORANGERY,
with the famous series of tempera paintings, the **Triumph of Julius
Caesar, executed by Mantegna in 1485–94 for the Duke of Mantua, and
bought by Charles I in 1629 for £10,500. This has been closed (so far for
ten years) while restoration is taking place.

Opposite, overlooking the river, is William III's *Banqueting House* (c. 1700),
decorated by Verrio (open Apr–Sept).

On the N. side of the palace is the *Wilderness*, laid out by William III, with a
celebrated *Maze*.

On the opposite side of Hampton Court Road is **Bushy Park** (1100 acres), noted
for its fine old trees. A herd of deer and cows graze here. Henry VIII used the park
as a royal hunting preserve. Near the Hampton Court gates is the *Diana Fountain*
(by Fanelli; c. 1640, now thought to depict Venus), beyond which is the triple
Avenue of chestnuts and limes, about 1 m. long, a beautiful sight in late spring
when the chestnuts are in bloom. 'Chestnut Sunday' (announced beforehand in the
newspapers) attracts crowds of visitors. *Bushy House*, at the Teddington (N.) end
of the avenue, first built in the reign of Charles II, was rebuilt in the early 18C. It
was for long occupied by Rangers of Bushy Park, who included Charles Montagu,
Earl of Halifax, Lord North, and William IV (while Duke of Clarence). Queen

Victoria lent the house to the Duc de Nemours (son of Louis Philippe). The house was converted for use by the *National Physical Laboratory*, which opened here in 1902 for scientific and industrial research.

On the Green w. of the palace-approach are the *Old Court House* where Sir Christopher Wren died in 1723, and *Faraday House*, where Michael Faraday died in 1867. Hampton Court Road continues w. between brick stables erected c. 1570 and (r.) the 18C Hampton Court House. From Terrace Gardens on the Thames is a view of *Tagg's Island* where 'Fred Karno' built his Karsino in 1913. A new hotel is rising on the site of the Hall where Charlie Chaplin, Stan Laurel, and Flanagan and Allen all performed. Farther on (l.) is *Garrick's Villa* occupied by the actor from 1754 until his death in 1779. He employed Robert Adam to remodel the house. The Temple (to Shakespeare) on the river bank was erected by Garrick.

42 CHISWICK, SYON, AND OSTERLEY

UNDERGROUND AND RAILWAY. For HAMMERSMITH and CHISWICK MALL: *Hammersmith* on Metropolitan, Piccadilly, and District lines; *Ravenscourt Park* on District line.—For CHISWICK HOUSE and HOGARTH'S HOUSE: *Chiswick Station* ($\frac{1}{2}$ m. w.) on S.R. from Waterloo; *Chiswick Park* and *Turnham Green* on District line (1 m. N.; bus E3 to Chiswick House); *Hammersmith* (bus 290 to Chiswick House).— For GUNNERSBURY PARK: *Acton Town* on Piccadilly and District lines.—For STRAND-ON-THE-GREEN: *Kew Bridge Station*.—For SYON: *Kew Bridge Station* on S.R. from Waterloo (then bus 267 or 117 to Brent Lea Gate); *Gunnersbury* on District line (then buses as above); *Syon Lane* and *Isleworth Stations* on S.R. from Waterloo.—For OSTERLEY: *Osterley* on Piccadilly line.—For BOSTON MANOR HOUSE: *Boston Manor* on Piccadilly line.

GREEN LINE coaches (Nos 704, 705) from Kensington viâ Chiswick Road and the Great West Road to Osterley.

CAR PARKING. At *Chiswick*: cars not admitted; parking space usually available in Corney Road, off Gt. Chertsey Rd.—Car Parks at *Gunnersbury Park*, *Syon*, and *Osterley*.

From central London to (3 m.) *Hammersmith Broadway*, see Rte 40. We continue on the Great West Road, taking the first turning left, Rivercourt Road, to reach HAMMERSMITH MALL on the Thames. To the left *Kelmscott House* (No. 26) was the home of William Morris, "poet, craftsman, socialist", from 1878 to his death in 1896.

Morris named the house after Kelmscott Manor, his country home near Lechlade. In 1891 he established here the Kelmscott Press. In 1816 Sir Francis Ronalds invented the first electric telegraph in this house, laying down 8 miles of cable in the garden. Before 1878 it was the home of George MacDonald (1824–1905), and Ruskin was a frequent visitor.

Number 19 Upper Mall is the old Doves Inn (Restaurant) in which tradition has it that James Thomson wrote part of 'The Seasons'. Beyond stretch *Furnival Gardens* named after Dr F. J. Furnival (1825–1910) the social reformer. Here *Hammersmith Pier* remains as a reminder of the harbour around which Hammersmith grew up, used by barges until 1929. Hammersmith Reach is still frequented by sailors and oarsmen. Across the gardens, the quaint and narrow Hammersmith Mall continues as a footpath (with several inns) to Hammersmith Bridge. A fashionable place of residence in the 18C and early 19C, it still retains a number of picturesque houses.

Upper Mall is continued w. by *Hammersmith Terrace*. At No. 7–8 De Loutherbourg, the painter, died in 1812, and Sir Emery Walker, topographer and antiquary, lived here from 1903 to 1933. Beyond we enter riverside **Chiswick,** the older part of which is both picturesque and interesting for its associations. CHISWICK MALL is another charming old riverside street with Queen Anne and early Georgian houses. Their gardens on the banks of the Thames look towards the island of Chiswick

Eyot. *Walpole House*, a fine example of the Restoration period, is supposed to be the original of Miss Pinkerton's establishment for young ladies in 'Vanity Fair'. Near the end of the Mall we turn right to skirt Fuller's Brewery (with its cobbled loading yard behind) and re-enter the Mall down the narrow Church Street. Here *St Nicholas* (rebuilt in 1884; 15C tower), stands in a large rural churchyard, in which are buried William Hogarth (1697–1764; large monument erected by Garrick on s. side of church), De Loutherbourg (1740–1812), William Kent (1684–1748), and the Duchess of Cleveland (1641–1709), mistress of Charles II. By the N. wall of the new burial-ground farther w. lies James McNeill Whistler (1834–1903).

The N. end of Church Street emerges on the busy *Hogarth Roundabout*. Before rejoining the traffic flow, just to the left may be glimpsed the tiny *Chiswick Square* with Boston House (1740) disputing the claim of Walpole House (see above) to be the scene of Becky Sharp's defiant departure from Miss Pinkerton's establishment. We continue down Great Chertsey Road to the main entrance (r.) of *Chiswick House* and Park.

The House is open Oct–March, Wed–Sun 9.30–4; April–Sept daily 9.30–5.30 or 7; fee. The Grounds are open daily throughout the year. An excellent Guidebook is available.

The Villa was built by the 3rd Earl of Burlington in the grounds of his principal residence (demolished in 1788). It was designed by him as a 'temple of the arts', modelled on Palladio's Villa Capra, near Vicenza. The Summer Parlour was built first, and later linked to the Villa which was begun in 1729. William Kent was employed to decorate the interior, and plan the gardens. Pope was a frequent visitor here.

James Wyatt was employed by the Dukes of Devonshire in 1788 to demolish the Jacobean mansion and enlarge the Villa by adding two wings to the N. and s. The Link Building was engulfed (though not demolished) during these alterations. Sir Joseph Paxton (1801–65), designer of Crystal Palace, worked as a boy in the garden. Charles James Fox died here in 1806, and King Edward VII spent much time at the Villa as Prince of Wales in 1866–79.

In 1952 when restoration work began, Wyatt's building was found to be in a serious state of disrepair, and so was demolished, and the Villa was returned to its original form in 1968.

The pleasing exterior design is centred on the upper storey and the dome above, surrounded by four obelisks (chimney stacks). Statues of Palladio and Inigo Jones (by Rysbrack, c. 1730) flank the elaborate double staircase. The Link building connects the Villa with the Summer Parlour.

We enter under the main portico on the GROUND FLOOR which housed Lord Burlington's library. It now contains an exhibition of drawings and prints relating to the house, including illustrations of works by Burlington, Kent, Flitcroft, Inigo Jones, and Palladio. The interesting parallel between Palladio's drawings of Roman baths here, and the design of many of the rooms in the Villa should be noted. The intricate form of the architecture, with its careful symmetry, on this floor is extended even to a basement wine cellar. Despite the low ceilings a feeling of spaciousness is given by the unexpected vistas on to the garden. Beyond the link building we reach the *Summer Parlour* (recently restored) with a fine ceiling and fireplace, and a portrait of the Earl of Dorset by Sir Godfrey Kneller.

We ascend a concealed spiral staircase to the UPPER FLOOR with the principal public rooms, richly decorated with ceilings by William Kent, fine chimney-pieces, and paintings by Sebastiano Ricci. The *Octagon Hall* has a superb domed ceiling. Around the walls are paintings by Kneller, Guido Reni, and (attrib.) Daniele da Volterra. The design of the *Gallery* is derived from the Roman Baths of Diocletian and of Agrippa. In the *Blue Velvet Room* are charming roundels painted by Dobson (portrait of Inigo Jones) and Kent (portrait of Pope).

The wooded *PARK of 66 acres was laid out by William Kent in an Italian style, and contains delightful avenues and walks through the woods. It is adorned with temples and a lake which has become a nesting place for wildfowl. The bridge was designed in 1788 by James Wyatt. A Gateway by Inigo Jones was brought from Beaufort House, Chelsea in 1736 (a gift from Sir Hans Sloane).

The Great Chertsey Rd. continues direct between sports grounds to join the Lower Richmond Rd. beyond Chiswick Bridge.

We return to the Hogarth Roundabout and rejoin the Great West Road (here called Hogarth Lane). Just beyond the laundry works (layby) **Hogarth's House** survives precariously on the very edge of the busy highway. It was the summer abode of William Hogarth from 1749 to 1764 (restored in 1951 after bomb damage). Its simple rooms contain a collection of Hogarth prints (adm. daily April–Sept 11–6, Sun from 2; Oct–March 11–4, closed Tues, Sun from 2; fee).

The Great West Road continues to (5½ m.) the *Chiswick Flyover* (comp Rte 40), diverging left from the motorway to descend to the roundabout beneath.

Gunnersbury Ave. (North Circular Rd.) leads N. from the roundabout towards Ealing past *Gunnersbury Park* (entrance left, off Pope's Lane). The Park is open daily, and the 19C Rothschild mansion contains a museum of coaches belonging to the Rothschilds, and local history collections. It is open daily,'2–4 or 5, Sat and Sun until 6.

We diverge left along Chiswick High Road. At the foot of Kew Bridge a narrow road descends to *Strand-on-the-Green* a delightful riverside walk, with boat houses and several inns. *Kew Bridge Road* branches right away from Kew Bridge (comp. Rte 40), and soon runs into BRENTFORD HIGH STREET. – 6 m. A church (r.) contains a *Piano Museum* (adm. Apr–Oct on Sat & Sun, 2–5.30; fee) devoted to 'automatic' pianos and other old instruments. – We cross the Grand Union Canal just before (7 m.) **Syon Park** pedestrian entrance. Cars skirt the long walls of the 300-acre estate (signposted) to reach the car park

Syon House is open at Easter weekend, then from May 14 to Sept 29, Mon–Thur, 2–5 (Sun 1–5; BH Mons 11–5), and closed Fri and Sat. The Gardening Centre in the park is open daily, exc. Christmas Day, Boxing Day, New Years Eve and Day, 9.30–5.15, Sun 10–5.45, winter closing usually 4.45. Fee. Camellia Restaurant and Bar.

SYON HOUSE, the seat of the Duke of Northumberland, was erected by Robert Adam c. 1760, and occupies the site of a Bridgettine nunnery founded in 1414 and granted to Protector Somerset at the Dissolution. Queen Catherine Howard was here confined between her trial and execution, and Lady Jane Grey was living here when summoned to the throne in 1553. The furniture, ceilings, and doorways are especially fine. – The *Gardening Centre* (plants, etc. for sale) includes a 6-acre rose garden. The Great Conservatory was built in 1830 by Fowler. It includes an aviary and an aquarium. To the N. of the house is the LONDON TRANSPORT COLLECTION (adm. 30p), transferred here in 1973 from Clapham and to be moved in 1979(?) to Covent Garden. This comprises buses, trams, and underground relics, together with maps, models, and documents. Here also are a fine exhibition 'History on Wheels' consisting mainly of vintage cars; and a Toy and Doll Museum.

Near the car park entrance, on a bend in the Thames, stands the pleasant little hamlet of *Isleworth*, with an old inn (Rest.). On the opposite bank extend Kew Gardens (comp. Rte 40). A new church (1967) by Michael Blee was erected here after a fire in 1943. The light interior has an unusual vaulted roof and tall windows through which the country churchyard and both arms of the river may be glimpsed. The delightful Joshua Chapel overlooking the Thames commemorates a child who died at the age of 2½ years. Part of the 18C aisle walls have been preserved and form an open court around a fountain between the new church and the fine 14C tower (view). A church has stood on this site since A.D. 695. The wharf farther upstream lies on the Duke of Northumberland River, constructed in the 15C and linked to the near-by river Crane. Mills established here were used in the making of gunpowder until the 1920s, and (until the late 19C) in the manufacture of swords, brass, copper, paper, etc.

We may now return to London Road which skirts the N. border of Syon Park. Spur Road, across London Rd., leads into Syon Lane which soon joins (8 m.) the Great West Road. Here we turn west.—9 m. ***Osterley Park.** Cars may follow the avenue to the car park, discreetly hidden from the house and grounds.

The House is open April–Sept, daily exc. Mon, 2–6; Oct–March 12–4; fee. The grounds are open free daily. Tea-room open April–Sept. Excellent Guidebook available.

Sir Thomas Gresham built a manor house at Osterley in the 1560s, and received Queen Elizabeth here in 1576. It was later owned by Sir William Waller, the parliamentary general, who died at Osterley in 1668. Francis Child (grandson of the founder of Child's Bank, comp. p. 206), employed Sir William Chambers to remodel the house. Work was begun c. 1756 and the old house with its four corner towers was encased in new walls. The Gallery and Breakfast Room were already completed when Robert Adam took over as architect in 1762. While keeping to the original design, he is responsible for the portico and magnificent decoration inside. He, and the cabinet-maker John Linnell, designed and made much of the furniture for each room. In 1949 Osterley was presented to the N.T. by the Earl of Jersey.

In the House much of the furniture and decoration designed by Adam for the state rooms remains in its original condition. The superb plasterwork, and detailed decoration on the furniture, doors, fireplaces, etc. are worth close examination. The Etruscan Dressing Room was painted, to Adam's design, by P. M. Borgnis. The ceiling paintings by Ant. Zucchi, the Beauvais (1786) and Gobelins (1775) tapestries, and paintings by Reynolds and Richard Wilson should all be noted.

In the grounds, the stables are only slightly altered since Gresham's day. The Garden House was added by Adam in 1780. Across the lawn is a Doric Temple by John James (c. 1720; interior probably by Chambers). Beyond fine cedars three lakes decorate the informal park.

Boston Manor House lies about 1½ m. E. (reached viâ the Great West Road and Boston Manor Road). A Tudor and Jacobean mansion (good ceilings) it is open May–Sept on Sat, 2.30–5 (fee). The park, now marred by the M4 motorway viaduct, is open daily.

We may return direct to London along the Great West Road which joins the M4 motorway.

43 WINDSOR AND ETON

GREEN LINE COACHES. Nos. 704 and 705 from Victoria and Hyde Park Corner viâ Great West Road in 1 hr 35 min.; No. 718 from Victoria viâ Kingston in 1 hr 40 min. All services run at half hourly intervals.

RAILWAY. From *Paddington* viâ Slough; and from *Waterloo* viâ Staines. Services every half hour in c. 40 min.

For COACH EXCURSIONS to Windsor, see p. 28.

The most direct approach by car to Windsor is described below. Alternative approaches: by the old Great West Road (A4), see Rte 48; viâ Richmond, see Rte 37.—By river from Kingston upon Thames, see Rte 38.

The M4 Motorway diverges from the old Great West Road (A4) at Chiswick.—At 12 m. it passes close to the N. side of London Airport (Rte 48). We by-pass *Slough*, an industrial town, on the s. Sir William Herschel (1738–1822) lived in Observatory House, and here his son Sir John (1792–1871) was born.—19½ m. *Slough West* exit. A spur of the motorway (*View of the Castle) serves (21 m.) **Windsor** (30,100 inhab.). Famous for its stately castle, which has been the chief residence of the sovereigns of England for 850 years, it is situated on the right (Berks) bank of the Thames and is connected by bridges with Eton and Datchet on the left (Bucks) bank. It was made a Royal Borough in 1922.

On the corner of Thames St., which ascends from the river, is a memorial (1937) to George V, by Lutyens. The street climbs round between the castle *Bastions and 18C houses refronted with shops. In High St., its continuation, beyond the statue of Queen Victoria at Castle Hill, is the *Guildhall* (adm. April–Oct daily 1–6; fee), designed in 1686 by Sir Thos. Fitch and completed by Wren (1707). It is adorned with statues of Queen Anne and Prince George of Denmark, and contains royal portraits, notably Prince Rupert, by D'Agar. The *Church*, farther on (rebuilt 1822), contains carving perhaps by Grinling Gibbons; and there are interesting houses in Market St. and Church St., both cobbled.

**Windsor Castle, on a chalk cliff rising abuptly above the Thames, was started in wood by William the Conqueror, continued in stone by Henry II, and though extended by Henry III and Edward III still preserves its original plan (two baileys and a mote-hill).

Henry I's marriage to Adeliza of Louvain (1121), was the first royal wedding to be celebrated here. Edward III was born here in 1312, and Henry VI in 1421, and three kings (David II of Scotland, John of France, and James I of Scotland) have been imprisoned within its walls; and from his cell window James first espied his future wife, Jane Beaufort. Edward III's queen, Philippa of Hainault, died in the castle in 1369. The present appearance of the building dates from the extensive restorations undertaken by Wyatville under George IV.

The *Lower Ward*, the *North Terrace*, and part of the *East Terrace* are open free daily (Guards' band on the E. terrace, 2–4 on Sun in June–Aug). In the absence of the Court (inquire beforehand) the *State Apartments* are shown on weekdays 11–3, 4, or 5 (according to season), also Sun in April–Oct from 1.30; fee. The *Round Tower* (April–Sept) and the *Albert Memorial Chapel* (closed 1–2, and on Sun) are open free at the same hours. *St George's Chapel* is open on weekdays 11–3.45 (Fri 1–3.45), Sun 2.30–4 (fee); free for services. The State Apartments and Round Tower are closed when the Queen is in residence; usually in April, and for periods during March, May, June, and December. In summer long queues for the State Apartments may be experienced, now somewhat alleviated by ticket machines at the entrance (5p and 10p coins necessary; change available at kiosks on North Terrace).

On entering the Lower Ward from Castle Hill by *Henry VIII's Gateway*, we have in front of us the entrance to the *Horseshoe Cloisters*, built under Edward IV, at the N.W. angle of which stands the *Curfew Tower* (shown by a Keeper), with a 13C interior. On the right are the houses of the *Military Knights of Windsor*.

This Order was founded by Edward III as the 'Poor Knights of Windsor' at the same times as the Order of the Garter; its present name was given by William IV in 1833. The central tower (1359) bears the arms of Philip and Mary.

*St George's Chapel (fee), dedicated to the patron saint of the Order of the Garter, was begun c. 1478 by Henry Janyns for Edward IV and continued in 1503–11 by William Vertue. It is one of the most perfect specimens of 15–16C Gothic work, ranking with King's College Chapel at Cambridge and Henry VII's Chapel at Westminster. The usual public entrance is by the s. door, whence the visit follows a controlled path through the nave and choir. The NAVE has a fine lierne vault with carved bosses. At the s.w. corner is the *Beaufort Chapel*, where the tomb of the Earl of Worcester (d. 1526) has a Flemish bronze grating unusual in Britain. The great w. window contains much fine glass of 1503–09. In the N.W. corner is the tomb by Lutyens and Reid Dick, of George V (d. 1936) and Queen Mary (1953), with the theatrical tomb of Princess Charlotte (d. 1817) in the Urswick Chapel behind.

The *CHOIR is separated from the nave by a Gothic screen (c. 1785) by Henry Emlyn. The organ, originally as at King's centrally placed, was rebuilt in flanking sections in 1930, to afford a clear view from the nave of the fan vaulting. We continue into the NORTH CHOIR AISLE off which (l.) is the *Rutland Chapel* (1481) containing effigies of George Manners (d. 1513) and his wife. To the right is the *Chantry Chapel of William, Lord Hastings* with contemporary paintings of his execution in 1483; to the left the memorial chapel of George VI (1969). To the N. of the High Altar a superb pair of gates (1482) front the tomb of Edward IV. Above is the Royal Pew, a splendid wooden oriel provided by Henry VIII for Catherine of Aragon. In the centre of the floor is a vault containing the remains of Henry VIII, Jane Seymour, and Charles I. The *Stalls (1478–95) in three tiers are surmounted by the helmets, crests, and banners of the Knights of the Garter, whose installations have taken place at Windsor since 1348. The reverse stalls are those of the Royal Family, the *Sovereign's Stall* marked by the Royal Standard.

We pass beneath the Screen, turn left past the Bray Chapel (with the cenotaph of the Prince Imperial, son of Napoleon III, killed in South Africa in 1879), and enter the SOUTH CHOIR AISLE. On the left is the *Chantry of John Oxenbridge* with paintings of 1522; the great sword of Edward III; and the simple slab marking the tomb of Henry VI. On the s. side of the altar is the tomb by Mackennal of Edward VII and Queen Alexandra. The S.E. Chapel, with the tomb of the Earl of Lincoln (d. 1585), is called the *Lincoln Chapel*, or *John Schorne's Tower*, from the relics of Sir John Schorne (d. 1314), brought here in 1478 from North Marston in Bucks.

The e. wall of the ambulatory once formed the w. front of Henry III's Chapel (1240–48) and retains its contemporary *Doors. Beyond the floor slab of Sir Jeffry Wyatville we pass through the N.E. door into the slype, leading (l.) to the *Dean's Cloister*, preserving arcading of Henry

III's chapel and a piece of fresco. To the N. is the *Canon's Cloister*, a picturesque corner of 1353–56.

The **Albert Memorial Chapel** was rebuilt by Henry VII as a burial-place for Henry VI, but, left unfinished, was completed by Wolsey. His magnificent tomb was never occupied and was broken up during the Civil War. Queen Victoria caused the chapel to be converted into a splendid memorial for her husband (d. 1861) who is buried, however, at Frogmore. It contains the cenotaph of Prince Albert, by Baron Triqueti, and the tombs of the Duke of Clarence (d. 1892), the elder son of Edward VII, by Alfred Gilbert, and of the Duke of Albany (d. 1884), Queen Victoria's youngest son.

Beneath the chapel are buried George III, Queen Charlotte, and six of their sons (including George IV and William IV).

To the left of the entrance to the N. terrace is the *Winchester Tower*, where Chaucer may have lived in 1390, when Master of the Works at Windsor.—A gateway leads on to the long *North Terrace* (*View of the Home Park, Eton, and Stoke Poges church).

Immediately below is *St George's School*, the choir school, in the building (1802) of *Travers College*, founded in 1795 from a bequest of Samuel Travers (d. 1725) for 'Naval Knights', an order corresponding to the Military Knights (see above) but disbanded in 1892.

From the North Terrace we enter the **State Apartments,** which occupy the N. wing of the Upper Ward. These are used mainly for royal func-tions and contain many notable paintings from the royal collections, superb *Furniture, and other treasures.

From the China Gallery we ascend the GRAND STAIRCASE, with a statue of George IV, by *Chantrey*, and armour made for Henry VIII and the sons of James I. CHARLES II's DINING ROOM has a ceiling by *Verrio* and carvings by *Grinling Gibbons*. In the *KING'S DRAWING ROOM, or RUBENS ROOM, is a series of noble works by *Rubens* (Holy Family, etc.) and a St Martin by *Van Dyck*. The STATE BEDCHAMBER contains a fine Louis Seize bed; the adjoining DRESSING ROOM, or LESSER BED-CHAMBER, a painting by *Van Dyck* (Charles I, from three points of view for use in the execution of a bust), and many of the smaller *Paintings: portraits by *Clouet*, *Memling*, *Dürer*, and *And. del Sarto*; by *Rubens* (of himself and of Van Dyck); and by *Holbein*. In the KING's CLOSET are Venetian views by *Canaletto* and portraits of David Garrick by *Hogarth* and *Reynolds*. The QUEEN's DRAWING ROOM contains an unequalled array of *Portraits by *Van Dyck*; Charles I, Henrietta Maria, their children, and members of the court; also *Dobson*, James II as Duke of York; 17C French and English furniture.

We pass into an older wing (renewed by Charles II), where the QUEEN's BALL-ROOM has more characteristic views by *Canaletto*. The QUEEN's AUDIENCE CHAMBER has *Gobelins* tapestries, and portraits of the Princes of Orange (by *Honthorst*) in frames carved by *Grinling Gibbons*; the QUEEN's PRESENCE CHAMBER continues the series of tapestries. Both these rooms have ceilings by *Verrio* glorifying Queen Catherine of Braganza. Here also is a bust of Handel by *Roubiliac*. The QUEEN's GUARD CHAMBER displays a fine suit of armour (1585), made for Sir Christopher Hatton, and busts (Philip II, Charles V) by *Leone Leoni*. Above busts of Marl-borough and Wellington hang the replica standards that constitute the annual rent paid for Woodstock and Stratfield Saye. A bust of Churchill was commissioned from *Oscar Nemon* (1953). The noble ST GEORGE's HALL, 185 ft long, in which the festivities of the Order of the Garter are held, bears on the ceiling and walls the coats-of-arms of the knights since 1348. The portraits of English sovereigns from James I to George IV are by *Van Dyck*, *Kneller*, etc. Among the parallel range of busts (by Nollekens, Chantrey, etc.), that by Roubiliac represents George II (*not* I). The GRAND RECEPTION ROOM has fine Gobelins tapestries; the THRONE ROOM or GARTER ROOM contains portraits of sovereigns in their Garter robes. The large *WATERLOO CHAMBER, constructed in 1830 inside a 12C court, contains portraits, mostly by *Lawrence*, of personages who were instrumental in the downfall of Napoleon. From the GRAND VESTIBULE beyond, with relics of Napoleon and the

Japanese surrender sword (early 15C) of 1945, we descend by King John's Tower to the Quadrangle.

In a room to the left of the entrance is *Queen Mary's Dolls' House* (add. fee), designed by Sir Edwin Lutyens on the scale of an inch to a foot, and furnished and decorated on the same scale by 1500 eminent artists and craftsmen (1922–23).— Reached also from the entrance to the State Apartments is a splendid *Exhibition of Old Master Drawings* from the royal collection (add. fee), including works of Holbein, Leonardo da Vinci, Raphael, and Michelangelo, the French School (Claude, Poussin, etc.), and 17–19C British artists, notably Hogarth and Paul Sandby.

Between the Upper and Lower Wards rises the **Round Tower** or *Keep*, in fact elliptical in plan, its lower half of 1170, heightened by Wyatville, which should be ascended (220 steps) for the extensive *View.—On the E. side of the Upper Ward (no adm.) are the *Private Apartments of the Queen*. The passage between the Round Tower and the Upper Ward leads through St George's Gateway to Castle Hill, near the entrance to the *Royal Stables*.

Immediately adjoining Windsor Castle on the N. and E. is the **Home Park**, in the s. part of which are *Frogmore House* and *Mausoleum*. The latter contains the remains of the Prince Consort and of Queen Victoria. Here, too, is buried the Duke of Windsor, King Edward VIII (1894–1972). It is open usually on the 1st Wed and Thurs in May, 10–dusk, and on the Wed nearest to 24 May (Queen Victoria's birthday), 11–4.—To the s. of Windsor lies **Windsor Great Park** (nearly 2000 acres), traversed by the road to Ascot and the *Long Walk*. The latter, planted with elms by Charles II and replanted after 1945 with horse-chestnut and plane, stretches straight from the castle to (2¾ m.) *Snow Hill*, which bears a huge statue of George III ('the Copper Horse') by Westmacott. On the right of the Ascot road stood *Cranbourn Lodge* (demolished), where the great Duke of Marlborough died in 1722.

Still within the park, but best approached from Windsor viâ Old Windsor village, along the winding Crimp Lane and past the hamlet of Bishopsgate (where Shelley had a cottage in 1816), is (4½ m.) the *Savill Garden* (adm. daily 10–6, March–Oct, fee; Restaurant), 20 acres of lovely woodland garden, named after a former park ranger. Wick Lane goes on to *Englefield Green*, on the A30 between Egham and Virginia Water. To the s. of the garden is *Smith's Lawn* where polo is played from late April to the end of August. Beyond are *Valley Gardens* (open all year). These lie on the N. side of *Virginia Water*, see the 'Blue Guide to England'.

The *Royal Windsor Safari Park*, 1½ m. s. of the town, is in the grounds (100 acres) of the 18C St Leonard's House. It is open daily 10–dusk (adm. with car, £1), and includes lion, cheetah, and baboon enclosures, a dolphinarium, etc.

Beyond Windsor Bridge (no cars) begins the long picturesque street forming the small town of **Eton** (4000 inhab.), lined with attractive shops (many of them dealing in antiques). It leads to (¾ m.) *Eton College, founded by Henry VI in 1440 and perhaps the most widely known of all English schools. The college, as founded, consists of the Provost, Vice-Provost, ten fellows, the Head Master, Lower Master, and seventy scholars.

On weekdays (unless required for school purposes) *School Yard* and *Cloisters* may be visited from 2 to lock-up (10–5 during holidays); the *Chapel* is open from 2.30–4.30 during the Lent and Michaelmas terms, and until 5.45 in summer term (10–5 during holidays). On Sundays the College is closed to visitors.

The pupils of Eton College consist of the 70 King's Scholars (K.S.) of the original foundation, who obtain scholarships by open competition, and about 1100 *Oppidans*, who live at the masters' house. The boys wear broad collars, and tailcoats, the last replaced for boys below a certain height by short jackets.

The main block, of fine mellow red brick, includes two courts, or quadrangles, the larger of which, *School Yard*, contains a statue of Henry VI (1719). On the entrance side a frieze commemorates 1157 Etonians who fell in 1914–19 and 748 killed in 1939–45. Above is the *Upper School* (1689–94), with busts of eminent Etonians, damaged in

1941, but restored; the panelled walls and staircase are covered with the names of boys going on to King's (earliest 1577), with wooden pillars of c. 1625. Opposite stands the *Chapel, a Perpendicular structure begun in 1441, and completed (though on a smaller scale than was intended) by William Orchard for William Waynflete in 1479–83. It was given a new fan-vault by Sir Wm. Holford in 1958 and contains a superb series of *Wall-paintings (1479–88) of British workmanship, discovered in 1847 (restored in 1927, and again in 1970–73), and a stained-glass E. window (1952) by Evie Hone. The clerestory windows are by John Piper.

A fine gatehouse of c. 1517, erected by Provost Lupton, admits to the original second court or *Cloisters*, with the Collegers' *Dining Hall* (1450) and the *College Library* (1725–29) above it.—In the playing-fields beyond is the 'wall', which gives name to the 'wall-game', a style of football peculiar to Eton (chief game on 30 Nov). The long list of famous Etonians includes Fielding, C. J. Fox, the elder and younger Pitt, the Walpole brothers, Gray, Shelley, Wellington, Canning, Hallam, Gladstone, Rosebery, and Roberts.

The High Street of Eton is prolonged N. by Slough Road, which passes beneath the M4 motorway.

V THE NORTHERN ENVIRONS

44 EPPING FOREST AND THE LEA VALLEY

GREEN LINE COACHES. Nos. 718 from Victoria, Hyde Park Corner, or Gt. Portland St. (via Walthamstow and Chingford), and 720 from Aldgate to *Woodford Wells*, *Loughton*, *Epping Forest*, and *Epping*, No. 715 from Bayswater Rd. or Oxford Circus to *Waltham Cross* and *Hoddesdon*.

BUSES from Central London, 279 to *Waltham Cross*; 149 to *Edmonton*. Also from Walthamstow Central (Victoria Line), 69 to *Chingford*; 20 to *Loughton* and *Epping*. No. 242 from Chingford to *Waltham Abbey* and *Cross*.

RAILWAYS. Central Line to *Woodford, Buckhurst Hill, Loughton, Theydon Bois*, and *Epping*, roughly parallel with the E. side of the Forest (every 12 min. to Loughton, every 24 min. to Epping); the branch from Woodford to *Hainault* is worked by the world's first automatic passenger trains (1964); E.R. from Liverpool St. to *Chingford*, for the S. part of Epping Forest, 10½ m. in 25 min.; from Liverpool St. (Hertford trains) to *Waltham Cross*, 13¾ m. in 30 min. (1–3 trains hourly).

The direct exit to N.E. London follows A104 from Islington (Rte 25), viâ Essex Road and Dalston, or from Shoreditch (Rte 30) we may diverge right by A107 through Hackney to join A104 at (3½ m.) *Clapton* pond.

To the S. lies HACKNEY, once a fashionable suburb, but now rather drab. In the centre, in Mare St., is the tower of the 16C restored church of *St John* and beyond is the new church built by James Spiller in 1792–97 with the tower and porches added in 1812–13; damaged by fire, it was restored in 1958. It takes the shape of a Greek cross, very spacious. The Urswick chapel, E. of the entrance, contains some interesting monuments. In S. Hackney, in Cassland Rd., is a delightful terrace of Georgian houses. *Sutton House* (N.T.; No. 2 Homerton High St.) is a fine 16C house (adm. free on written application to tenant).—To the S. between the Lea and the Lee Navigation extends *Hackney Marsh*, an area of flat grassland, 940 acres in extent, opened as a public park in 1894. In the football season it provides 110 pitches—more than any other sports arena in the country. Farther S. the Lee Navigation passes through Stratford (p. 261) and the industrial East End to join the Thames at Bugsby Reach.

At a huge roundabout we turn right into the long *Lea Bridge Road* flanked by reclaimed parkland, and soon cross the Lea just above its division into the Lea proper and the Lee Navigation. The disused 'Triples' Engine House (1891) of the old East London Water Works (on the l. bank) was restored for the Lea Valley Conference of 1964 which introduced the Civic Trust's scheme for a Regional Park (see below). The *Lea Bridge Centre* (riding school; circus) will have interconnected swimming pool, ice rink, and arts centre, set in river gardens.

Northwards most of the way to Waltham Abbey the tow-path (10m.; crossed by only 3 roads) passes between reservoirs and playing-fields, with the doomed landmark of Brimsdown power station on the w. In 1978 this provides the only N.–S. access to the Lea, but a new 'Park Way' has been started (comp. below).

5¾ m. *Leyton*. Hoe St. leads left through Walthamstow to Chingford (comp. below). We continue N.E. to (6½ m.) *Whipps Cross* at the S. extremity of Epping Forest. Here one of the *Hollow Ponds* has been transformed into a 'lido'. Near *Forest School* (475 boys; founded 1834 in a row of good Georgian houses), Snaresbrook Road (r.) affords a pleasant view across the Eagle Pond to the *Royal Wanstead School*, an early work of Gilbert Scott (1843). To the E. lies WANSTEAD (1½ m. from Forest School), where the wooded *Wanstead Park* once surrounded the first Wanstead House owned by Leicester and later by Essex, who used to retire here from the periodic wrath of Elizabeth I. Some outbuildings and ornamental waters remain of its Palladian successor (1715, demolished 1825), said to have surpassed Blenheim in magnificence, where the exiled Prince de Condé entertained Louis XVIII. The church of *St Mary*, by Thos. Hardwick (1790), recalls the classical heyday.—Beyond Forest School Woodford New Road bears N. and at (7½ m.) *Waterworks Corner* joins Forest Road, the approach from North London (A503) via Finsbury Park and Tottenham, which traverses Walthamstow from W. to E.

Walthamstow, with Chingford and Leyton now merged in the London Borough of Waltham Forest, has Saxon'origins. On A503 Ferry Lane and the Ferry Boat Inn recall an earlier method of crossing the Lea from Middlesex to Essex. The long Forest Road continues N.E., passing the *Water House* (c. 1750), home of William Morris (born near by) in 1848–56. It was opened in 1950 to house a *William Morris Gallery* and the Brangwyn Gift of pre-Raphaelite paintings; works of art and craft by many of Morris's circle are displayed. Lloyd Park, in which the house stands, has exotic water-fowl. Farther on (beyond Hoe St.; comp. below) are the *Town Hall* (1937–41), by P. D. Hepworth, flanked by an Assembly Hall with noted acoustics (concerts), much used by recording companies; a court house, originally intended to balance the composition, was completed in 1973 in a clashing, alien style. The huge Waltham Forest Technical College forms part of the East London Polytechnic.

Off Hoe St. Church Hill leads to *St Mary's*, with a monument by Nicholas Stone (1654). Adjacent is the original building of the Monoux School (1527; restored 1955), now an almshouse, and near by is the excellent *Vestry House Museum* (closed 1–2) of local history, containing the first British motor-car with an internal combustion engine (1892 Bremer).—North of Forest Road Hoe St. is continued by Chingford Road past the Monoux School (comp. above) and the site of Salisbury Hall (demolished 1952 to form the Stadium car park), where Roger Ascham wrote 'The Scholemaster' (1571).

At *Chingford*, to the N., *Pole Hill* (300 ft), once a retreat of Lawrence of Arabia, affords a good view of the huge King George V Reservoir. The Bank Holiday fair on *Chingford Plain* is vividly evoked by Somerset Maugham in 'Liza of Lambeth'. Queen Elizabeth's Hunting Lodge now houses the *Epping Forest Museum* (Thurs, Sat and Sun, 2–5). *Gilwell Park* to the W., is known as a camping ground to Scouts and Rovers throughout the world.

We cross the North Circular Road and, at (8½ m.) *Woodford Green* join Woodford High Road (A11; from Wanstead) near a statue, by David McFall, of Sir Winston Churchill erected in 1959 by his constituents. *Highams*, a mansion of 1768 now incorporated in the County High School for Girls, keeps the name of a pre-Domesday manor; *Highams Park* laid out by Repton, to the W. is now public and has given name to a district. At *Bancroft's School* (by Blomfield, 1887), in Woodford Wells, the road forks, the right branch passing close to the beautiful woodland known as *Lord's Bushes* (r.; 120 acres), descending *Buckhurst Hill*, and traversing (11½ m.) *Loughton* (comp. below), while the Epping New Road (l.) drives straight through the forest with branches (Rangers Road; l.) to Chingford and, farther on, to *High Beach* (⅜ m. l.), a popular viewpoint at weekends. Here a Conservation Centre provides information about the flora and fauna of the forest. The cave is shown where Dick Turpin hid in 1737.—At (13½ m.) the *Wake Arms Inn*, where the roads rejoin, ways diverge to Theydon Bois (E.) and Waltham Abbey (w.; 3 m.).

*Epping Forest, a delightful woodland of c. 6000 acres, occupies the high ground between the valleys of the Lea and the Roding, and has an extreme length of about 11 m., though only 1–2 m. broad. Its main portion lies between Chingford and Epping, though there are isolated strips both to the N. and to the S. The forest is the chief relic of the royal hunting forest of Waltham, saved from complete disafforestation in 1871 by the Commons Preservation Society supported by the Corporation of the City. The fallow deer of the forest are probably indigenous; badgers, foxes, squirrels, and weasels are found, and the bird-life and insect-life is extremely varied. Adders are not unknown. The characteristic trees are hornbeam, beech, oak, birch, and holly.

WALKS IN THE FOREST. Walkers are recommended to leave the beaten track and explore the forest with map and compass. A good plan for a day's walk is to start from Chingford and visit Connaught Water, High Beach, Loughton Camp (British), *Monk Wood, with fine beech trees, Ambersbury Banks, and Epping Thicks, and then walk W. past Copped Hall Green to Waltham Abbey (10 m. in all). In Baldwin's Hill, overlooking Monk Wood, Sir Jacob Epstein lived in 1920–40.

At *Debden*, a new suburb E. of Loughton (see above), is the Bank of England Printing Works, removed from St Luke's (Old St.) in 1956.

About 1m. beyond the Wake Arms Inn (r.) is *Ambersbury Banks*, a large and well-defined earthwork, the traditional scene of the defeat of Boudicca by Suetonius. *Epping Thicks*, to the E., is one of the wildest parts of the forest. To the W. of the road is seen *Copped Hall*, a mansion of 1753–57; William III once had an unexpected adventure in the vicinity. —16¼ m. **Epping,** with a long main street (Sat market), has an imposing 19C church.

Waltham Abbey, a fine early-Norman building, the burial-place of King Harold, slain at Hastings in 1066, lies to the W. in the Lea Valley. The present church consists of the *Nave begun by Harold, the Lady Chapel of 1316, and a W. tower of 1556–58. The massive columns of the nave, channelled with chevrons and spirals, recall Durham cathedral, which Waltham must have resembled before Henry II's vast E. extensions of 1177–84 were demolished at the dissolution. Thos. Tallis was organist until 1540. The fine windows in the Victorian E. end are by Burne-Jones. On the right the raised Chapel (in a position paralleled only at Rochester) has a fresco of the Last Judgment (c. 1430) and a W. window with tracery recalling the choir aisles of Bristol cathedral. The undercroft below contains a small historical display of the local archaeological society.

The walled Abbey Gardens, to the E., retain the form of an orchard and enclose a stone marking the site of the high altar and Harold's tomb, vestiges of the cloister, and near the E. end a square area still surrounded by a moat. To the N. are two monastic gateways (c. 1370) and the ancient little Harold's Bridge. Between the precinct and the N. relief road a Museum is planned, but the area is first to be systematically excavated. About 1½ m. S., on the Essex bank of the Lea, is the Royal Enfield Small Arms Factory, from which Lee-Enfield rifles supplied the army for nearly a century.

We cross the Lea near the Explosives Research and Development Establishment.—**Waltham Cross,** 1¾ m. W. of the Abbey and 14½ m. N. of central London, takes its name from the *Eleanor Cross* (heavily restored), the last but one of the series erected by Edward I in 1291 (comp. p. 73). A self-consciously re-erected inn-sign keeps it company in a dreary modern context. Anthony Trollope (1815–82) lived at Waltham House in 1859–71.

To the W. is the Georgian successor of *Theobalds*, the manor-house where James I died in 1625. Farther on, 1½ m. W. by Theobalds Lane and beyond A10, is old *Temple Bar*, re-erected here in 1888 as an entrance to Theobalds Park estate. Its neglected state provokes periodic but so far abortive suggestions for its return to the City.

Through Waltham Cross the old Cambridge Road (A1010) runs N. and S. in the **Lea Valley,** here characterized by gravel-pits and glass-houses beneath which flowers and tomatoes are grown. The Lea, King Alfred's frontier between Wessex and the Danelaw, was later the bound-ary between Essex, on the E., and Middlesex and Hertfordshire on the W., though above Hoddesdon the boundary follows the Stort, the Lea's main tributary. Izaak Walton fished the Lea. The LEE VALLEY REGIONAL PARK is a concept to regenerate the valley from Ware to the Thames. Derelict areas are being reclaimed and landscaped in the context of reservoirs and industrial uses. The Authority's terms of reference des-cribe the goal as "a place for the enjoyment of leisure, recreation, sport, games or amusements or any similar activity, for the provision of nature reserves, and for the provision and enjoyment of entertainments of any kind", and work will continue for c. 15 years.

Until Park Way the spinal access road is built, the piecemeal progress will not be conspicuous, and isolated completed attractions must be approached from the A1010. The road follows closely the line of Roman Ermine Street from Shoreditch to Edmonton; to the N. of Edmonton it deviates from the strict Roman line, and is particularly dreary, but it is still the road of John Gilpin's unwilling ride. The railway or the river give a better idea of the Valley's dismal past and happier future.

To the N. the road runs through (16½ m. from London) *Cheshunt*, where Richard Cromwell lived a quiet life from his return to England in 1680 until his death in 1712. The church of 1418–48, with its stone tower, stands opposite the huge and unattractive buildings that formerly housed Cheshunt College (transferred to Cambridge in 1905 and now defunct). Old gravel-pits here will be transformed into the National Rowing, Canoeing, and Regatta Centre. At (20 m.) *Wormley* our road is joined by the Great Cambridge Rd. (A10). — 22 m. **Broxbourne,** on a backwater of the Lea (boats for hire), has a fine 15C *Church* containing tombs of the Say family that built it and a tablet to John McAdam (d. 1836), the improver of British roads. Across the railway stands a fine 'Lido' (1977). Thence to Ware (and Cambridge), see the 'Blue Guide to England'.

RETURN TO THE CITY. To the S. of Waltham Cross the A1010 traverses the industrial E. fringes of Enfield, crossing Rte 45 at (2½ m.) *Ponders End.* To the S.E. (signposted l.) the first major leisure resort of the Regional Park, the *Picketts Lock Centre* (bus W8 from Lower Edmonton), was opened in 1973 between the railway and the William Girling Reservoir. This great sports centre is also linked to the North Circular Rd. by the planned Park Way. — In (5¼ m.) *Edmonton* we cross the North Circular Rd., which, to the E., gives access to the smaller *Banbury Reservoir*, used as a sail training centre for schools.

In (6½ m.) **Tottenham,** we pass (r.) White Hart Lane, synonymous with the 'Spurs football team, though their present ground is a little farther on to the left. Lordship Lane or Bruce Grove lead (r.) in 100 yds to BRUCE CASTLE, a much altered 16–18C manor house having shadowy associations with the Scots, where Rowland Hill kept a school in 1827–35. It houses a *Museum* of local and postal history. The collection, based on the Morten bequest (on permanent loan), includes material concerning the introduction of penny post, the display showing by letters and relics the development of mail-carrying from postboys of the 16C to the introduction of the postage stamp. The local archives include manor rolls from 1318.—*Tottenham High Cross* (17C) is not an Eleanor cross.

We cross A503 (comp. above) at Seven Sisters corner.—8 m. *Stamford*

Hill is the centre of a Hassidic Jewish community from Byelorussia.—8½ m. *Stoke Newington Station.* The southbound one-way system diverges viâ Rectory Road, passing Stoke Newington Common, but the centre lies to the right of the High Street. Church Street skirts *Abney Park Cemetery*, in which is buried Gen. Booth, founder of the Salvation Army. Former residents of **Stoke Newington** include Daniel Defoe ('Robinson Crusoe' was written in Church St.), John Howard, J. S. Mill, and Edgar Allan Poe. There is an attractive church, *Old St Mary's*, with a 16C s. aisle, restored in 1953; while the newer one by Sir Gilbert Scott (1858) has a spire added by his son.—As Kingsland Road A10 continues due s. towards the prominent spire of (11 m.) *Shoreditch Church* (comp. Rte 30).

45 FROM EPPING FOREST TO HARROW

ROAD, A110, A411, A409. 17 m. BUS 121 from Chingford to Enfield (not Sun); 107 from Ponders End to Elstree; 306 from Barnet to Elstree; 258 from Bushey fo Harrow (not Sun).

From Chingford (Rte 44) King's Head Hill descends steeply to the Lea Valley, here crossed between the William Girling and King George's reservoirs. The river is bridged at Ponders End Lock c. 1 m. N. of Picketts Lock (p. 319). We cross successively the A1010 and the Great Cambridge Road.

4 m. Enfield still has a town centre, though the one-way system has diminished the character of Church Street. Behind the *Market Place*, the *Parish Church* (14–16C), of battlemented flint and brick, contains the splendid tomb and brass of Lady Tiptoft (1404–46), with interesting details of costume; the elaborate monument of Sir Nicholas Raynton (d. 1646); and a good organ-case of 1752. The neighbouring *Grammar School*, refounded by Elizabeth I, still maintains its contemporary building. Pupils of Enfield schools include Capt. Marryat (1792–1848) and John Keats. Farther on at *Clarendon Cottage* (in the quiet Gentleman's Row, facing the Green) Lamb lived with his sister in 1829–32. Near by, many pleasant 18–19C houses are lapped by the original and later courses of the NEW RIVER, a 40-mile aqueduct completed by Sir Hugh Myddelton in 1613 to bring spring water to London (comp. p. 236).

Baker St. leads N. in 1½ m. to **Forty Hall** (car park; Easter–Sept, Tues–Fri 10–8, Sat & Sun 10–6; Oct–Easter daily exc. Mon, 10–4 or 5), a mansion built for Sir Nicholas Raynton in 1629–32 with a wooded park. It contains 17–18C furniture and pictures notably a portrait of Raynton by Dobson. Exhibitions are held in the adjoining Art Gallery. In the grounds have been found scanty remains of *Elsynge Hall*, a Tudor royal manor where, in the presence of the Princess Elizabeth, Edward VI was given the news of his accession in 1547.—The road continues to *Bull's Cross*, passing Myddelton House (1818), the headquarters of the Lee Valley Regional Park Authority.

Windmill Hill leads w. from the centre. At the top the bus continues straight on along the s. edge of Enfield Chase past Oakwood Station down into New Barnet. It is better to branch right on A1005 (the Ridgeway leading towards Potters Bar) and, after a mile, left to **Enfield Chase** (view). A royal hunting-ground from Henry IV to the 18C, the Chase has been much attenuated since Northaw and Southgate marked its N. and s. bounds. Beyond the pleasing Hadley Road Pumping Station (of the M.W.B.), the s. part of the chase, though enclosed as *Trent Park*, is still pleasantly wooded and natural. The house was refaced with materials from Devonshire House in 1926 and now serves as a teachers' training college; its last tenant was Sir Philip Sassoon. During the Second World War it was successively an interrogation centre and an internment camp for captured generals. The grounds, with a nature trail, are open to the public (entrance in Cockfosters Rd., l.; car park). — At *West Lodge* we cross Cockfosters Road. Beech Hill now traverses the well-to-do suburb of Hadley Wood with the thickets of *Hadley Common* extending across the main railway line to Cockfosters to the left.

9 m. *Monken Hadley Church*, in a picturesque rural triangle of old houses, has a fine flint tower (1494), surmounted by a unique cresset; within are 15–17C brasses and a good tomb (1616) by Nicholas Stone. Just beyond we reach **Hadley Green* preserving several duck-ponds and much of its rural tranquillity, though crossed near its w. side by the Old Great North Road. The attractive mansions of the 17–19C that surround it include the house (plaque) occupied by David Livingstone in 1857, and there is a pleasant low range of almshouses. An obelisk of 1740, just to the N., marks the site of the Battle of Barnet (1471) in which Edward IV defeated the Lancastrians and Warwick the Kingmaker was slain. The village all but forms an extension of **Barnet** (correctly Chipping or High Barnet) to which a steep hill rises from London. Barnet Fair for horses is still held in Sept, and a stall market flourishes (Wed & Sat; off the St Albans Rd.). The 15C *Church*, enlarged by Butterfield in 1875, has another flint tower and remains imposing on its commanding site at the parting of two ancient roads. Within is a Ravenscroft tomb of 1632. The *Tudor Hall* (1573), opposite, once part of Queen Elizabeth's Grammar School, now forms part of Barnet College, while the school has moved farther out. A few steps farther w. a small local *Museum* (Tues, Thurs, & Sat, 2.30–4.30, also 10–12.30 Sat) occupies the *Old Court House*.

Beyond Hadley Green A1000 continues N. *Wrotham Park* (l.), a Palladian mansion, was built in 1754 for the ill-fated Adm. Byng. *Potters Bar* (2½ m.) has a cross in its church made from the wreckage of the Zeppelin brought down here in 1916.

Wood St. continues the A411 w. towards *Arkley* where a toll-house survives of Barnet Gate. At (12½ m.) *Stirling Corner* (roundabout) we cross the A1, beyond which for about 2 m. the road forms the boundary between Greater London and Hertfordshire.—14 m. *Elstree* stands on Watling Street (r. of our road) and is known for its film studios, passed beyond Aldenham Reservoir just before we cross the Watford by-pass (A41) and pass beneath the M1. By the eccentric 19C *Caldecote*, a school, we bear left from A411 and turn s. past Bentley Priory (Rte 47) to (17 m.) **Harrow**.

46 HAMPSTEAD AND HIGHGATE

HAMPSTEAD. For Hampstead Heath and Old Hampstead the stations are *Hampstead* on the Northern line and *Hampstead Heath* on the North London railway; for Hampstead Garden Suburb and Golders Green, *Golders Green* on the Northern line; for South Hampstead, *Swiss Cottage* and *Finchley Road* on the Bakerloo line, and *Finchley Road* on the Metropolitan line.—BUSES: Nos. 2, 13, 113 traverse Finchley Road; Nos. 31 and 187 pass Swiss Cottage; Nos. 24, 187 to Hampstead Heath Station; No. 268 from Swiss Cottage to Hampstead Heath and Golders Green; No. 210 plies from Golders Green to Highgate across Hampstead Heath.

HIGHGATE. *Archway* and *Highgate* stations of the Northern line. BUSES: No. 210 to Highgate Village and Archway; Nos. 27, 41, 137, 143, 172, 263 to Archway Station.

CAR PARKING. For *Hampstead Heath*: Car parks at Heathbrow (behind Jack Straw's Castle) and on East Heath Road.

An alternative approach is viâ the drab HAMPSTEAD ROAD which continues Tottenham Court Road N. of Euston Road (comp. p. 174). At No. 263 George Cruickshank died in 1878, while No. 247 marks the site of Dickens' school in 1824–26 while he was living in 141 Bayham Street (parallel to the E.), his first London home. Camden High Street continues N. into CAMDEN TOWN.—3½ m. Camden Station. We diverge left along *Chalk Farm Road* across the Regent's Canal (comp. pp. 174, 162). Here is an embarkation point for cruises on the canal (W. to Little Venice and E. towards Islington). Beyond, an engine shed built in 1847 has been converted into the Roundhouse experimental theatre. Near the foot of Haverstock Hill, in Maitland Park Road (r.), Karl Marx died in 1883 at No. 41 (demolished). Opposite is the site of the white cottage where Steele wrote many numbers of 'The Spectator'.—4¾ m. Old Hampstead Town Hall. The names of various streets to the S.W. preserve the memory of the old manor of *Belsize*. In Howitt Road, Ramsay MacDonald lived from 1916–25. The *Royal Free* teaching hospital occupies a site on the E. side of Haverstock Hill.—We soon join (5¼ m.) Hampstead High Street (see below). On the left Green Hill and the Royal Soldiers' Daughters' School occupy the site of the house and grounds of Sir Henry Vane (1612–62).

Hampstead, a pleasant residential quarter N.W. of London, extends officially from the Edgware Road, on the W., to Highgate. But the Hampstead of literary and picturesque interest centres round the old village, near the top of Hampstead Hill. It may be approached from various points in the Finchley Road, and viâ Haverstock Hill.

To (2¾m.) St John's Wood Station, see p. 162. Finchley Road leads directly to Golders Green, skirting the W. base of Hampstead Hill.— 3½ m. SWISS COTTAGE. Here is the *Central School of Speech and Drama*, incorporating the Embassy Theatre. A statue (by Oscar Nemon) commemorates Sigmund Freud who spent the last 18 months of his life in Hampstead. Opposite are the Library and swimming baths (1964) of the *Civic Centre* which serves the Borough of Camden, in which Hampstead has been absorbed. The architects are Sir Basil Spence, Bonington, and Collins. On the other side of Finchley Rd. (in Alexandra Rd., reached viâ Adelaide Rd.) was the house in which Lily Langtry received Edward VII, when Prince of Wales. College Crescent and Fitzjohns Avenue lead N. to Hampstead High St. (see below), or we may continue (left) past Finchley Road Station.—4 m. *Frognal*, a winding street ascending to Old Hampstead diverges right. In Arkwright Road is the Camden Arts Centre. In Frognal we pass the buildings of *University College School*, erected in 1907, when the school was removed from the S. wing of University College. The school was founded in 1830, and among its famous pupils are Lord Morley, Lord Leighton, Joseph Chamberlain, Wm. de Morgan, and Lord Reading.—Upper Frognal Lodge (l.) was the last London home of J. Ramsay MacDonald (1866–1937). We turn right in to Church Row to *Hampstead Parish Church* (St John's), dating from 1745, with a chancel added on the w. in 1878. It contains a bust of Keats, by Anne Whitney, of Boston, Mass. (presented by American admirers in 1894). Coventry Patmore was married here to his first wife, the inspirer of 'The Angel in the House'.

In the s.e. corner of the churchyard, close to the wall, is the altar-tomb (surrounded by green railings) of *John Constable* (1776–1837), the landscape painter, who found many of his subjects in Hampstead. On the other side of the street are the graves of *George du Maurier* (1834–96) and *Sir Herbert Beerbohm Tree* (1853–1917), both seen from the road, *Sir Walter Besant* (1836–1901; w. side near the middle), and *Matthew Maris* (1839–1917), the Dutch painter.—Holly Walk ascends to Mount Vernon (comp. below).

At the end Heath Street runs N. to meet Holly Hill and Hampstead High Street opposite (4¾ m.) *Hampstead Underground station.*

Here we are at the crossroads of **Old Hampstead,** which deserves a visit for its Heath, its views, its literary associations, and its 18C houses and quaintly irregular streets. The attractive *Flask Walk,* diverging to the left (N.E.) from High St., immediately below the station, contains several second-hand bookshops. It leads to *Well Walk,* recalling the springs that made Hampstead fashionable in the 17C and 18C. Keats lived in Well Walk in 1816 (house near the pub at No. 30), and he returned to it in 1817 for a short time. Constable, the painter (see above), resided here (No. 5, now No. 40) from 1826 to 1837. Opposite is a chalybeate spring discovered in 1698.

HOLLY HILL, opposite the tube station, leads to an attractive secluded district at the foot of the Heath. On the left is the large National Institute for Medical Research. To the right, in Holly Bush Hill, is the house (much altered) built by George Romney, the painter, in 1796, and occupied by him till his death in 1802.

A steep footpath, Mount Vernon, leads w. past Holly Walk (see above) at the corner of which, in Abernethy House, the young R. L. Stevenson shared rooms with Sidney Colvin (1874). Below (l.) a R.C. Chapel was built in 1814 for French refugees. Frognal (comp. p. 322) beyond, contains some pleasant old houses. Frognal House was De Gaulle's temporary home in 1944–45. A footpath leads N. to Frognal Rise where another path follows Oak Hill Way to West Hampstead past an impressive block of flats (1961; by Michael Lyell Assoc.).

Hampstead Grove continues N. to the Heath past **Fenton House,* a gracious mansion of 1693 with a Regency loggia (N.T.; adm. 11–5, inc. BH Mon, Sun from 2, exc. Mon and Tues, Christmas Day, Boxing Day, and Good Friday; fee). Informal concerts are given in the Music Room (organized by the N.T.; for information, Tel. 435 3471).

The delightfully furnished rooms contain a notable collection of 18C porcelain (Chelsea, Worcester, Staffordshire, Meissen, Sèvres, Chinese, etc.), and a fine view of Hampstead Heath by Constable. The informal atmosphere of the house is often enhanced by the sound of a harpsichord, spinet, or virginal. The fine collection of keyboard instruments includes a harpsichord used by Handel. A charming garden extends to the N.; the entrance gates on Holly Hill date from c. 1707.

At New Grove House George du Maurier lived in 1874–95. *Admiral's Walk* leads left from Hampstead Grove. Here John Galsworthy (1867–1933) died at Grove Lodge. Beyond, in Lower Terrace, No. 2 was occupied by Constable in 1820–21. Windmill Hill climbs to *Judge's Walk,* a shaded terrace with a fine view over the West Heath, named from a doubtful tradition that assizes were held here during the Plague.

Hampstead Grove ends at (5 m.) *Whitestone Pond* (converted into an emergency water tank in 1940–44), where Shelley sailed paper boats for the Hampstead children. Near by, donkeys, may be hired; a pound for stray donkeys was set up here in 1871. Beyond is *Jack Straw's Castle* (altered), an old inn well known to Dickens. Between these is the highest point (443 ft) of *Hampstead Heath (825 acres)*, a wide, elevated, and sandy tract on the summit and N. slopes of Hampstead Hill. The Heath, kept in its picturesque natural state, is one of the most frequented open spaces near London, especially on Bank Holidays. The first 240 acres were secured for the public in 1871, the last 2¾ acres in 1958. The highest point in London, it was the main link in the chain of beacons from Romney Marsh on the s. coast, set up to warn of the landing of the Armada. Constable chose the Heath as the subject of many of his landscapes. Just beyond the inn the road forks: North End Way leads to the left; Spaniards Road (see below) runs straight on.

The WEST HEATH lies between North End Way and West Heath Road. On its N. side is *Golders Hill Park* (light refreshments), with a charming walled garden. North End Way passes (l.; viâ Inverforth Close) The Hill public garden, and (r.) the old *Bull & Bush Inn*, and the site of *Pitt House* (demolished in 1952), where the Earl of Chatham in 1766–67 lay disabled by illness while George III and his ministers were alienating the American colonies by their unfair taxation. A plaque at Ivy House, on the left farther on, marks the home of Pavlova (d. 1931). North End Road ends at *Golders Green Station*; to the N.E. is the *Hampstead Garden Suburb*, an idea conceived by Dame Henrietta Barnett in 1906 and realized by Raymond Unwin and Barry Parker. Golders Green Road runs N.W. to Hendon; while Finchley Road leads N. to Finchley and Barnet (comp. Rte 45).

Below the Spaniards Road extends the EAST HEATH, with the *Vale of Health*, a cluster of houses, where Leigh Hunt was visited in 1816 by Keats, Shelley, and Lamb. In North End Way Queen Mary's Maternity Home stands on the site of Upper Flask Inn, where the Kit-Cat Club often met (comp. pp. 85, 294). The *Hampstead Ponds* (S.E. corner of East Heath) were the subject of Mr Pickwick's 'Speculations'. On the edge of the Heath here fine willows adorn Gainsborough Gardens. The car park on East Heath Road becomes a fair-ground on Bank Holidays (Easter, Spring and August). The charming *Downshire Hill*, which leads from the Heath back towards Hampstead High Street, passes *St John's*, which retains its old box pews. Here in *Keats Grove*, once John St., stands *Wentworth Place*, later known as Lawn Bank, the house in which John Keats (1795–1821) spent a great part of the years 1818–20. This is now the **Keats Memorial House** and contains interesting souvenirs of the poet and his friends. Adm. free daily, 10–6, Sun 2–5. Keats and Charles Armitage Brown occupied the E. half of the house, the Brawnes the other. In the Chester Room, added on the E. in 1838, is a museum with MSS. and letters of Keats, personal relics of Keats and Fanny Brawne, books owned and annotated by Keats, portraits, early editions of his works, and letters of Shelley and others of his contemporaries. One letter refers to the wording for his tombstone ('Here lies One whose name was writ in Water'). In the garden a plum tree replaces one under which the 'Ode to a Nightingale' was written. Immediately adjoining is a branch public library containing early editions of Keats, and books relating to the poet (adm. weekdays, 9.30–5 or 8).

Hampstead Heath station is near by. To the E. an extension of the Heath is known as *Parliament Hill* (319 ft). Here an early British tumulus is popularly connected with Queen Boudicca.

From Jack Straw's Castle the high-lying *Spaniards Road*, raised to an embankment by sand quarrying on either side, runs N.E. across the Heath. At (5¾ m.) the road squeezes between an old toll house and the 18C tavern known as *The Spaniards*. The Gordon Rioters, on their way to burn Lord Mansfield's house (see below) in 1780, were overtaken at the inn by the military. Here Mrs Bardell was enjoying herself when she was arrested (see 'Pickwick Papers'), and inside are preserved Dick Turpin's (alleged) pistols.

Hampstead Lane continues to (6 m.) ***Kenwood,** once the seat of Lord Mansfield (1705–92), George III's great Chief Justice, for whom the mansion was reconstructed by Robert Adam in 1767–69. The wings were added to the N. front in 1793–96 by George Saunders. About 120 acres of the estate were acquired for the public in 1922, and in 1927 the house, with 74 acres more, was bequeathed to the nation by Lord Iveagh (1847–1927), along with a choice collection of paintings, fine furniture, and an endowment of £50,000. Adm. free, daily, Apr–Sept 10–7; Oct, Feb, Mar 10–5; Nov, Dec, Jan 10–4. Closed Good Friday, Christmas Eve, and Christmas Day. Refreshments in Coach House and Old Kitchen Restaurant.

In the Entrance Hall are works by *Reynolds*, and *Romney*. We turn left past the fine Staircase (exhibitions are held on the first floor), to the Marble Hall with French paintings (*Boucher*, *Pater*, etc.). The Dining Room contains a *Self-portrait by *Rembrandt* (c. 1665; restored 1969). Also: *Ferd. Bol* (attrib.), Portrait of a Lady; *Aelbert Cuyp*, View of Dordrecht; *Jan Vermeer*, Guitar Player. Beyond the Marble Hall (l.) is the sumptuous Adam *Library (ceiling paintings by *Ant. Zucchi*). In the Breakfast Room are works by the English School including *George Morland*, *Reynolds, and *Gainsborough.

The Parlour contains marine paintings by *Turner*, *Willem van de Velde the Younger*, *Jan van de Cappelle*, and *van Ostade*. Beyond the Old Tea Room with Adam designs for the decoration of the house, the Boudoir contains 17–18C Italian works, including two fine views of Venice by *Fr. Guardi*. The Orangery is dominated by *Stubbs*' magnificent painting of *Whistlejacket, and *Van Dyck*'s portrait of *Lady Goodwin. Beyond the Lobby, in the Music Room is a *Portrait of Mary Howe, by *Gainsborough*. The Harp by Erard of Paris dates from c. 1820, and the furniture is Hepplewhite.

The finely wooded estate includes a noble avenue of limes, a favourite resort of Pope (open 9–dusk). Dr Johnson's summerhouse from his home at Thrale Place was moved here in 1968. Concerts are given by the lake in summer (see p. 31).

The gaily-painted caravan (1905) outside the grounds, on the E., was acquired from the Bucklands, a family long associated with the fairs on the Heath (shown in summer).

Hampstead Lane continues E. to (6½ m.) **Highgate** which occupies the summit of Hampstead's 'sister hill' (426 ft). It takes name from the medieval toll gate which controlled the old North road's passage through the Bishop of London's estates. It retains many charming old houses and much of its village atmosphere. The most pleasant approach from Hampstead Lane is viâ *The Grove* (r.) with its fine houses. Roger Fry was born at No. 6 in 1866, and No. 3 was the home of Coleridge from 1816 till his death in 1834. Here, on the summit of the hill, is a reservoir of the M.W.B. Across West Hill is the well-sited church of *St Michael* (1832), with a conspicuous spire. The E. window is the work of Evie

Hone (1954). In the aisle is the tomb of S. T. Coleridge (1772–1834), removed from the chapel-crypt of Highgate School in 1961. A line on the vestibule wall shows the height of the top of the cross on St Paul's Cathedral.

South Grove leads hence to *Pond Square* with an attractive medley of buildings. At the end is HIGHGATE HIGH STREET with (l.) the Gate House inn (named from the toll-gate, see above) and *Highgate School* founded in 1565.

In *North Road*, which descends N. from the top of Highgate High St., A. E. Housman wrote 'A Shropshire Lad' at Byron Lodge (No. 17) in 1896.

Swain's Lane leads out of Pond Square and descends steeply to the s. past a tall radio mast between (l.) Waterlow Park and (r.) old **Highgate Cemetery**. In the old graveyard (fine view) Michael Faraday (1791–1867) and Mrs Henry Wood (1814–87) are buried. On the other side of the lane is the entrance to the newer portion. The crowded and overgrown tombstones give it a wild appearance. From the entrance a wide path leads s.; at the end of the left fork looms the huge bust (1956) on the grave of *Karl Marx* (1818–83). Opposite is the simple tomb of *Herbert Spencer* (1820–1903). Returning towards the entrance a small path (r.) leads past the tomb (with a grey obelisk) of *George Eliot* (Mary Ann Cross, 1819–80).

Beside the graveyard is the s.w. entrance to *WATERLOW PARK (29 acres) presented to the public in 1891 by Sir Sydney Waterlow as "a garden for the gardenless". It is beautifully maintained with fine lawns. Beyond the lake is *Lauderdale House* (restored), once the seat of the Duke of Lauderdale, the notorious minister of Charles II, who is said to have lent it frequently to Nell Gwynn. We emerge on *Highgate Hill* at its junction with Highgate High St. Here is the conspicuous dome of *St Joseph's Retreat*, the mother-house of the Passionist Fathers in England, with a large chapel. At the foot of Highgate High St. (r.) is Cromwell House (No. 104; no adm.), a fine building of the 17C built of red brick in the Dutch style. Francis Bacon died in 1626 at Arundel House which stood a little higher up the hill. Hornsey Lane leads to a viaduct (magnificent view of London, with St Paul's, etc.) built by Sir Alexander Binnie to replace the old 'Highgate Archway' in 1897. It crosses high above Archway Road constructed in 1812–29 to avoid the steep slope of Highgate Hill.

Highgate Hill descends to (7½ m.) Archway Station past (r.) the *Whittington Stone*, with a sculptured cat (1964), popularly supposed to occupy the site of the stone on which Dick Whittington sat and listened to Bow Bells chiming "Turn again, Whittington, Thrice Mayor of London".

Richard Whittington travelled to London in c. 1379 from Gloucestershire, after the death of his father. He became a mercer, wool exporter, and royal financier and was appointed by Richard II as Lord Mayor of London in 1397. He was subsequently elected to the office three times, and became an M.P. in 1416. In Elizabethan times popular myth attached a cat to this historical figure whose fame survived through the endowments he left to colleges, etc. from the fortune he amassed as a successful businessman.

Below, on both sides of the road are the grim buildings of Whittington Hospital. Archway tube Station (Northern line) is now submerged in a group of high shop and office blocks.

From *Highgate Tube Station* in Archway Road, Southwood Lane leads s. to Highgate Village, while Muswell Hill Rd. (buses Nos. 43, 134) runs N.E. between the two portions of *Highgate Woods* to *Muswell Hill*, on the E. side of which is **Alexandra Palace**, opened in 1878. In 1914–18 the palace was used first for Belgian refugees and later as an internment camp for enemy aliens, and after 1936 it became the principal transmitting station for the B.B.C. television programmes, with an interval of military service in 1939–46. It still furnishes studios for B.B.C. television news programmes. Exhibitions and concerts are also held here. The adjoining race-course was closed in 1970; it is now a recreational centre, with playing-fields.

47 HENDON AND HARROW

UNDERGROUND: *Hendon* and *Colindale* (for R.A.F. Museum) on Northern line; *Canons Park* and *Stanmore* on Bakerloo line; *Harrow-on-the-Hill* on Metropolitan line.

GREEN LINE COACHES: Nos. 706 and 708 to Hendon and Stanmore (No. 719 also runs to Stanmore).

BUSES: No. 113 along Finchley Road to Hendon; No. 183 from Hendon Central to Harrow.

The Edgware Road (A5; p. 173), following the line of the Roman *Watling Street*, runs N.W. through Cricklewood, while *Finchley Road* (A41) to the E., now the motorway feeder, traverses West Hampstead, crossing the North Circular Road at Brent Cross on a three-level flyover. Just w. of the A5's crossing of the North Circular extends the *Brent Reservoir* (1838), known as the *Welsh Harp* from a tavern close by, and now used for sailing.—6½ m. **Hendon**. The *Church* (r. of A41, by the Burroughs) contains a square arcaded Norman font and the tomb of Sir Stamford Raffles (1781–1826), founder of Singapore. Hendon Hall (farther E. on the Great North Way), an 18C house now a hotel, was bought by David Garrick c. 1756; a painted ceiling by Tiepolo was rediscovered here in 1954. On the opposing rise is an obelisk erected by Garrick.

From the Edgware Road, 2 m. beyond Brent Reservoir, Colindale Ave. leads E. past the Newspaper Library of the British Library (comp. p. 192) to *Royal Air Force Station, Hendon*, famous as an aerodrome for pioneer flying and for the public displays of the R.A.F. in the 1930s.

The factory and flying field set up by Claude Grahame-White was commandeered in 1914 by the Royal Naval Air Service and passed to the Royal Air Force in 1918. From Hendon in 1911 Pierre Prier made the first non-stop flight from London to Paris (3 hrs 56 min.), and from here the first official mail-carrying flight was made (to Windsor; 9 Sept 1911).

The splendid ***Royal Air Force Museum** (car park; adm. free 10–6, Sun from 2; rfmts), opened late in 1972, has been built to incorporate two hangars of 1914. These form the main EXHIBITION HALL in which c. 45 of the Museum's aircraft are displayed in chronological sequence; all have been superbly restored in R.A.F. workshops, except for part of a Gladiator dredged from a Norwegian fjord and left as a memorial. Most of the great names are represented, many by the last remaining example of its type: Blériot XI, S.E. 5A, Sopwith Triplane; the marvellous representative Hawker group arranged as a memorial to Sydney Camm, their designer, including a Hart in the colours of the Royal Afghan Air Force, a Hurricane, Typhoon, and Tempest; Wellington and Lancaster bombers; Lysander; a Spitfire of late 'Mark' (one example from a comprehensive range); the Meteor that held the airspeed record in 1946 (616 m.p.h.), the Canberra that won the England–New Zealand

air race in 1953; a Lightning; and Bluestreak missile.—Scale models (at
1:48) of *all* aircraft flown by the R.A.F. are on view in the museum in
dioramas reproducing particular airfields at various dates.

On the FIRST FLOOR (l. from entrance staircase) galleries demonstrate the history
of military flying from the balloon and box-kite, with recreated Royal Flying Corps
workshops and hangar benches of 1912 and 1914, aero engines, etc., to the end of
the First World War, followed by a section of original uniforms and decorations of
famous and royal flyers. Lord Trenchard, father of the R.A.F., is doubly remembered, for his Metropolitan Police College occupies the S.E. corner of the airfield.—
On the GROUND FLOOR: the R.A.F. since 1918; in the Middle East (note the huge
Rolls-Royce armoured car); control cabin of the R33 airship; relics of the Second
World War, including radar sets and gun turrets; a section on escapes from prison
camps; the development of jet propulsion and space flight; the R.A.F. today.

Also upstairs is the ART GALLERY (portraits and busts) and a CINEMA, where
historic films are shown from the LIBRARY AND ARCHIVES on the floor above.

Mill Hill, adjoining to the E., has a boys' public school, founded originally for
Nonconformists (1807). Conspicuous by its campanile is *St Joseph's College*
for Foreign Missions, founded by Card. Vaughan in 1866. In Mill Hill Park
is the London University Observatory. Highwood House, farther E., home of Sir
Stamford Raffles, is a convalescent home. From it the most attractive Totteridge
Lane runs E. through rural surroundings to Whetstone, a suburb on the old North
Road S. of Barnet (Rte 45).

8½ m. **Edgware.** Whitchurch Lane runs left to *St Lawrence*, the parish
church of *Little Stanmore* or *Whitchurch*, rebuilt (except the tower) by
the Duke of Chandos in 1715–20 and elaborately adorned with paintings
by Laguerre and Bellucci, and carvings in the manner of Gibbons. On
the N. side is the mausoleum of the duke, with two of his three wives; and
behind the altar is the little organ played by Handel, who was the duke's
private choirmaster in 1718–20, composing for him the 'Chandos
Anthems' and 'Esther'. Nothing supports the legend that the village
smith was the inspiration of the so-called 'Harmonious Blacksmith'.
Canons Park, to the N., now mostly cut up into building lots, was the
estate of the duke's magnificent mansion of *Canons*, demolished after its
sale by his heir in 1747. Here Dr Pepusch, the duke's first chapel master,
met John Gay.

Its successor at one time belonged to Dennis O'Kelly, owner of the undefeatable
racehorse 'Eclipse' (d. 1790) the skeleton of which is preserved in the Nat. Hist.
Museum. The house (much enlarged) is now occupied by the *North London Collegiate School for Girls*, established in 1850 in Camden Town by Frances Mary Buss
(1827–94), one of the pioneers in preparing women for university education.

Beyond Canons Park Stn. (Bakerloo line), we turn right and ascend
Marsh Lane.—10¼ m. **Stanmore,** properly *Great Stanmore*, has two
churches in its churchyard: the older a ruined Laudian building of 1632,
incorporating Saxon remnants from a predecessor; the newer (1849)
containing a font by Nich. Stone and a good wall-monument of 1605 in
the N. aisle. Outside is Gilbert's grave (comp. below). *Bernay's Gardens*,
just to the E., border some restored half-timbered buildings.

Stanmore Hill climbs N.W. On the right is *Stanmore Common* (car
park), thickly wooded with silver birch. To the left is the large park of
Bentley Priory, once a house of Austin Canons and later (from 1788,
when it was rebuilt by Sir John Soane) the home of the marquesses of
Abercorn and an important political rendezvous in the early 19C; here
Queen Adelaide died in 1849. It passed in 1926 to the Air Ministry and
since 1936 has been the headquarters of the R.A.F. fighter defence of
Great Britain.

We turn left (s.) at (11¾ m.) the Alpine and descend again between the park and *Harrow Weald Common*, on the far side of which stands *Grims Dyke*, by Norman Shaw (1872), where W. S. Gilbert died in 1911 as a result of rescuing a girl from drowning in his pool. Musical evenings (dinner and Gilbert and Sullivan selections) are held here on Sundays. A409 continues s. through *Harrow Weald*, with a printing works of H.M.S.O. and the Kodak works, and *Wealdstone*, to *Harrow* (3¾ m.). Well to the s. of the modern *Civic Centre* and the present-day shopping area rises the Hill, the prominent eminence, 200 ft above the plain and just 10 m. from London, on which stands **Harrow on the Hill.** The *Parish Church*, with a conspicuous spire, contains the brass of John Lyon (d. 1592; N. side of nave). In the churchyard (view) is the flat tombstone (railed in; tablet) on which Byron as a boy used to "sit for hours and hours", but the elm-tree is gone. Byron's daughter Allegra, refused burial in the church, lies in an unmarked grave in the churchyard. Grouped below the church are the principal (mainly 19C) buildings of *Harrow School*, one of the great public schools of England, which received its charter from Elizabeth I in 1572 by the offices of John Lyon, a yeoman of Preston, Middlesex. The boys live in Masters' houses and wear a special type of flat straw hat. Among famous pupils are Sheridan, Byron, Peel, Aberdeen, Palmerston, Manning, 7th Earl of Shaftesbury, Calverley, Dalhousie, Trollope, Galsworthy, Baldwin, Churchill, G. M. Trevelyan, Pandit Nehru, Lord Gort, and Lord Alexander; also Kings Ghazi and Faisal II of Iraq, and Hussein of Jordan. The school buildings (which may be seen most afternoons on application to Custos at the Old Schools) lie to the s. of the parish church; the Old Schools contain the 'Fourth Form Room' (1609) with panels scored with the names of former pupils. At the corner of Grove Hill a tablet recalls the first recorded fatal automobile accident here in 1899. The *High Street* contains many pleasant old buildings, mostly associated with the school.

Sudbury Hill descends to join the main road (A404) at Sudbury. The quickest return to London is made by bearing right almost at once on A4005 to join the A40 (Rte 48) at Hanger Lane. The old Harrow Road (l.) follows a circuitous course through **Wembley,** passing just s. of the huge *Wembley Stadium*, famed scene of international Association Football matches and Cup finals. Built for the British Empire Exhibition of 1924–26, it was opened early for the Cup Final of 1923, when so many people got in that the pitch had to be cleared by mounted police before the game could start. The Stadium is best remembered as the venue of the 1948 Olympic Games and for the victory of England in the World Cup of 1966. The near-by *Empire Pool*, opened as a swimming pool in 1934, is used for skating extravaganzas and show jumping. Beyond the North Circular Road, A404 continues through *Willesden*. The surprisingly attractive old parish church (l.) preserves a rare 14C traceried door, a Norman font, and six good brasses. Charles Reade (1814–84), the novelist, lies in the churchyard.

The Harrow Road, leaving *Wormwood Scrubs* to the right, passes Kensal Green Cemetery (p. 170) and in company with the *Grand Union Canal* enters Paddington (comp. Rte 15).

48 LONDON AIRPORT AND THE COLNE VALLEY

The direct route (14½ m.) to the *Airport* is now by the M4 which passes 1 m. N. of the entrance. For transport, see p. 13.

Uxbridge is on the Metropolitan and Piccadilly lines. BUSES: see Rte 42; bus 222 connects Hounslow and Uxbridge, and Green line No. 727 traverses the Colne Valley to Heathrow Airport.

The old Great West Road (A4) diverges from the motorway at Chiswick. To (9 m.) *Osterley*, see Rte 42. We continue w., passing *Heston* (r.), where the lych-gate (15C) is one of the oldest in England, and *Hounslow* (l.), a dull suburb preserving scanty remains of *Hounslow Heath*, once notorious for the highwaymen haunting the main w. road out of London. On the river Crane famous sword mills were established by the end of 16C, and gunpowder mills occupied the isolated Heath from the mid-16C until 1920. Here for a short time after the First World War was established London's first air terminal, whence (on 25 Aug 1919) took off the world's first regular commercial passenger flight, followed (11 Nov) by the first regular airmail service (both to Paris).— 12 m. *Cranford* church has 17–18C monuments, including a tablet to the one-time vicar, Thomas Fuller (1608–61) of the 'Worthies'. *Harlington*, 1 m. N., also retains its church, with a Norman doorway. To the s. is the vast expanse (2721 acres) of **London Airport** (*Heathrow;* hotels, services, etc. see pp. 13 and 19).

The airfield was first used in 1929 as a test flight base, and served aircraft in the Battle of Britain. It opened to international traffic in 1946, and by 1953 the volume of passenger traffic exceeded 1 million per annum. It is now the busiest airport handling international traffic in the world; in 1977 it served 23.7 million passengers.

On the North side of the airport the cannon was used in 1784 by General Roy to mark the terminal point of the first Ordnance Survey base line which he measured between here and Hampton. An R34 model airship commemorates the first two-way crossing of the Atlantic in 1919; and a statue (by William McMillan) of Sir John Alcock and Sir Arthur Whitten-Brown commemorates the first non-stop flight across the Atlantic, also in 1919. In 1952 B.O.A.C. began jet flights (using a DH Comet) from Heathrow to Johannesburg.

Building continues at the airport under the architectural direction of Frederick Gibberd. The three Terminal Buildings (with a separate Departures and Arrivals building for Terminal 3) are served by car parks and a restaurant (in Terminal 3 Departures). An inter-denominational underground chapel was opened in 1968. The *Queen's Building* Spectator Roof Garden (Rest.) provides facilities for sightseers (open 10–dusk; adm. 20p, children 10p). The spectators' car park is on the N. perimeter of the Airport (with a shuttle coach service to Queen's Building). Another viewing area at the car park is provided for the activity on the run-ways.

The villages which surround the airport retain a rural atmosphere and some fine churches. *Harmondsworth* church (½ m. N. of the perimeter road) is possibly of Saxon foundation, and has a Tudor brick tower and a splendid Norman doorway. Richard Cox, who gave his name to the Orange Pippin apple which was first grown near by, is buried in the churchyard. The s. end of the magnificent late-14C tithe-barn, which survives in the adjoining farm-yard, has been damaged by fire. *Colnbrook*, the first town in Bucks w. of the airport, is by-passed to the N. by the A4. It remains—but only just—in the appearance of Bridge Street and High Street, a typical coaching town of the old Bath Road with a fine series of inns (many already empty). It was the final stage for coaches bound for London. The Ostrich is said to have been founded in 1106, and used by Dick Turpin. At the fine old King John's Palace (no adm.) Edward III met the Black Prince when he returned with the King of France as captive.

At *Horton*, 1½ m. s., was the house of John Milton's father, where the poet wrote his greatest works. His mother is buried in the church. *Stanwell*, on the s. edge of the airport, has a good 14C church with a monument to Baron Knyvet, the magistrate who discovered Guy Fawkes in the cellars of Parliament. It also contains a painting attributed to Murillo. *East Bedfont* church (1½ m. e.) has a Norman door and a 16C Flemish oak panel.

We rejoin the A4 and cross a vast interchange beneath the M4. The first turning right (B470) leads to *Langley* where, in a porch attached to the old church, is the unique *Kenchington Library founded in 1631, and occupying a panelled room, adorned with paintings of Saints and prophets, views of Windsor, etc. We cross the Grand Union Canal and continue N.E. into **Uxbridge,** an ancient market-town on the Colne. Here an abortive meeting of the Commissioners to treat for peace between Charles I and Parliament took place in 1645. The *Treaty House* survives as an inn N.W. of the centre. In the ill-treated High Street is the attractive *Market House* of 1789 (still in use) in front of the Parish church, notable for its 15C roof. *Brunel University* was moved to Uxbridge in 1968 from Ealing where it had grown from a College of Technology.

The crowded old UXBRIDGE ROAD (A4020) returns towards the centre of London through *Hillingdon* where the church, inn, and 16C mansion opposite, form an attractive group. In the church (13–15C) are the fine brass of Lord Strange (1509) and good 17–18C monuments. Beyond Southall and Hayes End it traverses Hanwell; on the left is the fine brent Viaduct, where the railway crosses a pleasant stretch of the Brent. *Ealing* public library occupies Pitshanger Manor, built in 1801–02 by Sir John Soane for his own use. To the N. is St Benedict's School for boys attached to the neighbouring Benedictine Abbey, founded in 1897 and raised to the status of an abbey in 1955.

West Drayton 2¾ m. s. of Uxbridge, preserves the (restored) early 16C gatehouse of its manor house.

North of Uxbridge the busy A40 (Western Avenue) skirts *Northolt* Aerodrome (R.A.F.). A column (1948) at the s.e. corner crowned by a Polish eagle is dedicated to the memory of 546 Polish pilots killed in action with the R.A.F. in 1939–45. The A40 continues e. into London. The old Middlesex villages of Northolt, Greenford, and Perivale, on either side of the thoroughfare, preserve their churches.

Uxbridge lies at the foot of the **Colne Valley** traversed by the Grand Union Canal, with the charming villages of Denham on the Bucks side and Harefield on the Middlesex side. At the end of the fine old village street of *Denham* the church contains a brass to Dame Agnes Jordan, abbess of Syon (1544), one of only two extant brasses to an abbess. Denham Place is a notable 17C house. On the e. side of the valley *Swakeleys* (adm. Tues & Thurs 2–6) is a brick mansion of 1629–38. Beyond the little 14C church of *Ickenham*, Ruislip church has 14C mural paintings and a popular and well-equipped 'Lido' in the Ruislip Reservoir of the Grand Union Canal Company. The church of *Harefield* contains a particularly fine representative series of monuments of the

15–18C. The most imposing is the 'four-poster' of the Countess of Derby (d. 1636) who built the almshouses below the village in 1600. There are also many memorials to the Newdigate family, and a good three-decker pulpit. In the rural churchyard is an Australian Memorial Cemetery, with over 100 graves from the First World War.

INDEX

Topographical names, including buildings, institutes, etc. (whether existing or of the past), are printed in **Bold** type. Names of eminent persons are in *Italics*; statues and monuments are indexed under personal names; queens consort appear under their christian names whether born royal or commoners, e.g. *Jane Seymour, Queen*. Names beginning with Saint (St) are indexed under that heading. Other entries are in Roman type.

Printed litho in Great Britain
by W & J Mackay Ltd, Chatham

BLUE GUIDE
TO
LONDON

Atlas Contents

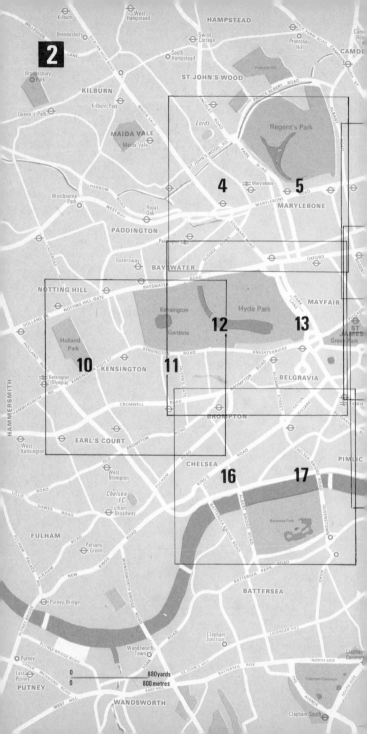

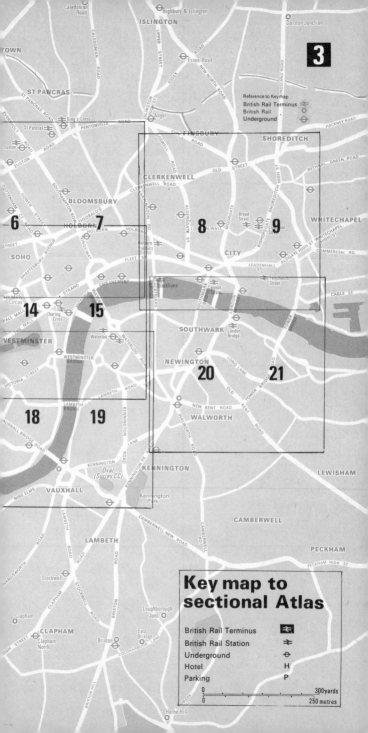

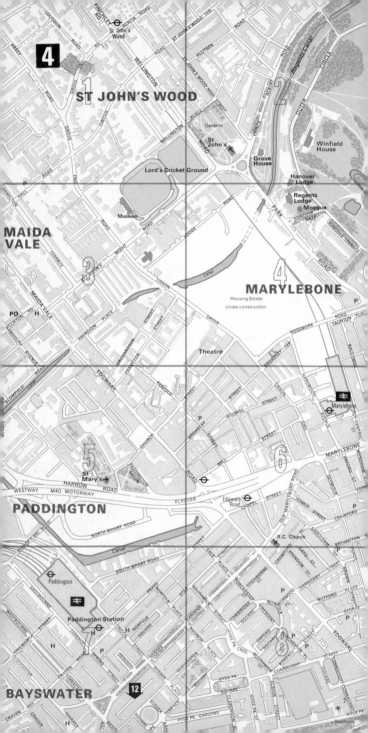

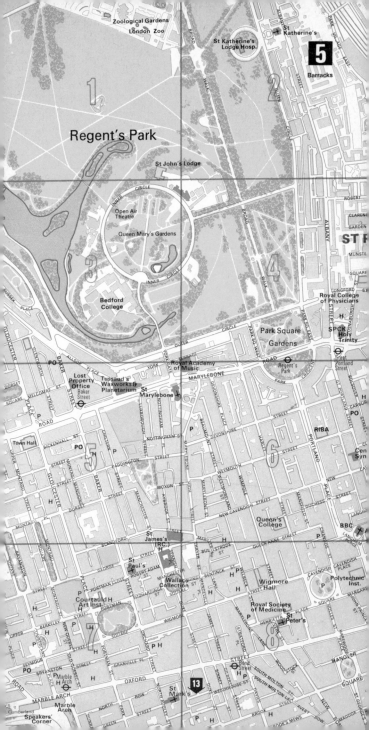

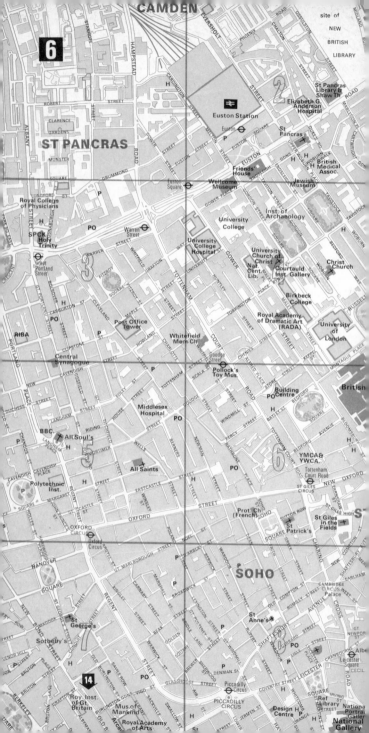

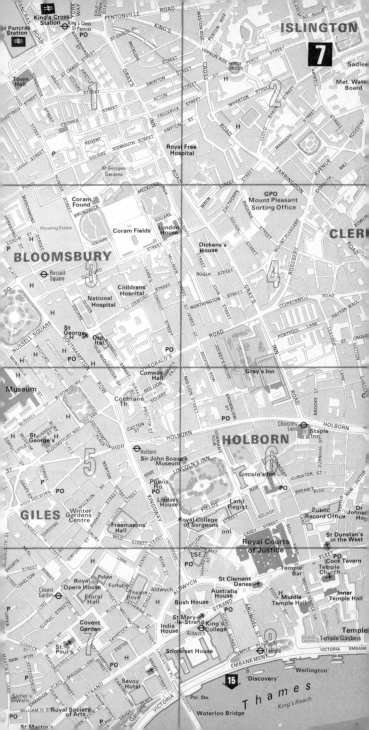

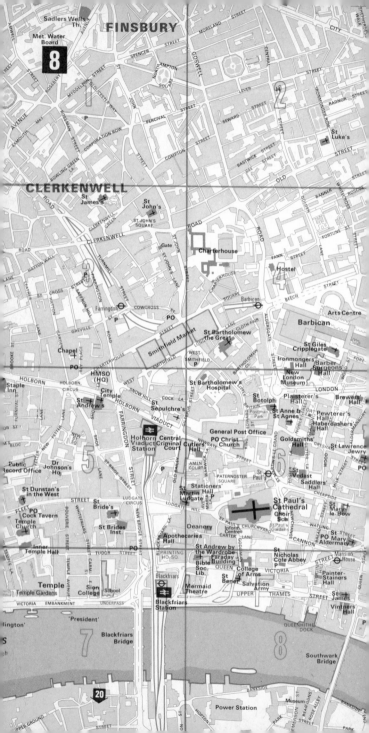

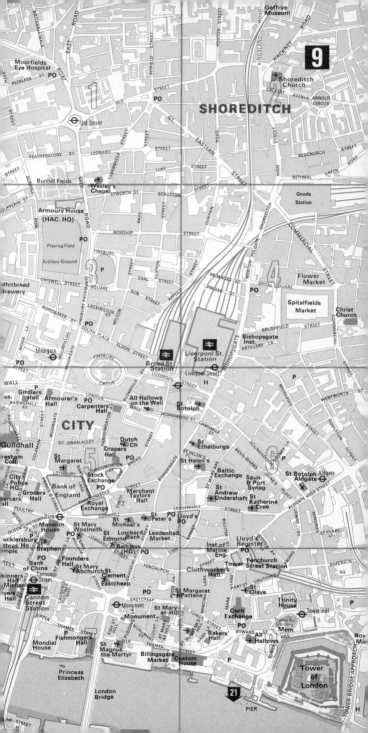

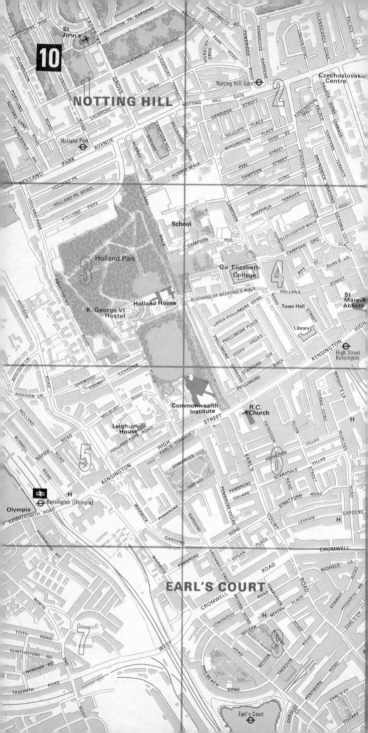

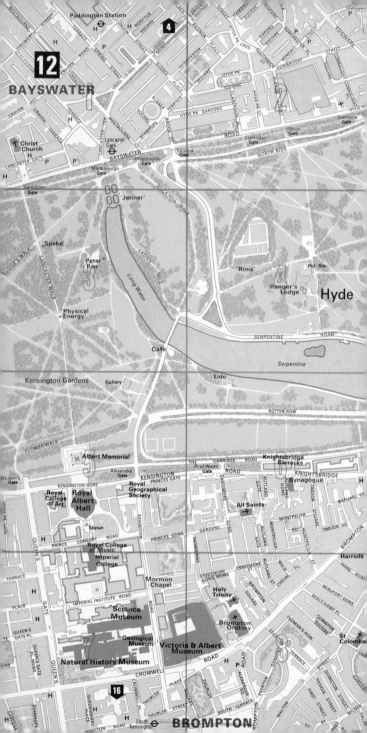

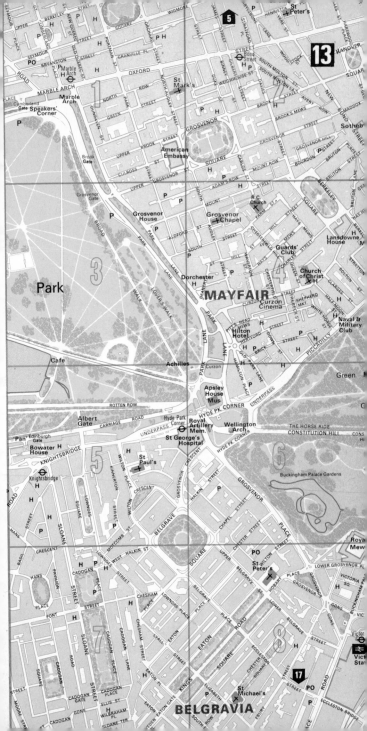

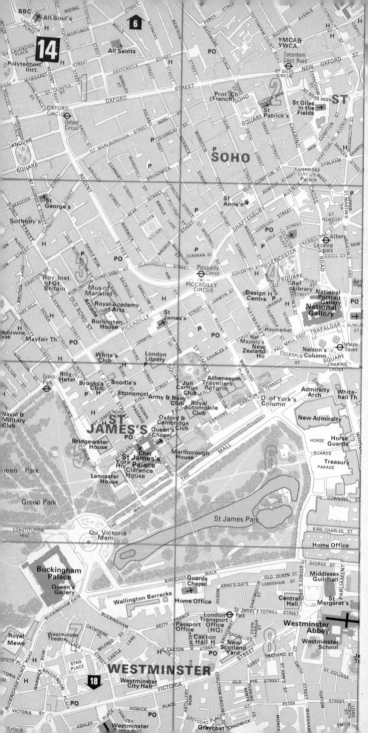

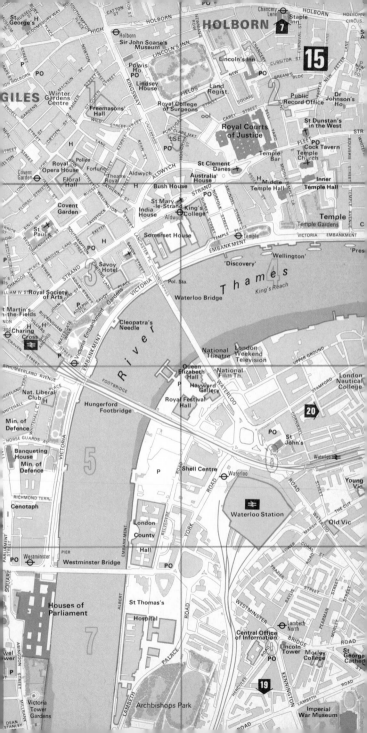

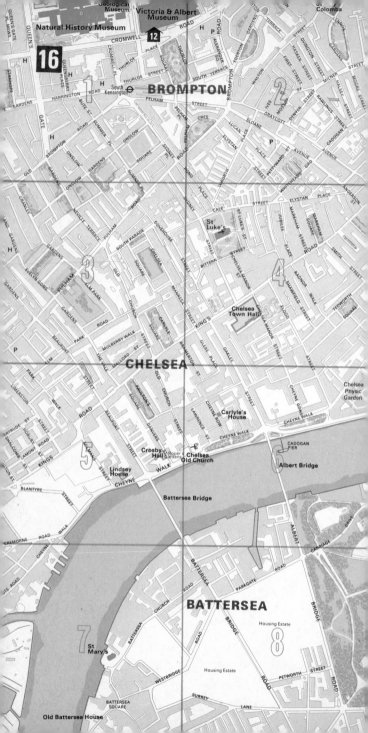

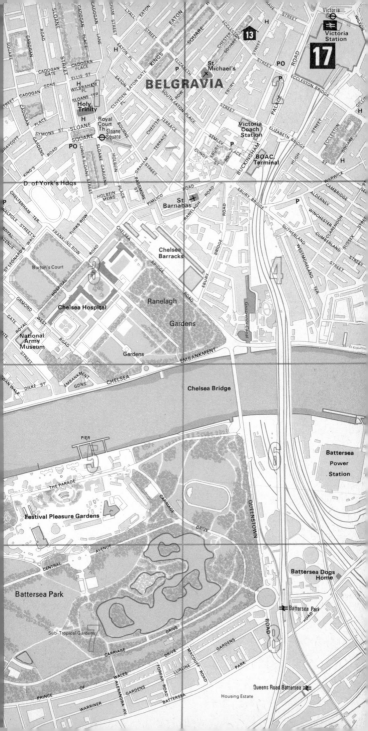

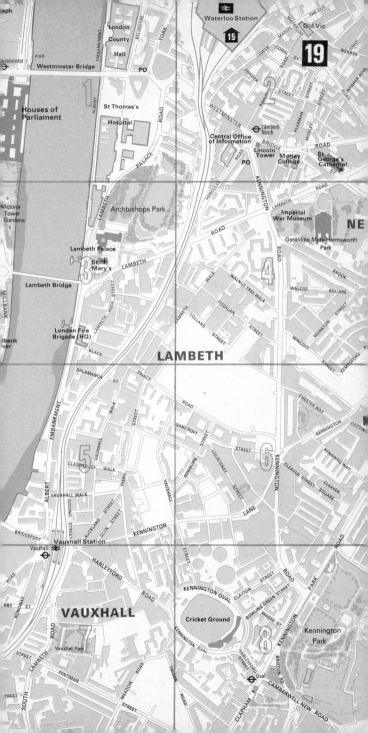

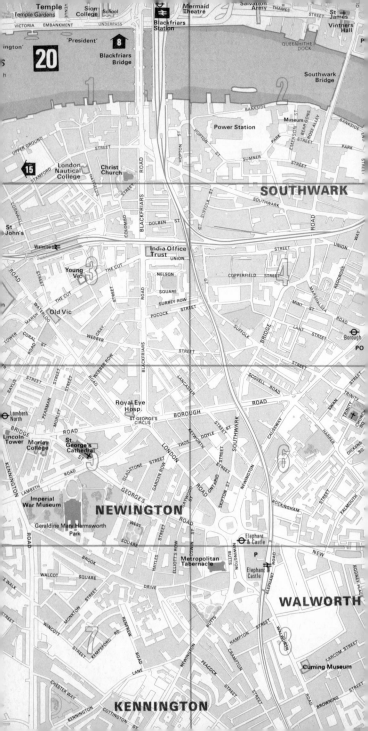

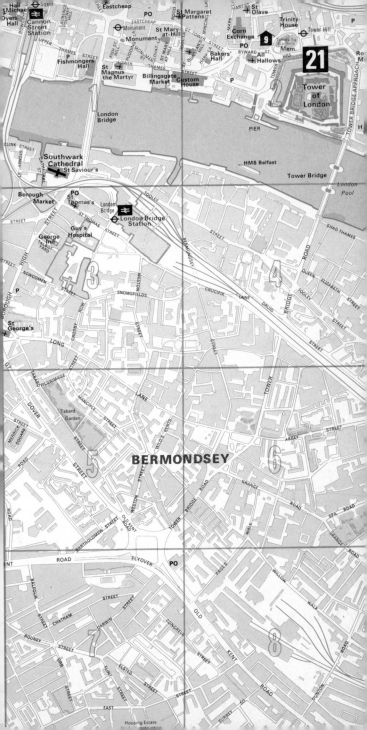

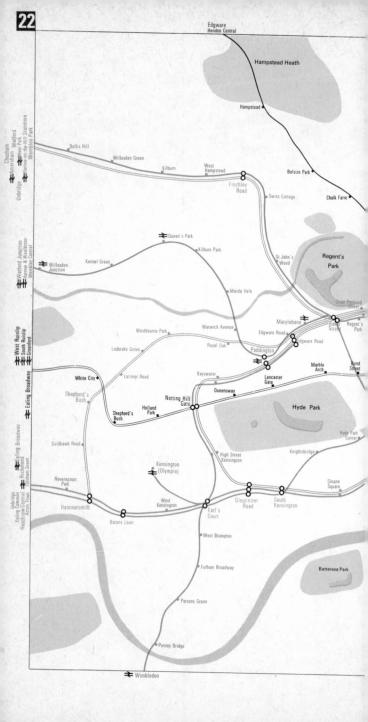

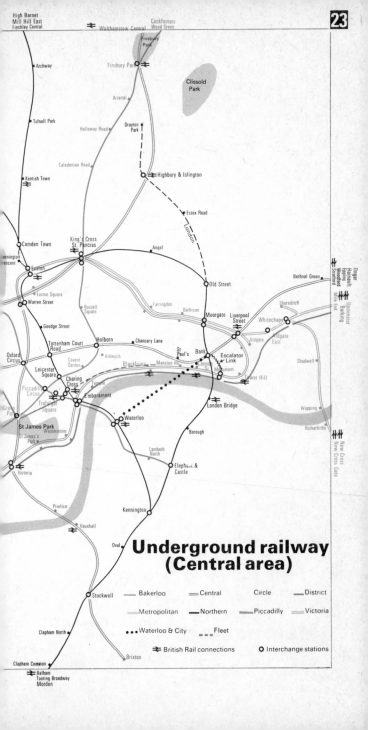

Underground railway (Central area)

Bakerloo	Central	Circle	District
Metropolitan	Northern	Piccadilly	Victoria
••• Waterloo & City	--- Fleet		
British Rail connections		O Interchange stations	

Hampstead Garden Suburb
Littleton Playing Fields
AYLMER
Big Wood

MEADWAY
KINGSLEY WAY
THE BISHOP'S AVENUE

Highgate
GC.

Jew's Cemetery

HOOP LANE

Garden of Remembrance

Hampstead Heath Extension

Hampstead GC.

FINCHLEY ROAD

HAMPSTEAD WAY

Turners Wood

HAMPSTEAD

North Wood

GOLDERS GREEN RD.

Golders Green

NORTH END ROAD

Kenwood

ROAD

North End

'The Spaniards'

Ken Wood

'Bull & Bush'

NORTH END WAY

Golders Hill Park

ROAD

Child's Hill

Hampstead Heath

FINCHLEY

West Heath

SPANIARDS

East Heath

Parliament

WEST HEATH ROAD

Pond

Jack Straw's Castle

Vale of Health

Hampstead Ponds

LANE

Pond

EAST HEATH ROAD

PLATT'S

BRANCH HILL

WINDMILL HILL

LOWER TERRACE

Qu. Mary's Hosp.

HEATH STREET

OAK HILL WAY

GREENHILL

FROGNAL

HOLLY HILL

WELL WALK

Old Hampstead

Fenton House

FLASK WALK

FORTUNE

St John's

DOWNSHIRE HILL

KEATS GRO.

Keats Mem. House

Hampstead Heath

Hampstead

HAMPSTEAD HIGH ST.

CHURCH ROW

St John's

POND STREET

FLEET

GREEN ROAD

FINCHLEY

FROGNAL LANE

FROGNAL

University College School

ROAD

FITZJOHN'S AVENUE

Pond Street

MILL LANE

WEST END

Belsize Park

HAVERSTOCK

ARKWRIGHT ROAD

AVENUE

West Hampstead

LANE

LYMINGTON

W. Hampstead, Midland

Finchley Road & Frognal

ROAD

BELSIZE

Belsize Park

West End Lane

Finchley Road

West Hampstead

COLLEGE

South Hampstead

CRES.

Swiss Cottage

Hampstead

FINCHLEY RD.

Civic Centre

0   1000 yds
0   1000 m

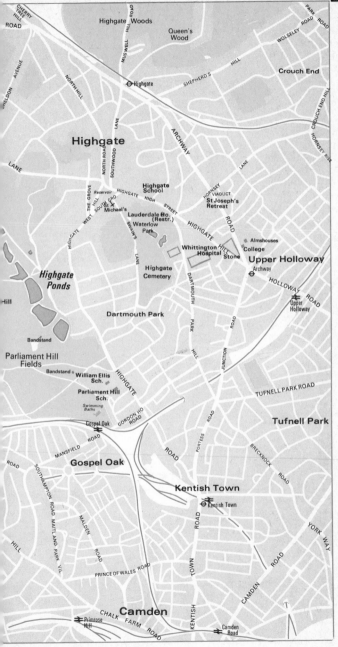

CHERRY TREE HILL ROAD

Highgate Woods

Queen's Wood

PARK ROAD

WOLSELEY ROAD

SHELDON AVENUE

NORTH HILL

MUSWELL HILL ROAD

SHEPHERD'S HILL

Crouch End

Highgate

HORNSEY RISE

CROUCH END HILL

LANE

LANE

NORTH ROAD

SOUTHWOOD LANE

ARCHWAY

Highgate

Highgate School

HIGHGATE HIGH STREET

HORNSEY LANE

HIGH VIADUCT

St Joseph's Retreat

Reservoir

HIGHGATE

THE GROVE

SOUTH GRO.

St Michael's

Lauderdale Ho. (Restr.)

HIGHGATE ROAD

HIGHGATE WEST HILL

SWAINS LANE

Waterlow Park

Whittington Hospital

HIGHGATE HILL

Hill Stone

Almshouses

College

Upper Holloway

Archway

Highgate Cemetery

DARTMOUTH PARK

HOLLOWAY ROAD

Upper Holloway

Highgate Ponds

Hill

Dartmouth Park

DARTMOUTH PARK HILL

ROAD

JUNCTION ROAD

Bandstand

Parliament Hill Fields

Bandstand

William Ellis Sch.

HIGHGATE

TUFNELL PARK ROAD

Parliament Hill Sch.

Swimming Baths

Gospel Oak

GORDON HO ROAD

FORTESS ROAD

Tufnell Park

MANSFIELD ROAD

ROAD

BRECKNOCK ROAD

ROAD

SOUTHAMPTON ROAD

MAITLAND PARK VIL.

Gospel Oak

Kentish Town

MALDEN ROAD

KENTISH TOWN ROAD

Kentish Town

CAMDEN ROAD

YORK WAY

HILL

PRINCE OF WALES ROAD

KENTISH TOWN

Camden

CHALK FARM ROAD

Primrose Hill

Camden Road

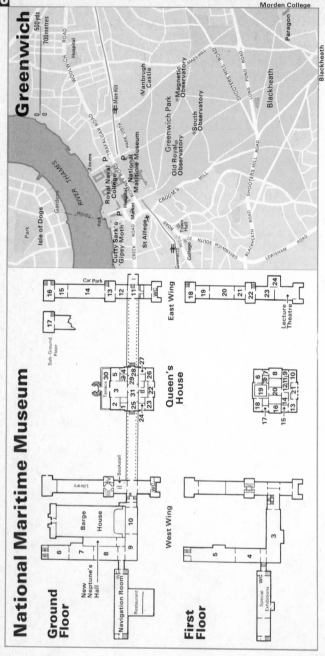

Greenwich

Morden College
Paragon
Blackheath
Blackheath

WOOLWICH ROAD
Hospital
Vanbrugh Castle
Magnetic Observatory
South Observatory
Greenwich Park
Old Royal Observatory
MAZE HILL
SHOOTERS HILL ROAD
LONG POND ROAD
HILL
SHOOTERS HILL ROAD
BLACKHEATH ROAD
LEWISHAM ROAD

Maze Hill
TRAFALGAR ROAD
PARK VISTA
ROMNEY ROAD
National Maritime Museum
Royal Naval College
Tavern
Hospital
Market
CROOM'S

RIVER THAMES
Isle of Dogs
Park
Gardens
Gardens
Tunnel
PIER
Cutty Sark
Gipsy Moth
St Alfege
CREEK ROAD
Greenwich HIGH ST
College ST
Town Hall
GREENWICH SOUTH ST
Blackheath

500 yds
700 metres

National Maritime Museum

Ground Floor

Car Park
16 15 14 13 12 11 WC
17 Sub-Ground Floor
Library
Barge House
New Neptune's Hall
Navigation Room
Restaurant
Bookstall
WC

Terrace 30
3 5
4
29 28
31
25 24
23 22
27
26
East Wing

Queen's House

West Wing

First Floor

18 19 20 21 22 23 24
Lecture Theatre

6
7
8
19 20 9
18
16 10
17 15
13 12 11

5
4
3
Special Exhibitions
WC

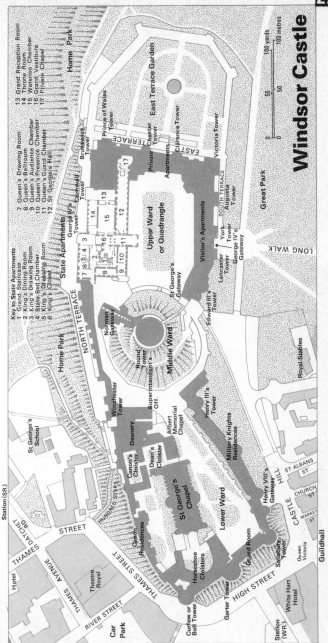

Windsor Castle

Key to State Apartments
1 Grand Staircase
2 King's Dining Room
3 King's Drawing Room
4 State Bed Chamber
5 King's Dressing Room
6 King's Closet
7 Queen's Drawing Room
8 Queen's Ballroom
9 Queen's Audience Chamber
10 Queen's Presence Chamber
11 Queen's Guard Chamber
12 St George's Hall
13 Grand Reception Room
14 Throne Room
15 Waterloo Chamber
16 Grand Vestibule
17 Private Chapel

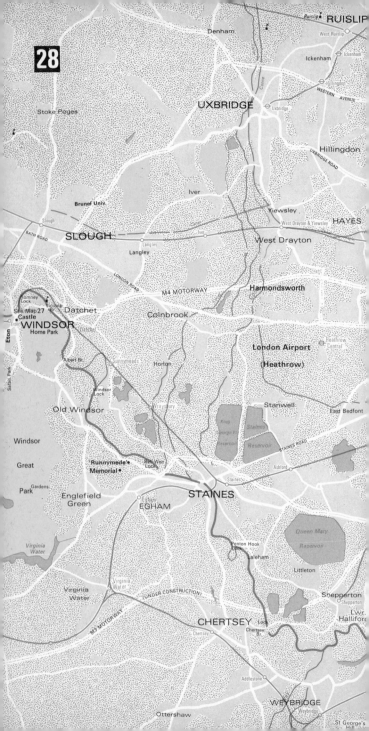